# White Sorrow

By

## Andrea Aviet

First published in Great Britain as a softback original in 2016

Copyright © Andrea Aviet

The moral right of this author has been asserted.

Typeset in Minion Pro

Design, editing, typesetting and publishing by UK Book Publishing

UK Book Publishing is a trading name of Consilience Media

www.ukbookpublishing.com

ISBN: 978-1-910223-69-7

# Acknowledgements

I would like to thank everyone who has helped me through my tough times in life and supported me throughout and all those who have helped make White Sorrow happen. I believe everything in life happens for a reason and that we each have a part to play.

1. Most important I would like to thank and give praise to God without whom nothing is possible. I know I had to go through all my trials in life so that I could reach out to others.
2. To my children who one day will know that being their mother gave me the determination, strength and will to fight against slavery and abuse and rise up so that they could have a happy, free life.
3. Hilary Hanson, a loyal and trustworthy friend who has always been there for me through all my tough times and supported me.
4. Marta Favret, who from a friend has turned into a sister and family. Our kids are like one big happy family. She has always been a source of great strength and encouragement.
5. A friend, Ann Wellington, who introduced me to a lovely pastor called Joan Morgan who has a heart of gold, from The Beacon of Hope Ministry.

The fantastic team in the north who helped produce White Sorrow:

6. Antonia Brindle from Get Brindled, who specialises in PR. She is very unique. I searched all over London to find someone I could connect with and my heart settled on Antonia, in the

North. She shared my same passion.
7. UK Book Publishing and the entire team for their amazing work and support.
8. Your Film for their fantastic videos.

# Early memories

Often I hear that the beginning of a story is the most important because it can either captivate the undying interest of the reader or make you just want to stop and walk away. I am going to do something very different, I am going to ask you not to stop here because it will be the biggest mistake of your life. This book is based on true events and though it pains me I'm writing with great sorrow. My heart's breaking and its 11.58pm. Why am I writing now, at this hour? Because I have tried to write many a time before but... The pain is too great, that I just could not. I need closure, I need the world to listen, learn what they can and to not do what I did for so long... This book will guide you and teach you things which people don't generally teach you – you can't read about it in classrooms or text books.

All too often people are suffering in silence for many reasons and there's only silence, torment, torture and victimisation.

This book will show you many unimaginable things – let it, keep reading. Learn from it and use it as a guide; it has complete and total disclosure. May it be an eye opener to all who read it... Let me start by introducing myself to you. **I am an ordinary person who has been forced to live through slavery and hell.** Like most people I belong to a good family, of four, consisting of my mother, father and elder sister. Me being the youngest I have always been adventurous and an extrovert. My sister has always been shy and passive.

However, Father has always been a very well known, honoured and well to do individual commanding high levels of respect in society. My father's ethnicity is Armenian and my mother is Anglo-Indian. It is a rare mix but this allowed us to have the best of both worlds.

Armenians are a very close community; we believe in helping each other and also providing for the less fortunate among the community. We are spread all over the world, like most others and are known to be the happiest people in the world. Since we grew up mostly among my father's people I can't really speak about my mother's race. We have an Armenian Sports club, Armenian College and Philanthropic Academy where the boys live – it's a boarding school and classes are held for all. The other side, we have The Davidian Girls School – this is where the girl boarders live. The main church located in the region is the Armenian Church of the Holy Nazareth.

My mother belonged to an ordinary middle class family; she was a very religious woman, kind hearted and always believed in helping others and doing lots of social service. Helping people with money and finances came very easily to her; since she was generous from her salary, she would donate to the church. She loved buying calendars painted by disabled children and adults. The money from the calendars being sold would go towards funding the charity-run school. It was her way of doing good and giving back to society. Mum worked for Indian Iron and Steel Ltd but it was not a strict working atmosphere. She loved to go to work, have a few laughs and spend her time. For Mum work was entertainment and a joy. She was always kind to everyone.

Going to church regularly every Sunday was compulsory. Although Mum was never forceful in nature, when it came to church there were no two ways about it. We had to go. I justify it by saying she was a staunch Roman Catholic believer. She was softly spoken and gentle, rarely got angry and was always calm. Yet if she did get angry you would definitely know that she was cross.

Our family life, growing up, was of a very high standard – we never faced any shortage, we were never left wanting, and we always had and had in abundance. Private drivers to take us around, servants to cook, clean, wash etc. We never had to do anything. Everything was done for us all; all we had to do was ask. Living a life like we did was brilliant; however, there were many who envied our lifestyle.

My father used to do plenty of voluntary work for the Y.M.C.A and for our Armenian Community. He is the President of a famous company and held a fantastic job there too. He has a reputation of being able to sell ice creams to Eskimos and combs to bald men.

Unlike my mother Dad was quite demanding; he loved to get his own way and often would not listen to anyone except Mum. Somehow she managed to get him to do whatever she wanted.

So our life was nothing short of spectacular but also very rigid; we had no freedom to do as we liked. We had rules which had to be followed and kept too.

We always had to lead a proper life, well dressed – most of our clothes were silks and satins and if we wore jeans it was all branded. We were well groomed; our behaviour had to be proper at all times lest it reflect badly on Father. Going to Governor House for Independence Day celebration, studying in the best of schools and colleges was all part of our lifestyle.

It is a beautiful experience to belong to different cultural, religious backgrounds. Not only does it help you mix and fit in easily with people from different backgrounds and walks of life but it also helps you to adjust and understand the sociological, religious, political aspects of people belonging to different countries.

My family used to make frequent trips to the UK to visit Grandma, my mother's mum and family. Mum has a huge family consisting of forty members here in the UK alone.

Whereas Dad's life was a lot more exciting – frequent trips to different countries and different parts of the world, meetings and generally meeting various people of importance and class. Mum was all heart, Dad was all business. Mum went to religious classes and Dad went to business meetings.

My sister being older was really lucky as I saw it – she was Mum's favourite and Grandma's too. That was my dad's mum's favourite. Whereas I really don't think I was anyone's favourite while growing up at least. My sister enjoyed coming on multiple visits with Mum to the UK and had seen all the family whereas I was not yet seen but my existence was known about. I was told I had to study first, that education is important.

# Coming to the UK

After I completed my Masters in Political Science Honours in 2007, I came to the UK for a holiday in 2008. Most of my mother's family residing here was one of the reasons for us to come to visit and have frequent family reunions.

This was my first visit though the family had always flown over. Meeting all the family was always a good, exciting time.

Before I came to the UK for my holiday, I was planning to go and do a second Masters in business management. It was something Dad was very much in support of me doing in Australia at Adelaide University. I have always loved Australia and been fascinated by the people, culture and way of life. That was my dream country, and in all honesty I could not wait to go and study and settle down there and I dreamt of having a nice home, maybe close to the beach.

But faith and destiny took me in an entirely different direction to what I had planned. From dreams of hot, sexy, sandy beaches in Australia to cold and rainy and majestic England.

Dad and Mum had planned a surprise visit for me to celebrate my doing well and completing my studies to a standard they approved of. They said I had made them proud.

# The surprise and rebellion

I still remember how shocked I was to find out that I was finally being allowed to come and visit here in the UK but it was a little, too late for my liking. I ended up sounding most ungrateful and fighting with my family. I wanted Australia – my friends were going there; I too wanted to go there and did not care for a family trip.

Kicking and screaming, I was told I could show as much temper as I wanted but the UK was our destination.

I still remember landing at the airport; it was quite a cold day with grey skies. I was in a foul mood and not talking to anyone. In all fairness Mum's brother, who came to collect us from Heathrow Airport, was really making a massive effort to try and break the ice with me and get me to respond. Nothing could change my mind, though – I was miserable on a holiday which I never wanted to be on.

I thought of Australia, the land of my dreams and felt my heart sink even more.

So the entire family on my mother's side saw how miserable I could be. I did, however, like both the wives of both of my mum's brothers. They were fun, friendly, young and simply nice. Grandma was in her eighties and full of fun and mischief. She loved to joke and she loved to be happy, always with a smile on her face.

# Uncle's house party

My life changed in 2008 when I met someone. I'll call him Mark. Well Mark was drinking at a gathering in my uncle's house party and the first thing I noticed was that every time he was offered something to drink he said yes. We were mainly invited to Uncle's house because he was attempting to lift me out of my misery.

We were all quite surprised at Uncle's cooking skills and that he was rather good. There was a good variety of food and since he loved to drink an even bigger collection and wide variety of alcohol.

It was not long before we started talking; Mark seemed alright and like a decent man. Very much like a kind looking gentleman – that was my first impression of him. We spoke a lot on various subjects but all these years later, I really can't recall the exact nature of the subject.

I actually found the entire event quite boring. Being an extrovert meant I never did like just staying indoors but rather I preferred to be outside. Sightseeing and taking photographs to capture every moment.

The party finished and I did not think much about it again. We were with family spending quality time. I was getting to know the others. Everyone was interested in my future plans for further education and seemed genuinely interested for my welfare.

Days passed visiting members of the family and being invited out for lunches and dinners but nothing made me happy. I hated coming half way around the world and having to just go from one house to another.

# Our first date

A few days passed and Mark called me, to ask me out on a date. You can imagine my surprise and shock. He had got my number from Uncle. Uncle James knew I was getting fed up and I think he was trying to help me enjoy my stay.

I decided to take Mark up on his offer. Well, I thought, instead of being at home and amongst family only, why not take him up on his offer to go sightseeing? After all I was on holiday; the family was ok with it.

So it was agreed, and the next day we went up to central London sightseeing; from then it continued every day for a while. We visited a few parks, the museums such as Science, Natural History, London Museum, British Museum, Buckingham Palace, Horniman Museum, St Paul's Cathedral, and the River Thames. While on our outings most of the time we ate out and food never seemed to be an issue. KFC, McDonald's, Subway and a few other places.

Well, on this holiday of mine I started to think about the direction in which my life was going. It was Mathew's wife who I really got along with. Mathew was Mum's other brother, his wife was friendly and being almost the same age we got along quite well. This developed into a good friendship. One day while Sandy and I were out together shopping she brought up the future in conversation. She had been married before and separated. Much later in life she found Mathew and he was the best thing that had ever happened to her. She spoke about her dreams, her change in plans and how nothing in life is ever guaranteed. Sandy seemed to think that taking chances was the only way to discover what life had in store for you, otherwise life would just pass you by and you would be left wondering what the future would have been.

The next morning as usual I was meant to meet Mark and while we were out the conversation, strangely enough, headed in the direction of future aspirations. He started talking about my future plans and seemed to be interested in them.

I belonged to an influential, strict, old fashioned family who were quite rigid in their ways. We had our own ways of doing things.

Anyway I was thinking of going to Australia, the country of my dreams, to do higher education, namely to do a second masters, in business. The first masters I had done was political science honours. I thought about my good job, friends and general things. So it was at this point in time, while all these thoughts were going around in my head, I was thinking about my future and about Mark, the present guy in my life that I was sort of dating, when something totally unexpected and strange happened that took me by surprise...

# The shocking proposal

Mark asked me while we were out all of a sudden what would I say if he were to ask me to marry him.

I thought Mark was joking but he, clearly, was not...

Was he really decent?

I was a hopeless romantic, yet I never believed that true love would ever come my way. I had seen too many friends fall in and out of love. Too many heartbreaks and so many crying because of their partners. Either the men were not faithful or they did not want to continue the relationship. I never ever wanted to have any of those problems.

Every woman dreams of meeting a perfect, nice guy and having a romantic wedding. It's something like a fairy tale or like something you would expect to happens in a movie. I must admit though, it's not something one does each time they want a change.

This was a real big change, it meant I had to trust him completely and know that he would be good to me, look after and take care of me. That when I was ill I could depend on him and rely on him for support and comfort.

I thought it over and then I made my decision. I was 28 and getting older; I had never thought of marriage before but he seemed really nice so why not? Plus I thought it would give me a life of more freedom, which I really longed for. By nature I am a hopeless romantic, so when the prospect of romance, love, and marriage became all intertwined my romantic nature just took over and took control of me.

However, life is never easy, destiny cannot be taken for granted and the future is definitely never what you dream it to be. I was about to embark upon my perfect, romantic, fairytale wedding with my newfound prince charming.

**These were the expectations from the eyes and soul of a naive young girl towards life.**

# The marriage preparations

**I accepted the marriage offer. Mark said he would prefer a small wedding. On the other hand, like everyone else I had always wanted a huge wedding. I had dreamt all my life of a big white wedding, with a coach and white horses etc. The entire Cinderella wedding would have been perfect for me, with a guest list going into the hundreds, Father calling everyone he knew over.**

But I decided to give in and jointly we decided not to waste money but rather to keep the money for necessities and things that were more important for after the wedding, instead of spending it lavishly on one day. It seemed the sensible option.

I informed my father that I was going to get married and that I really wished for him to come over for the first wedding in our family. That meant he had to rush over here with not much time to plan for anything big. Meanwhile, here on holiday we were staying with my mother's brother, wife and son. They were kind enough to put us up and keep us for our entire holiday.

My mum and dad could not understand the dramatic change in behaviour. Within me I was trying to reason and argue as to the benefits of a small wedding as Mark wanted. But I did like a lavish lifestyle and grandeur – that is how we were raised and that is what my true nature was.

However, I started the ball rolling and preparations began. Of course, being good at research, I did it all single handed. Mark said he wanted to get married yet he never contributed much at all. My first impression was that maybe Mark did not like doing all the work, he's just a little laid back but good at heart – or perhaps not confident as to what needed doing.

Being raised in our family gave me a lot of confidence. We were always out and about, meeting people. Besides, I saw how Dad was, always speaking in public, leading various events and giving speeches.

**The easiest part was done by Mark – he asked and that's where his input ended**.

It was left up to me to find out where we could get married because I was the one who desired a church wedding. That's one aspect I really would not compromise on. To me it was an exciting new challenge, to get what I desired. According to the rules of the Church of England, if you live within the parish you can get married in that church.

So, the first complication was to sort out where the wedding would take place. I was a Catholic, at least from my mother's side, but Mark was not a believer at all. He did not belong to any church but that was ok, the first hurdle was over. We managed to find a church and get permission to be married there. This was possible because Mark lived under the jurisdiction of the Church of St Michael's and All Angels.

Mark said that there would be no church wedding if he would have to go for classes; he was against having to go and learn about

Christianity. Usually, if someone is Catholic and would like to get married in a Catholic church, the other partner has to go for classes. Only then can the couple get married. But the Church of England didn't insist on classes, just a one day rehearsal for our big day. So each of us would know what to do and when. We meet the priest, Father David, who informed us about the entire procedure. He was most kind and helpful. A little later, we got permission for the church and the go ahead to get married – that's when all the plans started to come together.

The church was beautiful, huge and majestic looking. It had high ceilings and a beautiful altar. It would have been perfect for a big white wedding.

# The reception hall

Next on my to-do list was to find a small place to host the reception. I do believe that everything happens for a reason and it's true. God was good to us: the church had a small hall and they could cater for the wedding. That worked out quite well; we would have the wedding in church and go straight to the hall thereafter. This would be very convenient for everyone concerned.

The hall was a nice size, especially since there were only a few of us attending. Some from Mum's family but strangely enough none were to attend from Mark's side – something my mother questioned, as she could not make sense of the situation; it was too strange for her, that someone was getting married and did not want their family around. However, I did not want to pressurise Mark and felt if he did not want them around he must have had some reason for it. Yet for all that, I would have really liked it if they would attend.

The food arrangements were made by me again. The only alcohol was the champagne for the toast. We had a bar though where people could buy their own drinks if they wanted. I refused to put money behind the bar, especially since I was not having the exact wedding I had longed for.

The caterers were very good; I had gone for a simple roast English dinner. The music system had to be supplied and the cake I had pre-ordered from Marks and Spencer.

So everything from the Church, to the food and the service was taken care of by me alone.

**Mark was quite happy since he said he was nervous and preferred for me to do everything instead.**

**Somehow I was so caught up with the excitement of getting married that I failed to realise Mark had taken a back seat. Whereas I was stressing about getting things done and putting all my time and energy into planning for a marriage that should have been taken care of on a partnership basis. It was, after all, supposed to be a union of two coming together, right?**

# Finding accommodation

A major cause of concern was where we were going to live. Having only met Mark's mother once of course I did not want to live with them. It would naturally be uncomfortable for me, and I suppose for them too. Also I preferred to have my own living arrangements. All these plans were taking place in a very limited timespan because I was on holiday with my family.

So all this was stress beyond imagination. I contacted agents on the net, researched local places to live, agents in the local area and their ads; finally I came across Choices, the estate agent.

We went to view a local studio flat in Croydon, Surrey. It was on the ground floor. Not the world's best place, but it was a starter home and on short notice; its location served perfectly. The price was just right with all bills included. It was affordable, local and self contained, clean and had quite a good location. The studio had an open plan kitchen. There was room for a small TV stand, one wardrobe, a fridge, a bed and one armchair. It had large windows that allowed a lot of light to come in during the day. The walls were painted white; the floors were carpeted and brown. From the windows hung heavy white curtains and net lace curtains behind them. What I found difficult was that it had an electric hob and I had never cooked on an electric hob before. The kitchen cabinets were a light, pale oak colour. The bathroom had a standing cubicle with a shower and a light floral print shower curtain to stop the water from spilling out. It was a large, old Victorian house divided into small rooms. Each self contained flat had its own postbox. It was nice, different from what I was used to.

Well, considering the time restraints, the location, the affordability – which was 700 pounds including bills – it was perfect. Mark got his friend to stand as guarantor. The papers were signed, sealed and the deal made. Contracts drawn up, the keys were handed over to Mark. It was perfect, since he had to leave early most mornings for work and needed the trains. Being close to the station was a must for him and he was also thrilled that he did not have to live far from his mother's home. **Being close to his mother was always very important to Mark and in this studio flat he got all his wishes granted.**

My soon to be new mother-in-law had mentioned to Mark that on such short notice it would be impossible for us to get a place. But Mark had replied that I was confident I would get one, and I did. She was extremely surprised to learn about our newest development and find that we had settled all living arrangements. But being such a confident person with a go-getter attitude, which of course always helped me to do the things I desired, within my heart I knew all things could be achieved with a positive attitude. Research on the laptop made me extremely independent, helping me not to rely on anyone. These days, almost anything you want to discover can be found on the net.

**Truly speaking, knowledge is power...**

# Talking to Dad

**Well, me being a hopeless romantic, I decided to get married on the 28th September which was also Mark's birthday. That way I thought he would never forget our wedding anniversary, would he then?**

My poor dad rushed about, contacted everyone he could think of and managed to come to the UK for a week exactly, just for our wedding. The year was 2008, his little girl was going to get married and being the first wedding in the family he was definitely not going to miss it. When he landed I picked him up from Gatwick Airport and the next day we had a private father-daughter conversation.

Father asked me if I was sure that I wanted to get married, if I was sure I was doing this for the right reason and, of course, 'yes', at that time it seemed like a perfectly normal, natural thing for me to do.

Well, when my father was satisfied he said he wished for me to have a good and happy life. He hoped I knew what I was getting myself into but life teaches its own lessons and that he wanted me to be smart. Life was not a bed of roses – this was my father's advice to his very own little girl. He also wanted to warn me that I was on holiday with my sister and mum, that reality of life would be very different from when we were on holiday and that I must be prepared to start a life different from what I was used to. He hoped I realised that my present standard of life would be altered forever.

Of course every father and mother wants the best for their child. But in my heart I did not feel that Father was happy. He was always a man of few words, yet he always gave in to me. I guess I turned into being Dad's favourite although he would never admit it, while my sister remained Mum's favourite.

I listened to all his advice amidst the careful warnings and underlining concerns, yet being young and caught up in the moment my judgement was clearly clouded. I did not heed the well thought out concerns of Father.

# A mother's concerns

My mother, on the other hand, was very different in her approach. She was telling me off continuously, all the time saying she was not happy with my choice and that I was here on holiday only to meet her family, not to be getting married.

She did try her very best to convince me to rethink my decision and even went to the extent of fighting with Father, for she blamed him for giving into me all the time. The decision to get married was mine; I took it as an offence because Mum said I really did not understand what I was getting myself into and that I was far from ready to take on married life.

All my relations were brought into it; no one agreed with Mum. Her brothers thought she was just trying to be overprotective of me and controlling as usual. They seemed to think as a parent Mum would never find anyone good enough for us.

Numerous times she asked me to reconsider my decision, that in her heart she felt this was very wrong. She did not like or feel at all comfortable with the situation. She was not happy that he kept his family away and that he felt none of them would come to the wedding.

Very valuable arguments; although I loved my mother dearly we would always argue. If mum said left, I would say right; somehow the love was there but we just could not get along. I was too headstrong and always wanted my own way. Honestly, I did not pay any respect to maternal instincts and rather viewed it as the usual argument, paying no attention to it.

Mum just walked away saying I would remember her words one day, when it's too late which just got me angrier. The family decided we should stay apart a little, just until we both calmed down.

Mum said if I left and thought about it for a further month and then still felt the same way after that, she would not say another negative word to me.

Being hot headed though, I just viewed Mum's offer as some sort of manipulative, cunning deception to deviate me from my chosen path.

Besides, all the plans were made, the date set, my dress brought, cake ordered and studio flat paid for. I started to second guess, I began to rethink my decision but then I thought no, I am going ahead. I have done everything for this day, all the effort, the planning.

**What could be so terrible about getting married?**

**After all, Mark did say he did not believe in marriages breaking up. He believed in togetherness, working together, building a family life based on unity and hard work. He wanted to work together, he stressed.**

**So what could go wrong, I thought, I have a man who is willing to work together, who's willing to have a partnership.**

Is that not the basis of every marriage at the end of the day?

I believed him, wholeheartedly.

# The day before the Wedding Day

**I was very stupid and naive; there were signs which I did not see nor understand and take note of. That's the fault of being innocent and gullible.**

Although I kept asking Mark if his family were going to come for our wedding, he said no. But just in case they did turn up I had ordered more food with the caterers as advised by my wise mother.

Mark told me that they would not like to attend because I had no alcohol on offer and that it would be better if certain family members did not attend. Especially since after drinking they would not be able to keep themselves under control and just make a nuisance of themselves and cause embarrassment.

So I never pressurised him with the planning and getting organised for the marriage, since it was stressful enough just getting married, as he remarked. It seemed strange but I did not press the matter. However, I did think it strange with Mark being the second youngest in the family yet none wanted to attend the wedding. It's not often that people get married.

And indeed my busy father flew half way across the world, left his important work and came literally just for a week, for the wedding. Mark remarked that his father had long ago organised a fishing trip with a few friends and could not cancel since he was the designated driver on this occasion. As that seemed like a ridiculous excuse I felt Mark was hiding something and did not want to tell me or open up to what was really going on. The rest of the family were just busy.

However, we went for our rehearsals and I did not care to pursue the matter further with respect to guests from his side of the family.

# The Wedding Day

The day started well; it was a nice bright day. No rain but it was a busy day with much to be done. Last minute preparations, rushing about, getting ready. Even if it was a small wedding there were still things which needed taking care of. My relations were excited and happy for me.

Dad, in the morning, I noticed, had gone for a long walk. I went out to find him and join him on his walk. He seemed distant and far away, lost in thought. We walked together silently around the block of flats then he asked me turning silently and looking seriously at my face. I still remember him asking: Are you happy? Is this what you want?

Is this your final decision?

Oh, I was nervous, extremely nervous; it was my wedding day yet Mum's words kept playing in the deepest part of my subconscious mind.

I told Dad, "Yes I'm sure" and he left it at that. We returned to my uncle's home where we had breakfast for the last time all together. I could now see it was a very emotional time for my immediate family. Me getting married in the UK meant breaking away from them and living separately.

My sister was upset; for the first time I actually noticed her or maybe she was upset earlier but I really did not notice because I was so busy and self absorbed with everything that was happening in my life at the time. My sister refused to comment or say anything, all she did remark is "do whatever you want and what makes you happy". We were always much closer to each other than to our parents because of the busy lives they lived. Separating from each other was definitely going to be hard.

Mum sat with us during breakfast; she was really quiet. Not like herself. I could see in her eyes a thousand things that she wanted to say. Yet I could not understand why she hadn't, so far.

Later Sandy went with me, to get the cake, as one of Mum's brothers was held up at work. When we came back it was a bit of a rush.

Dad was angry as he said I should not have gone since I was the bride. I should have been getting ready instead of rushing around; someone else from the family could have gone instead.

Within a little while I came down the stairs of my uncle's house and as I sat on the couch a mix of feelings went through my heart. My stomach began to turn and I felt frightened and nervous.

Before my eyes flashed my father's face, his expression, the look which said a million words which were not spoken out loud; my mother's silence, which was not normal; my sister's looks, which for the first time in my life I did not understand or recognise what they meant.

Then within a few moments the living room was full of relatives. We were all travelling in cars together from Uncle's house. The silence quickly gone and filled with sounds of chatter, laughter but across the long hall my eyes fell upon a lonely figure staring, amidst the crowd, at me. I felt someone stare away; all I saw was the outline.

I got up and walked towards the figure – it was none other than my father.

He stared at me and said, "Though your dress is so simple yet you look radiant and beautiful, my daughter."

While he spoke I could hear sadness in his voice. It was at that moment Uncle came rushing in and said we had to leave right now, as there were road blocks and we might get held up or even be late if we did not make a move on it right now.

On entering the church my heart sank a little but bravely I walked in and stood at the main entrance and waited at the door for my father to come.

It was at that very moment my mother came and took me aside. She said, "It is never too late in life to realise that you have made a mistake. You can still turn back; you don't have to go through with this. We can still call off the wedding."

I could not understand Mum and she really surprised me. Though she did mention that the reason she was quiet was because Father had told her that I had made my decision and not to question me anymore on it. But nevertheless Mum thought it was worth one last try.

Just then Father walked in. I turned to Mum, kissed her cheek, took his arm and walked down the aisle. I know in my heart that Mum was trying her hardest to protect me the only way she knew how to, and in my own way I loved her too, dearly. We just had different ways of showing it.

As we entered through the main church doors, the organ started to play. Right at the top I spotted a slightly bigger gathering than expected; a few new faces that I did not recognise. To my surprise and happiness nearly all of Mark's family had attended. I never wanted his family to miss out on their brother's wedding nor for his parents to miss out. Being brought up to have strict family values and respect family life meant respecting family ties too and that's just the way we were brought up.

Everyone looked very happy and smart. This was the very first time, on the day of our wedding itself, that I actually got to see Mark's family. Strange, I agree, but until that moment the only person I had ever met – and then too just once – was Mark's mother, Ann. His mum, two brothers and two sisters attended, along with one of his nieces.

The service was short and sweet; once it finished we took a lot of photographs with both sides of the family.

Later, after signing the marriage certificate, we all went to the hall where there was music playing and the tables were lightly decorated. My uncle was the best man – Mark had decided on that because he had met me at Uncle's house party**. Soon after Mark gave his speech and said this was the happiest day of his life.**

We had an opening dance; I danced with Dad, Uncle and Mark. Then the rest of the families took to the dance floor. After cutting the cake and having dinner some of the children took to the floor, dancing and having fun. The gathering was small, warm and cosy.

One of Mark's sisters remarked that it would have been nice to meet me before the wedding, but little did they know that it was all Mark who had kept me away. It was never me who stayed away intentionally.

As we started to wish our guests goodbye we were simultaneously trying to sort out our travel arrangements. The gifts lay piled on a table at the side of the entrance. While I wished Ann goodbye I gave her some wedding cake to take home since Mark's father was away fishing, something for him to have from the wedding. I thought it would be a nice gesture.

My uncles, being most helpful, said they would take care of everything and that I had done enough. All I had to do now was relax. Mathew drove us to the little studio with all our presents. When Mark went to open the door, at that moment he realised that his mother had the keys. So outside the studio I waited with one uncle while the other drove Mark to his mother's house. By then I was extremely exhausted.

# The Wedding Night

Mark returned with the keys in his hand but was quite cross that his mother had gone off with them. He carried me across the threshold after Mathew teased him.

We were tired; I never quite understood why Mark was so tired because I had done lots before the wedding, and all he had to do was show up.

**Going into our new little studio flat for the first time as husband and wife had a nice feeling to it.**

Mr and Mrs. It's strange really, until that point in time I carried my father's name, I was his daughter – and now I was someone else. My name had changed; it gave me a sense of excitement and kind of a little pride. I was married and I was a Mrs, I had altered my identity a little. **Now I was a woman of the world, my own person, no longer under the shadow of my parents.**

This was a new phase of my life, a new journey from now on; I was going to be the lady of my very own house. I would look after all the dealings of the household with Mark and I was very excited, or so I thought. Little did I know what life had in store for me…

We opened our wedding gifts together. Mark was only impressed with envelopes which had money in it. Apart from that he never actually cared for what was given.

In all fairness Mark's family did get us a few utensils, a bed for us and he did say that the little studio had been cleaned by his mother before we arrived.

Later that night I really did not know whether Mark was going to become intimate that very same night as he had said he was very tired. At that time sex before marriage was considered a big no and living together was definitely out of the question. That was mainly because of my parents being so old fashioned.

We did end up consummating our marriage and in all honesty it was not that fantastic or great an experience.

Mark did not use any protection and instead told me, "Don't worry, you won't get pregnant so fast. I had not gone yet to the surgery to get my birth control pills and rather had reminded him to get some precaution but of course, being Mark, he ignored my request.

I don't know what a wedding night is supposed to be like but I found nothing romantic about it in the least.

Everyone usually talks about how exciting and special their night is but I could not find anything impressive. I don't think Mark tried to do anything romantic. There were no flowers, nothing special arranged etc.

I had thought he would take the time to make some special arrangements – after all I did do everything else so that was the least he could have done, not only to impress me but to make the night special. How often does one get married?

I would have ideally expected a bunch of flowers, some scented red candles. A rose on the bed and a bottle of wine with two glasses. Maybe a present of some nice nightwear wrapped in a box at the side of the bed. I am a romantic and felt at least some sort of effort could have been made, to do things.

The disappointing night passed quickly and I waited eagerly for morning to come. I knew I had only a few days remaining before my family left the UK. My father had work commitments to go back to.

They would not return until next year.

As soon as it was morning next day my family came to see us. It was our last few days together and Mark was quite good about it, he took it in good spirit. We all had morning tea and then I left with my family; Mark was to join us later. We went shopping. On our way out Mum decided to do what she did best. She wanted to know how our first night together had been and I told her, although I was clueless as to how it was supposed to be but I really did not find it anything special but rather a disappointment.

Well, Mum did try to explain that it was new to us both, we were a couple for the first time and couples need to develop and grow with time.

I guess that advice must have been the hardest, most neutral answer to give, especially since she did not want me to get married to Mark in the first place but I respected her effort.

# Farewell for now

Soon the days passed and it was time for my family to leave so we went to the airport Mark came too and we bade them farewell.

It was a very sad and emotional time for me. This was the first ever time I had been separated from them and the first ever time I had been separated from my sister. We were always close and although there was an age gap of six years we were always much closer to each other than to our parents so we were going to miss each other dearly.

After leaving the airport Mark decided to go and visit his mother so we went.

No one was home, it was quiet but peaceful. Mark's parents lived in a council house. It was clean, big and well maintained. As you entered the living room there were sofas and a TV. On the left was a staircase leading up to three bedrooms. The living room was divided into the living area and dining room. Beyond that lay the kitchen, bathroom and garden with a shed. Overall the house had been redone by Mark's father and it looked lovely. The garden had quite a few plants as Ann liked gardening and the shed contained quite a few tools as Mark's father loved breaking and reconstructing things.

Mark left me to go up to a room – I soon discovered that was his room of toys, as he called it. Curiosity got the better of me and I really wondered what Mark's toys were and what he was doing for such a long time upstairs.

To my surprise, that was the first introduction I was given to Mark's collection. He had loads of taxidermy, rocks and fossils, skulls of animals, different shapes and sizes. Lifesize skeletons, stamps, coins, different types of lizards, birds, rabbits and snakes. It was like walking into a small room in a zoo.

After a while, roughly two hours, Mark decided to leave; he had satisfied himself by spending time in his room and soon we started to head back to the little studio. Night had fallen, it was cold and dark and all I really wanted was to sleep so that I did not feel so sad and miss my family.

# Twist of faith

Married life together, a new start and a new journey. A promise of a lifetime of togetherness, that's what I was looking forward to. My family had reached India safely, Father returned to work and I was to live with my husband in love, peace and respect.

Our happy life together lasted only as long as we dated, went out during my holiday and until I said I do. I still remember Mark's speech that this was the happiest day of his life.

It's true a man will be all he can, do whatever you want until you are his and say 'I do'.

My life changed, and rapidly, like a rising tempest. I had to change fast, learn fast, in order to survive. It was not easy, it was not a fairy tale, and it was pure hardship and struggle. Kindness turned to nastiness, words and promises of working together were replaced by me slogging like a slave all by myself. All promises and dreams shattered like broken glass.

My earliest memory was soon after my family had left the next day. Quite early in the morning Mark asked me to make him a **sandwich with sardines in it**. Being a newly wedded bride I was excited to make breakfast for my husband. I went to the off licence and bought sardines in tomato sauce as I was instructed by him. Now let me make it clear so that you understand exactly what happened...

I got the small tin and came home. With great love and affection, I made the sandwich and put it in front of him. The next thing I knew all hell broke loose, I was being abused, shouted at and told off – "Come on, what shit is this, what the hell, do you think I'm a fucking cannibal?" – and the sandwich was not eaten but flung at me.

I was in shock and asked what had happened. Again he said, "This is shit; I'm not going to eat that shit."

**Well I wanted to know why I had been spoken to like that with such great rudeness.** I innocently asked how else the sandwich was to be made. And that I did not appreciate being addressed in that way...

This sparked a big argument between us. Mark began to raise his voice at me and talk over me. He said he did not 'fucking care' what I appreciated; I needed to keep my 'mouth shut'. He said he had no clue how his mother would make his sandwich and that I needed to go and find out from her and learn how she would do things for him. Being extremely upset I decided to wait patiently to see her...

I cannot explain what I felt at that moment, my insides shook with anger and I was terribly upset. What just happened?

Who was this man? I could not logically comprehend – surely this was not the man I married?

Horror gripped my soul and I hoped for some sort of answer to this sudden outburst. It was not normal; it must have been triggered by something, I thought. I tried analysing the events which had happened since morning but there was no reason at all, there was no magical answer, there was nothing to justify his irrational outburst.

Never ever had any servant in my parents' house ever been spoken to in such a degrading manner as Mark had spoken to me, his wife.

From my personal experience I have realised that life and situations never stay the same, changes always take place, even if it is not straight away, but eventually it does happen.

# Running frantically for help

Well I did meet Ann, soon after, and I told her how Mark had reacted recently. Ann was silent. She kept quiet and did not say anything although I narrated the entire incident to her.

I realised I was the daughter-in-law and that's exactly what I was: a stranger who no one in the family knew. I was a sudden addition brought forcibly by Mark.

Ann admitted later that she was afraid that this would happen but did not care to elaborate. **What this meant, I did not understand.** Soon one of her daughters came to visit and on seeing my rather upset face asked what the matter was.

I stood over the fireplace, teary eyed. She turned to me and said, "That's why the both of you should have taken your time and lived together first."

What was it that they were trying to imply upon made no sense to me? The man was perfectly well behaved when we were going around. People don't change all of a sudden, do they?

Then she said, "I was against you both getting married." Later she asked her mother to have a word with Mark in regards to his behaviour. What was rather surprising was that Ann did not show any signs of shock or surprise regarding her son and his behaviour. Rather her response was of someone who expected it or was used to this kind of behaviour.

While talking to Ann I realised that Mark had a history of behaviour which was not proper or appropriate. He had smashed his ex-girlfriend's house but paid for damages. He had previously had one too many drinks and got into fights at bars and smashed them too, gotten arrested and Ann most often had to go rescue him.

# The shock

As our conversation continued I questioned Ann as to what was the brand I needed for her son so that I didn't make the same mistake again and have to suffer that entire ordeal again.

**Ann still did not reveal the name of the product; instead she said "it's a bit dear"; and that she would get it for me**. Being innocent and naive I felt gratitude and light hearted. What I did not realise is how long it would be, for me to actually get the paste he so wanted.

Quite a while passed and my married life turned no better – rather it was up in turmoil.

Finally, one day, to my surprise, I was gifted with one little blue bottle the size of my thumb called sardines in tomato sauce; the company brand name was called Princess.

Strange, I thought to myself, this little thing must be very expensive. Later I hunted all over to try and find the cost and where I could shop for it. Oh my God, I was shocked beyond words; it cost just 50p from Sainsbury. I was surprised as this is not what I would call dear and I would certainly have been more generous if it was me who was buying things for them in respect to quantity. I always had a generous giving nature.

However, I let it pass, I had much to understand and learn about my new life.

Days went by and things just got worse. I would be terribly lonely not having anyone to talk to and no friends. All I had was Virgin Media TV to watch.

Eagerly I would wait for Mark to return every day from work. I would, during the day, try to keep the studio flat on the ground floor clean. Meals would be cooked for him so that after a hard day's work he would have something to eat.

**But strangely enough Mark never wanted to eat anything that I cooked**. I did not know what Mark was up to, where he ate, but it was not at home. Mark's work started early in the morning so I would make him packed lunch, then when he returned later he always said he was not hungry.

He would not want to communicate, he did not want to speak, and he never shared how his day was at work.

Mark would just come in, say "make me tea" and that's it.

The only sound was that of the TV...

Days passed in this manner.

# Worthless trash

One day, I put my arms lovingly around Mark from behind as he sat on the armchair watching the TV. It was an innocent, loving gesture; in return Mark asked me what did I want.

I said I wanted nothing from him. I was just being affectionate as he is my husband.

Mark remarked, "Take your hands off, are you after sex? Well you're not going to get any; even if you had to pay me I would not touch you..."

These words to a new wife hurt deeply.

It made me feel so awful and low, not to mention embarrassed. He gave the impression of wanting me to feel worthless and indeed he succeeded: that's exactly what I felt. I did not realise it then but that was the beginning of Mark starting to attack my self esteem. That was the start and continuation of him starting to break my confidence and chip away at my confidence level, just like a sharp butcher's knife slicing away at a raw piece of meat and cutting fine layers.

So many different thoughts and emotions ran through me mentally and emotionally. Was I inexperienced? Was I not good enough? What was it which made Mark turn against me and be so mean? I could not understand.

A thousand questions and no answers.

Mark made me feel worthless and like trash. It was a new marriage, we had not been dating very long, and we were not living together before marriage.

What makes a man turn away from his new wife?

# Cast Away

To make matters worse Mark would torment and torture me mentally with silence. He would come home and he would not speak a word, nor would he look at me, nor could I approach him for it would upset his mental peace and drive him mad with anger. The best way and appropriate behaviour was his way, his rules which had to be followed.

I started very soon, and at such an early stage in the marriage, to hate him.

When I tried to talk to Mark he would say, "Shush, woman, you talk too much, be quiet. Women should be seen but not heard. If you're lonely or want to talk to someone, get a ball, draw a face, call it Wilson and talk to it. I'm not interested. Leave me alone."

Does it sound familiar?

Yes, just like the movie Cast Away. When I would get upset somehow it made him very happy. Truly it was not a joke; he could stay all day long without communicating but I could see him watch my every move. It was like a sick game, the tormentor tormenting, waiting, watching, and studying my reactions to his actions. It was a mental game of the minds, to see how far he could take it. To what level and extent before I would cave and break down before him and he would look at me with arrogance and an air of superiority and victory.

Sometimes, I would have a sudden outburst at Mark because I thought, if this is what he had planned all along then why marry me?

What was the point? I did not understand – where was the equality and the promise of love and working together?

To love and to hold until death do us part.

Where were the vows we took, not so long ago?

# Mother-in-law

I openly admit to being a very naive and trusting young lady. One always looks at others and views them as you view yourself. I find this to be very common. Likewise I used to see everyone as good and I tried never to think badly or with negative thoughts in relation to others.

I would keep in contact with my family using a Lebara **connection** which worked out very economical but still I could not talk for as long as I would have liked. It did cost and they did have their own lives and responsibilities. This helped preserve my sanity to a certain extent because Mark was upsetting me and with each and every day he just got worse. Luckily I had some of the money from the wedding gifts, because we shared it between ourselves.

It felt as if Mark hated and despised my very presence.

My father told me before he left to treat my in-laws just like my very own parents, with respect and love.

So from my part I can say with a good conscience that I did. Through my conversation, although I tried to hide it from my family, they understood clearly that I was extremely unhappy. Since my early teenage days my mother had been sick and her health was not in a good condition. She had a cough which was awful; she would cough all day and all night. The doctors could not find any proper medication which could help her. She had various pumps and was diagnosed as having acute asthma. If Mum worried about anything and got upset it triggered this and sent her into coughing fits. I did not at any cost want my mother to suffer so I didn't want to tell my parents anything about what was going on behind closed doors.

But family is always family and no one can know you better than your immediate family. They knew things were not right and this upset my family and troubled them greatly. They knew I was hiding something from them. So finally I told them just a little bit, briefly, in regards to the issue I was facing.

My parents' advice was to take my mother-in-law into confidence since Mark loved her dearly and ask her for help. Maybe she could shed some light on this situation and help me understand how to deal with her son. Or try to understand what could be causing such a change in his attitude and behaviour towards me.

This seemed like really good advice, the only problem being I did not know the woman too well. Would she be open and honest or would she be like one of these other mother-in-laws who really did not like their new daughter-in-laws? Or she just might be fantastic and have all the advice ready for me.

I had only one way of finding out, **the direct approach.**

One day while Ann was making tea I told her I needed to talk to her. It was in total confidence. Somehow I think she knew I wanted to have a personal conversation with her. **Then I started to confide in her that I was going through a very tough time with her son and I was in desperate need of help.** I started by saying that food was a major issue because he wanted me to do things exactly the way she would do it and I had no clue what her style of cooking was.

She started laughing but nevertheless seemed to be supportive, saying she would have a word with him and calling him silly. I thought that she was listening and siding with me...

**To solve the first problem** I asked her to give me all the information in respect to what Mark liked.

Brands, places or supermarkets where I could go to, to get supplies for him so that he would be happy. I decided to give it a try because **the first excuse** I made for Mark was that he was not used to married life and that he was stressed. This is the excuse that I accepted which was given to me by Mark's mother and I simply went along with it.

The second problem that I faced in our relationship, which was a big problem, was the intimacy issue. It was a new marriage, very new, and there was no intimacy, no sex, no talking, there was nothing...

So what's going on?? This was my question. I could not make sense of it.

In relation to the lack of sex, Ann said, "Well there's nothing that great in it anyway, you're not losing out in any way."

I needed to understand how Mark was thinking at present. Up until now I was still trying to get to know what could have or what might have upset him so drastically as to cause a sudden shift and mental imbalance. That's the only explanation I could think of. I never wanted to blame Mark, rather I tried up until then to try to understand him. **Ann replied that Mark had grown up in an environment surrounded by and witnessing domestic violence and had seen things in his childhood which reflected in his present behaviour as an adult.**

I then realised that there were many factors behind Mark's irrational behaviour and sadly it occurred to me at that moment that Mark was an abuser not by choice but because that is what he had grown up witnessing.

# Uncle's revelation

Apart from everything that was going on simultaneously and making me miserable, I had a pleasant surprise. My uncle came over to visit me which was nice until ah...he came with more awful news.

Uncle worked for a company that used to supply staff to the railways which is how he and Mark became acquainted. They were work mates and drinking buddies.

He started by asking how everything was and if I was happy. He wanted to know if Mark was treating me right. When I questioned him as to why he was all of a sudden interested in my married life, Uncle just went silent...

I knew he had come for a reason – it was not just to visit. Uncle actually felt very embarrassed and did not know how to approach the conversation with me. **Recently at work, in the gents' toilet he had heard Mark, who was the centre of attention; he was surrounded with an audience of work mates while Mark stood and held the attention of all by mocking me, his wife, laughing, ridiculing me in a degrading manner.**

Mark was telling his work mates, how could a man have bigger tits than his wife?

Uncle did not want to say more...

Faith played a most horrific game with me as it was that morning that I had found out I was pregnant and then later on that very same day came my uncle's revelation. Only I knew I was pregnant at that moment.

No words could describe what I felt at that moment in time. This upset me a great deal. To me it meant not only did my married life behind closed doors remain awful but even people who were perfect strangers came to know what I looked like, despite never having seen me, with or without clothes on.

This made me go through a wide range of mixed feelings. I never ever wore false thick padded bras or manipulated the way I looked. Pride in myself was always a big part of my nature. What I had was what I had. I felt insulted, ashamed, angry etc.

That evening, when Mark returned home, I asked him about what I heard, was this true, that he had been making fun of me to his work mates?

I got no answer. Mark heard me but chose to ignore the question.

"Were you ridiculing me at work in the toilet?" I asked again. Louder this time. Mark did not want to answer and ignored me yet again. **Again, I repeated the question with a raised voice. He said, "Don't you dare fucking shout at me, you bitch." He got up, came at me and started to shout, "Yes I was. What you going to do about it, what you going to do? You better keep your mouth shut or I'll shut it for you."**

Then he remarked that the person who told me had a big mouth and it was not their business to tell me, they should stay out of it.

Mark was referring to my mother's brother James, who worked on the trains too and who had heard the entire conversation. Being my uncle he was upset to learn how my husband was ridiculing me, his niece. Of course he wanted to warn me.

I cried in anger when all I wanted to do was pick up something and hit him and call him a bastard, which he was. But me being nine stone and him being twenty stone was the main reason which kept me in control, because I knew if I were to be hit by him I would be severely crushed, injured or even killed.

# Meeting Ann again

Well I decided to throw caution to the wind and have yet another open conversation with his mum again. Maybe she could throw some light on all this, because I did not know what to make of it.

I had problems coping with Mark, understanding him and constantly being in a state of despair and uncertainty, not knowing how to react or what to expect. Each day held new challenges, every day had new problems; I dreaded each day, I hated having to run to Ann nearly every other day because there were problems – and how many times could I keep going to her?

How many times did I have to beg for help from the mother of my husband? I should not have had to keep doing this, or living like a dog. That's what I felt: as if I was being treated like a dog – but the main difference was the dog who was a pet in Ann's house was shown more care and respect than I was by all, including Mark himself.

For me this was not an easy conversation to have.

The reason being this was all new to me.

This lady was a stranger to me, she was the mother of my husband and I'm complaining about her son, to her. I'm the outsider but the reason I did this, was…Desperation. This man had promised to be a good husband, to work together in partnership and to do stuff as a family unit.

**The response Ann gave me first was, "Oh if you're not happy with him you can always leave and go back to your parents**." Not the response I was looking for. I would never be able to get married in church ever again? That meant, in other words, I had limited choices: to suffer, go back to my parents' house, or try to make the marriage work and hope for the better life of togetherness which he had promised only a few months ago.

**In response to the mockery at work and my physique** she was surprised but did not have much to say. Mark passed it off to Ann as if he was joking and she told him she did not want him being rude to me. Ann advised me not to pay any attention to his words and said he's not mature. **That justification did not satisfy me because I was only 28 and Mark was 34 – immaturity was no excuse for misconduct and the lack of respect I felt Mark had towards me.**

Mark had never been anything but respectful to his mother and sisters. When I reminded him of that, he said, "That's my mother, she's different, you're not..."

Then Ann went on to tell me that I should not worry about Mark. I should cook and clean and be a good wife. Do all my part and take no notice of him.

This kind of reminded me of Mark's famous sentence that a woman should be seen but not heard.

Looking back now I realise that this is the very same thing she did. Ann had endured a lot of abuse in her marriage and what she did and how she continued to live is the way she thought I should live. It seemed as if she wanted me to go through the same circumstances and follow her way of life in her footsteps. **But the main difference was I was not Ann and I would never be...**

Now at that time I knew no better, my family was in another country, miles away, and since I called Ann Mother and respected her as a mother I listened to what she said and took it as gospel truth.

Thinking she was not taking sides because she also tried to reassure me not to worry and that anytime I needed someone to talk to I could just come to her and she would straighten Mark out, gave me confidence.

# Fear of being pregnant

Strangely enough Ann's words comforted me at that time – it never really mattered who it came from, if the words were true and meant, or if it was just for show or hypocrisy. When you reach that point of an all-time low and have no one by your side, all you care for is a kind word of comfort, and unfortunately to keep getting that kindness you will do anything. I had some peace of mind; someone was there to talk to, someone whom I could rely on or so it seemed at the time... But still, I was annoyed, and to add to my awful life, **the secret I held within was that I was pregnant amidst all this misery.**

Being of mixed parents and having a staunch Roman Catholic mother at that time I was prohibited from having an abortion. The thought did cross my mind though.

But I was happy to be a mum – excited but also very worried because of the kind of husband I had. I wanted my baby but not him... Worries crept into my mind and fear too. What was to be a joyful occasion for me was going to turn into a long road of torment, anguish and torture.

I had hoped an innocent little baby would bring joy, peace and unity and would turn the heart of a beast into a gentle human being, but I could not have been more wrong.

I was going through a lot of mixed feelings: joy and fear, happiness and regret.

Yet at the end I was going to be a mum, one of the best decisions of my life.

When Mark returned home that evening, I gave him the news. Since that moment things took such a turn for the worse I can hardly find the words to describe the situation. He was in denial and would not accept that I was pregnant with his child. Mark said I was wrong, the pregnancy test was not right and that I needed to do it again. The second test came back positive and Mark was silent as usual but I could see that he was waiting to explode in anger. He looked like a caged, hungry lion waiting to spring to freedom and eat any obstruction in its way.

Just how horrible life was about to get I had not a clue... We broke the news to the entire family, starting with Ann first. I saw no signs of excitement or joy. Neither was I congratulated but I saw stress on Ann's face. She said she hoped I would have a girl because Mark would be worse if I had a boy. Truly I don't know why she said that or what she meant by the remark; he was not well behaved nor did he treat me right. Soon all of Mark's family had received the news that I was pregnant. Some were excited to have a new baby but others had no comment.

After a few weeks I started to become very ill. My body could not take the pregnancy. I was ill beyond imagination and could not keep any solid food or liquid down. I had regular visits to the GP; my body was swelling terribly because I was retaining a lot of fluid. As a result I looked very huge and fat. I was given medicines and arm bands but nothing seemed to be helping. My hands and feet were all swollen and blue. I had to keep my feet up, raised on the bed with pillows under it and the pain was terrible. The sickness lasted all day long and I had problems keeping food down. My spine would hurt and regular pain accompanied me throughout the pregnancy.

I made a mistake which I truly regretted – silly of me, really, why I did it I really don't know – but because of my spine pain I asked Mark if he would press my back for me. To this he replied, "Don't be stupid, woman, me press your back? You should be bending down on all fours and pressing my legs for me. In which world are you living that you think I am going to do anything for you? You are here to serve me, nothing else, not the other way around. Go make me tea, go now."

Inwardly, I hated Mark for how he treated me. I was trapped at that moment and I had seen so many others on the high street walking with their partners or husbands. Men supporting their woman. And yet for all that I on the other hand had Mark, selfish, rude, arrogant, an abuser and bully.

Nothing changed with each passing day: Mark's behaviour got worse, the language increased and his behaviour worsened. Cruelty reached a new level and I started to curse my life change from riches to this twenty first century slavery I had been reduced to. In this day and age I could never have imagined this was possible in Britain.

I was still kept in solitude and it was seen to in such a way that I could not talk to the rest of my family. Mark would get upset and said he wanted me to have nothing to do with any of them. I had to shop and carry the shopping up and down the high street. Hands swollen, I would spend the entire day cooking in pain and then Mark would come in and say I'm not hungry. This continued for a while... I had my suspicions that he was eating elsewhere but nevertheless due to fear of what might happen, I had to keep meals prepared for when he got home just in case if he wanted something to eat it would be ready for him.

Mark's behaviour was always irrational, never predictable; it was hard to know what to expect and he loved keeping me in mental agony. If he never wanted anything for days, the one day it was not there he would want it. If he wanted something no matter how hard I tried it was never good enough unless his mother did it. He was insanely torturous and tried to drive me to the point of mental insanity or a mental breakdown. **But my strength came from above and if I lived I lived for the little life I held inside of me.**

Mark resented me for getting pregnant – according to him it was my fault and I should have taken care not to get pregnant. The fact that at nine stone he found me fat, when pregnant and a larger size he despised my very size even more and said I had to leave the house on my own as he did not want to be seen with me on the streets.

# The fall of dark days

The money which my parents had left me with finally ran out and the money from the marriage gifts had all gone too – it was bound to, there was only a limit as to how far I could stretch it to. Mark would take care of all the bills which were the TV and phone basic package from Virgin Media and the studio flat which had all bills included in the rent. I knew he did not earn very much. Trying to still be the good and understanding wife, I had never asked Mark for any money all this time. I tried very hard to manage on the bare necessities with what I had.

I don't know where Mark thought I was getting money to manage on because food kept coming from whatever little I had. He never asked, nor did he care.

But unfortunately, the day soon came when my purse was empty. I checked and rechecked every compartment. I turned my handbag upside down and shook it vigorously – no, there was nothing, not even a penny. I told Mark, with dread filling my heart, that I didn't have any money, not even a penny to my name, and for the very first time I asked him if he would be kind enough to give me some. I knew I had to be kind, I knew I had to ask in a humble tone. Mark viewed and treated me not as his equal but as his slave, someone lower than himself, so I had to ask without looking at him for a little bit of money. It took everything out of me, the last of my self-pride, because within the deepest part of my soul I knew he would enjoy me asking and until now I had not had to ask him, I had kind of managed so far. I knew he would make me beg. But nothing mattered, only my baby did...so with this in mind I asked...

I was pregnant and felt extremely hungry. The day before was the last day of the last of the bread and I had one slice of crust left which I dipped in my cup of tea. That evening when I apologised to Mark saying I had not made anything to eat because I had nothing, I found it strange because he did not fly into a rage; he did not get upset but was rather calm.

But the next day on opening all the cabinets in the kitchen once again I could see in front of me empty shelves, apart from sugar, milk and tea – there was no food, not even scraps which I could put together so that baby and I did not starve.

I never cared for myself but what about my baby?

What had this innocent child done to deserve starvation? It had not even come into the world yet.

To my devastating horror Mark turned to me in the utmost unconcerned cold manner and said, "I don't have any money to give you." He added, "You can do with some starvation, it will do you some good, look at what you look like. Go take a look in the mirror; you're like a fat pig."

Such an evil, cruel, horrible man I had never seen in all my life. I was his wife, pregnant with his child inside of me and he said he had no money to give me.

This was the first time I had ever, ever asked Mark for money... I was in shock. I asked him again if he was serious or if this was a twisted way of him trying to wind me up.

I suspected cruelty; I suspected I would have to beg for my child for food from its father just so that he could watch me suffer. But never ever did I expect that a father would deny their wife food for their unborn child.

This was the start of our starvation days. With hands on my belly and tears rolling down my eyes in the bathroom, I told my baby I was so sorry. I wondered how I was going to feed baby. But I did not want Mark to see me cry.

# Not sex but rape

Meanwhile we were not going so often to Ann's house. Mark preferred to go without me before coming to the studio where we were living. After work he would go there while in solitude I would wait all day long, longing to talk to someone, anyone. Then Mark would return and shun me as usual. There Mark had his meals cooked for him, which I discovered much later on and that was the reason why he was never hungry and he never wanted anything accept tea. Even that too he would regularly throw away each time I made it.

The only time it started to be different is when he desired to have sex.

I don't know what brought about this sudden change because it was awful. As the days progressed my feelings changed – now at this point in time I had started to hate Mark. As such, the question that once had, much earlier in our marriage, crossed my mind as to the lack of intimacy at this stage in our marriage seemed to have no importance to me at all. I did not care for him. I bore his name and carried his child within me but we were strangers far apart living under one roof.

The relationship was of abuser and abused, stronger and weaker, tormented and tormentor. Mark had been controlling me and manipulating me mentally for a long time. He had become quite good at controlling me psychologically and belittling me.

Now I had no desire towards Mark at all, it was all long gone because of everything he had subjected me to.

But this changed, Mark changed: he suddenly started wanting to have sex. This was the cause of great grief for me. It was the most difficult situation for anyone to be in and I would not wish it upon my worst enemy either.

Not having any feelings for someone and having to sleep with them is awful. I used to tell Ann and Mark that one day my feelings will change, there is only so much someone can bear. Mark thought I was just talking, he never actually listened to anything I said and nor did he pay attention to anything I wanted.

Not having any feeling at all for someone except dislike, fear and repulsion and having to sleep and share an intimate moment with that person was nigh on impossible, willingly.

In fact it never mattered when I wanted to have sex. Never mattered what I wanted or did not want. Only what he did. He would say, "come on, get undressed" and I would just have to lie down and take it. He was never gentle nor loving. I don't think the art of love making existed ever between us. No foreplay, no tenderness, there was only pain. His hands on me and himself inside me. I would be still and in my head all I thought was go on and be done with it. I just waited for it to be over; anyway it never lasted long. He would use me, do himself and when he was finished he would give me a smack on my behind and say that's me done now. Time for bed.

Such was my life. I knew the routine; pretty much like a blow up doll I was used and abused. I cannot call this part a healthy sex life, how could I? There was no joy, only pain and disgust. I have the strength to term it as it is, rape, because being married does not mean sex can be forced upon someone, it has to be consensual.

I soon mastered the art of letting my mind go to other places while Mark lay on top of me; I was a vegetable, no response, but Mark never realised; then again Mark never ever took notice of me in the first place. How would he know anything that was happening or not happening?

The only one who Mark cared for was Mark himself.

I wanted too much by wanting to talk to him or wanting a relationship. He also said his mother would not be around forever and hence he needed someone to fill in for her when she was gone and to look after him, cook, clean and wash.

I do not write with joy in my heart. Rather, my experience of married life has been one of utmost misery and degradation. I write to help others learn from my mistake and free themselves. These are memories which neither time nor space can ever let me forget but one which is deep rooted within me forever.

# The penny jar

Money was never given to me. With each and every day passing by I was becoming more heavily pregnant and ravenous. The stomach pains were terrible; it felt like sharp, piercing pains and it was unbearable. Some days I would roll on the floor and could not stand. I would vomit but it was just white liquid first and then green bile.

Finally, when I could take no more and reached the point beyond hunger I went to the wardrobe.

There Mark had a penny jar. It was full of coppers, I took it down carefully, and counted it. In my mind I wanted to run as fast as I could to the off-licence but not being strong enough and weak I had to walk extremely slowly. As I walked I felt extremely dizzy and very faint but I had to get to the shop, I knew I did. There was enough to get a small bag of porridge. The shopkeeper asked if everything was okay. He asked if I needed to sit or if I was about to deliver. I said I was fine, just carrying big. All that seemed a priority at that moment was making the porridge with water and eating it quickly to fill my stomach so that baby would not starve any longer.

How could I tell perfect strangers what was going on? What if they too wanted to use and abuse me? No, at that moment I was scared, not knowing who to turn to. Hunger and starvation has a way of messing with your head. I told no one, I never saw Ann and nor did she care about my whereabouts, nor did she know anything about what was happening.

Ann knew the marriage was not right from the word go, or so she said it was doomed from the beginning. Mark was very particular and he knew that his jar had been touched. He asked me first if someone had come to our place; I said no. He asked if I had been in his wardrobe or if I had moved his jar. There was no point in lying so I admitted it. This made Mark very angry.

He started shouting and saying I had "no fucking business" touching his stuff and never ever as long as I live should I touch his things. I had no business to do that. Then he demanded to know what I went and bought so I told him it was porridge and I was so very hungry I could not take the hunger any more.

Mark said water is free, I should drink that and be full.

I recalled in my father's house we had servants for everything. Cooking, cleaning, washing and drivers to drive us around. Strange how life and situations can change from one extreme to another I did regret the choice I made to marry Mark every single day.

From riches to rags.

# Ten pounds too much

This continued. There was no way to get in touch with my family, no money to call and cry for help. My mum and dad thought everything was fine. Even I sometimes had problems believing what was happening. There was no way to travel to ask for food from other family members present. No oyster card. **I had nothing**, nothing at all, just my baby and I would pray to God to show me the way please... because I had had enough.

I was looking at the calendar eagerly, and on pay day I asked Mark, "Can I have just ten pounds please?" I knew what the answer would be but sometimes in life when you have nothing you have to ask; even if it's your abuser he might give you something.

He asked me, "For what?" I said, "My clothes don't fit me, it's extremely cold this winter, my shoes have fallen apart." I had been sticking them together and walking. I could not stick them anymore, they were too far gone. All I wanted was five pounds for a cheap pair of shoes and five pounds for a cheap pair of trousers.

My belly was growing, our baby was growing and my clothes did not fit me. My t shirts were rising up and my belly was hanging out. My short capris were the only thing that fitted me. Having to wear them every day was embarrassing, and soon they too would not fit me anymore. My shoes were held together by glue and many a time while walking on the road they would open up making me feel very awkward, so I would drag my feet so that others did not realise my shoes had opened up.

The most embarrassing time was while crossing a narrow road a car wanted to pass and I was dragging my feet. The man started shouting because I was really taking a long time to move across from one side to the other pavement. I took my shoe in my hand and crossed faster. It was just for one moment in time, yet the embarrassment stays with you for a lifetime. Crossing the road with one shoe on and holding the other all falling apart in my hand. I had no coat and when I would go for walks I would freeze. That winter was extremely cold especially since I had nothing warm or appropriate to wear to protect myself.

All hopes were up. I knew it was the 28th of the month, it was Mark's pay day. I did not ask for much. I thought he would have pity, show mercy and give me just ten pounds. I would make it last.

Mark turned to me and said, "I have no money for you..." I asked him what he meant; I was hungry, cold, freezing and very angry. He said, "Just what I told you – I have no money for you." I said, "You just got paid." Mark replied, "I spent it, it's all gone." I demanded to know what on because certainly I never saw any of it.

Mark had loved taxidermy ever since his teenage days; it was his hobby to buy taxidermy and collect them. His second love was the gym. He said, "I spent money on bills keeping a roof over your fat ass. Then I got money for my travel card and myself and the **rest I spent three hundred pounds on snakes.**"

As long as I live I will never forget that answer. Nothing could have prepared me for it. I starved, froze and Mark sat laughing loudly, saying, "Tough, too bad, I spent it, you don't need anything."

The evil, dark side I could see in Mark, who does that, who makes someone suffer in this manner, I thought. I started asking why he was torturing me so. Did he not want the baby? But each time something happened I was accepting it, submitting and not fighting back.

Married life continued as it did; there was no change at all. My mind was weakening even before I realised it was. From being a go-getter, strong minded, determined person I was changing. I did not even realise it. I was becoming weak, a victim of mental and physical abuse and I did not even realise it was happening to me. My mind, attitude and behaviour were all being reshaped to suit Mark's desires. He was very cleverly keeping me under bondage. Many a time he said no one would want me, I was useless, ugly, and fat and had nothing to offer anyone. It was mental imprisonment where psychologically I was bound and Mark was the only one holding the key.

Why I stayed with Mark is surprising. I think it's because I started to actually believe him; his words kept resounding even in his absence. It's a kind of brain washing, Mark was in my head. He made me feel useless, dependent and as if I had felt there would be no life without him and tomorrow would never come.

I was his wife, he provided the roof over my head. It's true, he did; if I left where would I go? On whose door would I knock, on strangers'?

What if that stranger took me straight back to him? Mark always said if ever he thought I was cheating on him he would kill me. The man had me afraid. There was no other place to be than where he could see me – that's the conclusion I came to. Stupid but I felt I had his protection. Protection from what I really don't know, maybe it was protection from himself.

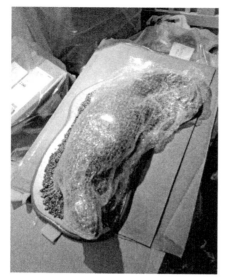

# A kindness to repay

A while after, together we went to see Mark's mother and I told Ann about Mark's taxidermy expenses. She was quiet, it was no surprise to her, she was used to it. Mark at that time asked Ann if she had anything spare that she could part with because I was grumbling too much that I was cold and getting on his nerves. He went so far as to say he just wanted to shut me up so that he did not have to put up with me.

Soon Ann came down from upstairs and she held a little, lightweight black coat in her hand; it was not very warm but it was something. I thought it was rather kind of her to give me one of her very own coats but later realised she had discarded it and kept it aside to be given away to charity...

A kindness which I would repay back many a time over in the years to come. Of course at that time none of us knew I would but I had hoped that I would be able to one day.

Later on, in the afternoon, I stood in the kitchen talking to Mark's mother about how things were going on between us. Ann wanted to know. She was not surprised at all, but gave me the usual answer not to bother about him but to keep on being a good wife and doing my part as she called it or chaos. This answer had stopped consoling me ages ago. It meant nothing to me, it was just the most well thought of neutral advice anyone could give which was meant to pacify me and maintain me under Mark's rule.

I did tell Ann that I thought it was not right that Mark spent so much on Taxidermy whilst he kept me starving. Ann said she was surprised to learn that. In relation to his expenses she agreed that now he had to straighten up his act and concentrate on being more of a father but he was too immature to do so. **She also went on to describe him as a big baby but that is not the words I would use to describe him.**

Later, one day during that week, one of Mark's elder sisters came to our little studio flat. She put in front of me a bag of really old looking shoes and sandals, though they were all big brands, and she said, "D**ig in, don't be shy**." But the shoes she gave me were really very old; and a shirt she offered me had a stain mark on it, but as the saying goes **beggars can't be choosers.**

And at that time and point in my life it was a question of survival so I could not refuse anything. I accepted humbly and with full gratitude. I remembered how ironic it was that in my father's house we would give away the best of clothes, silks and satins to charity and for the first time when I received charity it was in such a condition...

Never mind. I would not have ever dreamt of giving things away in such a condition. The bin would have been a better option for it. But I took her gesture in good faith, an act of kindness and thanked her genuinely.

As time went on things continued to worsen; I was getting heavier. But I believe God does send people to help in tough times and I had been asking plenty of times in prayers for help and a way out. Before this time I had completely stopped talking to my family when Mark made it so because he was getting upset with them calling and wanting to come and visit; he said it was annoying him.

My mother's brother would come over and give me his leftover food instead of throwing it in the bin.

This was food his mother-in-law would give to him and he and his wife did not want any of it. I was extremely grateful for the food, only I alone knew the value of it. This precious food put some amount of distance between me and baby starving. Uncle James was embarrassed to offer me the food but on seeing how delighted I was he remarked he would come as often as he could and when he had something spare to give me.

**I was hungry, so when the food would come my eyes would light up.** Maybe he realised or took note of my behaviour but never said a word. Only one day he commented that I looked very unwell, pale and hungry. I put it down to pregnancy and sickness.

For me he was an answer to my prayers.

Uncle James could not understand as he asked me once, "Why does Mark not give you any money at all? To go out, etc?" but **I was too ashamed to say out loud what my married life was like or what went on behind closed doors.**

Sadly, at that time I was not aware of soup kitchens, nor their locations. Care was taken to keep me in full darkness and ignorance. I was made to feel helpless, alone and vulnerable as if there was no choice – the only way was his way, their way or no way at all.

# The trip back

Feeling excited as the days passed by, I started counting down and eagerly awaiting my trip to return to my parents' home. This I welcomed with great joy in my heart. Since originally I was here only on holiday and to meet family, I had a return ticket to Kolkata. This was mainly because I was to return and then fly out to Australia to do a second masters. Since I changed plans on my holiday the ticket was never really cancelled so I decided I would travel later, visit family and then return back to join Mark. I did have all my personal belongings still back home which I wanted to bring back with me. Mark knew all along that I would be flying and would return later. So he never questioned it. We both believed marriage was for life until he started treating me terribly.

When I landed back in Kolkata though the heat was unbearable and my family had not seen me for a good few months. They were shocked at the sight of me; they could not believe that the person who stood before them was still me. They described me as wretched looking and said my face looked pale and tormented. The glow I once had was gone, my radiance dulled, the smile vanished, my eyes they saw were full of sadness and when my sister hugged me, at that moment I felt love and comfort. The first question she asked was: "Did you miss me?"

Tears rolled down my eyes uncontrollably. I missed them all, even Mum.

Mum knew when she looked at me that something was wrong but did not pursue the matter at that moment. Outside the airport stood the driver; he opened the door for me to get in. I was taken home and asked what I wanted to eat... That was the best part of being back home with family. It never mattered which country I was in, what mattered was that I was back with family. Anywhere they would have been at the time would have been home and a true delight for me to be with them.

We decided to go out and eat dinner outside.

Dinner outside?

Yes, my old life, my old ways: I was fed, I was looked after and got my hair and nails done, back massaged. Father had made arrangements to have me taken me to private doctors to have the baby monitored and checked and find out if the health and development of the foetus was going according to the expected growth rate. He was very concerned as to how his grandchild was doing especially since he had found out from Mum how I had suffered.

Yet what I never knew was that Mum was trying to keep the peace; she was very worried about what action my father would take in regards to Mark. So she tried to play it all down and did not narrate all that I said to her, to Father. Maybe he himself thought I was sick because of the pregnancy.

Every day I had a car at my disposal to go wherever I pleased. We would go out; all my favourite things were brought for me. Once again I was being spoilt by my family. I ate and ate as if I had never seen food before and everyone was surprised.

Forgetting all table manners, within me I felt as if I would never see food again – all that mattered was having large amounts of fresh fruits and food so that I could help provide all the necessary nutrients for the baby. My body was certainly not healthy; it was weak and needed to get replenished with goodness again.

The doctor prescribed iron and calcium tablets. Since I was having regular leaking from the embryo sack she gave me another medicine to keep baby in and stop any possible miscarriage from happening.

Father was not there – he was away on business – so Mum communicated from one side to another. During my stay with the family Mark never called, he never bothered at all. But suddenly, after three weeks, I got a call from Mark, saying he was missing me and wondering how long before I returned back to him. He also said he wanted the baby to be born in the UK and no other country because baby was English.

Mum was happy that he called. I had an argument with her because I did not want to return to the UK to Mark. But Mum was Catholic and I was very angry that she was old fashioned and quoting the Bible back at me. She said marriage is for life and she had tried to stop me from getting married to Mark but I was so headstrong and did not want to listen to her. She also said that I was going to be a mother and had to take responsibilities for my own actions.

While I still wanted to return to Australia, Mother said she was not going to look after the baby so I would have to. I had to make my own way. If Mark was saying he was sorry then maybe I should give him another chance just for the baby as he was the father.

She also said maybe he was scared of how to manage and was taking it out on me but once he saw the baby she was sure his heart would melt.

The main sentence which caught my attention was that Mum said I would be disgracing Father. Unfortunately it was Mother's wish to live in India, she loved the place, her entire family including her very own mother lived in the UK yet Mum loved it over there. As such I think the mentality of the people started to become part of her nature. She said Father would be very upset and embarrassed. Only a few months ago he had dropped his work and rushed from an important business meeting just to attend his daughter's wedding and then a few months down the line that very same daughter returns pregnant and does not want to go back to her husband.

She asked me for once to think about the family instead of myself, to think how many times the family had been there for me.

I did not agree with Mum but I soon realised this was a big mistake, one which I had gotten into and only I could get myself out of it.

Soon the time was drawing nearer; I was to get the last direct flight back to the UK. Dad unfortunately landed while I was preparing to leave. When we got to the airport I said my goodbyes to them and all I had was some clothes and a proper pair of shoes.

Before going up the stairs to the plane I ran out to wave my hands franticly at the glass window where people stood to see their loved ones off. I could not see them but I hoped they saw me wave goodbye. I was grateful for the care and affection they had showered on me and though I dreaded my return to Mark I cherished the short time with my family.

Dad still becomes emotional to this day when he thinks of me running out to say goodbye.

# Returning back to my persecutor

As the plane was landing in the UK I had begun to hope that maybe my absence from Mark would have changed him – back to when we first met – and I hoped he would be different in attitude and behaviour; perhaps Mum's words would turn out to be true, just maybe.

The journey back was horrible, it was long and did my back no favours. I took really ill on the flight and kept vomiting; the exact cause was not known – either it was because I ate something which did not agree with me or it was just the travelling.

The air hostess was extremely caring and helpful towards me. She organised for wheelchair facilities so that I did not have to walk unnecessarily.

Mark had arrived with his boss to pick me up from the airport and take me back to our house. This was the first time we had ever met. The boss, Raj, was kind and took me home. It was a long journey so I did get sick in the car too.

Finally on reaching the little studio and being exhausted all I wanted to do was sleep. Mark asked if I was hungry; this made me happy, how ridiculous of me. I thought maybe he has changed. Absence makes the heart grow fonder – was it true in my case?

Well, he said he was going to get me a KFC bargain bucket so I said, "Thank you."

It was mid afternoon, I was getting hungrier. All the cabinets were empty, there was nothing. Where once stood tea bags and sugar even they were not there and the shelves lay bare.

Oh my God, what had I come back to? Not even milk in the fridge, each and everything was spotlessly clean but empty as if no one had been living there.

Hours passed and from daylight it went to sunset; by now I was rolling on the floor, sick with hunger. I could not keep up with the hunger anymore and I am very sure that I passed out with the pain.

Much later, I came around to find Mark there sitting on the chair. He had actually got some chicken which really shocked me. I was extremely upset and forgot I had to keep my mouth shut, especially since I had just returned from home.

On asking Mark why he had taken so long as I was really hungry, he snapped; it was all of a sudden. One moment he was perfectly calm, sitting in darkness and watching TV quietly, the next moment he was all angry, aggressive and shouting. That I needed to be grateful to him, he had kept the studio while I was away although Ann told him to give it up until I returned. He had come and picked me up from the airport and never really did have to come and get me. He could have let me find my own way home.

**Lastly I needed to appreciate that I was given food, otherwise he would throw it on the floor and I would have to eat from there. Just like the dog that I was.**

Mark kept getting so angry that I had to apologise even if I did not want to, say "I am sorry" and keep quiet just to calm him down and maintain peace. **In the midst of it all he said it was Ann who was interested in my return because she wanted to see what his child would look like. As for him he was just happy to have his slave back.**

# Unknown children

A few days passed and Mark and I were walking through the shopping centre; we were on our way to see Ann. He wanted to check for a delivery he had ordered from eBay – all his deliveries and mail always went to Ann's house – and I just needed to get out for a little walk.

Surprisingly maybe it was meant to be: I could hear someone shouting out "Mark, Mark" very loudly. On turning back and looking all around, across the road there stood this lady. She was quite large and wore glasses on her face. She stared at me and tried to get my attention. I still remember her long, straight, light hair the colour of sand, pale complexion and decent looking.

From across the road she shouted, "This is his, ask him, this is his." All I saw was a little girl and a little boy.

On drawing Mark's attention to the lady and pointing her out to Mark he grabbed me. Putting his arm under my elbow he pulled me in the opposite direction. He told me not to pay attention to the lady. That was his ex and she was just trying to cause trouble between us. "Keep walking," he said, "and don't turn back."

Oh I really wanted to talk to her; this incident was still playing on my mind when we got to Ann's. I asked her about this lady. I was aware Mark had an ex but did he have children?

That I was not aware of at all. Ann did not want to respond; she was initially quiet and then said, "I don't know." Verbally she said she had no knowledge of anything I asked yet she could not look me in the eyes. So I understood either she knew and never wanted to reveal the truth to me or she was covering up for Mark – either way I knew she was deceiving me and hiding something from me. No one in the family ever revealed to me that Mark had other children out there. I was deceived into thinking that these were the only children Mark had. How can a marriage be based on so many lies?

Days passed and the incident still bothered me. I knew one day the truth would come out – it had to.

Nothing stays the same forever, nothing can be covered up, and the truth will always be uncovered.

# Traumatic delivery

Months passed and finally the baby was due to be born. I started getting pain on the 11th June 2009 which was the due date and it was getting worse.

I called Mark to inform him I was getting pains, to which he replied, "And? What do you want me to do about it??"

I told him I needed him to be there for me and the baby. I was scared but all he replied was, **"You're having a baby, don't be stupid, it's not that big a deal. I will get there when I get there."**

I was even more upset and in pain. He came back in the evening after doing his full shift. **When he got in he wanted to know where his food was.** I shouted back in pain and said, "I'm in pain." Hours went by and my contractions were getting stronger, it was excruciating, unbearable, and I started screaming.

Mark was getting angry; his rage, I realised amidst my pain, was gaining momentum. On the one hand I was suffering in pain, on the other hand I was in extreme fear of Mark. I tried not to make any noise; I tried to shut my mouth by holding a pillow in front of me. I knew he was losing control and could not take my groaning. No longer could I bear the pain and although I tried in terror to remain quiet due to fear of what Mark would do to me, I could be silent no more.

Mark started shouting and telling me to shut up and if I'm going to have this baby to have it quietly, to get a grip on myself and keep it down. Or he would come over and shut my mouth for me.

Throughout my groans he said I was pretending and that I could not take pain I was a pretender and drama queen. I was faking it and what I only really wanted was attention.

I begged him to call 999 for the ambulance, in-between when I could catch my breath, as I could not take the pain. When he finally did and when the paramedics heard me screaming in pain they decided to come and get me immediately.

I was thankful the ambulance came because Mark was getting angrier and was starting to threaten me because I could not stay quiet and my groans were upsetting him from resting. While I felt as if my insides were being ripped open and something huge was about to come out of me.

Trust me, at that point I just wanted my baby to come out.

On reaching the hospital the nurse told me I was too far gone, so all I was given was the gas to help with my delivery. The epidural could not be given as I was too far gone and I heard the nurses say I should have come in much earlier.

Mark was stressing me out at home; instead of being able to deliver in peace I was more petrified about what he was going to do to me because I was too loud. Continuous shouting and threats… I was shaking, trembling when I went in to hospital. As I went to the bed my waters broke.

But inside now, I was very glad to be there in a safe environment where people could take care of me. Mark never seemed to care, he stood without feeling, without emotion and with an attitude that said when is this going to be over.

Well a few hours went by and it was not going well; the nurses and the doctor were talking. They said if baby did not come soon they would have to use alternative means because it was not looking good. Baby was getting stressed, I was stressed and not in good shape. Every time they asked me to push I gave it my best, and although I felt faint I still pushed. It was difficult, really hard, but I wanted my baby in my arms. I needed baby out as I could feel my body giving up but the nurses and doctors kept encouraging me to "try once more, give us a big push, do it now, do it now". "That's it," I heard them say, sweat dripping down my forehead.

Thankfully eventually it happened, they could see my baby's head and pulled baby out using forceps. It was a girl; I had to have stitches as I tore. She was tiny, cute and all wrinkled up.

I fell in love with her and her smell straight away. She was worth the pain, every bit of it, she was my angel, the most beautiful sight I had ever laid my eyes upon and she was all mine.

# Worrying about baby stuff

Having no money meant being totally dependent on Mark to make arrangements for the baby and he would keep giving me disgusting answers such as, "baby will have to sleep on the sofa" or even worse, on the floor and I could sleep by its side.

Even having to go into hospital with just one set of clothes for myself and three baby changing bodysuits, that's all I had. Thankfully Mum's sister saw me on the road and gave me ten pounds to go and buy something for myself – it is that money I had used to get something small for us.

Mark said, "Don't worry about it, my family will get it all."

True enough, although I was stressed beyond imagination, they did get it all. The moses basket, baby bath, feeding bottles and some clothes.

Mark was going home to get it ready for baby, or so he said. I knew that meant to catch up on his sleep which he had missed out on. Meanwhile baby and I had to stay overnight in hospital. I must admit I was scared to change her, she had such tiny toes and fingers. Almost all night I stared at her. She was cute, so very cute, tiny and grumpy. My eyes closed, I don't know when exactly, and after that morning soon came.

Many a time I have heard people saying that children bring a couple closer and the bond of togetherness is strengthened. In my situation I silently foolishly hoped it would... not because I was in love with Mark any longer but simply because I don't like separating children from their biological father.

(We mothers always think about doing what's best for our kids. Yet staying with the wrong men, partners or husbands does no good for our children. I know this is the same thought many of us women have, and let me tell you it's the worst mistake anyone in our situation can make.)

Morning came and with each passing hour I grew impatient and each time I called Mark because I wanted to get out of the hospital. He said he was busy and I should wait and not bother him.

Finally he came with his sister; she drove us home. Well I had a little peace of mind after seeing things for my baby in the flat – baby would not suffer, that made me happy inside but that joy I did not dare to show openly because I feared Mark would try to take my joy away and spite her just to spite me.

Mark was a man who liked to feel powerful above others, physically and mentally. Sadly, he did not understand the power of love, children or a happy marriage with a loving wife. I think being mean and trying to hurt me over and over again in some way made him feel superior although inwardly inside he felt inferior and this was all like a big act. Which I only discovered much later.

Back in our little studio flat it was more crowded. I had longed to move before the baby was born but Mark had said it was not an option as there was no money to do so.

I quickly filled out all the forms for baby and sent off for Child Benefit too. I thought l could get little money for her milk and my priority was to make sure she never starved. I could go through anything but not my baby.

After having the baby, I was waiting to see how the marriage would turn out to be now. Would Mark change or would he remain just as he was?

# Mark's insanity

**There was not much change for the first few days but things got a little better** in the respect that Mark would wake up when Jane would. He would come home or make the milk if she was hungry.

I thought just maybe, maybe, he is repenting but very quickly that changed and it all stopped.

It was never easy to understand Mark – he was full of complications and sometimes I felt as if he had multiple personalities which could be triggered including being a good manipulator, aggressive abuser and yet a kind animal lover. He did have communication problems as he was more appreciative of his own company and only the world of history. He could spend hours with his Taxidermy but not with family. If he did he was the abuser and dictator. This is the best way I can describe the entire situation.

All day and all night, I looked after baby with no help, no breaks. When Mark would come home he would say, "It's my time to rest now." Well it continued like this for days.

I had no friends because he never liked me talking to anyone, family whom I had stopped talking to for complicated reasons, mainly Mark. He never liked them calling regularly, he did not like them coming around without prior arrangements. He was annoyed with Uncle telling me about what he did at work and even got fed up with him bringing food around. To keep the peace I decided to separate and keep away.

It was what Mark wished for.

So I was all alone with my baby which made me miserable and extremely lonely. I longed for mature company and someone to talk to.

I was stupidly excited to be going out somewhere at long last. When Baby was not even a week old Mark told me we would go and visit his mother. I was really excited.

Never did I imagine something could go wrong. We were all dressed to leave and suddenly my poor Jane, not even a week old, started crying and screaming – she was hungry, she wanted milk. I went to make a bottle up and the next thing I knew Mark was shouting. He said, "I'm ready to go now, right now, to my mother's house. What the hell are you doing, you stupid bitch?

"If you start feeding that fucking thing now we are not going. You choose. Let the fucking thing cry, it's not going to die. When we get there you feed her. It's good for her lungs to cry."

I could not do that. If you're a young mother or a loving parent how can you put off feeding a hungry, screaming baby not even a week old, for a twenty minute walk? It was not rational or logical and I could never ever do that.

So Mark lost his temper. He threw all the new clothes that had been given as gifts for the baby on the floor. He was raging with anger. I myself got angry and shouted at him for being stupid and wanting our baby to starve.

He started shouting abuse back at me and threatening. He wanted to smash the entire place. As he was drawing nearer to us with rage building up suddenly in the midst of all of this chaos of screaming and shouting, we heard a knock on the door.

It was Mark's mother and one of his sisters; they had come to visit.

Mark had always been a good pretender but as they entered they could tell something was not right by looking at my face and seeing the clothes on the floor.

Ann asked me what had happened. I could not be quiet, so I told her all this was the doing of her son and his irrational behaviour – he wanted us to walk to her house and put off feeding Jane until we got to her house. He behaved as if his mother's house was going to disappear all of a sudden. Mark just tried to bully me and take advantage; he could not bear the fact that I had stood up to him for the baby.

Mother and daughter were both quiet... said nothing and then left soon after. At which point Mark said there was nothing to talk about and it was not up for discussion.

# Stepping out

A few days passed; starvation was no longer an issue since I had registered for Working Tax Credit. This helped because there was a limited amount of food, and the money went into a joint bank account which I could use too. But what I found strange was that Mark never wanted to eat at home, he never seemed hungry and only wanted cups of tea.

I would get up early in the morning and make him sandwiches because he would leave at 3.30am to go to work. Mark worked only a few days in the week and the rest of the time all he ever wanted was to go to the gym and later to visit his mum – this was his regular routine. This pattern went on for a while but as much as I loved my baby I wanted to go out too and just have a little break and a little time for me.

Well... Jane suffered with colic pain which is so normal here amongst kids in the UK. Infacol was not much help. Something all of us mums can relate to, it becomes a little too much if you can't get a break and have some time off from the stress of the baby crying and the helpless feeling that although you are trying your best you still can't get baby comfortable or help her settle down.

My life at present was without breaks, without adult company; it revolved only around my crying Jane and a husband who cared not to have a relationship with me at all in any manner except for slavery.

So I was kept in solitude, my in-laws seemed to think I spoke too much. That's what Ann thought too. No one seemed to realise that I was dying from loneliness.

In the beginning I admit I would not go out with my Jane because I was so worried – what if I met with an accident? I asked Mark to come out with me just once so that I would have confidence. **That never happened because he was being vindictive. My uneasiness meant Mark had a greater hold over me. The more I was afraid the more Mark was happy, the more it gave him a sense of control and power. He enjoyed me being unhappy, he enjoyed me being trapped and most of all he enjoyed that I was his and he could do what he liked.**

**The day I said I do, from that day little did I know it was like signing a contract of slavery. To work, to serve and suffer till death do us part.**

One fine day I had had enough, it was long overdue – I was going to go out, come what may, that's what I decided. It was raining so I asked him for the last time, "Are you coming?" and he said, "no". I started to get the rain cover out and cover Jane, but he said, "Don't be stupid, you're not going out, it's raining." I said, "Yes I am." He told me to leave the baby behind with him to which I said no. **The whole purpose of this exercise was for me to gain confidence. Mark had stripped it all away from me but I felt suffocated and I could not live like that anymore, trapped in fear and confined to one room. I would step out even if it meant it was going to be fatal for me.**

That was my first step out into the world with my baby and it felt great.

It shocked Mark because he knew now I would go out for walks every day with her. One of his fear holds on me had broken. Because of loneliness and lack of money of my own to buy anything, I decided to **start looking for a job. After all I was more educated than Mark's entire family.**

What kind of a mother would I be if I could not protect and provide for my daughter?

# Desperate measures

Wanting to be able to provide for Jane and take care of her meant everything to me. The sense of parental duty and responsibility soon took hold of me and from within I knew the right to protect Jane, guard her from all harm, belonged to me and me alone. There was no one who could protect her as I could, my life had to change amidst all the misery; it was important to find a way to safeguard Jane. How I was to do that still was not known to me but this little child of mine would see no harm come her way – that I vowed to myself.

Silly me, I went straight to the nursery opposite my little studio flat. I went to find out about work. That was the first shock I got. They said I needed childcare qualifications. This meant more studies although I already had a Masters degree. No matter, I was willing to learn, and the lady informed me that they offered nursery training.

However, it was one year on-the-job training for free but to keep my Jane there I had to pay while training.

Sadness gripped my soul; I thought that she would keep my Jane for free while I learnt and offered my services in return. It just goes to show you how little I knew about the system and my lack of knowledge in regards to the entire situation. It would have been brilliant if that had worked but **in life things never go as one wishes them to. We have to keep trying. So I had to just say thank you and leave.**

The saddest part in relation to my lack of knowledge is that I went to my mother-in-law and told her what had happened. Innocently I said, "Mum, are they mad? Where would I get so much money to work for free and pay to keep my baby for a thousand pounds a month? I have nothing." Ann just became quiet as usual. She replied that she knew it was too much and that none of her six children had gone to nursery.

No one told me the government helps with childcare. Especially if you're on low income – you get benefits like Working tax credit and Child tax credit which can be found out from the government website or by calling them up and having them send out the forms to fill in. Even the online benefit calculator I never knew existed.

It's sad but true: if you don't ask you don't get; if you don't search and research on your own then no one is going to take the time to go out of their way to help you. Life doesn't work that way. Even in relation to my shock about nursery prices, Ann still never mentioned that her very own daughter put her child into nursery.

No one in the family, not even the in-laws said a word about benefits or solutions to the problems at hand and how to solve it. I tried to rely on myself to find a good job online, joining numerous online job sites, sending out as many applications as I could in a day because I was desperate to work and earn.

Mark would come home, he would say, "You're good for nothing. You're useless, you can't even get a job. What shit did you study?" Then he would go on to say, "I thought by marrying you I won't ever have to work, your dad will give me money but yet for all that, look at me, now my life has turned worse, I have you and a baby to look after.

"What did I gain by marrying you? You were the one who was supposed to get a good high-paying job so that I would not have to work and could relax. Marrying you was a waste of time and effort."

As each and every day passed I got more fed up, desperate, it was only my baby who kept me going. I looked at her and would tell myself this can't go on for long.

This can't be what my life was meant to be.

# Ann's ridicule

Every time I saw Ann she would tell me that I was being totally ridiculous. Why on earth did I want to work so much, Ann asked.

"Well who would look after my Jane?" I asked. Ann replied, "She will never go without, she will always have."

I somehow never saw Jane having anything except abuse, and how would she have when Mark never gave anything? Ann's comments were like twisted riddles – if she meant Jane would have, then what about me as Jane's mother? I still could not see myself having anything in life. Mark had not changed all this time, so I could not see any sudden miraculous change come over him.

I should stay at home to look after baby; after all I was the mother, she told me.

This would have been true in any normal circumstance but our married life and family situation was far from normal. The word normal did not exist.

It was a life of abuse, starvation, misery and a curse. Where every day Mark would remind me how miserable I made his life because he had to work. What a burden Baby and I were to him.

I longed to work to give my daughter a better life. I knew if she had to have a good life it would be up to me and no one else. I did not have the blessing of having a nice husband who wanted the same things as I did. I just had someone who wanted and wanted, nothing else mattered but just his wants.

Family life kept going downhill; nothing was going to change much, by now I was well aware of that. Most of the jobs I applied for replied saying I was too highly qualified. In reality the truth of the matter was I would have been willing to do anything just to start earning. It never mattered what I did, it never mattered to me where I did it or who was looking?

All that mattered is as a mother I knew I had to provide for my little girl – that's all that mattered.

I looked at cleaners' jobs and everything I could think of. Some jobs required qualifications which I did not have, others required different skill sets. Despite having previous banking experience I still did not find it easy – I never got a call back or reply from any banks. I needed money, that's all I could think of, so I decided since banks were not replying to me I would try anything and everything.

Ann told me on numerous occasions that she did not agree with whatever I was trying to do. She'd rather I stayed at home, I disagreed and she did not like it. I wanted more freedom, a better life. Money would make both of those desires of mine a reality yet Ann was unhappy. In all honesty I thought maybe as a mother she would be happy that I wanted to do something to help the family life but in return it seemed as if it upset her to a great degree, especially since she tried her level best to discourage me.

What was the real reason? I was well educated – did Ann fear I would gain my independence and they would lose their little slave girl? Or did it make her feel good that I kept begging, running to her for a decent chance at married life? Much later, all these questions which had started to arise in my mind were all answered so clearly.

True feelings and hidden deceptions were all unveiled.

# Finding work

I found work in a take away restaurant – it was the only place which gave me a call back. Thanks be to God I got a job! It was walking distance from my house; I was over the moon. Innocently I went dancing and telling Ann with great excitement, that I had got a job.

Ann would work very hard to pay all the bills since it was she who would have to pay for the upkeep of everyone in her household. Being a generous person and genuinely fond of her, I always wanted to help her out if ever I had the opportunity to do so. In my excitement I told her that now I could buy her things and take her on small holidays. To this she laughed hysterically, and her husband Jim asked what was the matter.

Ann replied, "She thinks she's got this little job so now we can all go on holidays." I left feeling hurt because it seemed like she was mocking me but I just let it pass. My first day at work gave me a sense of pride and joy; I really cannot explain how proud I felt that I had taken the first step towards Jane's and my future.

**This was like stepping out of the dark ages into the light. Silently I would keep telling myself my break would come one day. One day we would be free and earn our freedom. For now, Mark held the key, I had nowhere to go, no one to turn to, but I knew one day Jane and I would be walking happily somewhere together.**

This was my dream of the future: to break away from the bondage of ownership from my mental tormentor under the pretext of marriage.

No one could understand how symbolic getting this job was for me, no one paid attention to what I said.

Many a time I had warned both Mark and Ann that the day would come when I would walk away from them if life did not improve.

I still remember getting paid after two weeks' work – what a feeling of security it gave. I sat thinking I wish I could get a better job but in time I knew I would. I worked every evening from 6pm to 12 midnight.

It started with a few shifts, like three days a week, and I made sure I worked twice as hard because I wanted more shifts. There were not many females who did the closing – that's what this shift was known as. Not only during open hours would we serve customers but later after we shut, we would have to clean the entire place down and pull out all the heavy food trays, bins, coffee machines etc and clean everything down then restock, and keep everything prepared for the morning shift. By the time it was all done it would be midnight.

My bosses were pleased with me and soon the shifts started multiplying. The customers liked me; I would try to do as much as I could. Soon I started to close the store every day with the rest of the crew who were all male. I was permanently put on the list Monday to Sunday. This gave me joy in my heart as I very quickly started earning more. **The more I earned the better for Jane, I thought.**

I had started saving, so my bank account had some savings now. Mark was pleased that I was working because this meant I could sustain and look after baby and myself and also help him when he wanted anything. So he agreed that he would look after Jane, in the evenings, when I went to work. He seemed to enjoy the fact that I was working and he did not have to see my face. Mark had finally got what he wanted: money coming in and time for himself. Baby was good – she would sleep mostly throughout the night.

Simultaneously, I had applied for help with Housing Benefit by going online and finding out everything I was entitled to along with rebate on Council Tax – if the joint income was low enough help could be given. This helped with savings too. I tried to stay out of Mark's way as much as possible. This seemed to be working; Mark would go out early in the morning and when he returned it was time for me to leave.

It continued like this for a while but every night I came home my back would hurt after working; it was not easy work, it was hard. Yet never would I stop as I knew what I was working for.

The money brought us security, it kept me out of the house and Mark's way, it would help me get supplies for Jane's milk, nappies, jar food etc, it was a little blessing in a life filled with misery.

# Climbing up the ladder

Having worked in the banking sector previously for high end sales, credit cards and marketing, I had knowledge of the financial sector. I knew that getting a credit card was a must, as I needed to build up a good credit rating and as such that was my next step.

After a few months of regular income coming into my bank account **I applied for a credit card** and was approved for a limit of five hundred pounds.

This was yet another start to achieving something else in the future on a larger scale. So things were going my way a little. I can't say it was drastically transforming or improving things because it was not – my relationship with Mark stayed the same. There was just one little hint of improvement and a little better standard of living in respect to what I could offer Jane. I did not have to depend on Mark's mercy as much as before and be entirely under him.

It felt good to be earning again, it felt good to be able to buy things for my daughter and myself without having to beg, explain and wonder what the outcome would be of my begging.

It gave me such a sense of peace and security, to know that I had something saved for a rainy day.

**Strangely enough an incident from when I was pregnant came back to me at this point.** I remembered one of Mark's sisters had driven

Ann and me to her house. There Catherine had loads of pictures of her daughter Nancy on the wall. Her daughter was very sweet looking. However, one remark stood out to me: Ann commented that Catherine had dedicated an entire wall like a shrine honouring Nancy. To which Catherine remarked that of course I didn't know what a shrine was, did I?

Ann replied that of course I did.

The irony of this entire conversation was that it took place in front of me as if I were not present and never existed when in fact I stood in between both Catherine and Ann throughout the conversation.

While I was down, she regarded me as a lowly person. Although Catherine was hospitable to me I could nevertheless feel there was indifference. She had a superiority complex and looked down on me simply because I had nothing at that point of time in my life and was married to her brother.

Catherine tried very hard to make me feel low and inferior, in her remarks, mannerisms and in general the way she reacted to me.

Sincerely, I do believe that she felt jealousy towards me though at that time I had nothing in life to envy, yet it seemed that my very presence made her feel threatened.

**Jealousy is a very powerful emotion which can rule and drive someone crazy to the point of insanity. Sadly, human nature is such that at any given point of time anyone can feel envious of someone which can turn into hatred and vendetta. This became very obvious to me much later.**

Although I still suffered, I was trying to squeeze through the tiny gaps and narrow pathways which life threw to me. It was hard, like trying to climb up a slippery slope; I had to fall many times before I could get a strong grip and then pull myself up to the next level. Many trials and blizzards came my way yet I think that Catherine and Ann spotted my survival instincts and that's where the problem lay.

They both knew it was only a matter of time before I slipped away and their hold would be no more.

# Freezing to death at Mark's mercy

**Unfortunately, my rainy day came much faster than I anticipated...** A few months had passed. That year the winter was one of the worst England had ever witnessed, it was terribly cold. I remember not stepping out much because it was so cold.

Our small studio flat was operated by electricity only. **One day the electric company just came and turned our electricity off.** Having just stepped out with baby to buy some milk, on my return I could not do anything in the flat. The lights would not turn on and no one in the sharing house knew why this was. I asked around and then eventually came across a notice stuck on the door. It informed us all that EDF had turned off the electricity from the mains and it would not be turned back on until further notice.

I tried to get in contact with Mark but was unsuccessful. That evening when Mark returned to darkness and a pitch black house with only one candle burning at the side in front of the window, he saw that there was no proper way of continuing to live in our present accommodation but he did not want to shift and go anywhere else.

He tried calling the electric company and finally we learned that the landlord had been collecting rent from us monthly by direct debit but had not been paying the electric bill; as such the electric company had no choice other than to come and shut down the electricity supply.

Trying to call the landlord was of no use – calls just kept going to the answer phone; pleading from multiple families with young children fell on deaf ears.

The days passed by very slowly or at least it felt like that. The hours and minutes seemed to drag on. There was no television, no heating, there was nothing. **We were freezing, but above all my concern was in keeping Jane warm. Jane was so very cold. I was extremely upset, not wanting anything to go wrong with my precious baby. Trying to keep her warm was extremely challenging. I used to wrap her up with as many clothes as I could and hold her close to me so as to warm her up with my very own body heat.**

All my pleading and begging of Mark fell on deaf ears. I was petrified; the studio resembled a cold storage room. No matter how many times I begged that we needed to leave for Jane's sake, Mark ignored me. We needed to go where it was warmer. We could not stay in our present home because she might get very ill or even worse. I cannot write the words. It pains me too much to do so.

Mark did not want to go to his parents' house nor did he want to leave our studio. He argued that this present place was affordable and once the electrics were back up and running everything would be back to the way it was.

But my concern was only Jane – how long do we wait and what price was my daughter's life worth?

The entire situation was extremely stressful – a husband who was useless not only as a husband but as a father, provider and as a man, but who never failed to be other than the best tormentor. Even at that moment in time he stressed that if I were more capable, if instead of having a useless job I had a better one and was earning well, then we could have had a better and bigger house.

He made me feel useless, as if it was all my fault that we had to stay there and if I had tried more life would have been better for everyone.

I should have been paying for everything and his money should have been his alone to be used as he felt best, to go to the gym and do whatever else he pleased.

I really could not make sense of things. Mark's behaviour was that of a cruel tormentor, and did he still not care for his daughter?

Then I started to question why Ann, who knew her son's mentality – she called him her baby – did not tell him to come home with Jane.

They spoke daily, she was aware of the situation and yet not an offer to come and take refuge in their home. Mark said his mother had not invited us and he did not want to go and live with his parents again but no one but me seemed to be caring about my poor Jane.

Days passed and the electric company finally came and put a notice up, confirming the electricity would not be turned back on. The landlord was not paying the bills. So we all had to suffer and pay the price; we had to relocate.

This was the moment when Mark agreed to leave. I was happy about that but then he mentioned we would have to go and live with his mum because there was no other choice. We had tried to get help from the council but were told that we still had a roof over our heads so technically we were not homeless and as such we were not entitled to any emergency accommodation.

I felt uncomfortable staying with Mark's family, because at the end of the day no matter how small your own place is it's your own. Nothing like home as the saying goes. We got ready, packed and moved into my in-laws' place.

In all honesty I really did not feel comfortable but a mother's need to protect her child surpasses all.

# Living with the in-laws

Very generously we were given one room to ourselves. I hardly knew my in-laws; I must admit I felt uncomfortable and awkward... My father-in-law did tell me to go and help myself and to not be shy or awkward. Which I did appreciate and he did try to make conversation.

Since there was no one else who cared to hold any sort of conversation I would prefer to stay upstairs in my room. I would not be offered any breakfast and it was not in my nature to just be rude and go open the fridge and help myself in someone else's home. My upbringing was different, where manners mattered.

However, I did notice that Mark was always offered breakfast and other meals and it was even cooked and brought up to him. He never had to ask for anything. Yet no food would be offered to me, even out of courtesy.

In a way it worked out for the best – although we were staying with Ann temporarily, I realised that the entire situation was strange. Mark and Jane seemed to be made welcome but I was viewed as a nothing and non-existent.

Every evening as I waited for Mark to come we would say no you don't have to eat, come let's go up. The reason being Mark's dad would like to drink every day and then it would alter his behaviour which was not for the best. A few days passed like this in this manner and my restlessness grew.

I was getting fed up of being treated badly and not being given respect. After all I was supposed to be Mark's wife and the daughter-in-law? But all that existed in the eyes of the family were Mark and Jane.

Since we had been living in such awful conditions previously the cold had affected Jane; she was still not well and refusing to drink her milk. Her nose was blocked; it was at this time I went to hospital to get her checked. **Jane could not drink her milk and she was not her usual self – as a mother I could tell that my child was not well. There was something wrong but I didn't know what the exact reason was.**

The doctors said she was just unwell and she would get better – the body just needed time to fight and she would recover on her own. They told me to give her Saline drops to help her breathe.

So I was quite upset regarding Jane. The hospital's solution did not make any sense to me: **from a mother's point of view I knew my baby was not well and this was not going to do anything to help her in her distressed state.**

Simultaneously, I kept telling Mark that I wanted to leave and go to another place to live. Mark, however, was in no rush to leave – he was extremely happy to be back home with his mother who was doing an excellent job of looking after him.

However, after a while, things started to get too stressful between Ann and her husband Jim, since their own personal family life was not going too well. They had a spare room in which Ann would sleep. We were now occupying the spare room at this time, in which Ann would normally sleep, which caused a lot of inconvenience and friction. It meant that after Jim had one too many drinks Ann had no escape, she had to be in the same room where he would turn quite nasty, have arguments, fights etc, or she could sleep on the sofa in the living room.

As time passed Mark came to realise that us staying with his parents was not appropriate. Mark loved his mother dearly, so did not want to cause her grief in any way. Every decision had to be coming from Mark; even if I was right it would not be considered because I was deemed a low being.

# Death came to steal Jane

The estate agents whom I kept calling up regularly to find us another property were also responsible for the previous studio flat, and they finally called me back. They had an excellent Christmas gift for us: a one bedroom flat close to West Croydon and the Hospital which had come available. The building was called City of Angels. The estate agents reassured us that finally, they had found a good place for our family to live. l was very happy because of the location.

We were both delighted to see it was an open plan kitchen-cum-sitting room. It had a beautiful view from the window; you could see the sunrise and sunset. The only thing that concerned me was what if the lift stopped working then I would have problems. I would have to carry my Jane up six floors. The agent said there are three lifts and it would never be the case that all three were not working at the same time, and told us it was a fantastic place, communal gardens, security and a great location...The only negative aspect was that the flat was on the 6th floor.

However Mark laughed the most and told the agent not to listen to my ignorance and that I spoke out of turn on matters which did not concern me and which I did not understand.

Well we decided – or rather he decided – to take the flat. Mark liked it very much and made a point of telling me: **It was his decision, to take it.** It was bigger than our first studio, with a separate bedroom. The walls were white and the floor had a light brown carpet.

Sadly life is not what you always want or expect it to be. It can be quite the opposite. It's true that life is quite unpredictable. Problems can appear all of a sudden which has to be dealt with as priority.

So it was decided this would be our next home. Jane's health was still not improving though. On the news there had been so many cases of Swine Flu at the time that the hospitals had stopped doing swabs at the walk-in centres because there were too many coming in. My poor Jane was still feeling unwell, still not drinking her milk and I was getting upset with several attempts to go to the hospital which proved useless. All they did was send us back home with saline drops yet again; this happened quite a few times.

**The cold persisted and one day, very early in the morning, I was changing Jane. It was around 1 am and she was so lifeless.** She had a mark on her bottom which looked like a pinch. It was slightly purple. Quickly we got dressed and rushed her to hospital at that early hour. **The doctors took charge, they said they had to act immediately, there was no time to run tests as they felt it was meningitis and the treatment had to be started immediately with our permission, even before the test could be done or the results returned, in order to save her life.**

But nothing could prepare us for what we were about to hear – our daughter not only had got meningitis but swine flu too. Jane was fighting for her life, she was fighting to survive.

Oh God, not my baby, my heart was racing; I started shaking in fear, I could not lose my Jane. The fear growing so strong was almost suffocating me; before my very eyes I saw in a span of a few seconds doctors and nurses rushing around my baby all trying to help her live as with every passing second Jane was slipping away and turning colourless.

She was taken to hospital in London, children's Intensive care unit, where I prayed with all my heart for her to get better but each day the doctors would say we can't give you any guarantee, we are trying but we can't say anything yet.

As a mother it was terrible not being able to hold your child because she was covered in tubes from head to toe. She was so bloated that I could not even recognise my own baby. I could see from her face that she was crying, the facial expressions were there, it was clear, but I could not hear anything because my baby had tubes down her nose and mouth.

Those days were torture and hell on Earth; it was more terrible than anything, anything I have been through. Every day going through uncertainty and not knowing, would my baby girl open her eyes?

Would I be able to carry her without tubes, would she make it?

I prayed, I begged God to let her live and make her better. I prayed every hour of the day. I could not eat; I could not sleep though we were given a lovely clean room. All that mattered was my baby, she was just six months old and suffering so much, my heart longed, longed to somehow, somehow take all her pain away.

**It was okay for me to suffer, I was her mummy, I could take any amount of pain but just spare my innocent child – this was my prayer.**

Finally it happened, after monitoring Jane for days the doctors finally said they were going to take some of the tubes out, she was making a recovery, all thanks to God and the hard work of the medical team.

# Mark's temporary guilt

While we were in hospital Mark said he was thinking about Jane – she had not been out to see the world. She had never seen the beach, the sights of London. **I think he had started feeling guilty.**

I did tell Mark it was only his fault and he had himself to blame as I had many a time requested him to come out with us on family outings. But he said it's too much hassle with kids and nappies. Mark wanted to go out and leave the baby with his mum. I tried to appeal to his reasoning abilities, I asked Mark to take a look around – there were so many tourists travelling with kids, they made time not only for themselves yet still had their children along too.

**My heart's desire was to do things as a family, not to be dependent on anyone for my happiness.**

However, Mark only liked to go to museums and would say, "Oh I don't need to go anywhere else, I have eBay if I need to buy anything." His life revolved around himself.

**Well I had been working part time doing just nights after having the baby and had saved very carefully so the money which we needed up in London while we were in hospital all came from me.**

Jane took a long time to recover and I hoped that this heartbreaking traumatic period of our lives would bring us closer but sadly, no it did not. During the stay in the hospital we seemed to be ok, there was more progress in regards to improvement of behaviour, the insults, rudeness was down to minimal compared to before and all of us seemed to be getting along. **Baby recovered and we came back home.**

Unfortunately, so did all the old ways, life reverted back to how it had been and once again everything started like a vicious circle again. I somehow knew it would.

Sometimes in life you can keep giving someone chance after chance and the opportunity to change but unless they themselves have the desire to change they simply will not. All I could really and truly do is change myself.

# Slavery continued

Days went by...every day I had the same routine to do: the cooking, cleaning, washing, looking after baby and also do the household and grocery shopping. Sadly being on the 6th floor was indeed problematic because the residents would keep stealing parts of the lift, causing a fault and I would do the heavy shopping, carry it on my buggy and then be stranded when I returned. Sometimes I had to wait for hours until someone would come and be kind enough to help me carry the buggy up the stairs.

Living there was turning out to be a nightmare since sometimes I would be stranded with no more milk left **and baby wanting her next feed.**

Whenever I would ask Mark to do anything, he would say, "You fucking do it, I'm working." Many a time when I tried to discuss the lift issues he would say, "I don't care a fuck. You sort it out", even though he knew and was very aware that I could not sort this issue out. After work Mark would go to the gym. God forbid I would ever ask him to get anything – although we had Tesco just below at the entrance of the building he would say, "No I'm not going to get it."

"You got hands and legs, go your fucking self. I'm not going to do anything, why should I?" Countless number of times I had to go up and down, several trips, getting what I needed. Many a time, it was not possible to carry all that we required as it was very heavy; the lifts not working meant several trips to the store until I had everything we needed.

Up and down, up and down I would go, the shop keepers looking at me. Some friendly faces asked, "Can't someone help you? You have already come several times?"

No, no one could help me. I knew all I did was smile and avoid the question saying, "I needed it all today, I forgot it earlier." Actually I needed nothing, it was all to keep Mark quiet or else he would start on me again and I never wanted the baby witnessing anything.

I was the slave, to serve him as he so very often reminded me.

Desperation leads to many things. It gives you courage to overcome certain fears. Working nights was scary but I did not want to go back to starvation days again so it inspired me to work hard.

I needed to protect my Jane, so I decided to put my fears aside. Life continued with insults and abuse which kept getting worse. I got offered to work Sunday shifts and I did so to get more money and independence for my baby and me.

All my saving were gone after our stay in hospital; I had nothing left. So now once again, sadly, I had to start all over from scratch to work and to save for our future. Mark was happy since he never really wanted me around; he would rather prefer to take the baby to his mum's and go do his own stuff while she attended to the baby. **He never spent any quality father-daughter time with Jane.** Mark worked a few days a week and did not want to do anything else.

Well our situation was becoming unbearable again; I could not keep going up and down and slogging away. It was too much. I asked

Mark when we could move. His life was of comfort while mine was of persecution. I could not live like this and really wanted us to shift.

Mark sat like a king laying demands. He said a definite no and that the only way we would shift is when we would buy our house, "otherwise I'm not shifting," he said. He set impossible targets continuously which I had to keep achieving.

Ironically, when I look back and think, he had so many demands but the input into the relationship did not exist, he was useless. Mark wanted to suck the life out of me, for me to work so hard until I had nothing to offer any more.

I was getting frustrated.

# The start of changes

In the midst of all this I heard about a job for a team leader. I was quite excited and thought 'oh that's great, I could do that job'. I tried to go to the local nursery and found out for full time to keep a child it was around thousand pounds a month, as it was when I'd thought about training with the nursery.

At that time being a new mum and not knowing the system too well I remember having a conversation with my mother-in-law saying, "Childcare is so expensive – how do people manage to work?"

Being from a well to do family and never having to resort to a life of benefits, it was not something which was in my vocabulary. It was not something which I was familiar with. Yet I desired to do something more with my life and strive to improve my situation so I decided to try for this job. It was for a Leisure Group, dealing with bingo, slot machines, customer service etc.

I asked one of Mark's sisters, Kate, who was a stay at home mum, if I could keep my Jane with her while I worked and she agreed. I was happy.

Having quite a trek early in the morning I would go first to Kate's house to leave Jane then double back all the way to work. It was quite a distance; however, I thought there was no other way I could manage to work unless I had her help. So I did whatever I had to.

Every month I would give her two hundred pounds, though in the beginning she said she did not want anything, and also I would buy things for her three kids like sweets and bags of goodies. Since she was helping me, I thought it was only fair that I do something in return for her.

I used to do plenty for my mother-in-law. I got her a laptop, freezer, fridge and plenty of clothes from the charity shops, cosmetics – all this would go on my credit card and then I would pay it all back gradually.

Monthly shopping from Iceland, such as frozen goods, and bulk shopping from Tesco, along with regular and various trips to the off licence for groceries, electric and gas top ups, all added up.

I can honestly say I did more for Ann and Jim than most of their own children did including my very own husband. I had got my chance to repay the kindness tenfold over for Ann previously giving me her coat when I had nothing.

There was not enough money for them and me so I would go without and give them as long as they were helping me with my Jane – that's all that mattered to me. Quite a few months passed in this manner.

The situation at home was turning worse though, with me working. Mark always expected me to do the impossible, he wanted me to do everything. He expected me to work yet he was not happy. Me working meant that Mark would have to come back after work, pick Jane up from Kate's house and return back home.

He found that too much hard work. I was very desperate to leave City of Angels; it was in Croydon and a crowded area.

**Now I worked two jobs, Leisure Group and McDonald's. My timings were from 10.30am to 4pm. Then start back 5.00pm to 12.00 midnight OR 12.30. This continued for months, I worked seven days a week, no days off, no breaks, no holidays. I needed the money and had to do whatever it took to make ends meet. Yes, whatever it took.**

Mark had one job and refused to do anything else although I tried to get him to do security work. Three days a week, part time, that's all he did. Mark wanted me to drop my shifts because he wanted me to accommodate his work schedule which I did not agree with.

He was supposed to help look after the baby. What happened was entirely different: I still had to do all the housework and everything was left up to me.

The mental and physical pressure Mark put on me was unbearable and unimaginable. Many a time I felt like committing suicide; the only reason I had to live was for Jane. She was my only strength. I would think 'I have to be strong for her or she has no chance of survival'.

Every day I had to hear how lazy, fat and ugly I was. Every day I had to hear what a disappointment I was TO BE MARRIED TO and how my food tasted like dog shit and I was shit too.

By now, I had lost myself completely. Andrea did not exist anymore. I was just an outer shell, tired, confused, worried, tormented, and tortured. My mind was not mine anymore. Standing in front of the mirror the young girl full of confidence, radiance and determination was lost far away in the depths of time. It seemed so far away, like a lifetime ago.

Who was I now? I could not find me...

Mental abuse stole me from me, myself. It's the worst kind of abuse, you know not when it changes you, it happens like a silent killer and if you're not careful it will kill you.

I can't tell you when I changed; it was over time. I lost myself every day, a little more of me went.

Desperation made me do things which under normal circumstances I would not ever consider doing.

Mark as usual laid down his rules and demands; he said the only way he would leave our one bedroom apartment is if we had to buy a house. **That was the first condition**.

**The second condition was that it must be close to his mother's house.** When I spoke to Ann regarding our housing situation she said I was stupid to think I would ever get a place of my own and that I should stop torturing myself because it was never going to happen. I was just being silly.

While looking for comfort, instead what I got were words putting me down? And furthermore, negative feedback from someone who I valued as a mother.

Surprisingly Ann did not say anything in reference to Mark or his behaviour, all she said is I should not be stupid. In which world was I living in to think I could ever afford a house?

Nevertheless, it was me alone who was going through hell. I continued to persist in my search day and night with dedication and found one house which met all the demands he laid down in front of me.

I contacted the banks to try and find out how my credit rating was; Mark's credit was not at all good. Having worked in a bank previously – HSBC – I knew a fair deal about banking. The little cottage I looked at was in Surrey. It was small but looked cute and cosy. It met all of Mark's criteria, it was close to his mother's house, close to the station etc. Mark never had to do anything much apart from demand and then it was up to me; I had to provide for everything. The estate agents helped me to get my mortgage sorted out.

It took both my jobs' wage slips and Mark's to apply. The most important factor though was my father helping out and giving me the entire deposit for the house without even seeing it.

I was desperate not to live that life; I was desperate for change and to have a private garden in which Jane could run around and play. I longed to be on a quiet, child friendly street with less traffic and not have to struggle with heavy shopping.

A few months passed. I kept on top of things by chasing after and checking up on the agents, the brokers and the bank. Soon enough all the legalities went through and we soon moved into our new house.

The house needed a lot of repairs. The garden was overgrown like a wild forest, the fence was broken and almost falling apart. Briefly summarising, it needed a major makeover.

We had just shifted into our new home and decided to tell Mark's family that it was ours, when Catherine said, "I hope you have not bought that place – I will be very angry with you." I never did understand why she was so upset; I actually felt it was nothing to do with her. I was suffering, had worked hard to show affordability and Dad provided the deposit. It had nothing to do with anyone else.

It was ours and one day it would be Jane's. So all that mattered was that I secured my little girl's future.

In all honesty there seemed to be no hint of happiness in any of the family members' faces that we had achieved something good together. Yet this was a big responsibility and a huge step. The catch being it all fell on my shoulders. I had to make sure that my level of income did not fall so that the mortgage could be paid by me. There were other bills too which needed taking care of such as the Council Tax, electric and water bill. Buying groceries, toiletries and other household necessities etc. Keeping up working every day, doing double shifts throughout, takes its toll on the body.

A little later on I was becoming pressurised by my husband's family, **who kept trying to make me give up working, and cut down my shifts.** I really did not understand them especially since it was me who was doing everything. If the money was not enough we stood to lose everything and there was no way I was going to let that happen, no matter what they tried.

Doing things in regards to me was somehow bearable but in respect to my family or my child it was totally not acceptable. Especially not when my father had given me such a generous gift for his grandchild's future.

Clearly I could understand that none of Mark's side of the family cared for the loss of the house because there was no input from his family at all in regards to obtaining our little cottage.

While living in the little cottage my situation, which I thought would somehow improve miraculously by offering better future prospects, in actual fact deteriorated.

Somehow Mark's entire family's attitude seemed to have changed. And I cannot say it changed for the better. Although nowadays after Jane's birth before anything was given to me I think it was looked at first. While before I had started to work I was treated like a destitute victim, with clothes, shoes and food not given; later when I started to earn the way the family viewed me was with an air of envy which I could not see until much later on. It was the will and strength of determination to live and do for my daughter and myself which I believe annoyed them to no end. They wanted someone whom they could bully, take advantage of, control, dictate to and break.

Although they were getting the better of me, they were pulling me down but my true inner nature and survival instincts were always lurking in the background. It just needed a reason to come to the surface and help me break out of my present traumatic conditions of life.

# Taught to disrespect

Jane was growing up, although she was just a small little girl; she was sweet and my little angel of light and purity. Many a time Mark would take Jane to Ann's house to visit without me.

One Sunday, as usual we argued, and he was nasty and when my little girl was leaving to go to visit Ann, Jane turned lovingly to me and said, **'bye mummy, I love you'. Mark said, "You don't need to say anything to her. Just keep walking don't turn back…"**

So help me God, as I write these words to relate to you, the tears come streaming down my face again, the memories so strong as if it were only yesterday. I think I need to stop; I need to have a cuddle with my daughter. Before I can write anymore…

My hatred and resentment for Mark was growing. Not only was he nasty to me but now he was teaching our daughter not to respect me, her very own mother. Many a time he would be nasty and rude, and shout loudly in front of poor Jane who unfortunately witnessed everything.

When I returned home that night after work, I asked Mark whether, when our daughter started school, was he going to teach her?

He said, "No don't be stupid, you will. You're the educated one. You come home after work (which was past midnight) and teach her. I'm not going to do anything." But of course there was lots of abuse in between each and every word. He cared for no one and nothing. All he wanted was things for his own interest.

Once in a while Mark would say, "I'll ask Mum to keep baby and we will go out." Ann would say yes to keeping our little daughter but on the day itself she would always refuse saying, "no I have something else important to do" or "something has come up" yet for all that when we would go to her house she was always there and not doing anything. It felt too that they were all the same in respect that they liked messing about and toying with people's emotions. Somehow it seemed as if she never wanted to babysit so as to give us a chance to sort out our own differences.

Five very long years of marriage passed like this, **no babysitting, not even one day so that we could** go out together – never. The only babysitting was if I was going to work or for a job interview. This life was frustrating me; it was not the married life I had hoped for. It was no life at all.

Getting fed up, I told Mark one day, "We are going out." I had had enough.

So he agreed to go the museum again with us and then to his mum's. His mum was extremely shocked to learn that we had actually, finally gone out with Jane without her help. I really don't think she was too happy about it...

# The call

Next on the agenda was to try for a job with decent hours and good pay before my daughter started school so I could be there to teach her every evening, feed her, say a prayer, tuck her into bed and kiss her goodnight. I tried everywhere, every field and also to get back into the banking sector.

Finally after sending out plenty of application forms one bank did get back to me. My joy and excitement lifted me up to the heavens. Like everything else in my life though nothing came easily to me. The good news was that I was invited to an interview; the negative aspect was that because my phone was giving trouble the voicemail somehow appeared three days later. I returned the call but the bank informed me that people had already been invited for interviews and should no one be successful they would then give me a recall.

They asked for a contact number, so knowing there was always someone in my in-laws' house and they would take a message, I gave the bank their number.

Running across to my in-laws' house with tears running down the sides of my face – it was my chance that I had longed for – I explained to Ann what had happened. But she replied, "It does not mean you would have definitely got the job. Stop being silly."

I waited all day hoping, praying that I would get another call.

The cruelty of faith and destiny was that Mark rang to say he was coming home, so I left to return to the little cottage. The irony of the situation was that as I left, the bank called but instead of Ann taking that crucial message for me which could have been life changing for me, instead she told them that I had been waiting for them to call all day long and they should try my phone again.

The call never came. I called them back but it was useless – they had given me a recall but Ann did not take a message and instead had asked them to call my phone which was not working... The opportunity was lost forever, the chance gone...

I told Ann that all I needed was for her to listen to when they wanted me to come down for an interview.

She and her daughter told me it's no guarantee that I would have got the job but I knew I was good at high sales banking and if I got a second chance – which was lost because of their doing – then of course I would have gotten it.

So I had to stay with all my hurt and disappointment, but this was a much needed experience, a learning curve. Up until then I sincerely thought that Ann was all for me. Being a mother herself I thought we had a connection between us. Yet for all that I stand corrected: she was not truly fond of me. This situation was an eye opener for me.

My father had said, "Treat them like how you would treat us, your own parents." I did but... yet for all that I can't say that I received as much care as I put into the entire family circle.

Slowly but surely I started seeing things, noticing and realising what was actually happening and not seeing the entire situation from the way I always wanted to view things. In my heart and mind I always strived to not think badly of anyone. However, one has to call a spade a spade.

# Memories returning

The first time I met Ann when she heard I was mixed race she became very quiet and put her head down. I could not forget the obvious reaction.

Nearly every day I would go running to her complaining about Mark, seeking help in desperation and this was my desperate measure and cry for help. In return the advice she gave me was that she would talk to him and ask him to behave, yet in return Ann would turn to me saying, "he is my son and I still love him".

You do all that you have to, you be a good wife, take no notice of him but what about me, I thought? Was Mark doing right by me? Was he being good to me?

No he was not, ever since the day when I said 'I do'.

In respect to working, Ann was not happy that I wanted to work, yet Mark was not bothering to support me so how would he support a baby?

Worries kept on piling up upon my head and I was extremely stressed.

In respect to getting a house Ann would say, "You will never have one so why are you torturing yourself?"

During our married life, there was no babysitting so that Mark and I could even try to sort out our differences. Ann would commit to doing it and then on the day back out.

Almost always food was given to my daughter and Mark but there never seemed to be anything for me, yet in the kitchen I would see all dishes covered, plates covered and extras kept aside...

But the memories which got to me the most were in relation to Jane. That was the worst of all.

**Ann would tell my Jane all the time that I was not her mother**. This I did not like at all and when I would get upset Ann would say, "Of course she knows you're her mum." Countless remarks were always made as to how fair my children were in complexion.

Children are impressionable; a child knows only what it is taught by the ones closest to them. This was not acceptable yet because of the rotten life I was living and working like a slave to provide the best way I knew how for my little girl, it seemed like a good idea to be quiet for that moment until life improved.

Not having much at all for myself, once in a while I would like to get something small as a treat for myself. One day Ann saw me with false nails and straight away she turned to Jane commenting, "who does your mum think she is?".

That too I realised was quite a shallow comment.

Uncle's words came back to me, like a flash of lightning – it seems they are scared of you and want to keep you under them.

Who says that to a small innocent child who knows nothing about anything but only to play with their little toys?

Anyway my eyes started to open up; I began to see things for what they actually were.

Time passed and nothing seemed to get better, only worse. Mark and I were like strangers. We would not speak, just do what we each had to. It was very much like two strangers living under one roof.

The only conversation was when he wanted to buy something, for example like something of his interest. That's his history books, taxidermy or fossils, rocks etc. When he wanted money he would tell me to get it for him. Somehow it kept the peace so I just went along with it. Let the man have something, anything, as long as I had my peace of mind – that's what mattered to me.

Jane unfortunately was getting bigger and more aware of the family life situation. Many a time she would witness arguments, Mark coming at me, threatening and me being upset and crying. Once I still remember Mark saying he would kill me for getting angry and upset with him and that he could snap my neck effortlessly.

Every time I was upset Jane in all her little tiny tenderness would come my way. She would put her little arms around me and say, "Don't cry, Mummy, I love you. Naughty Daddy, making Mummy cry." It's sad to admit but the little gesture from Jane gave me strength to carry on with tearful eyes when I would look into her big blue eyes, so innocent, trying to understand and make sense of naughty Daddy and Mummy crying. How could I not get up to face another day, how could I not live even if it was in hell? I lived and survived just for Jane. Jane was my source of pure strength.

# Pregnancy again

On 18th January 2012, I found myself to be pregnant yet again. Nothing had changed between us to give any signs of hopes for a better or more promising future.

Jane and I had a discussion together. I tried to find out what Jane felt. Would she like to have another sister or brother? Jane in all her innocence said, "Yes, Mummy, I will look after baby and play with baby." When she said that her eyes beamed with joy, Jane was so excited. The decision was made. I wanted Jane to have someone to call her own; maybe I was planning far into the future and trying to make sure Jane was never alone.

I decided to have the baby but continue working. I had heard that the second pregnancy should be easier than the first one. Maybe it was because the body gets more used to it.

There was not much morning sickness, I felt fine. Only tired but I could handle that too, in comparison to my previous experience, and I retained a lot of fluid in my body. I had to go through the entire process again of Mark not wanting to accept that indeed I was pregnant once again. Mark's family was once again informed and some seemed happy but Catherine passed remarks saying we were stupid to be having another baby and we had no business having a second child. I worked extremely hard still, holding on and keeping my two jobs, knowing very well losing any of these jobs at the present moment would affect my life and be a source of great anxiety – who knows, even more horrific, compared to what Jane and myself were living through at the moment. Months passed by in this manner with me slogging, and Mark giving me tremendous amounts of problems and pressure all simultaneously.

But this time I was all prepared. I had arranged with Ann well in advance and informed her that if I could not speak and I needed help to call the ambulance, then she should call on my behalf. The sign would be me calling... I would not have to do anything else, not speak, not text nor have to explain anything. The call itself would mean urgent and that the baby was coming.

This was the arrangement made well in advance by me to prevent any fatal issues or repetition of the past. Particularly since I had nearly died the first time due to Mark's negligence and not wanting to call the ambulance for me. Ann had previously asked me if she could come for the delivery as she liked being present for the birth of a child. So I did not see the harm in it and maybe I would get more support this time, I thought, in comparison to the previous delivery.

# Baby's arrival

Soon the day came when the baby was due. My morning started well. Nothing out of the ordinary so I went about my normal day's work. Later during the day I began to feel uneasy and then started to have some dull sharp pains. The pains grew and the intensity kept increasing as the hours started to go by. I felt and saw the mucus plug come away.

It was then I knew, I knew baby was coming.

Well, as I had predicted, that was exactly what happened: Ann called the ambulance, Mark avoiding as usual and not wanting to take any responsibility. The ambulance came to get me and Ann accompanied me to the hospital. The ambulance did take long to get to me but then again I don't know when Ann actually called for the ambulance.

On reaching the hospital I could see everyone running around me to help. Second time, no epidural again; I was yet again too far gone.

Yet I could see Ann, and her face looked very pale so I knew I was not in a good way. Many a time I felt as if I were slipping in and out of consciousness and did not have the energy to push for baby to come but in the end, thanks to God, I did manage. Baby was finally here. I tore very badly and the delivery was hard. It was worse than the first pregnancy. The doctor had to use forceps. I had to take the gas again and again; in my mind I kept asking God to help me get through this. I just wanted to see my Jane again and my new baby.

As I lay on that bed feeling cold, drugged, going in and out of consciousness, I just kept begging God to let me live for my children, don't take me yet please, not yet.

I have much to do for them.

The delivery was not easy at all; it lasted for hours. The nurse showed no mercy – soon after she told me I had to go wash myself in the bathroom. The blood kept pouring down my legs; it was such an awful task to stand. I felt my insides ripped open, freshly raw and the skin so sensitive, burnt as if someone was putting salt on my wounds. Trying to go to the toilet to pass urine was terrifying. I would scream with tears in my eyes.

Mark told me I needed to get used to it and stop my whining. When Ann was getting ready to leave, Mark passed a comment to me saying even his mother frowned at my very sight and was repulsed, when I walked in the gown with my back open to the toilet. I thought how terrible having just gone through labour and the delivery and Ann was making gestures in regards to my physique to Mark but what upset me more was that Ann was a carer and I took her as a mother figure.

Having to stay in hospital was the usual procedure and overnight I was in intense pain. The night nurse explained to me it would be beneficial to purchase a soft pillow or cushion to sit on until I healed.

I still recall she said, "Why you don't ask your husband to get it for you; he looks like a nice man..."

Well I just smiled. How could I say what went through my mind at that point in time?

Suffering in silence, surrounded by darkness, the present looked lost to me without any hope for a brighter tomorrow.

The future was dull, dark and I could not see any signs or even a faint line of hope anywhere. I remember looking down at Jessica, fast asleep and so peaceful, tiny little hands and feet. So delicate and precious. I knew the love inside and bond was formed forever. **Yet while I looked at my precious, in my heart I knew the life Mummy lived at the moment was far from perfect for little Jessica and for my Jane.**

What was Mummy going to do? How was Mummy going to make both my little girls happy?

I would love you both; I would need to protect you both because I am Mummy. I helped create you and you both are my responsibility, just mine; no one else could do what a mother can do for her children.

Morning came soon and then much later Mark came with his sister to pick us up.

They were as usual without any thought or concern for my health and wellbeing and took us straight to Ann's house without asking me anything.

I still remember on entering everyone rushing to see the baby and even after the excitement had all calmed down still **no one apart from my very own Jane was happy and excited to see me walk in**. Jane was strangely enough so scared to see Jessica, the very first time inside the moses basket; when Jane saw her little sister she remarked, what is this? And ran far away.

It was the sweetest expression I had ever heard.

Slowly her curiosity got the better of her and she started to come closer. She soon wanted to feed Jessica and became very protective over her baby sister. Jane liked to role play mummy.

I have the sweetest, most precious memories which still make me smile and for a few moments forget the horror of the entire matrimonial situation. I remember Jane coming and covering Jessica with her little blanket, stroking her cheeks with one finger and saying 'sleep, baby'. Then when Jane would catch me looking, she would smile and hide her little face in my dress. She would go all shy and laugh...

These moments so pure, simple yet loving and precious still make me smile. It's just simple innocence, the love between mother, daughter and sister.

How does one ensure that the little laughter of pure love lasts as long as it can?

How do I, as the responsible adult, keep safe the mental, physical, emotional and psychological wellbeing of my little ones and ensure their safety in every way?

It's not enough to give life but that's just the beginning of a lifelong commitment.

# Heart of a beast

Very soon after we got back I needed to buy milk for the baby and Mark said, "Go then, do all the shopping. I'm fucking not going, get off your fat ass and go yourself. Don't be lazy." So although I could not sit or stand I struggled in pain to walk down the high street, shop and carry heavy bags. I had tears in my eyes, and people asking me if I was okay or about to deliver?

Just at that moment I saw a common friend from work. He could not believe that I had delivered only a few days previously and was carrying all this heavy shopping. Very kindly he carried all my bags for me and paid for my taxi to get me home.

When I got home I started to bleed terribly, the pain was unbearable and I just knew my stitches had re-opened because of the intensity of the burning and pain and the fact that I could not stand any longer. My hands became as cold as ice and white; I was shivering and shaking. Mark, looking at me, said, "Please, come on, I am sick of your acting, I don't care a shit about you. Make me a fucking cup of tea. I am toughening you up, and you need to be grateful to me."

And then he started laughing with great joy in his voice and said, "The served has now become the servant."

Mark got very excited at the thought that I was his slave and then he said when the girls would be old enough they too would do all the work for him while he would sit and rest.

I had taken only six months' maternity leave from work though legally I was entitled to almost a year. My parents were a blessing – they helped me out financially and that's how I managed to stay at home and look after Jessica, without having to worry about the mortgage since I was the main breadwinner. Apart from my parents I could not rely on anyone else.

I now understood very clearly in my life exactly how important financial security was. The importance for family life, securing a good future for the children and myself etc.

Sadly I did, but Mark was clueless, he took everything for granted. He lived in his own little world which revolved around his mother, himself and his collection of Taxidermy and collectables. Apart from that I don't think the real world in which we live held any meaning for him. **Mark's world was different to mine, very different.**

# Secret desires

The only circumstance when we thought alike briefly was in regards to the little cottage being done up. Though our reasons were as far apart as north and south.

While I was off work I decided it would be worthwhile to do up the little cottage. After all property was a good investment to have. **I had a silent dream in my heart which lay deep within and I dared not voice my longing desire to have a second home**. No matter how small but I thought if I could get a second home it would go to one of my girls. **One for Jane and one for Jessica.** At least Mum would have provided for each a roof over their head. I planned to wait for the property price to appreciate and take the equity out against the first house so as to go towards the second but for that I needed to show affordability which I hoped in time I would achieve.

However these were my secret desires which I cared not to share with minds that were not as pure as mine but rather twisted and cared only for self gain.

The entire family never ever understood me; what they did not understand or grasp made them think me to be a dreamer and not a realist. They viewed my ambition as ignorance and unheard of. My passion and drive to succeed and do better was viewed as a threat to their own life of comfort and lack of drive. Their set ways had no room to accommodate my ways.

I never believed in just being an ordinary worker, earning and living from hand to mouth. I wanted to be an achiever just like my father, the same passion and drive , the inner desire to be all that I could be and even better. **To be able to create my very own family legacy, not continue one which has been handed down from father to daughter but rather from mother to daughters.**

Neither did I want to set examples of life based on hardships, trials, debt, stress, anxiety and worry – like many in Mark's family and quite a few whom I had met.

My dream was to provide for my girls the same standard of life which my sister and I had received. A life of value, ethical, education and high morals.

With this goal in view, it gave me the silent strength to carry on, to go beyond the normal situation and work ten times harder for what I wanted for my kids. In front of me were examples of people who had ordinary lives, no will or ambition to succeed or do anything with their life. Mark's family, I looked at them all, many out of work, staying at home not wanting to work. Not caring about where food came from as long as it was provided by someone, somehow.

How could I lead and set proper examples for my kids amongst people who had bad ways and inappropriate behaviour?

# Renovations

I recall that when I was pregnant with Jessica, I had decided to not let it hold me back but rather to push me forward and strive harder. I knew in the depths of my soul that before I had the baby this was my chance to do all that was needed to get done or else my opportunity would be subject to serious delays, mainly because renovation cannot be done with a newborn around – it could cause baby to have serious health issues.

So the work had already started on the cottage from when I was pregnant with Jessica. It was a little old fashioned cottage. Though it was not easy to keep focused on renovating, even if you had a strong desire and goal but the pregnancy was getting to me.

Mark's father was a builder by trade. Self employed and worked mostly when he willed. If he fancied a job he would do it; if not, tough luck, he would not. Jim was a happy go lucky man and did not let anything bother him or upset him in anyway.

I had at this time no problems with the man, in fact I thought we got along rather well when he was sober and in his senses. He was a tall, slim man. Loved a drink, never seemed to have a care in the world and loved to smoke like a chimney.

Ann was a carer and worked all hours of the day to support her household. She was a short lady like myself, hardworking and loved all her children dearly but also spoilt her sons. She supported her sons, her husband and herself. Mark had three brothers and two sisters. He was the second youngest in the family and so he earned the name of being referred to as the baby of the family.

The house was like a family home, open to all who needed it but in this situation the mother was the provider and supporter for all including the grandchildren.

Jim was out of work and most of the time passed with him just sitting down and getting on Ann's nerves. So I would ask him if he could come do things in my place. I wanted to do it up before the baby came. Quite a few things were done to the cottage, all funded by myself and Dad.

I wanted to start with the rear garden first, the reason being it was like a wild forest, overgrown, infested with insects and I saw potential for development. Apart from me no one else could see the potential and importance of starting repairs from the outside and coming in.

The repairs went into months, draining me of funds, mentally and emotionally it was a drain completely.

The garden was cleared and needed three skips for it alone. But it looked much better after that temporarily, for the neighbour's fence was blown off and he was not getting it done, so I ended up doing that too – I valued my privacy too much. Mark wasn't bothered, for it was never his money. Once the fences were up, I asked for the next project to be done.

I had an outbuilding construction created and all while I was pregnant. It was built on decking and had a room made of wood, one window and it had several spotlights. It was very sweet and painted white. I wanted it as a little play room for my girls.

Double shifts, long hours from 10.30 am to 12.00 pm thoughout my pregnancy but I was not in a financial position to cut my shifts down. These long hours did my spine in and left me with terrible back pain.

Swollen feet and legs and hands too. I used to cry while I let the steaming, hot water from the shower run down my back. Though it hurt it was therapeutic simultaneously. The hot water helped. Mark never ever offered to press my back and I would not make the mistake of asking. For I knew what the answer would be. Abuse, abuse and more abuse.

Well, next step was to put a lovely lawn down but it did not last. The outbuilding was supposed to be a playhouse for the girls but Mark, being a bully, captured it. He started shifting all his Taxidermy into it and refused to keep it in his mother's house any longer.

By nature Mark was always selfish, self centred and was not capable of thinking about anyone else. However, he was quite cunning, he knew how to play with words and was brilliant at making people feel terrible. It was like an art with him. He was a very quick thinker, crafty, manipulative but had the face of an angel. Blond hair, green eyes, no tattoos, clean shaven and decently dressed all the time, with his glasses on his face made him look so decent, just like a regular, normal guy.

While the lawn was being done the house was in a mess because all the mud was being dragged through the house and it was very difficult to live in that situation, with those conditions. But I kept pushing because I wanted it decent for the girls.

Jim had extremely bad habits of negligence and not completing what he had started. He would undertake a project, soon lose interest and stop work for any amount of time and then come back to it when he felt it was appropriate.

So the garden had a lawn but it was not finished. Then we did some work inside the living room where I tried to level the floor but that again proved to be a big cause of concern and created issues with our neighbours.

Jim left all the stone and rubbish piled up, going up almost reaching my roof and the neighbours kept complaining. I too was getting upset with the ugly rocks in front of my door but my hands were tied. I had to keep my mouth shut. Eventually after weeks had passed, I decided to find a number of a skip and ask them to remove the rubbish myself.

The council too received complaints and had come around to inform me that I needed to have it removed. Every time I asked Jim he just refused saying, "I'll get it done when I get around to doing it." The frustration was growing mainly because as I would come out of the door, reaching up to my rooftop was gravel, stones, wooden floor boards and an area of constant worry and a public hazard. The neighbours were under the impression that I was breaking the entire house down and rebuilding it from scratch after seeing the outside rubbish and mess. But in fact all I was doing was lowering a floor.

**The kitchen was done again but unfortunately** the tap was put in the wrong place so every time the tap was turned on, the entire work surface would get wet and it would fall either side because it was placed in the wrong area and not over the sink directly. This would cause frequent fights at home.

Since Mark blamed me for everything, I was useless and could not wash, it was my fault, and it was even my fault that the house was tiny and needed doing up. The entire piping was fitted upside down causing the sink to block every week and frustrate me. I should have got a bigger house; I should have got more money, Mark said.

The flooring in both bedrooms was done again and the walls painted white. All this I had done again so that the little cottage would have a more modern look and feel to it. Spotlights ran throughout the house. The ceiling in the living room was very high and old fashioned to look at so I had it lowered down and again spotlights fitted as it gave a nice modern, cosy feel to it.

Yet there was much left to do, the reason being Jim had left each and everything incomplete, leading to more expense and a lot of things needing redoing.

# Cowboy builder

All over the house the plugs were left hanging out of the sockets. Jim said he would return to put new ones in but... he never did – I remained waiting.

Mark never wanted anyone else working in the house besides his dad, nor did he want to tell Jim to finish the work properly. I would try to ask sweetly without causing any more family issues about when my house would be safe, liveable and complete but instead I was nicknamed Mrs Want because I supposedly always wanted something done.

We decided that since the living room was tiny and Jim was offering to build an extension for us, we would go ahead and get one done.

After all, Jim was family, right... And certainly wanted everything in our best interests...

So it was agreed. Jim said he would break down our wall which divided the living room and separate it from the rear garden. The extension would not take long and would go on for a maximum of a week's time, if he devoted all his time to it.

Pretty much like everything else, what was promised and what was actually delivered were very different in reality.

The wall came down because Jim got a thrill from breaking stuff up yet the kids and I paid a very heavy price for it.

No big extension was done as promised; we were left still waiting on materials. The garden was left like a dangerous disaster zone with concrete slabs all over, sharp edges and holes and extremely unsafe. Although grass was laid down twice still each time it did not catch and then the condition it was left in with all the rubbish did it no favours.

I had the building inspector come round, not by choice but because of complaints by neighbours. What he saw shocked him beyond words. The expression on his face I still recall although it's very hard to write a description of it. He was speechless when he heard who the builder was since he thought it was just a local, ordinary builder but on learning it was my very own father-in-law he said this is unacceptable.

He informed me that we could not be living like this, it was a cause of concern and not safe at all. The division was a temporary partition of plywood held together with no insulation at all. The temporary door hung from the plywood frame with big gaps under the door and along the plywood partition were long gaps all over. The wall was made up of two pieces of plywood. Top and bottom put together, it was not even one long sheet of plywood.

A little heavy rain could flood our place and the water would come right in, explained the inspector from the council. I tried to reason with the inspector saying we had run out of finance and that it was all going to be done within a few days so he was happy with that and left.

There were glass slabs broken and kept all around the garden. Due to fear I would not want to let Jane out although she really wanted to go and play outside. I struggled and tried my best to put all the rocks to one side, picking them up one by one, by hand so as to try and clear the path but still it was too much.

I could not do it by myself. I needed help desperately but from whom?

No one came to mind; I had no one by my side.

Soon the weather started to get colder since there was no partition I had to keep the heating on day and night. Two additional, small electric heaters just to keep the rooms warm and prevent the kids from getting sick. Still it was cold, but when I complained to Jim he said, "No it's not, it's fine." Mark did not want to tell his father anything. **High electric bills and desperation led me to take tape and try to sellotape the plywood so as to cover all the gaps and try to keep the heat in and away from escaping. I had to try something and was willing to do anything. Heating bills were in the region of £350 upwards because there was nothing to prevent escape or trap the heat in.**

I often wondered with what conscience cowboy builders can do wrong to people, who work hard to give their life savings in the name of trust.

Yet I had no words to describe at this moment in time what thoughts were running through my mind. This was the man I called Dad out of respect and whom I liked and whose family I was supposed to be a part of. If not for me then at least for his very own grandchildren, he owed it to them to provide a safe, warm, sheltered environment. I tried hard to do everything on my limited budget but in all fairness my expectation was a safe environment at the very least.

Well, pleas fell on deaf ears so I stopped pleading. On one side physically the home was not good – it was not in any suitable condition to be called a home. Home is where the heart lies and where there is joy but I had neither.

On the other hand the marriage was a disaster... I knew it was only time. Before it ended...

There were so many things going on at the same time. Sometimes I was amazed at myself how on Earth I managed to hold on to my sanity. My world was crashing and crushing me from all sides. It was so hard to know where to turn, which path to take and simply how to live each day.

Who was I to go to for help? There was simply no one. My oppressors were trying their best to oppress me and crush the life out of me. If this was how my family was, how would strangers be?

Meanwhile both the girls were growing and my maternity leave had come to an end.

Kate had agreed to have both Jane and Jessica but I could see she was not that happy, even though she had said looking after a baby was no problem.

# Mental agony

My childcare problems started mounting up fairly quickly. Kate told me she could not keep my daughters on Saturdays, and then it was Wednesday too. Sometimes in the morning Kate would give me a call at the very last minute informing me that she could not help me with the kids.

This would put a lot of mental pressure on me. I would have to rush about when she was not available, to ask my mother-in-law if she was available to babysit and if that was not an option, then the only option was Jim. He was asked only as a last resort but it was becoming extremely stressful and under the pressure of work, our life at home with Mark and childcare, I was starting to have a nervous breakdown.

Kate told me once in a remark, "I will have to charge you more for the wear and tear of my legs". So I did start giving her a little extra but it was still not enough. She still could not keep my kids on a regular basis. I started to see all the inconsistency and the stress it caused which made me realise I had to do something. It was extremely difficult to continue like this. I had no more to give – that's the reason I could not afford to give her more. Both the jobs I did were just basic wage so after paying out for everything there was never anything left.

All Mark said was that it was my problem, I had to sort it out. If I could not handle it, then I could just give up working. That was not an option for me; under no circumstance was I willing to go back to starvation days nor was I going to let my children ever starve.

I dropped my Saturday shifts at work with great difficulty. Being a hard worker my bosses were not too happy for me to drop one of the busiest shifts of the week.

An incident which instigated this took place regarding Jessica. I still remember I had nappies and milk tins all piled up at Kate's, my sister-in-law's home for my baby and one day in the morning she told me she was not feeling well and would give the baby to her mum to look after for me, so that I could still go to work.

So naturally, I went to work thinking nothing negative of the family. Two hours into my shift Ann called, asking me for milk for the baby saying she did not have any. Let me explain: Kate's house was just down the road from Ann, five minutes on foot. At the top of Ann's road, another five minutes away, was a chemist and off licence.

What was most upsetting was not that my daughter needed milk and I was being called but **the underlying lack of care or thought.**

I had everything stacked up for my Jessica; the distance and time it would take me to travel back and get a tin of milk would be much longer than Ann just going to either her daughter's house or to the off licence.

Also knowing very well that when I was already doing so much for the family I would have paid for an extra tin of milk if they had got one for my little baby but they chose to call me instead. I rushed to my phone to ask Mark where he was; he said he was very close to his mother's home and would buy milk and take the baby home. I should continue my shift and I could pay him later. He also told me that his family were trying to make me give up working and so he wanted me not to return from work as he would not support us.

This incident hurt me to think I was depriving myself and giving my all, in the name of family, yet this is how I'm repaid. Every day there was some sort of problem, every day something new happening.

Kate kept making excuses about keeping the girls and work was getting very upset with me; they thought I did not want to work seriously – from being an asset I was turning into a liability.

Mark on the other hand was driving me insane. He kept grumbling at me constantly.

In the midst of all this I thought about being a childminder. It seemed like a good idea at the time, the reason being I thought if I was working from home I would not have to worry about childcare issues. So with my limited resources I decided to enrol in distance learning with ICS home learning and did a diploma course in Child Day Care. I also went to Croydon Council and decided to take several courses in regards to childminding.

Sadly, on becoming a registered childminder I found out it was not as easy as it seemed. Although Ofsted was very happy with me, finding children was not easy. I was ready to work but all the customers I was getting were just not right. Not wanting to take me seriously. Not wanting to sign contracts and haggling with already reasonable prices were some of the difficulties I faced. Soon realising that this was not meant for me, I decided not to pursue it further. Having spent enough time on this, I was not going to let this upset me. I would definitely try something else.

The only way to keep my mental sanity was to try to fight against every obstacle which kept coming my way. I knew full well that if I gave up, Jane and Jessica would have no one to fall back upon. I had to find another way out and I needed solutions quickly.

# Sorting childcare out

I decided not to suffer. I walked to the closest nursery and asked how it would work. They explained to me for the first time how childcare benefits worked. Strangers, not family members.

My mother-in-law believed that a mother should look after her baby and no one else should. Although her very own daughter Catherine put her child into care. However, I do believe this was only said because Ann never wanted me to work.

Sadly, if only I had known that my husband would provide for me and our children without ever having to starve again and history would not repeat itself, I would not have worked like a donkey.

The nursery was a blessing. They explained everything to me, the entire procedure, the income threshold, the number of hours available for childcare, example morning session, afternoon session or the entire day, the cost with or without food. They also had facilities available for term time or throughout the year and the help which was out there.

I called tax credits to confirm I would receive help in the form of child tax credit then I went and registered the kids in the nursery. I had to wait for a space to become available for my children.

The day I put my children into nursery was the day I told Kate that I was no longer taking my daughters to her house. I had kept it quiet because she kept having problems which were spreading throughout the week and I waited for the nursery to start. She was quite shocked and surprised and asked if both kids were going, to which I said yes. There was no point in not putting both in. The nursery was a blessing; they helped both children develop and grow. The teachers were amazing and dedicated; my only regret is that I had listened to Ann and I wished with all my heart I had not been manipulated and had put my children in earlier. I know by putting the kids into nursery this was a hold over me that they had lost since I was no longer dependent on them.

However, that was one problem solved – the nursery was just five minutes away from where we lived – but the marriage was still no better, in fact it was getting worse. Indeed, the word 'worse' does not begin to describe the exact intensity that married life was taking a turn for. **I was going through a bad phrase inside emotionally and at the same time turning dead inside.**

From time to time I would still occasionally ask Ann to help and intervene but soon found it was of no use; things never changed so eventually I stopped asking. I was long past caring but she was still interested to know what was happening at that moment. I failed to understand whether it was genuine concern or some sort of vindictive streak to try and find out how the marriage was coping, or failing. Ann asked how things were and I replied "same as always" and that there was "no change and no need to talk about it". **I was fed up of asking, I was fed up of tears being shed.**

Why did I have to beg to be treated rightly, why?

Many a time Mark would go over with my precious Jane and if I would start to get ready to go visit he would say what do you want to come for? They don't want to see your face; they just want to see the little girls. No one cares about you; you stay home and tidy up this mess or shit hole as he would like to call it. Sometimes Mark would even go so far as to call the house a shed or shoe box.

Some occasions, I would still go and Ann would say, "Oh, I never knew you were coming I only have dinner for them not for you..."

Well I got used to everything after a while. My main concern was my children and paying for bills to provide for them. **I was willing to go through everything and anything, it never mattered, all that mattered was my precious daughters**.

But things kept getting worse, he kept getting worse, more rude, more evil and nasty, and I was getting fed up. Fed up of picking up after him, cleaning after him, having to do everything and getting not even a kind word back in return; it was getting too much.

# Mental torment

The intensity of the mental abuse was increasing on a rapid, daily basis. The lack of respect grew. But when things keep happening, it forces change, it turns you and you just despise the person.

**An incident took place.** We had two sets of keys for our little home and the police inspector came to my door – he was trying to make the entire neighbourhood aware that there had been a robbery and told everyone to lock their doors.

Tired from working two jobs, a lack of sleep and stress, I was trying to rush around so by accident I locked both locks, forgetting that my husband only had the key to the top lock on the door. He would go to work early in the morning 4am and finish at 3pm that day; when he finished work he picked my daughters up from nursery and then went to his mother's. Every day at 4pm I would call to find out if everything was ok.

That day though I just got abused and shouted at over the phone; I was very upset. He said, "I don't have the keys, you locked the door." I told him he could have caught the tram to my workplace so I could have handed the keys over to him since I worked very close to home.

As usual the language was out of control; he was shouting abuse, calling me every name under the sun; it was terribly upsetting. Mark knew exactly what to say and he knew how to say it so that it would make my insides tremble since I was so upset and then I would not be able to function or concentrate properly.

When I met him on the road to give him the keys he was absolutely silent. No abuse but a sarcastic smile; he knew I was upset and he was so thrilled with what he had done. He was happy to see me as a wreck – that's what made Mark feel so very superior and was the highlight of his day. That is something else Mark would do – all the abusing was mostly when we were alone, but in front of people he would change and be very silent, he would be someone totally different. **You would never imagine that behind such an innocent face a monster lay hidden.**

So while everyone outside thought he was an angel it was only with the exception of Mark's family and myself who knew what he was really like.

If I had not called I would have gone home late in the night to find no one at home. My entire break went on going to get the keys to him and when I came back to work I was a wreck.

The marriage had taken away my mental peace. He thrived on making me feel weak, ugly, and fat, although I was only 9 stone and he was 20 stone.

When I returned my OM saw how upset I was, sobbing, shaking, terrified, crying uncontrollably. He was very kind and let me sit in the staffroom to get myself together. He took control of my department and handled it for me. **Later he tried to ask me what had happened. Until that moment in time no one at work knew anything; I had kept my problems well hidden from the rest of the world. Every day I had a smile on my face, I hid it well not wanting others to take advantage of me, laugh at my situation and also being too**

**scared to come out and say how married life really was. There were lots of different, mixed up feelings of worry, loss, fear of it coming out, his reactions, would I cope, where would I go. Who was I to turn to and take the kids to?**

I would tell my boss repeatedly what was happening at home and he would try to console me and be helpful. Everyone could see my tormented soul.

Well, after this incident with Mark happened, I was not happy that the entire workplace came to know what was going on but it gave me the courage to speak out nevertheless. Although I felt embarrassed I wondered what others thought about me. Did they laugh behind my back? Did they think I was weak? Many of them passed comment on what I should do, on how I could change my situation.

Yet it's so easy for strangers to look from the outside and comment. It's very different when you are living through that phase of tormenting terror.

When you suffer, it's good to speak out aloud because suffering in silence is like a silent killer. No one knows what's happening; everything stays suppressed inside and there's only so much one person can go through or take. Having a support system is very important. For me, my OM and my GM were a big source of support and strength for me along with a few others.

Mental abuse victims find it hard to communicate openly about their issues, especially because of the nature of abuse.

The abuser is like an artistic and a skilful thief. They steal your peace of mind, take control of you and hold you imprisoned within yourself. It's the worst kind of entrapment and cruelty one can face because to break out of that entrapment can take years. Some need help to be rescued by either a stranger or a friend. Or maybe you just need something which is more important to you than yourself – a cause or a person. In all cases the cycle of abuse has to be broken so that present and future generations can survive and have a chance at truly being happy and not living an existence of torment.

# Sources of inspiration

My OM had tried to find out what exactly was taking place at home. What he discovered was too shocking for him to comprehend. He felt bad and tried to encourage me as much as possible. He could not understand as to how someone could treat their wife the way Mark was treating me, since he would treat his wife with a lot of respect, love and care.

The General Manager was another source of inspiration. He said his office doors would always be open for me to come through. If I had any problems I could see him anytime and talk to him because he felt something was wrong but he was waiting for me to come to him. He gave me lots of useful advice, once I opened up and started talking to him in relation to my problems.

A security guard at work, who was like a brother to me, told me he was very upset in regards to my life. He gave me fantastic advice and said, **"If you have given the man multiple chances and he doesn't change, he will never change. But you're just like my sister. I don't want to hear that after ten years have passed and later I see you down the street and you are still crying. Only you can decide your future. Your future is only in your hands; no one else can decide or make you do something you are not ready to do. Take control of your life, you only have one life."**

So I decided to take control.

At work I had a lovely lady working with me from when I first started in 2011. She was pleasant, lovely and kind hearted. Although her health was poor she was a very hard worker and did her very best.

Later on in years to come it was this very same lady who was yet another great source of inspiration to me and someone who was like a guiding angel lighting up my path. She herself acted like a mirror into the future for me.

This lady had gone through a lot, forty years of abuse in a bad marriage and a horrible life. I was surprised about all that I learnt from Rose. Rose said that she had stayed only for her kids because she did not want them to have no father or lose out on being with their father.

Sadly although Rose was very much like me and suffered greatly, she lost a lot of her life. She lost her house that she had worked so hard for; she lost her family life, relationships and her health. Worst of all her kids blamed her for staying in a bad marriage.

Poor Rose has to keep going to hospital for regular breathing problems and check-ups since her health was so poor. **She believes in taking each day as it comes because she does not know if she will awaken to see tomorrow.**

Yet in the midst of all this suffering when Rose heard what was happening to me in my life, she decided to reach out to me. I hold the utmost respect and admiration for Rose – it takes true courage to reach out and make a difference.

She made a gentle approach and said she wanted to talk to me. Rose had much needed advice for me from which I learnt so many useful things. Sadly, to this day, she still lives in fear of her ex husband and refuses to disclose her location.

She advised me regarding, firstly, Victim Support. I honestly never knew that such an organisation existed or how to find them.

Secondly, Rose told me the GP was a good place to start too. If I had any worries it would be good to go to them since everything is kept confidential.

Thirdly, Rose said I should not hesitate to go to the police or call them at any time when I needed help.

Fourthly, I never knew of the existence of soup kitchens.

Fifthly, the Citizens Advice Bureau, who could give lots of free advice on many different things.

Sixthly, I learnt that certain lawyers give free twenty minutes' advice on the phone and also there are certain lawyers who will give you free advice for fifteen or twenty minutes in person.

Also legal aid for families on low income is very important – sometimes because income is so low they don't have to pay anything for legal procedures.

I know this sounds so simple, logical, but when you're in that situation of total despair and loss, confusion, you're struggling within yourself to come to grips with your life and understand or try to make sense of things, so it's not easy... The simplest solutions may be right in front of you and you still may not reach out because fear grips your soul.

Yes I can relate to the feeling, everything you do is wrong. You feel guilty for everything; all that you do or say is wrong.

You have to reach that point in your life where you need to find yourself again.

Until you are lost and want to be found again you cannot come out of the web of mental and emotional entrapment.

# Thinking of freedom and divorce

Many things lead to that decision: it's when you're tormented and can't take anymore, there's nothing left to take from you, you are willing to lose everything just so that you can walk away and start afresh. When you reach your breaking point and hit rock bottom – that's where I was.

Desperate, willing to do anything to end the misery, to survive and live at all costs, anywhere else as long as I had my children with me. I was going nowhere without them.

Ann had once long ago commented that since I was not happy with Mark all I had to do was leave the children and just go. Poor girls, what kind of a future would they have had, had I done so. Such evil thoughts asking a mother to abandon her kids to an environment and household that was a wreck and could not survive as a functioning family unit itself.

What would they have offered my children?

A friend asked me why, when I was so miserable, why did I choose to have a second child. The honest answer was I did not; sex between us was never consensual, it was never gentle nor a pleasure. It was for his pleasure, when he wanted, and I never enjoyed it even once.

My mother, I guess out of curiosity, asked me one day how things were between us sexually. She knew we had lots of issues between us but strangely I never thought she would ask that...

Maybe it was a mother's instinct or intuition, I really don't know.

Well, although I would talk to Mum about my difficult marriage I kind of never spoke about our sex life, I would leave that out. Mum was sick for years and had breathing problems so I did not want to make it worse or add to her stress which might cause her health to deteriorate even further. So although I suffered I never ever clearly stated the magnitude to which the relationship had reached in terms of cruelty.

This was the very first time I opened up to Mum and revealed that sex was never on mutual terms and because of how he was I hated it. The most uncomfortable conversation between a mother and daughter. She asked me if he was gentle and I said no. Mum asked was there any foreplay, and I said no.

Mum was silent for a long time. I tried to change the topic a little and divert from our present conversation but Mum would not deviate. She wanted to know more and asked me to open up without hiding anything.

So I disclosed to her that the brutally honest truth was that because of everything which had happened continuously between us from the start, I had pure hatred for him. He never said a kind word, never even gave me a little gift, not even a card for birthdays, anniversary, he did nothing. From the start of the marriage he said even if I had paid him money he would not touch me. Suddenly somehow when his cruelty got too much to bear and I had no feelings all of a sudden he wanted to have sex. But these times were when he wanted; when he was done he would say 'that's me done'.

Mum replied, "That's not the way it's supposed to be."

I was still with him because of the kids, that was all.

Mum never ever advised me in regards to the situation I was facing; she never said for me to leave him. I don't know if it's simply because of her being a staunch Roman Catholic and Catholics are against divorce or if it's just because she was shocked and speechless and could not comprehend what I was going through. As a parent it is very difficult to grasp the fact that your little girl is in an abusive marriage.

In fact, yes, it's not the way it was supposed to be; rather it was rape.

It does not matter if you're married, sex or love making should be gentle, loving, a pleasure and artful. An enjoyment between both parties and a deep fulfilment long after you have made love to your partner or husband.

If instead it's not mutual, full of pain and leaves you feeling violated, like a piece of meat or a commodity just used and put aside until next time, it's not love making, it is in fact rape and that's exactly how I would feel. Lying there dead and lifeless to the world, waiting for Mark to finish. No emotion, no reciprocation, nothing.

I know now that's not the way it's supposed to be.

I really never knew what each day had in store for me.

Men like this only get power from putting others down, making them feel belittled and like shit.

It never mattered what I wore, I always looked ugly to him; if I dressed up I would be insulted even more. He would say I looked like a prostitute and a slut. During our marriage he often said he had only married me for someone needed to take care of him and cook for him.

Other times he said he had only married me because he had heard I was well off and thought he would not have to do any work, he could have a comfortable life.

He thought I would be his slave. Other times he said, "When I first saw you, you were so confident I wanted to break you."

Well I'll say he definitely succeeded...

But with each and every day I was getting more aggravated, I was feeling the fear subsiding and was being taken over by a more powerful sense of rage, betrayal.

Finding that this man who had married me only did so because he wanted an easy life, he wanted a life of comfort and he wanted to feel all powerful by taking hold of my life and tormenting me, treating me like a puppet and pulling my strings empowered him…

Breaking me down every day, year after year gave him control over me; knocking me down gave Mark extreme excitement.

Mark broke my carefree, wild spirit and had me in captivity. No matter how many people said I was beautiful, I tried to keep changing the way I looked. I never felt comfortable within myself and every time I looked at myself I felt I was fat and ugly. Not because I was but because I was made to feel like that.

**I stopped eating and started literally starving myself. Weight became an obsession for me**. I joined Weight Watchers. I got a cheap value range scale from Argos and kept checking my weight regularly every day. Though everyone who saw me started to say I was not looking healthy, that I should stop losing weight, Mark was in my head saying I was still fat. I started looking for weight loss medicine to help burn the fat and visited Holland & Barrett to try to find the most efficient medicine and speed up my metabolism so as to burn fat. I needed to be slim.

My beautiful waist-long hair was coloured multiple times, the style was changed and permed and that's when it became damaged and finally I had to chop it off. All this was done in an attempt to look beautiful. To try to stop Mark from making me feel less miserable. I loved my hair, it was silky and long, and now that too was a symbol of my past.

Each day I stared into the mirror, I could not recognise myself. I never knew what was happening, I was just trying to survive, trying to get by each day. When I felt tired I would drink loads of coffee and many Red Bulls. That's what I survived upon.

Each time I felt that life was a curse and I could not go on, that my back was against the wall and I just wanted to give up, two little innocent sets of eyes peering up into my face as I looked over them at night kept me going. Many a time tears would stream down from my eyes and fall upon them softly as they slept. I thought why, my poor innocent children, why did I bring you into this world?

Mummy is so sorry, Mummy is very sorry but I love you both dearly.

Looking at my little ones I knew I had to protect them; life had to change, but when and how I did not know. Those answers I did not have yet...all I knew was that it was going to happen soon, within me I felt the strong desire awaken from within the depths of my soul to take my children and walk out. Find a better life for my kids and myself.

I started thinking about divorce because I wanted my sanity and my kids to be happy, and to set a good example for them. To have them educated, set good goals and provide the safe mental and physical environment they needed. To be able to supply them with emotional stability, help them achieve their true potential and be the best that they could be.

I wanted to be their rock yet I knew I could not be their rock when I myself was fragmented. Along with repairing myself and trying to find me again I would have to help the girls too, I understood this now. We had to get out one way or another so that we would be free to build the life we deserved as a family.

# Planning for freedom

My decision was made; that was the hardest step to take. Despite having been through so much, having to take this first step was the hardest decision since 2008. I knew that the road that lay ahead was going to be unknown; it was going to be new. The only person I would have to rely on was myself and I could make no mistakes because Jane and Jessica would pay the price, if I did.

I researched everything I could on divorce from Google at work and when Mark was not around at home sometimes. I researched so much that I knew every stage of the divorce procedure. Since I was on low income I could get help with divorce proceedings and that was a big help. I called a few lawyers after getting their details from the Citizens Advice Bureau to find out more.

It's true, knowledge is power, so I wanted to equip myself with as much information as I could so that nothing went against me. If I made any mistakes I am very sure I would not be alive to share my story with you today.

Next I made an appointment to see a lawyer because I needed to find out if all the information I had gathered was up to date. The lawyer was very patient yet her charges were too high. Not having £2,500 to pay for the divorce proceedings meant it was a certain no for me in respect to using her. Another £500 for each child and in respect to the house more money to get it claimed all in my name although I had paid for everything.

Overall the amount of money was going above and beyond what I could afford. Since I had a house she said I could not access legal aid.

The only option I had was to stay with Mark or have faith in myself and go ahead with the proceedings on my own. I wanted to wait until Jane was in school and then to start the process, hoping it would be easier.

Yet again though, fate had something else in store for me.

# Brutally attacked

One night while on my way home from work, I was attacked and brutally beaten by two men who wanted my phone. I was not willing to let it go and took the hammering because **it had my girls' snaps on it.** That was one of the most important things for me in my life at the moment. It had sentimental value; I could not let go. The GP gave me two weeks off from work since my head hurt severely.

While the police were taking my statement they got a call regarding another incident of someone else being attacked. The police drove me around the block but we could not see anyone. In the papers next day it was stated that two men were going around and attacking people and although they had a picture for identification still they were never caught.

My parents were on holiday in the UK; they came to visit me and they were upset. However, they asked Mark if he would go and pick me up at the station every day when I returned to work until they were present so the children would be looked after by them while he went to get me. Instead each day he would be late so I had to start walking up the lonely road myself, which made me very nervous.

A few days later, we had an argument over a staff party and me not returning home at an appropriate time, even though my family was there to look after the children for just one evening. Yet Mark was fuming and said he wanted to hit me and kill me because I had not returned on time. As we walked on the road together I thought we were both returning home but instead Mark walked off before me – where he went I had no clue. I came back to find Mum and Dad were upset because they said Mark was very angry and they feared for my safety.

Later in the day Ann came over; she told me it was not good that we argue and that we needed to get back together, if he returned home, especially for the children.

But that one little moment of freedom gave me a taste of both sides of my life.

My life was exactly like a coin and I felt as if I was flipping it in a way to see which path to take. On one side I was being able to breathe, to be me again and just be able to relax without looking over my shoulder.

In contrast, on the other side it was me looking over my shoulder, fear, worry, tension, stress, uncertainty, misery and slavery. Persecution and mental agony.

Under no condition did I want him back. Ann told my parents that I would be on the streets; the kids would be put on the streets too. We would all be homeless and that I could not manage without Mark. My parents never wanted to see a marriage breaking down. Ann went so far as to say now we know how serious the situation is. But that was a lie: they knew right from the start how serious the situation was, I never hid anything; instead it was Ann whose help I continued asking for and turning to so that the issues could be resolved.

My father had also told Ann that he was not pleased with the way

Mark spoke in regards to food. I had cooked food and Mark called it dog shit; Father heard it and was most upset. He got angry but Mum said not to say anything because they were on holiday and did not want to cause any more arguments in my home.

A few hours later Mark returned. He stayed silent; he sat on the sofa and watched the TV. No one except the kids spoke; the rest of us all had an uneasy silence.

The next day Mark brought me flowers and said he was sorry, that he wanted us to work and be a family, that things would be different. I never believed him for a moment. All these years he did nothing, then how come all of a sudden this change – it seemed like another game. Another twisted mental game and a strategic theory masterminded to keep me from fleeing with the kids.

Somehow I was the only one who could see it. Mum and Dad could not. They were blinded and kept nagging at me to give him a second chance for the children's sake. They said he is really trying and he is sorry. Against my better judgement I took him back. I really should not have but instead I was given the wrong advice.

Instead of me taking control of the situation, I reverted. Sadly when you're going through abuse it pulls you down and feelings of guilt take over even if you have nothing to feel guilty about. I was suffering, no one else, the decision should have been mine and people should have encouraged me to do the right thing, but instead misguided advice caused me more grief.

A few days later my family took off. No sooner had they left than Mark's behaviour reverted back to his normal ways, back to being nasty and selfish. He was becoming unbearable. In the meantime I was trying to get my father-in-law to do up our place but it was just not happening. Too many problems going on simultaneously.

In all honesty I was quite upset with my parents for telling me to take Mark back. Only much later, I could somewhat understand that they never wanted any harm to come to me. But were rather confused and could not comprehend what the best course of action should have been. Most parents go wrong there, they don't understand that this is the time they need to be supportive and a pillar of strength not only for their child but grandchildren too.

By that time I had started researching divorce...

# Mark's assault

Mark came home and we had the usual argument. I would always keep my phone on me close by since I was always uncertain about his irrational behaviour. At any given time Mark would suddenly switch off and go into one of his moods which were never pleasant. It never mattered if the kids were present.

Mark grabbed my phone out of my hands in the midst of shouting at me. The phone was our lifeline. I started asking for it back and he did not want to give it. I was scared and asked him again to return it. Unfortunately, with his twenty stone of pure muscle, Mark pushed me. At that moment Jane came rushing out and said, "Don't push Mummy," and Mark then pushed my Jane. That's when I could bear no more – Jane was only three. She was shocked and ran into my arms. I think at that moment Mark realised that things for him had changed forever. It was strange. He was angry, shouting, fuming but at the same time had a strange look; it's hard to describe.

As I held Jane my insides trembled. Jessica was asleep and knew nothing of what was happening. I had feared this day would come. No harm must ever come to my children – I was Mum. Feeling useless but nervous and terrified, I tried not to show Mark. I wanted him to leave, or I was ready to run myself; all I wanted was to grab the kids and run as far as I could go. No clothes, no shoes, no house; nothing mattered, just the girls and me at that moment.

Mark was shouting at me; he slammed my phone down but all this while Jane still clung to me. I don't quite understand why but Mark told me to stop him because he was leaving. If I did not stop him from leaving, we would be over.

But I had had enough so no more, I decided better he goes. But then I worried because I kept thinking of his rage. What would Mark do on his return? He would definitely return, I was sure of it.

I remember not too long ago I had had a chain put on the door because my big daughter could open the door and run straight onto the road. Our little cottage was on a side road and there was always traffic. It was early in the morning my husband's shift got cancelled so he was angry, it upset him. He always said he did not care about the road and that he never wanted the chain on the door to be on. I should sit and watch Jane. That's it and definitely no chains should be on the door for any reason.

That day Jane was not well so I had stayed at home to look after her. Mark got home earlier than expected. I knew Mark was back when I heard him at the door, so I called out saying I was coming. As I rushed to open the door, with great force the door was flung open. Mark had decided to break the door in and shouted, pointing his finger in my face, "I told you not to lock the fucking door." No amount of trying to reason with him or explain logically that it was for Jane's safety could get through his irrational behaviour.

As I turned I saw poor Jane standing in the corner quietly looking ill. I had never wanted Jane to experience any of this. She was a child and should never have had to witness her father acting in this way. Luckily the door did not hit me on my face, it just missed me.

My past experience and the knowledge of him breaking up his ex girlfriend's house was all frightening me so **I decided to call the police as I knew his capabilities.**

The police questioned me in regards to me being terrified and suggested it was better to have him arrested if I was really worried about our safety. They saw the chain broken on the door and questioned me in regards to it. They saw I had tried to build a barricade with Mark's Olympic weights to keep us safe from him.

The police asked what had led to the arguments and wanted to know the cause. I had to explain that the marriage was not going well and this was how Mark was. But today everything had changed, today he had laid his hand on my daughter. Just then Jane came and told the police in her little voice, "Daddy pushed Mummy and then Daddy pushed me."

I explained to the police that now Mark's behaviour all of a sudden radically changed once again. He was acting strange for a while. He suddenly stopped sharing the same bed as me; he slept on the sofa. His favourite insults were I cooked dog shit so I had to get large quantities of takeaway for him just to keep the peace. I told them everything that was going on behind closed doors in the privacy of my house.

**Well I got him arrested and felt peaceful for the first time in ages; I slept well**.

His mother and sister went to bail him out the next day. When Mark came out, I told him I wanted a divorce. He did not want to set me free. He said I was over-reacting and that I should not be silly. I was going to break up a family, take children away from their father and was being stupid; I "really need to be ashamed" of what I'm doing.

But I firmly stood my ground. Now was my second chance; I could not waver and had to be strong. For my girls and for me, this was it.

Making it clear to Mark was extremely difficult as usual – he did not want to accept that I had taken a decision to leave him yet he kept in check because now he knew he had a police record. Mark became boisterous; I tried to remain calm I needed to get my message across to him. It might be now or after a few years but the divorce would be inevitable...

No matter how much he would try to stop it.

Then after a while, like most incidents throughout the marriage, Mark agreed and said he did not want any contact with the kids. So I found out everything about our case, what I needed to do and how I had to proceed. The Internet was a great help, as well as the Citizens Advice Bureau and Gingerbread Helpline for single parents. When you're equipped with knowledge it makes life much easier.

# Flashback

Now that it was only the three of us I could sit down and just relax for a while. Something which I had not done in a long time for so many years. Going back to an earlier time while I was sitting down, quietly retracing my steps down memory lane...

I started to recall certain moments from the past like my mother-in-law saying when my husband and I were not getting on well, "You go back, leave the kids here." I could never get over those words – leave them with what and who, them? With no ambition, no future, no morals...for I saw what the entire family had turned out to be because of their own upbringing and issues. How can one tell a well educated, hard working mother "leave your children" when their son's the problem? No way on earth was I ever going to do that.

Then I recalled the multiple occasions Ann would tell my daughter that I wasn't her mother and when I would say something she used to say, "Oh of course you are, I'm only joking. She knows that." But I knew my daughter would get confused and call her grandma 'Mum'. I would have to correct Jane all the time.

I thought of the times, in the name of family, I had made sacrifices and given to them. That I had done things for Mark although none of them deserved all that I did. I did too much.

Recalling how the behaviour of the entire family got better with me showering gifts and doing things for them.

Mark himself was the biggest deceiver. He spoke so sweetly about marriage, how he never wanted it to break, how he believed in working together and doing things.

Five long years of marriage and yet he did nothing special for me, for us or the family. He got up very early and went to work and then did everything else he wanted. He never brought anything for the kids, not even a toy from the charity shop. **It was all me... Everything they had was because of me. Well, sad but very true, I was a lone parent right from the start. I was a house maker, mother, father, slave and provider all in one**.

Over Christmas we had separated for a while but got back together because my parents said he looked very sorry and to give him a chance for the kids... Then when I took him back as they left he started again. I remember fighting, and hating my parents at that moment because what I needed then was encouragement and support to do the right thing for me and the kids. Being with him would only mean suffering and leading a life of torment and pain.

At this moment I remembered Ann's words – "without him you will be on the streets for sure. In a half way house and the kids will not survive and will suffer". I also recalled how I had been lied to in the past about very important issues and they collectively tried to put fear into me. This was all done because I never knew the legal system.

But when you reach the point of no return and you know it has to end you will do whatever it takes. So I did...

# Divorce proceedings

Preparing for the divorce was quite unnerving. Throughout the proceedings I was on tenterhooks, not knowing at what given point of time Mark would come around to attack me just in case he felt like it. He did come, but just to have a civil talk – that's what he called it but he actually tried his best to guilt me into not going through the divorce for the sake of the children.

I decided to be calm and let him leave peacefully. I said later when I had the papers ready I would go to his mother's place to get it signed by him. When all the papers were ready and in order, I had also attached extra sheets with twenty additional points, added to explain to the judge the exact situation and reasons for the separation.

Before going to sign the papers I made it a point to inform Ann that I would be around and the purpose for my visit. As a precaution I also informed workmates so everyone was aware. This was done to safeguard myself just in case Mark snapped and I never made it out again.

When I entered Ann's house, she was very silent but said Mark was upstairs in one of the bedrooms. Though I was a bit wary of going up, not knowing what to expect, nevertheless I went. He looked paler than usual but I was not paying much attention to the way he looked. I lay the papers on the bed in front of him.

Mark turned to me and said he was sorry for everything and did not want us to end. He said he never meant for all this to happen and really wanted to be a good father and husband. He wanted me to give him another last chance to show he could be different and give us a chance at being a proper family.

My simple answer was that though I respected all he said there was no way I could stay any longer with him.

Realising Mark was trying to be calm about things, I needed to be very careful and tactful with my approach and what I said, because I was sat just two feet away from my abuser. This was extremely difficult knowing that if I said anything that did not please Mark not even Ann would be able to interfere and no one would be there to rescue me on time.

Mark confessed that he was jealous of me. I was too good compared to everyone he knew. More intelligent, capable, generous and he wanted to be like me but could not.

All Mark said felt like a speech carefully thought of and rehearsed with the hope of melting my heart and getting me entrapped yet again. But this time nothing Mark could say would get me back. My parents were not present, there was no pressure. The decision was entirely mine.

Later, Mark started getting agitated and Ann called us down, asking if we wanted tea. I guess Ann could hear the conversation taking a turn for the worse. We came down and Mark remarked why could not I be like his mother. She had been through everything and she still stayed with their father.

**I made it my point to say I was not Ann, I was Andrea and I would**

**never ever be Ann.**

**Mark got angry and was starting on me; he said he would not sign the papers and that I would have to suffer. So I told him that I was willing to lose everything, the house even, but we would never be together again. It did not matter if it was now or later after a few years, nothing was going to change my mind.**

**Mark was becoming imbalanced and his voice was changing. I decided leaving would be a good decision at the time.**

**So I left.**

While I was walking down the road suddenly I saw Mark coming up behind me. My breath stopped with fear, I thought, that's it, that's my end, he's coming for me. So I stopped just there on the road where I was and waited. Mark approached me. I stepped back and he said, "Don't be afraid, I am not going to hurt you. Come, I'll walk you home." I told Mark it was okay, I'd rather he did not and asked what he wanted.

He said he did not understand – if we wanted to get married again, could we? I seriously did not know how I should answer that question. So I kept silent instead.

As we stood on the road, Mark said, "Give me the papers." I never knew at that moment if he was just going to tear it up and throw it or actually sign them.

Shockingly Mark signed them and said, "I never wanted you to suffer, I love you," as he handed the papers back to me.

I said, "Thank you". He turned around and went back; I waited to see he was gone completely before I started to head back home.

# Going to court

**I filed for divorce on grounds of unreasonable behaviour.**

Still, I was very nervous because Mark was a very complex person to understand in all the time we were together. I can truly say his behaviour was irrational and not stable. At any given time he could just lose control and flare up. It could be any little thing which could set him off for no apparent reason. Throughout I prayed as each stage went on so that it would just go through; having suffered enough all I wanted was to be happy again and I waited eagerly.

**Since we agreed on everything it went through fast. Mark agreed to the grounds of divorce and even said he wanted no contact with the kids at all. Before my birthday in December it all came to an end – that was the best birthday gift I had had in five long years of hell.**

# The gift of freedom

Sincerely, I believe everything in life happens for a reason though we don't know why it happens to us. True I felt victimised, but it's true your life is yours. You alone can mould it and shape it.

You have to know what you're fighting for...

What's important to you?

I knew I never wanted my kids thinking this is the way a marriage is supposed to be: fights, arguments, abuse, fear, ridicule, insults. Seeing their mother work like a slave and their father relaxing like a king.

Fighting for the right to bring my angels up the right way, to set proper examples, and to provide a safe, healthy environment for them.

# Stressful days

Life after the divorce improved a lot; it finally came through on the 2nd of September 2013 and life took a turn finally for the positive. Time after that went on changing rapidly. Inner peace and a sense of happiness filled our home. The kids seemed more relaxed, happier and in general calmer. Finally I had the freedom to cook what we liked, eat what we wanted and do fun stuff together. We made a mess and then I tidied up after the kids. It was a taste of pure freedom at last.

**The days of slavery, bondage and mental and emotional trauma were finally over. We laughed, we giggled and we all jumped into bed and cuddled – it was the start of a new beginning and new life together for us.**

My work timings changed to 10.30am to 4pm, Monday to Friday. I was a single parent and had priority – something I never ever had before. Applying for all the help I could get for us which would help sustain us and get by gave us mother and daughters the opportunity to spend much needed meaningful time together.

The year was full of positives on the family side and us bonding together.

However, the year also went on fixing all the damage done to the house and it put me under tremendous pressure and stress. Having to take care of everything on my own and rectify all the damages was nothing short of a nightmare. Waiting for the benefits to be sorted out now as a single parent also took a while, so financially I was very stressed.

Mark, as usual, was very irrational and so he refused to take all his taxidermy back to his mother's house where he was living once again. He said to bin it. I recalled, that's what baby and I were kept starving for.

No I could not bin it; instead I went on to the internet, looked for people who were interested in taxidermy and then I sent them all the pictures I had. Since I never knew much about it people kept giving me different prices. Finally, luckily, I found a couple who had taxidermy as a business; they came to my little cottage and took it all off my hands.

I was so glad because the money they gave me helped keep us afloat and helped with the nursery cost and holiday club payments.

When a new claim is put into the tax department all existing finances stop coming in until the new claim is sorted out. So my credit cards were a blessing at that time. I never refused a credit card because I never knew when I might have problems and need cash instantly. It's funny but the people who bought Mark's taxidermy off me actually asked if he was alright or a bit weird since they had never seen such a big collection by a private collector at home. What they found more peculiar was that most of the taxidermy was never opened and was still in its packaging.

Jim had left lots of things undone and in a bad way so one by one I had to concentrate on doing it up. **I had to fix the back door which was my first priority.** I decided to call a professional company since

I knew not having the money to pay for it upfront meant it would probably need to be done on finance. The builders who came were surprised to see the back of the house; they said, "It looks like a cowboy builder has been in to do the job." I just kept silent. All my doors and windows were replaced on finance. I had lovely double glazed patio doors put in; this really helped remarkably to reduce the cost of heating and helped keep the kids warm too.

A few months passed and my **boiler stopped working;** there was no hot water. It was a cause of concern for me because to replace boilers are quite expensive and don't come cheap. Especially when you're a single mother trying to do everything yourself and on a tight budget. Thankfully I was able to access the government grants since I had young children. This helped me to qualify for help to get a free boiler. The engineer informed me that we were all very lucky to be alive. Someone had removed a stopper and all the fumes were coming into the house instead of going outside.

Next, I had to call an electrician because of my wiring. I discovered a burning smell every time the TV was switched on. Due to **faulty wiring** it could have caused a fire in the house. The sockets, which were hanging out of the wall, had to be changed and be fitted in properly. This is where Jim had unfortunately also done work for me – instead of wires hanging all around I wanted to have concealed wiring done. Everything he did for me was faulty.

Again, for the very last time, **I decided to give my garden a go; it had already been done thrice by Jim.** Lots of money had been spent but still it was not decent or safe.

**Ann had come to visit me after the divorce; she wanted to voice her concerns to me**. Her foremost worry was that although I was young she didn't want me to get another partner or husband in my life because she could not bear anyone being near the children. I actually thought that was quite ridiculous but decided not to say anything at that moment and hold my tongue. All I wanted was to get my life on track, keep my plans to myself and do what I had to do.

Ann at this point still underestimated me. She said she thought it would be better if yet again a fourth attempt by Jim was carried out to sort the garden once and for all. Otherwise there would be no way I could, on my own, be able to fix the mess out there. So I told Ann I would let her know.

Meanwhile I was fully aware of what had happened, and no amount of sweet talk and manipulation would work on me ever again.

I called another professional company in and they were happy to help me make the garden safe for the kids. They were absolutely brilliant; the garden was beautiful and transformed completely. It was a safe, fun area for the kids to play in.

My happiest moment was when Jane and Jessica went out to play on our lovely new lawn. The kids laughed as they ran up and down together playing catch. The girls had loads of fun watering the garden and trying to spray each other with water.

Special moments, children laughing, having fun; we take these for granted yet not too long ago my Jane and Jessica never had these moments of joy in their life.

**I stood smiling, looking on like a proud mum... until Jane decided to spray me with water as I stepped into the garden. I turned into a child myself joining in the fun with my two little**

girls. The garden, which once lay like a desolate graveyard, now had been transformed into a beautiful play area full of fun.

Their happiness to me meant everything; it was simply priceless.

I can happily say it was all done one by one, every hurdle overcome. It was a long and hard journey. But the end result speaks for itself. The kids being happy were music to my ears and gave me inner peace.

*New front door to replace the broken door.*

# Ann's return

Just after the house was done up, Ann decided to come and visit. She never called but rather just turned up at my doorstep. It kind of felt as if she was checking up on me and trying to see what I was up to. I did not appreciate it because it felt as if my privacy was being invaded – after all she had only ever come once before.

The only surprise visit was after Jessica was born, I remember it was when Mark and I were still together, Ann had come in my absence and Mark had taken one of the new sofas I had bought only the day before and agreed to give it away to his mother for his elder brother. The irony of the situation was it was not purchased by Mark, rather it was mine but I was not asked. All these negotiations went on in my absence without my consent.

However, Ann was surprised when she saw all the changes that I had managed to do without involving them. She turned to me and said that I was living her dream. She always wanted a little two bed cottage and two children and a happy life.

She sat for a while, had a cup of tea but was quite eager to take my daughters to her house. This is something I was totally against, especially considering my ex husband was living there. Also I had just fought for freedom for us all. I never wanted my children to be turned against me in my absence like before. Jim never came; Ann only came on birthdays and Christmas.

Eventually Ann understood I was not going to let the children be taken there. I was going to protect the mental and emotional wellbeing of my kids.

So everything was falling into place and life finally seemed to be on track.

# Mum's passing and my assault

**I thought I had everything under control but just then...**

**I received bad news from my father that my mother, who was terminally ill, had taken bad and that she had been given just 72 hours to live.**

Sadly, she was a strong lady who fought for many years to be with us and she finally passed away on the 7th January 2015. When Dad gave me the news my heart sank. He called me at 1 in the morning. I still remember being fast asleep and suddenly being woken up with a start and seeing Dad was calling me I knew something was very wrong.

I was extremely upset and I sat thinking of Mum and crying. She had gone and I would never again have a chance to talk to her. Mum was supposed to be coming to spend the summer with us; sadly she would never be coming ever again. Every night I used to pray for her and every day without fail I would make it a point to call and enquire as to how she was doing.

It is a strange feeling to know I could no longer reach for the phone and hold a conversation with her. Sadly it was now, when Mark was no longer in our life, I thought that having the family around would be different. It would be quality time spent together but it was too late, she was gone.

My father and sister were extremely upset but Father made all the arrangements in his grief. All the funeral arrangements were done. I could not go into work and remained in a state of total despair. I wondered why my life was so hard. Things kept happening to me one after another – was I never ever going to get a break in life?

How much does one person have to go through, one after the other? Feeling miserable and in a state of complete loss I found it hard to cope. I was grieving for Mum.

Father had asked me what I wanted from my mother's belongings. Some may say I am a sentimental fool – maybe. I did not want any jewellery, I did not want any of her clothes, perfumes, nothing. All I wanted was her old nightgown. There were some really old ones made from very soft cotton which Mum loved to wear. Mother was a simple lady, she loved simple things. That's all I wanted, just so that I could feel close to her and feel her by my side.

The strangest truth is that to this day Father can't understand why I refuse everything else of hers. The reality of the matter is it's too painful. Even today, at the bottom of my drawer, inside a sealed brown envelope lies my mother's old nightgown. Many a time I hold it in my hands when I miss her, many a time I cry but never have I, to date, had the strength to open it and I really don't know if I ever will be able to.

A wise friend brought me back to reality. I needed to stop, I must let go and move on, she said. My children needed me and I could not carry on grieving the way I was.

Going to church every morning and burning candles for Mum to rest in peace became my daily routine before going to work.

**Could I possibly have anything more go wrong in my life or done to me, to cause me any more grief and sorrow?**

The answer was yes. I was so upset walking down to work, after stopping to light candles in church for my mum to rest in peace. I felt great sadness and emptiness and after coming out of church I decided to call my sister whom I knew only too well was grieving too.

**While we were taking comfort in talking to each other all of a sudden I heard someone shouting, "You, I want to talk to you, you bitch." It was my ex husband's sister, Catherine.**

**As I recall, back on the 19th November 2014, I** had someone come knocking on my door and banging away very loudly as if they wanted to break my door down. Since I was talking to my mother on the phone, and had no eye spy I decided not to entertain whoever it was who was so rudely trying to get my attention. After 15 minutes I got a note saying 'call me please'; it had Catherine's number and name on it. You can imagine what thoughts ran through my mind. I was very wary about this whole situation.

Firstly, she did not have the best attitude, so being wary of the situation and the fact that there hadn't been any contact for a number of years I thought it's better to text rather than call. So this is what I did next. I sent a message stating that I don't open the door to anyone if I'm not expecting them. My number's still the same and I asked what she wanted.

In return I got a message saying she just wanted to have a chat with me, if that was ok. So I replied no need as all is well. I received no more messages and heard nothing more from her.

**That is until the 12th February 2015 when I was rudely called out to.** Well her behaviour resembled that of a mad woman, abusing and shouting, using language, saying how dare I not reply to her when clearly I did and gave her an open chance to text and get everything off her chest, whatever was upsetting her.

Not wanting to entertain her and in reaction to such absurdness I told her that I was busy and that I wouldn't entertain her when she was mouthing off and disrespecting me.

To this Catherine got angrier, agitated and outraged; she put her fist to my face and wanted to knock me out. She said she wanted to fist me and have me on the floor, flat on my back. When I tried to move off and away, she put both hands on my coat and pushed me onto the railings of a first floor shopping centre and wanted to throw me off.

I was completely clueless as to why Catherine was attacking me; all she did was keep coming at me aggressively. When I tried to get away it made her become more wild, somehow she just expected me to stand there and keep taking her abuse. I was only too familiar with this kind of behaviour. Where all of a sudden these people can turn and come at you for no apparent reason.

I tried to ask her what this was all about.

Well in the midst of all this she said her father had been diagnosed with cancer and she thought that I might want to bring the kids around to see him before he died. The approach was most uncivil.

To that I told her that my mum had just passed but I did not behave like her. I don't go around attacking people like a mad person and that she should spend quality time with her father while he was still around.

**Then she started calling me a money grabbing bitch and told me not to bother coming to her parents' house or ever asking for help.**

This was again absurd; the only help I had ever asked Ann for was in relation to Mark's behaviour. To ask for help to sort out my marriage. Since I felt being the mother she might have some influence over her children, which I knew Ann definitely had. In relation to money grabbing, well there was no money to grab. I worked two jobs and gave all that I had. It was my family who had provided the deposit for the house.

Also Catherine stooped lower in my opinion and fell even further in my eyes, when she brought up that she had helped when I was first married and gave baby equipment, a cot bed, and tried to help. She also made it a point to say that I did nothing for her in return.

Catherine had a good job and was earning more than I earned with both my jobs combined. I did as much as I could yet for all that my replies only fuelled her more. I did for her entire family more than what any of the others could have ever done.

I kept giving back for five long years not just one day. There was no getting away from Catherine, though, she refused to let go.

She was extremely shallow; unfortunately she still viewed me as the terrified, teary eyed young girl who once stood near the mantelpiece in her mother's home, begging for help and insight as to what was happening in her marriage.

Catherine could not see past that, and I sincerely believe, thinking that I was helpless, alone and still a victim of fate, she could attack me yet again. I always knew from the start that Catherine had a dislike for me and if I am being honest even some unknown jealousy.

People unfortunately can have everything and yet feel jealous and envious towards someone else for an insignificant reason.

A crowd gathered around looking. I stood calmly although inside I was very upset.

Well it ended with me informing Catherine that I was going to call the police on her and that I had had enough.

**Enough of being victimised for nothing. Catherine shouted back, "You do that, you do that. But don't you dare fucking send the police to my mum's house. I'll be in after four, send them to mine, you fucking bitch."**

I went into work and told my boss what had happened. I informed the police and logged a complaint. The police asked me what I wanted to do next. Since I was upset, grieving for Mum, I could not think properly. I asked them to go to Catherine's mother's house, call Catherine out of work and give her a severe warning. This time I was not pressing charges just because I had lost my mother and I respected that the father was ill. It was out of respect for the parents alone that I did not press charges and get her arrested.

**Well the police gave her a warning so that was the end of that, hopefully, I thought.** The police informed me that she had said it was just on the spur of the moment and that it would never happen again. She was very sorry. She was also told to have no contact with me and if anyone wanted to contact me it should only be the grandmother, no one else.

I do not agree that it was on the spur of the moment. I think it was a build up over the years of watching me, that led to this outburst of pent up jealously and envy.

Catherine, along with the rest of them, saw that from nothing and through struggles inflicted by them upon me, I still fought through everything, managing to hold onto my kids, my house and my job and walk away from them.

**They saw a slave rise to have a home and start to reach for the skies.**

# Life goes on

Jane started school and was very happy. She had a lot of friends; the teachers were friendly and understanding.

But soon Father's Day came around. Yes, the day on which most children who don't have dads make things for their mums instead. Somehow with everything going on I just never paid any attention to it. When I went to pick Jane up from school, while she stood in line I saw a few children around her. They held things in their hands which had Happy Fathers' Day written on it. It was different from Jane's.

**I don't really know what the kids were talking about but when I got close to Jane she said, "I don't have a daddy, Mummy."**

**Her little friends stood smiling and Jane just looked at me. We both knew there was no Daddy around, it was just Mummy. But I knew my Jane was always happy, never caring about a daddy but today when I saw her with her little friends, I knew something had been said by looking into her eyes.**

Sadly, sometimes little children can be quite cruel and unmindful though it is unintentional. I never wanted anything upsetting my Jane.

Looking down and smiling at Jane, I told Jane we don't have another daddy because Mummy is Mummy and Daddy. All the children looked at me; a little boy gave me the sweetest, strangest of looks and asked me, "You are Mummy and Daddy too?"

**I replied, "Yes I am Mummy and Daddy." Jane's teachers standing close by looked at me and smiled. Jane hugged me and said, "Here, Daddy, I made this for you." Giving Jane a kiss, I said, "Thank you, baby."**

**Ever since then my girls refer to me as Mummy and Daddy and I am extremely proud to be both and I would have it no other way.**

Jessica was in nursery. Both the kids were doing exceptionally well, while I was very careful budgeting and keeping a strict eye on my expenses to provide more for my kids with limited resources.

Shopping around for the best deals and trying to keep a check on every expense. Shopping in places and using delivery services to do bulk shopping from Tesco, Everyday Value, and Sainsbury Basic range and Iceland gave me good value for money. Poundland and 99p Store were excellent sources of entertainment for the kids. Primark was the best for clothes shopping as it was the most affordable.

Sticking to my routine helped me cope and put a little bit aside for the future and emergencies. I did not want to rely on my father anymore – the man had cleared several debts of mine which I had got into as a result of being with Mark and had helped me already in the past on several occasions.

Jane and Jessica both go to dance classes. Jane being the oldest has been doing a lot of other activities too like swimming and going for maths classes along with several fun clubs after school. Jessica will do the same when she comes of age too.

Neither of them would have gone for all these classes if I was still with Mark, the girls would have had nothing. Since Jane had witnessed a lot more arguments, fights and Mark coming at me, I had to work a lot more with her to build up her confidence. The poor child was very shy, backward, nervous and timid. She was nervous and afraid but putting her into dance and drama classes really helped her develop, build her confidence, throw her voice and step out of her shell.

It helped Jane find herself especially since she naturally loved to sing and act. The first show my baby did was to the song 'Let it go' from Frozen. She was amazing. While all the parents were clapping and stood in pairs, husbands and wives, I stood alone carrying Jessica, but the pride I felt inside cannot be described – that's my little girl centre stage.

**Later Jane ran to me full of excitement. I kissed her, gave her a little hug and said "Mummy loves you" with tears of joy and pride; it was a very emotional moment.**

As life went on I had decided to keep writing about everything that had happened during the five years of marriage. I had several reasons for doing this. Self help and inner healing was one, trying to let go of the past and have closure. The next reason that came to mind was that one day my children might want to know what actually happened and this would be a good way to give them an insight into what I went through. Also I hoped that in their life they never ever had to face anything like I had gone through.

It was hard to write all this down; many a time I wanted to just stop and not carry on but what can I say, I knew it had to be done.

Mum, before she passed, had told me "write it all down but don't go publishing anything. Don't have people laughing at you and don't go making things worse for yourself in any way".

So I decided to write but never actually got round to finishing because different negative situations kept on reoccurring. After Mum's passing I just stopped; too much had happened.

Wanting to forget all the negatives of the past I decided maybe it's time just to stop...

**But my inspiration to finish it was reignited, once again, when my attacker decided to come at me again.**

# After Mum's passing

I asked Dad and my sister to come over just so that we could spend some quality time together. It was sad when they did finally come over to visit as there was a strong sense of emptiness surrounding us all. Going to pick them up from the airport was always a happy time. But this was the first year we were all very emotional. **This year there was no Mum.**

**The journey to my house was a long and quiet one mainly because we were all teary. Dad remarked how strange it felt; usually coming to visit me was a joyful occasion but today he felt so lost, alone and sad.**

How cruel life can be. Mum longed to go to Lourdes in France. She very much wanted to go but was waiting until she was well enough to travel. Sadly, she never got the chance. She wanted to spend the summer with us in 2015 but that too never happened.

My parents had completed forty years of marriage on the 4th January 2015. Dad showed me all the snaps of the burial and I felt miserable. How do you console a man who has lost his wife after all these years?

I tried to be patient; I tried to help him though my very own heart was broken inside. Being a good daughter meant that now it was my turn to be there for Dad when he needed me.

I think we needed to spend that time together just so that we could use that time to heal and help each other.

The days passed and Dad started to become more understanding of the fact that my life had changed. I was determined to work and do things on my own. He offered to look after the children for me, if I wanted to go and do some extra shifts at work. That was fantastic – childcare was quite expensive so I was more than happy to get free, reliable help.

I had always wanted a front garden with a brick boundary put up with a little black iron gate. Doing extra shifts finally meant I had enough money to have that done for myself. It gave the little cottage a nice, private feel to it.

The days passed quickly and it was soon time for Dad to return to his work and life. Six months had passed quite fast. He was sad to go but was happy for us to have spent time together. Since he was always busy with work, we hardly got to spend much quality time together. We all saw him off at the airport and life returned to the same routine, work and home, until one day led to a very new chapter in my life.

# Justice prevailing

Getting up in the morning and feeling rather sick I decided to call my GP and ask for an appointment. After visiting the GP, on my way back home I had an unpleasant incident of seeing Catherine in her car at the signal waiting to move on.

**As I passed by she put her window down and shouted out at me, "You fucking bitch!" The incident took place on the 14th January 2016, yes this year itself.**

**Not paying any attention to her directly and not wanting to have any arguments on the street, I nevertheless decided I needed to do something about this. This incident happened on the street in public during the middle of the day.**

After this incident I now realised that although such a long time had passed since Catherine had been close enough to me, she still held extreme resentment towards me. She would use even the slightest of opportunity to attack me in any manner of form whether it be physical, verbal, emotional or mental, she would definitely try.

What I really can't understand is how ridiculous the entire situation was. Mark had other women in his life, other children somewhere out there before mine. Yet this woman kept coming at me year after year as if I was married to her instead of her brother. Every year there was an incident forming into a recurring pattern. I longed to move, but being a single parent with house prices rising it was certainly not easy at all to shift. Catherine was now taking advantage of the fact that I was alone and she knew where I lived. The family never bothered and all stayed away apart from Catherine who seemed to be obsessed with me.

It was time to make a stand. No more letting things pass. The marriage broke down because of unreasonable, irrational behaviour, it was long gone. Ended. Yet Catherine persisted in making my life a living hell. I forgave her once and showed mercy but today again she had targeted me. Reasoning with myself as to what should be my course of action I wondered what if we had both been on foot – would history repeat itself? If I didn't put in place any precautionary safety measures would things get worse?

Who knows the mind of an unstable individual, who is driven by sudden impulse? With this in mind and past occurrences, I decided to call the police and reported the incident once again.

The lady officer was very caring and considerate; she advised me that if I was feeling unsafe I could potentially go to court to see if any sort of order could be put in place. She even drove me to court.

Going into court, I was informed that from the family court I could fill out a form and see a judge before 2pm that very same day. That was fantastic since all I wanted was to get this situation resolved once and for all. However, after filling out the form when I returned to see a judge the clerks informed me that it had to go through the civil court and not the family court.

Since I was working the only day of return would be after one week. So I returned and met a judge, who said that no decision could be taken without the other party being present. Respectfully I left and was told that I needed to give notice to the other party so that she could also attend.

On my way home, after going over the situation in my head, I decided it was better not to go on my own but to take along someone with some sort of legal status. All the barristers were quite expensive but after going into great length and continuous searching. I found one barrister who was affordable. The firm took my case on. Stewart agreed to represent me and the first date of the court hearing was set for the 5th February 2016. Unfortunately due to error and miscommunication, Catherine was not present nor did she have any knowledge of what was going on. There was miscommunication between me and the clerks – I thought they were going to inform Catherine but in fact I was supposed to do it.

So we both genuinely apologised to the judge for wasting her time and rescheduled for the 15th of February 2016 which was good for both the Judge and Stewart.

When we next returned to court, I saw Catherine sitting in the waiting room and she was staring at me. I tried to pay no attention to her since I was waiting eagerly for Stewart to come and was stressed as he was running late. No way did I wish to enter and sit in front of the judge without him.

Luckily he arrived just in time and we were able to have a quick run through of the events.

The judge was very fair in her proceedings and heard both sides. She asked Catherine first if she wanted representation and if she was aware of the reason for being summoned. To which Catherine acknowledged that she was aware of the reason and did not think she required representation. So the judge continued...

The judge wanted to know all about the attacks. Catherine stated that previously she had attacked me, and that she was sorry, it was a one off and on the spur of the moment. She also admitted that she told the police she would do nothing ever again.

The judge asked if she had abused me recently on the road. First Catherine did not agree then later she did.

**The judge told Catherine in a calm voice, "So after you promised to stay away from Andrea you still abused her on the streets."**

**The reason for doing that was she felt I was a nasty piece of work and because she did not like me, as she admitted.**

She further went on to tell the judge that I don't call the grandparents over and I could, for a cup of tea, so that they could see the children. The judge said I was under no obligation to do so and if the grandparents really wanted they could go to court.

To which Catherine said they won't do that and that because we live close by it was ridiculous to go to court.

Stewart, the barrister, told the judge that I had never stopped the grandparents from coming around but there were many underlying factors however.

The learned judge, after hearing everything, calmly said that in light of the facts she could handle the matter with two different approaches.

One would be where Catherine would willingly have to undertake an oath to the judge promising to behave and not make any contact with me, physical, verbal etc. Not to come near my house or near me. And not try to interfere with me directly or through anyone else.

The next course of action the judge could take was to force an injunction upon Catherine; the choice was entirely hers.

**The judge said she did not feel comfortable leaving the situation as it was without putting anything in place.**

**Catherine said she understood and that she would comply and be respectful and sign whatever the judge wanted her to sign.**

The judge asked Stewart to draw up an undertaking for Catherine to sign it, which we were to bring back to the judge when she called us back in.

While we sat at the table outside the judge's room Stewart tried to introduce himself and be civil to Catherine but once again she was being really nasty and rude. While I tried to speak to Stewart, Catherine was trying to direct a remark towards me. So after we were done drawing up the agreement Stewart said, "Come, let's move to another table."

He was surprised at the intensity of hatred which he could feel Catherine had towards me. He said he could feel it from her, the dislike and it was really strange behaviour.

The judge called us in after a while and Catherine read and signed it all. If Catherine does try to come for me before a year is up, not only will she be arrested but can be fined heavily and her assets taken.

**We thanked the judge and left.**

I thanked Stewart from the bottom of my heart for this protection being put in place for a year; sadly there is no way to have it in place permanently.

**Well, thanks to God, Stewart and the Judge, justice prevailed.**

# Collective abuse

Like every other woman, I too wanted a fairytale wedding with a happy ending but instead I got something entirely different.

My experience of mental and physical abuse, trauma and violence started with Mark as an individual and from there it turned into collective abuse. Each one wanting and trying to see how they could take advantage of an innocent, gullible and naive young lady.

Being around that family was literally suffocating and I felt my very life was being stripped away from me. It was like being caught in a web of deception and manipulation. **From taking everything I had, to wanting to turn my very own children against me and brainwashing them that I was not their mother. This was the height of cruelty.**

Somehow it gave them contentment and happiness seeing me struggle and go through hardship. The best way I can describe the relationship was like they were wanting to punish me for something I had done wrong yet the reason was never mentioned.

I was meant to be there, not as an equal part of the family but as someone much lower and not worthy to be part of them. There were a lot of false airs and graces which I never quite understood at that time.

I was made to suffer for wanting to rise above the status that they so desperately wanted me to maintain.

I know the family had their own issues of domestic violence and abuse and that's the reason, I feel, in some way, for inflicting the harshest standard of life and misery upon me, to act as unification between them. It gave them common ground and a bond of unity.

**Collective abuse is terrible – you really don't know who to trust**. On faith, I took my in-laws to be just like my parents, loving them and doing everything I could without expecting anything from them except respect, understanding and love.

**It's quite sad really, what provokes another human being to treat someone else so badly. How can they have sleep soundly at night – do their consciences not prick them?**

Several questions come to mind in trying to understand their psychological disposition. Their behavioural pattern has certain common trends. There is a build up and the best description of their nature is calm yet very unstable and volatile.

**It took me five long years of this entire nightmare to understand that they themselves were not in a comfortable place within themselves...**

None of them have true inner peace and joy in their hearts.

In fact I remember Mark saying I was too good and although he wanted to be like me he would never be. He also admitted that he was jealous of me for being better than him in every way and he knew that but just did not want to admit it earlier. He also said he found it hard to live like that.

Ann had mentioned she envied my life; I had my own house, my kids and a job. I had managed to keep it all together. That would have been her perfect life.

Catherine, apart from once admitting that I was lucky to have kids and a husband, never said anything else. Catherine was a single parent and suffered from excessive rage; she liked to cause fights and arguments. Yet for all that it has been only Catherine who until today, persists to keep coming year after year to harass me and be a cause of grief.

Jim always had an attitude to say he cared for no one. I actually thought he was alright until I could not comprehend how a grandfather could let his grandchildren live in an unsafe environment caused by him. Most of the damages were health hazards and detrimental as I discovered a year later.

I feel that because of low self esteem, arrogance, envy and pride my abusers abused me. With the view to giving themselves mental satisfaction. Somehow their very own past was triggered when they saw me break down mentally and go into a state of loss, panic and desperation.

Because their past could in no way be altered, they decided to turn into exactly the same thing which they saw, knew and feared.

**They turned into the abuser and abused me, the victim, so that they could feel empowered.**

# Domestic violence and mental abuse

Domestic violence and mental abuse has its birthplace at home, behind closed doors where many a truth lies silenced.

Unfortunately, just like with Mark, it's more about being in control, dominating and terrorising. Mark had a fear that no one would be there to look after him but nevertheless preferred to be alone, fearful of losing and not being able to handle affection or being true to longstanding commitment. Mark grew up not knowing or recognising what it meant to be a father.

When a child is subjected to abuse from birth that's what it recognises. Children learn from what they see; the mind is a very powerful tool. It records everything and later enacts it all in time.

Mark was of the opinion that his strength and the fact that he was twenty stone gave him power.

He thrived on others staring at him in the gym. Maybe that's what made him feel safe. Yet on the other side, he thrived on belittling me. He unconsciously was trying to re-enact that which he had seen happening so many times through growing up at home. It was only fair that he do the same. That's what he recognised, understood and followed; the examples which were set before his very own eyes in childhood.

**The past does determine the future. With this in mind I never wanted my life with Mark to determine Jane and Jessica's future.**

As a mother I had to make sure no harm came to either of them from within the family circle and external forces too. So many times we mothers do wrong by not making the right decision. Taking a stand is often hard; it is never easy but it's the first step which matters. Allowing the suffering to continue is the biggest wrong that someone can allow to happen. The vicious circle of abuse has to be broken otherwise it will be passed down from one generation to another forming somewhat like a tradition.

We cannot make excuses for the abuser and say he is sorry. He cannot say he had a bad past or childhood. Nor can we say it will get better. It never does. Ignoring the reality of what life actually is like or recognising it to be what it should not only stems from denial of not wanting to do what is right.

How many chances do you give an abuser before you lose your very own self or worse?

How many years of being tormented, threatened, bullied before the threats become reality and death ends it all?

I was lucky: before I got hammered or killed, I got out. I made my stand and had Mark arrested. Why did my poor Jane have to be subjected to all the misery? She was an innocent child. Yet it was my very own fear of Mark and what he might do to me, which held me back, entrapped. My mind was weakened yet the love for my two girls, a better life for them, gave me the inner strength to break away from all abuse.

I needed to be stronger and wiser, better, confident and turn my very own way of thinking around. Building up my inner strength and changing the way I viewed my life.

Did I want to be a weak slave tormented and battered or did I want to rise and be a symbol of strength for my little ones to follow and be proud of and to lead them, to aspire to reach for the stars one day?

I recalled one day I had returned from work nearing midnight, and Mark was sat looking at his eBay as usual, relaxing, not speaking a word. His clothes flung on the floor. Wrappers of crisps and chocolates lay scattered...

It angered me to see him sitting while I withered away. I asked why he didn't at least put things in the bin. Mark replied, "That's what you're here for."

I don't have a slave and do things myself.

Just then I noticed a black piece of toast on a plate with butter. It looked more like coal to me. I asked Mark, "Who is that for?" He said he had made it for Jane but then she never wanted it once he gave it to her.

I got very cross. Every morning I had food prepared. Mark hadn't a clue; he never bothered about anything, he never opened his eyes to see what was there. Of course my Jane would not eat that – how could she?

I asked Mark, "Would you eat that? I will make that for you next time." Mark's laughter stopped when in anger I passed my comments. He said I needed to be careful and to watch it; I was stepping out of my place.

On going into Jane's bedroom as I kissed her forehead while I was about to leave, I felt something hold on to my dress. Jane in her little voice whispered to me, "Mummy, hungry." My heart sank; my baby was hungry. She said it so quietly I knew she did not want Mark to hear. I asked Jane to come down with me and I would give her food. Jane would not come; she said, "Daddy said if I don't eat what he gave me then I need to sleep. I won't get anything."

My poor child, that's something I never wanted. Never ever for my baby to go hungry.

I looked at Jane and went and heated up some food, took it up to her and fed her in bed. Mark never cared; he sat looking at his eBay still while I cleaned the house. Inside I knew this would be the last time my little girl went without.

I was going to get out; it was only a matter of time. Every incident that happened in relation to my kids, no matter how insignificant, added fuel to my burning desire to leave. I just needed to break away.

Looking down into my sweet angels' faces and having them looking innocently back up at me, led me to realise no matter what happens in life, I cannot back down. I have to fight and I can't give up. Should I fail, my kids stand no chance of succeeding. Their happiness depends upon mine alone.

Seeing them gives me the drive and determination to face new challenges each and every day.

# The fairytale

There have been many trials and tribulations but the future looks bright and beautiful.

Today my kids are happy, safe; they play together and love each other. Our tiny house resounds with laughter and we have peace. I am a proud mum and feel blessed to have overcome my own trials in life. Though as long as there is life there will be problems but I am sure every challenge I will face head on.

My clever children are close to each other and have been raised by me to have manners and dreams. This year my little girl starts school. They are growing fast. For now we do everything together, I still play the role of mummy and daddy. That has not changed.

My goal is to let our story come out so that no one else needs to live in fear and isolation. Speaking out, standing up for what we believe and making a positive change is very important for moulding the minds of future generations. If we all stand together, united, great things can be accomplished. The first step in my opinion is to want to change, is to want a better life.

The next is to step out and ask for help.

Later know what you're fighting for. No one should have to live in fear during a marriage or after coming out of it or in a relationship.

Jane wants to be an actress and Jessica she is still too young. Both of them now have the freedom to live freely and are free to choose the life they desire.

There's a big beautiful white church which stands in the distance. A white horse drawn carriage pulled by four white horses. I can hear in the distance the organ playing. The voices of people merrymaking carry over far into the wilderness.

The church is decorated with colourful bunches of flowers around the majestic pillars. Inside the church is laid with red carpet. Every aisle has red ribbon bows at the ends. The church is filled with hundreds of guests and I can see everyone looking so happy.

My girls are dressed in little red dresses holding flower baskets filled with petals. Their faces are radiant and beaming with joy.

It's time and everyone takes their places, my dress has so many different layers. It's my dream wedding that I have always wanted. One day my dream will become a reality, as long as there is positive energy, hope, love and freedom.

I do believe in fairytales and one day my children will have a father again and me my soul mate but until then my responsibility is to hold the fort up.

To all the many woman out there I write for us all. Follow me: stepping out and speaking up is the best freedom of all. Do not be embarrassed, ashamed or feel guilty by what you go through. Silence must be broken. It does not matter who is on your side. It does not matter who helps you. All that matters is what you do. There is help out there. Of course I never knew about it. Sadly misguided by my own parents I did previously go back to Mark. Yet I would say standing up for what you believe in is what is important. My life is blessed today, I am not rich monetarily but I'm very rich mentally. There is no price you can put on the freedom of your children or yourself. I refuse to be quiet any longer.

I continue to work hard to this day to support my kids and do whatever is necessary. Yet I do still have Catherine who out of jealously keeps attacking me as she did admit to the judge that she just does not like me and thinks I am nasty. Personally I think because I continue to do things to better my life that is what stirs up more envy and hatred.

All women must be treated with respect and dignity. No woman must be made to suffer like I did or even worse due to any relationship. We are all equal and deserve to live with respect and freedom from slavery and exploitation.

My belief is that truth and justice shall prevail and set you free. May my own true life story with full disclosure give you the strength to know that you too can break the circle of abuse – all you have to do is reach out. xxxx

Written by

*Andrea Aviet*

Contact:

*www.whitesorrow.com*
*www.facebook.com/whitesorrow1*

Printed in Great Britain
by Amazon

19405748R00139

# An Introduction to Statistical Analysis for Business and Industry

## A Problem Solving Approach

**Michael Stuart**

*Department of Statistics, Trinity College Dublin, Ireland*

A member of the Hodder Headline Group
LONDON
Distributed in the United States of America by
Oxford University Press Inc., New York

First published in Great Britain in 2003 by
Hodder Arnold, a member of the Hodder Headline Group,
338 Euston Road, London NW1 3BH

**http://www.arnoldpublishers.com**

Distributed in the United States of America by
Oxford University Press Inc.
198 Madison Avenue, New York, NY 10016

*British Library Cataloguing in Publication Data*
A catalogue record for this book is available from the British Library

*Library of Congress Cataloging-in-Publication Data*
A catalog record for this book is available from the Library of Congress

ISBN 0 340 80844 6

1 2 3 4 5 6 7 8 9 10

Typeset in 10 on 12 Times by Phoenix Photosetting, Chatham, Kent
Printed and bound in Malta

What do you think about this book? Or any other Arnold title?
Please send your comments to feedback.arnold@hodder.co.uk

# Contents

Preface                    ix
Acknowledgements         xii
Website                    xiii

| 1 | **Introduction** | **1** |
|---|---|---|
| | Learning objectives | 2 |
| 1.1 | Sales and shortages in a sports and social club | 2 |
| 1.2 | Statistical variation in the Stock Exchange | 10 |
| 1.3 | Variation in manufacturing: charts, graphs and stratification as aids to understanding | 15 |
| 1.4 | Chance and assignable causes of variation, the Normal model for chance variation and frequency distributions | 19 |
| 1.5 | Modelling assignable causes; relations between variables | 23 |
| 1.6 | Introducing the multiple regression model for forecasting postage stamp sales; a case study in problem formulation | 32 |
| 1.7 | A strategic forecasting problem | 45 |
| 1.8 | Researching youth technology markets; sample surveys | 50 |
| 1.9 | Statistical assessment of a process change; design issues in experimentation | 54 |
| | Appendix | 58 |

| 2 | **Data display and summary** | **60** |
|---|---|---|
| | Learning objectives | 61 |
| 2.1 | Graphical display of measured data | 61 |
| 2.2 | Numerical summaries of measured data | 72 |
| 2.3 | How to read a table | 74 |
| 2.4 | How to make a table | 77 |
| 2.5 | Graphical display of summary data | 85 |
| 2.6 | Review exercises | 92 |

**3    The Normal model for chance variation**                                    **95**
Learning objectives                                                                 96
3.1    Calculating non-conformance rates                                         96
3.2    Using the Normal model; the standard Normal distribution              100
3.3    Normal model calculations using Excel                                   103
3.4    'What-if' analysis                                                      105
3.5    Models and data; parameters and statistics                             107
3.6    Checking the Normal model; the Normal diagnostic plot                  109
3.7    Review exercises                                                        114
3.8    Laboratory exercise: 'What-if' analysis for non-conformance rates     116

**4    Process monitoring, control charts and statistical inference**         **117**
Learning objectives                                                          118
4.1    Process monitoring using control charts                               118
4.2    Mean and range charts                                                 127
4.3    The statistical basis for X-bar charts; the sampling distribution
       of the mean                                                           131
4.4    Assessing process capability; statistical estimation                 141
4.5    Monitoring counts                                                     148
4.6    Review exercises                                                      152
4.7    Laboratory exercise: Estimating $\sigma$ from data with possible
       exceptional cases                                                     157

**5    Principles of statistical inference**                                 **159**
Learning objectives                                                          159
5.1    Statistical significance testing                                      160
5.2    False alarm rates and significance levels                             167
5.3    Detection rates and power                                             170
5.4    Confidence intervals                                                  175
5.5    Review exercises                                                      186
5.6    Laboratory exercise: Simulating sampling distributions,
       significance tests and confidence intervals                          188

**6    Simple linear regression**                                            **190**
Learning objectives                                                          190
6.1    The simple linear regression model                                    191
6.2    The regression control chart                                          199
6.3    Reporting the results of simple linear regression                     204
6.4    Correlation                                                           207
6.5    Pitfalls with regression and correlation                              212
6.6    Review exercises                                                      213
6.7    Laboratory exercise: Exploring and explaining computer
       maintenance costs                                                     219

**7    Frequency data analysis**                                             **221**
Learning objectives                                                          227

7.1   A market penetration study                                       224
7.2   Statistical inference for frequency data                         227
7.3   The chi-square test                                              231
7.4   Multiply classified frequency data                              238
7.5   Review exercises                                                 242
7.6   Laboratory exercise: Frequency data analysis                    247

**8   Multiple linear regression                                       248**
Learning objectives                                                    248
8.1   A prediction problem                                             249
8.2   The multiple linear regression model                            253
8.3   Regression diagnostics                                           260
8.4   Iterating the analysis                                           264
8.5   Alternative measures of goodness of fit                          268
8.6   Outlining the model fitting and testing procedure               269
8.7   Another application: the stamp sales case study                 270
8.8   General issues                                                   285
8.9   Review exercises                                                 288
8.10  Laboratory exercise: Prediction of meter sales                  296

**9   Time series                                                      297**
Learning objectives                                                    297
9.1   A sales forecasting problem                                      298
9.2   Modelling trend and seasonality                                  300
9.3   Smoothing for exploratory analysis                               307
9.4   Forecasting with smoothers; the Holt–Winters method             312
9.5   Advanced time series analysis                                    320
9.6   Review exercises                                                 323
9.7   Laboratory exercise: Housing completions                        324

**10  Simple statistical models in finance                            326**
Learning objectives                                                    326
10.1  The random walk model for variation in the Stock Exchange       327
10.2  Risk and return                                                  333
10.3  The capital asset pricing model                                 335
10.4  Evaluating $\beta$                                              337
10.5  Testing the CAPM                                                339
10.6  Laboratory exercise: Statistical analysis of a portfolio of stocks  340

**11  Data production; surveys, experiments, archives                 342**
Learning objectives                                                    342
11.1  Sample surveys                                                   343
11.2  The survey process                                              346
11.3  Errors in surveys                                                346
11.4  Observational studies and experimentation                       356
11.5  Multi-factor experiments                                         359

11.6  Implementing experiments                                      364
11.7  Archive data                                                  366

**12  Statistical analysis in context**                             **368**
Learning objectives                                                 368
12.1  The management context                                        369
12.2  The role of mathematics                                       373
12.3  The role of computing                                         374
12.4  Extensions and developments                                   375
12.5  Conclusion                                                    377

**Appendix A    Areas under the standard Normal curve**             **378**

**Appendix B    Selected critical values of the chi-square distribution**    **379**

**Index**                                                           **381**

# Preface

Statistics is the science of variation. Statistical analysis is concerned with gaining an understanding of variation and what causes it, with a view to exploiting it when we can and containing it when we have to. Statistical analysis for business and industry is concerned with problem solving and assisting decision making. This is achieved through the definition, production, analysis and interpretation of data in context. A key to this achievement is what has come to be called statistical thinking. Statistical thinking involves a focus on processes, the recognition that all processes are subject to variation and that identifying, characterising, quantifying and reducing process variation are keys to business success. Within this broader focus, the contribution unique to the statistical analyst lies in characterising and quantifying variation and in specifying data sources and designs for data production which will provide the most suitable information for these purposes. At a technical level, this involves the use of models which reflect structure and relationships in variation as well as models for unstructured variation, which may be ascribed to chance.

Statistical analysis has become an essential tool in problem solving and process improvement. The statistical approach to problem solving involves:

- identifying the information requirements for solving the problem;
- arranging the necessary data acquisition;
- analysing the data to determine the key patterns and relationships;
- quantifying the uncertainty involved;
- reporting the results in readily interpretable form;
- advising on interpretation and on solution implementation.

The intention in this book is to assist students to begin to develop the skills used by the statistical analyst at all stages of the decision making/problem solving process. To this end, the statistical ideas, concepts and methods are introduced through a series of case studies and examples drawn from such areas as manufacturing, market research, accountancy, finance, forecasting and quality improvement. There is a series of short problems integrated into the text, intended to be completed as the student works through the text. There are also case study, workshop and computer laboratory exercises which complement the text and review exercises at the end of each chapter designed to test progress. Ideally, students will work together on all but the review exercises. This will assist students in the learning process. It will also develop their understanding of teamwork which is so important in business problem solving.

The conceptual focus of the book is on statistical variation in business and industrial processes. The treatment is largely non-mathematical; in particular, formal probability theory does not feature. The fundamental notion of repeated sampling which underlies classical statistical inference is developed naturally in a process setting. The classical approach to statistical inference involving statistical significance testing and statistical estimation is developed from statistical process control and process capability assessment.

Data analysis in the broad sense is covered, with an emphasis on modern tabular and graphical methods of presentation and analysis, as well as on the more formal traditional approaches. In this respect, the book reflects modern developments in the practice of statistical methods, emphasising simple and direct methods of data analysis, interpretation and display.

## Outline

The book opens with a series of case studies which introduce the reader to all the key issues and methods dealt with later in the book. Chapter 2 covers data summary and display, the latter based on sets of guidelines whose use is explained and illustrated. Chapter 3 covers the Normal frequency distribution, a basic model for statistical variation. Chapter 4 begins the study of statistical inference, using process monitoring, control charts and process capability analysis as bases on which to develop the key ideas. These are more fully developed in Chapter 5 and then applied in a series of chapters devoted to different kinds of applications including simple and multiple linear regression, frequency data analysis, time series and forecasting and a short chapter on simple models in finance. Chapter 11 reviews issues related to the production of data. Chapter 12 concludes by placing statistical thinking and analysis in context.

## Laboratories

An essential feature of the book is the use of a statistical software package in laboratory exercises. Most chapters end with a laboratory exercise which requires extensive use of statistical software. To facilitate and encourage the use of these exercises, detailed instructions on proceeding through the exercise are available on the website associated with the book. Also available to instructors is a series of feedback documents on the exercises. The address is www.tcd.ie/Statistics/Stuart/StatisticalAnalysis.

There are a number of suitable software packages available. The material in the text and in the exercises was developed with the package Data Desk in mind. Data Desk is user friendly, graphics oriented and interactive. However, other packages such as Minitab may be used. The laboratory exercise instructions on the website have been implemented in versions suitable for Data Desk, Minitab and an add-on for Microsoft Excel derived from Data Desk called DDXL. Other versions will be added as soon as they become available.

**Teaching aims**

The teaching aims in preparing this book were to develop in students an appreciation of and ability for statistical thinking about business and industrial processes and an ability to apply statistical thinking in the solution of business and industrial problems. This means that students should be able to

- recognise statistical variation in processes;
- apply a statistical problem solving strategy for process improvement;
- select and apply appropriate statistical analysis methods

in addressing problems arising in business and industry.

**Learning objectives**

Students who have completed a course based on this book should be able to

- appreciate the application of statistical analysis to solving problems in a range of substantive areas, through case studies, illustrations and exercises;
- understand the sources and nature of statistical variation as it arises in business and industry;
- understand the purposes of data summary and display, the importance of guidelines for good data display, the definition/construction of basic graphs and numerical summaries and the use of the Normal model for modelling chance variation;
- construct and use control charts for process monitoring and process capability assessment based on process observation and process sampling;
- explain the nature and purpose of statistical inference and the key statistical concepts underlying statistical inference;
- arrange frequency data in informative displays and apply statistical inference to frequency data;
- calculate simple and multiple linear regressions and correlations, select and interpret relevant graphical and tabular summaries and diagnostics and apply statistical inference to regression results;
- recognise types of variation in time series, select and use some simple methods for time series analysis with a view to forecasting, and recognise some problems and pitfalls with time series forecasting;
- explain the requirement for data in problem solving, acquire data from archives and the internet, explain the uses, advantages and limitations of observational studies, sample surveys and experiments and describe the conditions required for their validity;
- understand the development, application and limitations of simple models for variation in financial data, including the random walk model and the capital asset pricing model;
- give an account of the role of statistical analysis and statistical thinking in business and industry and an outline of the management and organisational requirements for their effective deployment.

## Genesis of the book

The approach taken in this book is radically different from that found in traditional service courses in statistics. The traditional approach emphasised methods, with illustrations, and was bedded in formal probability theory. In this text, the emphasis is on problem solving and statistical thinking and formal probability is not required.

There has been steadily increasing interest in reforming the teaching of elementary statistics, reflected in a series of conferences, research papers and textbooks. The approach taken here draws heavily on such sources. It parallels approaches advocated in a series of conferences on the theme 'Making statistics more effective in schools of business', starting in the University of Chicago in 1986. The emphasis on statistical thinking reflects the efforts of American industrial statisticians to promote more appropriate teaching and practice of statistics as well as of some academic researchers who have been developing a coherent theory of statistical thinking.

## Acknowledgements

I am grateful for the feedback received from the many students on whom various versions of the material in this book have been tested over the years. In particular, I am grateful to the following students who participated in course quality improvement teams: Sarah Chadwick, Alan Clarke, Lee Clements, Darina Colhoun, Sarah Downing, Ciaran Doyle, Naomi Gough, Suzanne Greely, Kevin Hopkins, Deirdre Kelly, Linnet Kuhnke, Emma McKenna, Rael McNally, Fiona Molloy, Michelle Murphy, Mark Pender, Ciara Rogerson, Dominic Smith, Owen Travers, Sinead Walsh, Grainne Wells. Paul Rafferty, Paul McNicholas and Ciara Fitzmaurice provide valuable research assistance.

Pat McKerr, Larry Breen, Brian O'Connor, Paddy Banks, Michael Chadwick, Ed Crotty, Corona Naessens and Bettina MacCarvill all provided case study material and considerable advice and assistance on case background. Colleagues Myra O'Regan, Dermot Duggan and Cathal Walsh read parts of the manuscript and provided helpful comments. Liz Gooster, Lesley Riddle, Christina Wipf and Tiara Misquitta provided continuing assistance with the publishing process. Mike Nugent and Jenny Dewhirst provided valuable editorial assistance.

My biggest debt is to long standing colleague Eamonn Mullins. Eamonn read the entire manuscript and provided detailed and invaluable comments on all aspects of the material, as well as specific suggestions and models for the treatment of some topics. The form and style of the book have benefited incalculably from the many conversations and debates that Eamonn and I have had over the years, occasionally in the company of our mutual friend, Arthur Guinness. Needless to say, any faults remaining are attributable solely to the author.

Finally, my wife, Ita, has given constant support over many years and our children Eoghan, Deirdre, Elaine and Gerry provided a form of encouragement by asking questions such as 'how is it going?' and 'when will it be finished?'

Michael Stuart
Dublin, July 2003

**Website**

There is a website associated with this text. The address is:

**www.tcd.ie/Statistics/Stuart/StatisticalAnalysis**

In addition to the laboratory exercise and feedback material referred to in the Preface, the website also includes solutions to the exercises in the text, additional exercises with solutions, a bank of multiple choice questions with answers and explanations, all the data sets referred to in the text and selected supplements and extensions to the material contained herein. It is intended to add further features, including slide presentations, in due course.

# 1

# Introduction

Statistical analysis for business and industry is concerned with problem solving and assisting decision making. This is achieved through the definition, production, analysis and interpretation of data in context. A key to this achievement is what has come to be called statistical thinking. Statistical thinking involves a focus on processes, the recognition that all processes are subject to variation and that identifying, characterising, quantifying and reducing process variation are keys to business success. Within this broader focus, the contribution unique to the statistical analyst lies in characterising and quantifying variation and in specifying data sources and designs for data production which will provide the most suitable information for these purposes. At a technical level, this involves the use of models which reflect structure and relationships in variation as well as models for unstructured variation, which may be ascribed to chance.

The rest of this chapter is concerned with putting some flesh on this rather abstract skeleton with the aid of a series of examples, illustrations and case studies, ranging from simple but revealing graphical analysis of data arising in a small retailing venture through similar analyses of data arising in finance, manufacturing, business administration, market research and forecasting. Along the way, the so-called Normal model for chance variation and the multiple regression model for structured variation will be introduced, along with a formal framework for statistical problem solving.

The rest of this book is concerned with extending and elaborating on the ideas introduced and illustrated in this first chapter. The examples and case studies introduced here will be further developed and further case studies introduced. The intention is to develop the ideas and methods of statistical analysis in a problem solving and decision making environment. To this end, most chapters will include computer laboratory exercises and some will include teamwork exercises, a feature which plays a significant role in modern business and manufacturing.

**Learning objectives**

After completing this chapter, students should understand the nature of statistical variation, understand the role of some important statistical models in explaining statistical variation and in solving substantive problems, and begin to develop an understanding of and capacity for statistical thinking and demonstrate this by being able to:

- define, illustrate and distinguish between chance and assignable causes of variation;
- illustrate and distinguish between the process view and the histogram view of statistical variation;
- describe and characterise typical sources of chance variation;
- describe and illustrate the Normal model for chance variation;
- explain frequency distribution and its relation to histogram and Normal curve;
- describe and illustrate the random walk model;
- explain simple implications of the random walk model for variation in financial data;
- illustrate by example the relationship between two variables, distinguishing between response and explanatory variables;
- define, construct and explain the uses and advantages of line charts and scatterplots;
- define and illustrate the simple linear regression model, incorporating the Normal model;
- illustrate, by example, the relationship between a response variable and several explanatory variables;
- illustrate, by example, problems in the definition of variables;
- demonstrate the role of line charts and scatterplots in learning about relationships between a response variable and several explanatory variables;
- define the multiple regression model and use a multiple regression prediction formula;
- list the main steps in an approach to statistical problem solving and illustrate selected steps by example;
- illustrate, by example, sources of error in questionnaire design.

## 1.1   Sales and shortages in a sports and social club

A sports and social club runs a drinks bar for its members, the proceeds of which help fund its sporting activities. To assist with proper management and control of this business, some key figures are monitored. One of these is total weekly sales. Some years ago, on a (more or less) regular basis, the Treasurer presented a report on weekly sales to the bar management committee. Extracts from management meeting minutes summarising some of these reports are given in Table 1.1.

**Table 1.1**  Weekly sales reports for eight weeks in 1992

| Date of meeting | Week ending | Bar takings |
|---|---|---|
| February 27, 1992 | 16/2/92 | £5,700 |
|  | 23/2/92 | £6,038 |
| April 9, 1992 | 29/3/92 | £4,584 |
|  | 5/4/92 | £4,822 |
| May 5, 1992 | 26/4/92 | £6,353 |
|  | 3/5/92 | £5,917 |
| May 28, 1992 | 17/5/92 | £6,553 |
|  | 24/5/92 | £5,390 |
| June 11, 1992 | 31/5/92 | £6,484 |
|  | 7/6/92 | £5,585 |
| July 30, 1992 | 19/7/92 | £6,437 |
|  | 26/7/92 | £7,821 |
| August 27, 1992 | 16/8/92 | £6,000 |
|  | 23/8/92 | £7,596 |
| September 24, 1992 | 13/9/92 | £6,500 |
|  | 20/9/92 | £8,532 |

The reports are in 'last week/this week' format, with attention focusing on the week to week change. Almost invariably, the Treasurer made a brief comment complimenting the staff when reporting an increase. Equally invariably, when reporting a decrease, the Treasurer spent some time recounting the details of a conversation he had had with the bar manager, including the explanations that had been advanced by the bar manager for the drop in sales, and then engaged the committee in a discussion about remedies for these ills. Careful examination of the table[1] reveals that takings were up from the previous week on five occasions and down on three. In fact, the takings for the week ending 20/9/92 included around £3,000 taken on one night when the club was celebrating a famous victory by one of its competitive teams; when this is taken into account, the takings for that week are down on those for the previous week, so that takings are up as often as they are down, in these data. In light of observations such as this, one or two members of the committee occasionally suggested that the Treasurer not take up the time of the committee with such lengthy discussions and sort out any problems there might be with the bar manager, but to no avail, until another view of the bar takings emerged.

## The process view

As part of a review of club activities, with a view to preparing a business plan in connection with a proposed extension of the club premises, daily bar takings over a two year period were extracted from the club records. A graph was prepared showing weekly sales over the two year period (Figure 1.1). Two immediately striking characteristics of the data displayed here are the seasonal pattern, high in summer and low in winter, and a few exceptionally high values.

---

[1]  The fact that careful examination is required reflects the inadequacy of this table for data display. This issue will be taken up in Chapter 2.

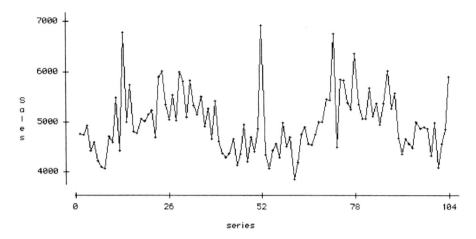

**Figure 1.1**   Weekly sales in a sports and social club for two years, 1990–1.

The graph in Figure 1.1 is shown again in Figure 1.2 enhanced by adding a computer generated 'smoother', which follows the seasonal pattern.

The remaining variation in sales, having allowed for the seasonal effect and the exceptional values, is now revealed as having no systematic pattern, with deviations above or below the seasonal pattern occurring apparently haphazardly. This phenomenon is emphasised by calculating the actual deviations of the sales figures from the values corresponding to the computer generated seasonal pattern. These deviations, called the 'rough' by the computer, are shown in Figure 1.3. Apart from the exceptional values, which persist in this graph, the weekly deviations appear to oscillate around 0 and appear just as likely to be up as down.

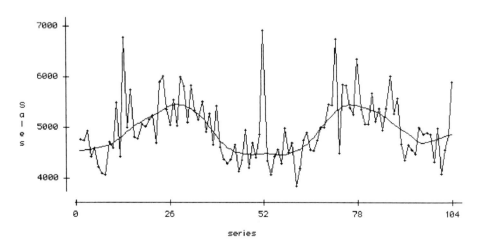

**Figure 1.2**   Weekly bar sales with seasonal effect emphasised.

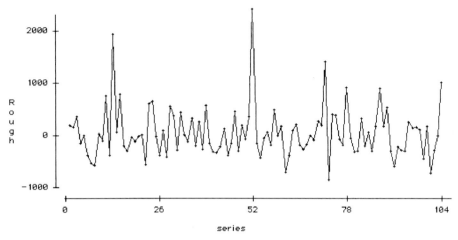

**Figure 1.3** Deviations of weekly sales from seasonal pattern.

### Advantages of the process view

There are important lessons to be learned from the contrast between the two views of the data shown here, the 'this week/last week' view of Table 1.1 and the time oriented process view of Figures 1.1–1.3. The latter reveals important features of the variation in the weekly sales process. On the one hand, there are the seasonal pattern and the exceptional values, on the other, the remaining apparently haphazard week to week variation. Each of these has important management consequences. For example, the presence of the seasonal pattern indicates spare capacity outside of the summer season which could profitably be filled by introducing regular events designed to draw customers during that period. The exceptionally high values correspond to Christmas week or to long weekends (incorporating public holidays) when special events with late opening bars are organised. The irregular occurrence of the latter suggests an opportunity to increase business by organising more special events.

Turning to the remaining apparently haphazard week to week variation, there is a different kind of lesson to be learned, which is that there is little or no value in worrying about week to week variation, precisely because it is haphazard and unpredictable. Further than that, there may be considerable negative consequences to such activity. In this case, not only was much time being wasted at the management meetings but also the bar manager was likely to waste more time looking for explanations for the drop in sales and, possibly, acting on such explanations. Since the 'explanations' were almost certainly spurious, acting on them is likely to make things worse rather than better. Furthermore, the constant useless interventions by the Treasurer were likely to create an uneasy relationship between management and staff, which is unlikely to improve business.

On seeing Figure 1.1, the club Treasurer ceased commenting on week to week variation at management meetings and also ceased discussing them with the bar manager.

Far too many companies make use of the 'this week/last week' approach described here or variants such as 'this week/last week/same week last year' or 'this week/same week last month/same week last year'. Invariably, this leads to lost opportunities, through not seeing the whole picture, and wasted effort (or worse) through reacting to haphazard variation. By contrast, the graphical view of process variation shows up important patterns which provide important information to management. Of central importance is the distinction between haphazard unstructured variation, which is best left alone (at least in the short term), and structured variation where the structure can be related to key features of the process, understanding of which inevitably leads to better management.

Anticipating seasonal patterns and 'special event' patterns is, essentially, an act of prediction. In later chapters, we will see how to quantify such predictions and, in particular, how to quantify the allowance in such predictions that must be made for haphazard variation.

## Monitoring cash variances

Another key activity associated with running a business is financial control. As part of this control activity in the sports and social club, the till/cash variances, that is the differences between the cash in the till at the end of each day's trading and what was recorded on the till roll, as entered through the keys, are monitored. (Modern tills are programmed so that the value of each transaction and their total value over a day's trading can be printed on the till roll at the touch of a button at the close of business. In larger retail organisations, till records may be routed electronically to a central database.) Once again, the Treasurer took a keen interest in this and was continually annoyed when variances exceeding a few pounds occurred. He expressed the view that anything more than one pound was excessive, but had reconciled himself to seeing variances of £5 and more fairly regularly.

What is a reasonable maximum for such variances, beyond which we should take corrective action? We can begin to see an answer by looking at the *process* of till/cash variances, as in the graph in Figure 1.4.

What we see is a pattern of more or less haphazard variation around 0, with a few possible exceptions. Such variation is to be expected. Small errors in making change or in entering cash amounts on the till keys are inevitable in a busy retail outlet. Such errors will occur more or less haphazardly, may be plus or minus, and will build up over a period of time. In the presence of such inevitable haphazard variation, the best that can be hoped for is that the cash variances will centre around zero. The key question is how much of a deviation should we allow for.

For the process displayed in Figure 1.4, it may be reasonable to suggest that the negative variance of around –£20 in week 34 is exceptional, by comparison with the bulk of the rest. We might also suspect week 51 and, perhaps, week 41. The larger positive variances in week 11 and week 44 may also be suspect, although positive variances are usually not of great concern. But why stop there? Why not investigate all variances exceeding, say, £5? In fact, such a policy had been applied at an earlier stage but was abandoned when too many investigations led nowhere and made the bar manager and staff resentful of such close but apparently pointless scrutiny. What

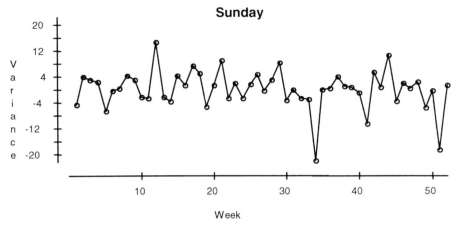

**Figure 1.4**   Till/cash variances, in £IR, for Sunday trading for one year.

is needed is a rational approach to deciding what is inevitable haphazard variation and what is exceptional variation. A solution to this problem was developed by Walter Shewhart in the mid-1920s and named by him the *control chart*. The formal development of Shewhart's solution is taken up in Chapter 4 and leads into what statisticians refer to as *statistical significance testing*. Shewhart developed his work more broadly during the 1920s and later, and his ideas became a key element in the development of the modern quality improvement movement in business and industry.[2]

### The histogram view

We can get a preview of Shewhart's thinking by looking at another view of the cash variance data. Figure 1.5 shows a *histogram* of the Sunday cash variances discussed above. Each vertical bar in the histogram represents the number of variances whose values fall in the corresponding interval on the horizontal axis.

This histogram shows a preponderance of relatively small values around 0 with decreasing numbers of larger values, positive and negative, with some exceptional values showing up as separated from the bulk of the rest. This alternative display of the data gives a different view of the way in which the variances are spread around 0. The particular pattern seen here is a classic pattern which recurs regularly in practice. In fact, it occurs so regularly that mathematicians have developed a special *model* for variation which follows such a pattern, called the *Normal* model, and characterised by the smooth curve shown added to the histogram in Figure 1.6. In later sections, we will see more about the construction of histograms from data and we will review the genesis of the corresponding theoretical Normal curves.

Put in the context of this example, Shewhart's key idea was that, in practice, variances do not occur beyond the bounds corresponding to the top and bottom bars

---

[2]   See the historical note on page 9.

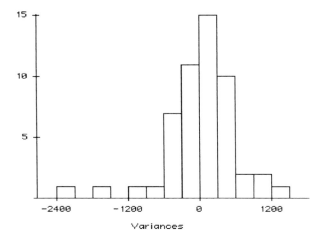

**Figure 1.5**   Histogram of Sunday cash variances in pence IR.

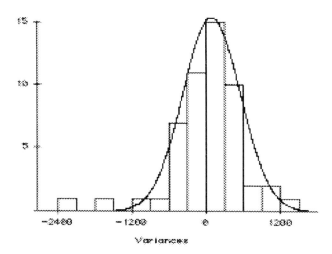

**Figure 1.6**   Histogram of Sunday cash variances with Normal curve.

of the bulk of the variances, unless exceptional circumstances cause exceptional values. When such exceptional circumstances occur, they should be investigated with a view to eliminating their causes. On this simple idea rests a large part of modern statistical quality control and, by extension, statistical significance testing and estimation, the details of which will be presented in Chapters 4 and 5.

## The band around the trend

When referred to the process view, this idea translates into placing a band above and below the line at 0, as illustrated in Figure 1.7. In normal circumstances, data points

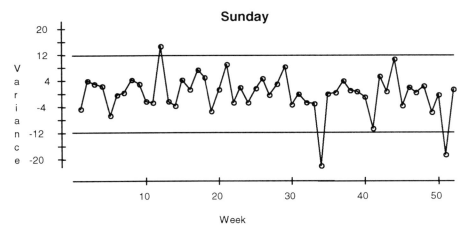

**Figure 1.7** Till/cash variances, in £IR, for Sunday trading for one year with Shewhart control limits.

are expected to fall haphazardly within this band and such data points are unremarkable. Data points falling outside the band suggest exceptional circumstances and indicate the need for investigation and, possibly, action. Figure 1.7 constitutes the simplest form of what Shewhart termed a control chart. It will be further developed in Chapter 4.

## Historical note

The control chart idea was developed by Walter Shewhart, a research engineer working with Bell Telephone Laboratories in New Jersey, USA, in 1924. He was part of a team charged with ensuring the quality of manufacture of telephones and related equipment, who quickly realised that statistical variation in manufacturing was a key issue and that it needed control. Subsequently, the control chart idea was extended in many ways and to many applications. Shewhart himself went on to pioneer and promote ideas of quality improvement and made several key contributions in this area. Many of his ideas were published in his book *The Economic Control of Quality* in 1931. He may be regarded as the 'father' of the modern quality movement in business and industry, although other quality 'gurus' have seemed to lay claim to his mantle.

By a remarkable coincidence, the same ideas that were put to use by Shewhart in 1924 in a manufacturing setting were being put to use in another context by the English statistician and geneticist, Ronald Fisher. At that time, Fisher worked in an agricultural research station at Rothamstead, north of London, where he advised agricultural research scientists on statistical aspects of the design of their experiments and on statistical analysis of the subsequent data. He made a number of fundamental contributions to the theory and practice of statistics and many regard him as the 'father' of modern statistics. His account of statistical significance and the ideas behind it was published in his book *Statistical Methods for Research Workers* in 1925.

## 1.2   Statistical variation in the Stock Exchange

Variation in financial data is a remarkable feature of modern daily living for a great many people. Virtually every broadsheet newspaper devotes large areas of print to detailed tables of prices of company shares and government bonds, exchange rates and interest rates, along with more or less extensive commentaries on the main movers as well as stories about company developments, government initiatives and views expressed by apparently important people in the world of business and finance. In some cases, whole newspapers such as the *Financial Times* and the *Wall Street Journal* are devoted to such matters. Almost every prime time radio and television news programme devotes some time to reporting on changes in the major Stock Exchange indices, the main movers on the Stock Exchange and the main stories about business and finance. In recent years, internet service providers have made available up to the minute data on Stock Exchange prices, for a fee (with fifteen minute old data available free). Presumably, this wealth of detail is valuable to a great many people, else media market researchers would long ago have advised that they be abandoned. We will see in Chapter 10 that relatively straightforward statistical analysis of historical financial data can lead to useful guidelines for broad investment strategies. However, to go beyond that it appears that extremely detailed and fundamental research is needed to take full advantage of the vagaries of financial variation. Here, we note two important characteristics from which important lessons may be learned.

**FTSE 100**

The *Financial Times* index of the leading 100 company shares traded on the London Stock Exchange, known as FTSE 100 ('footsy 100'), is one of the main financial indices. It is, essentially, a weighted average using a carefully designed set of weights of the share prices of the top 100 shares chosen according to carefully specified criteria.[3] We can begin to get some understanding of the variation in FTSE 100 by looking at historical data such as that illustrated in Figure 1.8 which shows a line plot of the daily closing values of FTSE 100 for the five years 1996–2000.

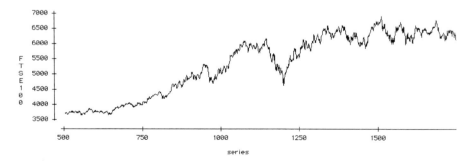

**Figure 1.8**   The FTSE 100 index, daily, 1996–2000.

---

[3]   Full details can be found on the FTSE website at www.ftse.com

There appears to be a strong increasing trend in the value of the index over the five year period. We can see that someone who had invested in the 100 shares that make up the index at the beginning of the period, when its value was just over 3,500, would have almost doubled the value of the investment at the end of the period, by which time the index had increased to almost 7,000. Allowing for general price inflation in the UK economy which amounted to 15% over the five year period, this represents reasonable growth in the assets invested, comforting for an investor prepared to let the investment stand for a substantial period. Along the way, the investor might have had some uneasy moments when the index dropped sharply, particularly in the period near the middle of the graph (mid-July to early October, 1998) when the index fell by an alarming 25% of its value, 6,174 to 4,649. However, this was still more than 25% up on the value in January 1996, while investors who held their nerves would have been satisfied to see the value rise again and pass out the previous high, although levelling off somewhat in the last year or so, and having an increasing number of ups and downs.

## Daily changes in FTSE 100

A rather different view of the variation is seen in Figure 1.9. This shows the daily changes in the value of FTSE 100, that is, each day's closing value less the previous day's closing value. There are two striking aspects to this graph; the variation in daily change appears to be haphazard around 0 and the spread in the variation appears to be steadily increasing up to late 1998 and stabilising after that.

These features can be seen in more detail in Figure 1.10, which shows each year's changes separately. Note the changes in the vertical scales, moving through the years, reflecting the change in spread, or *volatility*, as it is referred to in the world of finance. Also, the variation in 1996 shown in Figure 1.10a looks just like the haphazard unstructured variation we saw in both bar sales and cash variances in Section 1.1, with perhaps a few exceptional changes. Similar patterns appear in the other plots in Figure 1.10. This view is corroborated by the histograms for each year's changes shown in Figure 1.11, which show patterns similar to that seen in the cash variances as shown in Figure 1.5. These views suggest that changes from day to day are essentially unpredictable. For example, it suggests that we are as likely to

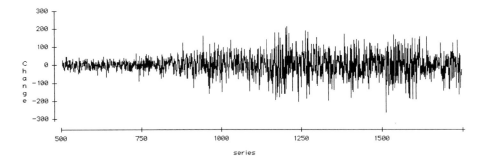

**Figure 1.9**  Daily changes in FTSE 100, 1996–2000.

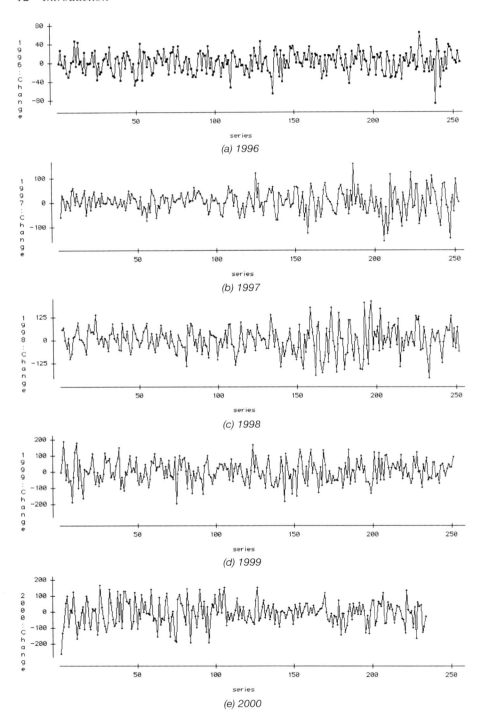

*(a) 1996*

*(b) 1997*

*(c) 1998*

*(d) 1999*

*(e) 2000*

**Figure 1.10**  Daily changes in FTSE 100, 1996–2000.

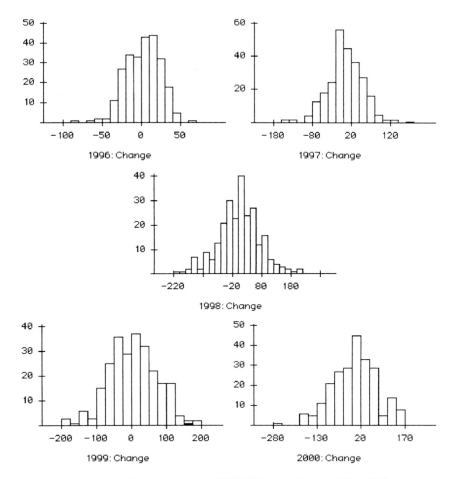

**Figure 1.11**   Histograms of daily changes in FTSE 100 for each year, 1996–2000.

have as much success in predicting the direction of tomorrow's change, up or down, as in predicting the result of tossing a coin, head or tail. If this is so, it has important implications for the way we view short term trading on the Stock Exchange.

For example, if this view prevails then the daily reporting of changes in Stock Exchange indices may be as helpful as reporting the change from last week's National Lottery number (all six strung together) to this week's. If such a view applies to individual shares as well as stock market indices, it suggests that short term trading is a hazardous venture, with outcomes being largely determined as if by chance.

## A simple mathematical model of daily change

Financial analysts like to describe the pattern of variation seen here in the FTSE 100 as a *random walk*. It is as if the index tracks across the graph by taking steps whose direction and length are unpredictable: sometimes up, sometimes down, sometimes long, sometimes short. There is a simple mathematical representation of such variation: if successive values are denoted by $X_1$, $X_2$, $X_3$, etc., then the value on day $t$ may be represented as

$$X_t = X_{t-1} + \varepsilon_t,$$

where $\varepsilon_t$, which represents the change from day $t - 1$ to day $t$, is determined entirely by chance. This representation is referred to as the *random walk model*.

There has been considerable debate in the financial community, among both practitioners and academics, on the consequences of considerations such as this. On the one hand, purists argue that the markets are (or should be) efficient in the sense that any useful information, such as a profit announcement, becomes quickly available to the whole market so that no individual can take advantage of it. If so, then the random walk model applies and forecasting further change, after the useful information has been accounted for, is like forecasting next week's National Lottery.

On the other hand, it is well established that the random walk model does not apply exactly; no mathematical model ever does. The task then is to locate the inefficiencies in the market that will allow clever analysts to make a profit on short term transactions. The problem is that the gains to be made in an almost efficient market are very small and may be swamped by the risk involved in dealing with that part of the market variation which is subject to the random walk model. That challenge has been taken up by highly qualified and highly paid financial analysts.

## Reducing the risk of investment

The first big step was the introduction of the notion of *diversified portfolios* as a method of risk reduction. The classic illustration is a portfolio consisting of two investments: shares in an ice cream company and shares in an umbrella company. Profits from both vary through the year; the first rises in the sunny season and falls in the rainy season, the second does the opposite. However, when the two are combined and viewed as a single investment, the opposing variations cancel out. The shares combine to form a diversified portfolio with steady more or less unvarying profit at all times. The key to extending this idea to forming diversified portfolios of many shares is the important statistical idea of *correlation*. The ice cream and umbrella shares are said to be *negatively correlated* which means that when one rises in value, the other tends to fall. The trick is to seek a variety of negatively correlated investments. Development along these lines leads to the *capital asset pricing model* (CAPM). This is closely related to what statisticians call *simple linear regression,* which is introduced in Section 1.5 and developed in detail, along with correlation, in Chapter 6.

Further developments along these lines, in which statistical ideas played a central role, led to achieving substantial reduction in the risk of investment, while protecting profits. However, risk could not be eliminated by these methods and some of the practitioners got badly burnt, through over-confidence.

The next big step in risk reduction involved inventing new types of investments, called *derivatives,* and then finding complex combinations of such investments which could take advantage of identified inefficiencies in the market while virtually eliminating risk. These have worked spectacularly well for some traders who have made enormous profits as a result. However, they have also failed spectacularly, as in the case of Long-Term Capital Management (LTCM), a financial management company employing the best mathematical and financial brains that money could buy, including two former academics who had won an economics 'Nobel Prize' for their contributions to financial theory. Their theories did not allow for what happened in the world's financial markets between July and October, 1998, as illustrated in Figure 1.8.

Specifically, the mathematical models they used had a *liquidity* assumption built in. In practice, this required that there would always be sufficient money invested in the market. However, the slump in 1998 meant that more and more investors were taking their money out of the market, thus undermining LTCM's strategy. As a result, the 14 biggest investment banks in the world, who were tied in to LTCM through extensive trading and enormous loans, almost collapsed and only survived by taking concerted action to support LTCM and by relying on the US Government to reduce interest rates.[4]

Chapter 10 will review some of the simpler ways in which statistical thinking and statistical models can assist understanding of stock markets and suggest principles of risk reduction.

## 1.3 Variation in manufacturing; charts, graphs and stratification as aids to understanding

In this section, we look at a manufacturing process through data collected in a trouble shooting exercise designed to assist in solving a problem which affected a critical characteristic of the product involved. We take the opportunity of introducing some problem solving tools including the flow chart as an aid to understanding the process, stratification to study a key source of variation and using histograms to summarise differences between strata.

### Variation in tennis ball manufacturing

The International Lawn Tennis Federation sets standards and specifications which manufacturers of tennis balls must meet in order to have their products approved for official competitions. Key quality characteristics for tennis balls include diameter, weight, bounce, breaking strength and fluffiness. However, it is a fact of manufacturing life that almost all manufacturing processes are subject to variation which, to some extent, is unpredictable. The control and reduction of such variation so that the end product meets the required specifications is a major concern in modern manufacturing. Here, we look at the results of a special study of tennis ball core diameters

---

[4]   A readable account of the rise and fall of LTCM can be found in *Inventing Money; the Story of Long-Term Capital Management and the Legends Behind it*, by Nicholas Dunbar, published by John Wiley, 2000.

which was part of a quality improvement project designed to bring the finished tennis ball diameters within more stringent specifications that had been introduced by the International Lawn Tennis Federation.

*Flow charting the process*

The first step in reducing the variation in any process is to gain some understanding of the sources of variation. We start by developing some understanding of the process itself through the *flowchart* shown in Figure 1.12.

The process raw materials are natural rubber and chemical additives, some in trace quantities, some in larger quantities, which are loaded into a mixing hopper and mixed at a raised temperature. The mixed material is extruded into long sheets which are cut into 'pellets', each of sufficient material to make a half tennis ball core, or 'cup' as it is called. The pellets are placed in hemispherical moulds which, again at a raised temperature, create the cups. To make a complete core, two cups must be glued together. As the cup edge surface is completely smooth it must be roughened to allow the glue to bond; this is achieved by hand using a grinding wheel, called an 'edge buffer'.

Pairs of cups are glued together in four special presses, 186 pairs per press at a time. The balls are pressurised at this stage also; each press is closed to the outside

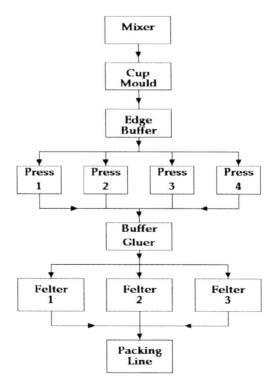

**Figure 1.12**   Flow chart for a tennis ball manufacturing process.

before the cup pairs come together, the pressure in the press is raised and then a second stage closure brings the cup pairs together. Finally, the glue is set, or 'cured', for 20 minutes at a raised temperature.

The outside cover, or 'felt', is glued onto the core on one of three felting machines by skilled operatives, the outside surface of the core having been buffed and glued in a 'buffer and gluer'. Finally, the finished tennis balls are packed under pressure in plastic or metal containers (cans).

*Sources of process variation*

This view of the process makes us aware that there are many potential sources of variation in the process. For example, the diameter of a ball could be affected if

- the main raw material, rubber (a natural product), varied slightly in different parts of the mixture;
- the chemical additives varied slightly in their properties or in the amounts of each in different parts of the mixture;
- the size of the pellets placed in the moulds varied;
- the extent of edge buffing varied;
- the ambient temperature of the presses varied, perhaps from end to end of a press;
- the press pressure was slightly different;
- the measuring instrument was slightly differently adjusted;
- the instrument reader made slight measurement errors; etc.

**Variation between and within presses**

In the quality improvement project, the focus of attention was variation arising in the four presses. To study this, the diameters of the 744 cores produced by the four presses in one run were measured and recorded. The data are given in the appendix at the end of this chapter (and in data file Tennis.xls on the book's website). They are *stratified* into four *strata* corresponding to the four presses. The data analysis task then is to study the variation *between* the four strata, in the context of the inevitable variation *within* strata that can be ascribed to all the other variation sources listed and many others that we have not thought about. Stratified graphical analysis is used to reveal the key features of the data simply and effectively; Figure 1.13 shows histograms of the core diameters in the four presses.

Within each press, the data are spread across the horizontal scale in no particular pattern, apart from tending to be concentrated in the middle and sparse at the edges.[5] We are not able to pinpoint a specific cause for such patternless variation; rather, we may regard such variation as the combined effect of the very many individually negligible and unpredictable sources of variation, such as those listed above, which could arise at any stage of the process.

Now, consider the variation between presses. Presses 1 and 2 produce cores with rather similar measurements, the press 3 cores are clearly more spread and may be,

---

[5]   There may be a suggestion of measurement problems in the data from presses 1 and 3. This suggestion will not be pursued immediately, and does not seriously affect our interpretation of these data.

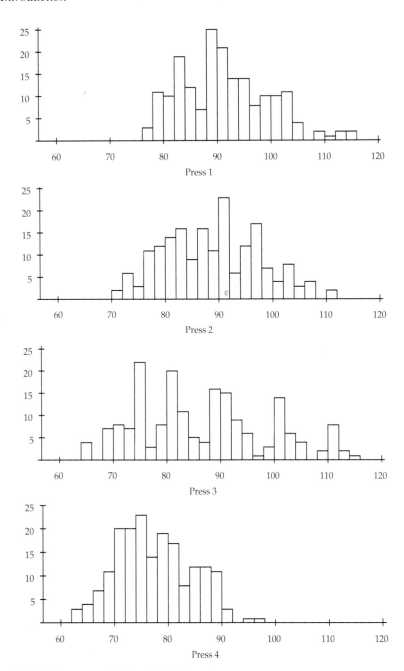

**Figure 1.13**  Histograms of the tennis ball diameters.

as a whole, smaller than those of presses 1 and 2. The cores of press 4 have dispersion similar to that in presses 1 and 2 but are, as a whole, considerably smaller.

It is tempting to suggest that the differences described are due to differences between the presses, as such, and that physical causes can be found for these differences whose discovery and elimination will also eliminate the statistical differences described. Thus, it may be surmised that a simple adjustment to the pressure in press 4 will raise the diameters to be more in line with presses 1 and 2, assuming these to be more or less satisfactory. Reducing the spread in press 3 may be a more difficult problem, since spread is usually related to the combined effect of the very many individually negligible and unpredictable sources of variation which affect the process. A more intense investigation of the factors affecting variation in press 3 may be required.

## 1.4 Chance and assignable causes of variation, the Normal model for chance variation and frequency distributions

In all the examples we have encountered so far, we have attempted to understand process variation in terms of two types of variation. On the one hand, we find a few identifiable sources of variation which correspond to definite patterns in graphical representations of process data. For example, we saw a seasonal effect and the effects of special events on sales in Section 1.1. We also saw there the effect of staff errors on cash–till variances. Stock Exchange data are subject to dramatic falls which may be regarded as the result of such factors as overheating of the economy. Different conditions in the tennis ball presses appeared to have noticeable effects on tennis ball diameters. Shewhart referred to this kind of variation as being due to *assignable* causes.

On the other hand, we have seen another type of variation, which appears to have no single identifiable source and seems *haphazard* when viewed in the process view, although it assumes a more or less recognisable global pattern in the 'histogram' view. A convenient model for this kind of variation is to regard it as having been generated by what Shewhart referred to as *chance* causes.

### Chance and assignable causes defined

We can formalise a definition of chance and assignable causes as follows.

- Chance causes of variation are the *many individually negligible* and *unpredictable* but *collectively influential* factors that affect a process or system.
- Assignable causes of variation are the *few individually influential* and *predictable effect* factors that affect a process or system.

### Chance variation in tennis ball diameters

Recall the tennis ball manufacturing process where we were able to list a number of factors, virtually imperceptible variations in which together could cause noticeable if unpredictable variation in the diameters of tennis ball cores. While we could, in theory, determine the individual effects of each individual source of variation, by using sufficiently precise investigative techniques, this is not feasible in practice. Lacking such detailed information, it appears to us *as if* the variation was due to a combination of chance mechanisms. We might imagine tossing a fair coin to decide the contribution of each of the many factors affecting the diameter; a head indicates a positive (if tiny) contribution leading to an increased diameter, a tail leading to a reduced diameter. The resulting diameter of a tennis ball core may be thought of as the result of combining these very many apparently chance contributions. Repeating such an exercise for a succession of tennis balls will produce a succession of diameters which are unpredictable from one to the next, leading to the haphazard quality of the variation noted in many processes.

It will also lead to the pattern seen in the histograms of Figure 1.13, where the actual diameters tend to be concentrated towards the middle and sparse at the edges. In practice, it will be rare for all or almost all the many contributing factors to contribute positively, thus producing a very large diameter. Equally, a very small diameter corresponding to almost all negative contributions is unlikely. In our coin tossing analogy, this corresponds to the rather small chance of almost all heads or almost all tails in a long succession of coin tosses. In practice, the contributions from the many individual factors will be more in balance, leading to less extreme variation and a greater concentration of diameters towards the middle of the possible range. This is echoed in coin tossing by the higher chances of similar numbers of heads and tails in a long series of tosses.

### The Normal model for chance variation

This pattern is very common in applications. In fact, an important mathematical model for this form of variation is called the *Normal* model for chance variation. This model may be represented graphically by a *Normal frequency curve,* which is an idealized histogram where the bases of the rectangles making up the histogram are so small that the tops of the rectangles merge into a smooth curve, given by a well defined mathematical formula,[6] and having a characteristic 'bell' shape such as that illustrated in Figure 1.14. A version of this curve was displayed earlier in Figure 1.6.

In Figure 1.15, the Normal curve is used to model the variation in the three sets of measurements of tennis ball diameters from presses 1, 2 and 4 shown in 'histogram' view in Figure 1.13. In this case, the model is adapted to the three datasets simply by moving its centre.

Figure 1.16 illustrates its further adaptability in accommodating sets of measurements with different spreads as well as different centres. The low wide spread curve corresponds to the data from press 3. It has a different centre to the others and its spread is approximately 1.5 times as large as the spread common to the other three presses. By contrast, the tall thin curve represents data whose spread is approxi-

---

[6]    The height of a standard version of this curve at value $x$ is $\dfrac{1}{\sqrt{2\pi}}\,\mathrm{e}^{-\frac{1}{2}x^2}$.

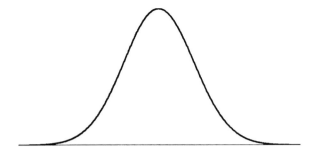

**Figure 1.14** A Normal frequency curve.

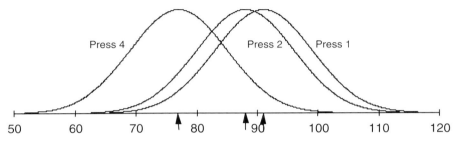

**Figure 1.15** The Normal model for chance variation in tennis ball cores, presses 1, 2 and 4.

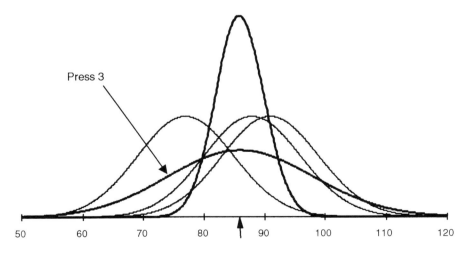

**Figure 1.16** Normal curves with different spreads.

mately 1.5 times smaller than that in presses 1, 2 and 4. This might represent a target spread to be achieved in a quality improvement programme.

We will see many applications for the Normal model later in this text. We will examine its development and application in Chapter 3. In particular, we will see how to identify the two model characteristics, centre and spread, with quantities to be introduced then called *mean* and *standard deviation.*

## Frequency distributions

Underlying the usefulness of the histogram as a graphical summary of chance variation and the Normal curve as a model for chance variation is the key idea of *frequency distribution.* We have seen that measurements which reflect chance variation tend to be more frequent towards the centre and less frequent towards the extremes. More precisely, the rectangles constituting the histogram represent the frequencies with which measurements occurred in the corresponding intervals on the horizontal axis. In fact, in order to construct the intervals in the first place, these frequencies must be determined. As an illustration, Table 1.2 shows these frequencies in the case of press 4.

The first column shows the intervals on the horizontal axis using a special notation: 60– means measurements of 60 or more but less than 62; 62– means measurements of 62 or more but less than 64, etc. From the second column, we find that there were no measurements of 60 or more but less than 62, three measurements of 62 or more but less than 64, etc. The second column shows the *frequencies* of measurements in the different intervals or, alternatively, shows how the total frequency of 186 is *distributed* across the intervals. Technically speaking, the second column shows the *frequency distribution* of the 186 measurements across the 20 intervals in the first column.

**Table 1.2**　Frequency distribution of tennis ball core diameters for press 4

| Interval | Frequency | Relative frequency | Frequency (%) |
|---|---|---|---|
| 60– | 0 | 0 | 0 |
| 62– | 3 | 0.016 | 1.6 |
| 64– | 4 | 0.022 | 2.2 |
| 66– | 4 | 0.022 | 2.2 |
| 68– | 9 | 0.048 | 4.8 |
| 70– | 15 | 0.081 | 8.1 |
| 72– | 21 | 0.113 | 11.3 |
| 74– | 25 | 0.134 | 13.4 |
| 76– | 16 | 0.086 | 8.6 |
| 78– | 17 | 0.091 | 9.1 |
| 80– | 19 | 0.102 | 10.2 |
| 82– | 11 | 0.059 | 5.9 |
| 84– | 11 | 0.059 | 5.9 |
| 86– | 13 | 0.070 | 7.0 |
| 88– | 11 | 0.059 | 5.9 |
| 90– | 5 | 0.027 | 2.7 |
| 92– | 0 | 0 | 0 |
| 94– | 1 | 0.005 | 0.5 |
| 96– | 0 | 0 | 0 |
| 98– | 1 | 0.005 | 0.5 |
| Total | 186 | 1.00 | 100 |

The third column expresses the frequencies in relative terms, taking the whole 186 measurements as a single unit and expressing the frequencies in the intervals as fractions or proportions of this, adding to 1. This gives the *relative frequency distribution* of measurements in intervals, relative to a base of 1. The fourth column shows the proportions of the third column expressed as percentages, that is, it shows the relative frequency distribution relative to a base of 100 rather than 1.

*The Normal frequency distribution*

The curve we have used to represent the Normal model for chance variation is a graphical representation of that model. As with the histogram, there is an equivalent numerical representation, called the *Normal frequency distribution*. Indeed, in order to be able to use the Normal model effectively, we will need to be able to calculate Normal frequencies, given data on the centre and spread of the Normal curve. In principle, these may be calculated directly from the *Normal frequency function*, given in footnote 6, page 20. In practice, reference is made to a pre-computed table of the Normal distribution or to an appropriate spreadsheet function. Details will follow in Chapter 3.

## 1.5   Modelling assignable causes: relations between variables

The US Post Office is organised in administrative districts, each served by a major post office. In one such district, a project was undertaken to set up a system for monitoring the cost of handling the mail that passed through the post office. The main cost involved was labour, which the project team decided to measure in terms of manhours[7] required. Experience indicated that the labour requirement varied with volume of mail handled and that volume itself varied from time to time. Thus, any cost monitoring system would have to allow for variation in volume from time to time. It would be helpful if management knew *by how much* the labour requirement should change for any given change in volume, for then they could say whether the labour cost incurred in a particular instance, when a particular volume was processed, conformed to that pattern, thus giving themselves a criterion for *cost control*.[8]

There is a bonus in quantifying the relationship between cost of production and volume in this way: it allows management to predict labour requirements as soon as they have an idea of anticipated volume. Such a prediction capability could have a variety of applications including strategic review, planning and budgeting, evaluating the effects of planned change and of unplanned interventions. For example, management may be able to anticipate the expected increase in volume in the weeks before Christmas and increase the labour force accordingly. Or, in the event of the sudden closure of a mail order company in the district, with a consequent substantial drop in volume, management will be in a position to decide on the extent

---

[7]   This case dates from 1962–3, when all the relevant workers were male.

[8]   Establishing a criterion for cost control, the topic of this example, is relatively easy, compared with the management task of establishing control, as such.

of redeployment required.

Relationships of the kind discussed here arise in many settings, for example:

1  Service times are related to machines serviced;
2  Service costs are related to machine age;
3  Recorded account balances are related to audited accounts;
4  Sales are related to costs of sales.

Such relationships are described as *response relationships;* a *response variable,* for example, cost of production, is seen as *responding* to changes in an *explanatory variable,* for example, volume of production; variation in the latter may be seen as *explaining* variation in the former.

## Looking at data

Having decided on the need to quantify the relationship between cost and volume, the need for data arose. In this case, there were detailed historical records on manhours (these data pertain to 1962–3) and volume for 26 four week accounting periods over two years. These were assembled in a table, shown as Table 1.3.

> **Exercise 1.1**    Discuss the reasonableness of 'pieces of mail handled' as a measure of volume and of 'manhours used' as a measure of cost, in the context of a study of the relationship between the two. Suggest and discuss alternatives, where appropriate.

**Table 1.3**    Data on mail processing hours and volume for the ABCD Post Office (fiscal years 1962–63)

| Fiscal year 1 | | | Fiscal year 2 | | |
|---|---|---|---|---|---|
| Four-week accounting period | Pieces of mail handled (in millions) | Manhours used (in thousands) | Four-week accounting period | Pieces of mail handled (in millions) | Manhours used (in thousands) |
| 1 | 157 | 572 | 1 | 154 | 569 |
| 2 | 161 | 570 | 2 | 157 | 564 |
| 3 | 168 | 645 | 3 | 164 | 573 |
| 4 | 186 | 645 | 4 | 188 | 667 |
| 5 | 183 | 645 | 5 | 191 | 700 |
| 6 | 184 | 671 | 6 | 180 | 765 |
| 7 | 268 | 1,053 | 7 | 270 | 1,070 |
| 8 | 180 | 675 | 8 | 180 | 637 |
| 9 | 175 | 670 | 9 | 172 | 650 |
| 10 | 193 | 710 | 10 | 184 | 655 |
| 11 | 184 | 656 | 11 | 179 | 665 |
| 12 | 179 | 640 | 12 | 169 | 599 |
| 13 | 164 | 599 | 13 | 160 | 605 |

Inspection of the data as laid out in the table does not convey much insight. More revealing is a graphical view of the mail handling process as shown in Figure 1.17.

There are strong similarities between the two graphs but both are dominated by exceptional values that occur in period 7 of each fiscal year. Period 7 corresponds to the weeks before Christmas; the fiscal year starts in mid-June. As this exceptional period does not conform with the rest of the year, it makes sense to exclude it and redraw the graphs. This results in Figure 1.18.

There are strong seasonal patterns in both curves and a close, if not perfect, relationship between the two variables. It appears that volume of mail provides a good, if not perfect, explanation for variation in mail processing hours. However, this qualitative correspondence provides no help in deriving a quantitative relationship which would allow management to say by how much the labour requirement would change for any given change in volume. To make progress in this direction, an alternative graphical form, the *scatterplot*, is helpful.

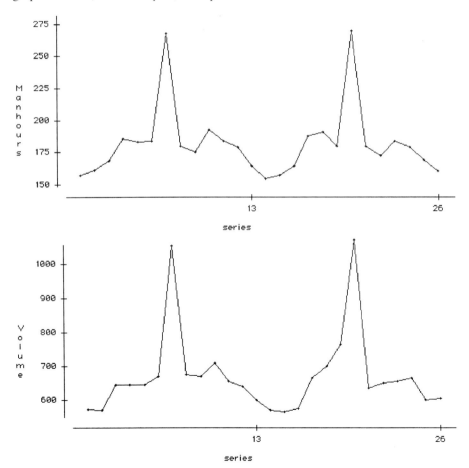

**Figure 1.17**   Line plots of manhours, in thousands, and numbers of pieces handled, in millions, for fiscal years 1962 and 1963.

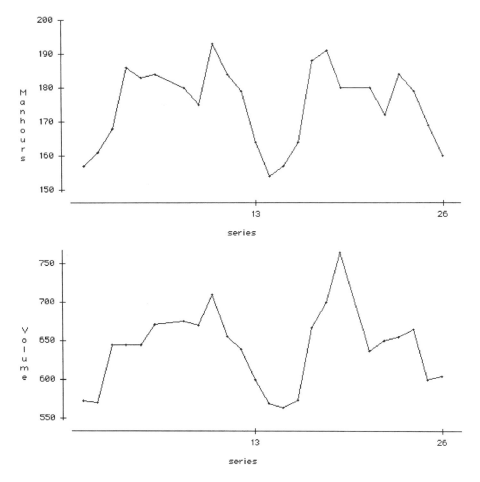

**Figure 1.18**   Line plots of manhours, in thousands, and numbers of pieces handled, in millions, for fiscal years 1962 and 1963, Christmas excluded.

*The scatterplot view*

Figure 1.19 shows the scatterplot of manhours against volume, a graph made by plotting points corresponding to each pair (*x, y*) of values of volume, *x*, and manhours, *y*. There appear to be three distinct subsets of data; the two points in the top right corner, the isolated point near (180, 800), and the remaining set of 23 points. The two points in the top right corner correspond to the two Christmas periods, already identified as exceptional in Figure 1.17. It may be suggested that the set of 23 points conform to a pattern in that they are all close to being in a straight line. Figure 1.20 shows the scatterplot enhanced with a computer generated straight line applied to the set of 23 points. It suggests a simple model for the variation in manhours relative to volume: for a given volume of mail, the line determines the corresponding manhours, apart from some haphazard variation which may be positive or negative.

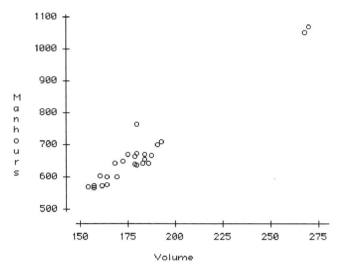

**Figure 1.19**  Scatterplot of manhours against volume.

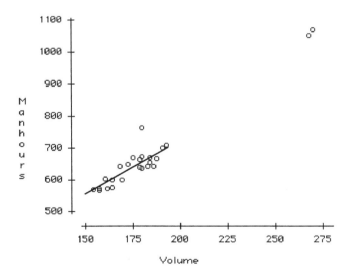

**Figure 1.20**  Scatterplot of manhours against volume enhanced with computer generated line.

In the light of this view of the data, the isolated point near (180, 800) appears exceptionally high. In fact, if we apply Shewhart's idea first introduced in connection with the cash variances discussed in Section 1.1, we can envisage a band around the straight line within which we anticipate all points on a scatterplot of manhours versus volume will fall, in normal circumstances. On the evidence of the data to hand, the band shown in Figure 1.21 may be reasonable. A point that does not fall within this band may be regarded as exceptional, and an explanation sought.

The isolated point near (180, 800) corresponds to period 6 in fiscal 1963. It so happened that equipment used in the mail sorting process was faulty during part of that period with the result that manhours accrued when no volume was being processed, thus giving a considerably higher manhours value than would be anticipated in normal circumstances. A bonus from this analysis is the availability of an estimate of the loss incurred through equipment downtime, that is, the vertical deviation of the isolated point from the line. Visually determined, this appears to be around 100,000 manhours.

If we assume that the computer generated line and its associated band can validly be extended towards the exceptional points associated with Christmas, as shown in Figure 1.22, we might infer that actual manhours then were higher than they ought to be, again by around 100,000 hours, estimated visually.

A plausible explanation for this is that substantial numbers of temporary workers, with little training and no experience, are hired during this period, thus leading to reduced productivity. However, caution is needed in extrapolating from the data on which our 'straight line' model of the relation between manhours and volume is based to cases which are considerably different and where little evidence about the relation is available. For example, it could well be that the relationship, while appearing approximately linear in the volume range 150–200, becomes non-linear for increased volume values. One possibility is that, with an expanded properly trained work force, increased volume would bring productivity returns to scale, reflected in a downward bending curved relationship, as suggested in Figure 1.23. Of course, if such a model is appropriate, the estimated loss in productivity during the Christmas period is very much increased.

For many practical purposes, the graphical analysis we have undertaken here is

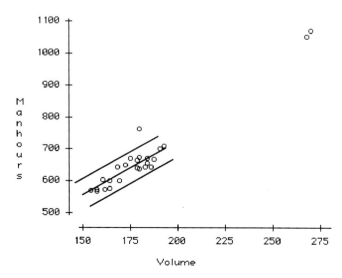

**Figure 1.21**   Scatterplot of manhours against volume enhanced with a computer generated line and a band corresponding to chance variation.

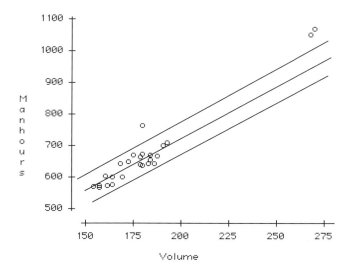

**Figure 1.22**   Scatterplot of manhours against volume enhanced with a computer generated line and a band corresponding to chance variation, extended to encompass the Christmas period.

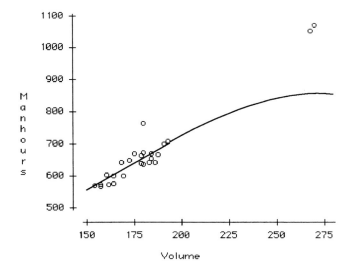

**Figure 1.23**   Scatterplot of manhours against volume enhanced with curve representing return to scale.

entirely adequate. The one mysterious aspect, the computer generated line and the associated band, can be replaced in practice by hand drawn lines. However, a more quantitative approach is required when more precise assessments of conformity to a linear relationship and of departure from conformity are sought. More significantly, when faced with more complex relationships, which may be non-linear or involve several variables rather than just two, the simple graphical approach breaks down. It is desirable, therefore, to have a quantitative version of the linear model we have introduced here.

### The simple linear regression model

The standard algebraic representation of the graphical linear model shown above is:

$$Y = \alpha + \beta X + \varepsilon.$$

If $\varepsilon$ were not there, the equation $Y = \alpha + \beta X$ would represent a line on the scatterplot whose slope was $\beta$ and whose intercept with the vertical ($Y$) axis was $\alpha$; given a value of $X$, the equation (and the line) determine a corresponding value for $Y$. However, as is evident from the scatterplot, the data to hand do not correspond to a well-defined line; $\varepsilon$ represents the deviation away from the line that varies haphazardly from point to point.

At this point, it may be helpful to revise ideas about graphs, coordinates, points on graphs, lines, etc.

---

**Exercise 1.2**   On a rough graph of $y$ against $x$, plot the points (3, 4), (0, 3), (9, 6) and the line with equation $y = 3 + \frac{1}{3} x$.

---

To complete the specification of the model, we might assume that $\varepsilon$ follows the Normal model for chance variation with mean 0 and standard deviation $\sigma$, to be determined. This version of the model, restricted to the 23 points already discussed, is illustrated in Figure 1.24.

The description of the relation between manhours and volume in the terms outlined above is referred to as the *simple linear regression model.*[9] The model attempts to *explain* the variation in manhours in terms of an assignable cause of variation, represented by the linear relation to volume, and chance causes of variation, represented by $\varepsilon$. The *parameters* of the model are $\alpha$, $\beta$ and $\sigma$. Different values for $\alpha$ and $\beta$ give us different straight lines; different values of $\sigma$ give different amounts of spread around the line. To make effective use of this model, we need to determine appropriate values for the parameters. For this example, we will find later that the values 50 and 3.3 for $\alpha$ and $\beta$ are appropriate; these values correspond to the 'computer generated line' used earlier. This leads us to use the formula

$$\hat{Y} = 50 + 3.3X$$

---

[9]   The term 'regression' arose in a particular context (see, e.g., *Introduction to the Practice of Statistics*, by D.S. Moore and G.P. McCabe, page 174, footnote); its use in general applications, however inappropriate or mysterious, is now universal.

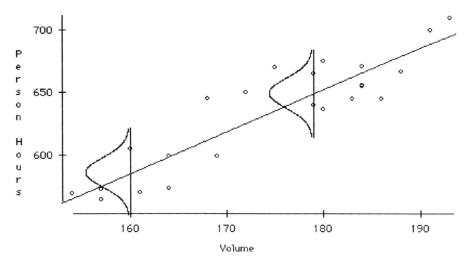

**Figure 1.24**   The simple linear regression model with Normal error.

to predict manhours when volume $X$ is expected. Furthermore, recognising the presence of chance variation, we will find that an allowance of $\pm 20$ for prediction error is appropriate. Thus, the full prediction formula is

$$\hat{Y} = 50 + 3.3X \pm 20$$

The prediction formula can also be used in retrospect, as suggested at the outset, by asking did the actual manhours conform to what would be anticipated given the actual volume? A non-conforming value suggests that there is a problem that needs to be investigated and, if necessary, corrected. Predictions can also be used by anticipating a given volume and making provision for the manhours to handle it. For example, at the start of this section, we envisaged management being able to anticipate the expected increase in volume in the weeks before Christmas and increase the labour force accordingly. However, this example also shows us the caution needed in making such predictions and, in particular, the danger of extrapolating beyond the range of the data on which the prediction formula is based. As noted in Section 1.4, model assessment is a critical necessity. A model can be assessed only against data. There are no reliable data against which to assess the validity of the simple linear regression model during the pre-Christmas period.

---

**Exercise 1.3**   Use the prediction formula to estimate the loss incurred through equipment breakdown in period 6, fiscal 1962, and to predict the *extra* manpower requirement during the Christmas period, based on the experience of period 7, fiscal 1962 and 1963.

The detailed development and application of the simple linear regression model is taken up in Chapter 6. Also developed there is the closely related idea of *correlation*.

## 1.6   Introducing the multiple regression model for forecasting postage stamp sales; a case study in problem formulation

In this section, we introduce a case study on sales forecasting in which many practical issues arise and where some relatively sophisticated statistical analysis techniques are required to make sense of the problem. As part of the case study, we will introduce a broad approach to statistical problem solving. Issues such as the choice of characteristics to study, definition of variables, index numbers, relationships between variables and other issues will be dealt with. We will also introduce a model which represents an extension of the simple linear regression model introduced in the previous section, the *multiple linear regression model*.

### Introducing the case

In January 1984, the Irish government established An Post as a commercial semi-state body to provide a postal service in the State, a service which up to then had been provided by the civil service Department of Posts and Telegraphs. At an early stage, they sought to develop a sales forecasting system to assist them in their business planning activities. As a basis for such forecasts, they had available historical data on sales going back as far as 1949, as shown in Table 1.4. Realising that they needed technical assistance, they approached a statistical consultant, whose first step was to graph the existing data.

### Looking at the data

A multiple time series plot of the data is shown in Figure 1.25 on page 34. Stamp sales and meter sales show opposite overall trends; presumably, as more companies use metered mail, less use stamped mail. Stamp sales show a sharp decline from 1961 to 1962. This is reflected in the total sales. Total sales dip sharply from 1970 to 1971, reflecting moderate dips in each of its components. All three graphs dip sharply in 1979, coinciding with an industrial dispute that occurred in the postal service during that year.

For prediction purposes, one might consider a straightforward extrapolation of the trends in the graphs shown in Figure 1.25. There are problems with this, however. Thus, while the trend in meter sales appears quite smooth up to 1977, apart from one or two dips, its behaviour is more erratic after that, even allowing for the industrial dispute in 1979. This hardly provides a basis for confident prediction. Also, there are two (or maybe three) separate trends in stamp sales, increasing up to 1961 (more or less constant up to 1968) and decreasing thereafter, allowing for the dip in 1979. There is no basis for assuming that the latter trend will continue past 1983; trend projection is thus not a feasible basis for prediction. To make any further progress with this problem, the consultant (and his clients) needed to understand more about the

**Table 1.4**  Annual sales of stamps and metered mail, 1949–83

| Year | Stamp sales[1] | Meter sales[1] | Total sales |
|------|------|------|------|
| 1949 | 245.2 | 42.0 | 287.2 |
| 1950 | 224.4 | 48.6 | 273.0 |
| 1951 | 241.3 | 52.1 | 293.4 |
| 1952 | 251.3 | 60.9 | 312.3 |
| 1953 | 236.7 | 65.8 | 302.5 |
| 1954 | 231.6 | 69.1 | 300.7 |
| 1955 | 235.8 | 75.1 | 310.8 |
| 1956 | 253.0 | 90.4 | 343.4 |
| 1957 | 262.6 | 98.1 | 360.7 |
| 1958 | 265.4 | 104.6 | 370.0 |
| 1959 | 266.0 | 107.5 | 373.4 |
| 1960 | 278.4 | 112.4 | 390.8 |
| 1961 | 277.7 | 116.9 | 394.6 |
| 1962 | 235.9 | 105.0 | 340.9 |
| 1963 | 230.0 | 105.2 | 335.2 |
| 1964 | 234.8 | 121.3 | 356.1 |
| 1965 | 228.8 | 149.0 | 377.8 |
| 1966 | 230.1 | 153.7 | 383.8 |
| 1967 | 234.3 | 162.8 | 397.1 |
| 1968 | 238.6 | 169.3 | 407.9 |
| 1969 | 242.7 | 186.5 | 429.3 |
| 1970 | 226.4 | 197.5 | 423.9 |
| 1971 | 199.4 | 172.2 | 371.6 |
| 1972 | 205.4 | 192.8 | 398.2 |
| 1973 | 201.6 | 195.9 | 397.4 |
| 1974 | 191.1 | 199.6 | 390.8 |
| 1975 | 181.0 | 213.3 | 394.3 |
| 1976 | 174.9 | 240.9 | 415.8 |
| 1977 | 181.0 | 258.4 | 439.3 |
| 1978 | 188.2 | 240.8 | 429.0 |
| 1979 | 112.5 | 163.5 | 276.0 |
| 1980 | 163.7 | 211.5 | 375.2 |
| 1981 | 162.1 | 195.3 | 357.4 |
| 1982 | 148.9 | 228.5 | 377.4 |
| 1983 | 151.2 | 259.7 | 410.9 |

[1] Sales are recorded as millions of standard stamp equivalents, that is, total revenue in a year divided by the price of a stamp for a standard sealed letter for internal delivery, and divided by 1,000,000.

causes of variation in sales over time. To assist in this, they might enquire what factors may have influenced sales during the study period.

**Influential factors**

First of all, clearly, the price of stamps is likely to affect sales; an increase will discourage sales, a decrease will have the opposite effect. Secondly, the prices of

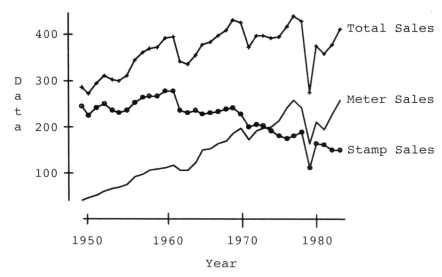

**Figure 1.25**    Annual sales of stamps and metered mail, 1949–83.

alternative services[10] are also likely to affect sales of stamps; an increase in the price of facsimile services, for example, is likely to make postal services seem more attractive. Thirdly, an increase in general economic activity in the country is likely to increase stamp sales, for at least two reasons: first, the increased activity will need increased communication to sustain it and, second, there will be more available for expenditure.

Actual variables must be chosen to represent these sources of variation. Following some brainstorming between consultant and client, they chose Real Letter Price (RLP), Real Phone Charge (RPC) and Gross National Product (GNP). RLP is the price of a standard sealed letter for within-Ireland delivery and RPC is the cost of a local telephone call, both adjusted for inflation. GNP is, informally, the total value of goods and services produced by Irish people and companies. Table 1.5 shows data on these three variables, along with the sales data. Further detail on what these variables are and why they were chosen will be discussed later.

### Viewing the relationships

Graphs again provide an effective first view of the relationship of sales with the 'explanatory' variables. For brevity, we focus here on stamp sales. Figure 1.26 on page 36 shows multiple time series plots for stamp sales and Real Letter Price. In broad terms, the pattern accords with intuition; as RLP decreases, as in the early years, sales increase, and vice versa in the later years. Careful examination will show some deviations from this pattern and will also show that the degree of increase or decrease of one relative to the other is not always the same. However, the pattern suggests that

---

[10]  Note that alternative services were limited in 1984. In more recent years, however, this situation has changed dramatically; see Chapter 8 for further comment.

**Table 1.5** Annual postal sales, GNP, Real Letter Prices and Real Phone Charges, 1949–83

| Year | Stamp sales | Meter sales | Total sales | GNP | RLP[a] | RPC[b] |
|------|-------------|-------------|-------------|-----|--------|--------|
| 1949 | 245.2 | 42 | 287.2 | 552.6 | 1.047 | 0.419 |
| 1950 | 224.4 | 48.6 | 273 | 557 | 1.031 | 0.413 |
| 1951 | 241.3 | 52.1 | 293.4 | 564.3 | 0.957 | 0.383 |
| 1952 | 251.3 | 60.9 | 312.3 | 580.1 | 0.88 | 0.352 |
| 1953 | 236.7 | 65.8 | 302.5 | 598.1 | 0.946 | 0.501 |
| 1954 | 231.6 | 69.1 | 300.7 | 603.9 | 0.998 | 0.499 |
| 1955 | 235.8 | 75.1 | 310.8 | 616 | 0.974 | 0.487 |
| 1956 | 253 | 90.4 | 343.4 | 608.3 | 0.934 | 0.622 |
| 1957 | 262.6 | 98.1 | 360.7 | 611.8 | 0.897 | 0.598 |
| 1958 | 265.4 | 104.6 | 370 | 600.9 | 0.859 | 0.572 |
| 1959 | 266 | 107.5 | 373.4 | 626.6 | 0.859 | 0.572 |
| 1960 | 278.4 | 112.4 | 390.8 | 658.9 | 0.855 | 0.57 |
| 1961 | 277.7 | 116.9 | 394.6 | 690.9 | 0.832 | 0.554 |
| 1962 | 235.9 | 105 | 340.9 | 716 | 0.997 | 0.532 |
| 1963 | 230 | 105.2 | 335.2 | 749.6 | 1.039 | 0.519 |
| 1964 | 234.8 | 121.3 | 356.1 | 780.7 | 1.113 | 0.73 |
| 1965 | 228.8 | 149 | 377.8 | 800.7 | 1.158 | 0.695 |
| 1966 | 230.1 | 153.7 | 383.8 | 806.8 | 1.124 | 0.675 |
| 1967 | 234.3 | 162.8 | 397.1 | 848.4 | 1.09 | 0.654 |
| 1968 | 238.6 | 169.3 | 407.9 | 919.4 | 1.04 | 0.624 |
| 1969 | 242.7 | 186.5 | 429.3 | 970.7 | 1.164 | 0.582 |
| 1970 | 226.4 | 197.5 | 423.9 | 1,002.6 | 1.206 | 0.714 |
| 1971 | 199.4 | 172.2 | 371.6 | 1,037.3 | 1.57 | 0.655 |
| 1972 | 205.4 | 192.8 | 398.2 | 1,112.5 | 1.453 | 0.603 |
| 1973 | 201.6 | 195.9 | 397.4 | 1,154.5 | 1.464 | 0.541 |
| 1974 | 191.1 | 199.6 | 390.8 | 1,201.7 | 1.526 | 0.557 |
| 1975 | 181 | 213.3 | 394.3 | 1,223.5 | 1.616 | 0.544 |
| 1976 | 174.9 | 240.9 | 415.8 | 1,229.7 | 1.764 | 0.626 |
| 1977 | 181 | 258.4 | 439.3 | 1,316.2 | 1.677 | 0.551 |
| 1978 | 188.2 | 240.8 | 429 | 1,388.4 | 1.598 | 0.639 |
| 1979 | 112.5 | 163.5 | 276 | 1,422.8 | 1.526 | 0.564 |
| 1980 | 163.7 | 211.5 | 375.2 | 1,462.2 | 1.607 | 0.577 |
| 1981 | 162.1 | 195.3 | 357.4 | 1,492.6 | 1.835 | 0.58 |
| 1982 | 148.9 | 228.5 | 377.4 | 1,473.2 | 2.114 | 0.601 |
| 1983 | 151.2 | 259.7 | 410.9 | 1,462.6 | 1.993 | 0.651 |

[a] The Real Letter Price is the price of a standard sealed internal letter divided by the Consumer Price Index (CPI).
[b] The Real Phone Charge (RPC) is the price of a local telephone call divided by the CPI.

there is a fairly consistent relationship. How to exploit this relationship for prediction purposes is another matter; we will deal with that question in some detail, later.

Figure 1.27 shows multiple time series plots for stamp sales and Real Phone Charge. The relationship is not so clear in this case.

Finally, Figure 1.28 on page 37 shows the relationship between GNP and stamp sales. There may be a relationship here. The initial upward trend in sales corresponds to a slow increase in GNP; the later downward trend in sales corresponds to a faster rate of growth of GNP. Note that this is counter to our earlier intuition. More detailed exploration and possible exploitation of this relationship will follow later.

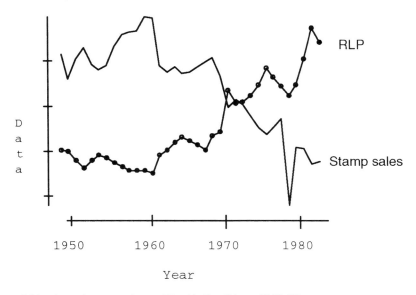

**Figure 1.26**   Annual stamp sales and Real Letter Prices, 1949–83.

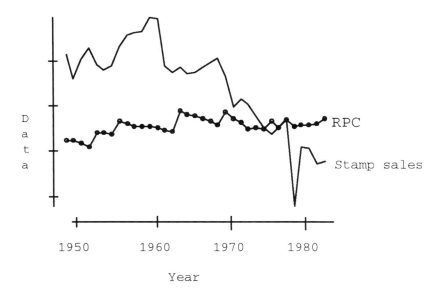

**Figure 1.27**   Annual stamp sales and Real Phone Charges, 1949–83.

### What are these data?

Before arriving at any conclusions on the basis of this graphical analysis or contemplating alternative analyses, we need to understand what these data represent. The first step is to understand the units of measurement.

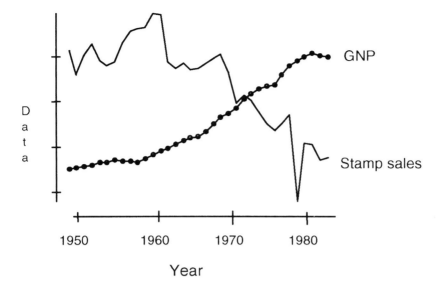

**Figure 1.28**   Annual stamp sales and GNP, 1949–83.

*Sales*

The footnote to the original data table says that 'sales are recorded as millions of standard stamp equivalents, that is, total revenue in a year divided by the price of a stamp for a standard sealed letter for internal delivery, and divided by 1,000,000'. Why is this complicated definition of sales used? We could just study the revenue from stamp sales. However, since the price of stamps changed from time to time, this would not allow fair comparisons from time to time; sales may have increased just because the price went up and not because of any real improvement in performance. Technically, the revenue is said to be subject to inflation.

Revenue divided by the price of a stamp gives a measure of the *volume* of sales; if all stamps were the same price, this would be just the total number of stamps sold. However, stamps are sold at a range of different prices and different postal services cost different amounts. Separately calculating volume of sales for each of the many categories would be a formidable task as the data were stored on paper. As a compromise, total revenue was divided by the price of a stamp for a standard sealed letter for delivery within Ireland. Such a stamp was taken to be a standard unit, called a *standard stamp equivalent* by An Post. Other postal services, for example, over-weight sealed letters, unsealed letters, parcels, overseas delivery, may be thought of as requiring an appropriate number of standard units.[11] This number may be less than 1. For example, an unsealed standard letter for delivery internally cost 28p in 1993, while a standard unit cost 32p. Thus, the stamp for an unsealed standard letter for

---

[11]   This is similar to the *standard call unit* used by telecom service providers representing a local call of fixed duration. Long distance and overseas calls for varying durations are evaluated in terms of numbers of standard call units, and charged accordingly.

delivery internally is 28/32 = 0.875 standard stamp equivalents. Dividing by 1,000,000 merely gives the count as millions of stamps (or standard stamp equivalents), and saves us having to peruse eight or nine digits in each number in the table.

*Real Letter Price*

Having defined the standard stamp equivalent, it seemed sensible to use the price of a stamp for a standard internal letter to represent stamp prices in general. A problem with using price is that part of the change in the price of a stamp is related to changes in prices of goods and services as a whole; there is a tendency for them to increase over time, reflecting inflation. What is important is the relative change in the price of a stamp, relative to changes in the prices of other goods and services. This is usually established through the use of a price index to *deflate* the nominal price of a stamp. The Consumer Price Index (CPI) is an average price of a suitably representative range of goods and services, compiled and published by the Government Central Statistics Office (CSO) at regular intervals. Relative changes from year to year are important. Usually, the CPI for a chosen base year is adjusted to be 100 and CPI values for subsequent years are adjusted *pro rata*. Then, the adjusted CPI in any given year shows immediately the *percentage* change since the base year. Thus, in the table in Exercise 1.4 below, the CPI in 1950 was 1% higher than in 1949, the CPI in 1951 was 9% higher than in 1949.

The ratio of the nominal price of a stamp (the price that appears on the stamp) in a given year to the CPI for that year is called the *real price* of a stamp. It was calculated for each year in the time period covered by the data, 1949–83, and used in the analysis.

---

**Exercise 1.4**   The nominal price of a standard stamp and the CPI for each of the years 1949–54 (1949 CPI = 100) were as follows:

| Year | 1949 | 1950 | 1951 | 1952 | 1953 | 1954 |
|------|------|------|------|------|------|------|
| Nominal price | 2.5p | 2.5p | 2.5p | 2.5p | 3p | 3p |
| CPI | 100 | 101 | 109 | 118 | 124.8 | 125.2 |

Calculate the real price of a standard stamp for each year.

---

*Real Phone Charge*

The second set of factors referred to above as possible influences on stamp sales was prices of alternative services. In recent years, there has been a proliferation of such services, with facsimile, electronic mail, express mail, couriers and companies doing their own local message deliveries all increasing dramatically and all, presumably, competing with the postal service. For the period covered by the data, however, the main competitor to the postal service was the telephone service. As with the postal service, there is a range of services and prices. The price of a local telephone call from a private telephone was chosen to represent the general level of telephone prices, and the nominal price was deflated by the CPI adjusted to 100 in 1949.

*General economic activity*

There are several ways of measuring the level of general economic activity. We can measure total income, total expenditure or total production, totalled across all people and companies in the country. For the purposes of this project, such measures will be so closely related to each other that it does not much matter which is used; a change in one is accompanied by a similar pattern of change in others so that the relation of changes in stamp sales to changes in general economic activity level will be similar for any of the standard measures of the latter. In this case, Gross National Product (GNP), a production measure compiled by the CSO, was used.

**Final problem formulation**

At this stage, the consultant had enough information to proceed to the task of producing a numerical formula for forecasting stamp sales, given possible values for the other variables for which data were available. The next step was to study the relationship between sales and the other variable in some depth. He proposed using *multiple linear regression* to model this relationship; from this modelling exercise would emerge a suitable prediction formula. He explained that this was an extension of simple linear regression which involved modelling the relationship of one variable to *one* other variable. He produced scatterplots to indicate that there was some evidence of linear relations, but with some unusual patterns present; see Figure 1.29.

These suggested that sales were most strongly related to RLP, followed by GNP, and that RPC appeared to have a weak relationship. By using multiple linear regression, the consultant hoped to extract from the data more information about the relationships than would be possible using just simple linear regression. He indicated, however, that some relatively sophisticated methods would have to be used to identify and validate an appropriate prediction formula.

*Terms of reference*

Having come this far in the process of *formulating* the prediction problem, consultant and clients agreed to formalise their relationship by specifying *terms of reference* which would lay down what the consultant undertook to complete and deliver. The terms of reference finally agreed were as follows:

1. Identify and collect the relevant macro-economic data.
2. Establish a database containing the data needed for model building.
3. Identify, estimate and check a dynamic regression model suitable for the following purposes:
   (a) medium-term (one to five years) forecasting of aggregate demand for postal services;

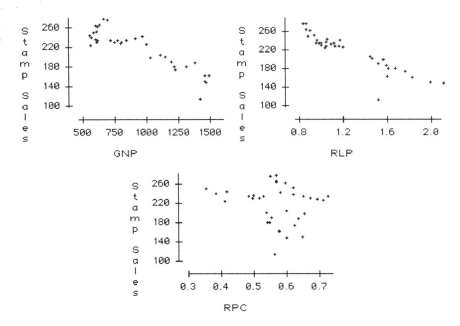

**Figure 1.29**   Scatterplots of stamp sales versus GNP, RLP and RPC.

(b) analysis of the effects of levels of general economic activity, postal prices and the prices of competing services, on aggregate demand for postal services;

(c) use as a benchmark for the analysis of the effects of demand stimulation activities.

---

**Exercise 1.5**   These terms of reference may be criticised in that they use over-elaborate language and refer to tasks already completed, twice in one case. Simplify.

---

## Multiple linear regression

When reporting results to the client, it is appropriate to give an overview of the technical analysis used to produce the results, without getting into the technical details. Here, we give a brief outline of the multiple linear regression model before specifying and illustrating a prediction formula derived from an application of the model to the available data. (Multiple regression is treated in more detail in Chapter 8.) Note that several versions of the model were tried and tested before one was chosen and that not all the data was used in determining the final model.

Following the notational style established in Section 1.5 for the simple linear regression model, the variables being considered are denoted as follows:

| Stamp sales | denoted by | $Y$; |
| Gross National Product (GNP) | denoted by | $X_1$; |
| Real Letter Price (RLP) | denoted by | $X_2$; |
| Real Phone Charge (RPC) | denoted by | $X_3$. |

The multiple linear regression model is represented by the equation

$$Y = \alpha + \beta_1 X_1 + \beta_2 X_2 + \beta_3 X_3 + \varepsilon.$$

Here, $X_1$, $X_2$ and $X_3$ are referred to as *explanatory* variables, $Y$ is the *explained* variable, $\alpha$, $\beta_1$, $\beta_2$ and $\beta_3$ are the *regression coefficients* and $\varepsilon$ is referred to as the *error variable* or *disturbance term*. If we assume that $\varepsilon$ is centred on 0 and has standard deviation $\sigma$, then $\alpha$, $\beta_1$, $\beta_2$, $\beta_3$ and $\sigma$ are the *parameters* of the model; different values for the parameters give different versions of the model. Choosing values for these parameters appropriate to the data to hand is an iterative process of successively trying and testing different versions of the model, in the process identifying possible exceptional cases which do not conform to the multiple regression model. The end result of this process is a prediction formula which incorporates *estimates* of the regression coefficients as well as *error bounds* which reflect what we may regard as chance variation in the stamp sales process.

It would be inappropriate here to use Shewhart's term *assignable causes* in connection with the $X$ variables. It cannot be assumed that changes in GNP, for example, have a direct causal influence on stamp sales. Causal relationships in socio-economic systems are notoriously complex. In this case, for instance, stamp sales constitute a part (if a very small part) of GNP. Frequently, relations between variables change over time, through the influence of other variables which may not affect relations in the short term.[12] The idea of cause and effect is hotly debated in socio-economic circles.

## Using the prediction formula

The prediction formula, including error bounds, that emerged from the regression modelling exercise in this case was

$$\text{Sales} = 340 - 0.0316 \text{ GNP} - 70.2 \text{ RLP} \pm 8.$$

It is noted that RPC did not contribute to the formula.

A simple application of the formula is to measure the effect of the industrial action in 1979. The 'prediction' formula, with the 1979 values for GNP and RLP substituted, should give a value for sales that might have been anticipated without the industrial action; the difference between 'forecast' and 'actual' measures the effect of the industrial action. The relevant values were:

$$\text{GNP}(79) = 1422.8, \qquad \text{RLP}(79) = 1.526$$

leading to a prediction of

---

[12] In Chapter 8, where this case study is explored in more depth, we will see that it is plausible to assume that two different multiple regression equations applied to these data over different time periods.

$$340 - 0.0316 \times 1422.8 - 70.2 \times 1.526 \pm 8 = 188 \pm 8.$$

Actual sales were 112.5. The difference is 75.5. Allowing for prediction error, this may be reported as

$$75.5 \pm 8 \text{ million standard stamp equivalents.}$$

*Predicted sales for 1984, 1985*

A difficulty that arises when we attempt actual prediction is that the values of the X variables are not known in advance and must themselves be predicted. Thus, in 1984, the GNP for 1984 is not known. (In fact, the GNP for 1984 is not finally known until late 1985; the data required for its computation do not become available to the Central Statistics Office until then. The CSO produces a provisional value early in 1985, based on the data then available, but subject to change when all the data are in.) Fortunately, reasonably accurate predictions are available from a number of agencies. For present purposes, the prediction made by the Central Bank of Ireland is used. Also, the value of RLP is not known in advance; it depends on the inflation rate also compiled by the CSO when all the necessary data are available. Again, fortunately, the Central Bank provides predictions of the inflation rate.

The Central Bank predictions for 1984 and 1985 were as follows:

|  | 1984 | 1985 |
|---|---|---|
| GNP | + 1.5% | + 1.5% |
| Inflation | + 8.6% | + 5.5% |

From Table 1.5, page 35, GNP(1983) = 1462.6. Hence the predicted GNP(1984) is

$$1462.6 \times 1.015 = 1484.5.$$

An Post was proposing to make no change to the nominal stamp price (26p) in 1984 or 1985. An inflation rate of 8.6% for 1984 meant that the 'average' price of all goods and services would rise by 8.6%. If the nominal stamp prices was to stay fixed then, relative to all (other) goods and services, its real price would fall by 8.6%. Hence, the Real Letter Price was predicted to fall by a factor of 1.086 in 1984. From Table 1.5, RLP(83) = 1.993 so the predicted RLP(1984) is

$$1.993/1.086 = 1.835.$$

Substituting these values in the prediction formula gives predicted sales for 1984 of

$$340 - 0.0316 \times 1484.5 - 70.2 \times 1.835 \pm 8 = 164 \pm 8.$$

---

**Exercise 1.6**   Calculate the predicted stamp sales for 1985; note that the predicted changes in GNP and inflation are applied to the predicted 1984 figures.

A caveat must be applied to the error bounds reported here. These reflect anticipated chance variation in the stamp sales process. There are, however, other sources of prediction error including, in this case, the errors involved in predicting the $X$ variables. One approach to this is to use 'scenario' forecasting, specifying high and low values for the $X$ variables (which may be obtained from the Central Bank) and making predictions using all combinations of these values. However, we will not pursue this issue here.

Although An Post did not propose raising their own prices in the short term, they could anticipate the effects of raising prices with the assistance of the prediction formula. For example, a 5% rise in nominal stamp price in 1984 would mean a predicted RLP(1984) of

$$1.835 \times 1.05 = 1.927.$$

Substituting this instead of 1.835 in the prediction formula leads to a prediction of

$$340 - 0.0316 \times 1484.5 - 70.2 \times 1.927 \pm 8 = 158 \pm 8,$$

that is, a drop of around 6 million standard stamp equivalents. Further 'scenario' forecasts can be made, as in the following exercise. Indeed, these scenarios can be combined with scenario forecasting of GNP and inflation rates to provide a more comprehensive guide for decision making.

---

**Exercise 1.7**   Predict the effects on stamp sales in 1984 and 1985 of 1%, 5% and 10% increases in stamp prices and 1% and 5% decreases in stamp prices.

---

*Interpreting regression coefficients*

Rather than recalculate the full prediction formula to find the effect of changing stamp prices, there is a more direct calculation, which also leads to a useful interpretation of individual regression coefficients. Note that the only change in the prediction formula when the price was increased by 5% was to replace the RLP value of 1.835 with the 5% higher value of 1.927, that is, an absolute increase of 0.092. This is then multiplied by $-70.2$ to gave a decrease in sales of

$$-70.2 \times 0.092 = -6,$$

as noted above. More generally, whatever An Post adds to RLP is multiplied by $-70.2$ to find the predicted change in stamp sales.

This leads to the formal interpretation of a regression coefficient as:

the change in $Y$ when the corresponding $X$ is increased by 1 unit
*while the other X variables remain unchanged.*

The last restriction is unimportant in the present example; a change in stamp prices will have a negligible effect on GNP. However, if RPC had been included in the prediction formula, then a change in stamp prices by An Post could well induce Bord Telecom (who ran the telephone service) to change their prices and those changes would also affect predicted stamp sales. With more complicated prediction equations, there may be more complicated relations between the $X$ variables and, in those circumstances, the individual interpretation of individual regression coefficients becomes problematical.

## Monitoring prediction performance

Having constructed a prediction formula based on historical data, it is important that its performance be monitored over time by comparing predicted sales with actual sales figures when they become available. As an example, note that actual stamp sales for 1984 were 163.6 million standard stamp equivalents which is 3.9 million higher than the predicted value of 158, well within prediction error. It also turned out that actual GNP was 1487.5, marginally higher than the predicted 1484.5, while actual RLP was 1.835, identical to the predicted value. This performance lends some confidence to the validity of the prediction formula in the short term.

If it turned out that actual was substantially different from predicted, then either the regression model did not adequately reflect the stamp sales process up to 1983 or the process and its relations with GNP and RLP had changed since 1983. Either outcome should prompt a review of both the model and the process, with a view to identifying important changes.[13] Of course, short term changes may be difficult to identify but knowing that they exist is better than not knowing.

## An approach to statistical problem solving

In this case study, we have gone through (or referred to) a range of activities involved in finding a statistical solution for a management problem. Here, we identify such problem solving activities and group them under four broad headings:

- Formulation;
- Data production;
- Data analysis;
- Implementation.

A more detailed listing is:

- Formulation
  - Define objectives
  - Identify variables
  - Specify model
  - Determine data requirements
- Data production
  - Existing source
  - Observational study
  - Sample survey
  - Controlled experiment

---

[13]  Revision of economic forecasts is all too frequent. A cynic once described an economist as someone who can tell you tomorrow why yesterday's forecast didn't work out today.

- Data analysis
  - Initial data analysis
  - Model estimation
  - Inference
  - Interpretation
- Implementation
  - Reporting
  - Consulting
  - Monitoring
  - Updating

Some of the activities listed have not arisen in this study. Thus, the data were available from existing sources; special data collection exercises such as sample surveys or controlled experiments were not required. Model estimation was deferred, inference about model parameters will also be considered in some detail later. However, all other activities did arise in some form.

---

**Exercise 1.8**   Review the stamp sales case study and identify each point arising with one or more points in the above list.

---

## 1.7   A strategic forecasting problem

Grafton Group plc is an independent, profit growth oriented company operating in Great Britain and Ireland whose main activities are builders and plumbers merchanting, DIY retailing and strategic manufacturing in related areas.

The group aims to achieve above average returns for its shareholders. Grafton strategy is to maintain strong positions in business serving the British and Irish building sectors, to develop in other British and Irish markets, and to grow in businesses with which it is familiar.

A key factor affecting the Group's trading level is the number of new houses being built. This has strategic implications for the development of the company. Knowledge of this will assist in determining future levels of investment and consequent staffing levels. It will also provide assistance in making profit projections required by the Stock Exchange.

In 2001, the company embarked on a project to better understand the new housing market in Ireland. As a first step towards strategic decision making, a company executive had acquired data on numbers of housing completions in Ireland, quarterly from 1978 to 2000. The data are shown in Table 1.6.

**Initial data analysis**

Figure 1.30 shows a line plot or time series plot of quarterly housing completions for the 92 quarters, numbered 1–92, of the 23-year period, 1978–2000, enhanced with a

**Table 1.6**   Housing completions, quarterly, 1978–2000

| Quarter | 1978 | 1979 | 1980 | 1981 | 1982 | 1983 | 1984 | 1985 |
|---------|------|------|------|------|------|------|------|------|
| Q1 | 5,777 | 7,276 | 3,538 | 6,642 | 5,981 | 4,859 | 5,129 | 4,947 |
| Q2 | 4,772 | 4,510 | 6,001 | 4,710 | 4,883 | 5,862 | 4,671 | 5,188 |
| Q3 | 4,579 | 4,278 | 5,879 | 5,570 | 5,354 | 4,663 | 4,947 | 3,930 |
| Q4 | 4,243 | 4,274 | 6,383 | 6,314 | 4,894 | 4,564 | 3,195 | 3,360 |

| Quarter | 1986 | 1987 | 1988 | 1989 | 1990 | 1991 | 1992 | 1993 |
|---------|------|------|------|------|------|------|------|------|
| Q1 | 5,186 | 4,144 | 3,682 | 3,554 | 4,296 | 4,692 | 4,155 | 3,684 |
| Q2 | 3,719 | 3,363 | 3,298 | 3,985 | 4,477 | 3,898 | 5,603 | 4,487 |
| Q3 | 4,533 | 4,391 | 3,747 | 5,277 | 5,011 | 4,600 | 5,919 | 5,121 |
| Q4 | 3,726 | 3,478 | 3,477 | 4,484 | 4,752 | 5,282 | 5,305 | 6,009 |

| Quarter | 1994 | 1995 | 1996 | 1997 | 1998 | 1999 | 2000 | |
|---------|------|------|------|------|------|------|------|------|
| Q1 | 4,291 | 5,770 | 6,582 | 7,434 | 8,010 | 9,930 | 10,302 | |
| Q2 | 5,266 | 6,149 | 7,203 | 8,799 | 9,506 | 10,227 | 11,590 | |
| Q3 | 6,871 | 6,806 | 7,634 | 9,140 | 10,103 | 10,788 | 11,892 | |
| Q4 | 7,160 | 7,879 | 8,713 | 10,081 | 11,474 | 12,079 | 12,873 | |

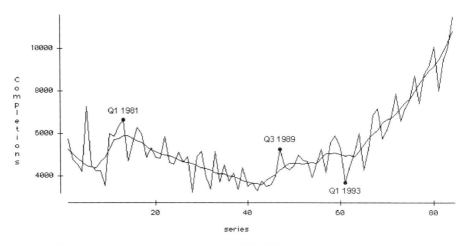

**Figure 1.30**   Housing completions, quarterly, 1978–2000.

'smoother'. This smoother is a version of the smoother used in Figure 1.2 to emphasise the seasonal effect in weekly bar sales.

Visual inspection of the plot suggests four distinct patterns. During the first three
years, the number of housing completions per quarter appeared erratic. From 1981
until 1988, there appeared to be a strong negative trend. This coincided with a period
of weak performance by the Irish economy. At the end of this period, there appeared
to be a large jump followed by a period of relative stability, from the third quarter of
1989. Then, starting in 1993, there was a very strong upward trend. This coincided

with the phase in the Irish economy popularly referred to as the 'Celtic Tiger Economy', during which the country moved from being regarded internationally as underdeveloped to being more fully developed.

In principle, much may be learned by studying the trends in the data and changes therein and relating them to changes in key economic variables and to Government interventions in the housing market, such as providing housing subsidies to first time buyers and changing tax allowances relating to house mortgage interest payments. On the other hand, it may be argued that the conditions that applied in earlier periods were not relevant to the strategic forecasting problem being addressed by the Grafton Group. This led to a decision to study recent trends initially, with a view to making short to medium term forecasts, and subsequently turning to the earlier data, to see what lessons might be learned that might suggest qualifications to forecasts made on the basis of recent trends.

Figure 1.31 shows the housing completions data for the period of the Celtic Tiger Economy. Clearly, there is a strong positive trend. Closer examination reveals that, within each year, completions increase each quarter but fall back at the start of the next year. Figure 1.32 shows the same data with separate quarterly trends, to emphasise the strong trend and the strong quarterly effects.

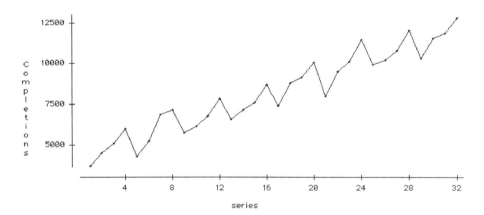

**Figure 1.31** Housing completions, quarterly, 1993–2000.

## Model formulation

Given the dominance of the underlying trend, it is reasonable to start with a simple linear regression model, as introduced in Section 1.5, of the form

$$\text{Completions} = \alpha + \beta \times \text{Time} + \varepsilon.$$

Here, the time variable simply measures the time in quarters, starting from the first quarter in 1993; its values are shown in the third column of Table 1.7, page 49. Computer analysis, such as that used to produce the manhours prediction formula discussed in Section 1.5, in this case leads to estimated values of 3,937 and 259 for $\alpha$ and $\beta$, and the prediction formula

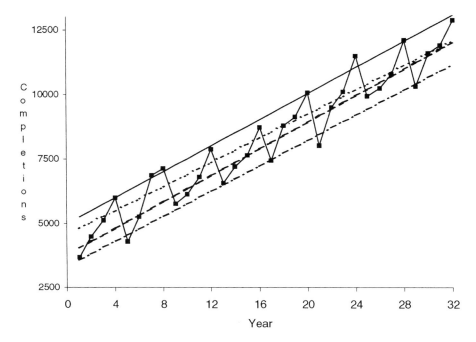

**Figure 1.32**    Housing completions, quarterly, 1993–2000, with quarterly trends.

$$\text{Predicted completions} = 3{,}937 + 259 \times \text{Time}.$$

This is of limited value, since it ignores the obvious quarterly effect. However, it does tell us that completions have been growing at an average rate of around 260 houses per quarter, or $4 \times 260 = 1{,}040$ houses per year.

It is tempting to suggest that the quarterly trends are, in fact, parallel and that the slight differences in slope seen in Figure 1.32 may be explained by chance variation. If this is so, then a relatively straightforward multiple regression model may be fitted to these data and used to produce a simple quarterly forecasting formula. The model will have a common slope, or $\beta$ value, and separate intercepts, or $\alpha$ values, for each quarter. To specify this model, we introduce special variables called *indicator* variables.[14] The new variables are labelled Q1, Q2, Q3 and Q4, one corresponding to each quarter. Their values are shown in Table 1.7, alongside the corresponding values for Housing Completions and Time. Note that Q1 has the value 1 in every first quarter and 0 in quarters 2, 3 and 4. Thus the indicator variable Q1 indicates by its values whether the corresponding data points are first quarter points, value 1, or not, value 0. The values of Q2, Q3 and Q4 are similarly interpreted.

The model may now be specified as

$$\text{Completions} = \alpha_1 \times \text{Q1} + \alpha_2 \times \text{Q2} + \alpha_3 \times \text{Q3} + \alpha_4 \times \text{Q4} + \beta \times \text{Time} + \varepsilon.$$

---

[14]    Econometricians refer to them as *dummy* variables.

**Table 1.7**  Housing completions and quarterly indicators, 1993–2000

| Year | Quarter | Time | Completions | Q1 | Q2 | Q3 | Q4 |
|------|---------|------|-------------|----|----|----|----|
| 1993 | 1 | 1 | 3,684 | 1 | 0 | 0 | 0 |
| 1993 | 2 | 2 | 4,487 | 0 | 1 | 0 | 0 |
| 1993 | 3 | 3 | 5,121 | 0 | 0 | 1 | 0 |
| 1993 | 4 | 4 | 6,009 | 0 | 0 | 0 | 1 |
| 1994 | 1 | 5 | 4,291 | 1 | 0 | 0 | 0 |
| 1994 | 2 | 6 | 5,266 | 0 | 1 | 0 | 0 |
| 1994 | 3 | 7 | 6,871 | 0 | 0 | 1 | 0 |
| 1994 | 4 | 8 | 7,160 | 0 | 0 | 0 | 1 |
| 1995 | 1 | 9 | 5,770 | 1 | 0 | 0 | 0 |
| 1995 | 2 | 10 | 6,149 | 0 | 1 | 0 | 0 |
| 1995 | 3 | 11 | 6,806 | 0 | 0 | 1 | 0 |
| 1995 | 4 | 12 | 7,879 | 0 | 0 | 0 | 1 |
| 1996 | 1 | 13 | 6,582 | 1 | 0 | 0 | 0 |
| 1996 | 2 | 14 | 7,203 | 0 | 1 | 0 | 0 |
| 1996 | 3 | 15 | 7,634 | 0 | 0 | 1 | 0 |
| 1996 | 4 | 16 | 8,713 | 0 | 0 | 0 | 1 |
| 1997 | 1 | 17 | 7,434 | 1 | 0 | 0 | 0 |
| 1997 | 2 | 18 | 8,799 | 0 | 1 | 0 | 0 |
| 1997 | 3 | 19 | 9,140 | 0 | 0 | 1 | 0 |
| 1997 | 4 | 20 | 10,081 | 0 | 0 | 0 | 1 |
| 1998 | 1 | 21 | 8,010 | 1 | 0 | 0 | 0 |
| 1998 | 2 | 22 | 9,506 | 0 | 1 | 0 | 0 |
| 1998 | 3 | 23 | 10,103 | 0 | 0 | 1 | 0 |
| 1998 | 4 | 24 | 11,474 | 0 | 0 | 0 | 1 |
| 1999 | 1 | 25 | 9,930 | 1 | 0 | 0 | 0 |
| 1999 | 2 | 26 | 10,227 | 0 | 1 | 0 | 0 |
| 1999 | 3 | 27 | 10,788 | 0 | 0 | 1 | 0 |
| 1999 | 4 | 28 | 12,079 | 0 | 0 | 0 | 1 |
| 2000 | 1 | 29 | 10,302 | 1 | 0 | 0 | 0 |
| 2000 | 2 | 30 | 11,590 | 0 | 1 | 0 | 0 |
| 2000 | 3 | 31 | 11,892 | 0 | 0 | 1 | 0 |
| 2000 | 4 | 32 | 12,873 | 0 | 0 | 0 | 1 |

This model provides a separate prediction formula for each quarter. For example, to predict completions for a future first quarter, where Q1 = 1 and Q2, Q3 and Q4 are all 0, the prediction formula is

$$\text{Completions} = \alpha_1 + \beta \times \text{Time},$$

a simple linear regression formula, with suitable values for $\alpha_1$ and $\beta$. For the first quarter of 2001, when Time is 33, the formula becomes

$$\text{Completions} = \alpha_1 + \beta \times 33.$$

To predict a future second quarter value for Completions, note that Q2 is 1 while Q1, Q3 and Q4 are 0, so the prediction formula becomes

$$\text{Completions} = \alpha_2 + \beta \times \text{Time},$$

another simple linear regression formula with the same slope coefficient, $\beta$, but a different intercept.

---

**Exercise 1.9**   Write down the prediction formulas for future third and fourth quarters.

---

### Generating a prediction formula

A modelling exercise similar to that carried out in the stamp sales forecasting problem of Section 1.6 may be applied here; the values displayed in Table 1.7 are entered into appropriate statistical software, instead of the values displayed in Table 1.5. Further details are the subject of the Laboratory Exercise in Chapter 9. As a result of such an exercise, the following general prediction formula emerged:

Predicted completions

$$= 3{,}248 \times Q1 + 3{,}901 \times Q2 + 4{,}174 \times Q3 + 5{,}031 \times Q4 + 250 \times \text{Time} \pm 500.$$

---

**Exercise 1.10**   Write down separate prediction formulas for each of the four quarters. Make predictions for each quarter of 2001 and of 2002.

---

## 1.8   Researching youth technology markets; sample surveys

The growth in the spending power of young people and the concurrent growth in their interest and expertise in communications technology, viz., mobile phones (cell phones) and the internet, has led to considerable interest in the youth market for communications related products. It is suggested that the current youth market is the first generation to have the opportunity to integrate technology across all aspects of their lives, from education and information to entertainment and personal communications. For companies interested in supplying this market, relevant market research is vital.

### Generation T

Amárach[15] Consulting, a specialist in predictive market research, consumer trend analysis and business forecasting, provides a market research service called Generation T which tracks the impact of new technologies on Irish youth markets in terms of usage, buying intentions and branding. Every six months, Amárach conducts interviews with a sample of 15–24 year olds in which they seek answers to questions such as

- What is the current and forecast penetration of mobile phones among the 15–24 year old age cohort?
- What is the market share of the different mobile phone service providers?
- How are mobile phones used: specifically, what is the extent of text messaging, ring tones, use of WAP service, games, etc.?

---

[15]   The Gaelic language word for 'tomorrow'; pronounced 'amawruck'.

- What is the average monthly expenditure of youth mobile owners?
- What is the level of interest in future mobile propositions – attitudes to and interest in using a range of new mobile services?
- What are the attitudes to online and mobile marketing?
- How many 15–24 year olds use PCs and the internet?
- What is the internet used for?
- How many are currently transacting online – specifically, online shopping and internet banking?
- What are general attitudes to marketing communications?

In addition, they provide a demographic overview of the 15–24 year old market, with data on age, gender, working and education status, region, spending power, etc., background information which is vital for exploiting the answers to the substantive questions.

Amárach makes the results of this research available to a range of clients including some of Ireland's main telecommunications suppliers (fixed and mobile) and financial institutions. Their clients have varying interests and research objectives. For example, a client financial institution is concerned primarily about the opportunities these new channels offer for communicating and transacting with the youth market, that is, will youth mobile owners use their mobiles to check their bank balances, how will they react if they get a text message from a bank advertising a special offer, are they interested in online banking, are they buying online, and if not, do they need a credit card to buy online, etc.

*Exploiting the results; identifying a business opportunity*

A clear conclusion emerging from these surveys is that mobile phones are considerably more important to the youth market than fixed lines are. They prefer using a mobile and if they had to choose between a fixed line and a mobile a majority would opt for a mobile. How does a fixed line company react to this and prevent loss of fixed line minutes to mobiles? Specific questions were asked regarding interest in using a fixed line handset that offers much the same functionality as mobile handsets, in particular, new fixed line handsets which have a text messaging function. The results from this research combined with other research conducted suggested a market existed for fixed line handsets with mobile handset features. Encouraged by this, a client telecommunications company started to market cordless fixed line handsets with a text messaging facility, caller display and phone book storage, that is, similar in design and functionality to a mobile handset. The marketing campaign was directed at the youth market. The aim was to ensure that when a fixed line is available, i.e. when the mobile phone owner is at home, they will be more inclined to use a fixed line rather than a mobile phone.

*Exploiting trends, changing emphasis*

A key conclusion emerging from tracking trends over time is that mobile ownership among this age cohort is reaching saturation levels. Figure 1.33 shows the numbers, per cent, of 15–24 year olds that have a mobile phone primarily for their own use,

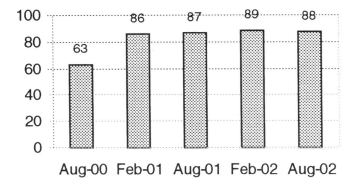

**Figure 1.33**  Mobile phone ownership, per cent, August 2000–August 2002.

according to five six-monthly surveys from August 2000. Following an apparent surge from 63% between August 2000 and February 2001, there seems to have been a levelling off at just under 90% in the later periods. This suggests that the market is very close to saturation level.

It is likely that future growth in the marketplace, in terms of new users, will be limited. In such circumstances, mobile phone service providers need to turn their attention to increasing average revenue per user, rather than relying on new users for revenue growth. For Amárach, this means that ongoing market research should be designed to identify mobile services that mobile phone owners are willing to pay for, in addition to simply voice and text messaging.

**Sample surveys**

The research methodology used by Amárach is called *sample surveying*. In designing and conducting the sample survey, the aim is to ask appropriate questions of a small sample of 15–24 year olds with a view to providing information that is representative of the full population of 15–24 year olds in the country. To achieve this, considerable care is needed in

• specifying objectives and identifying data requirements;
• questionnaire design;
• sample design;
• field work; and
• data processing, analysis and reporting.

Substantial issues arise in each of these stages of survey design, implementation and analysis. Thus, considerable consultation with clients will be needed to elucidate objectives and data requirements. This parallels the formulation stage in the approach to statistical problem solving outlined in Section 1.6.

*Questionnaire design*

In questionnaire design, the key requirement is to match the questions asked in the questionnaire with the research questions such as those posed earlier. This may be straightforward for simple factual questions but may not be for other questions. For example, it is relatively easy to establish how many use mobile phones, which service providers they use and what mobile phone features they use, as in the first three research questions listed above. However, it may be more difficult to establish monthly expenditure; memory retrieval is notoriously error prone when it comes to such matters. Also, establishing attitudes to and interest in using a range of new mobile services is not straightforward. Great care is needed with the wording of such questions. Consider, for example, one of the questions used by Amárach whereby interviewees are asked to state their levels of interest in

buying a can of coke/chocolate bars/snacks from a vending machine by sending it a text message and having the money added to your phone bill/debiting your phone credit available.

and compare to asking for levels of interest in

buying a can of coke/chocolate bars/snacks from a vending machine by sending it a text message,

where the reference to cost is omitted. On the basis of extensive research carried out into the effects of varying question wording, it is reasonable to expect a considerably higher expression of interest to result from the alternative wording; making the question more specific by adding the reference to cost, as in the Amárach wording, is likely to result in a lower level of interest being expressed. However, the Amárach question is more realistic and more closely in line with the research interests of their clients, who want to identify services that young people are willing to pay for.

*Sample design*

Amárach Consulting described their February 2002 sample of 15–24 year olds as 'nationally representative (with) inter-locking quota controls set in terms of age and gender, additional controls for region and social class (with) 309 face-to-face interviews'. This describes one of several approaches to sample design that are available. Virtually all sample designs aim to be 'representative'. In this case, the implication is that quantities, percentages, etc., calculated from the sample will be similar to the same quantities, percentages, etc., calculated from the population. The *quota controls* which feature in the design are intended to achieve this for the variables indicated. For example, the male/female balance in the 15–24 year old population is 51%/49%. When selecting interviewees, the numbers of males and females in the sample are chosen in the same proportions.

To aim for such representativeness for the research variables, an element of *random selection* is used. In its simplest form, *simple random sampling* from a population means that all individuals in the population have the same chance of being selected for inclusion in the sample. Then, the possibility that there might be a few more or a few less mobile phone owners in the sample than there are in the target population is a matter of chance. This chance element helps us to quantify how close a sample percentage is to a target population. The other key element in this regard is the *sample size*. With a sample of 309, as in the Amárach survey, we could have a high degree of confidence (conventionally quantified as 95% confidence) that the percentage of mobile phone owners in the population of 15–24 year olds is within around 3.5 percentage points of the 89% reported in the February 2002 sample survey.

In theory, simple random sampling is required to produce a sample that is representative in the sense just described, allowing us to make *inferences* about the population based on the evidence in the sample. The theory involved parallels that for processes, as discussed in more detail in Chapters 4 and 5. The application to percentages from sample surveys is discussed in Chapter 7.

In practice, simple random sampling is prohibitively expensive and alternatives are used which are intended to approximate the ideal. Devices such as quota controls contribute to this, although great care is required to ensure that other aspects of quota sampling, in which considerable discretion in interviewee selection is allowed to interviewers, do not detract from the ideal.

Other issues relating to sample design and sample surveys in general are deferred to Chapter 11. Other applications are introduced there also, including applications in auditing and accounting.

## 1.9   Statistical assessment of a process change; design issues in experimentation

Dr. Gerald J. Hahn of Corporate Research and Development at General Electric described a simple experiment to evaluate the effect of making a change in a process for the bulk manufacture of an electronic component.[16] The old and new processes were run on alternate days for a period of eight weeks, switching the sequence (old followed by new or new followed by old) from week to week. Thus, during the first week, the new process was run on Monday, Wednesday and Friday with the old process being run on Tuesday, Thursday and Saturday while, during the second week, the old process was run on Monday, Wednesday and Friday with the new process being run on Tuesday, Thursday and Saturday, and continuing this pattern in subsequent pairs of weeks. On each day, a sample of 50 components was checked and the number of defective components counted. The counts on successive *pairs* of days were recorded and tabulated as in Table 1.8.

On this evidence, it appears as if the new process is slightly better than the old. However, there is always the possibility that this apparent improvement is consistent with chance variation and that there is no *real* or long term improvement. An informal assessment of this may be made using a version of the *control chart* introduced in Section 1.1 and illustrated in Figure 1.7. Figure 1.34 shows a line plot of the differences in the last column of Table 1.8, with 'control limits' representing a band

---

[16]   Full details are given in Dr. Hahn's article, 'Statistical assessment of a process change' in the *Journal of Quality Technology*, Volume 14, Number 1, pages 1–9, January 1982.

**Table 1.8**   Results of comparison of two processes over eight weeks (24 pairs of days)

| Week | Day pair | Old process | New process | Difference (New–Old) |
|------|----------|-------------|-------------|----------------------|
| | | Number of defectives in samples of 50 Units | | |
| 1 | 1 | 0 | 0 | 0 |
| 1 | 2 | 6 | 3 | −3 |
| 1 | 3 | 3 | 3 | 0 |
| 2 | 4 | 1 | 4 | +3 |
| 2 | 5 | 2 | 0 | −2 |
| 2 | 6 | 0 | 0 | 0 |
| 3 | 7 | 1 | 0 | −1 |
| 3 | 8 | 3 | 1 | −2 |
| 3 | 9 | 0 | 2 | +2 |
| 4 | 10 | 1 | 0 | −1 |
| 4 | 11 | 0 | 2 | +2 |
| 4 | 12 | 3 | 1 | −2 |
| 5 | 13 | 0 | 0 | 0 |
| 5 | 14 | 0 | 2 | +2 |
| 5 | 15 | 0 | 0 | 0 |
| 6 | 16 | 1 | 1 | 0 |
| 6 | 17 | 0 | 0 | 0 |
| 6 | 18 | 2 | 0 | −2 |
| 7 | 19 | 2 | 0 | −2 |
| 7 | 20 | 0 | 0 | 0 |
| 7 | 21 | 0 | 0 | 0 |
| 8 | 22 | 0 | 1 | +1 |
| 8 | 23 | 0 | 2 | +2 |
| 8 | 24 | 0 | 0 | 0 |
| | Total | 25 | 22 | −3 |
| | Average | 1.04 | 0.92 | −0.13 |
| | Per cent | 2.08 | 1.83 | −0.25 |

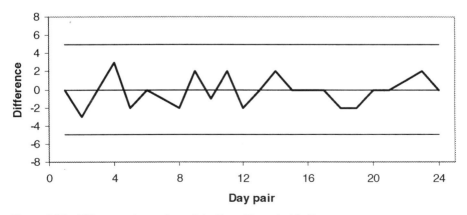

**Figure 1.34**   Differences in numbers defective with control limits.

of chance variation around a centre line at 0. These limits are based on the same idea as that illustrated in Figure 1.7. This is Shewhart's idea that, in normal circumstances, we can expect some haphazard or chance variation in processes but that we can put more or less well defined limits on such variation and that, if such limits are breached, then we must conclude that there is some assignable cause for the exceptional variation.

Figure 1.34 reveals no evidence for assignable causes of variation. This is entirely consistent with the hypothesis that the process change has no effect on process quality, showing, as it does, a pattern of chance variation around the centre line at 0. A more formal test of this hypothesis (details of which will be introduced in Chapter 7) supports this conclusion.

### An alternative experimental design

The protocol used to implement the experiment described above was quite complicated and resource intensive requiring, as it did, a process change every one or two days. A much simpler approach would be to monitor the old process for a four week period, then introduce the new process and monitor it for a further four weeks, with a simple comparison of defect rates to be made at the end of the eight week period. In fact, this is what the engineers who were considering the process change proposed to do. However, this approach suffers from a serious flaw. Conceivably, the process could be affected by some other factor that changes with time. For example, if the defect rate is sensitive to changes in ambient temperature, then the normal seasonal change in temperature, taken over a two month period, could influence the results of the experiment, so that any *perceived* difference between the old and new processes could well be due to seasonal change rather than process change.

Figure 1.35 shows that some such effect appears to have influenced the manufacturing process. The figure shows the numbers of defectives in time order, day by day, irrespective of which process, old or new, was used. Also shown is a computer generated 'smoother', similar to that used in Figure 1.2 to emphasise the seasonal effect there and in Figure 1.30 to assist with exploratory analysis there. Here, the smoother suggests that the daily numbers of defectives were higher during the first four-week period (days 1 to 24) than they are during the second. They were considerably higher during the first week, appeared to remain reasonably steady or perhaps rise slowly for the next three weeks and then seemed to reduce slowly over the second four-week period.

Table 1.9 shows the difference in defect rates between the first four weeks and the second four weeks, for both processes and for each separately.

The pattern is remarkably consistent, irrespective of the process. We can see that the defect rate decreased by around 2% between the two periods. If the old process had been run in the first period and the new in the second, the experimenters would have been inclined to conclude that the new process was better.[17]

---

[17]   The difference of 2.1% for both processes is 'highly statistically significant', according to the standard criteria, which will be introduced later.

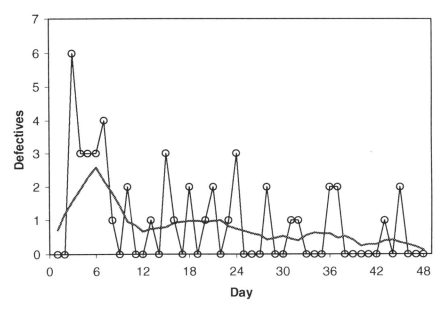

**Figure 1.35**   Numbers defective in time order.

**Table 1.9**   Defect rates, per cent, with differences, for the first and second four week periods

|  | First period | Second period | Difference |
|---|---|---|---|
| Both processes | 3.0 | 0.9 | 2.1 |
| Old process | 3.3 | 0.8 | 2.5 |
| New process | 2.7 | 1.0 | 1.7 |

## Attaining homogeneous experimental conditions

The design of even a simple experiment such as the one described here may be critical to permitting valid conclusions to be drawn from the results of the experiment. A fundamental principle is that comparisons be made in the most *homogeneous* conditions possible. Clearly, conditions were not homogeneous across the two four-week periods and the simple design that allocates the old process to the first period and the new to the second would have failed because of this. An improved design would be to alternate processes between successive weeks; successive pairs of weeks are likely to be more homogeneous then successive four-week periods. However, the evidence in Figure 1.35 indicates that the first week seemed quite different from the rest. The obvious next design improvement in this case would be to alternate the processes on a daily basis. As it happened, the production line was shut down nightly and restarted each day, so that daily changes were feasible and convenient.

However, within the daily pairing arrangement, there is still room for improvement. If, as the evidence suggests, there is a trend in defect rate in some weeks, then putting one process first each successive pair of days means that process will appear worse if the trend is downward, or better if the trend is upward. To counteract this, the sequence of old and new process was alternated each week.

### Randomisation

An alternative to the systematic alternating of weeks adopted in this case, with a view to avoiding time related biases, is *random* allocation of processes to days within pairs. Then, if there are trends or other systematic patterns that affect the system, the chances that such systematic patterns affect the results of the experiment are very small; in fact, the chances are the same as the chances of finding a systematic pattern in the results of 24 successive tosses of a coin.

The great advantage of random allocation is that, not only does it avoid biases arising from systematic patterns that we might anticipate, but also it avoids biases arising from systematic patterns that we might never think of.

In Chapter 11, further details on the design of experiments are presented. In particular, considerations arising when more than one factor may affect a response will be dealt with.

## Appendix: Diameters of tennis ball cores in four presses

| Press 1 | | | | | | Press 2 | | | | | |
|---|---|---|---|---|---|---|---|---|---|---|---|
| 109 | 104 | 100 | 100 | 102 | 102 | 98 | 96 | 94 | 102 | 90 | 103 |
| 114 | 112 | 100 | 102 | 112 | 100 | 101 | 106 | 90 | 98 | 101 | 96 |
| 100 | 115 | 110 | 94 | 90 | 98 | 106 | 106 | 111 | 104 | 104 | 89 |
| 82 | 102 | 86 | 94 | 102 | 94 | 90 | 89 | 90 | 95 | 90 | 91 |
| 96 | 98 | 85 | 94 | 102 | 96 | 97 | 96 | 92 | 87 | 110 | 98 |
| 90 | 92 | 83 | 88 | 85 | 98 | 96 | 93 | 87 | 86 | 83 | 88 |
| 94 | 102 | 101 | 98 | 104 | 102 | 87 | 91 | 96 | 88 | 90 | 76 |
| 90 | 97 | 96 | 90 | 95 | 88 | 97 | 96 | 99 | 96 | 99 | 84 |
| 88 | 80 | 80 | 90 | 78 | 92 | 85 | 78 | 82 | 90 | 88 | 81 |
| 92 | 88 | 92 | 100 | 100 | 88 | 84 | 80 | 90 | 87 | 90 | 95 |
| 88 | 90 | 92 | 90 | 77 | 90 | 105 | 97 | 91 | 91 | 85 | 71 |
| 90 | 90 | 90 | 88 | 80 | 88 | 76 | 74 | 80 | 83 | 84 | 85 |
| 88 | 88 | 92 | 85 | 94 | 92 | 89 | 86 | 92 | 90 | 96 | 96 |
| 90 | 80 | 78 | 84 | 85 | 84 | 88 | 91 | 86 | 80 | 76 | 73 |
| 88 | 78 | 88 | 93 | 78 | 82 | 78 | 77 | 79 | 76 | 87 | 91 |
| 98 | 82 | 92 | 82 | 84 | 82 | 81 | 100 | 94 | 102 | 99 | 95 |
| 82 | 77 | 78 | 85 | 88 | 78 | 94 | 82 | 72 | 74 | 73 | 77 |
| 94 | 80 | 78 | 90 | 82 | 88 | 83 | 83 | 80 | 83 | 81 | 87 |
| 95 | 88 | 88 | 89 | 76 | 88 | 103 | 87 | 96 | 103 | 103 | 83 |
| 82 | 78 | 86 | 78 | 82 | 82 | 76 | 77 | 77 | 76 | 82 | 80 |
| 82 | 82 | 84 | 94 | 100 | 91 | 80 | 87 | 86 | 92 | 102 | 96 |

Press 1 (cont.)

| 84 | 92 | 80 | 84 | 80 | 80 |
|----|----|----|----|----|----|
| 82 | 82 | 88 | 88 | 86 | 91 |
| 88 | 92 | 94 | 102 | 88 | 98 |
| 92 | 91 | 80 | 88 | 82 | 80 |
| 87 | 90 | 87 | 94 | 90 | 86 |
| 102 | 94 | 96 | 90 | 90 | 82 |
| 82 | 86 | 82 | 88 | 79 | 92 |
| 90 | 97 | 108 | 105 | 98 | 100 |
| 98 | 102 | 98 | 94 | 96 | 78 |
| 98 | 97 | 92 | 84 | 88 | 104 |

Press 2 (cont.)

| 85 | 80 | 82 | 73 | 78 | 79 |
|----|----|----|----|----|----|
| 78 | 82 | 71 | 73 | 79 | 83 |
| 89 | 88 | 97 | 103 | 94 | 88 |
| 90 | 79 | 80 | 78 | 77 | 79 |
| 82 | 72 | 81 | 91 | 95 | 94 |
| 90 | 86 | 74 | 90 | 83 | 78 |
| 79 | 83 | 80 | 82 | 86 | 87 |
| 95 | 93 | 106 | 101 | 95 | 90 |
| 84 | 90 | 86 | 80 | 96 | 90 |
| 89 | 85 | 94 | 93 | 97 | 98 |

Press 3

| 100 | 112 | 100 | 102 | 104 | 110 |
|----|----|----|----|----|----|
| 111 | 108 | 110 | 114 | 112 | 101 |
| 100 | 100 | 79 | 90 | 90 | 92 |
| 100 | 82 | 92 | 94 | 100 | 100 |
| 104 | 90 | 90 | 90 | 92 | 86 |
| 80 | 102 | 90 | 88 | 97 | 98 |
| 94 | 100 | 102 | 110 | 110 | 92 |
| 88 | 84 | 88 | 88 | 80 | 90 |
| 82 | 77 | 82 | 92 | 92 | 94 |
| 102 | 108 | 110 | 110 | 100 | 88 |
| 80 | 82 | 80 | 80 | 80 | 77 |
| 88 | 88 | 92 | 100 | 110 | 102 |
| 82 | 84 | 86 | 88 | 82 | 68 |
| 80 | 78 | 74 | 84 | 74 | 88 |
| 90 | 100 | 99 | 104 | 104 | 88 |
| 80 | 82 | 80 | 72 | 78 | 72 |
| 72 | 64 | 75 | 80 | 82 | 88 |
| 94 | 102 | 100 | 78 | 88 | 88 |
| 74 | 74 | 70 | 68 | 74 | 74 |
| 72 | 88 | 72 | 79 | 90 | 90 |
| 94 | 98 | 82 | 87 | 74 | 80 |
| 68 | 68 | 70 | 72 | 72 | 70 |
| 80 | 79 | 84 | 90 | 92 | 86 |
| 81 | 82 | 79 | 69 | 69 | 74 |
| 68 | 74 | 70 | 74 | 76 | 64 |
| 74 | 80 | 88 | 80 | 100 | 81 |
| 90 | 74 | 70 | 74 | 74 | 78 |
| 64 | 74 | 70 | 74 | 94 | 74 |
| 80 | 92 | 82 | 88 | 80 | 80 |
| 90 | 64 | 74 | 70 | 74 | 70 |
| 74 | 74 | 80 | 84 | 90 | 90 |

Press 4

| 78 | 74 | 86 | 81 | 89 | 86 |
|----|----|----|----|----|----|
| 86 | 86 | 84 | 88 | 86 | 84 |
| 88 | 82 | 89 | 78 | 74 | 77 |
| 75 | 81 | 72 | 76 | 79 | 80 |
| 66 | 64 | 76 | 72 | 74 | 76 |
| 88 | 81 | 80 | 72 | 80 | 70 |
| 73 | 76 | 81 | 77 | 71 | 76 |
| 74 | 85 | 62 | 80 | 88 | 84 |
| 75 | 73 | 73 | 72 | 75 | 79 |
| 75 | 73 | 64 | 67 | 67 | 69 |
| 71 | 82 | 87 | 79 | 86 | 69 |
| 71 | 73 | 72 | 70 | 74 | 69 |
| 68 | 71 | 64 | 72 | 75 | 71 |
| 74 | 79 | 74 | 76 | 78 | 66 |
| 73 | 74 | 72 | 72 | 73 | 66 |
| 62 | 62 | 69 | 68 | 80 | 80 |
| 78 | 74 | 79 | 74 | 78 | 71 |
| 74 | 80 | 74 | 69 | 72 | 68 |
| 88 | 77 | 82 | 84 | 80 | 68 |
| 70 | 66 | 70 | 70 | 71 | 70 |
| 68 | 67 | 70 | 70 | 76 | 78 |
| 84 | 80 | 70 | 70 | 75 | 74 |
| 82 | 75 | 68 | 73 | 64 | 76 |
| 76 | 88 | 86 | 84 | 78 | 88 |
| 78 | 81 | 80 | 78 | 71 | 78 |
| 79 | 74 | 71 | 72 | 86 | 90 |
| 77 | 73 | 71 | 74 | 82 | 78 |
| 80 | 85 | 80 | 74 | 77 | 72 |
| 79 | 78 | 84 | 88 | 97 | 94 |
| 86 | 84 | 86 | 90 | 87 | 90 |
| 83 | 84 | 83 | 82 | 88 | 85 |

# 2
# Data display and summary

Many of our examples suggest that clarity and excellence in thinking is very much like clarity and excellence in the display of data. When principles of design replicate principles of thought, the act of arranging information becomes an act of insight.

Edward R. Tufte
*Visual Explanations*[1]

Statistical analysis of a problem is inevitably based on data associated with the problem. The data may be collected specially for the purpose or may be extracted from some already existing data source. The analyst must interact with the data in order to solve the problem. This may require the analyst to form several 'views' of the data, which may involve different kinds of summary, involving different levels of detail. Some analytical methods may require sophisticated numerical methods of data processing before arriving at an appropriate summary or 'view' of the data. Some of these will be discussed later. When the analysis is complete, the analyst must make a report presenting the results of the analysis, and this will involve presenting appropriate 'views' of the data. Here, we address questions concerning the display of data in tables and graphs, whether for analysis or presentation. (In fact, these two aspects generally overlap. Thus, a good presentation display will allow, even lead, the viewer to conduct an appropriate analysis.)

As with any product, the most important person to please when producing a data display is the consumer, the intended viewer of the display. We will examine the problem of data display from that perspective. That there is a problem may be shown convincingly by examining some of the numerous very bad displays that exist.

---

[1]  Edward R. Tufte *Visual Explanations: Images and Quantities, Evidence and Narrative*, Cheshire, Connecticut; Graphics Press (1997).

**Learning objectives**

After completing this chapter, students should understand the purposes of data summary and display, the importance of guidelines for good data display, the definition/construction of basic graphs and numerical summaries and the concepts of frequency distribution, centre and spread and demonstrate this by being able to:

- read data displays effectively;
- illustrate by example common display inadequacies and difficulties in interpretation of inadequate displays;
- illustrate by example the role of perception in data display construction and interpretation;
- list guidelines for good data display and apply them to table and graph construction and reconstruction;
- construct and interpret dotplots, boxplots, histograms, line plots;
- define and calculate simple numerical summaries of sample data;
- define and construct a frequency distribution of sample data.

## 2.1   Graphical display of measured data

In this section, we introduce dotplots and boxplots and revisit histograms, time series plots and scatterplots already seen in Chapter 1.

**Dotplots**

First, consider the dotplots shown in Figure 2.1. In these dotplots, each dot represents a diameter value. Dotplots may be seen as forms of histograms in which all the data points are shown. The interpretation of the dotplots in Figure 2.1 is similar to that of the histograms in Figure 1.13; within each press, the data are spread across the horizontal scale, tending to be concentrated in the middle and sparse at the edges. In Chapter 1 such patterns were thought to suggest chance variation. Between presses, differences in centre and spread are revealed. These suggest assignable causes of variation.

*Making dotplots*

The dotplots shown in Figure 2.1 are simple to interpret and effective in revealing the nature of the variation in the diameters. They were made using computer software, the only feasible way to produce them with relatively large datasets. For smaller datasets, however, dotplots are easy to make by hand, as follows:

(i)   determine the largest and smallest values;
(ii)   draw an appropriately scaled horizontal line;
(iii)   make a dot above the line at the point corresponding to the value of the first measurement;

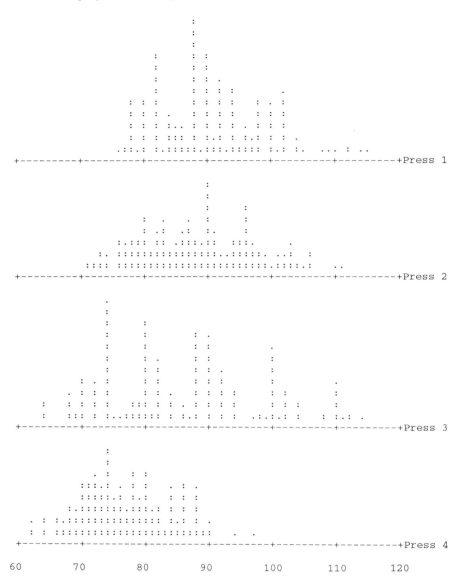

**Figure 2.1**   Dotplots of tennis ball diameters.

(iv)  continue with second and subsequent measurements; if two measurements have the same value, place the second dot above the first.

When data are stratified, as in the tennis ball problem, separate plots are made and stacked one above another, making sure that all use the same horizontal scale. To avoid clutter, only the bottom scale is labelled.

**Exercise 2.1**   A department store chain regularly audits its transaction documentation, receipts, invoices, credit notes, etc., to monitor and control errors made in completing the documents. As part of the audit, a team of inspectors checks a batch of invoices for errors and reports the number of errors discovered. To check on the adequacy of the audit inspection process, the company carried out a special study which involved putting a specially prepared batch of invoices, having exactly 21 errors, into the inspection stream without the knowledge of the inspectors. This was repeated six times at suitable intervals for each of four inspectors. The inspectors' error counts were as follows:

| Inspector | Counts | | | | | |
|---|---|---|---|---|---|---|
| 1 | 22 | 19 | 21 | 24 | 22 | 24 |
| 2 | 19 | 22 | 15 | 24 | 26 | 14 |
| 3 | 26 | 25 | 27 | 26 | 28 | 30 |
| 4 | 21 | 19 | 22 | 19 | 31 | 20 |

Make dotplots for each inspector. Provide an interpretation of the result.

## Boxplots

Dotplots are intended for small datasets where they can be produced quickly by hand. They have the virtue that they preserve the original data while arranging them in a graphical display that reveals the variation pattern. With larger datasets such as the tennis ball data, it may be argued that dotplots are too extensive, both physically on the page and in the effort required to produce them if done by hand. An alternative plot which involves summarising or condensing the original data while preserving key features of the variation pattern is the *boxplot*. A boxplot display of the stratified tennis ball data is shown in Figure 2.2.

The vertical bar in the middle of each box represents the *median* of the sample, that is, the sample value which has half the values smaller (or equal) to it and the other half larger (or equal), or the 'middlemost' data value. The bar at the left end of the box represents the *lower quartile,* defined to have one quarter of the values smaller than it and three quarters larger. Correspondingly, the bar at the right end of the box represents the *upper quartile,* defined to have three quarters of the values smaller than it and one quarter larger. The lines extending on either side of each box (called *whiskers*) extend to the extremes (largest and smallest) of the datasets.[2]

The four boxplots in Figure 2.2 clearly convey the main features of the variation pattern present in these data, already described. They achieve this in a more

---

[2]   In more elaborate versions of the boxplot, extreme values that would not be expected from a 'reasonable' data set are separately identified.

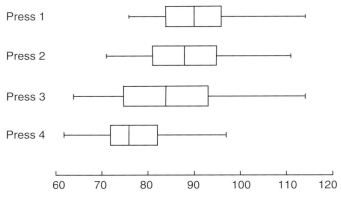

**Figure 2.2**   Boxplots of tennis ball diameters.

condensed fashion. This is important from the point of view of assimilating the information in the display. The fact that they *summarise* the data means that details are not revealed.

---

**Exercise 2.2**   A sample of 20 measurements from each of the four presses resulted in the following data:

| | | | | | | | | | | | | | | | | | | | | |
|---|---|---|---|---|---|---|---|---|---|---|---|---|---|---|---|---|---|---|---|---|
| Press 1 | 90 | 101 | 81 | 84 | 87 | 93 | 81 | 83 | 86 | 85 | 89 | 82 | 87 | 91 | 95 | 94 | 99 | 71 | 91 | 85 |
| Press 2 | 102 | 77 | 81 | 76 | 77 | 88 | 96 | 81 | 101 | 88 | 96 | 73 | 94 | 95 | 69 | 89 | 86 | 86 | 95 | 84 |
| Press 3 | 103 | 100 | 87 | 76 | 77 | 92 | 83 | 90 | 97 | 110 | 67 | 92 | 77 | 78 | 85 | 95 | 93 | 93 | 76 | 109 |
| Press 4 | 70 | 84 | 80 | 76 | 70 | 78 | 84 | 75 | 85 | 73 | 74 | 70 | 64 | 73 | 90 | 74 | 67 | 77 | 76 | 73 |

Find the median of each: list each dataset in increasing order of magnitude and count to the middle value. Note that there are not unique middle values; 10th and 11th are equally 'middle'. By convention, set the median to be their average. Find the quartiles and extremes. (The quartiles may be found as the medians of the upper and lower halves of the data, as determined by the overall median.[3]) Construct the corresponding boxplots. Interpret and comment.

---

## Histograms

A graph form widely used for illustrating statistical variation patterns in measured data is the *histogram.* Figure 2.3 reproduces the histograms for the stratified tennis ball diameter data, already shown as Figure 1.13. In form, the histograms are similar to dotplots and they convey their message similarly. The main difference is that individual

---

[3]   Alternative rules exist for determining the box ends. In the context of interpreting data, the choice between such rules is not important.

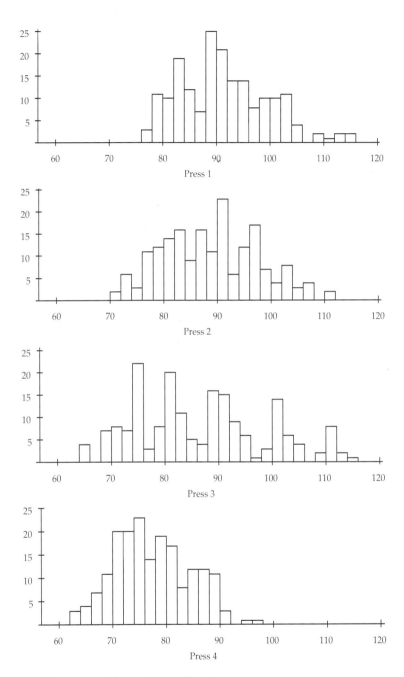

**Figure 2.3**   Histograms of the tennis ball diameters.

measurements are distinguishable in the dotplots while measurements are grouped into intervals in the histograms. Histograms are also much more difficult to construct.

*Making histograms*

The steps involve in constructing a histogram may be listed as:

(i)    determine the largest and smallest values;
(ii)   draw an appropriately scaled line;
(iii)  divide the line into an appropriate number of neighbouring intervals;
(iv)   count the number of values in each interval;
(v)    draw a rectangle based on each interval whose area is proportional to the corresponding count.

Some of these steps require elaboration. Thus, in step (iii), care is needed in choosing the intervals. The number of intervals or the width of each interval is chosen to achieve a suitable degree of smoothness in the resulting graph while, at the same time, giving convenient end-points or mid-points for identifying and labelling the intervals. There is considerable scope here and many recommendations, some conflicting, are available for making these decisions.

Step (iv) may be achieved with the aid of a *tally sheet* such as that shown in Figure 2.4. The measurements are tallied as follows. Each measurement is assigned in turn to its appropriate interval, this being recorded by placing a stroke in the space beside the interval. The fifth point in an interval may be represented by a horizontal stroke through the first four upright strokes, giving a 'five-bar gate' effect, e.g., *卌*. Subsequent measurements in the same interval may be grouped in fives, in this way, thus facilitating the count made at the end of the tally.

---

**Exercise 2.3** Complete a tally sheet for each of the datasets of Exercise 2.2.

---

**Histogram Tally Sheet**

| No. | Interval | Mid | Tally | Count | Percent |
|-----|----------|-----|-------|-------|---------|
| 1   | 76–80    | 78  |       |       |         |
| 2   | 81–85    | 83  |       |       |         |
| 3   | 86–90    | 88  |       |       |         |
| 4   | 91–95    | 93  |       |       |         |
| 5   | 96–100   | 98  |       |       |         |
| 6   | 101–105  | 103 |       |       |         |
| 7   | 106–110  | 108 |       |       |         |
| 8   | 111–115  | 113 |       |       |         |
| 9   |          |     |       |       |         |
| 10  |          |     |       |       |         |

**Figure 2.4**   A histogram tally sheet.

Assuming that all the intervals have equal width, step (v) is implemented by drawing rectangles whose heights are proportional to the counts.[4] It is suggested that the completed histogram be adjusted so that it fits into a square with side 2 or 3 inches. If it is allowed to be any larger, then the eye will have a harder job of taking in the general shape. Perception is all important when interpreting graphs, of any kind.

---

**Exercise 2.4**  Make histograms for each of the datasets of Exercise 2.2.

---

As an illustration of this construction, the result of tallying the 186 press 1 diameters is the tally sheet shown in Figure 2.5 and the corresponding histogram shown as Figure 2.6. Note how the tallies in the tally sheet suggest the shape of the final histogram, on its side. For exploratory purposes, when working by hand, this view of the data is often sufficient and the extra effort of producing the final histogram is not needed.

*Interpreting histograms*

Histograms should be interpreted with caution, particularly because the shape of the histogram can change dramatically simply by changing the number of classification intervals. Consider the three versions of the 186 press 3 tennis ball diameters shown in Figure 2.7. The first, a slight variation on the histogram of the same data shown in Figure 2.3, suggests a measurement problem, where the measurer, when reading a scale, rounds most values that fall between scale marks, but attempts to read between

| No. | Interval | Mid | Tally | Count | Percent |
|-----|----------|-----|-------|-------|---------|
| 1 | 76–80 | 78 | ℋℋ ℋℋ ℋℋ ℋℋ //// | 24 | 13 |
| 2 | 81–85 | 83 | ℋℋ ℋℋ ℋℋ ℋℋ ℋℋ ℋℋ / | 31 | 17 |
| 3 | 86–90 | 88 | ℋℋ ℋℋ ℋℋ ℋℋ ℋℋ ℋℋ ℋℋ ℋℋ ℋℋ ℋℋ | 50 | 27 |
| 4 | 91–95 | 93 | ℋℋ ℋℋ ℋℋ ℋℋ ℋℋ ℋℋ / | 31 | 17 |
| 5 | 96–100 | 98 | ℋℋ ℋℋ ℋℋ ℋℋ ℋℋ // | 27 | 15 |
| 6 | 101–105 | 103 | ℋℋ ℋℋ ℋℋ / | 16 | 9 |
| 7 | 106–110 | 108 | /// | 3 | 2 |
| 8 | 111–115 | 113 | //// | 4 | 2 |

*Total*  186  100

**Figure 2.5**  A tally sheet of the press 1 tennis ball diameters.

---

[4] If the intervals are not all of equal width, it is the areas that must be proportional to the counts; if heights are used, then wider intervals will look as if they have relatively more values than they actually have. There is no need to use unequal width bases if starting from raw data. However, in some cases, the data may have already been grouped using unequal width bases. This arises with age and income distributions, for example, where long standing conventions exist for the definitions of the bases.

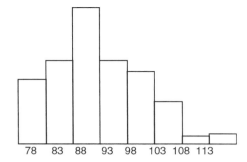

**Figure 2.6**   A histogram of the press 1 tennis ball diameters.

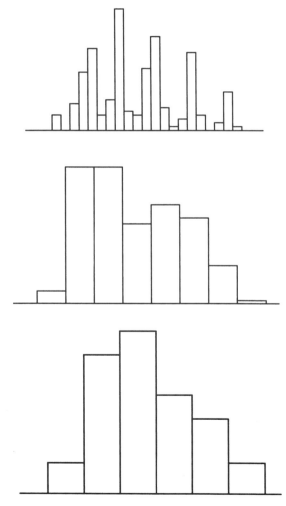

**Figure 2.7**   Three histograms of the press 3 diameters.

the scale marks in a few cases. The second and third show the same press 3 data, but with smaller numbers of intervals and two quite different shapes. The second, with its two peaks, suggests that the data are a mixture of data from two processes, each with its own set of chance causes of variation, that is, its own set of very many individually negligible and unpredictable sources of variation. The third suggests just one such process.

To cope with this problem, guidelines relating the number of intervals to the sample size are given by various authorities. Unfortunately, the guidelines conflict. The best advice is to study the data carefully, trying different histograms, and pick the one which best shows the features of the data that you think are important.

---

**Exercise 2.5**   Dotplots, boxplots and histograms graphically convey information concerning frequency distributions. Which of the three conveys the most information? Which conveys the least?

---

*Frequency distributions*

Typically, histograms are made using appropriate computer software. Here, the details of making histograms by hand have been emphasised to show their link to the data through the *frequency distribution*, an important construct in its own right, as will be seen later. The frequency distribution, already introduced in Section 1.4, is defined as the set of counts of values in each histogram interval, shown on the right hand side of the tally sheet in Figure 2.5. It shows how the 186 values are *distributed* among the histogram intervals by giving the *frequency* of values in each interval. Alternatively, the *relative frequencies,* got by dividing the frequencies by their total, 186 in this case, show how the entire data, regarded as a unit, are distributed among the intervals. In Figure 2.5 the relative frequencies are given as percentages, adding up to 100; they may also be given as proportions, adding up to 1.

The concept of frequency distribution is fundamental to statistical theory and practice in ways which will emerge gradually. In the first place, it does provide a comprehensive numerical summary of the pattern of variation in our data. Indeed, when we interpret the more usual summaries which will be introduced in the next section, we should think in terms of the frequency distribution pattern that they summarise. The standard deviation, in particular, has a direct interpretation in terms of the *Normal frequency distribution* to be discussed in Chapter 3.

We will also find that the frequency distribution plays a fundamental role in the theory and practice of *statistical inference,* which is concerned with drawing conclusions about processes from data sampled from those processes. Specifically, we will be able to use frequency distributions to quantify the frequency of errors in such inferences. Such errors are inevitable in the presence of chance variation; one of our objectives is to learn how to minimise them. Statistical inference will be introduced in Chapter 4, developed more formally in Chapter 5 and applied in a range of applications in subsequent chapters.

## Line charts, scatter diagrams

Line charts (time series charts) and scatter diagrams are used to display data concerning relationships between two measured variables; several examples were seen in Chapter 1. A key feature which can influence interpretation of such charts is the *aspect ratio,* that is, the ratio between the (physical) lengths of the axes. As an illustration of the issues involved, consider the comparison between Figures 2.8 and 2.9. These show two versions of a time series plot of sunspot numbers. Sunspots are the result of explosions in the sun which occur at regular (approximately 11 year) intervals. Immediately after such an explosion, there is a sharp rise in the number of sunspots observed, followed by a somewhat slower decline, until the next explosion. This pattern of a quick rise followed by a slow fall is clearly evident in the first version but not at all evident in the second. Yet, the only difference between the versions is the length of the vertical axis and, hence, the aspect ratio.

The problem here is that the pattern is perceived through comparison of slopes, that is, of angles. As will be discussed in Section 2.5, data encoded as angles are relatively difficult to decode. This difficulty is compounded when the slopes involved are either very steep, as in Figure 2.9, or very shallow. An example of the

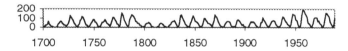

**Figure 2.8**   Sunspot numbers; aspect ratio = 0.1.

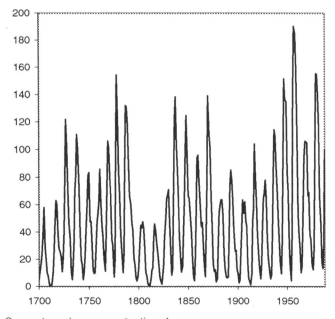

**Figure 2.9**   Sunspot numbers; aspect ratio = 1.

latter will arise in Section 2.5; see Figure 2.22. The solution to this problem is to adjust the aspect ratio so that typical or important slopes correspond to an angle of around 45°. Figure 2.8 conforms to this convention.

The implication of this convention for scatterplots which reflect a straight line relationship between the two variables involved is that the aspect ratio should be around 1. However, for aesthetic reasons, an aspect ratio of a little less than one may be used.

Figures 2.10 and 2.11 illustrates another issue relating to graphical perception and correct interpretation. Figure 2.10 shows a modern version of a classic economic

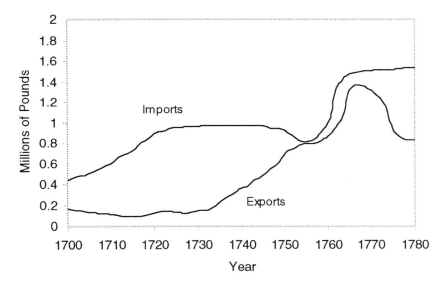

**Figure 2.10** Imports to and exports from England in the eighteenth century.

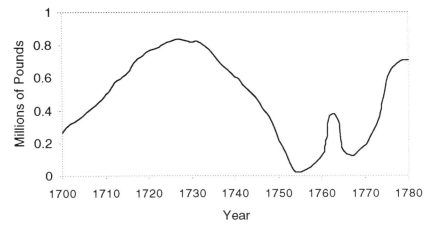

**Figure 2.11** The English balance of trade with the East Indies in the eighteenth century.

graph, originally made in the eighteenth century by the economist William Playfair, who is considered by many to be the founder of statistical graphics. The graph shows eighteenth century trade figures between England and the East Indies. We can see that, for the first half of the eighteenth century, there was a considerable excess of imports over exports. The excess appeared to become very small between 1755 and 1765, growing again after that. However, looking at Figure 2.11, which displays the excess, we can see that appearances are deceptive, at least for the period 1760–5. For this period, the trade gap appears almost constant in the first graph but obviously not so in the second. The problem here is that the viewer naturally compares the curves of Figure 2.11 in terms of closest pairs of points, whereas the correct comparison is in terms of contemporary pairs of points. In terms of the perceived distance between the curves, the natural perception is of *minimum* distance whereas the correct perception is of *vertical* distance.

## 2.2   Numerical summaries of measured data

Differences in the variation patterns in the four presses were clearly revealed by the graphical data displays. We have discussed these differences in terms of the centre of measurements in each press, some presses producing balls with larger diameters 'as a whole', and others smaller. We have also discussed the measurements from each press in terms of the spread of measurements within the press, one appearing to have larger spread than the others. Traditionally, these ideas have been quantified through the use of appropriately defined numerical summaries. We have already encountered two sets of numerical summaries, the frequency distribution displayed as part of the histogram tally sheet in Figure 2.5 and the so-called *five number summary* which forms the basis for making boxplots:

*median*

*lower quartile*                    *upper quartile*

*lower extreme*                              *upper extreme*

As a numerical summary, the frequency distribution conveys a quantitative version of the more qualitative graphical view shown in the histogram; we can see how much more frequent are values in the middle intervals and how much less frequent the values at the extremes. However, the frequency distribution is cumbersome as a numerical summary. More compact summaries are needed for practical use. One such summary is easily derived from the five number summary.

### Median, range, interquartile range

Viewed in terms of location of (the bulk of) the data along a scale, the *median* identifies the centre of the data. If the median is small, it indicates that the measurements 'as a whole' are small; if the median is large, it indicates that the measurements 'as a whole' are large. The spread of the data is obviously measured by the *range,* that is, the difference between the extreme values. A problem with the range is that it is distorted by exceptional values, which may not conform to the bulk of the data and may need to be dealt with separately. Alternatively, the *interquartile range*, that is, the difference between the quartiles, may be used. As a measure of spread, this is insensitive to exceptional values.[5]

**Exercise 2.6** Find the medians, ranges and interquartile ranges for the datasets of Exercises 2.2.

The values of these numerical summaries for the four sets of 186 tennis ball diameters are given in Table 2.1. Note that the numerical patterns in the columns accord closely with the patterns already seen in the graphical displays.

**Table 2.1** Medians, ranges and interquartile ranges for the 186 tennis ball core diameters of presses 1 to 4

| Press | Median | Range | Interquartile range |
|-------|--------|-------|---------------------|
| 1 | 90 | 39 | 12 |
| 2 | 88 | 40 | 14 |
| 3 | 84 | 50 | 20 |
| 4 | 76 | 35 | 10 |

**Mean, standard deviation**

A more traditional numerical summary is in terms of the *mean*, $\bar{X}$ and *standard deviation*, $s$ (or root mean square deviation, r.m.s.) of the values. These are formally defined in terms of a set of $n$ numbers, denoted $X_1, X_2, X_3, \ldots, X_n$, by

$$\bar{X} = \frac{1}{n}\sum_{i=1}^{n} X_i \quad \text{and} \quad s = \sqrt{\frac{1}{n}\sum_{i=1}^{n}\left(X_i - \bar{X}\right)^2}$$

Typically, the mean will be near the centre of the set of values, similar to the median. The standard deviation measures the spread of the set of values. It does this through a form of average of the 'spread' of individual values from the middle. The fact that the form of average is rather complicated, involving squaring, averaging and 'square rooting' again, is, perverse as it seems, related to mathematical simplicity.[6]

**Exercise 2.7** Calculate the means and standard deviations for the datasets of Exercise 2.2. Compare the variation pattern in these summaries with those calculated in Exercise 2.6.

---

[5] In statistical jargon, it is referred to as a *robust* statistic.
[6] Underlying this is Pythagoras's theorem concerning the sides of right angled triangles; if $x$ and $y$ are the lengths of the sides adjacent to the right angle and $z$ is the length of the hypotenuse, the relation between $x$, $y$ and $z$ is simply expressed through their squares; $x^2 + y^2 = z^2$. The idea of representing spread as sums of squared deviations turns up repeatedly and is fundamental in the mathematical theory of statistics.

Table 2.2 is an extension of Table 2.1, with means and standard deviations added. Note that, while the values of the median and mean have direct interpretations in terms of the quantity being measured (and both have similar values for each press), the measures of spread do not; they are interpreted comparatively. Thus we can say that presses 1, 2 and 4 have similar spread and press 3 has considerably greater spread, irrespective of which measure of spread we use. However, as we will see in Chapter 3, the standard deviation does have an interpretation in terms of the *Normal frequency distribution*.

**Table 2.2**   Measures of centre and spread  for the 186 tennis ball core diameters of presses 1–4

| Press | Mean | Median | Standard deviation | Range | Interquartile range |
|-------|------|--------|--------------------|-------|---------------------|
| 1 | 91 | 90 | 8.3 | 39 | 12 |
| 2 | 88 | 88 | 8.9 | 40 | 14 |
| 3 | 86 | 84 | 12.1 | 50 | 20 |
| 4 | 77 | 76 | 7.0 | 35 | 10 |

## 2.3   How to read a table

Data are frequently displayed as tables, in which the raw data or data summaries such as means, standard deviations, counts, proportions, etc., are classified by one or more categorical variables. In the next section, a set of guidelines designed to assist with the production of good tables will be introduced. Ultimately, tables are produced to be used. To assist in establishing a user's perspective, it may help to go through the steps a typical user takes in reading a typical table and, from the lessons learned there, proceed to a set of guidelines for table making.

### Example 1: An easily read table

Consider Table 2.3. The first step is to decode the title. It tells us that the basic variable is 'workers' absence rate', the basic measurement unit is 'per cent' (though we are not

**Table 2.3**   Absence rates, per cent, for the workers in a company, classified by sex, age and whether management or shop floor workers

| Age (years) | Management | | | Shop-floor | | | Both | | |
|-------------|------|--------|------|------|--------|------|------|--------|------|
| | Male | Female | Both | Male | Female | Both | Male | Female | Both |
| 14 to 24 | 1.2 | 0.5 | 0.8 | 7.2 | 1.4 | 3.9 | 1.8 | 0.6 | 1.2 |
| 25 to 34 | 0.8 | 0.6 | 0.7 | 9.7 | 3.8 | 6.4 | 1.6 | 0.9 | 1.2 |
| 35 to 44 | 1.2 | 0.5 | 0.8 | 7.5 | 5.9 | 6.6 | 1.7 | 1.0 | 1.3 |
| 45 to 54 | 2.2 | 1.4 | 1.8 | 12.8 | 10.4 | 11.5 | 3.2 | 2.3 | 2.7 |
| 55 to 64 | 3.6 | 3.4 | 3.5 | 19.4 | 16.9 | 18.1 | 4.7 | 4.4 | 4.5 |
| 65 and over* | 5.6 | 4.4 | 5.0 | 35.8 | 31.2 | 33.3 | 7.6 | 6.2 | 6.9 |
| 14 and over | 2.1 | 1.5 | 1.8 | 12.7 | 8.2 | 10.2 | 3.0 | 2.1 | 2.5 |

* The official retirement age was 70 years.

told of what), and the factors classifying the variation are sex, age and employment type. The next step is to note the layout of the table, with respect to the classifying factors. Rates are classified in columns by type of worker (management or shop floor), and by gender (male or female), with summary columns, as well as being classified in rows by age, in 10 year age groups (except for the last), with a summary row at the end.

The next step is an assessment of a 'typical' value of the variable and the extent of variation around that value. In this case, the table layout directs us to the bottom right corner, where we find an overall value of 2.5%. A quick look at the body of the table reveals variation from as low as 0.5% to more than 30%. (This immediately suggests some asymmetry in the distribution of the values in the table; we might make a note of this, for possible later explanation.)

Noting the structure of the classifying factors, with age having the most categories, we look next at the simplest breakdown of the overall percentage; rates of 3.0% for males and 2.1% for females. Moving further left (using the next simplest breakdown), we note the disparity between management and shop floor workers. (We might more or less naively begin to formulate explanations for this disparity such as, for example, that shop floor workers are inherently more absence prone or, alternatively, that management has provided bad working conditions for shop floor workers. This should be resisted by all except those with an intimate knowledge of the causative factors associated with absenteeism in this organisation; others should note the disparity for possible explanation later.)

Within each worker category, however, we note that the ratio of male to female absence rates is about the same for management and shop floor workers. This marks the emergence of a *pattern*.

Finally, looking at the breakdown by age, we note from the right-most column that absence rates are roughly constant for lower age groups but increase rapidly in the older age groups. Moving left, a similar pattern seems to apply in the other columns.

There emerges from this reading of the table that there are definite *patterns* of variation of absence rates. If this table was being presented as part of a report on an investigation into absence rates, these patterns should be summarised verbally, perhaps as follows.

> Absence rates are consistently higher among males than among females, are consistently much higher among shop floor than among management workers, and show a consistent and increasing tendency to be higher for older age groups.

This table was relatively easy to read. Not all tables are so; the following example highlights some problems.

## Example 2: A hard-to-read table

Tables 2.4 and 2.5, which are concerned with changes in income tax rates as income increases, are taken from a paper published in a reputable academic journal. In Table 2.4, *average rate progression* is the change in a typical person's average tax rate when income increases by £1, while in Table 2.5, *liability progression* is the change in average tax rate when income increases by 1%. For example, in 1946, the average tax rate of persons with income in the £1,000–1,500 range increased by 0.000 076% when income increased by £1 and by 2.868 852% when income increased by 1%.

The task of describing the contents of these tables is not easy.

> **Exercise 2.8**   What trends and patterns in average rate progression and liability progression do you see displayed in Tables 2.4 and 2.5?

Following the steps taken in reading Table 2.3, the titles are reasonably clear and the classifying factors appear reasonably well defined. Closer examination, however, reveals a curious gap in the income ranges; £2,000–2,500 is omitted. Also, the years are evenly spaced up to 1971, with one year spacing from 1974. This makes for difficulty in interpreting patterns.

There is not a 'typical' value to use as a reference point for the values in the body of the table. Also, there is no simple breakdown, by rows or by columns, which would allow the reader to begin to see some structure in the variation before proceeding to study the body of the table.

When it comes to the body of the table, the most obvious feature is the blur of digits. It takes some time to realise that not all the entries in Table 2.4 are zero and, then, comparisons among the entries are not easy because of the proliferation of zero digits. Comparisons in Table 2.5 prove to be even more difficult; there are too many apparently non-negligible digits in each number.

**Table 2.4**   Average rate progression, selected incomes, every five years 1946–71, 1974–6; single person

| (1976 £s) | £500 to £1,000 | £1,000 to £1,500 | £1,500 to £2,000 | £2,500 to £4,000 | £4,000 to £5,000 | £5,000 to £10,000 |
|---|---|---|---|---|---|---|
| 1946 | 0.000052 | 0.000076 | 0.000078 | 0.000030 | 0.000014 | 0.000010 |
| 1951 | 0.000072 | 0.000106 | 0.000069 | 0.000025 | 0.000013 | 0.000014 |
| 1956 | 0.000068 | 0.000102 | 0.000075 | 0.000034 | 0.000018 | 0.000018 |
| 1961 | 0.000000 | 0.000154 | 0.000064 | 0.000024 | 0.000012 | 0.000013 |
| 1966 | 0.000092 | 0.000144 | 0.000058 | 0.000021 | 0.000011 | 0.000020 |
| 1971 | 0.000160 | 0.000140 | 0.000045 | 0.000019 | 0.000026 | 0.000013 |
| 1974 | 0.000166 | 0.000118 | 0.000047 | 0.000036 | 0.000021 | 0.000021 |
| 1975 | 0.000184 | 0.000112 | 0.000050 | 0.000047 | 0.000024 | 0.000024 |
| 1976 | 0.000198 | 0.000108 | 0.000059 | 0.000043 | 0.000022 | 0.000029 |

**Table 2.5**   Liability progression, selected incomes, every five years 1946–71, 1974–76; single person

| (1976 £s) | £500 to £1,000 | £1,000 to £1,500 | £1,500 to £2,000 | £2,500 to £4,000 | £4,000 to £5,000 | £5,000 to £10,000 |
|---|---|---|---|---|---|---|
| 1946 | 0.000000 | 2.868852 | 2.297118 | 1.543971 | 1.319452 | 1.284495 |
| 1951 | 0.000000 | 2.876106 | 1.979186 | 1.429743 | 1.284308 | 1.365059 |
| 1956 | 0.000000 | 2.894737 | 2.066351 | 1.546624 | 1.361991 | 1.422503 |
| 1961 | 0.000000 | 0.000000 | 2.025641 | 1.452617 | 1.290381 | 1.377682 |
| 1966 | 0.000000 | 2.937220 | 1.705024 | 1.335430 | 1.228334 | 1.459555 |
| 1971 | 0.000000 | 2.377049 | 1.473684 | 1.270629 | 1.486664 | 1.288660 |
| 1974 | 0.000000 | 2.195946 | 1.514223 | 1.498442 | 1.366492 | 1.416000 |
| 1975 | 0.000000 | 2.070064 | 1.523013 | 1.595618 | 1.379147 | 1.430108 |
| 1976 | 0.000000 | 1.986301 | 1.582620 | 1.529101 | 1.338071 | 1.483516 |

**Suggested improvements**

The contrasts between these two tables and Table 2.3 suggest some immediate steps that could be taken to improve the design of Tables 2.4 and 2.5. These are incorporated in Exercise 2.9. Consideration should also be given to graphical display; suggestions are made in Exercise 2.10. In the next section, a more comprehensive set of guidelines for table making is presented.

---

**Exercise 2.9**  Tables 2.4 and 2.5 are available in Word table format in Progression.doc on the book's website. Copy the Average Rate Progression and Liability Progression data into separate Excel worksheets. Note the immediate formatting of the '0' column in Table 2.5. Select the remaining columns of Table 2.5 and format the numbers to have two decimal places. Enter formulas to calculate suitable summaries of data in rows and columns and of all the data; median is suggested. Comment on the patterns of variation in the data.

Multiply Average Rate Progression by 1,000,000. Note the simplification. Enter formulas to calculate suitable summaries of data in rows and columns and of all the data. Comment on the patterns of variation in the data.

---

**Exercise 2.10**  Use the Excel Chart Wizard to make *XY(scatter) plots* of the Average Rate Progression data columns against Year; select the data, click on the Chart Wizard button, select XY(Scatter), select the *scatter with data points connected by lines without markers* and go straight to Finish. Note the immediate revealing of patterns, with exceptions, and the correct treatment of year spacing. Repeat with the Liability Progression data.

---

## 2.4  How to make a table

Andrew Ehrenberg[7] introduced a series of rules and procedures for table making. He illustrated their application using Table 2.6. The data are not clearly identified, but may be taken to be quarterly·sales in each of four sales areas. In this section, the application of the guidelines is discussed and illustrated using Table 2.3 concerning absence rates on page 74 and also, in a series of exercises, Ehernberg's Table 2.6.

Ehrenberg's rules and procedures may be summarised as follows.

---

[7]  A.S.C. Ehrenberg, *Data Reduction; Analysing and Interpreting Statistical Data*, London, John Wiley (1975).

**Table 2.6**   Data in four areas and four three-month periods
in 1969

|   | 13–15 | 16–18 | 19–21 | 22–24 |
|---|-------|-------|-------|-------|
| A | 97.63 | 92.24 | 100.90 | 90.39 |
| B | 48.29 | 42.31 | 49.98 | 39.09 |
| C | 75.23 | 75.16 | 100.11 | 74.23 |
| D | 49.69 | 57.21 | 80.19 | 51.09 |

## Guidelines for table making

1. Use two effective digits; avoid unnecessary digits.
2. Use spaces as separators to facilitate comparison; avoid unnecessary lines.
3. Use summaries and ordering, of rows and/or columns, to reveal patterns; avoid unnecessary summaries.
4. Use columns to show simple patterns; use comparison of columns to show elaboration of pattern.
5. Use short but informative titles, labels and footnotes (where appropriate); avoid unnecessary text.

## Discussion of the guidelines

### 1.   Use two effective digits; avoid unnecessary digits

The tax rate data of Tables 2.4 and 2.5 illustrate the difficulty of discerning anything in a table where each number has several digits. Seeing patterns requires scanning several numbers and retaining their values in short term memory for mental comparison. Psychological experiments as well as much practical experience indicate that short term memory is ineffective in retaining numbers with more than two digits, in such circumstances. In some cases, numbers will contain digits which are necessary for adequate representation but ineffective for comparison purposes. For example, consider the list

123.67, 133.63, 154.13, 129.18, 136.52, 145.99, 137.42, 125.17

Here, the initial 1, while redundant for comparing the numbers, is necessary to establish their magnitude and so should not be deleted. The digits after the decimal point are unhelpful; the *effective* digits, for mental comparison purposes, are the two preceding the decimal point. The conclusion is that the numbers should be rounded to whole numbers:

124, 134, 154, 129, 137, 146, 137, 125

In Table 2.3, the absence rates are already reduced to two effective digits.

---

**Exercise 2.11**   Amend Table 2.6 by rounding the sales data to whole numbers. (This is easily done in Excel.) Does this improve readability?

While it is clear that the two digit guideline can improve tables considerably, it may be feared that the rounding necessary to achieve such an improvement may cause inaccuracies. In the case of Table 2.6, the maximum error involved in rounding to the nearest whole number is 0.5. However, the values in the data range from 37.39 to 100.90, a spread of 63.51. Relative to this, the rounding error is at most $0.5 \div 63.51$, or about 0.8%. For almost all practical analytical uses of tables, this is negligible.

On the other hand, the effects of rounding errors can be magnified if the rounded data are used in supplementary computation. For this reason, rounding should be avoided in data, such as census data or detailed results of market research surveys, which is published as a record for use by others.

**2. Use spaces as separators to facilitate comparison; avoid unnecessary lines**
Unnecessary ink in a data display distracts attention from the quantitative information in the display. In particular, lines in a table can interfere with comparison of numbers on either side. They are often unnecessary; white space can be used effectively as a separator. Thus, in Table 2.3 the vertical lines serve to inhibit comparisons between columns. By contrast, the revised version in Table 2.7 makes column comparisons easier.

**Table 2.7** Absence rates, per cent, for the workers in a company, classified by sex, age and whether management or shop floor workers

| Age (years) | Management | | | Shop floor | | | Both | | |
|---|---|---|---|---|---|---|---|---|---|
| | Male | Female | Both | Male | Female | Both | Male | Female | Both |
| 14 to 24 | 1.2 | 0.5 | 0.8 | 7.2 | 1.4 | 3.9 | 1.8 | 0.6 | 1.2 |
| 25 to 34 | 0.8 | 0.6 | 0.7 | 9.7 | 3.8 | 6.4 | 1.6 | 0.9 | 1.2 |
| 35 to 44 | 1.2 | 0.5 | 0.8 | 7.5 | 5.9 | 6.6 | 1.7 | 1.0 | 1.3 |
| 45 to 54 | 2.2 | 1.4 | 1.8 | 12.8 | 10.4 | 11.5 | 3.2 | 2.3 | 2.7 |
| 55 to 64 | 3.6 | 3.4 | 3.5 | 19.4 | 16.9 | 18.1 | 4.7 | 4.4 | 4.5 |
| 65 and over* | 5.6 | 4.4 | 5.0 | 35.8 | 31.2 | 33.3 | 7.6 | 6.2 | 6.9 |
| 14 and over | 2.1 | 1.5 | 1.8 | 12.7 | 8.2 | 10.2 | 3.0 | 2.1 | 2.5 |

* The official retirement age was 70 years.

Note also the use of wider white spaces to separate the 'Management', 'Shopfloor' and 'Both' groups, achieved in Table 2.3 by heavy (and therefore even more interfering) lines. In Table 2.7, horizontal lines are used to separate headings from the data, to bracket subheadings, and to separate the last summary row from the body of the data. This last separation is desirable, since the entries in the last row are not part of the pattern evident in the columns.

**Exercise 2.12** Continuation of Exercise 2.11. In Table 2.6, insert a blank row between the column header row and the data. Alternatively, insert a line underneath the header row. Try both. Which do you prefer? Why?

### 3. Use summaries and ordering, of rows and/or columns, to reveal patterns; avoid unnecessary summaries

In Table 2.7, summaries have already been included. Those in the last row are quite helpful; they allow a quick mental calculation to show that the male/female ratio is similar among both types of worker; a pattern begins to emerge. We note from the right-most column that overall absence rates are roughly constant for lower age groups but increase rapidly in the older age groups. Having identified this pattern from the summary column, it can be seen that a similar pattern seems to apply in the other columns. However, there is some redundancy in the five 'Both' columns. It may be suggested that all but the right-most be deleted, as shown in Table 2.8.

**Table 2.8**   Absence rates, per cent, for the workers in a company, classified by sex, age and whether management or shop floor workers

| Age (years) | Management | | Shop floor | | Overall |
|---|---|---|---|---|---|
| | Male | Female | Male | Female | |
| 14 to 24 | 1.2 | 0.5 | 7.2 | 1.4 | 1.2 |
| 25 to 34 | 0.8 | 0.6 | 9.7 | 3.8 | 1.2 |
| 35 to 44 | 1.2 | 0.5 | 7.5 | 5.9 | 1.3 |
| 45 to 54 | 2.2 | 1.4 | 12.8 | 10.4 | 2.7 |
| 55 to 64 | 3.6 | 3.4 | 19.4 | 16.9 | 4.5 |
| 65 and over* | 5.6 | 4.4 | 35.8 | 31.2 | 6.9 |
| 14 and over | 2.1 | 1.5 | 12.7 | 8.2 | 2.5 |

\* The official retirement age was 70 years.

It is easier to make comparisons between numbers if they are ordered than if not. Compare the unordered row of data used in the discussion of guideline 1,

$$124, 134, 154, 129, 137, 146, 137, 125$$

with the same data ordered from smallest to largest,

$$124, 125, 129, 134, 137, 137, 146, 154$$

Being able to establish the range quickly assists in evaluating other comparisons. Also, it may seem that there is more spread at the top end.

While it does not make sense in a table to order individual columns, it is often helpful to order row or column summaries. If there are corresponding patterns in the columns, then the ordering in the summary will be reflected in the individual columns, at least approximately. The same applies to rows. These effects are illustrated for the case of Table 2.6 in Exercise 2.13 below

In Table 2.8, the absence rates in the 'Overall' column are already in increasing order. If this column was not so ordered, it would not be appropriate in this case to order the table according to the data in the 'Overall' column, because there is a natural order in the age categories; it is not appropriate to upset a natural order. As there are only two categories within each of the other categorisations, the order in which these are presented is not critical.

Having noted the similarity of the ratios of male to female absence rates in management and shop floor workers, it may be worth exploring whether this persists in the different age groups. This could be achieved by inserting extra columns, perhaps in italics, with the calculated ratios. However, this may be achieved at the cost of loss of clarity. It may be advisable to display the additional columns in a separate table. This is left as an exercise. Note, however, the danger of using rounded data in supplementary calculations.

---

**Exercise 2.13**  Continuation of Exercise 2.12. Calculate row and column averages for the data in Table 2.6. Noting that the columns are in a natural (time) order, sort the rows according to the row averages. To what extent is this ordering preserved between rows? What pattern is perceived within rows? How would you describe this pattern verbally? What exceptions are evident?

---

**Exercise 2.14**  Absence rate data are available in datafile Absence.xls in the book's website. Calculate male–female ratios for management and shop floor workers in each age category. Comment. Are there similarities? Are there exceptions? Show the calculated ratios as additions to the existing table and also in a separate table. Discuss the merits of each approach.

---

4. **Use columns to show simple patterns; use comparison of columns to show elaboration of pattern**

Compare the row of data used in the discussion of guideline 1, ordered as above,

124, 125, 129, 134, 137, 137, 146, 154

with the same data arranged in a column,

124
125
129
134
137
137
146
154

The 1 in the first column is quickly seen to be constant and can be ignored in comparisons. Scanning down the second column of digits gives a quick impression of the variation in the numbers, with three 2's, three 3's, a 4 and a 5. By contrast, the corresponding sets of digits are not as close together physically and so take longer to scan; the initial digits in the row format do not stand out as clearly and so take more time to deal with while the pattern in the second digits does not emerge as quickly.

Again, compare scanning the 'overall' column in Table 2.8 with scanning the same data displayed as a row:

1.2  1.2  1.3  2.7  4.5  6.9.

In the column format, numbers to be compared are closer so that the eye does not have to travel as much, while digits in corresponding positions (for example, leading digits) are aligned and are scanned without interruption. These features make the scanning task easier. Also, comparison of the columns in Table 2.8 shows that similar patterns of increasing absence rates occur in the different columns.

---

**Exercise 2.15**  Continuation of Exercise 2.13. Rearrange the data of Table 2.6 by switching rows and columns. Note the almost constant pattern within rows, seen by scanning down first digits.

---

5.  **Use short but informative titles, labels and footnotes (where appropriate); avoid unnecessary text**

There is much scope allowed within this guideline, depending on circumstances and personal taste. When a table is part of a report, and is discussed in the body of the report, it is probably wise to reduce to a minimum any text attached to the table. On the other hand, if the intended readers are unlikely to want to (or have time to) read detailed discussion, extra text designed to make the table more or less complete in itself, may be added. Preparing such text is an art form. If Table 2.8 were to stand alone, one might replace the title by something like that in Table 2.9, and insert a heading, 'Absence rates, per cent', on the line underneath the title, as shown.

**Table 2.9**  Absence rates are higher among men, among shop floor workers and among older people

Absence rates, per cent

| Age (years) | Management | | Shop floor | | Overall |
|---|---|---|---|---|---|
| | Male | Female | Male | Female | |
| 14 to 24 | 1.2 | 0.5 | 7.2 | 1.4 | 1.2 |
| 25 to 34 | 0.8 | 0.6 | 9.7 | 3.8 | 1.2 |
| 35 to 44 | 1.2 | 0.5 | 7.5 | 5.9 | 1.3 |
| 45 to 54 | 2.2 | 1.4 | 12.8 | 10.4 | 2.7 |
| 55 to 64 | 3.6 | 3.4 | 19.4 | 16.9 | 4.5 |
| 65 and over* | 5.6 | 4.4 | 35.8 | 31.2 | 6.9 |
| 14 and over | 2.1 | 1.5 | 12.7 | 8.2 | 2.5 |

* The official retirement age was 70 years.

*Redrawing Table 2.6*

Applying the guidelines to Table 2.6 leads to Table 2.10. The columns have been arranged in decreasing order of magnitude, thus easing overall comparison of columns. The rows have not been reordered; a natural order already exists.

**Table 2.10**  Quarterly sales in each of four sales areas

|       | North | East | South | West | Average |
|-------|-------|------|-------|------|---------|
| Q 1   | 98    | 75   | 50    | 49   | 68      |
| Q 2   | 92    | 75   | 57    | 42   | 67      |
| Q 3   | 101   | *100* | *80*  | 50   | 83      |
| Q 4   | 90    | 74   | 51    | 39   | 64      |
| Average | 95  | 75*  | 53*   | 45   | 67      |

* Averages based on three quarters only.

The (almost) constant columns indicate that there is little quarterly variation. Note the exceptions in the pattern identified with italics. Omitting these from the corresponding column averages means that the latter summarise normal regional differences. They have not been omitted from the row averages and hence show up the third quarter exception.

## Graphical displays

The information in each of the tables discussed above may also be displayed graphically. Figure 2.12 shows the absence rate data. It clearly shows the difference between males and females, the much larger difference between management and shop floor workers and the increasingly higher rates for the older age groups. It also reveals quickly and clearly the relatively high rates among young male shop floor workers, an aspect of the pattern not as immediately obvious from the tabular version. The apparent slight irregularity of the management rates, by comparison with shop floor rates, not readily visible in the table, may be ascribed to the fact that the former rates are based on smaller numbers of workers than the latter.

Figure 2.13 shows immediately and very clearly the pattern already seen in Table 2.10.

## Graphs versus tables

These comparisons of graphs and tables bring out certain contrasts between the two display styles. Graphs are clearly better at conveying qualitative information; they reveal such information much more quickly than tables and they can reveal detailed patterns in data that may be less quickly seen in tables. There is also evidence to suggest that patterns in data are more memorably conveyed by graph than by table.

By contrast, tables are better at conveying information quantitatively and accurately. As a consequence, once the data to be displayed have been chosen, tables are less susceptible to distortion than are graphs; examples of distortions in graphs abound.

Also, tables are limited in the amount of information that they can convey and generally are limited to one or very few variables, whereas graphs can convey information from much larger volumes of data, including multiple variable patterns.

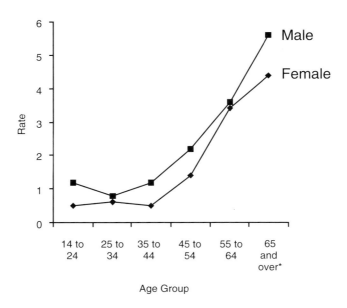

**Figure 2.12**   Absence rates, per cent.

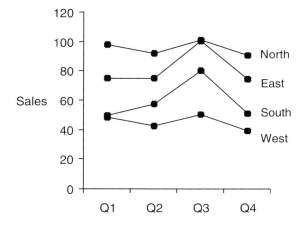

**Figure 2.13** Quarterly sales in four regions.

## 2.5　Graphical display of summary data

Because there is so much scope for variety in graphical design and so relatively little knowledge of the factors governing graphical perception, it is less easy to prescribe guidelines for good graph making than it is for good table making. Indeed, there is much debate on the topic. Two basic guidelines are:

1. Use graphical codes which are easily decoded.
2. Maximise the data-to-ink ratio.

The first refers to the encoding of numbers as lengths, as in bar charts; areas, as in histograms; angles, as in pie charts, etc., and the comparative difficulty in subsequent decoding. The second recognises that unnecessary ink in a graph (and in a table) distracts from the parts of the graph that encode the data. Some examples are used to illustrate both points, and recommendations on the choice of graphical form follow. Most of the examples are concerned with frequency data but the guidelines apply equally well to graphs displaying measurement data.

### Bar charts versus pie charts, lengths versus angles

In the pie chart shown in Figure 2.14, which of segments 2 and 3 is bigger? Which of segments 2 and 4 is bigger? What proportion of the total is any of segments 1 to 5?

　By comparison, consider the same quantities displayed as a bar chart in Figure 2.15. It is quite clear that the values are in ascending order. The reason for this is that lengths referred to a common base, the horizontal axis in this case, are considerably easier to decode than are angles. Furthermore, the values can be read reasonably easily from the vertical scale, although it should be noted that graphs are not ideal for decoding values.

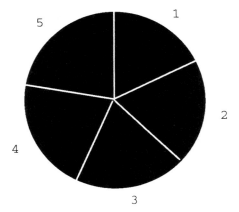

**Figure 2.14**   Values encoded in a pie chart.

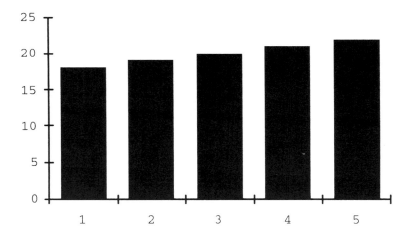

**Figure 2.15**   The same values encoded in a bar chart.

### Improving the bar chart; reducing the ink

The bars in Figure 2.15 are very prominent; they may serve to distract from neighbouring text or figures, unnecessarily. Figure 2.16 shows a much 'quieter' version on the left, using considerably less ink. By removing just a little more ink, a grid which helps in decoding values is seen, as in Figure 2.16, right.

### 'Enhanced' pie charts

Figure 2.17 is a classic pie chart showing how the total expenditure in a university is divided between several categories. The graph has been enhanced by giving it a three-dimensional look. Note the visual mismatch between the 3%, 4% and 5% slices

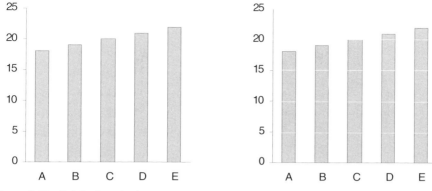

**Figure 2.16**   Quieter bar charts.

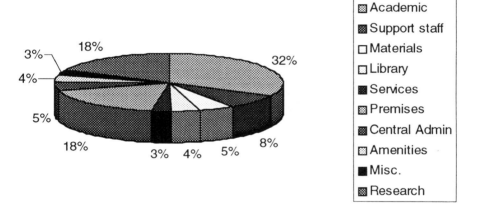

**Figure 2.17**   College expenditure displayed as a 'three-dimensional' pie chart.

corresponding to Miscellaneous, Amenities and Central Administration, on the left, compared with the same slices for Services, Library and Materials, at the bottom. By contrast, no such mismatch is visible in Figure 2.18, which shows the same data but without the third dimension[6].

The mismatch is due to tilting the circular pie into an ellipse, a consequence of creating the three-dimensional look, with consequent distortion. It is added to by the fact that the base of the chart is visible at the front but not at the back.

---

[6]   The fact that different shades of grey are insufficiently distinguishable adds to the difficulty in reading this graph. A full colour version is included in the Supplements and Extensions page of the book's website.

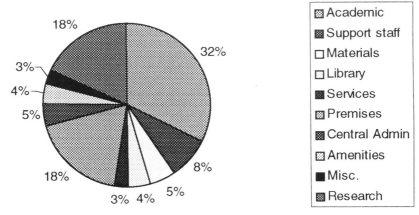

**Figure 2.18**   College expenditure displayed as a standard pie chart.

## Charts with two classifying variables

Table 2.11 shows the market share of seven brands of a product over a four year period.

**Table 2.11**   Market share, per cent, of seven brands over a four year period

| | | | | Product | | | |
|---|---|---|---|---|---|---|---|
| Year | A | B | C | D | E | F | G |
| 1999 | 29 | 44 | 5 | 2 | 6 | 10 | 4 |
| 2000 | 26 | 51 | 4 | 3 | 5 | 9 | 2 |
| 2001 | 21 | 56 | 5 | 3 | 4 | 8 | 2 |
| 2002 | 25 | 55 | 5 | 1 | 3 | 8 | 2 |

Figure 2.19 shows the same data in a popular chart format.

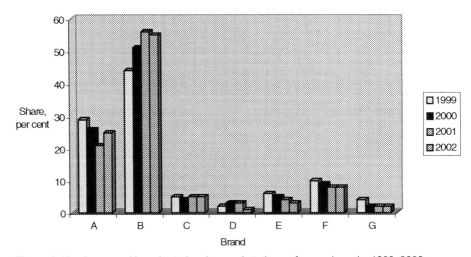

**Figure 2.19**   A grouped bar chart showing market share of seven brands, 1999–2002.

> **Exercise 2.16** What trends and patterns in brand share per cent do you see displayed in Figure 2.19. Make comparisons within brands across time and between brands at the same time.

There are several problems with this graph. Overall comparisons of the bigger brands with the rest and year to year comparisons of shares for a given (bigger) brand are relatively straightforward. However, it is more difficult to compare brand shares for a given year and to compare the smaller brands overall. Comparing changing patterns is even more difficult. Switching the roles of the categorising variables, making Year the horizontal axis variable and Brand the legend on the right, makes it easier to compare brand shares for a given year but at the expense of greater difficulty in year to year comparisons of shares for a given brand.

Apart from this, the artwork is unnecessarily distracting, and may be misleading. We are shown a three-dimensional depiction of a two-dimensional display; there is no information in the 'depth' dimension and the chosen perspective may mislead by hiding parts of some bars while revealing others. Also, the shading used to differentiate bars corresponding to different times may distract and mislead; some shading styles are more prominent than others, and so may register more strongly, making a bar appear bigger (however slightly) than it actually is, thus possibly distorting the overall image of the information.

Some suggestions for variations on this graph are made in Exercise 2.17.

> **Exercise 2.17** The data in Table 2.11 are in datafile Marketshare.xls in the book's website. In the row underneath the data, enter the average formula applied to each set of four brand shares. Select the data and the averages and sort by average. This has the effect of sorting the brands by a measure of size. Use the Excel Chart Wizard to make a new grouped bar chart (or clustered column chart, to use the Excel terminology), with no 3-D effects and quieter shading or colours to differentiate years. Also, make a new chart with the roles of Year and Brand switched. Discuss the improvements and disimprovements resulting from ordering by size, removing 3-D effects, changing shading, switching Year and Brand.

A commonly used alternative to the grouped bar chart is the split bar chart, exemplified in Figure 2.20. This makes year to year comparison of brand share relatively easy for the largest brand. However, this task is less easy for the other large brands. The reason for this is that the bar segments showing shares for Brand B, the largest brand, have a common base, the horizontal axis, and the comparison involves comparing just the bar heights. However, the bars segments for Brand A, the second largest brand, do not have a common base; comparison of lengths that are not

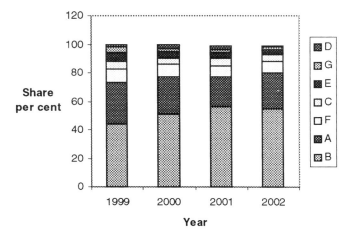

**Figure 2.20**   A split bar chart showing market share of seven brands, 1999–2002.

referred to a common base is a more difficult task than comparison of lengths with a common base.

The conventional graph form for displaying parts of a whole, such as market share, is the pie chart. However, this is virtually useless for comparison; see Figure 2.21. The main reason for this is that angles are much more difficult to evaluate and compare than line lengths or distances. The main virtue of the pie chart is that it draws

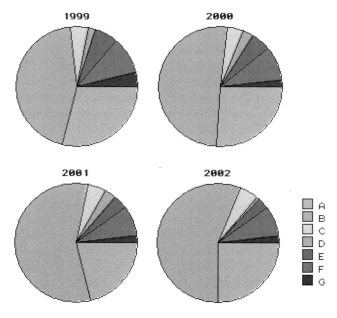

**Figure 2.21**   Pie charts showing market share of seven brands, 1999–2002.

attention to the fact that parts of a whole are being displayed. Other than that, its virtues are less obvious.

## Conclusions on graphical coding of data

The conclusion that emerges from these comparisons of chart forms is that some forms of data encoding are easier to decode than others. In particular, lengths referred to a common base are easier to compare than lengths that do not have a common reference base; angles are more difficult to compare than lengths.

## Profile charts

A chart form which may be more effective in some circumstances is the *profile chart* used in Figure 2.22 to display the market share data. This makes comparison of the same brand share at different times very simple; all are referred to a common (vertical) scale, with a common base. Comparison of different brands at the same time is made easier as the comparisons are now made vertically; the eye does not have to travel across the page to compare heights from the horizontal axis.

The problem of mixing large and small brands, with brand shares of differing orders of magnitude, is solved by using two charts, with the small brands shown as a more or less undifferentiated group in the first, to allow comparison of large and small. The key difference between the two charts is the *aspect ratio,* that is, the ratio

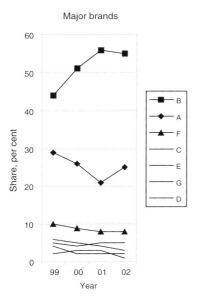 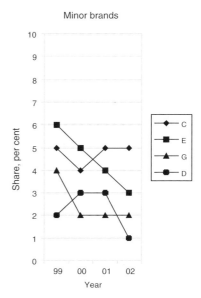

**Figure 2.22** Profile charts of market share for major and minor brands, 1999–2002.

between the (physical) lengths of the axes; recall the discussion at the end of Section 2.1. Rescaling the vertical axis makes brand differences more distinct. Making the key angles of the line segments that make up the profiles closer to 45° makes the profiles more distinctive. This is another example of encoding data in ways which are more easily decoded.

The second guideline, maximise the data-to-ink ratio, has also been employed in producing Figure 2.22; all unnecessary borders have been removed, axes and grid-lines have been lightened, bold print titles and legends have been unbolded.

Note that the profile chart works whether the categorizing variable on the horizontal axis is quantitative, as here, or qualitative. An example of data with two qualitative categorizing variables is given in Review Exercise 2.3.

## 2.6   Review exercises

2.1   Recall the data of Exercise 2.1, page 63:

| Inspector | Counts | | | | | |
|-----------|----|----|----|----|----|----|
| 1 | 22 | 19 | 21 | 24 | 22 | 24 |
| 2 | 19 | 22 | 15 | 24 | 26 | 14 |
| 3 | 26 | 25 | 27 | 26 | 28 | 30 |
| 4 | 21 | 19 | 22 | 19 | 31 | 20 |

Calculate the mean and standard deviation for each inspector. Make a small table of the numerical summaries. Prepare a short commentary on comparison of inspectors.

Recall the exceptional count for inspector 4. Recalculate the mean and standard deviation for inspector 4 excluding this value. Revise your commentary in the light of this.

Discuss the relative sensitivity of mean and standard deviation to the presence of exceptional values.

2.2   A building society (savings and loan association) branch manager is concerned about computer maintenance charges in his branch and decides to investigate. As a first step, he retrieves from the branch accounting system the monthly maintenance charges for the previous twelve months. They were, in euros:

588,  880,  608,  699,  817,  546,  707,  504,  732,  664,  584,  599

The system also yielded values for the mean and standard deviation of €660.67 and €11.47, respectively. For comparison, he telephones a fellow branch manager and persuades her to give him her monthly maintenance charges for the previous six months. They were, in euros:

354,   512,   432,   421,   568,   724.

He calculates the mean and standard deviation for the other branch, finding $\bar{X} = $ €501.83 and $s = $ €131.99.

(i)   Check his calculation.
(ii)  Make a small table to assist comparison.
(iii) Make dotplots of both datasets.
(iv)  Make a short report on comparisons between the branches, including any reservations you have about numerical comparisons.

2.3   A market research company has reported on approval ratings, per cent, of a sample of drinkers to a selection of products, in the table below. The data are the numbers, per cent, who associate corresponding attributes with products.

| Attribute | Product | | | | | |
|---|---|---|---|---|---|---|
| | Guinness | Smithwicks | Harp | Budweiser | Furstenburg | Fosters |
| Good taste | 55.4 | 33.3 | 20.3 | 6.8 | 76.7 | 10.7 |
| Consistent | 17.3 | 10.9 | 7.4 | 3.4 | 17.1 | 4.5 |
| Good ads | 61.1 | 27.4 | 4.3 | 4.9 | 53.8 | 2.1 |
| For RKPs* | 9.0 | 6.2 | 11.1 | 1.1 | 9.8 | 2.3 |
| Good value | 34.0 | 21.6 | 13.8 | 4.6 | 36.3 | 35.7 |

*RKP stands for Right Kind of Person

Make a new table, or tables, to facilitate analysis and reporting. Prepare a commentary on the improvements you have made.
    Make a graph or graphs for the same purpose. Prepare a commentary on your choice of graph form, referring to other possible choices. Prepare a report for the beer company sales manager based on a combination of tables and graphs.
    Compare and contrast the relative merits of tables and graphs for the purpose of analysis and presentation in this case.

2.4   The table overleaf gives audience duplication figures for selected pairs of television programmes during a particular week. Each figure in the body of the table is the percentage of viewers of the corresponding column programme who also viewed the corresponding row programme. Data such as these are used in planning television advertising campaigns.
    Construct another table from the one given so as to discover and present the main features of the information in the table, and the main departures from the pattern you discover. Construct a graph for the same purpose. Report on your conclusions. What reservations do you have about your conclusions? Suggest how these data might be used to assist in the design of television advertising campaigns.

| | Day and time | Viewers of | | | | | | | Rating* |
|---|---|---|---|---|---|---|---|---|---|
| | | 6 pm News | World in Action | Tues. Film | Coron. Street | Adventurers | News at 10 | 6 pm News | |
| Percentage who also watched | | % | % | % | % | % | % | % | % |
| 6 pm News | Mon 6 pm | 100.0 | 24.6 | 29.1 | 23.2 | 26.8 | 25.2 | 46.1 | 15.1 |
| World in Action | Mon 8 pm | 49.0 | 100.0 | 49.8 | 54.2 | 51.3 | 47.6 | 47.4 | 30.1 |
| The Tuesday Film | Tue 11 pm | 21.2 | 18.3 | 100.0 | 20.9 | 19.1 | 40.0 | 17.1 | 11.0 |
| Coronation Street | Wed 8 pm | 53.6 | 63.4 | 68.5 | 100.0 | 59.1 | 54.7 | 53.3 | 34.9 |
| The Adventurers | Thu 8 pm | 47.7 | 44.7 | 46.3 | 44.8 | 100.0 | 42.9 | 44.7 | 26.9 |
| News at Ten | Fri 10 pm | 25.2 | 23.1 | 54.2 | 24.4 | 23.8 | 100.0 | 25.0 | 15.1 |
| 6 pm News | Fri 6 pm | 46.3 | 23.9 | 23.6 | 23.2 | 25.3 | 25.2 | 100.0 | 15.2 |

* % of all adults who watched the programme.

2.5    The table that follow shows per capita consumption of a range of beverages of different types in several European countries.

| Litres per Capita | Tea (kg) | Coffee (kg) | Carbonated Drinks | Mineral Water | Fruit Juices | Beer | Wine | Spirits |
|---|---|---|---|---|---|---|---|---|
| Belgium | 0.1 | 6.8 | 75.3 | 74.3 | 16.0 | 125.3 | 23.8 | 3.2 |
| Denmark | 0.4 | 10.8 | 44.8 | 10.7 | 18.7 | 125.0 | 21.9 | 3.8 |
| France | 0.2 | 5.7 | 35.3 | 68.3 | 7.0 | 38.8 | 88.4 | 5.6 |
| Germany (E) | 0.2 | – | – | – | – | 139.3 | 11.5 | 5.0 |
| Germany (W) | 0.2 | 8.4 | 88.1 | 76.3 | 38.5 | 141.6 | 26.1 | 6.1 |
| Greece | 0.0 | 3.1 | 32.9 | 17.0 | 4.4 | 24.3 | 30.3 | 14.7 |
| Ireland | 3.1 | 1.7 | 55.6 | 3.1 | 10.2 | 90.0 | 10.5 | 4.0 |
| Italy | 0.1 | 4.5 | 31.7 | 79.9 | 6.3 | 21.3 | 72.3 | 3.4 |
| Luxembourg | – | – | – | – | – | – | – | – |
| Netherlands | 0.7 | 9.2 | 56.2 | 11.7 | 16.3 | 87.5 | 15.8 | 6.9 |
| Portugal | 0.0 | 2.6 | 31.2 | 25.9 | 3.4 | 45.3 | 56.3 | 2.6 |
| Spain | 0.0 | 4.0 | 42.6 | 31.2 | 9.4 | 71.3 | 37.0 | 6.5 |
| U.K. | 2.7 | 2.3 | 124.7 | 5.4 | 18.7 | 108.1 | 12.9 | 4.3 |
| **EC Average** | **0.6** | **5.3** | **64.2** | **49.7** | **16.1** | **81.2** | **42.5** | **5.3** |

*Source: Adapted from Euromonitor, European Marketing Data and Statistics 1992, 27th Ed.*

Prepare a report, intended for a general readership, which describes the main features of interest in the table, using appropriate data displays to illustrate the features you describe. The report should not exceed two A4 pages, including displays and text; one page is preferable.

Separately, justify each choice of display in terms of principles of good data display and explain the corresponding shortcomings of the table above. Use at most half an A4 page.

# 3

# The Normal model for chance variation

Everybody believes in the law of errors, the experimenters because they think it is a mathematical theorem, the mathematicians because they think it is an experimental fact.

quoted by Harald Cramér
*Mathematical Methods of Statistics*[1]

The Normal frequency distribution, sometimes referred to as the Normal law of errors, has a long history as a widely applicable model for what is referred to here as 'chance variation'. Its mathematical properties have long fascinated theoreticians who have studied its properties and its provenances. In response to the quotation above, Cramér noted: 'It seems appropriate to comment that both parties are perfectly right, provided that their belief is not too absolute: mathematical proof tells us that, *under certain qualifying conditions,* we are justified in expecting a normal distribution, while statistical experience shows that, in fact, distributions are often *approximately normal.*'

Shewhart's term 'chance causes of variation', invented in the 1920s, has been defined in Section 1.4 as the many individually negligible and unpredictable but collectively influential factors that affect a process or system. Shewhart noted that the frequency distribution of a set of measurements which followed such a prescription may be expected to be well approximated by a Normal distribution. One can imagine engineers, business analysts, medical scientists or others reassuring themselves that their variables of interest are subject to chance causes of variation and that was why their empirical frequency distributions appear Normal. Such considerations will enhance their confidence in using standard methods for the statistical analysis of their data.

---

[1] Harald Cramér, *Mathematical Methods of Statistics*, Princeton, Princeton University Press (1946), page 232.

In Section 1.4, the Normal model for chance variation was introduced as an idealised histogram. Different versions of the curve were used to model the chance variation evident in different production conditions. In Section 2.1, we saw how to construct a histogram from the underlying frequency distribution. To use the Normal curve effectively, we must be able to deal with the corresponding Normal frequency distribution. In this chapter, we develop the tools to allow us to do this, in the context of calculating non-conformance rates in the tennis ball manufacturing process. We also develop some key modelling concepts

**Learning objectives**

After completing this chapter, students should understand the characteristics of the Normal model for chance variation, its application in calculating non-conformance rates for manufacturing processes, its estimation through sample statistics and its assessment using Normal diagnostic plots, and demonstrate this by being able to:

- superimpose a Normal curve on a histogram reflecting chance causes of variation;
- calculate non-conformance rates from sample data;
- read the standard Normal table and draw Normal curves to illustrate;
- standardise a given value of a process measurement in terms of standard deviations from the mean;
- calculate Normal frequencies for arbitrary means and standard deviation;
- use the Excel NORMDIST function to calculate non-conformance rates and tables of non-conformance rates for varying means and standard deviations;
- use tables of non-conformance rates to identify improvement targets and requirements;
- explain the correspondence between model and process parameters and the distinction between both and sample statistics;
- explain the idea behind Normal diagnostic plots and describe their application;
- explain the use of simulated Normal diagnostic plots as reference plots in assessing Normality.

## 3.1   Calculating non-conformance rates

Recall Figure 1.13, reproduced here as Figure 3.1, which showed histograms reflecting the variation in tennis ball core diameters produced by four presses in one production run. In Chapter 1, we noted that presses 1 and 2 produced cores with rather similar measurements, and the press 3 cores were clearly more spread and may have been, as a whole, smaller than those of presses 1 and 2. The cores of press 4 had dispersion similar to that in presses 1 and 2 but were, as a whole, considerably smaller. It was surmised that a simple adjustment to the pressure in press 4 would raise the

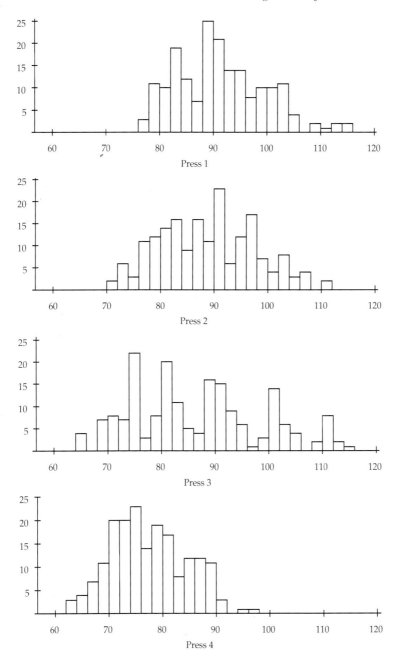

**Figure 3.1**   Histograms of the tennis ball diameters.

diameters to be more in line with presses 1 and 2, assuming these to be more or less satisfactory. It was also suggested that a more intense investigation of the factors affecting variation in press 3 might be required to bring its spread into line with the others.

Implicit in this account is that the tennis ball cores produced by presses 1 and 2 are more or less satisfactory. To make this more explicit, we need *specification limits* for tennis ball core diameters, which will allow us to calculate the *non-conformance rate* appropriate to each press. From limits on tennis ball diameters specified by the International Lawn Tennis Association, it is possible to derive specification limits for tennis ball core diameters on the coded scale being used here. In this case, the limits are 70–100.[2] By sorting the data in Excel, the numbers of tennis balls outside these specification limits may be found by subtracting row numbers, and non-conformance rates may be found by dividing these numbers by 186, the number of tennis ball cores produced in each press in one run.[3]

---

**Exercise 3.1**   The tennis ball core diameter data are in datafile Tennis.xls on the book's website. Copy the data to a new worksheet, sort each column separately, count the numbers less than 70 and greater than 100 in each and calculate the non-conformance rates.

---

It appears that press 2 is best with a non-conformance rate of 11%, followed by press 1 at 12%. Note that both of these err on the upper limit only. Press 3 has 6% below the lower limit and 13% above the upper limit, giving a total non-conformance rate of 19%, while press 4 has 13% non-conforming, all below the lower limit. Contrary to suggestions made in Chapter 1 that the core diameters of presses 1 and 2 were 'more or less satisfactory', these calculations show that none of the presses is satisfactory and that considerable improvement is needed. In all cases, a combination of moving diameter centres and reducing diameter spread will improve matters.

### Non-conformance rates and the Normal model

In Chapter 1, it was suggested that the Normal model for chance variation could be used to *model* the variation represented by the histograms. Figure 3.2 shows the four histograms with Normal curves superimposed. Assuming that the Normal model provides an adequate representation of the variation in the data, the Normal curves provide an alternative approach to evaluating non-conformance rates. The big advantage of the Normal model, assuming it provides an adequate fit to the data, is that it allows the variation to be represented by just two numbers, the mean and standard deviation, representing centre and spread, respectively. Thus, if we calculate values for the mean and standard deviation from data, the frequency distribution of the data

---

[2]   Note that a specification range of 30, at least 30% of the permitted values, is unrealistic. In this case, the original data were 'coded'; the two leading digits in each value, which were the same for all the data, were deleted.

[3]   This 'quick and dirty' method is adequate for our purposes here. More efficient methods may be used, including dedicated commands in specialised software, for example, the Capability Analysis feature in Minitab.

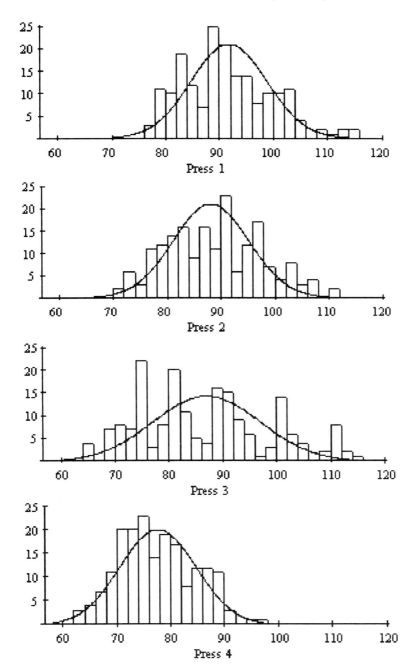

**Figure 3.2** Histograms of the tennis ball diameters with Normal curves superimposed.

being modelled can be reproduced reasonably accurately by substituting these values into the appropriate mathematical formula. This can be done using a computerised version of the formula such as the NORMDIST function incorporated in Excel or by using a special table which gives relevant values for what is called the *standard* Normal curve. Details are explained in the next section.

Apart from providing an alternative approach to assessing non-conformance rates in particular instances, the Normal model also provides us with a tool for evaluating process non-conformance rates in a much wider range of circumstances. Thus, we can easily evaluate the improvements that can be achieved by moving the centre or reducing the spread by different amounts, that is, a 'what-if' study. Alternatively, given specification limits and acceptable non-conformance rates, we can calculate target centre and spread values to achieve these. Illustrations are given in Section 3.4. We can use such calculations to assist decision making in a quality improvement context, given the costs and benefits involved.

We will find other uses for the Normal model in later chapters. In particular, we will see its role in statistical inference introduced in Chapters 4 and 5 and illustrated repeatedly thereafter.

## 3.2   Using the Normal model; the standard Normal distribution

To identify the Normal curve corresponding to a given centre and spread, we need numerical measures of centre and spread. A key feature of the Normal curve and Normal frequency distribution is that the values of the mean and standard deviation completely determine the frequency distribution. To illustrate, Figure 3.3 shows the Normal frequencies within 1, 2 and 3 standard deviations of the mean; approximately 68% of the values in a Normal frequency distribution lie within one standard deviation of the mean, 95% within two standard deviations and 99.7% within three standard deviations. Note the horizontal scale; the numbers represent numbers of standard deviations from the mean with 0 in the middle representing the mean.

More generally, the proportion of values within any distance of the mean is uniquely determined by the number of standard deviations from the mean, irrespective of the values of the mean and standard deviation. This permits any Normal frequency distribution to be determined from the so-called *standard Normal frequency distribution* having mean 0 and standard deviation 1. A table for this distribution can be found in Appendix A at the end of the book. As indicated at the head of the table,

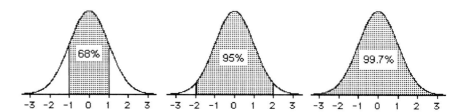

**Figure 3.3**   Standard Normal curves.

the table gives the proportion of the area under the Normal curve to the left of $z$, as illustrated in Figure 3.4.

The total area, representing all the values in the frequency distribution, is 1, so the area left of $z$ gives the proportion of values in the frequency distribution that are smaller than $z$. Values of $z$ up to one decimal place are listed in the left column; values of the second decimal place are in the top row. For example, the area to the left of 1.23, the shaded area in Figure 3.4, is 0.8907. Since the total area is 1, the area to the right of 1.23 is $1 - 0.8907 = 0.1093$, the unshaded area in Figure 3.4.

This works for positive values of $z$. For values of $z$ less than 0, the symmetry of the Normal curve is used. The unshaded area to the left of $-1.23$ in Figure 3.5 is the same as the area to the right of $+1.23$ in Figure 3.4, that is, 0.1093, as already calculated.

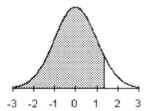

**Figure 3.4**  Area under the standard Normal curve.

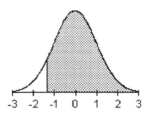

**Figure 3.5**  Area under the standard Normal curve for negative values.

**Exercise 3.2**  From the table in Appendix A, find the areas less than 1.08 and −2.53. Illustrate your calculations using standard Normal curves.

It is easy to extend this to find the proportion of values that lie between any two values, $z_1$ and $z_2$; assuming $z_1$ is less than $z_2$, find the proportion less than $z_1$ and the proportion less than $z_2$ and subtract the former from the latter.

**Exercise 3.3**  From the table in Appendix A, find the area between −2.53 and 1.08. Illustrate your calculations using a standard Normal curve.

## Standardisation

To extend this to a Normal frequency distribution with mean and standard deviation different from 0 and 1, the important device of *standardisation* is used. In standard notation, we designate the mean by the Greek letter $\mu$ (Greek for m) and the standard deviation by $\sigma$ (Greek for s). To calculate the proportion of values less than a given value, say $x$, in a Normal distribution with mean $\mu$ and standard deviation $\sigma$, first calculate

$$z = \frac{x - \mu}{\sigma},$$

and then use the standard Normal table to find the proportion of values less than $z$ in a standard Normal distribution. The process of subtracting the mean and dividing by the standard deviation is referred to as *standardisation*; $z$ is the *standardised value* of $x$. The value of $z$ may be interpreted as the number of standard deviations by which $x$ deviates from the mean. Equivalently, $z$ measures the deviation from the mean in *standard deviation units*.

## Illustration

Recall from Chapter 2 that the means and standard deviations of the data in the four presses were:

| Press | Mean | Standard deviation |
|---|---|---|
| 1 | 91 | 8.3 |
| 2 | 88 | 8.9 |
| 3 | 86 | 12.1 |
| 4 | 77 | 7.0 |

If these are taken as representative of the corresponding processes (where each press is regarded as corresponding to a separate process), we can calculate the non-conformance rates to be expected from each process, assuming that they continue to produce in this way. In the case of press 1, taking $\mu$ to be 91 and $\sigma$ to be 8.3, let $x_1 = 70$ and $x_2 = 100$ and calculate

$$z_1 = \frac{x_1 - \mu}{\sigma} = \frac{70 - 91}{8.3} = -2.53$$

and

$$z_2 = \frac{x_2 - \mu}{\sigma} = \frac{100 - 91}{8.3} = +1.08.$$

This is illustrated in Figure 3.6, showing a Normal curve with alternative labels for the horizontal axis. (The $x$ labels are not evenly spaced, due to rounding.) The shaded area on the right shows the area right of 1.08 or the proportion non-conforming above 100. That on the left, barely visible, shows the area left of –2.53 or the proportion non-conforming below 70.

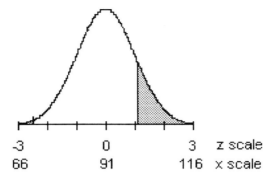

**Figure 3.6**　Standardisation as a change of scale.

From the result of Exercise 3.3, we find the area between −2.53 and +1.08 is 0.8542, that is, a conformance rate of 85.42%. Subtraction from 100% gives a non-conformance rate of 14.58%.

---

**Exercise 3.4**　Assuming a Normal frequency distribution for the diameters of presses 2, 3 and 4, with means of 88, 86 and 77 and standard deviations of 8.9, 12.1 and 7.0, respectively, use the standard Normal table to calculate the proportion of non-conformances for each press.

---

The press 1 and 2 rates of 14.5% and 11% are close to those observed in the data, the press 3 and press 4 rates of 22% and 16% are not quite so close. It is inevitable that different approaches to calculating process non-conformance rates from limited process data will provide somewhat different answers; the presence of chance causes of variation will ensure that. Whether these differences can be partially ascribed to a deficiency in the Normal model or to some other causes cannot be decided at this stage.

## 3.3　Normal model calculations using Excel

The Excel NORMDIST function provides an alternative to using the standard Normal table for calculating quantities such as non-conformance rates. The NORMDIST function has four arguments, x, Mean, Standard_dev and Cumulative. The last is a logical argument, which may be TRUE (corresponding to numerical value 1) or FALSE (corresponding to 0). When Cumulative is TRUE, as it will be in all applications here, the NORMDIST function gives the proportion of the area under the Normal curve with the given mean and standard deviation which lies to the left of the given value of $x$. As a mathematical function, it is referred to as the *Normal cumulative distribution function*. The use of the function is illustrated here to calculate the non-conformance rate for a process with mean and standard deviation as in press 1.

## Illustration

From the Insert menu, select Function. The following dialog box appears.

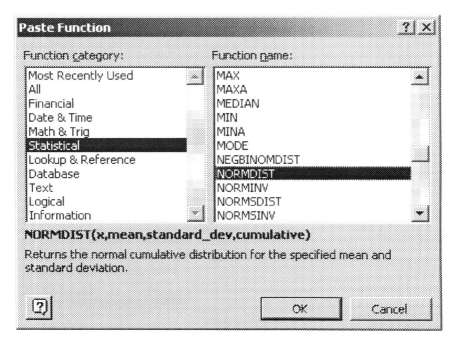

In the Function category window, select Statistical. In the Function name window, scroll to NORMDIST and select. Note the function description that appears underneath.

Click OK; in the Function palette that appears, enter 70, the lower specification limit, for **x**, 91 for **Mean**, 8.3 for **Standard_dev** and 1 for **Cumulative**, so that it appears as below.

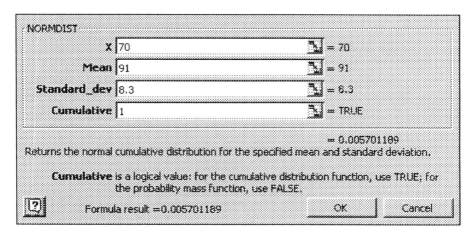

Note the confirmation of the entries to the right of each box and the result underneath. It appears that just over 0.5% of press 1 diameters are less than 70, according to the Normal approximation.

To calculate the proportion above the upper specification limit, first edit the function palette by replacing 70 by 100. This gives the proportion of diameters *less than* 100 as 0.8609. Subtracting this from 1 gives the proportion exceeding 100, that is, 0.1391. Combining the two percentages gives a non-conformance rate of 14.5%.

---

**Exercise 3.5**    Use Excel to calculate the approximate non-conformance rates for presses 2, 3 and 4, using the Normal model with means and standard deviations as given above.

---

## 3.4    'What-if' analysis

The flexibility of the Normal model makes it useful in answering questions such as

- How will the non-conformance rate change in response to a range of changes in centre and spread?
- How will the non-conformance rate change in response to possible changes in customer specifications?
- What change in centre and reduction in spread are needed to achieve an acceptably low non-conformance rate?
- What change in centre and reduction in spread are needed if the customer demands tighter specifications?

Assuming we know the costs involved in making such improvements to the process, 'what-if' analyses of this form are an essential component of rational decision making.

To illustrate, we use Excel to construct a simple table showing how the non-conformance rate changes in response to a range of changes in centre and spread. First, however, we note that the symmetry of the Normal curve allows us to reduce the range of mean values we need to explore. In the case of tennis ball core diameters where the specification range is 70–100, non-conformances rates for means less than 85, the centre of the specification range, are mirror images of those for means exceeding 85. Thus, with standard deviation 8, if the mean is 83, two units below 85, the lower non-conformance rate is 5.2% while if the mean is 87, two units above 85, the upper non-conformance rate is also 5.2%. This is illustrated in Figure 3.7 (and may be checked by extending the Excel table whose construction is described below; try it). It also follows that the non-conformance rate is smallest when the mean is in the middle of the specification range.

### Illustration

We will explore the effect of allowing the mean to vary from 85 to 90. Our calculations to date suggest that non-conformance rates for means above 90 are likely to be

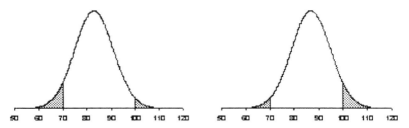

**Figure 3.7**    Illustrating non-conformance rates for mean 83 (left) and mean 87 (right).

very high. Also, we allow the standard deviation to range from 8 down to 4; engineering considerations suggest that reducing the spread to less than half of what is currently achieved would be very optimistic, using existing technology.

To start construction of the table in an Excel worksheet, enter the mean values 90, 89, 88, 87, 86, 85 in cells B1 to G1 and standard deviation values 8, 7, 6, 5, 4 in cells A2 to A6. Next, enter the formula

$$=100*(NORMDIST(70,B\$1,\$A2,1)+1-NORMDIST(100,B\$1,\$A2,1))$$

in cell B2. This calculates the non-conformance rate, per cent, for a process with mean 90 (in cell B1) and standard deviation 8 (in cell A2), assuming a Normal distribution of diameters:

- the first NORMDIST function gives the proportion of diameters below 70;
- the second gives the proportion below 100; 1 minus this is the proportion exceeding 100;
- the two are combined to give the proportional non-conformance rate; and
- multiplied by 100 to give the rate per cent.

Next, copy the formula to the cell range B2:G6 to complete the table.

Standard cell formatting makes the table difficult to read. Applying the guidelines for table making (Chapter 2) to the individual cells results in a table such as Table 3.1.

Observe that the non-conformance rates decrease across each row, that is, as the mean moves towards the mid-specification range, and down each column, that is, as the standard deviation decreases. It may help comprehension of this qualitative pattern to view it graphically, as shown in Figure 3.8.

**Table 3.1**    Non-conformance rates, per cent, for Normal processes with means 85–90 and standard deviations 4–8; specification limits 70–100

|  |  | Mean | | | | | |
| --- | --- | --- | --- | --- | --- | --- | --- |
|  |  | 90 | 89 | 88 | 87 | 86 | 85 |
|  | 8 | 11 | 9.3 | 7.9 | 6.9 | 6.3 | 6.1 |
| Standard | 7 | 7.9 | 6.1 | 4.8 | 3.9 | 3.4 | 3.2 |
| deviation | 6 | 4.8 | 3.4 | 2.4 | 1.7 | 1.4 | 1.2 |
|  | 5 | 2.3 | 1.4 | 0.84 | 0.50 | 0.32 | 0.27 |
|  | 4 | 0.62 | 0.30 | 0.14 | 0.059 | 0.026 | 0.018 |

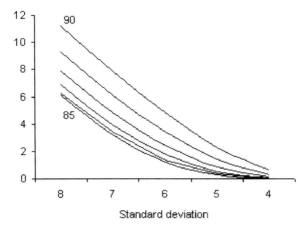

**Figure 3.8** Non-conformance rates for a range of means and standard deviations; curves arranged in order of means, highest 90 to lowest 85.

We can draw a variety of conclusions from the table. For example, the lowest non-conformance rate achievable without reducing the standard deviation is around 6%. We can do considerably better by reducing the standard deviation from 8 to 6; almost as low as 1% can be achieved. If we halve the standard deviation, then we can achieve as low as 0.02%, or 2 in 10,000, provided we can maintain the process 'on target', that is, with the mean in the mid-specification range. This is not always possible.

We can answer questions such as 'what changes in centre and reduction in spread are needed to achieve an acceptably low non-conformance rate' at least approximately using tables such as Table 3.1. For example, if a non-conformance rate of less than 1 in 1,000 is required, the standard deviation must be reduced to 4 and the mean must not move much above 87 or much below 83.

---

**Exercise 3.6**   Use Excel to make a table of non-conformance rates for specification limits of 75 and 95, using the same ranges of means and standard deviations as in the preceding Illustration. Prepare a brief report on the main conclusions to be drawn. Extend the standard deviation range down to 2 and report on what is needed to achieve a rate of less than 1 in 1,000. Revise your work to reflect a change in specification limits to 80 and 90.

---

## 3.5   Models and data; parameters and statistics

In our 'what-if' analysis, essentially we studied the effect of varying the *mean* and *standard deviation* that we used as inputs to the Normal cumulative distribution function, NORMDIST, in calculating non-conformance rates. By changing the mean and standard deviation, we change the Normal model being used to represent chance variation in the tennis ball process. Recalling the discussion of model parameters of the simple linear regression model introduced in Section 1.5, we describe the mean and standard deviation here as *parameters of the Normal model*. As we did in Section 1.5 (and in Section 3.2 above), we use Greek letters to designate the model parameters; $\mu$ for the mean and $\sigma$ for standard deviation.

**Process parameters**

If we were to measure every tennis ball core produced by the manufacturing process, assuming the process remained stable, we could calculate the mean and standard deviation of those measurements. These would then be referred to as the *process mean and standard deviation*. To the extent that the Normal model represents chance variation in the process being modelled, we may identify the Normal model parameters, $\mu$ and $\sigma$, with the process mean and standard deviation. Thus, we also refer to $\mu$ and $\sigma$ as *process parameters*. By changing the process parameters, we change the process. The 'what-if' analysis involving changes in model parameters gives us a guide to desirable changes in the process parameters, thus leading to process improvement.

**Parameter estimation**

The values of the model parameters used in calculating non-conformance rates for the four presses were chosen in the light of the data available from the presses. However, it is important to make a clear distinction between values of $\mu$ and $\sigma$ regarded as model parameters and values of the mean and standard deviation calculated from data. The available data are regarded as the result of *sampling* the process. The values of the mean and standard deviation calculated from the four *samples* are referred to as *sample statistics* and designated as $\bar{X}$ and $s$, as defined in Chapter 2, Section 2.2:

$$\bar{X} = \frac{1}{n}\sum_{i=1}^{n} X_i \qquad \text{and} \qquad s = \sqrt{\frac{1}{n}\sum_{i=1}^{n}\left(X_i - \bar{X}\right)^2}$$

While we never know the actual values of real process parameters, we can substitute calculated values of the sample statistics $\bar{X}$ and $s$ for the parameters $\mu$ and $\sigma$. $\bar{X}$ and $s$ are referred to as *estimates* of the model or process parameters.[4]

The fact that data sampled from a process are subject to chance variation means that any values of the parameter estimates $\bar{X}$ and $s$ calculated from such data are also subject to chance variation. This means that the values of $\mu$ and $\sigma$ cannot be determined with certainty; parameter estimation is subject to uncertainty. *Statistical inference* is concerned with quantifying the uncertainty involved. In the classical

---

[4]    When estimating the process standard deviation, $\sigma$, it is conventional to use a slight variation on $s$ in which the divisor, $n$, in the formula defining $s$ is replaced by $n - 1$. This is because the deviations $X_i - \bar{X}$ tend to be smaller than the deviations of the $X_i$ from $\mu$, the process mean, which are the deviations we would ideally use. Dividing by $n - 1$ instead of $n$ helps counteract this downward bias in the estimate of $\sigma$. In practice, this adjustment makes little difference, unless $n$ is very small.

approach to statistical inference, a range of plausible parameter values surrounding the corresponding sample statistic is calculated and referred to as a *confidence interval*. Details are discussed in Chapter 5.

## 3.6   Checking the Normal model; the Normal diagnostic plot

A well-known saying among professional statisticians (and other professionals) is that 'all models are wrong but some are useful'.[5] The extent to which models are useful depends on how well they approximate the phenomenon being modelled. The Normal model for chance variation has been proven to be very useful in a range of applications. However, its usefulness is undoubtedly sensitive to its accuracy. Predicting the non-conformance rates of manufacturing processes will not be very accurate if the Normal model does not fit well. The catastrophic failure of LTCM discussed in Section 1.2 is partly related to the fact that the Normal model for variation in financial series does not sufficiently allow for extreme fluctuations. Furthermore, the theoretical validity of many standard methods of statistical analysis to be introduced later depends on the practical validity of the Normal model.

It is important, therefore, to have an effective means of assessing the validity of the Normal model. In this section, we introduce a graphical approach to this task involving the *Normal diagnostic plot*.[6] The idea is very simple.

- Values sampled from a Normal process tend to be bunched towards the middle and increasingly spaced out towards the edges.
- Using an appropriate mathematical formula, it is possible to calculate a set of pseudo-values, called N-scores, with the theoretical spacing pattern expected from a Normal sample.
- A scatterplot is made of sampled values against N-scores, pairing smallest with smallest, second smallest with second smallest, etc.
- If the sampled process follows the Normal model, the similarity of the spacing patterns will lead to a straight line scatterplot pattern, with some chance variation.
- If the scatterplot pattern is *not* a straight line with some chance variation, then the conclusion is that the sample process does not conform to the Normal model.

All serious statistical software includes a facility for making Normal diagnostic plots. In theory, it is possible to make them by hand, using a table of the Normal distribution to assist in calculating Normal scores; in practice, this is infeasible for all but very small samples. However, it is relatively straightforward to make the plots using Excel. Details may be found in the Supplements and Extensions page of the book's website.

---

[5]   Attributed to G.E.P. Box.
[6]   This plot is more usually referred to as the Normal probability plot. However, as formal probability does not feature in this text, the simpler designation is preferred here.

## Illustration

Data on samples of twenty tennis ball core diameter measurements from each of the presses were the subject of Exercise 2.2 in Chapter 2. To illustrate the use of the Normal diagnostic plot, consider the twenty press 2 measurements. Figure 3.9 shows a dotplot which exhibits some bunching towards the middle and increasing spacing towards the edges.

**Figure 3.9**   Dotplot of a sample of 20 measurements from press 2.

Figure 3.10 shows a dotplot of twenty N-scores. Note the regularly increasing spacing between dots left and right of centre.

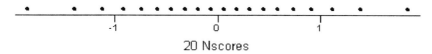

**Figure 3.10**   Dotplot of 20 N-scores.

Figure 3.11 shows the scatterplot of the twenty press 2 measurements of Figure 3.9 against the twenty N-scores of Figure 3.10, with smallest measurement paired with smallest N-score, second smallest with second smallest, etc.

This suggests a strong linear relationship, in turn suggesting that the data were sampled from a process that conforms to the Normal model.

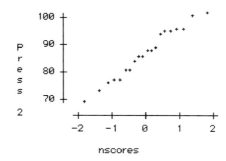

**Figure 3.11**   Normal diagnostic plot for press 2 measurements.

## Diagnostic plots for presses 1, 3 and 4

The diagnostic plots for the data from presses 1, 3 and 4 are shown in Figure 3.12. The press 4 measurements appear linear. Those from presses 1 and 3 show evidence of non-linearity. In the case of press 1, the non-linearity involves just one

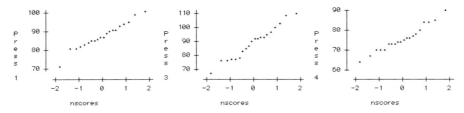

**Figure 3.12**   Normal diagnostic plot for measurements from presses 1, 3 and 4.

measurement; the smallest of the press 1 measurements appears exceptional, an 'outlier'. This suggests dealing with the exception separately and treating the rest as if the process did conform to the Normal model. The smallest press 3 measurement may also be exceptional and there are some strange bends in the pattern of the rest. It is tempting to conclude that the data do not conform to the Normal model.

### Reference plots

A problem with this informal style of evaluating Normality is the difficulty in deciding whether suggested deviations from linearity are more than 'some chance variation'. One approach to dealing with this is to use computer simulation to generate 'random' samples of twenty simulated measurements that behave as if they were measurements on a process that *does* follow the Normal model, make Normal diagnostic plots for these samples and then check whether the variation pattern in the diagnostic plot of real measurements is consistent with the variation patterns seen in the simulated plots.

Figure 3.13 shows the three plots from presses 1, 3 and 4 followed by a block of nine simulated diagnostic plots. Judged in the light of these, it seems that none of presses 1, 2, 3 or 4 appear non-Normal.

### Assessing the complete datasets

In the case of the tennis ball core diameters, we have available more extensive data, the 186 measurements made in each of the four presses. Diagnostic plots for presses 1, 2, 3 and 4 are shown in Figure 3.14, followed by nine reference plots, each based on 186 values, for comparison.

There are suggestions of non-linearity in the plots corresponding to presses 1 and 3. Each plot shows some curvature at the lower end, with the smaller values appearing less spread out than the rest. This corresponds to what is referred to as a 'skew' frequency distribution; a schematic skew frequency curve is shown in Figure 3.15.

Comparison with the reference set suggests that the patterns in presses 2 and 4 are consistent with a Normal model with 'some chance variation'.

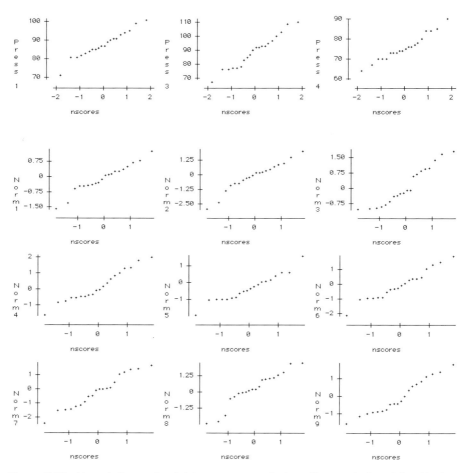

**Figure 3.13**   Normal diagnostic plot for measurements from Presses 1, 3 and 4, with nine simulated Normal diagnostic plots based on samples of 20.

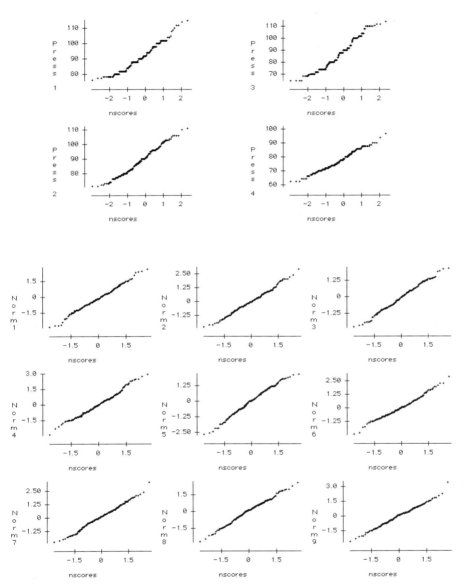

**Figure 3.14** Normal diagnostic plots for complete data from Presses 1, 2, 3 and 4, with nine simulated Normal diagnostic plots based on samples of 186.

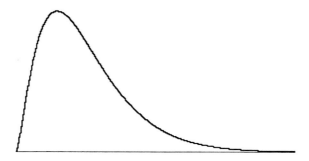

**Figure 3.15**    A skew frequency curve.

## 3.7    Review exercises

3.1    Over the past years' trading in the sports and social club referred to in Section 1.1, the difference between the total daily takings in the bar, as recorded by the cash register, and the total cash, as counted by the bar manager, averaged –50c, that is an average daily shortfall of 50c. The standard deviation of the differences was €2.00. Would you be surprised if today's shortfall was €2? €4? €6? What are the chances of getting a *surplus* of €2? €4? €6?

3.2    The time to complete each of 100 bank counter transactions was measured. The average transaction time was five minutes and the standard deviation was one minute. Assuming that the Normal model for statistical variation applies to bank counter transaction times, calculate

(i)    the percentage of transactions which take more than five minutes;
(ii)   the percentage of transactions which take more than six minutes;
(iii)  the percentage of transactions which take between four and six minutes;
(iv)   the percentage of transactions which take more than seven minutes.

3.3    Daily changes in the FTSE 100 were displayed in Figure 1.10 of Chapter 1. The mean change and standard deviation for 1996 were 2.00 and 20.82, respectively. On how many trading days would you expect a daily change of more than 50, more than 75, more than 100, assuming the Normal model for variation in daily change. Note that there were 265 trading days on the London Stock Exchange in 1996.

For the first half of 1997, the mean and standard deviation of daily changes in the FTSE 100 were 5 and 30, respectively. On how many trading days would you expect a daily change of more than 50, more than 75, more than 100, assuming the Normal model for variation in daily change. Note that there were 131 trading days on the London Stock Exchange in the first half of 1997.

For the second half of 1997, the mean and standard deviation of daily changes in the FTSE 100 were 3 and 56, respectively. On how many trading days would you expect a daily change of more than 50, more than 75, more than 100, assuming the

Normal model for variation in daily change. Note that there were 130 trading days on the London Stock Exchange in the second half of 1997.

Comment on the effect of increasing volatility.

3.4  A manufacturer of drinking glasses makes glasses of varying nominal sizes. According to regulations administered by a national metrology agency, not more than 0.5% of glasses should have size less than nominal. To comply with the requirements of the metrology agency, the manufacturer takes a sample of fifty glasses from each production run. To ensure that the samples are representatively spread across time, one glass is sampled every five minutes until the sample of fifty is made up. Summary statistics calculated from data sampled from eight production runs of half litre glasses were as follows.

| Run | 1 | 2 | 3 | 4 | 5 | 6 | 7 | 8 |
|---|---|---|---|---|---|---|---|---|
| Mean | 505.1 | 505.9 | 504.8 | 504.9 | 504.2 | 503.5 | 502.5 | 505.4 |
| SD | 1.90 | 1.83 | 1.56 | 1.52 | 2.18 | 1.96 | 1.74 | 1.32 |

The measurement unit was 1 millilitre.

Based on these data, estimate the percentage of non-conformances (glasses less than nominal size) in each run, assuming variation in glass size follows the Normal model.

According to an informal convention, actual glass sizes should exceed nominal by no more than 1%. On the evidence of the eight runs, what percentages of glasses conform to this convention?

3.5  A printing company routinely examines a number of quality characteristics of paper. The company specifies that the paper should be within ± 5% of 200 microns in thickness. Company records show that the standard deviation of paper thickness has been 3.8 microns. What proportion of paper would you expect to comply with the company specifications assuming:

(i)  that the supplier was 'on target'?
(ii)  that the average thickness of paper supplied was 195 microns?

3.6  Learn more about the cumulative Normal distribution by drawing its curve. In an Excel worksheet, enter the range −3 to 3 in steps of 0.1 in Column A and the cumulative NORMDIST function with mean 0 and standard deviation 1 in Column B. Use the ChartWizard to make the corresponding graph.

Describe the resulting curve; its range, its shape, notable values, etc.

Set the tick marks and labels on the horizontal axis to be at 0, ±1, ±2, ±3. Read (approximately) the corresponding cumulative distribution values. (Stretch the vertical axis to improve the accuracy of your readings.) From the values you have read, calculate the Normal frequencies between ±1, ±2, ±3. Refer to the corresponding values given in Chapter 1 or to calculations from your worksheet.

## 3.8    Laboratory exercise: 'What-if' analysis for non-conformance rates

A supplier to the automobile industry manufactures retainer clips using a machine which cuts a strip of metal from a roll and bends it into a clip shape. The key parameter is the gap between the ends of the clip; if the gap is too small, the clip will not fit on the intended part, if it is too large, it will not grip the intended part. You are part of a quality improvement team charged with improving the clip gap process. You are asked to calculate the non-conformance rates currently being achieved, given process mean values that appear to range from around 65–75 mm, a standard deviation of 7.3 mm and specification limits of 50–90 mm. You are also asked to find out what process mean and standard deviation values are required to achieve a non-conformance rate of 1 in 1,000 and 1 in 1,000,000. Your approach is to set up a table giving non-conformance rates for mean values ranging from 65 mm to 70 mm in steps of 1 mm and standard deviation values ranging from 8 mm down to 4 mm in steps of 1 mm. Implement this in Excel using the NORMDIST function. Use cell formatting to set appropriate numbers of significant digits.

Prepare a brief report on what is required to achieve non-conformance rates of 1 in 1,000 and 1 in 1,000,000.

Extend your table to include the range 71–75 mm for the mean value. Note the symmetry in the table, which makes the additional range redundant in practice. Explain why this happens, with the aid of an illustration which includes the symmetric Normal frequency curve.

# 4

# Process monitoring, control charts and statistical inference

In Chapter 1, we introduced the idea of process as a key idea in approaching problems in a wide range of areas. We encountered several examples of processes including business processes, manufacturing processes, and financial processes which, we observed in all cases, were subject to variation. We focused on two basic kinds of variation, chance variation and variation due to assignable causes.

We visualised chance variation in terms of the *band around the trend*. We noted the importance of realising the existence of this 'band' and saw several examples of the dangers of ignoring it.

We also visualised chance variation through a histogram in which small deviations from the centre of the 'band' occurred more frequently than larger deviations, which led us to the important concept of a *model* for chance variation and, in particular, the *Normal* model, in which the empirical frequency distribution of chance deviations from the trend is approximated by the theoretical Normal frequency distribution. This allows us to make predictions about the extent of chance variation in terms of the anticipated frequency of deviations of various sizes. In particular the chances of getting a deviation greater than two *standard deviations* is small, less than 1 in 20, while the chances of getting a deviation greater than three standard deviations is smaller still, less than 3 in 1,000.

We also need to be able to make statements about assignable causes of variation such as being able to say whether or not there *is* an assignable cause of variation and, if there is, being able to quantify its extent. Indeed, this is usually of greater immediate interest than quantifying the extent of chance variation but is complicated by the presence of chance variation in data.

These ideas lead naturally to process monitoring and control and, in particular, to the definition and use of the *control chart* for this purpose. We will find that the same body of ideas lies behind what statisticians refer to as *statistical inference*. In this chapter, we introduce the control chart, develop the basic statistical ideas that underlie it and re-express these ideas in the language of statistical inference, particularly in the guise of *statistical significance*.

**Learning objectives**

After completing this chapter, students should understand the statistical basis for and application of control charts and their correspondence to statistical testing and estimation, and demonstrate this by being able to:

- describe the benefits of being able to make the distinction between chance and assignable causes of variation;
- construct and use control charts based on individual process measurements, explain their statistical basis and describe their connection with statistical significance testing;
- explain and implement a procedure for constructing an estimate of process standard deviation based on individual process measurements;
- construct and use control charts based on means and ranges of samples of measurements;
- define the sampling distribution of the sample mean and standard error of the sample mean;
- describe the computer simulation of a sampling distribution through repeated simulation of a stable process;
- describe the role of sampling distribution and standard error in determining control limits;
- describe the statistical implications of increasing sample size for improved knowledge of the process;
- explain and implement procedures for constructing estimates of process standard deviation and process mean based on samples of process measurements;
- describe the correspondences between the use of control charts and statistical significance tests;
- explain the distinction between a process and data sampled from a process and between process characteristics and sample statistics;
- use sample data to estimate process characteristics;
- explain the limitations of sample statistics as estimates of process characteristics;
- provide illustrations of the need for control charts based on counts;
- describe the use of the Normal model as an approximation to the sampling distribution of an error count, including its mean and standard deviation, and calculate corresponding control limits.

## 4.1  Process monitoring using control charts

Consider the problem of monitoring cash variances in the till of a retail outlet. At the end of each day's trading, the cash in the till is counted. Then, the till is set to compute the total cash entered through the keys, which is printed on the till roll. The cash variance is the difference between cash and till roll totals. Small errors in making change or in entering cash amounts on the till keys are inevitable in a busy retail outlet. Such errors will build up over a period of time, leading inevitably to chance variation in the cash variance. Ideally, the cash variance will be zero. In the presence of inevitable chance variation, the best that can be hoped for is that the cash variances will centre around zero. In other words, the cash variance process is ideally expected to be a pure chance process with a process mean of 0.

A widely used device for process monitoring is the control chart. A control chart covering Sunday cash variances for a year in the sports and social club discussed earlier is shown in Figure 4.1. The variances are recorded in pounds and pence. Three horizontal lines are marked on the chart. The line marked 'CL' is the *centre line,* here placed at zero, the desired process mean. The lines marked 'UCL' and 'LCL' are the *upper* and *lower control limits,* respectively, intended to mark the limits of chance variation. These are placed at ±£12. For the record, the 52 variances displayed in the chart are shown in Table 4.1.

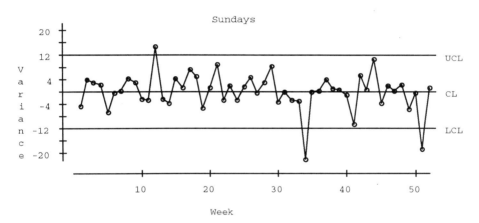

**Figure 4.1**   Sunday cash variances control chart.

**Table 4.1**   Sunday cash variances (£) for 52 weeks

| Week | Variance | Week | Variance | Week | Variance | Week | Variance |
|------|----------|------|----------|------|----------|------|----------|
| 1 | −4.72 | 14 | −3.67 | 27 | −0.37 | 40 | −0.95 |
| 2 | 3.99 | 15 | 4.21 | 28 | 3.01 | 41 | −10.62 |
| 3 | 3.06 | 16 | 1.20 | 29 | 8.35 | 42 | 5.23 |
| 4 | 2.17 | 17 | 7.31 | 30 | −3.22 | 43 | 0.73 |
| 5 | −6.63 | 18 | 4.90 | 31 | 0.14 | 44 | 10.78 |
| 6 | −0.47 | 19 | −5.26 | 32 | −2.75 | 45 | −3.75 |
| 7 | 0.28 | 20 | 1.43 | 33 | −3.16 | 46 | 1.89 |
| 8 | 4.26 | 21 | 10.13 | 34 | −22.08 | 47 | 0.47 |
| 9 | 3.06 | 22 | −2.74 | 35 | −0.09 | 48 | 2.40 |
| 10 | −2.23 | 23 | 1.91 | 36 | 0.25 | 49 | −5.56 |
| 11 | −2.60 | 24 | −2.76 | 37 | 3.87 | 50 | −0.18 |
| 12 | 14.83 | 25 | 1.56 | 38 | 1.05 | 51 | −18.63 |
| 13 | −2.34 | 26 | 4.77 | 39 | 0.60 | 52 | 1.42 |

As may be seen from the chart, this process was well behaved for the most part; apart from three points outside the control limits, the rest resemble a 'band around the trend', the trend in this instance being horizontal.

On observing points such as the three referred to, the process is judged to be *out of (statistical) control* and an investigation should follow. In the first case, week 12, value £14.83, the excessive positive cash variance indicates too much cash or not enough entered through the till keys. When the bar manager queried this, one of the bar assistants indicated a vague recollection of the possibility that a customer had been given change out of £5 instead of out of £10. On enquiring of the customer involved on her next visit, she indicated that she had suspected a cash shortage on that night. The £5 was reimbursed.

In the second case, week 34, value −£22.08, an assistant bar manager who was on duty that night paid a casual bar assistant £20 wages out of the till but did not follow the standard procedure in such cases of crediting the till with the relevant amount on the reconciliation sheet, and indicating a debit on the Staff Wages subaccount. Normally, the book-keeper, who processes the reconciliation sheet on the following day, makes appropriate entries in the books. In this case, she drew the cash variance to the attention of the Club Treasurer who subsequently instructed the assistant bar manager in proper procedure.

The last case, week 51, value −£18.63, was unexplained at first. However, other out of control negative cash variances on other nights of the week were observed, and these continued into the following year. Suspicion rested on a recently employed casual bar assistant. An investigation revealed that these cash variances occurred only when that bar assistant was on duty and such a coincidence applied to no other bar person. The services of that bar assistant were no longer required and the cash variances returned to Normal.

## The control chart principle

In its simplest form, a control chart involves making observations on a process at regular intervals, plotting the observed values on a line chart and checking each time whether the plotted value is inside or outside control limits, intended to indicate the limits of chance variation associated with the process. If we encounter an observed value outside the control limits, we conclude that this degree of variation is due to more than chance causes and that there must be an assignable cause which we proceed to seek. The assumption is that, if this cause persists, the process average will be affected and the operation of the process will not be as intended.

## Benefits of process monitoring using control charts

The benefits include the following. In the case that a process is in control, there is no point in wasting time and other resources in discussing and investigating what are no more than inevitable chance deviations. In particular, one should not unnecessarily interfere with a process when the evidence, properly evaluated, suggests mere chance causes of variation. The practice of doing so on a regular basis will disimprove the process. For example, regularly reprimanding bar staff for till variances that are due to chance causes of variation will irritate staff who are doing their best and create tension between management and staff which will not enhance the level of service. In a manufacturing process, unnecessary adjustment merely adds to the chance variation in the process, thereby making control more difficult to achieve.

On the other hand, when a process does go out of control, it is wise to have a rational method of detecting this, so that the situation can be corrected as soon as possible.

Along with such operational benefits, control charts also provide strategic benefits. Thus, in the course of investigating a genuine out-of-control signal and finding and fixing its problem, the opportunity can be taken to review the process and change it so that the problem cannot occur again. Also, when carrying out a strategic review, control charts provide clear evidence of process behaviour which can inform and provide a context for such a review, allowing the review to be based on fact and not just opinion.

## Statistical basis for control limits

The statistical basis for control charts rests on the Normal model for chance variation. The control limits are placed at distances of three standard deviations above and below the centre line:

$$UCL = CL + 3\sigma;$$

$$LCL = CL - 3\sigma.$$

Here, 'standard deviation' is the process standard deviation, or, equivalently, the standard deviation of the Normal model representing chance variation in the process.

We have already seen (Section 3.2) that 99.7% (in fact, slightly more) of values under a Normal curve are within three standard deviations of the centre. This means that slightly less then 0.3%, or 3 in 1,000, are more than three standard deviations from the centre. Thus, if the cash variance process is a pure chance process that follows the Normal model and is centred on 0, then the chances are less than 3 in 1,000 that an observed cash variance plotted on the control chart will be outside the control limits. This is such a small chance that, in practice, we do not expect to find points on our control chart outside the limits. Conversely, if we do observe such a point, then we conclude that more than chance causes are at work, in other words, we conclude that there is an assignable cause of variation.

Paraphrasing, since the pure chance model makes observing a point outside the control limits highly improbable, observing such a point makes the pure chance model highly implausible.

Putting it another way, we anticipate a certain *pattern* of variation from data generated by in-control processes. If we observe an *exception* to that pattern, then we conclude that the process is no longer in control and take appropriates steps. The control chart set-up described here provides us with a rule for distinguishing between pattern and exception, on the basis that the pattern conforms more or less to the Normal model for chance variation.

The choice of the multiplier 3 for determining the control limits through the formula $CL \pm 3\sigma$ means that, in approximately 3 cases in 1,000 when the process is in control we will be wrong in detecting an exception, that is, in declaring the process to be out of control. Three in 1,000 is the *false alarm rate* associated with the control chart procedure. The multiplier 3 was chosen by Shewhart because he deemed the corresponding false alarm rate suitably low that control chart users would not be upset by too frequent occurrence of false alarms, leading to unnecessary investigations and possibly inappropriate actions if an investigation leads to a spurious assignable cause. This *3σ rule* has now become conventional in control charting although other rules are possible. In fact, in statistical significance testing, discussed in the next chapter, there is a popular convention which is approximately equivalent to using a 2σ rule.

---

**Exercise 4.1**   Calculate the false alarm rate for a 2σ rule; how many values are expected to fall more than two standard deviations from the centre of a Normal curve?

---

**Exercise 4.2**   Assuming that cash variances are monitored daily, how often will a false alarm occur using the 3σ rule? The 2σ rule? Discuss the acceptability of each to a busy bar manager.

---

**Statistical significance**

Statisticians have developed a parallel approach to the problem of detecting exceptions from an expected (or hoped for) pattern of variation. In the language of statisticians, the occurrence of an 'out-of-control' point on the control chart when the process being monitored is assumed to be in statistical control is said to be a *statistically significant* event. The rule used to make the distinction, the 3σ rule in the control chart context, is called a *test of significance* by statisticians although, as mentioned above, it is more conventional among statisticians to use the equivalent of a 2σ rule.

The ideas underlying the use of the control chart also underlie *statistical significance* and, by extension, the whole area known as *statistical inference,* which has been applied in many guises in a wide range of application areas including science and technology, business and industry, economic and social studies, medicine, etc. Statistical inference is developed formally in the next chapter; applications will form a recurring theme throughout this text.

**Calculating σ**

A value for σ is needed to calculate the control limits from the formulas given earlier. There are varying approaches to this task. Here, we adopt a combined visual and numerical method to identify a band that may reasonably be deemed to represent chance variation and then calculate the standard deviation of the points within the band. The basic idea is to recognise that exceptional points, those substantially separated from the 'band' pattern, may not be part of the same 'band around the trend' as the rest and including them in the calculation of σ will give an inflated value of σ that reflects more than just chance variation. The procedure is first described and then exemplified using the cash variances data of Table 4.1.

The first step is to make a line plot of the data with a trial centre line drawn at the actual average of the cash variances. This differs from the centre line used for control purposes, the target value of £0 cash variance. Here, we are assessing the properties of the process as it is, which may differ from what we would like it to be. The method proceeds in steps as follows:

- visually identify the most extreme data point, furthest from the trial centre line;
- calculate trial values for μ and σ from the remaining points;
- calculate trial centre line and control limits and display them on the line plot;
- check whether the most extreme and any other data points lie outside the limits:
  ○ if none are outside, recalculate σ including the most extreme point;
  ○ otherwise, exclude the points outside the limits and repeat the whole process with the remaining points.

Three iterations of this procedure lead to a value of σ = £4.15, as illustrated in Figures 4.2–4.5. The first trial centre line in the line chart, Figure 4.2, is placed at the average variance, £0.07 (70p). The most extreme point may be identified from Figure 4.2 and Table 4.1 as week 34, with a value of −£22.08. Calculating the mean and standard deviation from all the data excluding this point gives trial values of μ = £0.50 (50p) and σ = £5.29.

Figure 4.3 shows the control chart with the corresponding trial control limits placed at £0.50 ± 15.87, that is, £16.37 and −£15.37. The two lowest points (weeks 34 and 51, values −£22.08 and −£18.83) are below the lower limit and so are excluded.

Repeating the process, the mean and standard deviation are calculated from all the remaining points except for the highest (week 12) which is now the most extreme.

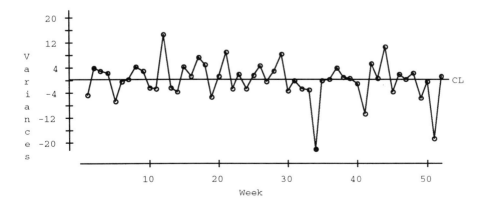

**Figure 4.2**   Line chart of Sunday cash variances, centre line at μ = 70p.

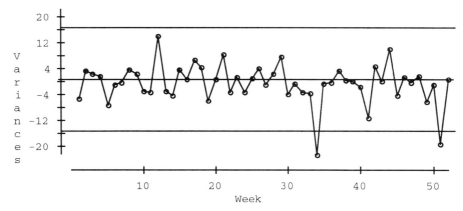

**Figure 4.3**   Sunday cash variances control chart using trial limits with week 34 deleted.

The recalculated trial values of μ and σ are £0.60 and £4.15, respectively; the recalculated trial control limits are £13.05 and −£11.85. The latter are shown in Figure 4.4. The current most extreme point (value £14.83) is above the upper limit and so is excluded, and the process repeated.

The next most extreme point corresponds to week 41, value −£10.62. Deleting it from calculations gives trial values μ = £0.83 and σ = £3.86 and control limits £12.41 and −£10.74, as shown in Figure 4.5.

The deleted case does not appear 'out of control', by comparison with the rest, and so it seems reasonable to consider it part of the same 'band' as the rest. This leads back to the previously calculated value of σ = £4.15, with case 41 included, and the control limits shown in Figure 4.4.

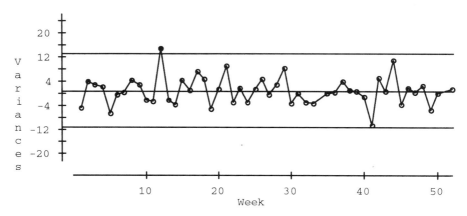

**Figure 4.4**   Sunday cash variances control chart with weeks 34 and 51 excluded; trial limits with week 11 deleted.

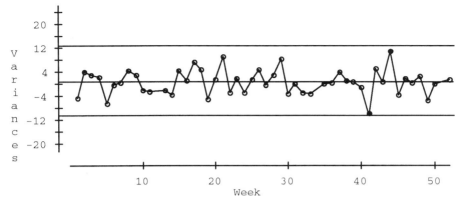

**Figure 4.5** Sunday cash variances control chart with weeks 11, 34 and 51 excluded; trial limits with week 41 deleted.

**Exercise 4.3** Retrace the steps of the above procedure. In each case, draw the corresponding control lines on a copy of the line chart of the Sunday cash variances that follows. Note that the line chart has been scaled and gridded to facilitate hand drawing of control lines.

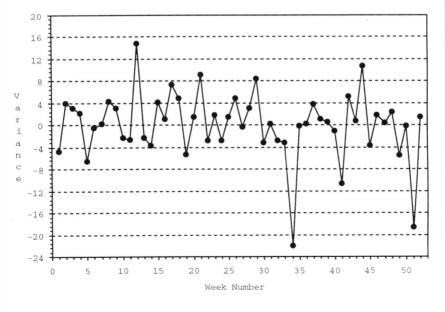

## Determining the limits

The final value of σ may now be used to calculate control limits centred on 0 for control purposes:

$$0 \pm 3 \times £4.15 = \pm £12.45.$$

In practice, it makes sense to use convenient control limits. It usually pays to simplify procedures as much as possible, particularly when it is a control procedure such as this which may be regarded as peripheral by some staff. In this case, control limits of ±£12.00 may be recommended.

---

**Exercise 4.4**   A line plot of data for Monday cash variances for the same year as those for Sunday discussed above follows.

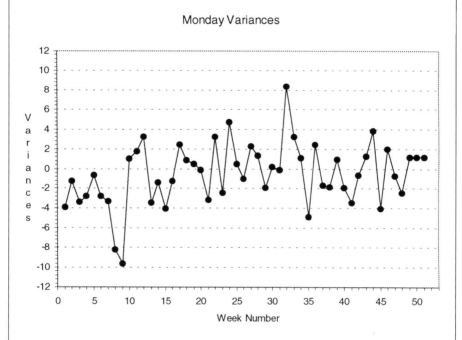

The value for σ was calculated to be 2.37. (This is the subject of a laboratory exercise.) Calculate control limits and draw them on a copy of the line chart. Comment on the state of control of the Variance process. What are the chances of getting nine negative variances in a row below target, as in weeks 1–9, if the process is on target? What action is suggested? Suggest why this estimate of σ is smaller than the Sunday variance standard deviation estimate.

---

## 4.2   Mean and range charts

While the use of control charts for monitoring business processes is relatively recent, their use in monitoring manufacturing processes goes back to the 1920s. A typical application is in mass production, where components and finished products are produced in large numbers. Frequently, in such cases, inspecting the entire process output is not feasible. Instead, the process is sampled at regular intervals, with a relatively small number of items being inspected and measured. Also, instead of plotting the individual measurements on a chart, their average is calculated and plotted on a chart with suitable control limits. The result is an X-bar chart, the most widely used type of control chart.

Typically, along with the X-bar chart, a range chart is also made. The range, $R$, of each sample of measurements, that is, the difference between largest and smallest, is calculated and plotted on a second chart marked with suitably chosen control limits. This is used to monitor the extent of chance variation, which also needs to be kept under control.

Many companies produce standard chart formats for use within the company and by suppliers. For example, the big three American motor manufacturers, Chrysler, Ford and General Motors, collaborated in producing such a format as part of a general effort to standardise their supplier assessment systems. The three companies, although direct competitors in the American market, felt the need to combine their efforts to meet the quality challenge provided by Japanese motor manufacturers. To this end, they formed the Automotive Industry Action Group (AIAG) in an effort to simplify and minimise variation in supplier quality requirements.

### Illustration

The control chart shown in Figure 4.6 is a combined mean and range (X-bar and $R$) chart, partially completed, on a standard form for such charts produced by AIAG. The chart gives a view of the operation of a process for making a retainer clip by bending a straight piece of metal into a clip shape. The key parameter is the gap between the ends of the clip; if the gap is too small, the clip will not fit on the intended part; if it is too large, it will not grip the intended part.

According to the engineering specification, the clip gap is required to be between 50 mm and 90 mm.[1] It is indicated that samples of five clips were collected every two hours. For each sample of five, the resulting clip gap measurements were recorded in the column provided at the end of the form; the mean of the five values, $\bar{X}$, and their range, $R$, were calculated, and then each calculated value was plotted with reference to the relevant vertical scale. The result is two graphs, one of sample mean against sample number and the second of sample range against sample number. Charts such as this may be used in ongoing process control, ideally by the machine operator who takes the samples, makes the measurements, records the data and plots the graphs in 'real time'.

---

[1]   Clearly, the data recorded here have been 'coded'; a permitted variation of over 50% of a typical value is unrealistic. The original clip gap measurements must have been considerably larger, perhaps of the order of 1,050–1,090 mm. Unfortunately, the source for these data does not say.

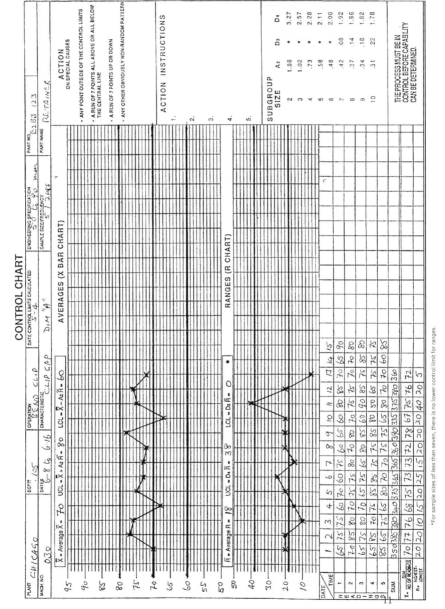

**Figure 4.6** AIAG chart form.

It is evident that there was some variation in the process during the period of recording of these data. While some variation is inevitable in almost all processes, the crucial question is 'how much variation is OK?' Shewhart's approach to this question, outlined in Section 4.1 above, may be applied to X-bar and *R* charts. The idea is to draw control limits on the charts such that a point on the chart outside these limits is regarded as exceptional for an in-control process and hence is regarded as a signal that the process is out of control.

While the basic principle is identical, its implementation for X-bar and *R* charts is somewhat more complicated than it is for individual measurements as described in Section 4.1. To facilitate its implementation, AIAG have included on the chart all the elements for carrying out the necessary calculations, along with instructions for action on an out of control signal. Here, we show how the procedures work. In Section 5.3, we investigate the statistical basis for the procedures.

### The X-bar chart

The X-bar chart is the upper chart in Figure 4.6. There is a centre line at 70, halfway between the specification limits of 50–90 mm indicated in the top row of the chart form. This is a target process mean value, appropriate for 'real time' process monitoring. When the objective is to study the process through historical data, the historical mean value would be more appropriate as a centre line.

The chart also has an upper control limit (UCL) and a lower control limit (LCL). Note that these statistical process control limits are different from the engineering specification limits. A formula for the control limits is given on top of the chart. In the formula, the centre line (CL) is taken to be a historical data average, labelled $\bar{\bar{X}}$. As already indicated, we will vary this here and take the centre line to be the target value for the process, that is, 70 mm. The control limits are given as

$$CL \pm A_2 \bar{R}.$$

Values for $A_2$, which depends on sample size, here 5, are given in the table in the bottom right corner of the chart; here, $A_2 = 0.58$. $\bar{R}$ is an 'expected' or 'typical' value for the range, which may be derived from historical data as will be seen later. For the moment, for this application we take $\bar{R}$ to be 17.8. Thus, the control limits are

$$70 \pm 0.58 \times 17.8$$

that is

$$70 \pm 10.32$$

that is

$$LCL = 60; \quad UCL = 80,$$

to the nearest millimetre.

On the right side of the chart form, there is a list of four 'action' rules:

- any point outside of the control limits;
- a run of seven points all above or all below the central line;

- a run of seven points up or down;
- any other obviously non-random pattern.

The first of these parallels the rule used in Section 4.1. According to Shewhart's argument, the control limits are such that, assuming the process was on target, finding a point on the $\bar{X}$ plot which fell outside the control limits would be very unlikely. Then, if such a point actually occurred at some time, it would suggest that the process was off target at that time. If indeed the process was substantially off target in the sense that the *process* average was substantially different from 70, then it is likely that too many clips are being produced with gaps outside the engineering specifications.[2] In such a case, action is needed to discover the *assignable cause* of this and make the appropriate adjustment.

The rationale behind the first action rule is identical to that used in Section 4.1 in the case of the control chart for monitoring cash variances. Also, the statistical basis is essentially the same as that outlined in Section 4.1. However, the formulas for the control limits given there need to be adapted to the situation here where the process is being monitored through the average of five measurements, rather than just one at a time as in the cash variances problem. The necessary adaptations are discussed in Section 4.3.

Similar arguments apply in the case of the other action rules. For example, the chances of finding seven points all above or all below the centre line are quite low if the process is in control; they are the same as getting seven heads or seven tails on tossing seven fair coins.[3] Consequently, if it happens, we are inclined to believe that the process mean has shifted, up or down as appropriate. Referring to the third action rule, a run of seven points up or down is equally unlikely if the process is in control; seeing such a run suggests that the process mean is gradually moving up or down.

The fourth action rule is not specific. In fact, its application can be dangerous. Purely random patterns quite often contain subpatterns that appear non-random to naive observers. Accordingly, this rule should be used sparingly, if at all.

### The range chart

A similar rationale is used for the $R$ chart control limits. Values of $R$ are taken to be centred on an 'expected' or 'typical' value for the range, which may be derived from

---

[2]   This amounts to saying that the *non-conformance rate* is too high. Procedures for estimating non-conformance rates are introduced in Section 4.4; see Exercises 4.6 and 4.7.

[3]   If two fair coins are tossed, the possible outcomes are $H_1H_2$, $H_1T_2$, $T_1H_2$, $T_1T_2$, where $H_1$ represents head up on the first coin, $T_2$ represents tail up on the second coin, etc. Two of these four equally likely outcomes correspond to all heads or all tails, thus the chances of this eventuality are 2 in 4, or 1 in 2. If three fair coins are tossed, the possibilities are $H_1H_2H_3$, $H_1H_2T_3$, $H_1T_2H_3$, $H_1T_2T_3$, $T_1H_2H_3$, $T_1H_2T_3$, $T_1T_2H_3$, $T_1T_2T_3$. Now, two of these *eight* equally likely outcomes correspond to all heads or all tails, that is 2 chances in 8 or 1 in 4. With four coins, the number of equally likely outcomes doubles again, to 16, and the chances of all heads or all tails are halved, to 2 in 16 or 1 in 8. Continuing, we find that the chances of all heads or all tails are 1 in 16 with five coins, 1 in 32 with six coins, 1 in 64 with seven coins.

Those equipped with knowledge and understanding of elementary probability theory will be able to apply its rules to derive these results more expeditiously. However, such knowledge is not assumed here.

historical data. The lower and upper control limits are then given as multiples of this central value. The appropriate multiples are tabled as $D_3$ and $D_4$ in the bottom right corner of the AIAG chart form. For the example to hand, taking the central value for $R$ to be 17.8, as above, with sample size 5 the value for $D_4$ is 2.11, so the upper control limit is

$$\text{UCL} = 2.11 \times 0.18 = 0.38.$$

Note that there is no corresponding value for $D_3$ in this table. This is because the rationale on which the calculation of control limits is based would lead to a negative LCL in this case. This applies for sample sizes up to 6. In these circumstances, an LCL is not used.

Finding a point outside the upper control limit on the range chart would indicate that the process was subject to excessive chance variation. Such a situation is likely to result in too many clips being produced with gaps outside the engineering specifications and action to investigate and correct is required. Similar considerations apply to rules 2–4 as with the X-bar chart.

**Applying the rules**

Up to sample number 13, there was no 'out of control' point on the X-bar chart, while there was one at sample 11 on the range chart. As it happened, the 'out of control' point at sample 11 led to an investigation and it was concluded that the extra variability in the process at that time, as indicated by such a large value of the sample range, was due to the presence of a trainee operator; the effect was only temporary and vanished once the new operator had gained some experience.

The runs rules are not violated on either chart.

---

**Exercise 4.5** Data for the next two samples have been entered in the chart on page 128. Calculate the sample mean and range in each case and plot the resulting values on the graphs. Interpret the extended charts in the light of action rule 1.

---

## 4.3 The statistical basis for X-bar charts; the sampling distribution of the mean

The rationale for control charts described in Section 4.1 applies here; since the pure chance model for variation in values of $\bar{X}$ makes observing a value of $\bar{X}$ outside the control limits highly improbable, observing such a value makes the pure chance model highly implausible. The only difference is that the pure chance model for $\bar{X}$ is not the same as that for a single measurement made on the process.

Intuition suggests that $\bar{X}$ values are likely to be centred on the process mean; if individual values are equally likely to be above or below the process mean, then so are means of samples of individual values. On the other hand, in the averaging process, deviations of individual values above and below the process mean tend to cancel each other, so that $\bar{X}$ values tend to be closer to the process mean than individual values. Hence, values of $\bar{X}$ subject to chance variation tend to vary less than values of corresponding individual measurements. We can confirm this intuition in two ways. We can use computer simulation to simulate repeated sampling from a stable process and then study the variation in the individual values and the $\bar{X}$ values so generated. We can also refer to results of mathematical theory.

Studying the results of repeated sampling from a stable process leads to the fundamentally important statistical concept of the *sampling distribution* and the related *standard error formula* from which follows, in turn, a formula for control limits which corresponds with the formula used in Section 4.2. Some important consequences of the standard error formula are noted here and developed in Chapter 5 and later chapters.

### Simulation of process sampling

We can *simulate* measurements from the clip gap process by using a computer random number generator. Virtually all statistical software and spreadsheets have a facility for generating numbers that behave as if they followed the Normal model for chance variation.[4] By choosing appropriate values for the mean and standard deviation, we can simulate repeated sampling from any stable Normal process. With the clip gap process in mind, the simulation process can be tailored to produce numbers as if from a Normal process centred on 70 and with standard deviation 7.3. Recall that 70 is the target value for the clip gap process, half-way between the specification limits of 50 and 90. The value 7.3 for the standard deviation results from a study of historical data; details will emerge later.

The result of such a simulation is illustrated in Figure 4.7 which shows two superimposed plots. One is a plot of individual measurements made on a process; the other

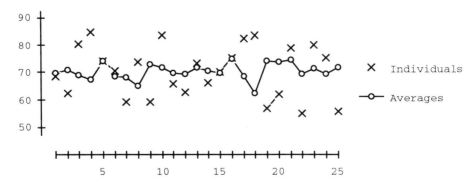

**Figure 4.7**    Plots of 25 individuals and 25 averages of five.

---

[4]    Exercises in simulation will follow. Simulation of this kind has many uses. Similar methods are used extensively in management science and operations research.

a line plot of $\bar{X}$ values calculated from samples of five measurements made on the same process. The 'band around the trend' is narrower for the $\bar{X}$ values.

The sequence of figures on the following pages give alternative views of the sampling and averaging processes and also show the effect of averaging with different sample sizes. We show the results of simulating 25 samples of five, along with their sample means, repeated for samples of 10 and 20.

Dotplots of 25 samples of five values sampled from a clip gap simulation process are shown in Figure 4.8 along with a dotplot of the 25 sample averages. While there is considerable variation within the samples, with more in some and less in others, there is much less variation in the dotplot of sample averages. This is because each sample average is close to the centre of the sample and this centring effect produces less variation in the dotplot of sample averages.

This exercise was repeated, with 25 new samples of five values each being generated by the same simulation process. The dotplot view of the results is shown in Figure 4.9.

The simulation was carried out again, this time with samples of 10, twice. Boxplots provide a neater view of the data with the larger sample sizes; boxplot views of the two simulations are shown in Figures 4.10 and 4.11.

A further 25 simulated samples of size 20 are shown in Figure 4.12; the spread of the means is further reduced. Further simulations with larger sample sizes will provide further confirmation.

Figures 4.8–4.12 show the results of repeated sampling from a stable process, each time averaging the resulting sample values. The conclusion in all cases is that averaging reduces spread, the reduction increasing with sample size, here samples of 5, 10 and 20.

In Figures 4.8–4.12, the simulation was restricted to 25 samples each time, due to space limitations. More extensive simulations, with a more compact display, can provide more convincing evidence. Figure 4.13 shows the results of 1,000 repetitions of the sampling process, with different sample sizes. It shows a histogram of 1,000 individual measurements and histograms of 1,000 means of samples of 5, 10, 20 and 40 measurements from the same process, all drawn to the same scale. The narrowing of the spread as sample size increases is obvious.

## Simulation summary

Figure 4.7 showed that samples of five measurements on a process show less variation around a centre line than individual measurements from the same process. An immediate consequence of this observation is that control limits for X-bar charts should be closer to the centre line than control limits for charts based on individual measurements; a key question is by how much.

Figures 4.8–4.12 show in more detail the relationship between the spread in a series of samples of individual measurements and the spread of the means of those samples, for varying sample sizes. It is clear that the spread of sample means is smaller than that of individuals and, furthermore, that it decreases as the sample size increases.

Finally, Figure 4.13 focuses on the frequency distribution of sample means, this time based on many more repetitions of the sampling process. It confirms that the

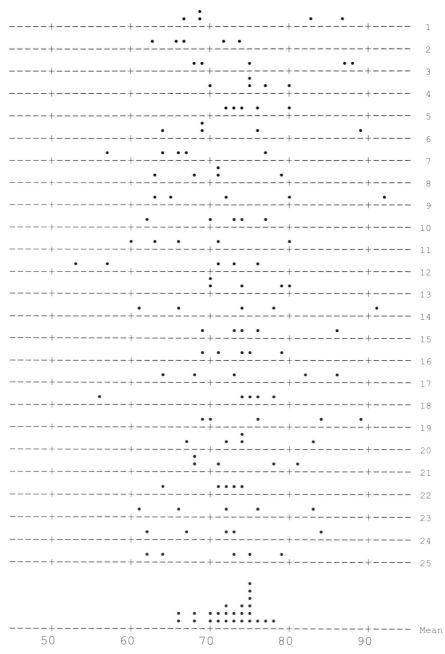

**Figure 4.8**   Dotplots of 25 samples of five and a dotplot of the sample means.

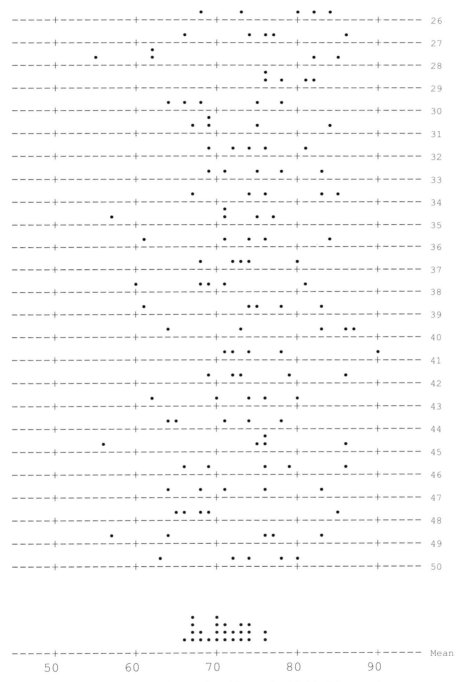

**Figure 4.9**   Dotplots of another 25 samples of five and a dotplot of the sample means.

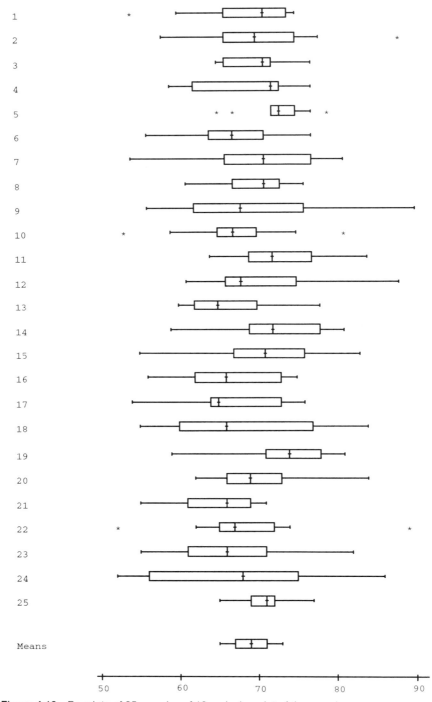

**Figure 4.10**    Boxplots of 25 samples of 10 and a boxplot of the sample means.

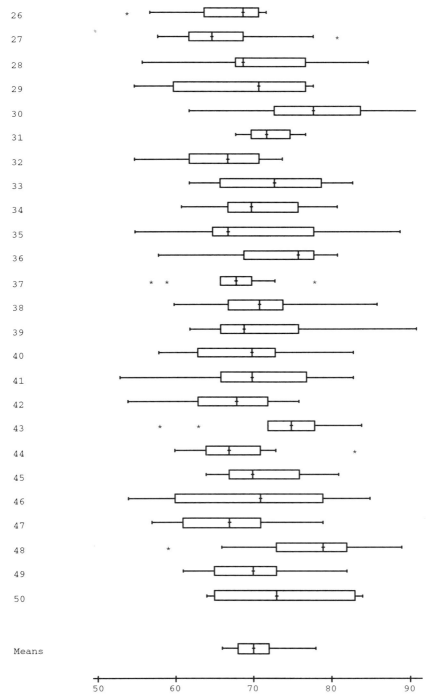

**Figure 4.11** Boxplots of another 25 samples of 10 and a boxplot of the sample means.

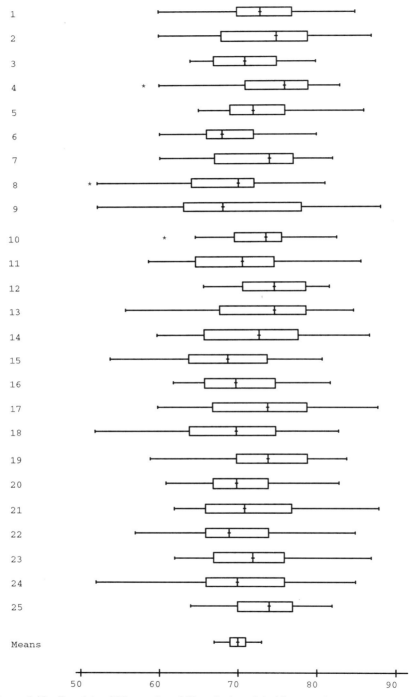

**Figure 4.12**   Boxplots of 25 samples of 20 and a boxplot of the sample means.

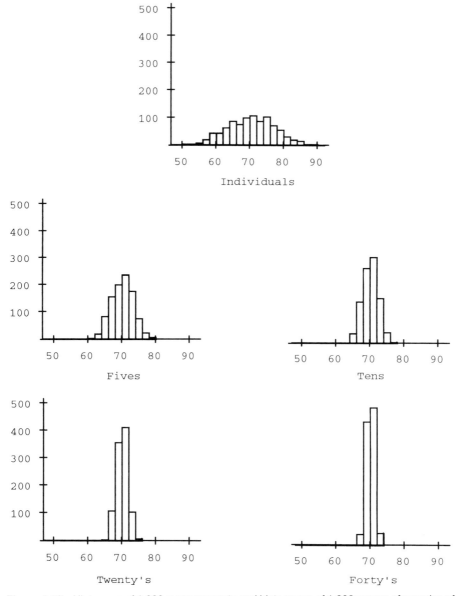

**Figure 4.13** Histogram of 1,000 measurements and histograms of 1,000 means of samples of 5, 10, 20 and 40 measurements.

spread of sample means is smaller than that of individual measurements sampled from the same process. Figure 4.13 suggests further that the Normal model for chance variation, which applies by design to the individual measurements, also applies to sample means.

## The Normal model for variation in $\bar{X}$

More extensive simulations, with many more than 1,000 repetitions of the sampling process, will result in smoother histograms than those shown in Figure 4.13, even more suggestive of the Normal model. The Normal model can be made plausible in another way by regarding the sampling process, including calculation of the sample mean, as an extension of the clip manufacturing process involving three further steps;

- five clips are sampled;
- their gap sizes are measured;
- the average of the gap sizes is calculated.

Consequently, if the Normal model for chance variation applies to the clip manufacturing process, we may anticipate that it will also apply to the process of generating $\bar{X}$ values; if chance causes of variation apply to the individual clip gaps, they will also apply to their averages.

The evidence displayed so far indicates that the mean of the $\bar{X}$ process corresponds to the mean of the original manufacturing process while its standard deviation is considerably reduced. Mathematical analysis confirms that the mean of the $\bar{X}$ process is the same as that of the clip gap process and also provides a simple formula for the standard deviation of the $\bar{X}$ process:

$$\sigma/\sqrt{n},$$

where $\sigma$ is the standard deviation of the clip gap process and $n$ is the sample size, that is, the number of measurements in each sample, five in this case.

## Alternative formula for control limits

Control limits for the X-bar chart may be calculated in essentially the same way as those for the individual measurements chart discussed earlier except that $\sigma$, which measures chance variation for a single measurement, is replaced by $\sigma/\sqrt{n}$, which measures chance variation for the mean of a sample of $n$ measurements. Thus the control limits are given by the formula:

$$\mathsf{CL} \pm 3\sigma/\sqrt{n}.$$

The formula

$$\mathsf{CL} \pm A_2\bar{R}$$

used in the Automotive Industry Action Group chart form is a variant on this, designed to give approximately the same results. It is based on using range as a measure of spread rather than the more complicated standard deviation. The simplicity of the range as a measure of spread is an important consideration in making the use of control charts accessible at all levels in a company. The more complicated formula involving the standard deviation is likely to be a considerable deterrent to those whose strengths are other than mathematical.

### The sampling distribution of the mean

The frequency distribution of sample mean values resulting from indefinitely repeated sampling of a stable process is a key element of the theory behind X-bar charts. In statistical terminology, it is called the *sampling distribution* of the sample mean. Its standard deviation, $\sigma/\sqrt{n}$, is called the *standard error* of the mean.

The sampling distribution concept is a central concept of classical statistical inference which has wide application in statistical analysis. It will be considered in more detail in Chapter 5.

### Implications of the standard error formula

Some very important implications flow from the formula $\sigma/\sqrt{n}$ for standard error, in particular from the fact that $n$, the sample size, appears in the denominator.

First, note that making a single clip gap measurement tells us something about the process average, $\mu$, provided we know something about $\sigma$. Thinking in terms of the Normal curve, with mean $\mu$ and standard deviation $\sigma$, we know that the measurement is unlikely to be more than, say, two standard deviations from $\mu$ and even less likely to be more than three standard deviations from $\mu$. Hence, we can be reasonably confident that $\mu$ is within $2\sigma$ of the measured value and even more confident that $\mu$ is within $3\sigma$ of the measured value.

Next, suppose that we sampled four clips, measured their gaps and calculated their average. Following the same logic, thinking in terms of the Normal curve, with mean $\mu$ and standard deviation $\sigma/\sqrt{n} = \sigma/2$ in this case, we know that the calculated value is unlikely to be more than two *standard errors* from $\mu$ and even less likely to be more than three *standard errors* from $\mu$. Hence, we can be reasonably confident that $\mu$ is within $2\sigma/2$ of the measured value and even more confident that $\mu$ is within $3\sigma/2$ of the measured value. Thus, by basing our estimation of $\mu$ on the average of four measurements instead of just 1, we have halved the interval which reflects our uncertainty about $\mu$.

This analysis shows why it is sensible in circumstances such as this to plot averages rather than single measurements; we get better quality information about the process mean and therefore can make better quality decisions about the process.

Taking this to its logical conclusion, we see that we can reduce the deviation of $\overline{X}$ from $\mu$, and therefore the deviation of $\mu$ from $\overline{X}$, as much as we wish by taking a large enough sample. If we make $n$ very large, we make $\sigma/\sqrt{n}$ very small and so make the difference between the calculated value of $\overline{X}$ and the actual value of $\mu$ very small. Hence, by making $n$ sufficiently large, we can determine $\mu$ effectively without error simply by calculating the value of $\overline{X}$. In practice, however, cost and logistics prevent this.

## 4.4   Assessing process capability; statistical estimation

Once we know that our process is in statistical control, we can ask questions such as 'how well does it work?', 'Is it working satisfactorily?', 'Does it need to be improved?' The key to answering these questions lies in using historical data to *estimate* the process parameters μ and σ. Then, assuming that the process remains in statistical control, we can predict how well the process will perform in the future. For example, if we set a standard for till cash variances of 'not more than £10', then we can calculate how frequently that standard will be met, the *conformance rate,* and, complementarily, how frequently that standard will not be met, the *non-conformance rate.* The metal clip manufacturing process introduced in Section 4.2 has engineering specification limits of 50–90 mm for the gap across the ends of the clip. Given the current performance levels of the process, is it capable of meeting those specifications or to what extent is it capable of meeting those specifications?

---

**Exercise 4.6**    Assuming a value of 7.3 mm for σ, use the Normal table to predict the proportion of clips whose gaps fail to meet the specification limits of 50–90 mm:

(i)    when the process mean is 70 mm;
(ii)   when the process mean is 74 mm;
(iii)  when the process mean is 67 mm.

---

### Estimating σ

When estimating the process standard deviation for till variances in Section 4.1, we used an iterative approach which allowed us to identify potential assignable causes of variation, delete the corresponding data and calculate the final estimate of σ from data which we judged were subject to pure chance variation.

When sampling the clip gap process, several (that is, five) measurements were made at each of several time periods (every two hours). In that case, a more direct approach is available. Note that each sample is assembled in a short period of time. If it can be assumed that the process is not changed by an assignable cause of variation during that short time, then the data within each sample are subject to pure chance variation only. Note that this assumption is easily checked by inspecting the range chart. Making this assumption, we can calculate a valid estimate of σ from the data within each sample. This gives us several estimates of σ, one from each sample. Naturally, these estimates will vary from sample to sample. By averaging these estimates,[5] we get a combined estimate which is likely to be better than the individual sample estimates. This approach gives us an estimate for σ which is unaffected by assignable causes of variation which may occur between samples and reflects pure chance variation as measured within samples.

The calculations involved in this procedure are relatively complicated, involving calculation of several sample standard deviations. It is to avoid such calculations that

---

[5]    Mathematical considerations suggest averaging the *squares* of these estimates and taking the square root of this average. The mathematical considerations are related to those which led to the *root mean square* definition of the sample standard deviation, *s,* in Chapter 2; see footnote 6, page 73. When the individual sample standard deviations are not too different from each other, the values of the combined estimate calculated either way will be similar.

the range chart is used to monitor spread in the chart form prescribed by the Automotive Industry Action Group, as discussed in Section 4.2. Fortunately, there is a conversion factor which allows us to move from range to standard deviation. In this section, therefore, we focus on deriving an appropriate range value from historical data and then converting this to an estimate of $\sigma$.

## The average range

To illustrate the procedure, consider the set of 25 samples of clip gap measurements which became available when the control chart form illustrated in Figure 4.6 was filled. They are shown in Table 4.2, with the sample ranges appended.

The average of the range values is 17.8. Before accepting this as a valid measure of process spread, we can check the assumption of within-sample homogeneity, that is, that variation within samples is due to chance causes only, by inspecting a range chart. Analogously to the procedure used to identify potential assignable causes when estimating $\sigma$ for till variances, we should

- identify the largest sample range value;
- calculate the average range from the remaining points;
- calculate a trial upper control limit and display the centre line and UCL on the line plot;
- check whether the largest and any other range values lie outside the limits:
  - if none are outside, recalculate the average range including the most extreme point;
  - otherwise, delete the points outside the limits and repeat the whole process with the remaining points.

**Table 4.2**   Clip gap measurements (mm) in 25 samples of five measurements each

| Sample | 1 | 2 | 3 | 4 | 5 | 6 | 7 | 8 | 9 | 10 | 11 | 12 | |
|--------|---|---|---|---|---|---|---|---|---|----|----|----|--|
| | 65 | 75 | 75 | 60 | 70 | 60 | 75 | 60 | 65 | 60 | 80 | 85 | |
| Clip | 70 | 85 | 80 | 70 | 75 | 75 | 80 | 70 | 80 | 70 | 75 | 75 | |
| gaps | 65 | 75 | 80 | 70 | 65 | 75 | 65 | 80 | 85 | 60 | 90 | 85 | |
| | 65 | 85 | 70 | 75 | 85 | 85 | 75 | 75 | 85 | 80 | 50 | 65 | |
| | 85 | 65 | 75 | 65 | 80 | 70 | 70 | 75 | 75 | 65 | 80 | 70 | |
| Range | 20 | 20 | 10 | 15 | 20 | 25 | 15 | 20 | 20 | 20 | 40 | 20 | |

| Sample | 13 | 14 | 15 | 16 | 17 | 18 | 19 | 20 | 21 | 22 | 23 | 24 | 25 |
|--------|----|----|----|----|----|----|----|----|----|----|----|----|----|
| | 70 | 65 | 90 | 75 | 75 | 75 | 65 | 60 | 50 | 60 | 80 | 65 | 65 |
| Clip | 70 | 70 | 80 | 80 | 85 | 70 | 65 | 60 | 55 | 80 | 65 | 60 | 70 |
| gaps | 75 | 85 | 80 | 75 | 70 | 60 | 85 | 65 | 65 | 65 | 75 | 65 | 70 |
| | 75 | 75 | 75 | 80 | 80 | 70 | 65 | 60 | 80 | 65 | 65 | 60 | 60 |
| | 70 | 60 | 85 | 65 | 70 | 60 | 70 | 65 | 80 | 75 | 65 | 70 | 65 |
| Range | 5 | 25 | 15 | 15 | 15 | 15 | 20 | 5 | 30 | 20 | 15 | 10 | 10 |

The largest sample range value is 40, the range of sample 11. The average of the remaining sample ranges is 17. Using the multiplier $D_4$ given in the bottom right corner of the AIAG chart form, Figure 4.6, calculate

$$UCL = 2.11 \times 17 = 36.$$

The resulting range chart is shown in Figure 4.14.

Sample 11 exceeds the UCL and so we judge that there was a potential assignable cause of variation and the sample is deleted. The largest remaining sample range value is 30, the range of sample 21. The average of the remaining sample ranges is 16.3. The trial upper control limit is

$$UCL = 2.11 \times 16.3 = 34.$$

The resulting range chart is shown in Figure 4.15. All points are below the limit so we revert to the previously calculated value, $\bar{R} = 17$, as the appropriate range value for control chart construction.

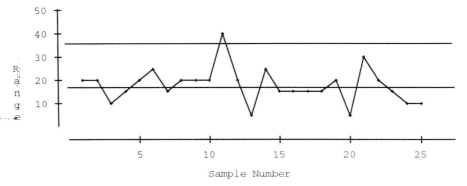

**Figure 4.14**   Clip gaps range chart using trial limits with sample 11 deleted.

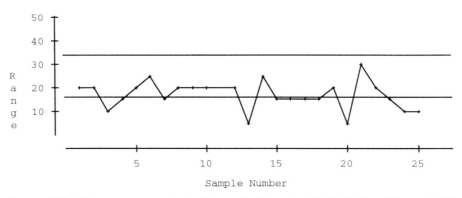

**Figure 4.15**   Clip gaps range chart with sample 11 excluded; trial limits with sample 21 deleted.

*Converting to σ*

To convert this value of $\bar{R}$ to an estimate of σ, the process standard deviation, we need an appropriate conversion factor. The AIAG chart form does not supply a conversion factor for this purpose. However, we can easily work out what it must be from the equivalence of the two formulas for X-bar chart control limits:

$$CL \pm 3\sigma/\sqrt{n}$$

and

$$CL \pm A_2\bar{R},$$

already noted in the subsection 'Alternative formula for control limits' on page 140. This implies

$$3\sigma/\sqrt{n} = A_2\bar{R}$$

from which it follows that

$$\sigma = \frac{A_2\sqrt{n}}{3} \times \bar{R},$$

where the values for $A_2$ are given in the bottom left of the AIAG chart form. With $n = 5$ so that $A_2 = 0.58$, we find that the conversion factor is

$$\frac{0.58 \times \sqrt{5}}{3} = 0.43$$

so that

$$\sigma = 0.43 \times 17 = 7.3$$

## Estimating $\mu$

Given the historical data of Table 4.2, what can we say about the process mean, $\mu$? If the process was stable throughout the period during which the data of Table 4.2 were observed, then the obvious estimate of $\mu$ is the mean of all the data. If not, then the standard approach is to examine an X-bar chart for all the data, attempt to identify a subset of the data which reflects a stable process and base an estimate of $\mu$ on the subset. As a starting point, we use the mean of all the data (excluding sample 11 which we have already identified as out of control) as our centre line and derive control limits from this using the formula of Section 4.2, page 129. From Table 4.2, we calculate the mean of all the data as

$$\bar{\bar{X}} = 71.5$$

and recalculate the control limits as

$$UCL = 71.5 + 10 = 81.5$$

and

$$LCL = 71.5 - 10 = 61.5.$$

The resulting chart is shown in Figure 4.16.

Applying the rules given in the AIAG chart form, we see immediately that the mean of sample 15 exceeds the upper control limit, suggesting that the process was out of control at that time. The process log sheet had no record which might indicate an explanation for this signal. Looking further we see a number of points below the centre line from sample number 18 on, in fact eight in all. According to the second

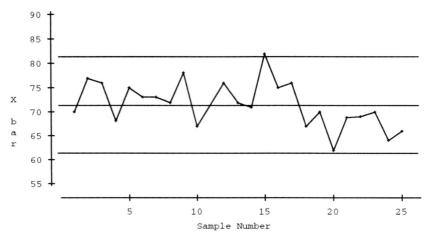

**Figure 4.16**   X-bar chart for clip gaps with historical centre line, sample 11 excluded.

rule for action in the AIAG chart form, this suggests that the process was out of control. Specifically, it suggests that the process mean had shifted downward. In fact, it had been noted in the process log sheet that a new roll of the steel raw material from which the clips are made had been started after the time that sample number 17 had been taken.

This suggests that the process had been operating at two different mean levels during the time that the data were recorded. If so, it does not make sense to use a common centre line representing a constant process mean. The data need to be re-analysed. Calculating mean values for the data up to sample 17 (excluding sample 11) and after sample 17 gives values of 73.8 and 66.75. For the purpose of drawing control lines on a chart, these may as well be rounded to 74 and 67. Recalculating control limits for the two subsets gives

$$UCL = 74 + 10 = 84$$

and

$$LCL = 74 - 10 = 64$$

for samples up to sample number 17, and

$$UCL = 67 + 10 = 77$$

and

$$LCL = 67 - 10 = 57.$$

The X-bar chart for clip gaps is shown in Figure 4.17 with redrawn centre lines and control limits which reflect the re-analysis of the data.

From this, we see that the process appeared to be in *statistical* control throughout both periods covered by the sampling, up to sample number 17 and after sample number 17. There is no evidence to suggest anything other than a 'band around a

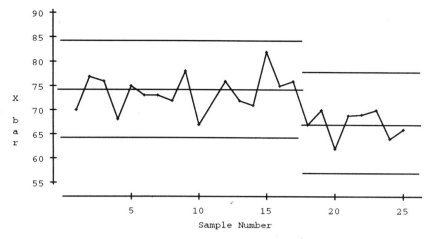

**Figure 4.17**   X-bar chart for clip gaps with redrawn control lines.

trend' within each period. However, there is a question concerning *engineering* control; a process whose mean is 3 or 4 mm off target is producing more nonconforming
items than one centred on target. Recall Exercise 4.6, page 142, in which the non-
conformance rates at all three levels were sought. For an on-target process, the rate
is 0.6%; with process mean 67 mm the rate is 1.1%; and with mean 74 mm it is 1.5%.

Whether non-conformance rates which are almost double or more than double the
'on-target' rate are acceptable is a management issue. If they are not acceptable, then
steps must be taken to ensure that the process mean is on, or at least closer to, target.
In this case, where it appears that the change in process mean is due to a change in
raw material, the manufacturer will seek a decrease in batch to batch variation from
the supplier.

Indeed, in modern motor manufacturing, the on-target rate of 0.6% is unlikely to
be acceptable. In this case, improvement requires a reduction in process standard
deviation. Conceivably, this could be achieved through appropriate changes to the
clip bending process. In the light of the batch to batch variation in the raw material,
it is likely that the supplier would be invited to improve within-batch variation as
well as between-batch variation.

---

**Exercise 4.7**   In anticipation of a quality improvement initiative to
improve control over the process mean and reduce the process standard deviation, calculate the non-conformance rates to be anticipated
if the process mean stays at 70 mm and the process standard deviation
is reduced to (i) 6 mm, (ii) 4 mm.

---

## Statistical estimation

The process of deriving values for the process mean and standard deviation from data
sampled from the process is referred as *statistical estimation.* The resulting values

are called *estimates*. It is convenient to have a suitable notation for estimates of process parameters. A widely used convention is to denote an estimate of the process mean, $\mu$, by $\hat{\mu}$ and an estimate of the process standard deviation, $\sigma$, by $\hat{\sigma}$. These are referred to as 'mu-hat' and 'sigma-hat', respectively.

Because statistical estimates are based on data which are subject to chance causes of variation, the estimates themselves are also subject to chance variation. Simply reporting a single number as an estimate, a *point estimate,* does not recognise this source of variation. The statistical approach is to report an *interval estimate.* The necessary ideas are developed in Chapter 5 and will be applied repeatedly throughout the text.

## 4.5  Monitoring counts

In many applications of process monitoring, observation of the process results in a 'yes–no' response, rather than a more or less continuous measurement such as length in centimetres or value in euros or dollars. In financial auditing, the distinction is made between *compliance testing* (was the correct value entered in the form) and *substantive testing* (what was the (accountancy) variance of the value entered in the form). In manufacturing, process inspectors may use a 'Go–No Go' gauge to assess whether a sampled part meets specifications or not, rather than the more demanding (and usually more expensive) task of measuring the part. In such cases, an alternative form of control chart is appropriate. A frequently used chart form is the so-called *np chart*, illustrated in the following example.

### An np chart for clerical error counts

As part of a procedure for monitoring clerical errors in order forms, a company examines a sample of 100 forms from those completed each week, records the number of forms with errors in them and maintains a control chart for the number of errors per sample, or *sample count* of errors, for each week. Details of such weekly counts over a 30 week period are shown in Table 4.3.

An np chart based on the sample counts listed in Table 4.3 is shown in Figure 4.18. The same basic principles of chart design and interpretation apply here as before. The centre line for this chart is at 5; management opinion suggested that, on average,

**Table 4.3**  Clerical error counts in weekly samples of 100 forms for a 30 week period

| Week No. | Error Count | Week No. | Error Count | Week No. | Error Count | Week No. | Error Count | Week No. | Error Count |
|---|---|---|---|---|---|---|---|---|---|
| 1 | 5 | 7 | 12 | 13 | 5 | 19 | 3 | 25 | 6 |
| 2 | 5 | 8 | 10 | 14 | 6 | 20 | 4 | 26 | 5 |
| 3 | 4 | 9 | 6 | 15 | 8 | 21 | 6 | 27 | 5 |
| 4 | 6 | 10 | 3 | 16 | 8 | 22 | 7 | 28 | 8 |
| 5 | 3 | 11 | 8 | 17 | 6 | 23 | 5 | 29 | 4 |
| 6 | 9 | 12 | 3 | 18 | 5 | 24 | 7 | 30 | 7 |

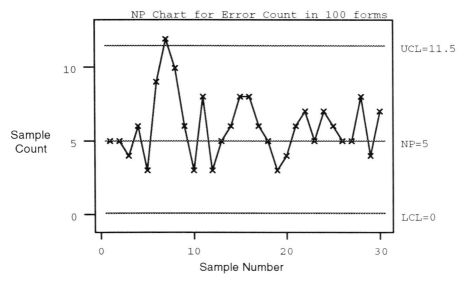

**Figure 4.18** A count control chart.

no more than 5% of order forms should have errors in them. The upper control limit is at 11.5, so that a sample count of 12 or more suggests that the target of a 5% average error rate is not being achieved. The data showed that this occurred in week 7 and prompted a review of the form filling process.

Following this review, conducted by a problem solving team, some simplifications were introduced to the design of the form and the redesigned form was introduced after Week 30. Error counts in weekly samples of 100 forms were recorded for a 20 week period; the resulting data are shown in Table 4.4.

**Table 4.4** Clerical error counts in weekly samples of 100 forms for a further 20 week period

| Week No. | Error Count | Week No. | Error Count | Week No. | Error Count | Week No. | Error Count |
|---|---|---|---|---|---|---|---|
| 31 | 1 | 36 | 4 | 41 | 4 | 46 | 2 |
| 32 | 1 | 37 | 4 | 42 | 1 | 47 | 1 |
| 33 | 4 | 38 | 4 | 43 | 6 | 48 | 5 |
| 34 | 4 | 39 | 1 | 44 | 5 | 49 | 2 |
| 35 | 1 | 40 | 6 | 45 | 1 | 50 | 3 |

Figure 4.19 shows the chart of Figure 4.18 extended to include the 20 week period following the change in form design. It is clear that a substantial improvement took place following the improvement in form design. In fact, an inspection of the chart from week 31 onwards suggests that the average error rate being achieved is somewhat less than 5%. This being so, it would make sense to move the centre line down and, with it, the upper control limit.

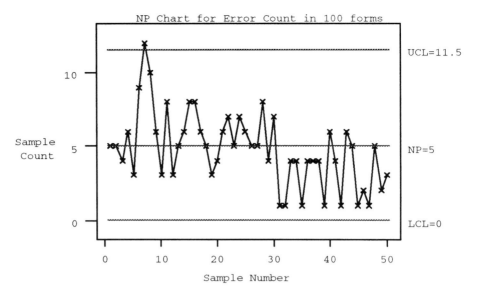

**Figure 4.19**   The count chart extended.

### The statistical basis for the np chart

The basis for setting control limits for charts based on counts is essentially the same as before. As with any quantity whose value is based on a sample of observations of a process, repeated sampling of the process will produce varying values for the error count. The frequency distribution of such values resulting from a long run of repeated sampling, assuming the process remains stable, is called the sampling distribution of the error count. The Normal model is not the theoretically correct model for chance variation in this case; the correct model is the *Binomial* model.[6] However, when the sample size is sufficiently large and error rates are not very small, the Binomial frequency distribution may be approximated by the Normal frequency distribution. The required conditions are satisfied here, so we need not develop the details of the Binomial model;[7] we can use the Normal model as an approximate model for chance variation in the error counts.

The key parameter in the error count process is the process mean error rate, expressed as a proportion or percentage. Here, the original target process mean error rate is 0.05, or 5%. If this is the actual process mean error rate, then the number of errors in a sample of 100 from a process with average error rate 0.05 is expected to be about

---

[6]   So called because the items counted are divided into *two parts* (Greek, *bi nomos*), correct and incorrect in this example.

[7]   Discussion of the Binomial model for chance variation (the Binomial *probability distribution*) may be found in many traditional statistics texts.

$$100 \times 0.05,$$

that is, the process mean error rate is applied to the sample size. This serves as the mean of the (approximating) Normal model for chance variation in the error count process and, therefore, as the centre line for the error count control chart.

More generally, if the process mean error rate is denoted by $p$, for proportion, and $n$ is the sample size, the error count is expected to be about

$$n \times p,$$

whence the name 'np chart'.

To complete the specification of the Normal model, we need its standard deviation, that is, the standard deviation of the error count sampling distribution or, briefly, the error count standard error. With measurement data, this was based on a second model parameter, $\sigma$, typically estimated from sample data. In this case, the standard error is determined differently, as a function of the process mean error rate, $p$. The formula for the error count standard error is

$$\sqrt{np(1-p)}$$

and so the control limits are given by

$$\text{UCL} = np + 3\sqrt{np(1-p)};$$
$$\text{LCL} = np - 3\sqrt{np(1-p)}.$$

With $p = 0.05$, these evaluate as

$$\begin{aligned}
\text{UCL} &= 5 + 3\sqrt{100 \times 0.05 \times 0.95} \\
&= 5 + 3\sqrt{4.75} \\
&= 5 + 3 \times 2.18 \\
&= 5 + 6.54 \\
&= 11.54
\end{aligned}$$

and

$$\begin{aligned}
\text{LCL} &= 5 - 6.54 \\
&= -1.54.
\end{aligned}$$

Note that the upper control limit may be placed anywhere between 11 and 12. A sample error count of 11 or less leads to no action, a count of 12 or more is an action signal. Conventionally, the limit may be placed half-way between the two nearest counts, that is, at 11.5.

Note also that the formula for the lower control limit gives a negative value. Since a negative error count is not possible, there is, effectively, no lower control limit. Conventionally, the lower control limit is placed at 0. This situation arises because the Normal distribution is not the exact sampling distribution for a sample count. The exact Binomial model, mentioned above, excludes negative values. However, since what is needed here is a rough guide for action or not, such fine points as the goodness of the Normal approximation to the Binomial model need not trouble us now.

**Reviewing process performance post-improvement**

As noted earlier, it appeared from the extended count chart shown in Figure 4.19 that the process was performing better than target after the improved form design was implemented. It was suggested that a lower centre line would be more appropriate for monitoring the improved process. It would be sensible to base the new centre line on the data we have already observed following the improvement. The numbers of errors found in the 20 samples following the improvement were:

1   1   4   4   1   4   4   4   1   6   4   1   6   5   1   2   1   5   2   3.

These total 60, out of a total of 20 times 100 forms examined. The sample mean error rate,

$$\hat{p} = \frac{60}{20 \times 100} = \frac{60}{2000} = 0.03,$$

that is, 3%, provides an estimate of the process mean error rate.

---

**Exercise 4.8**   Use the formulas on the previous page to calculate the control limits for the np chart for the number of errors in samples of 100 when $p = 0.03$.

---

The redrawn chart for the last 20 samples with recalculated limits is shown in Figure 4.20.

It is seen that the process is now under statistical control with an improved process mean error rate of around 3%.

---

**Exercise 4.9**   From the data in Table 4.3, calculate the mean sample error rate during the period of the first 30 samples and use this as the basis for recalculating control limits. Draw the recalculated centre line and control limits on the chart for the first 30 samples. What is your conclusion? Why is this conclusion different from that drawn from the review of the chart in Figure 4.17? Can you differentiate between the different *forms* of control being assessed in the two charts?

---

## 4.6   Review exercises

4.1   Recall Review Exercise 3.5, page 115. The printing company decided to set up a Shewhart control chart to monitor the quality of incoming paper. Based on the data given in Review Exercise 3.5, calculate the control limits for a mean chart for thickness, based on samples of size 4. Prepare a blank chart as if for routine use. Explain the routine use of the chart, as if to a worker assigned the task of maintaining it.

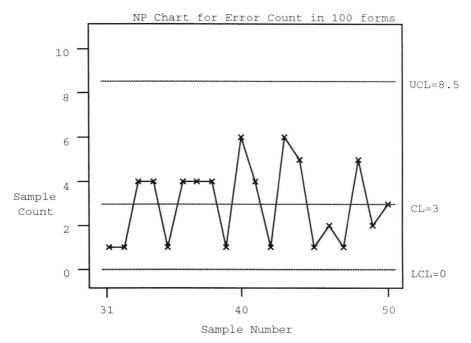

**Figure 4.20** Post-improvement count chart with new limits.

4.2 Recall Exercise 3.4, page 115. The data on volume measurements for the run 1 sample of 50 glasses follow.

| Sample | 1 | 2 | 3 | 4 | 5 | 6 | 7 | 8 | 9 | 10 |
|--------|---|---|---|---|---|---|---|---|---|----|
| Volume | 503.5 | 507.7 | 506.1 | 505.6 | 504.1 | 504.2 | 504.3 | 503.0 | 504.2 | 507.1 |

| Sample | 11 | 12 | 13 | 14 | 15 | 16 | 17 | 18 | 19 | 20 |
|--------|----|----|----|----|----|----|----|----|----|----|
| Volume | 500.2 | 509.2 | 506.2 | 501.3 | 506.4 | 506.0 | 506.1 | 505.0 | 504.4 | 504.0 |

| Sample | 21 | 22 | 23 | 24 | 25 | 26 | 27 | 28 | 29 | 30 |
|--------|----|----|----|----|----|----|----|----|----|----|
| Volume | 505.0 | 502.8 | 502.4 | 506.5 | 504.0 | 503.5 | 502.2 | 502.5 | 505.3 | 507.8 |

| Sample | 31 | 32 | 33 | 34 | 35 | 36 | 37 | 38 | 39 | 40 |
|--------|----|----|----|----|----|----|----|----|----|----|
| Volume | 507.7 | 506.2 | 506.9 | 502.5 | 505.0 | 505.4 | 507.3 | 506.2 | 507.6 | 506.5 |

| Sample | 41 | 42 | 43 | 44 | 45 | 46 | 47 | 48 | 49 | 50 |
|--------|----|----|----|----|----|----|----|----|----|----|
| Volume | 504.1 | 506.5 | 505.2 | 504.9 | 503.6 | 506.5 | 506.6 | 503.4 | 504.3 | 507.7 |

The mean and standard deviation were calculated as 505.1 and 1.9, respectively. Calculate control limits, make a control chart for the individual measurements and plot the run 1 values on it. Report on the state of statistical control of the process.

4.3    Continuation of Exercise 4.2.
Line charts for the individual measurements made in production runs 2–8 follow.

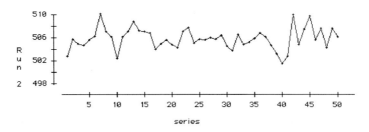

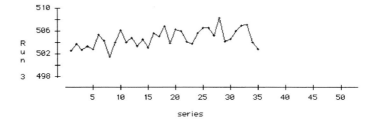

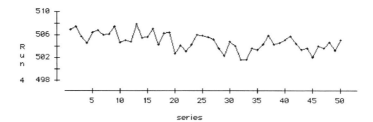

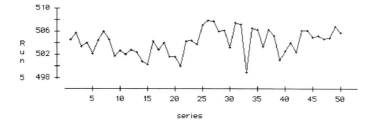

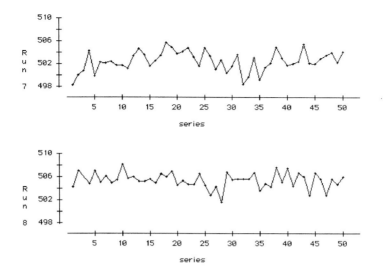

In each case, use the run 1 limits as a basis for monitoring. Report on the state of control using all four AIAG rules where appropriate.

4.4    In an effort to improve its quality of service, a large mail order company monitors the times it takes to complete certain activities. One of these is the time taken from receipt of a customer's order to the time the order is dispatched to the customer. This dispatch time will vary for many reasons, including current work-load, time taken to assemble the order, time taken to order stock from suppliers, etc. The company aims for an average of 20 days to dispatch orders. The dispatch time is determined on the day the order is dispatched by checking the customer's order form, which is date-stamped on receipt. As this would be impractical to do for every order, the company has decided to do a special exercise on the first Monday of every month, when a clerk will determine the dispatch times of the first six orders dispatched on that day and plot them on X-bar and *R* charts. To get started, they create charts based on the first week's data:

$$23, 26, 19, 16, 26, 16.$$

They use the target, 20, as centre line for the X-bar chart and base the remaining control lines on the range of the data.

(i)    Calculate the control limits for the X-bar and *R* charts. Create blank charts for ongoing monitoring purposes.
(ii)   The chart was updated monthly for a 12 month period. The corresponding means and ranges were:

| X-bar | 21.00 | 22.00 | 15.83 | 18.17 | 21.00 | 22.00 | 25.17 | 19.83 | 16.33 | 16.67 | 20.17 | 19.33 |
|-------|-------|-------|-------|-------|-------|-------|-------|-------|-------|-------|-------|-------|
| Range | 10 | 17 | 15 | 18 | 13 | 20 | 11 | 13 | 13 | 7 | 18 | 8 |

Plot these values on the charts you have prepared. After plotting each month's data, make a report on the current state of control of the process.

(iii) At the end of the first 12 months, the procedure was reviewed. New control limits were calculated based on all the data to date. Calculate the new limits and draw them on your chart. Review your monthly reports in the light of the new limits.

(iv) Summary data for the next 12 months follow.

| X-bar | 20.17 | 21.50 | 17.83 | 23.50 | 24.83 | 19.17 | 22.83 | 21.33 | 24.83 | 18.50 | 21.83 | 18.00 |
|-------|-------|-------|-------|-------|-------|-------|-------|-------|-------|-------|-------|-------|
| Range | 17 | 12 | 5 | 19 | 13 | 14 | 13 | 10 | 9 | 20 | 16 | 16 |

Plot these data on your revised chart, extended if necessary. After plotting each month's data, make a report on the current state of control of the process. Calculate new limits based on the 24 months' data, plot on your chart and make a revised report.

(v) Comment on the practice of calculating control limits on the basis of a single sample. Also, comment on the practice of observing the dispatch times of the first six orders dispatched on the first Monday of every month. Can you think of any source of bias that might arise? If so, can you think of a way of minimising the bias?

4.5   As part of a preliminary study of the bill-paying behaviour of its customers, a mail order company collected data on the number of days to collection of accounts receivable. Rather than observe every account, the first five accounts received on Monday morning each week were taken as a sample of the process. A line chart for the sample means calculated from 30 such samples follows. The overall average number of days to collection for the 150 accounts is 34. The process standard deviation is calculated as 3.

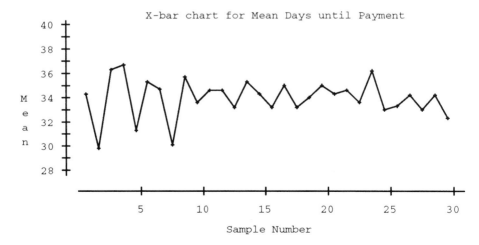

(i)   Calculate control limits for the means and plot them on a copy of the line graph.
(ii)  Interpret the resulting control chart. Does the process appear to be in control with respect to both variability and mean level?

(iii) In the light of your answer to part (ii), suggest how new control limits might be calculated for going forward.

4.6 A distributor of ball point pens receives regular complaints from clients that too many pens are being returned as not working. When the distributor takes this up with the manufacturer, the latter insists that the defect rates in their products are minimal, no more than 1%. The distributor decides to collect some data. From each of 50 batches delivered by the manufacturer, the distributor samples 100 pens and tests them by drawing them across a sheet of paper yielding the following defect numbers:

| | | | | | | | | | | | | | | | | | | | | | | | | |
|---|---|---|---|---|---|---|---|---|---|---|---|---|---|---|---|---|---|---|---|---|---|---|---|---|
| 2 | 4 | 2 | 1 | 6 | | 2 | 4 | 1 | 0 | 0 | | 4 | 5 | 3 | 2 | 3 | | 2 | 3 | 0 | 3 | 1 | | 2 | 3 | 1 | 2 | 1 |
| 2 | 0 | 4 | 2 | 1 | | 0 | 3 | 1 | 2 | 1 | | 2 | 1 | 5 | 3 | 0 | | 2 | 2 | 1 | 3 | 1 | | 1 | 3 | 0 | 2 | 1 |

Plot these on a line chart.

Suppose the value for $p$ in the ball point pen manufacturing process is taken to be 0·01, or 1%. Draw the corresponding control lines on your chart. What do you deduce?

The total number of defectives in the 50 samples is 100. Calculate the mean sample error rate. Calculate the corresponding centre line and control limits and plot them on your chart. What is your conclusion?

## 4.7 Laboratory exercise: Estimating σ from data with possible exceptional cases

Data on Monday cash variances in the sports and social club discussed earlier are in an Excel file, Mvariances.xls, in the book's website. In this laboratory, you will implement the procedure given in Section 4.1, pages 122–24, for estimating process standard deviation from historical data.

Make a time series plot (line plot) of the data. Calculate the mean and standard deviation of the data. Set up a formula to calculate upper and lower control limits from the calculated mean and standard deviation.

In the line plot, identify the data point furthest from the mean, mark it for deletion and recalculate mean, standard deviation and control limits.

Check if the deleted point is outside the new control limits. If not, undelete the deleted point, recalculate and report the recalculated standard deviation.

If the deleted point is outside the new control limits, exclude it from further calculation, along with any other points outside the new control limits and recalculate.

Repeat the deletion, recalculation, checking and exclusion process until the deleted point is inside the recalculated control limits. Then, undelete the deleted point, recalculate and report the recalculated standard deviation.

Keep a log of your iterations, recording successive deleted values, re-calculated parameter values, recalculated control limits and exclusions and record your final estimate of σ.

Prepare a brief report on the results of your calculation, including references to exceptional values, the final estimated value of $\sigma$ and control limits for monitoring Monday cash variances. Include in your report an account of why you think the standard deviation of Monday variances differs from that for Sunday.

# 5

# Principles of statistical inference

In Chapter 4, we developed an approach to monitoring process performance through the use of control charts. The basic idea is that process variation is characterised by a trend and a band around the trend and if we observe values beyond this band, then we conclude that the process is misbehaving. If so, action may be needed to discover the assignable causes of such misbehaviour and adjust the process accordingly.

Related to this is the idea of assessing process performance in the light of historical data. If the process appears stable over some period of time, on the basis of historical data plotted on a control chart, then we can use those data to provide estimates of process characteristics such as process mean, standard deviation, and non-conformance rate.

In either case, the conclusions we come to are subject to chance variation, since the process which generated the data is subject to chance variation. We need to qualify our conclusions to allow for the presence of such chance variation. The key statistical concept which allows us to do this is that of the *sampling distribution.*

Statisticians have developed a vocabulary for dealing with these ideas, under the general heading of *statistical inference.* Along with the sampling distribution concept, the main ideas are those of *statistical significance,* corresponding to process monitoring, and *confidence intervals,* arising out of process performance assessment. In this chapter, we will re-express the ideas of Chapter 4 in terms of this vocabulary, thus providing a theoretical framework and a basic set of guidelines for dealing with uncertainty in problem solving which is due to the presence of chance causes of variation. Then, in this and later chapters, we will see how the ideas may be applied in a wide variety of problem solving settings.

### Learning objectives

After completing this chapter, students should understand the nature and purpose of statistical inference and the key statistical concepts underlying statistical inference, and demonstrate this by being able to:

- implement the standard Z tests for assessing the statistical significance of the deviation of a sample mean from a target, the difference between two sample means, the deviation of a sample proportion from a target;
- set out the formal steps involved in implementing such tests, as tests of hypotheses;
- explain the basis for statistical significance in terms of sampling distributions;
- describe the correspondences between Z tests of deviations from target and control charts;
- explain the meaning of statistical significance in terms of false alarm rates;
- define and interpret p-values or 'observed significance levels';
- define and interpret the statistical power of a test and explain its meaning in terms of control chart detection rates;
- explain the relation between significance level, power and sample size;
- calculate confidence intervals for process means, proportions and percentages based on sampled process data;
- explain the need for confidence intervals and the role of the sampling distribution in their construction and interpretation;
- explain the relation between confidence level, interval width and sample size;
- explain the correspondence between significance tests and confidence intervals.

## 5.1   Statistical significance testing

We saw in Chapter 4 that a point outside the control limits on a control chart set up to monitor process variation signalled a possible assignable cause of variation which typically needed investigation and possible action. In Section 4.1, we described the observation of such a point as *statistically significant,* and we described the rule which is used to make the distinction between in-control and out-of-control points as a *test of statistical significance.* Identical considerations apply in the case of the X-bar chart, the range chart and the np chart developed in later Sections of Chapter 4; while the details of the rules used are adapted to the particular circumstances, the basic ideas and justification are essentially the same. Here, we develop a formal language and structure for significance testing in the context of the X-bar chart.

### The Z test

Consider the X-bar chart. The 'in-control' assumption that the process mean $\mu$ coincides with the chart centre line is referred to in the language of statistical theory as the *null hypothesis,* the term *'null'* indicating *no* difference between process mean and centre line. The *alternative hypothesis* is the assumption that the process mean differs from the centre line, that is, that the process is out of control in this regard.

If sample data suggest that the null hypothesis is implausible, the departure from the null hypothesis assumption is said to be *statistically significant.* The test applied to the data, that is, 'is $\bar{X}$ inside or outside the control limits?', is called a *test of statistical significance* or significance test.

The control chart test is conventionally formalised as follows. A point on the chart is outside the control limits if its $\bar{X}$ value deviates from the centre line by more than three standard errors. If $\mu_o$ is the process mean value corresponding to the centre line, this is equivalent to saying that the value of $\bar{X}$ satisfies

$$\bar{X} - \mu_o > 3\sigma/\sqrt{n} \quad \text{or} \quad \bar{X} - \mu_o < -3\sigma/\sqrt{n},$$

that is

$$\frac{\bar{X} - \mu_o}{\sigma/\sqrt{n}} > 3 \quad \text{or} \quad \frac{\bar{X} - \mu_o}{\sigma/\sqrt{n}} < -3$$

that is, the calculated value of

$$\frac{\bar{X} - \mu_o}{\sigma/\sqrt{n}}$$

exceeds 3 in magnitude. Here,

$$\frac{\bar{X} - \mu_o}{\sigma/\sqrt{n}},$$

usually denoted by $Z$, is referred to as the *test statistic* and the number 3 is called the *critical value* for the test statistic. It is critical in the sense that the deviation of $\bar{X}$ from $\mu_o$ is statistically significant or not according as the calculated value of the test statistic exceeds the critical value or not.

The null hypothesis is *rejected* if the test statistic exceeds the critical value in magnitude, corresponding to an 'out-of-control' signal from the control chart. Otherwise the null hypothesis is *accepted,* at least provisionally.

The correspondence between the control chart test and the $Z$ test is illustrated in Figure 5.1. This shows the sampling distribution of $\bar{X}$ or $Z$, as appropriate, assuming the null hypothesis holds. For $Z$, this is the standard Normal distribution with mean 0 and standard deviation 1, for which appropriate tables are available. Recall that the sampling distribution of a sample statistic[1] is the frequency distribution of values of the statistic that arise from repeated sampling of the process, calculating a new value of the statistic from each sample. Assuming that the process is in control, a value of $\bar{X}$ outside the control limits is improbable; finding such a value makes an in-control process implausible. Equivalently, assuming the null hypothesis, a value of $Z$ exceeding $\pm 3$ is improbable; finding such a value makes the null hypothesis implausible.

---

**Exercise 5.1**   List the correspondences between all relevant aspects of the X-bar chart and the associated $Z$ test.

---

[1]   In statistical language, any quantity whose value is calculated from sample data is called a *statistic.*

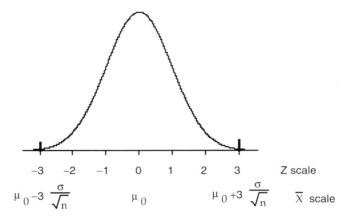

**Figure 5.1**   Normal curve for control chart test and *Z* test.

**Exercise 5.2**   Express as a series of statistical significance tests the use of the control chart for monitoring cash variances introduced in Section 4.1; refer to Table 4.1 in Chapter 4 for the corresponding variance values, and assume that $\sigma = £4.00$, as in the construction of the control chart. Apply the test to the cash variances recorded in weeks 1, 2 and 3, when the process appeared in statistical control, and in weeks 12, 34 and 51, when it appeared to be out of control. Plot the corresponding variance values on a graph illustrating the null hypothesis sampling distribution.

**An extension of the control chart Z test**

In our analysis of the capability of the clip gap process in Section 4.4, we concluded from the graphical evidence (Figure 4.16, page 146) that the process had gone through two phases, the first up to sample 17 and the second after sample 17. Figure 4.17, reproduced here as Figure 5.2, suggested means of around 74 mm and 67 mm, respectively. This is despite the fact that, in the original control chart with centre line at 70 mm, just one of the individual control chart tests suggests rejection of the null hypothesis that the process mean is 70 mm. It seems we have used our graphically informed good sense, based on the combined evidence of several quality control samples, to arrive at these conclusions.

We can complement these graphically based assessments with formal significance tests based on extending the control chart *Z* test to combinations of the quality control samples.

First, looking at the samples up to sample 17, suppose we combine all the quality control samples (excluding sample 11 where the process was operated by a trainee) into one big 'capability assessment' sample. We now have a sample of 80

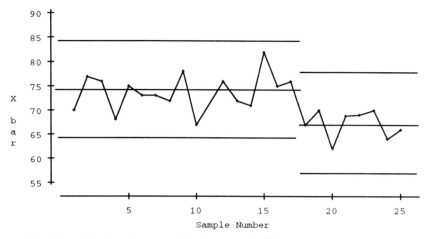

**Figure 5.2** X-bar chart for clip gaps with redrawn control lines.

measurements whose mean is 73.8 mm, as noted in Section 4.4, page 145. We can apply the ideas of statistical significance testing by asking 'Is the sample mean within three standard errors of the null hypothesis value' or by computing an appropriate Z statistic and comparing it to the critical value, 3. It is as if we had a quality control sample of 80, so that the standard error of $\overline{X}$, based in this case on 80 sample values, is

$$\sigma/\sqrt{n} = 7.3/\sqrt{80} = 0.8$$

Clearly, a sample mean value of 73.8 mm is considerably more than three standard errors, that is, 2.4 mm, away from 70 mm. Equivalently, we can calculate the corresponding Z statistic,

$$Z = \frac{\overline{X} - \mu_0}{\sigma/\sqrt{n}} = \frac{73.8 - 70}{7.3/\sqrt{80}} = \frac{3.8}{0.8} = 4.75.$$

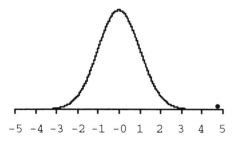

This exceeds the critical value for Z, 3, whence we reject the null hypothesis. On a picture of the null hypothesis sampling distribution of values of Z, as shown above, the calculated value appears extreme.

**Exercise 5.3** Test the significance of the difference between the sample mean of samples 18–25 combined, 66.75 mm, and the null hypothesis value for the process mean, 70 mm. Illustrate the result on a picture of the relevant sampling distribution. Compare and contrast with the result found up to sample 17; explain any differences.

### Discussion

There appears to be a conflict between the results of the tests based on samples 1–17 and samples 18–25. The first test suggested a shift in the process mean, the second, the subject of Exercise 5.3, did not, in spite of the fact that the graphical evidence in Figure 5.2 appears stronger in the latter case.[2]

There are two contributory reasons for this. In the first place, the second sample mean is closer to the centre line than the first, giving a smaller numerator to the $Z$ statistic. More critically, however, the second test is based on a considerably smaller sample, 40 as compared to 80. Thus, there is less evidence on which to base a decision in the second sample. This is reflected in the $Z$ statistic through the presence of $\sqrt{n}$ in the standard error formula in its denominator; smaller $n$ means bigger standard error which results in smaller $Z$. This reflects the discussion in the subsection 'Implications of the standard error formula' in Section 4.3, page 141.

**Exercise 5.4** Following analysis of the 52 cash variances observed over the year, it was concluded that three of the values were exceptional and that the remaining values represented a process in statistical control, with standard deviation £4.15; see page 124, Chapter 4. The estimated mean value, based on the in-control variances, was £0.60. Based on these data, test the null hypothesis that the cash variance process mean was £0. Make a detailed report of the test and its result, referring to

- the null hypothesis;
- the test statistic;
- the critical value for the test statistic;
- the calculated value of the test statistic;
- a comparison of these values; and
- the test result.

Illustrate the result on a picture of the relevant sampling distribution.

---

[2]  In fact, the second action rule on the control chart form, 'a run of seven points all above or all below the central line' (see Figure 4.6), gives a numerical version of our graphical test. While this does not occur in samples 1–17, there is a run of 8 below the line in samples 18–25, stronger evidence than is required by the rule. Note that this action rule may be formally represented as a statistical significance test where the test statistic is the run length above or below the line and the critical value is 7.

### A Z test for the difference between two means

While the $Z$ tests of the previous subsection addressed questions concerning deviation of the process mean from the target, there is another question of interest, that is, did the change in raw material after sample 17 have a statistically significant effect on the process mean? In other words, the question is 'Was the change in raw material an assignable cause of variation?' More formally, denoting the process mean during the first period, up to sample 17, by $\mu_1$ and the process mean after that by $\mu_2$, we seek to test the null hypothesis

$$H_0: \mu_1 = \mu_2$$

or, equivalently

$$H_0: \mu_1 - \mu_2 = 0$$

The sample evidence for a possible difference between the process means is contained in the difference between the sample means,

$$\bar{X}_1 - \bar{X}_2$$

However, each of these is subject to chance variation, as reflected in the corresponding standard error formulas,

$$\frac{\sigma_1}{\sqrt{n_1}} \text{ and } \frac{\sigma_2}{\sqrt{n_2}}$$

(Here, we have allowed for the possibility that the process standard deviation might also change with the change in raw material.) Thus, the difference between the sample means is subject to a combination of the two sources of variation. Consequently, the two standard error formulae must be combined to get a standard error for the difference between sample means. Mathematical considerations dictate that the individual standard errors are squared first, then added, then the square root of the sum is calculated, leading to the formula

$$\sqrt{\left(\frac{\sigma_1}{\sqrt{n_1}}\right)^2 + \left(\frac{\sigma_2}{\sqrt{n_2}}\right)^2}$$

or

$$\sqrt{\frac{\sigma_1^2}{n_1} + \frac{\sigma_2^2}{n_2}}$$

Finally, this leads to the test statistic

$$Z = \frac{\bar{X}_1 - \bar{X}_2}{\sqrt{\dfrac{\sigma_1^2}{n_1} + \dfrac{\sigma_2^2}{n_2}}}$$

In practice, we substitute estimates, $s_1$ and $s_2$, for $\sigma_1$ and $\sigma_2$, calculated from the two subsets using one of the methods described in Section 4.4. Using the 'average range' method, the estimated values are 7.6 and 6.75, respectively; see Exercise 5.5. Thus, the calculated value for $Z$ is

$$Z = \frac{73.8 - 66.75}{\sqrt{\dfrac{7.6^2}{80} + \dfrac{6.75^2}{40}}} = \frac{7.05}{1.36} = 5.2.$$

This is very highly significant. Hence, we *reject* the null hypothesis that the process mean was the same before and after the raw material change and conclude that there was a real affect, that changing the raw material was an assignable cause of variation.

---

**Exercise 5.5**   Verify the calculations of $\sigma_1$, $\sigma_2$; calculate the average ranges of subgroups 1–17 (excluding subgroup 11) and subgroups 18–25 of the clip gap data and multiply by the conversion factor $0.58 \times \sqrt{5/3} = 0.43$. Subsequently, verify the calculation of $Z$.

---

**Application to the np chart; a Z test for proportions**

The $Z$ test approach may be applied to the np chart introduced in Section 4.5. As indicated there, the key process parameter (or characteristic) is the process average error rate expressed as a proportion, which we will denote by $p$. The null hypothesis is the assumption that the process achieves a target error rate, to be denoted by $p_0$. In the context of a control chart based on the error count in a sample of $n$, this translates into a centre line at $np_0$; the sample error count should be roughly a proportion, $p_0$, of the total sample total count, $n$. Using the control chart test consists of checking whether or not the sample error count exceeds the control limits,

$$np_0 \pm 3\sqrt{np_0(1 - p_0)};$$

the test statistic is the error count and the critical values are the control limits.

The $Z$ test statistic is the 'standardised' count,

$$Z = \frac{X - np_0}{\sqrt{np_0(1 - p_0)}},$$

where $X$ represents the sample count, and the test consists of checking whether or not the calculated value for this test statistic exceeds the critical value, 3, in magnitude.

---

**Exercise 5.6**   List the correspondences between all relevant aspects of the np chart and the associated $Z$ test. Apply the $Z$ test in the cases of week number 7, when the process appeared out of control, and week number 8, when it appeared in control; refer to Table 4.3, page 148, for the error count data. Illustrate on a diagram of the relevant sampling distribution.

---

**Exercise 5.7** The evidence of the last 20 samples as shown in the extended count chart of Figure 4.18, page 149, suggests that the process mean error rate had shifted from 5%. Using the data of the last 20 samples combined to form one larger sample with $n = 2,000$, test the null hypothesis that the process mean error rate was 5%, or 0.05. Illustrate the result.

---

## 5.2 False alarm rates and significance levels

It must be recognised that statistical significance tests are subject to error because of the presence of chance variation. We can reject a null hypothesis when we should not or we can fail to reject a null hypothesis when we should.[3] In either case, the consequences can be serious. In a quality control context, possible consequences of incorrect rejection are:

- the process may be stopped unnecessarily;
- a costly investigation may be undertaken unnecessarily;
- the process may be adjusted unnecessarily, thus adding to the chance causes of variation.

Possible consequences of incorrect acceptance are:

- non-conforming products may occur, needing special attention, 'quarantine', rectification, scrapping;
- non-conforming products may be shipped to customers, leading to returns, claims for replacement, loss of goodwill, possibly loss of custom or, worse still, loss of reputation.

It is desirable, therefore, to minimise the chances of occurrence of such incorrect decisions. In the standard approach to control charting and statistical significance testing, the chance of incorrectly rejecting a null hypothesis is predetermined, while the possibility of not rejecting a null hypothesis when it does not hold is rarely considered. We will consider the former here and return to the latter later.

We have seen in Section 4.1 that the chances of a false alarm are less than 0.3% or 3 in 1,000 or, equivalently, the false alarm rate in the long run is less than 3 in 1,000. Shewhart chose to use *three* standard error limits because they gave such low false alarm rates. This choice has become conventional in control charting.

### Significance levels

In conventional statistical significance testing, it is common, following the English statistician R.A. Fisher, to set at 5% the chance of incorrect rejection of the null hypothesis.[4] This corresponds to a critical value of 2 for a standard $Z$ statistic;

---

[3]  These two types of error are often referred to as 'type I error' and 'type II error'.
[4]  See the historical note at the end of Section 1.1, page 9.

approximately 5% of the values in a Normal frequency distribution are more than two standard deviations from the mean.[5]

In statistical language, the chance of incorrect rejection of the null hypothesis is called the *significance level* of the test. Using the Shewhart convention, the significance level, synonymous with the *false alarm rate,* is 0.0027. Using Fisher's convention, the significance level is 0.05.

The formal theory of statistical significance tests requires that the significance level be *fixed in advance*. Little general guidance is given for this choice. Fisher offered a choice of three values:

$$0.1, \quad 0.05 \quad \text{and} \quad 0.01$$

The corresponding critical values for a $Z$ test statistic are

$$1.64, \quad 1.96 \quad \text{and} \quad 2.58,$$

respectively. An elaboration of this convention is to describe results which are significant at the 10%, 5% and 1% levels as 'almost significant', 'significant' and 'highly significant', respectively.

### Significance levels as error rates

Shewhart proposed his 'three standard error' control limits on the basis that the relatively low false alarm rate of less than 3 in 1,000 would be tolerable in the context of the frequent sampling typically involved in parts manufacturing. By contrast, a false alarm rate of approximately 1 in 20 (5%) would quickly lead to lack of confidence in using a procedure which led to frequent shut downs, investigations, etc. which later proved unnecessary. For example, sampling every two hours, as in the clip gap example, and using 'two standard error' control limits would mean getting a false alarm roughly once a week in the case of a 40 hour work week or three or more times a week with shift working. This would quickly kill the use of control charts.

On the other hand, in a process capability analysis based on historical data, the data on which significance tests are based involve combining several samples over a longer period of time. Thus, a combined sample of 80 clip gap measurements which involves combining 16 two-hourly samples covers a period of 32 hours. Assuming a 40 hour week, the Fisherian prescription of 5%, or 1 in 20, would lead to a test error roughly every 16 weeks, in that case. Such an error rate is less likely to cause upset.

It may be worth noting that Shewhart set up the control chart for use on a regular and frequent basis whereas Fisher initiated the systematic use of significance tests in the context of scientific, specifically agricultural, experimentation, where the perspective was over a much longer term. The chosen error rates make sense in these contexts.

---

[5]   More exactly, the percentage is 4.55%. Alternatively, the percentage is exactly 5% if the multiple of $\sigma/\sqrt{n}$ is 1.96, rather than 2. Since the Normality assumption is at best approximate, the use of the multiple 1.96, widely advocated in standard textbooks, lends an air of precision which is somewhat spurious; the 'two standard errors' rule is preferred here.

**Exercise 5.8** Repeat Exercise 5.3, page 164, using a 5% significance level. Illustrate the result. Compare the result with that found in Exercise 5.3.

### The 'observed significance level'

Instead of choosing fixed significance levels or critical values, the *observed signifi-cance level* or *p-value* may be calculated. (It is referred to as 'p-value' because some authorities use the expression 'observed significance probability'.) This is the area in the tail of the sampling distribution determined by ± the observed value.[6] Thus, in the clip gap control chart example, if a value of 74 were observed for $\bar{X}$, then the value for the corresponding test statistic would be

$$Z = \frac{74 - 70}{7.3/\sqrt{5}} = 1.2.$$

If this value of 1.2 were taken to be the critical value of the test, then the correspon-ding significance level, calculated as the area outside ±1.2 under the standard Normal curve, is 0.22; see Figure 5.3. Such a p-value would generally be regarded as non-significant.

**Exercise 5.9** Use the tables of the standard Normal distribution or the Excel NORMDIST function to confirm the calculation of the p-value of 0.22 above.

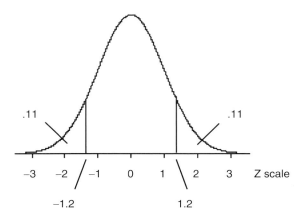

**Figure 5.3** p-value corresponding to $Z = 1.2$.

---

[6] It is also the chance or *probability* that the same test, *applied to data that satisfied the null hypothesis*, would produce a test statistic value that exceeded the value calculated from the actual data, whence the name 'observed significance probability'.

> **Exercise 5.10**    Calculate the p-values for the significance tests of Exercises 5.3–5.7.

As noted earlier, the formal theory requires that the significance level be chosen beforehand. By using the same significance level repeatedly, as is the case with control charts, we control the long-term error rate (false alarm rate) of the control chart procedure. By contrast, the p-value may be interpreted as a measure of statistical significance *in a particular instance*: the smaller the p-value, the greater the statistical significance.

## 5.3    Detection rates and power

When designing control charts, the control limits are set so that the false alarm rate is suitably small. There is another possibility of error using a control chart, that is, no signal is given even though the process actually is out of control. As noted in Section 5.2, the consequences of such an error can be serious. Given that control charts are based on data which are subject to chance variation, it is not possible to avoid such consequences completely; the best that can be hoped for is to minimise the chances of their occurring. Equivalently, we should seek to maximise the *detection rate* when the process is actually out of control.

In this section, we will see that the detection rates for conventionally designed charts can be undesirably low. We will also see how to modify the chart design so as to improve the detection rate. The basic requirement is to increase the sample size; more information equates with better decisions.

There is a parallel development in statistical significance testing. Earlier, we noted two types of error in applying significance tests, namely, incorrect rejection and incorrect acceptance. The significance level is the chance of incorrect rejection, and users of significance tests tend to concentrate their attention on it. This may be misleading, however, unless due attention is given to minimising the chance of incorrect acceptance. Equivalently, we should seek to maximise the chance of correct rejection, that is, the chance of rejecting the null hypothesis when it actually is false (and should be rejected). This chance is called the *power* of the statistical test.

### Calculating detection rates and power

To illustrate, recall the clip gap example where the target value (null hypothesis) was 70 mm and the assumed value of $\sigma$ was 7.3 mm. We may ask 'What are the chances of getting the other kind of incorrect signal, that is of not detecting that the process is out of control?'. As there are many ways in which a process can be out of control, we need to make this question more specific. For example, we may think it important to detect a shift in the clip gap process average from 70 to 75. It may be shown that, according to the Normal model for chance variation, the predicted non-conformance rate in that case is 2%, which would be regarded as unacceptably high for most modern manufacturing processes.[7]

The sampling distribution of $\bar{X}$ is centred on the process mean, $\mu$, whatever that is. Figure 5.4 shows the two possibilities corresponding to $\mu = 70$, the null hypothesis, and $\mu = 75$, an alternative of interest.

The shift to $\mu = 75$ is detected if $\bar{X}$ is less than LCL = 60 or greater than UCL = 80. It is clear from the figure that there is little or no chance of getting a value of $\bar{X}$ less than 60 when $\mu = 75$. The chance of $\bar{X}$ exceeding 80 when $\mu = 75$, represented by the shaded area in Figure 5.4, may be found by calculating

$$Z = \frac{80 - \mu}{\sigma/\sqrt{n}} = \frac{80 - 75}{7.3/\sqrt{5}} = 1.53$$

and referring that value to the Normal table. We find that the chance of getting a value of $\bar{X}$ which is more than 1.53 standard errors above the process mean is 0.063, or 6.3%. Clearly, if we regard it as important that we should be able to detect a shift in the process average which causes 2% non-conformances, then a procedure which gives us a 6.3% chance of detecting such a shift is unsatisfactory.

A simple calculation shows that the non-conformance rate when $\mu = 80$ is 8.5%, extremely high by modern standards, while there is just a 50% chance of detecting a shift in the process mean from 70 to 80.

---

**Exercise 5.11**   Confirm that the clip gap process non-conformance rate is 8.5% when $\mu = 80$ (specification limits are 50–90 mm), and the chance of detecting a shift to $\mu = 80$ is 50% (control limits are 60 and 80). Draw a picture to illustrate your calculations. Is calculation necessary to find the detection rate when $\mu = 80$?

---

It seems that the detection rate of the chart as designed is too low. Equivalently, the power of the corresponding statistical test is too low.

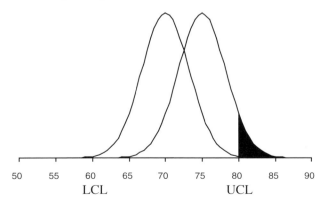

**Figure 5.4**   Null and alternative sampling distributions; $n = 5$.

---

[7]   Recall Exercise 4.6, page 142, which called for similar calculations.

## Improving detection rates and power

There are three ways of improving the detection rate of a control chart or the power of the corresponding test:

- reduce the process variation;
- reduce the critical value; or
- increase the sample size, $n$.

Reducing the process variation is typically not a short-term option for increasing detection rates. It is highly desirable that process variation be reduced, however. The modern approach to quality emphasises quality improvement, in which reduction of process variation is a key element.

Reducing the critical value makes it easier to reject the null hypothesis, thus decreasing the chance of acceptance. When the null hypothesis is not true, this means increasing the power of the test, as desired. On the other hand, increasing the chance of rejection also increases the chance of incorrect rejection, that is, the significance level. This may not be satisfactory. Exercise 5.12 provides numerical illustrations.

---

**Exercise 5.12**   Calculate control limits using a '1.5 standard errors' rule using the formula

$$CL \pm 1.5\sigma/\sqrt{n}.$$

Calculate the corresponding detection rates for $\mu = 75$ and 80. Compare with the detection rates for the 'three standard errors' rule. Calculate the false alarm rate corresponding to the '1.5 standard errors' rule; compare with the false alarm rate corresponding to the 'three standard errors' rule. Discuss.

---

## Increasing sample size

Increasing the sample size, $n$, reduces $\sigma/\sqrt{n}$, the standard error of $\bar{X}$, thus increasing the concentration of the sampling distribution of $\bar{X}$ around the process average and thereby making it easier to distinguish between cases where the null hypothesis is correct and where it is not. We can view this graphically, beginning with Figure 5.4 which illustrates the corresponding sampling distributions when $n = 5$. A sample value of $\bar{X}$ in the overlap of the two curves shown in the figure, say between 65 and 80, could plausibly correspond to either curve. Thus values in this wide range give no basis for discriminating between the two possibilities, $\mu = 70$ or $\mu = 75$; the test has low power.

By increasing the value of $n$, we reduce the width of these curves and therefore the overlap range. For example, if our two sampling distributions looked like those shown in Figure 5.5, almost all sample values of $\bar{X}$ would allow us to discriminate between the two cases; a value of $\bar{X}$ below 71 (and above 66) would almost certainly indicate that the process was on target, as opposed to centred at 75, while a value above 74 (and below 79) would indicate the opposite.

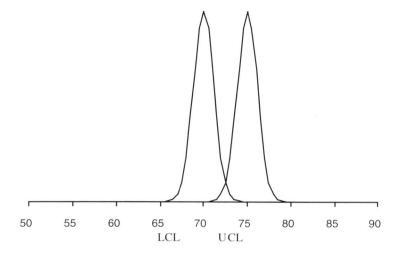

**Figure 5.5**   Null and alternative sampling distributions; larger *n*.

Thus, increasing the sample size improves the power of the $\bar{X}$ chart to discriminate between good and bad quality. On the other hand, increasing the sample size also requires more resources.

### Choosing a sample size

Having agreed that a detection rate of 6.3% for a 2% non-conformance rate is unacceptable, and that an increase in sample size will improve matters, the next question is what sample size to choose? The simplest approach to this question is trial and error or 'what-if' analysis. Thus, we might try doubling the sample size, try $n = 10$.

The first step is to recompute the control limits, which depend on *n*:

$$\text{LCL} = 70 - 3\sigma/\sqrt{n} = 70 - 3 \times 7.3/\sqrt{10} = 70 - 6.9 = 63 \text{ approximately;}$$

$$\text{UCL} = 70 + 3\sigma/\sqrt{n} = 70 + 3 \times 7.3/\sqrt{10} = 70 + 6.9 = 77 \text{ approximately.}$$

Note that these are closer to the centre line (at 70) than the sample size 5 limits of 60 and 80, reflecting the change in the sampling distribution of $\bar{X}$. Note also that the false alarm rate remains the same; they are still 'three standard error limits', even if the limits themselves have changed.

The next step is to calculate the detection rate when the process mean is 75 mm, that is, the chances that $\bar{X}$ exceeds the control limits when $\mu = 75$. The situation is illustrated in Figure 5.6.

Visually, we can see that the detection rate, represented by the shaded area under the right-hand curve to the right of the UCL, is still rather small. Calculation (see Exercise 5.13) shows the detection rate to be almost 20%, still unsatisfactory. It would seem that a considerably higher sample size is required.

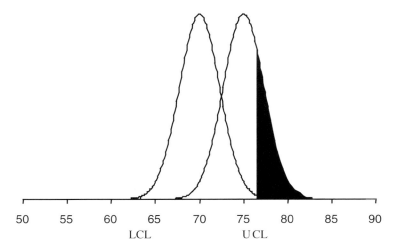

**Figure 5.6**   Null and alternative (μ = 75) sampling distributions; *n* = 10.

**Exercise 5.13**   Confirm that the detection rate using a 'three standard error' rule with *n* = 10 is 19.22% when μ = 75. Calculate the detection rate when μ = 80.

A series of such calculations leads to the graph shown in Figure 5.7. From it, we can see immediately that the marginal returns to increasing sample size diminish rapidly once *n* exceeds 40 or 50.

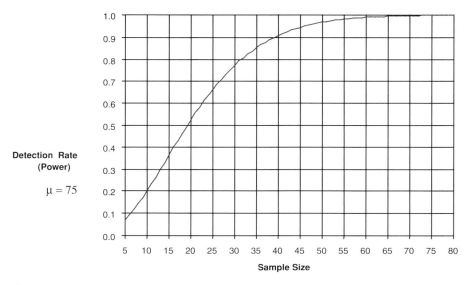

**Figure 5.7**   X-bar chart detection rate, equivalently, *Z*-test power, when μ = 75, as a function of sample size.

We can also use the graph to determine the sample size required to achieve a desired detection rate. Conventionally, a 90% detection rate is suggested. From the graph, we read that a sample size of approximately 40 is required to achieve this. This far exceeds the sample size of 5 used in the construction of the AIAG chart shown in Figure 4.6, page 128.

If we want to use a detection rate more in balance with the false alarm rate, we need even larger samples. Further inspection of the graph shows that a sample size of $n = 70$ is required to achieve a non-detection rate of 0.3%, that is, a detection rate of 99.7%.

### Balancing significance level, power and sample size

In practice, sample sizes of the order of 40 or 70 are likely to be regarded as prohibitively large in a busy manufacturing environment. On the other hand, detection rates achievable with smaller samples are likely to be regarded as unacceptable. This suggests striking a balance between the two views. It also suggests the possibility of reconsidering the false alarm rate and significance level and factoring it into the balance. What is required is a management analysis of the costs and benefits associated with changing all three, keeping in mind the costs involved in increasing sample size as well as the consequences of false alarms and non-detection already listed on page 167.

Most of the inputs required for this management analysis are non-statistical in nature. What is contributed by a statistical analysis is the language and frame of reference in which management can discuss such issues on a rational basis as well as relevant calculations that can quantify the issues. In particular, by specifying a particular significance level (false alarm rate) and power (detection rate), we are specifying in terms of error rates how well the test procedure performs in repeated applications, and these error rates, combined with the costs associated with test procedure error, will give us a handle on overall cost involved in using the procedure. However, it cannot be stressed too strongly that this cost must be balanced against the benefits to be got from using effective control and improvement procedures.

## 5.4   Confidence intervals

In Section 4.4, we saw that, assuming the process is in statistical control, it makes sense to *estimate* the process mean and standard deviation by corresponding *statistics* calculated from the observed data. For example, in a case where the mean of the till cash variances of Section 4.1 differs significantly from 0, we will want to know *what is* the cash variance process mean. Knowing this, we can then, for example, predict the total cash variance over a year's trading. But any estimate we derive from data which is subject to chance variation is itself subject to chance variation. We need to be able to allow for this.

Again, in our process capability assessment of the clip gap process, we saw that the average clip gap measurement seems to be different from the target value of

70 mm, with possibly two different values. Calculations suggested that the process mean was about 74 mm up to the time that the new batch of raw material was introduced and about 67 mm afterwards. In each case, however, we need to allow for the fact that both of these estimates were derived from data which were subject to chance variation. Thus, while an estimated process mean of 74 mm (and a standard deviation of 7.3 mm) suggests a non-conformance rate of 2%, allowing for chance variation means that the non-conformance rate could be somewhat higher or lower; Management will want to know by how much.

As another example, in Section 4.5 we found the post-improvement process error rate for clerical errors in completing order forms to be 3%, based on the 20 samples of 100 observed since the improvement was put in place. But the process and these sample observations of it are subject to chance variation. So, how sure can we be that the process error rate is 3%?

The standard approach to allowing for the uncertainty involved in estimates such as these is to calculate a *confidence interval*. The basic idea is implicit in the discussion of implications of the standard error formula contained at the end of Section 4.3, page 141. There, we noted that the calculated value of a sample mean was unlikely to be more than two standard errors from the process mean and even less likely to be more than three standard errors from the process mean. We concluded that we could be 'reasonably confident' that the process mean was within two standard errors of the calculated value of the sample mean and even more confident that the process mean was within three standard errors of the calculated value of the sample mean.

In fact, with repeated sampling from the process, $n$ at a time and calculating a new value of $\bar{X}$ each time, we expect 95% of the calculated values of $\bar{X}$ to be within two standard errors of the process mean, as illustrated in Figure 5.8.

Changing the emphasis, we expect that in 95% of samples from a stable process, the value of $\mu$ will be within two standard errors (that is, $2\,\sigma/\sqrt{n}$ units) of the calculated value of $\bar{X}$.

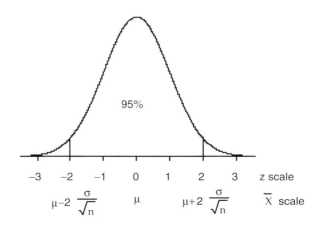

95%

| -3 | -2 | -1 | 0 | 1 | 2 | 3 | z scale |

$\mu-2\,\dfrac{\sigma}{\sqrt{n}}$ $\quad\mu\quad$ $\mu+2\,\dfrac{\sigma}{\sqrt{n}}$ $\qquad\bar{X}$ scale

**Figure 5.8**  Sampling distribution of $\bar{X}$.

Referring now to the specific value of $\bar{X}$ calculated from the sample of $n$ observations of the process available to us, we can be reasonably confident that it is one of the 95% of possible values of $\bar{X}$ which fall within two standard errors of $\mu$. Hence we can be confident that $\mu$ falls within two standard errors of that specific $\bar{X}$ value or, more concisely, that $\mu$ belongs to the interval

$$(\bar{X} - 2 \, \sigma/\sqrt{n} \, , \bar{X} + 2 \, \sigma/\sqrt{n} \, ).$$

This interval, with relevant values substituted, is called a *95% confidence interval.* The ends of the interval, $\bar{X} \pm 2 \, \sigma/\sqrt{n}$, are called *confidence bounds.* 95% is a measure of our confidence that the interval actually contains $\mu$ and is called the *confidence level.*

Of course, it is always possible that the specific interval we calculate is not one of the 95% of possible intervals which contain $\mu$, in which case our confidence statement will be in error. This is the chance we have to take when making inferences about processes which are subject to chance variation. This view parallels the view of significance level as error rate; in repeated applications of confidence interval calculations, using the 95% confidence level, we will be right in 95% of cases and wrong in 5% of cases. Thus, the confidence level is a property of the confidence interval procedure, just as the significance level of a test is a property of the test procedure.

**An example**

Imagine that we had just started the clip gap control chart shown in Figure 4.6, page 128. The mean of the first sample of n = 5 measurements was calculated as $\bar{X} = 70$, as shown in the bottom left of Figure 4.6. If we take the process standard deviation, $\sigma$, to be 7.3 mm., as we did in Chapter 4 on the basis of historical records, then we can calculate a 95% confidence interval for the process mean, $\mu$, as

$$70 \pm 2 \times 7.3/\sqrt{5},$$

that is

$$70 \pm 2 \times 3.26$$

that is

$$70 \pm 6.5,$$

that is

$$(63.5, 76.5);$$

we are 95% confident that the process mean is somewhere between 63.5 mm and 76.5 mm.

---

**Exercise 5.14**   The mean of the second sample in Figure 4.6 was 77. Calculate a 95% confidence interval for $\mu$ assuming that the data in sample 2 are the only data available. Compare with the interval calculated from the first sample. Discuss the comparison.

## Increasing the sample size

Imagine now that we had observed the first 13 samples as shown in Figure 4.6. Assuming that the process has remained stable in the period during which these data were collected, that is, the process mean $\mu$ remained constant, whatever its value, and process standard deviation remained at 7.3 mm, we can calculate an improved confidence interval based on these more extensive data. The '$n$' involved here is $65 = 13 \times 5$, rather than 5, and $\sigma/\sqrt{n}$ should be considerably smaller, so that the 95% confidence interval we calculate should be considerably narrower.

The mean of this extended sample of 65 measurements on the process is $\bar{X} = 73.2$ mm. Hence, the 95% confidence interval is

$$73.2 \pm 2 \times 7.3/\sqrt{65},$$

that is

$$73.2 \pm 2 \times 0.9,$$

that is

$$73.2 \pm 1.8,$$

that is

$$(71.4, 75.0);$$

we are 95% confident that the process mean is somewhere between 71.4 mm and 75.0 mm.

Note the dramatic reduction in the standard error, from 3.26 to 0.9, and the consequent reduction in the width of the interval; we get much greater precision from the much increased sample size. Note also that the interval is centred differently; $\bar{X}$ changes from sample to sample.

**Exercise 5.15**  Recall the completed clip gap chart showing 25 samples shown in Figure 4.17, reproduced as Figure 5.9.

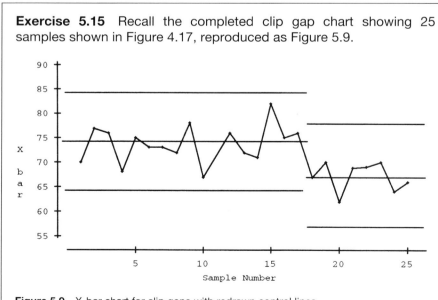

**Figure 5.9**   X-bar chart for clip gaps with redrawn control lines.

The average of the clip gaps in samples 1–17 excluding sample 11 was 73.8 mm. The average of the clip gap measurements in the last eight samples was 66.75 mm, as noted earlier. Assuming the value 7.3 mm for the process standard deviation, calculate 95% confidence intervals for the process mean both before and after the introduction of new raw material. What sample size (*n*) did you use in each case? Compare the interval widths. Relate your comparison to your comparison of the significance tests applied to the same data in Exercise 5.3, page 164.

---

**Exercise 5.16**   While analysing the cash variances data in Section 4.4 with a view to establishing a value for σ, we came up with a value for μ, which was the value we used for our final trial centre line, £0.60 or 60p. This was after we had concluded that the process variation was stable around a centre line, with a standard deviation of £4.15, following removal of the three exceptional values.

Based on the remaining values, calculate a 95% confidence interval for the process mean cash variance. Hence, calculate a 95% confidence interval for the total annual Sunday cash variance, assuming 52 Sundays in the year.

### Simulating confidence intervals

To assist in understanding the basis for confidence intervals, we can simulate a large number of confidence intervals from a process with known mean and standard deviation and see how many correctly contain the known process mean. If we simulate 100 intervals, we would expect around 95 to include μ; if we simulate 1,000 intervals, we would expect around 950 to include μ.

The results of such a simulation are shown in Figure 5.10. In it, the flat curve represents a Normal frequency distribution of values produced by a stable process which is repeatedly sampled. The narrow curve represents the sampling distribution of mean values calculated from such repeated samples.

The computer simulation consists of generating sets of values as if they were samples from a stable process, calculating a sample mean value in each case and then calculating an interval representing the calculated value ± 2 standard errors. Each calculated interval is represented in the figure by a horizontal line segment. The vertical line represents the position of the process mean. From our knowledge of the sampling distribution of the mean, we would expect 5% of the intervals not to cover the mean. In fact, in this simulation, two intervals did not; as indicated, the remaining 48 did, as desired.

Further simulations will provide additional support for the interpretation of confidence intervals; see the Laboratory Exercise at the end of the chapter.

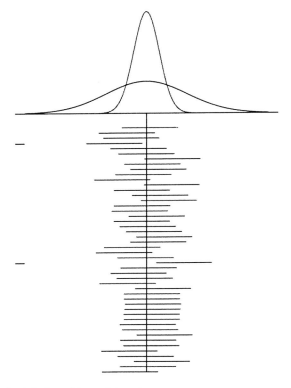

**Figure 5.10**   50 simulated confidence intervals.

## Alternative confidence levels

We may wish to have an interval estimate in which we have greater confidence. We can achieve this by widening the interval, the extent of widening depending on the level of confidence we wish to achieve. For example, we may read from the table of the Normal frequency distribution that 99% of possible values of $\bar{X}$ fall within 2.58 standard errors of $\mu$. We deduce that

$$\bar{X} \pm 2.58 \times \sigma/\sqrt{n}$$

gives a 99% confidence interval for $\mu$.

Applying the 99% confidence interval formula to the data in the first 13 samples in the clip gap control chart leads to

$$73.2 \pm 2.58 \times 7.3/\sqrt{65},$$

that is

$$73.2 \pm 2.58 \times 0.9,$$

that is

$$73.2 \pm 2.3,$$

that is

$$(70.9, 75.5);$$

an increase in interval width of about 30%.

---

**Exercise 5.17** Calculate 99% confidence intervals for the clip gap process mean before and after the introduction of new raw material.

---

**Exercise 5.18** Calculate a 90% confidence interval for the clip gap process mean based on the first 13 samples as shown in Figure 4.6. Compare with the 95% and 99% confidence intervals calculated from the same data.

---

**Reducing interval width**

If we want a narrower interval estimate, we can achieve this by:

- reducing the process variation, i.e. reducing $\sigma$; or
- reducing the confidence level; or
- increasing the sample size, $n$.

As noted earlier, the first of these is typically not a short-term option, albeit highly desirable in the long term. The second is usually not a satisfactory solution. Thus, while we can achieve an interval as narrow as we please by choosing a suitably low confidence level, there is little value in an interval in which we have low confidence.

Turning to the sample size option, suppose we want a 95% confidence interval whose width is the same as that of the 90% confidence interval of Exercise 5.18. The simplest approach is to equate the 'half-widths' of the two intervals, that is, set

$$2 \times 7.3/\sqrt{n} = 1.5,$$

that is,

$$\sqrt{n} = 2 \times 7.3/1.5 = 9.73,$$

or

$$n = 94.7$$

which, rounded to the nearest integer, gives $n = 95$.

Note that this requires 19 samples of size 5. With samples being taken every two hours, a sample of 95 will take 38 hours, or almost a full working week, to assemble. Assurance is needed that the process remains stable over such a period; a control chart used to monitor the process can provide this.

---

**Exercise 5.19**  Engineering management has specified that it needs to know the mean of the clip gap process to an accuracy of ±1 mm, with confidence level 99%. What sample size is required to achieve this? How long would it take to assemble a sample of this size using the current process sampling scheme? Discuss the process stability requirement in this context. Can you suggest an alternative sampling procedure?

---

### Confidence intervals for proportions and percentages

As with significance tests, the standard formula for a confidence interval for a process mean based on measured data can be adapted for proportions and percentages, provided the sample size is not too small.

Recall the data on clerical error counts in Section 4.5. Following the improvement to the form, 60 errors were noted on examination of 2,000 forms (20 samples of 100 forms each). Estimating the process mean error rate, $p$, by the sample mean error rate gives $\hat{p} = 0.03$. The standard error associated with this estimate is given by the formula

$$\sqrt{\hat{p}(1 - \hat{p})/n}$$

Note that this is a variation on the formula for the standard error of the error count, in which the factor $n$ appeared in the numerator. The error rate or proportion is calculated from the count by dividing by the sample size, $n$; the standard error is adjusted accordingly.

A 95% confidence interval for the process mean error rate is given by

$$\hat{p} \pm 2\sqrt{\hat{p}(1 - \hat{p})/n},$$

that is,

$$0.03 \pm 2 \times \sqrt{0.03 \times 0.97/2000},$$

that is,

$$0.03 \pm 2 \times 0.004,$$

that is,

$$0.022 \text{ to } 0.038$$

or

$$2.2\% \text{ to } 3.8\%.$$

The interpretation of this interval is as before. If the sampling exercise were to be repeated indefinitely with a new interval calculated each time, and the process remained stable, then 95% of the calculated intervals would include the process mean error rate, that is, the confidence interval method is correct in 95% of the repetitions. This makes us 95% confident that the single interval we calculated using the method does include the process mean error rate.

**Exercise 5.20** Calculate a 95% confidence interval for the process mean error rate for the 30 week period prior to the improvement of the form. Recall that 3,000 forms were sampled during that period, and a total of 179 clerical errors were discovered.

If we prefer to work directly with percentages, then the standard error formula must be adapted accordingly to

$$\sqrt{P(100-P)/n}.$$

Thus, a 95% confidence interval for the percentage of clerical errors is

$$\hat{P} \pm 2\sqrt{\hat{P}(100-\hat{P})/n},$$

that is,

$$3 \pm 2 \times \sqrt{3 \times 97/2000},$$

that is,

$$3 \pm 2 \times 0.4,$$

that is,

$$2.2\% \text{ to } 3.8\%,$$

as before.

## Sample size for estimating proportions and percentages

If we want to estimate a proportion or percentage to a given precision, we can choose a sample size that will ensure this by ensuring that the standard error is sufficiently small. There is an extra complication in this case, however, because the standard error formula depends on the parameter being estimated. In practice, we have evaluated the standard error formula by substituting the proportion or percentage with the value estimated from the data. Since we cannot know this before the data becomes available, there seems to be a problem. The solution to this problem is to substitute a 'worst case' value in the formula.

As an illustration, consider the problem of choosing the sample size for an opinion poll. Reports of such polls in the popular press frequently quote an accuracy of ±3% for reported percentages. Typically, such polls are based on samples of around 1,000 respondents. The level of accuracy reported is loosely related to a 95% confidence statement. More precisely, if the sample size is 1,111, then a 95% confidence interval for a reported percentage will not exceed the ±3% limits.

To see why this is so, consider the part of the standard error formula which depends on $P$,

$$\sqrt{P(100-P)}.$$

Figure 5.11 shows the graph of this as a function of $P$.

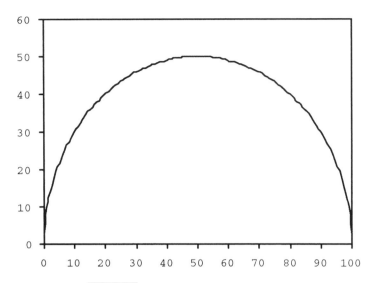

**Figure 5.11**   Graph of $\sqrt{P(100-P)}$ as a function of $P$.

The maximum of this function occurs at $P = 50$ so that this is the worst case for confidence interval width. To find a sample size that gives a 'worst case' width corresponding to ±3%, set the confidence interval 'half-width' to be 3, substituting $P = 50$ in the formula, that is,

$$2 \times \sqrt{50 \times (100-50)/n} = 3,$$

that is,

$$2 \times \sqrt{50 \times 50}/\sqrt{n} = 3,$$

that is,

$$\sqrt{n} = 2 \times 50/3,$$

that is,

$$n = 1{,}111$$

---

**Exercise 5.21**   What sample size is required to ensure that a percentage is estimated to within ±1% with 95% confidence?

---

**Exercise 5.22**   Frequently, 1.96 is used as the multiple corresponding to a 95% confidence level (but see footnote 5, page 168). Show that the sample size required to ensure that a percentage is estimated to within ±1% with 95% confidence is 1067. This calculation is the original basis for the commonly used opinion poll sample size of 1,000.

From the graph in Figure 5.11, it is clear that percentages which are smaller or larger than 50% can be estimated more precisely than the worst case. Frequently, something is known in advance concerning a percentage to be estimated. For example, in recent years in Irish election poll surveys, the percentage support for the largest party, Fianna Fail, has rarely exceeded 40%. It is probably safe to say that, in the next election poll survey, the percentage support for Fianna Fail will not exceed 45%. If so, 45%, represents the worst case. In order to ensure a 95% confidence interval width of ±3% for the Fianna Fail percentage, therefore, we repeat the previous calculation with 50 replaced by 45, that is, we set

$$2 \times \sqrt{45 \times 55/n} = 3,$$

that is,

$$2 \times \sqrt{45 \times 55}/\sqrt{n} = 3,$$

that is,

$$\sqrt{n} = 2 \times \sqrt{45 \times 55}/3,$$

that is,

$$n = 4 \times 45 \times 55/9 = 1{,}100$$

This reflects very little saving relative to a sample size of 1,111 reflecting, in turn, the flatness of the graph of $\sqrt{P(100 - P)}$ in the region around $P = 50$.

On the other hand, the graph falls off considerably as $P$ moves away from 50%. This may be viewed from two different angles. First, assuming the typical sample size of approximately 1,000 which gives a 95% confidence interval width of 3% for the worst case, we will get much narrower intervals for the percentage support for the smaller parties. Second, a smaller party commissioning a private poll can use a much smaller sample and still expect an accuracy of ±3%.

---

**Exercise 5.23**   In a recent election poll survey based on a sample of 1,000, the percentages of respondents supporting the second and third largest parties, Fine Gael and Labour, were 25% and 10%, respectively. Calculate the corresponding 95% confidence interval. Comment on the respective interval widths.

---

**Exercise 5.24**   Assuming that support for the Fine Gael party will not exceed 30% in the next poll, calculate the sample size required to give a 95% confidence interval width of 3%. Repeat this exercise in the case of the Labour party, assuming its support will not exceed 15%. Comment on the respective sample sizes.

---

## Confidence intervals and significance tests

There is a close correspondence between confidence intervals and significance tests. Given a sample of data from a process:

- a null hypothesis concerning the value of the process mean is accepted at the 5% level of significance if the sample mean is within two standard errors of the hypothesised process mean value;
- a 95% confidence interval for the process mean is made up of all those values within two standard errors of the sample mean.

It follows from this that an alternative way to implement a significance test is to calculate the corresponding confidence interval and check whether the null hypothesis value is included or not.

---

**Exercise 5.25**   Refer to Exercises 5.3, page 164 and 5.15, page 179. Use the intervals calculated in the latter to confirm the results of the former.

---

Some argue that the confidence interval is the preferred form of statistical inference and should supersede the significance test which may be implemented by simple reference to the confidence interval; if there is interest in some particular value of the process mean, then it is easy to check whether or not that value is included in the interval. While this argument is appealing, we will encounter problems later with a more complicated structure, where the confidence idea is not easily implemented in a readily interpretable form.

## 5.5   Review exercises

5.1   The catering manager in a hotel suspects that the weight of loaves of bread delivered daily by a bakery is consistently below the nominal weight of 800 gm. To test this, 10 loaves chosen at random from a day's deliveries are weighed. The mean and standard deviation of the ten weights are 792 gm and 25 gm, respectively. Carry out a formal significance test. List the steps involved in this test, from null hypothesis specification to conclusion. Illustrate the result of the test.

5.2   Calculate a 95% confidence interval for the average weight of loaves produced by the baker in Exercise 5.1. Comment on the correspondence between the interval, as calculated, and the result of the test in Exercise 5.1.

5.3   A company with a large number of debtors claims (for the purpose of negotiating a bank loan) that the average amount owed is £100. An evaluator acting on behalf of the bank looked at a sample of 25 of the company's outstanding accounts and found an average amount owed of £94.56. She found the standard deviation to be £8.50. Formally test the statistical significance of the deviation of the sample average from the company's claimed average. Indicate what you take to be the *null hypothesis*, the *test statistic*, the *critical value(s)*, and explain the basis for your test in terms of the *sampling distribution* of the test statistic. Illustrate the result with an appropriate diagram. Calculate the observed significance level for the test and relate its value to the formal conclusion of the test and to the illustrative diagram.

5.4    Recall Review Exercise 2.2, page 92. Test the statistical significance of the difference between the mean maintenance charge for the two branches. Make a formal report, referring to the null hypothesis, the test statistic, the chosen significance level, the corresponding critical value for the test statistic, the calculated value, the comparison and the formal conclusion. Calculate the observed significance level for the test and relate its value to the formal conclusion of the test.

Recalling the existence of a possible exceptional value in the data from the other branch, re-calculate the test statistic with the exceptional value excluded. Note the effect on the value of the test statistic, through both mean and standard deviation.

5.5    In the manufacture of tennis balls, a standard test for the finished product is the rebound test. Recent quality control inspections have indicated a substantial incidence of failures. In the most recent inspection, there were 15 test failures in a sample of 100 tennis balls, a failure rate of 15%.

Following a consultation between the Test Laboratory Manager and the Production Manager, the pressure inside the tennis balls was raised in an attempt to correct the problem. Following the increase in pressure, a second sample of 100 tennis balls was tested. This time, there were seven failures. This seems to indicate an improvement. However, to be sure, the Test Laboratory Manager decided to assess the statistical significance of the improvement.

(a)  Write down the formula for an appropriate test statistic, substitute the relevant values into the formula and calculate its value. Test the statistical significance of the difference in percentage failures before and after the process adjustment; present your answer in the form of a short (two or three lines) report of the result for the Test Laboratory Manager, incorporating a (very brief) explanation of the basis for your conclusion and a recommendation for action.

The Test Laboratory Manager is surprised and somewhat disappointed by the result of the statistical significance test. A colleague notes that the actual rebound heights are recorded and suggests that a test of the statistical significance of the difference in mean rebound heights would be more informative. The sample means of the 'before' and 'after' values were 104.5 cm and 107.5 cm respectively; the corresponding standard deviations were 4.7 cm and 5.4 cm.

(b)  Write down the formula for an appropriate test statistic, substitute the relevant values into the formula and calculate its value. Test the statistical significance of the difference in average rebound heights before and after the process adjustment; present your answer in the form of a short (a few lines) report of the result for the Test Laboratory Manager, incorporating a (very brief) explanation of the basis for your conclusion and a recommendation for action.

(c)  Explain the apparently increased statistical significance associated with the second test.

(d)  Explain what is meant by the standard error of the difference between two sample means. Explain the structure of the standard error formula. Discuss the correspondence between the standard error formulas in the denominators of the two test statistics above

5.6 A natural gas utility company is engaged in extending its pipe network to a number of urban areas surrounding its traditional area of operation. Before deciding to extend the supply to each area, the company tests the market. In one area, the company commissioned a survey of 500 households in order to estimate the percentage take-up, that is, the percentage of households in the area that would switch to gas if a pipe network was installed. One hundred and seventy three positive responses were received. Calculate a 95% confidence interval for the percentage take-up. Explain the basis for your confidence.

Subsequently, having installed a pipe network, the company found a take-up rate of 25%. Assuming that the sample of 500 was a proper random sample, test the statistical significance of the difference. Provide a formal report in which you state the null hypothesis, show the test statistic, the critical value and the formal conclusion.

5.7 An internal audit on over-the-counter transactions is carried out by a bank. A sample of 150 transactions from all transactions in a given year reveals 30 errors. What is the 95% confidence interval for the transaction process error rate?

Suppose the sample size is 600 and the number of errors revealed is 120. What happens to the confidence interval?

Suppose the sample size is 600 and the number of errors revealed is 30. What happens to the confidence interval?

Briefly explain the effect, on confidence intervals, of changing the sample size, assuming that the estimated error rate stays the same.

5.8 The marketing director of a bank would like to make a 'special offer' to personal customers whose accounts turn over more than €100,000 in a year. He guesses that such customers account for no more than 10% of all the banks customers, and costs the 'special offer' accordingly. The financial controller believes that there are over 20% of such customers and suggests that the cost will be too high. To resolve the issue, the accounts department is asked to estimate the percentage of large customers. What sample size is needed to estimate this percentage to within (i) 1%, (ii) 2%, with (a) 90% confidence, (b) 95% confidence.

## 5.6 Laboratory exercise: Simulating sampling distributions, significance tests and confidence intervals

The key to understanding classical statistical inference, including statistical significance tests and confidence intervals, is the concept of the *sampling distribution*. This is concerned with the behaviour of statistics, such as a sample mean, calculated from sample data. Such data is produced repeatedly in statistical process control through repeated sampling of the process. By simulating such repeated sampling, we can see how the statistic, repeatedly calculated, behaves.

In Review Exercises 5.1 and 5.2 above, the catering manager looked at just one sample. In this simulation exercise, you will look at many simulated samples, as if the catering manager repeated his sampling exercise day after day. Assume that the bakery is producing at the required nominal weight, and see what results the catering manager gets from a series of simulated tests.

Using random number generation, generate 100 samples of 10 values each, as if from a process following the Normal model with mean 800 and standard deviation 25.

Compare the first two samples; make dotplots, calculate summary statistics. Are the samples different? Are you surprised by the difference?

Calculate the means of all 100 samples and study their frequency distribution. Make a histogram of the 100 mean values. What did you expect? What did you get? Discuss.

Which of the following would you expect to approximate to the *range* of the 100 sample mean values?

$$790–810, \quad 775–825, \quad 760–840, \quad 750–850, \quad 725–875.$$

Explain your choice.

For comparison with the 100 sample means based on ten values each, simulate 100 individual values. Make a histogram of the 100 individual values. Make boxplots, using a common scale, of the 100 means and the 100 individual values. Make line plots using a common scale, of the 100 means and the 100 individual values. Calculate summary statistics for the 100 individual values.

What did you expect? What did you get? Write a brief report highlighting the main points of comparison.

To simulate significance tests and confidence intervals, copy the 100 simulated samples of ten values each into the first ten columns of an Excel worksheet. If an Excel function was used to generate the samples, make sure to use Paste Special and copy values only; else, the simulated values will change every time a function of them is calculated.

Enter the formula for the Z statistic for testing the hypothesis that $\mu = 800$ in cell K1 and copy to cells K2:K100. Count the number of values of Z that exceed 2. What did you expect? What did you get?

Confirm your count by entering an appropriate IF function in column L and summing the results.

Enter the formulas for lower and upper confidence intervals in columns M and N. Count the intervals that do *not* cover 800; scan down the lower confidence interval column looking for numbers beginning with 8, scan down the upper confidence interval column looking for numbers beginning with 7. What did you expect? What did you get? Discuss.

Confirm your count by entering an appropriate IF function in column O and summing the results. Compare columns L and O. Explain correspondences.

Repeat the entire exercise: simulate another 100 samples of 10 values each and paste into columns A to J. Review the changes in columns K to O. Repeat several times; each time note the number of 'reject' results from the significance tests. If you used Excel to generate your random numbers, use ordinary Paste and then press F9 to generate new samples.

Make a frequency distribution of the numbers of 'rejects'. What did you expect? What did you get?

# 6

# Simple linear regression

Simple linear regression is an approach to studying relations between pairs of continuous variables which aims to produce a simple prediction formula, based on historical data, to predict the value of one of the variables, given a new value for the other, allowing for any uncertainty due to chance variation. It seeks to achieve this through a combination of a simple graphical representation of the relation as reflected in historical data, the scatterplot, and a simple mathematical model of the relation which also allows for deviations due to chance causes of variation. The scatterplot also serves as a diagnostic tool, indicating the extent to which the historical data fit the pattern of the mathematical model by drawing attention to exceptional data. The related concept of correlation is introduced and developed.

The ideas involved are developed in this chapter in the context of the US Post Office case study introduced in Section 1.5 involving the relation of production costs, as measured through number of manhours employed, to volume of production, as measured by number of pieces of mail handled.

## Learning objectives

After completing this chapter, students should understand the basis for and application of simple linear regression and correlation, and demonstrate this by being able to:

- illustrate the need for a prediction formula relating a response variable to an explanatory variable;
- draw a scatterplot and recognise an underlying linear relation, if present, and exceptions from linearity, if present;
- explain the variation in linear scatter in terms of a line representing an assignable cause of variation and deviations from the line representing chance causes;
- write down an equation representing the simple linear regression model and identify the parameters of the model;

- motivate and describe informally the least squares approach to choosing estimates for the linear parameters;
- explain the formula for estimating standard deviation;
- produce scatterplots and calculate parameter estimates;
- explain computer regression output and calculate a prediction formula with error bounds from the output;
- construct a regression control chart, explain the basis for it and describe uses for it;
- explain what is measured by a correlation coefficient and sketch scatterplots corresponding to different values;
- describe the relation between regression and correlation;
- illustrate problems and pitfalls with simple linear regression and correlation.

## 6.1 The simple linear regression model

Table 1.3, page 24, shows data on manhours used and number of pieces of mail handled in a US Post Office for 26 successive four week accounting periods in 1962 and 1963. The scatterplot of manhours versus volume shown in Figure 1.19, and reproduced here as Figure 6.1, suggests an approximately linear relationship between the two variables, apart from three clearly exceptional data points.

Focusing on the cases suggesting the linear relation leads to Figure 1.24, reproduced as Figure 6.2, with the implicit suggestion of a straight line relationship with deviations which conform to the Normal model.

This may be expressed through the equation

$$Y = \alpha + \beta X + \varepsilon,$$

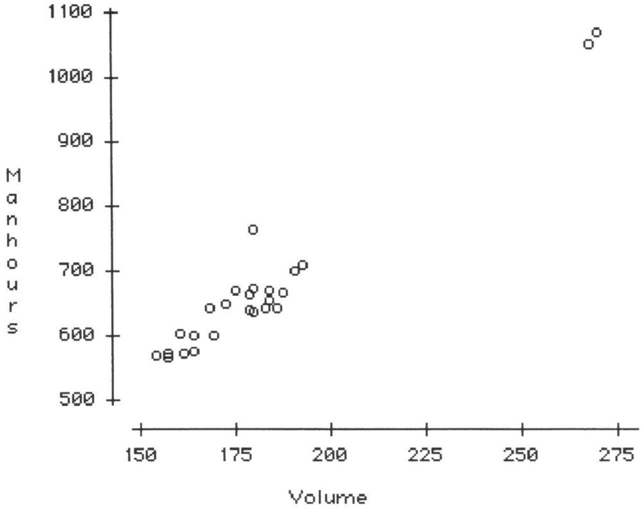

**Figure 6.1**   Scatterplot of manhours against volume.

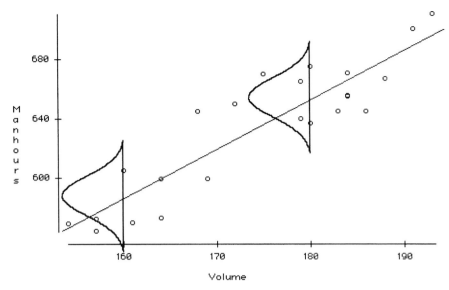

**Figure 6.2**   The simple linear regression model with Normal error.

the *simple linear regression model*. Typically, it is assumed that ε, which represents uncertainty in the relation between *Y* and *X* ascribed to chance causes of variation, conforms to the Normal model with mean 0 and standard deviation σ. α, β and σ are the *parameters* of the simple linear regression model meaning that different values of α, β and σ give rise to different versions of the model. To make effective use of the 'model', we need to determine appropriate values for the *linear coefficients* α and β, and to measure the uncertainty inherent in ε. In Section 1.5, we saw how a particular choice of parameters could be used to make predictions which, in turn, could be used for strategic review, planning and budgeting, evaluating the effects of planned change and of unplanned interventions, and process control.

### Choosing values for the regression coefficients

One way to select values of α and β appropriate to the data to hand is to draw a line on the scatter diagram which, we judge, fits the 23 points as well as possible, in the sense that it comes as close as possible to all 23 points. Necessarily, it will be closer to some than to others.

---

**Exercise 6.1**   On a copy of the scatter diagram in Figure 6.3,[1] draw the line you think best fits the data. Determine the corresponding values for α and β. (Pick two values for *X*, read off the corresponding values for *Y* as determined by your line, substitute your *X* and *Y* values in the equation of the line, and solve for α and β.) Compare your answer with your neighbours' answers.

---

[1]   Copies may be reproduced from the Resources page of the book's website.

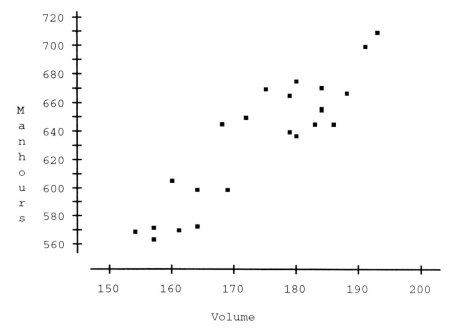

**Figure 6.3**   Scatterplot of manhours against volume, exceptions deleted.

While the 'eyeball' method for choosing a line is perfectly satisfactory in many practical problems, it suffers from its subjectivity; different analysts will choose different lines. This subjectivity has two important consequences: different analysts will make different predictions of manhours for the same volume; and it is virtually impossible to assess the uncertainty associated with an individual prediction. A more formal approach which yields unique predictions as well as a procedure for assessing prediction uncertainty makes use of the *method of least squares* to find values for $\alpha$ and $\beta$.

## The method of least squares

The method of least squares is a mathematical optimisation technique which chooses a line which is closest in a sort of average sense to the points in the scatter diagram. Given a value for $X$, the volume of mail, any two values for $\alpha$ and $\beta$ will give a value for $Y$ as determined by the equation for the corresponding line, $Y = \alpha + \beta X$. In particular, given the 23 values of $X$ to hand, 23 values of $Y$ may be so determined. If the values of $X$ to hand are referred to as $X_1, X_2, X_3, \ldots, X_n$, where $n = 23$, the values of $Y$ determined by $\alpha$ and $\beta$ are

$$\alpha + \beta X_1, \alpha + \beta X_2, \alpha + \beta X_3, \ldots, \alpha + \beta X_n.$$

Finding the line which fits as closely as possible to all the points on the scatterplot could be interpreted as finding the values of $\alpha$ and $\beta$ which minimise the set of deviations

$$Y_1 - \alpha - \beta X_1, \ Y_2 - \alpha - \beta X_2, \ Y_3 - \alpha - \beta X_3, \ \ldots, \ Y_n - \alpha - \beta X_n,$$

which are deviations of the *observed* values of Y, the actual manhours, from the *fitted* values of Y, the values determined by the line with equation $Y = \alpha + \beta X$. Two examples are shown in Figure 6.4, with the deviations represented as the short vertical lines joining the 23 points to the fitted lines. Neither of these fitted lines is very good.

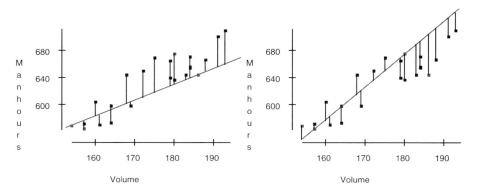

**Figure 6.4**   Possible regression lines based on trial values for $\alpha$ and $\beta$.

The method of least squares seeks values of *a* and *b* which minimise the *sum of squares* of these deviations,

$$\sum_{i=1}^{n} (Y_i - \alpha - \beta X_i)^2.$$

The solution to this mathematical optimisation problem may be found using differential calculus or appropriate algebraic manipulations. Details may be found in the Supplements and Extensions page of the book's website. The corresponding line, with deviations, is shown in Figure 6.5. The resulting line is called the *fitted line;* it is the line which *best fits* the points in the scatterplot. Formulas for the minimising values of $\alpha$ and $\beta$, here labelled $\hat{\alpha}$ and $\hat{\beta}$, are given by

$$\hat{\alpha} = \bar{Y} - \hat{\beta}\bar{X};$$

$$\hat{\beta} = \frac{\frac{1}{n}\Sigma(X_i - \bar{X})(Y_i - \bar{Y})}{\frac{1}{n}\Sigma(X_i - \bar{X})^2}.$$

Since 'scientific' calculators and computer software which incorporate the formulas for $\hat{\alpha}$ and $\hat{\beta}$ are widely available, the computational aspects of these formulas will not be pursued here. For the data to hand, excluding the three exceptional points, the values of $\hat{\alpha}$ and $\hat{\beta}$ corresponding to the fitted line are

$$\hat{\alpha} = 50, \ \hat{\beta} = 3.3.$$

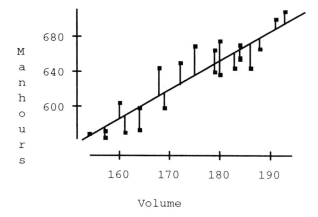

**Figure 6.5**   The least squares line, with deviations.

**Exercise 6.2**   Plot the line corresponding to these values of $\hat{\alpha}$ and $\hat{\beta}$ on the scatterplot of Exercise 6.1. How does it compare to your subjectively chosen line? Compute the $Y$ value determined by the line when $X = 180$. How does this compare?

### Interpreting the fitted line

The numbers 50 and 3.3, estimates for $\hat{\alpha}$ and $\hat{\beta}$, are the *estimated regression coefficients*. They may be interpreted as follows. The number 3.3 is the estimated marginal change in manhours when the volume increases by 1 unit. Thus, recalling the units in which volume and manhours are measured, an increase in volume of 1,000,000 pieces of mail is expected to be accompanied by an increase of 3,300 manhours.

When there is no mail to process, that is, when the volume ($X$) is 0 in the regression equation, the fitted equation indicates $Y = 50$, that is, 50,000 manhours are required. This might be ascribed to administrative overheads, rent, light and heat, or similar.

However, one should be very cautious about these interpretations, particularly of the value for $\hat{\alpha}$. The value $X = 0$ is far removed from the set of values for $X$ in Table 1.3. There is no guarantee that the straight line relation, which appears to hold for the range of data available, also holds for $X$ values far removed from that range, and about which we have no evidence. The scatterplot in Figure 6.6 shows the scales extended to include the point (0,0). The straight line is an extension of the calculated regression line. Either of the two curves, or many other lines and curves, would be entirely plausible in the light of the evidence in the available data.

The interpretation of the value $\hat{\beta} = 3.3$ is reasonable, provided we restrict its application to the range of $X$ values on which its estimation has been based.

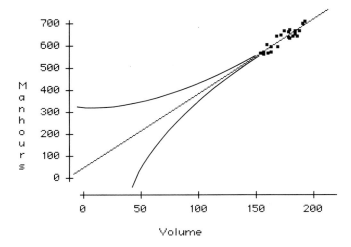

**Figure 6.6**   Scatterplot of manhours against volume, extended.

## Using the fitted line: prediction

Once we have values for $\hat{\alpha}$ and $\hat{\beta}$, we can use the formula $Y = \hat{\alpha} + \hat{\beta}X$ for a variety of purposes, including prediction and control as referred to earlier. For example, if we know what next month's volume is going to be (perhaps from past experience, perhaps from market research information), and if we can assume that the relation between volume and manhours remains stable, then we can use the fitted regression equation to make a prediction of next month's labour requirement. If volume $X$ is anticipated, then the obvious prediction for manhours is

$$Y = \hat{\alpha} + \hat{\beta}X.$$

However, there are (at least) two sources of prediction error. First, the fitted line is based on data which was subject to chance causes of variation. Secondly, the fitted line predicts a $Y$ value corresponding to a point on the line, while an actual value will deviate from the line because of chance causes of variation. In many practical problems, including the present one, the dominant source of prediction error is the deviation of actual values from the fitted line; the contribution to prediction error of the uncertainty about the fitted line is relatively negligible.[2] Following ideas developed in Chapter 5, we may specify a confidence interval for prediction, called a *prediction interval*. With (approximately) 95% confidence, we can predict that the labour requirement at volume $X$ will be in the interval

$$\hat{\alpha} + \hat{\beta}X \pm 2 \times \sigma,$$

---

[2]   Discussion of the standard error formula, incorporating both sources of error, may be found in the Supplements and Extensions page of the book's website.

where the standard deviation, σ, measures the extent of chance variation associated with ε.

To find a value for σ, we use an elaboration of the approach taken with control charts.

## A model for chance causes of variation

The Normal model for chance variation was developed in the context of processes where the process mean was thought to be constant, in the absence of assignable causes of variation, and deviations from the process mean were thought of as being due to chance causes. In the simple linear regression model, the mean of the manhours process is not constant; there is an assignable cause of variation, namely volume, which causes the manhours to change linearly as the volume changes. It is the deviations from that linear relation that are thought to be due to chance causes. These deviations are represented by the variable ε in our model; they are reflected in deviations of points from the straight line in the scatterplot.

In many problems, it is reasonable to assume that the Normal model for chance variation applies to the values taken on by ε, implying that they are sampled from a process whose values have a Normal frequency distribution with mean 0 and some standard deviation, σ, to be estimated from the data to hand. It may be imagined that, whenever a value of $X$ is given, the corresponding value of $Y$ is the value determined from the regression line with a value of ε added. Figure 6.2, page 192, shows this graphically.

In Figure 6.2, each point on the scatterplot may be thought of as made up in two steps: first, an $X$ value, e.g. 160, is given and the line determines a corresponding value of $Y$, then a value is chosen at random from the 'error' process and added to the $Y$ value. In the case of the point (160, 605) corresponding to period 13, 1963, the 'error' value is about two standard deviations. There are two points with $X = 179$, (179, 665) and (179, 640), corresponding to period 12, 1962 and period 11, 1963. In the first case, there is a positive 'error' of just under two standard deviations; in the second, the 'error' is negative and about one standard deviation in size. (Note that the 'tail ends' of the Normal curves in the diagram are about three standard deviations from the regression line.)

---

**Exercise 6.3** On the scatter diagram of Exercise 6.1, draw a Normal curve representing the 'error' process on the vertical line through $X = 180$. How many standard deviations from the regression line are the two corresponding points? Replot the deleted point corresponding to period 6, 1963. How many standard deviations from the regression line is this point? Comment.

---

## Estimating σ

The deviations of the 23 points on the scatterplot from the regression line may be regarded as realisations of sampling the 'error' process. Their standard deviation provides an estimate of the 'error' process standard deviation, $\sigma$. The formula for estimating $\sigma$ is developed as follows.

The 23 values given by the regression formula, referred to as the *fitted values*, are found by substituting the 23 $X$ values into the regression formula:

$$\hat{Y}_1 = \hat{\alpha} + \hat{\beta} X_1;$$
$$\hat{Y}_2 = \hat{\alpha} + \hat{\beta} X_2;$$
$$\hat{Y}_3 = \hat{\alpha} + \hat{\beta} X_3;$$
$$\vdots$$
$$\hat{Y}_n = \hat{\alpha} + \hat{\beta} X_n;$$

The 'hat' (circumflex) on the $Y$'s is the accepted notation used to distinguish the fitted values from the observed $Y$ values. The subscript '$n$' in the last equation represents the number of observations; $n = 23$ in this case.

---

**Exercise 6.4**   Calculate the fitted values for periods 1, 6 and 7 of fiscal year 1963. Visually compare with the corresponding observed values. Comment.

---

The deviations of 'observed' from 'fitted' may now be calculated as

$$e_1 = Y_1 - \hat{Y}_1;$$
$$e_2 = Y_2 - \hat{Y}_2;$$
$$e_3 = Y_3 - \hat{Y}_3;$$
$$\vdots$$
$$e_n = Y_n - \hat{Y}_n;$$

The $e_i$ are called the *residual values* and may be thought of as *estimated errors*.

---

**Exercise 6.5**   Calculate the residuals for periods 1, 6 and 7 of fiscal year 1963. Comment.

---

An estimate for the error process standard deviation may be based on the sample standard deviation of these residuals,

$$\hat{\sigma} = \sqrt{\frac{\sum\limits_{i=1}^{n} e_i^2}{n-2}}$$

This formula differs from conventional standard deviation formulas in two ways. First, the average of the residuals, $\bar{e}$, is not subtracted from each residual before squaring. This is because the average is always 0, a result of the mathematics involved with the least squares estimation method. Second, because these $n$ residuals involve *two* estimated parameter values, $\hat{\alpha}$ and $\hat{\beta}$, two 'degrees of freedom' are lost;[3] hence the divisor $n - 2$ rather than $n$. Looking at this in another way, although it appears that we have a sample of $n$ 'estimated errors' on which to base our estimate of $\sigma$, some of the information in the sample has been used to estimate $\alpha$ and $\beta$, leaving an 'effective' sample size of $n - 2$ for estimating $\sigma$.

Computation of this formula for $\hat{\sigma}$ is tedious; it is best left to a computer. Details of typical computer regression output are discussed later. For this example, the value of $\hat{\sigma}$ is 19. Once this value is available, we are in a position to calculate predictions with error intervals.

---

**Exercise 6.6**   Given the volume figures for periods 1, 6 and 7 of fiscal year 1963, what predictions, including prediction errors, would you make for the manhours requirement? How do these relate to the actual manhours used? Comment.

---

## 6.2   The regression control chart

Exercise 6.6 contains the essentials of an important idea, that of monitoring processes where inputs may vary and outputs vary accordingly. Here, the volume of mail measures an input to the mail handling process; manhours measure cost which may be regarded as an output. The idea is that, given the volume of mail for the current period, the manhours used are expected to fall within the calculated prediction interval. If not, something unexpected has occurred and warrants an investigation.

As an example, consider the sixth period of 1963. Then, the volume was 180, so that one would have expected the manhours to have been between 606 and 682, that is, $\hat{\alpha} + \hat{\beta}X \pm 2\hat{\sigma}$. In fact, the actual manhours were 765, considerably outside the anticipated interval. Following the reasoning used with control charts, one should declare the 'process' to be 'out of control', and seek 'assignable causes'. In this case, investigation showed that there was an abnormal amount of machine downtime during that period; recall the discussion in Section 1.5, page 28.

Here, we have used a historical data point to illustrate the control procedure. In practice, one might maintain a *regression control chart* on an ongoing basis, designed as follows. On a sheet of graph paper, mark out and label horizontal and vertical axes for volume and manhours, respectively. On it, draw the fitted regression line, $y = 50 + 3.3\ x$, to act as a centre line for the control chart. Draw an upper control line parallel to the centre line and 38 vertical units above it, and a lower control line 38 units below. (Thus, the equation for the upper control line is $y = 88 + 3.3\ x$.)

---

[3]   The mathematical derivation leading to the formulas for $\hat{\alpha}$ and $\hat{\beta}$ includes two equations involving the residuals: $\Sigma e_i = 0$ and $\Sigma e_i X_i = 0$. The residuals can, in principle, take on any values. However, the first equation says that their sum must be 0, so that, once $n - 1$ of them are assigned values, the last one is determined as minus their sum and thus the last one is not free to vary; one 'degree of freedom' is lost. Similarly, because of the second equation, a second 'degree of freedom' is lost.

At the end of each four-week accounting period, obtain the volume and man hour figures, plot the corresponding point on the graph and declare the 'process' to be 'in control' or 'out of control' according as the point is inside or outside the control lines.

---

**Exercise 6.7** Make a blank regression control chart for the mail handling process according to the above prescription. Discuss your choice of ranges of values for the axes; in particular, do you include or exclude the 'Christmas' values? Regard each period in Table 1.3 in turn as the current period and plot the corresponding points on the regression control chart, noting your decision in each case. How do you handle the 'Christmas' values?

---

Figure 6.7 shows a computer drawn regression control chart with the observed sample points added. The completed chart may be used retrospectively for process performance analysis. Period 6, 1963 shows up as 'out of control'. The 'Christmas' points cannot be plotted on this chart. On the following chart in Figure 6.8 whose axes are scaled to allow for those points, they show up as 'out of control'. We have already dealt with the reason for these 'out of control' points; see Section 1.5, page 28.

The conclusion of the process performance analysis is that the mail process was

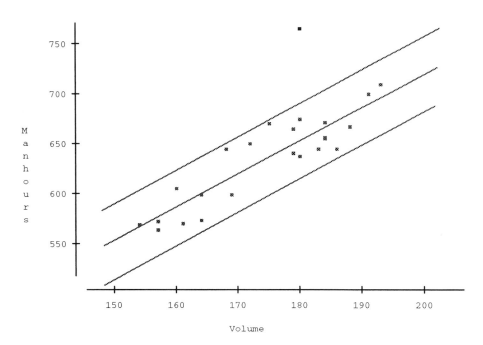

**Figure 6.7**   A regression control chart.

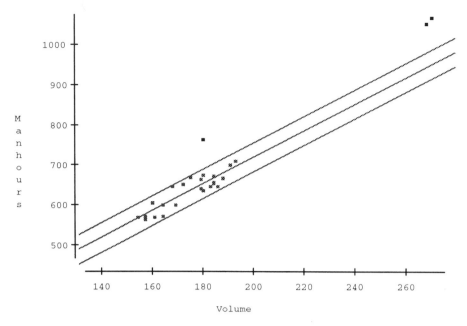

**Figure 6.8**   A regression control chart, extended.

'in statistical control' during the two years except for three periods for which well defined 'assignable causes' were found.

## Advantages of performance control

The regression control chart provides management with a tool for administrative control which has a rational basis and avoids arbitrary decisions. Thus, a manager who observes below average productivity during a four-week period may decide to institute tighter controls on the work force. If, in fact, the level of productivity, though below average, is within control limits, in the regression control chart sense, then the implication in the manager's decision that the workers are to blame is very likely to be incorrect and the manager's action may be counter-productive, since the workers' performance is adequate by historical standards; the dip in productivity is just a chance event.

On the other hand, a point falling outside the control limits indicates an unusual event which *should* be investigated. It could be due to poor worker performance, poor manpower scheduling, equipment breakdown, an unusual mail mix (such as a high proportion of parcel post) or, simply, a reporting error. All but the first of these are management problems; the first may well have a management component.

## An alternative display: the 'variance' control chart

The regression control chart display has the advantage that it explicitly embodies the basis for decision making about manhours, that is, its relation with volume. An alternative display would be a 'variance' (in the accountancy sense) plot, where each 'variance' or deviation from predicted manhours, referred to as 'residual' in the regression context, is plotted against time. The centre line is placed horizontally at 0 and the control limits are at $0 \pm 2\sigma$. This has the appearance of a traditional Shewhart $\bar{X}$ chart. The points appear on the chart in time order, and not in 'volume' order. Points with similar volumes lead to clutter on the regression chart; this is avoided on the 'variance' chart. Also avoided is the scaling problem encountered with the regression control chart.

The 'variance' chart form of display is essential if more than one variable affects the variable being controlled. This situation requires the use of *multiple regression analysis*, a topic to be taken up in Chapter 8.

The choice between the two forms of display will depend on individual circumstances.

---

**Exercise 6.8**   Repeat Exercise 6.7, with a variance control chart instead of a regression control chart.

---

### 2σ or 3σ?

The Shewhart chart discussed in Chapter 4 had control limits at Centre Line $\pm 3\sigma$. Here, we have used $\pm 2\sigma$. It is reasonable to ask which is more appropriate. Recalling the discussion in Section 5.2, page 168, the key is the false alarm rate, approximately 5% with $2\sigma$ limits and less than 0.3% with $3\sigma$ limits. The latter is appropriate for mass production processes which are frequently monitored, where frequent stoppages for no good reason would undermine confidence in the use of control charts. If $2\sigma$ limits were used with such a process, then approximately one in 20 samples (5%) would produce a false alarm. For example, if a process is sampled every two hours, there will be a false alarm roughly every 40 hours, which is once a week given a five day, eight hours per day working week, or four times a week with a continuously running process. On the other hand, a process such as the mail handling process which is sampled just once a month will produce a false alarm roughly every 20 months.

There is a benefit in using the narrower limits. Narrower limits lead to more 'out-of-control' signals. While this means more false alarms when the process is 'in control', it means more correct signals when the process is not 'in control', which is clearly desirable.

### Other administrative applications

The regression control chart may be used as a basis for budgeting. Manhour targets, and associated costs, can be set for the coming year, or other planning horizon, given information about anticipated volume. This information may simply be an extrapolation of historical data or it may reflect recent marketing efforts or knowledge about a local population increase or the opening (or closing) of a large business enterprise in the neighbourhood.

**Exercise 6.9** Calculate the average volume for period 1 over the two years 1962 and 1963. Use this as input to predict the manhour requirements for 1964.

Once a budget has been formulated for some planning period, the regression control chart may be used to review the outcome over the entire period. This is over and above the regular month by month monitoring role of the chart, and may lead to strategic, rather than operational, changes in procedures. If such strategic changes are made, with a view to permanently improving productivity, the regression control chart may be used to measure the effect of the changes.

**Exercise 6.10** Suppose a new sorting machine designed to speed up the mail handling process had been introduced at the end of fiscal year 1962. The effect may be viewed in the scatterplot in Figure 6.9, where the points corresponding to fiscal year 1962 and fiscal year 1963 are + and ×, respectively. Corresponding approximate regression lines have been added, the upper line corresponding to fiscal 1963.

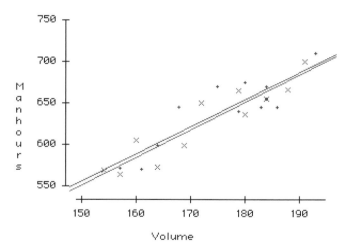

**Figure 6.9**

Visually assess the effect of the process change. Note that, with the aid of multiple regression, we will be able to conduct a more formal analysis of the effects of process changes such as this.

When exceptional events occur, the extra associated cost may be estimated as the deviation of their actual cost from the prediction given by simple linear regression.

---

**Exercise 6.11** For each of periods 7 1962, 6 1963 and 7 1963, calculate the deviation of the observed manhours from those predicted by the simple linear regression equation, using the corresponding volumes. Average the two period 7 deviations to get an improved 'Christmas' effect.

---

## 6.3 Reporting the results of simple linear regression

A standard set of results is reported following a regression analysis. The form in which the report is presented may vary. For the data of Table 1.3, with the exceptional values omitted, the following is one form of report.

$$\text{The regression equation is:}$$
$$\text{Manhours} = 50 + 3.3*\text{Volume};$$
$$\qquad\qquad (60) \quad (.34)$$
$$\hat{\sigma} = 19.$$

The numbers in parentheses underneath the estimated regression coefficients are the standard errors of these estimates; each estimate is based on sample data and is, therefore, subject to uncertainty, which is measured via their standard errors. The formula for the standard error in this case is relatively complicated; its computation may safely be left to the computer.

The last item in the report is the value of $\hat{\sigma}$, which is calculated from the formula given on page 198, and is an estimate of the standard deviation of the chance variation in the regression model. Its role in prediction has already been explained. $\hat{\sigma}$ is incorporated in the formulas for the standard errors of the estimated regression coefficients.

### Interpreting computer regression output

Computer programs have their own styles for reporting on the results of a regression. The following is the standard report produced by Data Desk.

```
Dependent variable is:              Manhours
No Selector
26 total cases of which 3 are missing
R squared = 82.2%     R squared (adjusted) = 81.3%
s =  18.93  with  23 - 2 = 21  degrees of freedom
```

| Source | Sum of Squares | df | Mean Square | F-ratio |
|--------|----------------|-----|-------------|---------|
| Regression | 34668.8 | 1 | 34668.8 | 96.7 |
| Residual | 7525.24 | 21 | 358.345 | |

| Variable | Coefficient | s.e. of Coeff | t-ratio | prob |
|----------|-------------|---------------|---------|------|
| Constant | 50.4394 | 59.46 | 0.848 | 0.4058 |
| Volume | 3.34544 | 0.3401 | 9.84 | ≤ 0.0001 |

The third line indicates that a special procedure was used to exclude the exceptional points from the calculations. R squared and R squared (adjusted) may be ignored for present purposes.[4]

$s$ is $\hat{\sigma}$. The number of 'degrees of freedom' is the effective sample size on which the estimate of $\sigma$ is based, as discussed earlier; see page 198.

The middle block is a report on a technical analysis called the 'analysis of variance', which need not concern us here.

The first three columns of the last block give the values of the estimated regression coefficients, with their standard errors. The estimated regression coefficients are used to construct the prediction formula. They are, of course, subject to uncertainty themselves. The standard errors measure the extent of this uncertainty. The estimated regression coefficients, being based on data subject to chance variation, are themselves subject to chance variation, in much the same way as a value of $\bar{X}$ calculated from data sampled from a process for control chart purposes. In much the same way as for $\bar{X}$, we regard $\hat{\beta}$ as having been sampled from a process. Repeated sampling from that process would yield a frequency distribution of possible values, called the sampling distribution of $\hat{\beta}$. The standard error of $\hat{\beta}$ is the standard deviation of that frequency distribution. The standard error of $\hat{\alpha}$ has a similar genesis.

---

**Exercise 6.12** Review the steps leading to the development of the sampling distribution concept and standard error in Chapter 5. Make a list of correspondences between that development, in terms of $\bar{X}$, and the corresponding development for $\hat{\beta}$. How do you handle the idea of repeated sampling?

---

## A confidence interval for marginal change

Recall that $\hat{\beta}$ was interpreted as the estimated marginal change in manhours for a 1 unit change in volume. As such, it estimates the actual marginal change, $\beta$, which characterises the mail handling process. Assuming that the data are representative of process behaviour, we can expect the actual $\beta$ to be reasonably close to the estimated $\hat{\beta}$. As with the estimation of process means in Chapter 5, we can calculate a confidence interval for $b$. The formula is

$$\hat{\beta} \pm 2 \times \text{SE}(\hat{\beta}).$$

---

**Exercise 6.13** Calculate a confidence interval for marginal change for the mail handling process. Calculate a confidence interval for the change in manhours corresponding to a 10,000,000 increase in pieces of mail handled.

---

[4] They are related to correlation, introduced later, but are more appropriate to multiple linear regression, the subject of a later chapter. They are briefly discussed in the Supplements and Extensions page of the book's website.

---

**Exercise 6.14**    Discuss point by point the correspondences between the confidence interval calculated here and the confidence interval for a process mean discussed earlier. Include a discussion of the interpretation.

---

### Testing the statistical significance of the intercept

From the Data Desk output, we notice that $\hat{\alpha}$ is actually smaller than its standard error. This suggests that its value can be entirely attributed to chance variation and, therefore, it could reasonably be omitted from the prediction formula, thus making it simpler. Formally, this is equivalent to testing the null hypothesis that $\alpha$, the actual intercept characteristic of the process, is 0. Recalling the formal statistical significance testing procedures of Chapter 5, the test statistic for this null hypothesis is

$$Z = \frac{\hat{\alpha} - 0}{\text{SE}(\hat{\alpha})}$$

which simplifies to

$$\frac{\hat{\alpha}}{\text{SE}(\hat{\alpha})}.$$

This is, in fact, what is labelled as the t-ratio for the so-called 'Constant' variable.[5] The corresponding 'prob' value is the 'observed significance level'; see Chapter 5 for a discussion of 'observed significance levels'.

---

**Exercise 6.15**    Verify that the test statistic $Z$ equals the corresponding t-ratio for the mail handling process data.

---

**Exercise 6.16**    List the steps for testing a null hypothesis concerning a process mean as in Chapter 5. Make a corresponding list for the test involved here.

---

[5]    When the process standard deviation, $\sigma$, is estimated from the data, as in this case, the sampling distribution of test statistics such as that used here is not the Normal distribution, rather, it is another distribution called the $t$ distribution which is somewhat more spread out than the Normal. The extra spread in the sampling distribution corresponds to the extra uncertainty due to estimating $\sigma$ from data which were subject to chance variation, rather than assuming that the value of $\sigma$ is known. However, for all but very small samples, the extra uncertainty is negligible and, in parallel with this, the $t$ distribution is well approximated by the Normal. For example, with a sample of 23 as we have here, the 5% critical value for $t$ is 2.08, not much different from the conventional value 2 nor from the 5% critical value for a Normal distribution, 1.96.

While it is possible to carry out the formal test, as we have done, it is not clear that it is meaningful. In fact, we have already seen that the meaningfulness of $\alpha$ and of $\hat{\alpha}$ is questionable; there is no evidence that the relation between manhours and volume is linear when the volume is 0. There is another aspect to this also. The substantive significance of an added 50 in the prediction formula is considerable; over the observed range of manhour values, 564–710, 50 represents 7–9%.

---

**Exercise 6.17** Calculate the regression of manhours on volume assuming $\hat{\alpha} = 0$. Calculate the percentage deviation of the fitted values from the fitted values corresponding to the regression with $\alpha$ included. Comment.

---

Generally, it is advised that an intercept be included, unless there are specific substantive arguments, other than statistical, to the contrary; testing the statistical significance of $\hat{\alpha}$ is not recommended unless there is a reasonable theoretical basis for interpreting $\alpha$ and there are data close to the point (0,0). The blind application of statistical significance tests without having regard to substantive significance is all too prevalent and can lead to nonsense results. Ultimately, substantive significance is far more important than statistical significance.

## 6.4 Correlation

Simple linear regression is concerned with making predictions of values of one variable, given values of another, to which the first is related. In the US Post Office productivity case study, the manhours required to process mail is seen as related to the volume of mail to be processed and the prediction equation developed provides predictions of manhours, for given volumes. There is a clear direction associated with the relation between manhours and volume; values of volume are seen as determining, to a large extent, corresponding values of manhours. Implicit in this is an assumption of cause and effect.

For the purpose of general discussion, especially when several such relations are involved, it is convenient to have a measure of the predictive power of such relations. In cases where the direction of cause and effect is not clear, it is desirable to have a measure of the strength of the relation between a pair of variables.[6] Here, we develop such a measure, called the correlation coefficient. We will see that it is closely related to the slope coefficient in simple linear regression. For this reason, the correlation coefficient is often quoted in problems where simple linear regression is appropriate. Common alternative approaches to the interpretation of the correlation coefficient may be found in the Supplements and Extensions page of the book's website.

---

[6] A case in point is the relationship between sales and advertising. In that case, there is an issue as to whether increased advertising causes increased sales or whether increased sales (and, presumably, increased income) causes increased advertising, or both.

## The correlation coefficient formula

Given $n$ pairs of values, $(X_1 , Y_1), (X_2 , Y_2), \ldots , (X_n , Y_n)$, of variables $X$ and $Y$, the correlation coefficient, typically labelled $r$, is formally defined as

$$r = \frac{s_{XY}}{s_X s_Y},$$

where

$$s_X = \sqrt{\frac{1}{n} \sum_{i=1}^{n} \left( X_i - \bar{X} \right)^2},$$

the standard deviation of the $X$ values,

$$s_Y = \sqrt{\frac{1}{n} \sum_{i=1}^{n} \left( Y_i - \bar{Y} \right)^2}$$

the standard deviation of the $Y$ values, and

$$s_{XY} = \tfrac{1}{n} \Sigma (X_i - \bar{X})(Y_i - \bar{Y}),$$

referred to as the *covariance*[7] of $X$ and $Y$.

While this formula may seem formidable at first sight, we will see that it has a relatively simple interpretation. In the first place, a reference back to the formula for $\hat{\beta}$ on page 194 shows a remarkable similarity. In fact,

$$r = \hat{\beta} \times \frac{s_X}{s_Y} \qquad \text{or, equivalently,} \qquad \hat{\beta} = r \times \frac{s_Y}{s_X}.$$

We can see immediately that a zero value for $r$, implying $\hat{\beta} = 0$, means that there is no *linear* relation between $X$ and $Y$. Note that the linear qualifier here is important. It is easy to construct examples where a strong non-linear relation exists between $X$ and $Y$, but $r = 0$; see Exercise 6.19, page 211.

## r and reduction of prediction error

The scatterplots in Figure 6.10 provide a visual guide to the meaning of different values of $r$.

It may be seen that, when $r$ is high, knowledge of the value of $X$ narrows the range of variation of $Y$, and vice versa, while, when $r$ is low, or close to 0, this does not happen to any appreciable degree. Indeed, viewing the scatter diagrams in Figure 6.10, it may be suggested that, when $r$ is less than, say, 0.4 or 0.5, knowing the value of one variable gives no appreciable reduction in the range of variation of the other. On the other hand, when $r$ exceeds, say, 0.6 or 0.7, there is clear visual evidence in

---

[7] The meaning of this term is discussed in the section on alternative approaches to the interpretation of the correlation coefficient in the Supplements and Extensions page of the book's website.

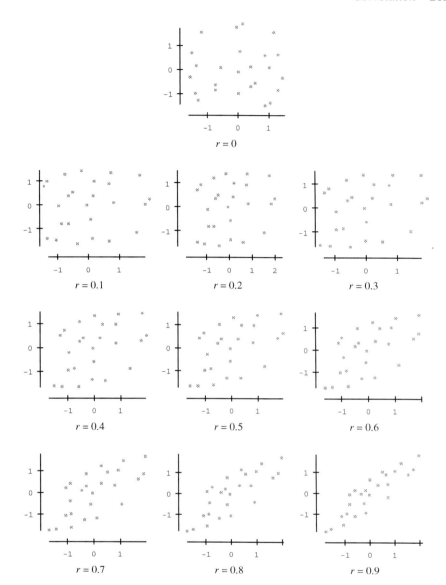

**Figure 6.10** Scatterplots for variables with varying correlations illustrating the increasing strength of the relation between X and Y as r goes from 0, in steps of 0.1, to 0.9.

the corresponding scatter diagrams that knowing $X$ gives more precise knowledge of $Y$ than not knowing $X$.

Alternative evidence for this is the picture of variation and variation reduction contained in the regression control chart of Figure 6.7. If the volume is not known, the next value of manhours could well be any value on the vertical axis as drawn on the chart while, knowing the volume, the control limits give reasonable and much narrower bounds on the range of variation to be expected from the manhours.

This idea may be formalised through the (approximate) equation

$$\hat{\sigma} = \sqrt{1 - r^2} \times s_Y$$

where $\hat{\sigma}$ is the (approximate) standard error of a simple linear regression prediction, as discussed earlier, and $s_Y$ is the sample standard deviation of the observed $Y$ values. If $r = 0$, then $\hat{\sigma} \cong s_Y$. Also, if $r = 0$, then $\hat{\beta} = 0$, so the prediction formula for $Y$ reduces to $\overline{Y}$, irrespective of the value of $X$. It is as if we predict the next value of $Y$ to be

$$\overline{Y} \pm 2s_Y.$$

As $r$ increases from 0, $\sqrt{1 - r^2}$ decreases from 1 and so the value of $\hat{\sigma}$ decreases from $s_Y$ until, when $r$ reaches 1, $\hat{\sigma}$ becomes 0, that is, prediction is perfect. Thus, $r$ may be interpreted as indirectly measuring the *decrease* in prediction error achieved by using the simple linear regression prediction formula as opposed to using $\overline{Y}$, ignoring $X$.

### Positive and negative correlation

Relationships between two variables where one tends to increase with the other are described as *positive*; the slope of the regression line will be positive in such cases. From the equations above, so will the correlation coefficient.

Similarly, relations where one variable tends to decrease when the other increases are described as *negative*; the slope of the regression line will be negative in such cases, as will the correlation coefficient.

The scatterplot of manhours versus volume, reproduced on the left of Figure 6.11, shows a positive relation with a positive slope and a positive correlation coefficient. If the scatterplot had looked like that on the right of Figure 6.11, slope and correlation would have been negative.

### Perfect correlation

As noted above, prediction is perfect when $r = 1$. In fact, it can be shown that $r$ cannot exceed 1 in magnitude, that is,

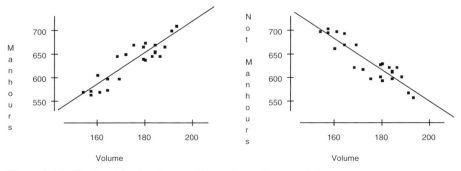

**Figure 6.11**  Scatterplots showing positive and negative correlation.

$$-1 \le r \le +1.$$

$r = +1$ indicates a perfect positive linear relation between $X$ and $Y$, with no scatter, that is, all points in the scatterplot lie on the line, as in the plot on the left of Figure 6.12. Similarly, $r = -1$ indicates a perfect negative linear relation, as on the right of Figure 6.12.

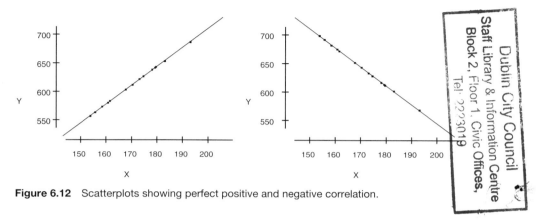

**Figure 6.12** Scatterplots showing perfect positive and negative correlation.

**Exercise 6.18** The fitted values in a simple linear regression are calculated from the formula for the line and so the corresponding points on the scatter diagram lie on the line. Calculate the fitted values from the regression of manhours on volume. Make a scatterplot of fitted values versus volume. Calculate the coefficient of correlation between fitted values and volume.

**Exercise 6.19** Set up an $X$ variable with values going from −10 to 10 in steps of 1 and a $Y$ variable equal to the square of $X$. Make a scatterplot. Add the simple linear regression line. Calculate the correlation coefficient. Comment.

### Conventional interpretations of values of $r$

There is a tendency for physical scientists and technologists to regard $r$ values exceeding 0.9 as interesting and smaller values of lesser interest. Econometricians tend to view 0.7, or 0.5, in the same sort of way. Sociologists tend to regard an $r$ value as small as 0.3 as interesting. It may be suggested that these differences in outlook reflect the difficulty of measuring things; physical measurements may be extremely precise, economic ones less so, while sociological measurements are extremely difficult to establish.

In practical applications in business and industry, where prediction is invariably of prime importance, such arbitrary designations are of little value. The interpretation of $r$ as measuring the reduction in prediction error is rather more concrete. In practice, the direct comparison of $\hat{\sigma}$ to $S_Y$ has much to recommend it.

## 6.5   Pitfalls with regression and correlation

It is easy to be deceived by the values of regression coefficients, correlation coefficients and the like. Consider the four sets of data, in Table 6.1, each consisting of 11 pairs of values of $X$ and $Y$.[8] Calculating the regression of $Y$ on $X$ yields the same results (apart from negligible rounding errors) in all four cases. It may also be checked that all four sets of $X$ values have the same mean and standard deviation, as have all four sets of $Y$ values.

**Table 6.1**

| $X_1$ | $Y_1$ | $X_2$ | $Y_2$ | $X_3$ | $Y_3$ | $X_4$ | $Y_4$ |
|----|-------|----|------|----|-------|----|-------|
| 10 | 8.04  | 10 | 9.14 | 10 | 7.46  | 8  | 6.58  |
| 8  | 6.95  | 8  | 8.14 | 8  | 6.77  | 8  | 5.76  |
| 13 | 7.58  | 13 | 8.74 | 13 | 12.74 | 8  | 7.7   |
| 9  | 8.81  | 9  | 8.77 | 9  | 7.11  | 8  | 8.84  |
| 11 | 8.33  | 11 | 9.26 | 11 | 7.81  | 8  | 8.47  |
| 14 | 9.96  | 14 | 8.10 | 14 | 8.84  | 8  | 7.04  |
| 6  | 7.24  | 6  | 6.13 | 6  | 6.08  | 8  | 5.25  |
| 4  | 4.26  | 4  | 3.10 | 4  | 5.39  | 19 | 12.50 |
| 12 | 10.84 | 12 | 9.13 | 12 | 8.15  | 8  | 5.56  |
| 7  | 4.82  | 7  | 7.26 | 7  | 6.42  | 8  | 7.91  |
| 5  | 5.68  | 5  | 4.74 | 5  | 5.73  | 8  | 6.89  |

**Exercise 6.20**   Calculate the regression of $Y$ on $X$ and the coefficient of correlation between $Y$ and $X$ for each of the four datasets shown above. Round all results to two significant figures and compare the four sets of results. Comment.

It might be concluded from this that all four sets share the same relation and are statistically indistinguishable. However, viewing the corresponding scatterplots tells a different story.

---

[8]   These datasets and the related demonstrations were developed by F.J. Anscombe and published in 1973 in *The American Statistician*, a professional journal published by the American Statistical Association, Volume 27, Number 1, pages 17–21.

**Exercise 6.21**   Make scatterplots for each of the four datasets shown above. Interpret each scatterplot. Comment, in the light of the comparisons of calculations in Exercise 6.20.

In summary, it is ill-advised to rely only on computational results when dealing with regression and correlation. The relation may be non-linear, in which case linear regression and correlation, which measures the strength of *linear* relations, are inappropriate. The relation may be linear, but with exceptions; a simple linear regression model cannot cope with exceptions. The data may have large gaps, in which case the nature of the relation is indeterminate where there are no data. This point also applies to attempts to extrapolate beyond the range of available data.

These examples again emphasise the power of pictures in coming to an understanding of variation. In this case, the simple scatterplot distinguishes between pattern and exception, highlighting the presence of the latter and revealing the nature of the former.

## 6.6   Review exercises

6.1   In a study of a wholesaler's distribution costs, undertaken with a view to controling cost, the volume of goods handled and the overall costs were recorded for one month in each of ten depots in a distribution network. The results are presented in the following table.

| Depot | 1 | 2 | 3 | 4 | 5 | 6 | 7 | 8 | 9 | 10 |
|---|---|---|---|---|---|---|---|---|---|---|
| Volume (£ thousands) | 48 | 57 | 49 | 45 | 50 | 62 | 58 | 55 | 38 | 51 |
| Costs (£ hundreds) | 20 | 22 | 19 | 18 | 20 | 24 | 21 | 21 | 15 | 20 |

The simple linear regression of costs $(Y)$ on volume $(X)$ was calculated, and resulted in the following numerical summary.

Dependent variable is:   Costs
No Selector
R squared = 93.1%   R squared (adjusted) = 92.3%
s = 0.6676 with 10 - 2 = 8 degrees of freedom

| Source | Sum of Squares | df | Mean Square | F-ratio |
|---|---|---|---|---|
| Regression | 48.4344 | 1 | 48.4344 | 109 |
| Residual | 3.56555 | 8 | 0.445694 | |

| Variable | Coefficient | s.e. of Coeff | t-ratio | prob |
|---|---|---|---|---|
| Constant | 2.98160 | 1.646 | 1.81 | 0.1077 |
| Volume | 0.331743 | 0.0318 | 10.4 | ≤ 0.0001 |

Draw a scatterplot for these data. Comment. Interpret the numerical summary in context. Make a regression control chart for monitoring costs in future months.

During a later month, two depots recorded volumes of £40,000 and £51,000 and costs of £1,700 and £2,300 respectively. Plot these on your chart and comment in each case. Provide formal calculations to support your comments.

6.2   The sales for the past year of nine sales persons operating in nine sales regions are recorded below, along with the population of each region. Also shown are (partial) results of the simple linear regression of sales on population and a corresponding scatterplot.

| Sales person | Sales ($) | Population |
|---|---|---|
| 1 | 2,687,224 | 247,826 |
| 2 | 3,543,166 | 412,830 |
| 3 | 3,320,214 | 454,766 |
| 4 | 3,542,722 | 612,540 |
| 5 | 2,251,482 | 236,775 |
| 6 | 5,149,127 | 684,183 |
| 7 | 2,024,809 | 179,003 |
| 8 | 1,711,720 | 138,791 |
| 9 | 3,260,464 | 231,855 |

Dependent variable is:   **Sales $m**
No Selector
R squared = 79.7%      R squared (adjusted) = 76.8%
s =  0.5004  with  9 - 2 = 7  degrees of freedom

| Source | Sum of Squares | df | Mean Square | F-ratio |
|---|---|---|---|---|
| Regression | 6.86816 | 1 | 6.86816 | 27.4 |
| Residual | 1.75253 | 7 | 0.250361 | |

| Variable | Coefficient | s.e. of Coeff | t-ratio | prob |
|---|---|---|---|---|
| Constant | 1.37173 | 0.362 | 3.79 | 0.0068 |
| Population (... | 0.00473503 | 0.000904 | 5.24 | 0.0012 |

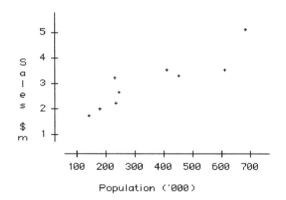

The sales director suggested that sales person 9 deserved special praise because her sales were considerably higher than those of two other sales persons whose sales regions had similar populations. He also suggested that sales person 4 was performing rather poorly because he had only marginally higher sales than sales person 3, though with a much bigger population, while he had considerably smaller sales than sales person 6, whose population was not much bigger.

Are the sales director's comments justified? Show details of the statistical analysis which supports your answer.

6.3   A company with a contract to service a particular brand of personal computer keeps records on the number of machines serviced and length of service calls. For 18 recent calls, the following were recorded:

| Machines Serviced | 7 | 4 | 5 | 1 | 5 | 4 | 7 | 2 | 4 | 2 | 8 | 5 | 2 | 5 | 7 | 1 | 4 | 5 |
|---|---|---|---|---|---|---|---|---|---|---|---|---|---|---|---|---|---|---|
| Length of Service (Minutes) | 97 | 57 | 78 | 10 | 75 | 62 | 101 | 27 | 53 | 33 | 118 | 65 | 25 | 71 | 105 | 17 | 49 | 68 |

The simple linear regression of length of service (minutes) on number of machines serviced resulted as follows:

```
Dependent variable is:    Time
No Selector
R squared = 98.1%      R squared (adjusted) = 98.0%
s =  4.419  with  18 - 2 = 16  degrees of freedom
```

| Source | Sum of Squares | df | Mean Square | F-ratio |
|---|---|---|---|---|
| Regression | 16407.2 | 1 | 16407.2 | 840 |
| Residual | 312.447 | 16 | 19.528 | |

| Variable | Coefficient | s.e. of Coeff | t-ratio | prob |
|---|---|---|---|---|
| Constant | -1.94737 | 2.431 | -0.801 | 0.4348 |
| Machines | 14.693 | 0.5069 | 29 | ≤ 0.0001 |

Is a simple linear regression equation appropriate? Display the evidence.

Estimate the change in mean service time when the number of machines serviced increases by one. Calculate a 95% confidence interval.

The service manager would like to have a simple formula to predict the length of individual service calls, with an allowance for prediction error. What formula would you suggest? Explain the basis for your suggestion. What is your prediction of the service time required for the next call to service five machines?

Discuss how these data and analysis could be used in maintaining routine administrative control on productivity. Indicate the advantages of the procedure you recommend.

6.4   As a check on production costs, a specialist computer manufacturer records the number of computers produced each week and the costs involved in that production. For one 18 week period, numbers produced and costs were as follows:

| Week no. | Number produced | Cost (£ thousands) | Week no. | Number produced | Cost (£ thousands) |
|---|---|---|---|---|---|
| 1 | 22 | 3,470 | 10 | 30 | 3,589 |
| 2 | 30 | 3,783 | 11 | 38 | 3,999 |
| 3 | 26 | 3,856 | 12 | 41 | 4,158 |
| 4 | 31 | 3,910 | 13 | 27 | 3,666 |
| 5 | 36 | 4,489 | 14 | 28 | 3,885 |
| 6 | 30 | 3,876 | 15 | 31 | 3,574 |
| 7 | 22 | 3,221 | 16 | 37 | 4,495 |
| 8 | 45 | 4,579 | 17 | 32 | 3,814 |
| 9 | 38 | 4,325 | 18 | 41 | 4,430 |

A scatterplot and a report of a simple linear regression analysis follow.

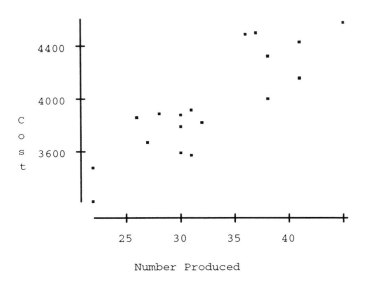

Number Produced

| Variable | Coefficient | s.e. of Coeff | *t*-ratio |
|---|---|---|---|
| Constant | 2272.07 | 243.3 | 9.34 |
| Number Prod | 51.6612 | 7.347 | 7.03 |
| s = 198.6 | | | |

Does the scatterplot support the use of simple linear regression? Say why or why not.

Which is the response variable? Which is the explanatory variable? Explain.

Is the simple linear regression statistically significant? Say why or why not.

What average increase in weekly cost would you estimate for each additional computer produced in a week? What is the standard error of that estimate?

What weekly cost would you predict if you planned to produce 40 computers next week? Calculate a prediction interval with 95% confidence.

Suppose the weekly cost for producing the 40 computers referred to in the last question amounted to £5,000,000. How would you react? Explain.

6.5 The shelf-life of packaged foods depends on many factors. Dry cereal (such as corn flakes) is considered to be a moisture-sensitive product, with the shelf-life determined primarily by moisture. In a study of the shelf-life of one brand of cereal, packets of cereal were stored in controlled conditions (23 °C and 50% relative humidity) for a range of times, and moisture content was measured. The results were as follows.

| Storage time (days) | 0 | 3 | 6 | 8 | 10 | 13 | 16 | 20 | 24 | 27 | 30 | 34 | 37 | 41 |
|---|---|---|---|---|---|---|---|---|---|---|---|---|---|---|
| Moisture content | | 2.8 | 3.0 | 3.1 | 3.2 | 3.4 | 3.4 | 3.5 | 3.1 | 3.8 | 4.0 | 4.1 | 4.3 | 4.4 | 4.9 |

Draw a scatter diagram. Comment. What action is suggested? Why?
Following appropriate action, the following regression was computed.

```
Dependent variable is:                Moisture Content
No Selector
14 total cases of which 2 are missing
R squared = 99.2%       R squared (adjusted) = 99.1%
s = 0.04935  with  12 - 2 = 10  degrees of freedom

Source       Sum of Squares   df    Mean Square    F-ratio
Regression   3.05231           1     3.05231       1.25e3
Residual     0.0243518        10     0.00243518

Variable      Coefficient   s.e. of Coeff   t-ratio    prob
Constant      2.86122        0.02488         115       ≤ 0.0001
Storage Ti…   0.0416603      0.001177        35.4      ≤ 0.0001
```

Calculate a 95% confidence interval for the daily change in moisture content; show details.

Predict the moisture content of a packet of cereal stored under these conditions for 30 days; calculate a prediction interval. What would be the effect on your interval of not taking the action you suggested on studying the scatter diagram? Why?

Taste tests indicate that this brand of cereal is unacceptably soggy when the moisture content exceeds 4.1. Based on your prediction interval, do you think that a box of cereal that has been on the shelf for 30 days will be acceptable? Explain.

Was the action you suggested on studying the scatter diagram in the first part of the exercise justified? Explain.

6.6 Recall Review Exercise 5.5, page 187. According to product specifications, the minimum rebound height when applying the rebound test to tennis balls is 100 centimetres (cms). The rebound height can be increased by increasing the pressure inside the ball which, in turn, is achieved by adjusting the pressure in the presses in which rubber cores are produced from pairs of half-cores. The adjustment is made by turning a dial. The dial has a scale consisting of 10 evenly spaced marks, labelled 1 to 10.

In the experiment reported on in Review Exercise 5.5, 100 balls were sampled from production with the dial set to 3 and a second sample of 100 was taken from production with the dial set to 4. While the experiment indicated an improvement, it did not completely cure the problem; there was still a substantial proportion of failures. It was decided to experiment further with a range of dial settings to attempt to find a pressure level that would enable the product specification to be met, keeping in mind that the increase in pressure should be kept as small as possible, because increased pressure meant increased diameter, which had its own specification limits. Five further experimental runs were made with the dial set at 5, 6, 7, 8, 9, in succession, with twenty balls sampled from each run and rebound tested. The results, along with the results from the earlier experiment with the dial set to 3 and 4, were entered into a computer file for analysis. The Test Laboratory Manager made a scatterplot of rebound height against setting, to use as a basis for a recommendation to the Production Manager regarding the appropriate pressure setting.

The scatterplot of rebound against setting is shown below. Also shown are the corresponding simple linear regression line and the horizontal line at rebound = 100. Make a short comment, interpreting the scatterplot for the Production Manager, recommending a dial setting and justifying your recommendation.

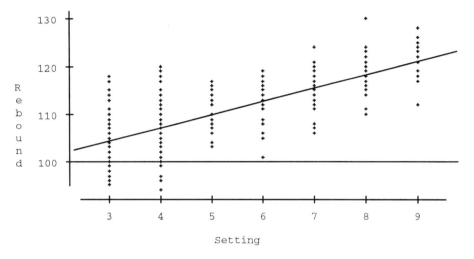

A more formal approach may be based on the use of simple linear regression and making an assumption that no rebound values will be more than three standard deviations below the mean rebound value. The results of regressing rebound height on setting follow.

Dependent variable is:     Rebound
No Selector
R squared = 53.8%     R squared (adjusted) = 53.6%
s = 4.883  with  300 - 2 = 298  degrees of freedom

| Source | Sum of Squares | df | Mean Square | F-ratio |
|---|---|---|---|---|
| Regression | 8269.59 | 1 | 8269.59 | 347 |
| Residual | 7106.73 | 298 | 23.8481 | |

| Variable | Coefficient | s.e. of Coeff | t-ratio | prob |
|---|---|---|---|---|
| Constant | 96.1662 | 0.7526 | 128 | < 0.0001 |
| Setting | 2.78437 | 0.1495 | 18.6 | < 0.0001 |

Use the simple linear regression results to

(i)   estimate the mean rebound value that ensures (almost) no test failures, and
(ii)  calculate the corresponding setting value.

Allowing (informally) for chance error in the regression output and subsequent calculations, make a conservative recommendation of pressure dial setting and incorporate it in a short report for the Test Laboratory Manager and the Production Manager explaining what you have done and why.

## 6.7   Laboratory exercise: Exploring and explaining computer maintenance costs

Recall Review Exercise 5.4, page 187. Following comparisons of computer maintenance charges in two branches of a building society, it was suggested that the observed difference could be explained by different computer usage. The study was extended to eight other 'well managed' branches, to explore this suggestion further, with a view to setting a benchmark for other branches. Data were collected on total usage, in hours, for a single week and total maintenance charges, in hundreds of pounds, incurred during the previous six months in each of the 10 branches. The data were:

| Maintenance cost (£ hundreds) | 17 | 22 | 30 | 37 | 47 | 49 | 31 | 33 | 40 | 29 | 52 | 41 |
|---|---|---|---|---|---|---|---|---|---|---|---|---|
| Usage (hours) | 13 | 10 | 20 | 28 | 32 | 15 | 17 | 24 | 31 | 0 | 40 | 38 |

Make dotplots and a scatterplot of these data. Describe what you see in terms of pattern and exceptions. What does the scatterplot reveal about pattern and exceptions that the dotplots do not?

Calculate a simple linear regression of cost on usage. Report the values of the key summary statistics. Write down a prediction equation, with prediction limits. Predict the cost when the usage is 0, 15; record the prediction and the lower and upper prediction limits along with the corresponding exceptional observed values of cost.

On investigation, it was found that a major problem had occurred in branch 6 during the previous six months, adding to the maintenance charge while, in branch 10, there had been a fault on the copy of the logging software installed there, so that no logging took place. Recompute the regression with the exceptional cases excluded; record the new prediction and the lower and upper prediction limits. How does deleting the exceptional values affect the predictions and their relation to the exceptional values?

Study the effect of deleting one exceptional case at a time; repeat the calculations with one exceptional case excluded and the other included, alternately. Noting the positions of the exceptional cases relative to the rest of the data, record the effect on the intercept and slope estimates of excluding the exceptional cases separately and together.

Check the validity of the simple linear regression; make a scatterplot with the exceptional cases deleted.

Calculate a 95% confidence interval for the average increase in maintenance charge for each extra hour of usage per week.

Draw a regression control chart for application to the other branches of the society. Explain the statistical basis for your chart and describe the connection with statistical significance testing. Following further data collection exercises in other offices, the results for one branch were:

| | |
|---|---|
| Usage | 20 hours |
| Maintenance cost | 45 (£4,500) |

Plot the corresponding point on your chart. What conclusion do you draw? Explain. What conclusion would you have drawn if the maintenance charge had been £3,500? Explain.

# 7

# Frequency data analysis

Up to now, the variables we have studied have been, for the most part, *quantitative* variables which resulted from measuring some quantity of money, of time, of labour, of production, etc. Here, we consider forms of statistical analysis appropriate to *qualitative* or *categorical* variables whose 'values' are categories rather than numbers. For example, the variable 'gender' has values 'male' or 'female'.

Many of the variables in the Generation T surveys introduced in Section 1.8 are categorical. Data on such categorical variables typically are reported in the form of relative frequency distributions across the categories. For example, of 306 respondents to the August 2002 Generation T survey, 269 or 88% were categorised as mobile phone owners and 37 or 12% were categorised as non-owners. For the purpose of the survey, the country was divided into four geographical regions, here labelled A, B, C, and D.[1] There was some regional variation in ownership levels, as shown below.

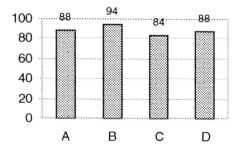

Ownership, per cent

---

[1] They were Dublin, Rest of Leinster, Munster and Connaught-Ulster, four traditional administrative regions in the Republic of Ireland.

Before asking whether these regional differences were of substantive business interest, the first question to be asked is whether they are statistically significant; if not, then discussion of possible business implications is a waste of time, as it amounts to discussing chance variation. In this chapter, a test of statistical significance is presented, called the *chi-square test*.[2]

Mobile phone users were asked several questions regarding their attitudes towards mobile phone use. Among these was one which asked whether they thought their use was 'just enough', 'too much' or 'too little'. These may be regarded as 'values' for the variable 'Perceived extent of use'. The response pattern could influence the style of advertising. The response pattern of 269 mobile phone users in the August 2002 survey is illustrated below.

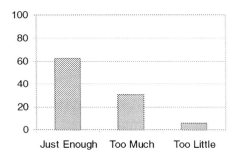

**Perceived extent of use, per cent**

There is little doubt about the statistical significance of these differences. What may be of interest is whether the pattern evident here persists in all regions, or whether perceptions change from region to region, thus suggesting varying approaches to local advertising. A regional breakdown of the pattern shown above is illustrated below.

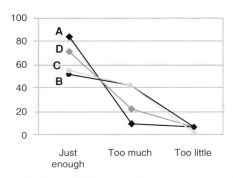

**Perceived extent of use, per cent, by region**

---

[2]    Chi, pronounced ky, is the representation in English for the Greek letter $\chi$.

Clear differences in regional patterns are apparent. The patterns in regions B and C are almost indistinguishable. The A and D patterns are not dissimilar, but both appear distinctly different from the B and C patterns. However, before taking action on such apparent similarities and differences, we need to be sure that the observed differences are not due to mere chance variation and would not be reproduced in another sample. A variation on the chi-square test referred to above is required to test the statistical significance of the observed regional differences in the patterns.

In Chapter 5, we saw how to construct significance tests and confidence intervals for proportions and percentages. In this chapter, we review these ideas and extend them to comparison of two or more percentages and comparison of sets of percentages, such as the comparisons of ownership and perceived extent of use patterns shown above. This will require the extension of the Z test of Chapter 5 to the more complicated chi-square test.

The comparisons and tests are developed in the context of another marketing research survey designed to produce information on *market penetration* of a particular product. As above, the data come in the form of frequency distributions which are reported separately for different regions. We will see how to make formal comparisons between these and thus assess the extent to which the frequency patterns are subject to regional variation.

It is helpful to view the first and third examples discussed above in terms of *response relationships*. The 'response' in the first case is ownership per cent and in the third case perceived extent of use pattern. In both cases, the 'explanatory' variable is region.

Problems of display and interpretation arise when frequency data are categorised by more than one explanatory factor. The issues arising will be explored in the context of a study of bank loan default rates, which may depend on size of loan (bigger or smaller than £10,000) and type of loan (commercial or non-commercial).

## Learning objectives

After completing this chapter, students should be able to undertake simple statistical analysis of frequency data, understand the basis for the analysis and demonstrate this by being able to:

- compare and contrast relative frequencies of responses at varying levels of an explanatory variable;
- carry out a test of the difference between a single sample percentage and a given value;
- describe the approximate sampling distribution for a sample percentage, including the formula for its standard error;
- calculate a confidence interval for a percentage based on a sample percentage;
- explain the formula for the standard error of the difference between two sample percentages and test the statistical significance of the difference;

- test the statistical significance of the difference between several sample percentages and explain the chi-square formula used for the test;
- test the statistical significance of the difference between several conditional frequency distributions and outline the chi-square formula used for the test;
- explain and illustrate Simpson's paradox.

## 7.1    A market penetration study

One of the factors which may help to explain variation in sales of a product in different regions is the level of market penetration achieved for the product through promotion, advertising, etc. One way of assessing this is to carry out an appropriate marketing research survey. In one such survey, potential purchasers randomly sampled in each of three sales regions were interviewed, 200 from region A, 150 from region B and 300 from region C. Among the questions were the following:

| | |
|---|---|
| Have you ever heard of this product? | ☐ Yes |
| | ☐ No |
| If 'No', skip to next Question. If 'Yes', | |
| Did you ever buy this product? | ☐ Yes |
| | ☐ No |

The results of the survey were entered into a database. Some data on the first twenty cases are shown in Table 7.1.

The variables 'Hear?' and 'Buy?' record 'Yes' (Y) or 'No' (N) answers to the corresponding questions; a 'No' answer to the first question entails a blank for 'Buy?'. The variable 'Level' records one of the three levels of penetration that may be deduced from the answers to the questions asked:

N ↔ 'Never heard of product';
H ↔ 'Heard of product, did not buy';
B ↔ 'Bought product'.

This variable was derived from the 'Hear?' and 'Buy?' variables by entering an appropriate function in the database.[3]

Typically, there will be many more questions on the questionnaire, resulting in many other variables in the database, both other primary variables recording answers

---

[3]    The appropriate function is an 'if/then/else' type function such as:

if 'Hear?' = 'N' then 'N' else if 'Hear?' = 'Y' and 'Buy?' = 'Y' then 'B' else 'H'.

The details of the syntax vary from one database package to another.

**Table 7.1** Marketing research survey data base, first twenty cases

| Case No. | Region | Hear? | Buy? | *others* | Level | *others* |
|----------|--------|-------|------|----------|-------|----------|
| 1 | A | N | | ... | N | ... |
| 2 | A | Y | Y | ... | B | ... |
| 3 | A | Y | Y | ... | B | ... |
| 4 | A | Y | Y | ... | B | ... |
| 5 | A | Y | N | ... | H | ... |
| 6 | A | Y | Y | ... | B | ... |
| 7 | A | Y | Y | ... | B | ... |
| 8 | A | Y | Y | ... | B | ... |
| 9 | A | Y | N | ... | H | ... |
| 10 | A | Y | Y | ... | B | ... |
| 11 | A | Y | N | ... | H | ... |
| 12 | A | Y | Y | ... | B | ... |
| 13 | A | Y | Y | ... | B | ... |
| 14 | A | N | | ... | N | ... |
| 15 | A | N | | ... | N | ... |
| 16 | A | Y | N | ... | H | ... |
| 17 | A | Y | Y | ... | B | ... |
| 18 | A | Y | Y | ... | B | ... |
| 19 | A | Y | Y | ... | B | ... |
| 20 | A | Y | Y | ... | B | ... |

**Table 7.2** Responses at each penetration level, per cent in each region

| Region | Bought product | Heard of product, did not buy | Never heard of product | Sample sizes |
|--------|----------------|-------------------------------|------------------------|--------------|
| A | 55 | 28 | 18 | *200* |
| C | 56 | 26 | 18 | *300* |
| B | 33 | 37 | 30 | *150* |
| Overall | 50 | 29 | 21 | *650* |

to questions and other derived variables derived as functions of the primary variables.

Summary results of the market penetration study, as produced by the database, are presented in Table 7.2, using a popular presentation format. It shows the relative frequencies of penetration levels within each region.

> **Exercise 7.1**   Read Table 7.2. Provide a verbal description of its contents. Provide a brief verbal summary of the comparisons of penetration levels between regions.

Note the similarity of the penetration patterns in regions A and C, and their difference from that in region B. To improve the presentation in the light of this, the order of the rows has been changed. Also, the database used to produce Table 7.2 ordered the levels of penetration in their order of entry as table headings. The marketing department would prefer to see the positive 'Bought product' heading first, rather than the negative 'Never heard of product'. Finally, the percentages have been rounded to two significant figures. Typical database and statistical software will show at least four significant figures. As we have seen in Chapter 2, the extra figures hide information.

The regional patterns are more vividly seen in the profile chart in Figure 7.1.

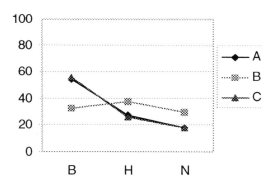

**Numbers responding, per cent**

**Figure 7.1**   Responses at each penetration level, per cent in each region.

### Relationships between categorical variables

Apparently, there is a relationship between penetration pattern and region. For example, survey respondents in regions A and C appear more likely to have bought the product than respondents in region B. Correspondingly, the percentage of the respondents in region B who have never heard of the product is greater than the corresponding percentages in regions A and C. If the observed differences between regions were real, the marketing manager might wish to seek an explanation for these differences and an improvement in performance in region B.

The relationship described here may be viewed as a *response relationship*. The variable 'region' may be viewed as an *explanatory variable,* with varying responses in different regions, as summarised in the varying penetration patterns. This is analogous to corresponding relationships between continuous variables such as those introduced in Section 1.5 and discussed in Chapter 6.

> **Exercise 7.2** What explanations are likely for the observed differences in penetration patterns? What kinds of solutions might the marketing manager consider? It may help to think in terms of a particular product or type of product. Would your answers be the same for all products? Try thinking in terms of different products.

> **Exercise 7.3** Why, do you think, was the survey 'stratified' among the three regions? Why were the sample sizes chosen as they were?

## 7.2   Statistical inference for frequency data

While regional differences in the sample data are obvious in Table 7.2 and Figure 7.1, it is conceivable that these differences are due to chance causes of variation. The respondents to the market research survey were randomly sampled within each region; a different sample would have produced different responses. We need to be able to assess the possibility that the observed differences are due to chance variation. Correspondingly, we need to be able to quantify the degree of uncertainty associated with the different percentages in Table 7.2. For these purposes we need to adapt the ideas of statistical inference developed earlier.

In Section 4.5, we showed how to set up a control chart for the percentage of non-conformances in an industrial or business process. In Section 5.1, we showed how this corresponded to a test of the statistical significance of the departure of an observed percentage from a target or hypothesised percentage. In Section 5.4, we showed how the idea of a confidence interval provided a solution to the problem of estimating the capability of a process as measured by error rate. Here, we apply these ideas to the market penetration example and extend them to making inferences about differences between percentages and differences between patterns of percentages.

### Has the target been achieved?

Based on previous experience with similar products and marketing campaigns, the marketing manager has aimed for a target 'Buy' percentage of 60%. He seems to have come close in regions A and C. In fact, such relatively small deviations from target typically would not be regarded as substantively significant. On the other hand, he seems to have missed badly in region B. In the light of previous analyses, however, we should address the question of whether such a deviation from target is also statistically significant, as well as being substantively significant.

Following the formulation of Chapter 5, Section 5.1, we test the null hypothesis that the actual 'Buy' percentage in region B is 60% by calculating the value of the test statistic

$$Z = \frac{\hat{P} - P_0}{\sqrt{\dfrac{P_0 \times (100 - P_0)}{n}}}$$

and comparing it to the critical value of 2. If the calculated value exceeds 2, we conclude that the deviation from target is statistically significant, in that it is unlikely to have happened by chance.

This is a modified version of the test statistic introduced in Section 5.1 for testing hypotheses about proportions, using sample counts. Here, we are testing a hypothesis about a percentage, using a sample percentage.

Substituting the relevant values in the formula for $Z$ leads to

$$Z = \frac{33 - 60}{\sqrt{\dfrac{60 \times (100 - 60)}{150}}} = 6.75$$

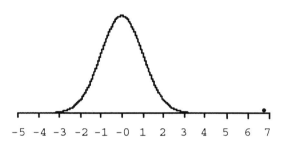

Here, the calculated value is almost 7, very highly significant by the usual criterion. Above, the calculated value and the sampling distribution of $Z$, assuming the null hypothesis, are displayed on the same graph. Clearly the two are not compatible, whence we reject the null hypothesis.

In many cases, the 'Buy' percentages observed in the samples from regions A and C would not be regarded as *substantively* significantly different from the target if they accurately reflected the 'Buy' percentages in the regions as a whole. Consequently, in such cases there is no practical value in testing the *statistical* significance of the observed deviations from the target. In the following exercise, however, you are asked to carry out the tests and make appropriate observations concerning technical aspects of the tests.

---

**Exercise 7.4**   Test the statistical significance of the deviation of the region A sample 'Buy' percentage from target and report on the result.

**Exercise 7.5** In the light of the result of Exercise 7.4, discuss whether a corresponding test for region C is needed. Note that the region C 'Buy' percentage is closer to 60 while the region C sample size is bigger. Carry out the test and comment on the result.

### Estimating purchase percentages

We must bear in mind that the reported percentages buying the product in the three regions, 55% and 56% in regions A and C, respectively, and 33% in region B, are based on samples, albeit representative samples. Consequently, we must be aware of sampling error and make allowances for it when interpreting the survey results. Thus, the 55% reported for region A is an estimated percentage for the region; to allow for its uncertainty, we need to calculate its standard error and report a confidence interval, as in Chapter 5. Recall from Section 5.4, page 183, that an approximate 95% confidence interval for the actual percentage, $P$, is

$$\hat{P} \pm 2\sqrt{\frac{\hat{P} \times (100 - \hat{P})}{n}}.$$

For region A, this is

$$55 \pm 2\sqrt{\frac{55 \times 45}{200}},$$

that is,

$$55 \pm 2 \times 3.5 = 55 \pm 7,$$

that is, we can be 95% confident that the percentage who bought the product in region A is somewhere between 48% and 62%. This is quite a wide interval, an expression of the uncertainty inherent in a percentage based on a sample as small as 200. While a sales director may not be too concerned about a 5% shortfall from target, the possibility that the 'Buy' percentage in region A might be as low as 48% may well cause concern.

**Exercise 7.6** Calculate 95% confidence intervals for the percentages who bought the product in regions B and C. In what respects are the intervals different? Why? (Refer to Exercise 7.5.)

### Statistical significance of regional differences

Clearly, with such a level of uncertainty, there can be no question of a statistically significant difference between the estimated percentages buying in regions A and C. Indeed, some argue that the *significant sameness* of these percentages should be emphasised and the substantive or commercial significance of that sameness should be pursued.

But what about the difference between these regions and region B? As a rough guide, the fact that the region B confidence interval does not intersect with either of the other two intervals can be taken to indicate that the corresponding differences are statistically significant.[4] A more formal test is based on the two-sample $Z$ statistic

$$Z = \frac{\hat{P}_1 - \hat{P}_2}{\sqrt{\dfrac{\hat{P}_1 \times (100 - \hat{P}_1)}{n_1} + \dfrac{\hat{P}_2 \times (100 - \hat{P}_2)}{n_2}}}.$$

The numerator measures the size of the difference between the two percentages; the denominator is the estimated *standard error* of this difference which measures the chance variation associated with the difference. By the usual convention for values of $Z$, if the calculated value exceeds 2 in magnitude we conclude that the difference between the percentages reflects more than chance variation and we will be interested in finding an assignable cause of variation.

Substituting the figures for regions A and B in this formula ($\hat{P}_1 = 55$, $n_1 = 200$, $\hat{P}_2 = 33$, $n_2 = 150$) gives $Z = 4.2$, very highly significant by any standards.

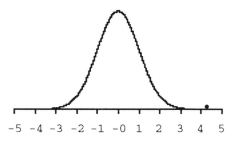

More precisely, *assuming equal population purchase percentages in the two regions,* the sampling distribution of the test statistic $Z$ would approximate the standard Normal distribution, illustrated here with the sample value of $Z$ indicated. Such a value is so extremely unlikely that it calls into question the assumption of equal population percentages. In other words, the sample percentages are statistically significantly different.

---

**Exercise 7.7**   Formally test the statistical significance of the difference between the sample percentages in regions A and C. Calculate a 95% confidence interval for the actual percentage in the combined regions. Comment on the interval width.

---

**Exercise 7.8**   Test the statistical significance of the difference between the sample percentages in region B and the combined regions A and C.

---

4   The complementary conclusion, that intersection of the intervals implies that the corresponding differences are *not* statistically significantly, is not true.

**Standard error of a difference between percentages**

The formula for the standard error of the difference between percentages,

$$\sqrt{\frac{\hat{P}_1 \times (100 - \hat{P}_1)}{n_1} + \frac{\hat{P}_2 \times (100 - \hat{P}_2)}{n_2}},$$

looks formidable. However, it does bear some resemblance to the formula for the standard error of a single percentage. In fact, if square root signs are ignored, the formula here is just the sum of the formulas corresponding to the two individual percentages. This merely reflects the fact that there are two sources of chance variation in the numerator of Z, $\hat{P}_1$ and $\hat{P}_2$, and the total chance variation is the sum of the parts. It is a mathematical technicality that the 'parts', the individual standard errors, are squared before being summed and the square root of the sum is then calculated.[5]

---

**Exercise 7.9** Develop a correspondence between this formula and that for the standard error of the difference between two sample means

$$\sqrt{\left(\frac{\sigma_1}{\sqrt{n_1}}\right)^2 + \left(\frac{\sigma_2}{\sqrt{n_2}}\right)^2}$$

developed in Chapter 5; see page 165. Make correspondences between the significance test described here and the corresponding test for the difference between two sample means.

---

## 7.3 The chi-square test

We have already carried out more than enough significance tests on the 'Buy' percentages in this example, and our conclusion is clear: regions A and C have similar 'Buy' percentages, between 53% and 58% with 95% confidence, and region B has considerably lower percentage, between 29% and 37% with 95% confidence. However, the pattern of differences between such percentages may not always be as clear cut. Suppose, for example, that the numbers in the regional samples who had bought the product had been

$$109, \quad 68, \quad \text{and} \quad 149,$$

for regions A, B and C, respectively, rather than the reported

$$109, \quad 49, \quad \text{and} \quad 168.$$

Conceivably, the former could have been typed into a spreadsheet in error, with two pairs of digits being accidentally transposed. Table 7.2 would change to Table 7.3.

---

[5] The square of the standard deviation is called the *variance*. In mathematical statistics, it is more convenient to work with variances than with standard deviations. However, for practical interpretability, the standard deviation is favoured.

**Table 7.3**  Frequency of responses, classified by penetration level and region

| Region | Never heard of product | Heard of product, did not buy | Bought product | Totals |
|---|---|---|---|---|
| Region A | 36 | 55 | 109 | 200 |
| Region B | 45 | 56 | 68 | 150 |
| Region C | 54 | 78 | 149 | 300 |
| Totals | 135 | 189 | 326 | 650 |

(Here, we have assumed that the row totals were transcribed exactly although they are not row totals for the modified table.) The 'Buy' percentages, as calculated from Table 7.3, now become

$$55\%, \quad 45\%, \quad \text{and} \quad 50\%,$$

respectively, and the question of statistically significant differences between them is not as clear-cut. It may well be that all three regional percentages more or less coincide. We need a test that compares all three sample percentages simultaneously.

### Testing homogeneity of percentages

If the null hypothesis that all three regional population percentages are the same is true, then the differences between the sample percentages can be ascribed to chance variation. In that case, it makes sense to focus on a single overall percentage and to estimate this by the overall sample percentage based on all three regional samples combined, that is,

$$\hat{P} = 100 \times \frac{326}{650},$$

that is, 50%, as shown in Table 7.2, page 225.

Assuming the null hypothesis, the deviations of the sample regional percentages from this overall percentage can be ascribed to chance variation. Accordingly, the individual regional percentages,

$$\hat{P}_1 = 55, \quad \hat{P}_2 = 45 \quad \text{and} \quad \hat{P}_3 = 50$$

could be compared separately with this estimated overall percentage through the test statistics

$$Z_i = \frac{\hat{P}_i - \hat{P}}{\sqrt{\dfrac{\hat{P}_i \times (100 - \hat{P}_i)}{n_i}}}, \quad i = 1, 2, 3.$$

Here, $n_1$, $n_2$ and $n_3$ are the regional sample sizes for regions A, B and C, respectively: 200, 150 and 300.

**Exercise 7.10**  Calculate the values of the test statistics $Z_1$, $Z_2$ and $Z_3$.

The individual tests do not provide a test of the overall null hypothesis that all three regional population percentages are the same. To get a single test statistic for that hypothesis, we combine the individual test statistics by summing their squares to give

$$Z_1^2 + Z_2^2 + Z_3^2 = \sum_{i=1}^{3} \frac{(\hat{P}_i - \hat{P})^2}{\dfrac{\hat{P}_i \times (100 - \hat{P}_i)}{n_i}}.$$

This is usually expressed in the form

$$\chi^2 = \sum_{i=1}^{3} n_i \frac{(\hat{P}_i - \hat{P})^2}{\hat{P}_i \times (100 - \hat{P}_i)},$$

called the *chi-square statistic for testing homogeneity.*

Thus, the test of the statistical significance of the deviations of the sample percentages from each other is made up as a combination of Z tests of the significance of the deviations of the sample percentages from the estimated overall percentage.

---

**Exercise 7.11** Calculate the value of the chi-square statistic for testing the homogeneity of the 'Buy' percentages both as the sum of squares of the Z statistics calculated in Exercise 7.10 and by direct substitution in the chi-square formula shown above.

---

**Exercise 7.12** Calculate the value of $\chi^2$ from the original 'Buy' percentages as reported in Table 7.2.

---

### The sampling distribution of chi-square

Having calculated the value of the test statistic, the standard significance testing procedure requires us to compare this value to a suitable critical value. In this case, the standard Normal distribution is not a suitable reference distribution. In fact, another distribution called the 'chi-square distribution with two degrees of freedom' is needed. Its graph is shown in Figure 7.2, with the values calculated in Exercises 7.11 and 7.12 indicated. One clearly is highly significant, the other can be explained by chance. Thus, if the numbers buying the product had been as reported incorrectly in Table 7.3, the differences between the corresponding sample 'Buy' percentages would have been ignored. On the other hand, the correctly reported sample 'Buy' percentages are highly statistically significantly different and management action is called for.

### Degrees of freedom for chi-square

To apply the formal chi-square test, we need a critical value for the chi-square distribution. In fact, we need several critical values because there is a whole family of

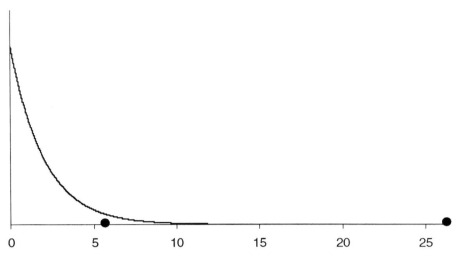

**Figure 7.2** Frequency distribution of chi-square with two degrees of freedom, showing calculated values 3.5 and 24.

chi-square distributions, indexed by the number of 'degrees of freedom'. We have already encountered this idea in the context of simple linear regression, where the residuals were 'constrained' by two equations and so 'lost' two degrees of freedom; see Chapter 6, footnote 3, page 199.

Here, the deviations $\hat{P}_1 - \hat{P}$, $\hat{P}_2 - \hat{P}$ and $\hat{P}_3 - \hat{P}$, which are the basic building blocks of the chi-square statistic, are constrained by the equation

$$\sum_{i=1}^{3} n_i\left(\hat{P}_i - \hat{P}\right) = 0.$$

**Exercise 7.13** Substitute the values for $n_i$, $\hat{P}_i$ and $\hat{P}$ in the above equation and verify that it is correct apart from rounding error.

The *three* deviations 'lose' *one* degree of freedom through this mathematical constraint and so are regarded as having *two* degrees of freedom: $2 = 3 - 1$.

More generally, the chi-square statistic for comparing $r$ percentages,

$$\chi^2 = \sum_{i=1}^{r} n_i \times \frac{(\hat{P}_i - \hat{P})^2}{\hat{P}_i \times (100 - \hat{P}_i)}$$

which involves $r$ deviations $\hat{P}_i - \hat{P}$, $1 \leq i \leq r$, has $r - 1$ degrees of freedom.

Appendix B at the end of the book gives critical values corresponding to a range of significance levels, labelled $\alpha$ (Greek 'alpha') and a range of numbers of degrees of freedom, labelled ν (Greek 'nu'). Using the conventional 5% significance level, α = 0.05, and noting that ν = 2 in this case, the critical value is 6.

Note that, because $\chi^2$ measures departures from the null hypothesis in terms of sums of *square* deviations, which are always positive (or at least non-negative), a large value suggests a large departure. Hence, the null hypothesis is rejected if the calculated value is *larger than* the critical value.

---

**Exercise 7.14** Formally apply the $\chi^2$ test to the original 'Buy' percentages as reported in Table 7.2, reproduced in Table 7.4, and also to the alternative percentages discussed above.

---

**Exercise 7.15** Calculate the degrees of freedom and find the 5% critical value for a chi-square test comparing *two* percentages. Calculate the square root of the critical value. Can you make the connection between this value and the 5% critical value for a $Z$ statistic?

---

### Testing homogeneity of penetration patterns

Market penetration is not just about purchase percentages, the percentages who heard of the product and who never heard of the product are also important. Table 7.2, reproduced on Table 7.4, suggests that the overall patterns in regions A and C are similar and both are quite different from that in region B. How can we assess the statistical significance of such regional variation in the overall pattern?

**Table 7.4** Responses at each penetration level, per cent in each region

| Region | Bought product | Heard of product, did not buy | Never heard of product | Sample sizes |
|--------|---------|---------|---------|---------|
| A | 55 | 28 | 18 | 200 |
| C | 56 | 26 | 18 | 300 |
| B | 33 | 37 | 30 | 150 |
| Overall | 50 | 29 | 21 | 650 |

The chi-square test for comparing percentages can be extended to a test for comparing patterns of percentages or, equivalently, comparing frequency distributions. Essentially, a slightly modified version of the test statistic for percentages is applied to each column of Table 7.4, and then combined into one chi-square test statistic.[6] The null hypothesis of interest here is that the three regional penetration patterns, or frequency distributions, are the same, apart from chance variation. If so, then the best estimate of the overall pattern is given by the overall sample percentages, 50, 29 and 21 in this case. The test of the null hypothesis is based on the deviations of the regional sample percentages from the corresponding overall sample percentages.

---

[6] Details of this and an alternative approach, via *contingency tables,* are available in the book's website.

**Table 7.5**   Frequencies of responses, classified by penetration level and region

| Region | Never heard of product | Heard of product, did not buy | Bought product | Totals |
|---|---|---|---|---|
| Region A | 36 | 55 | 109 | 200 |
| Region B | 45 | 56 | 49 | 150 |
| Region C | 54 | 78 | 168 | 300 |
| Totals | 135 | 189 | 326 | 650 |

The test statistic is the sum of the statistics for testing homogeneity of each of the three sets of column percentages, slightly modified.

*Computing chi-square*

Computation is best left to suitable computer software. Typically, standard statistical software includes a *contingency table analysis* facility. A contingency table is a two way table of actual frequencies, rather than the relative frequencies or percentages which have featured here. For example, Table 7.5 shows the contingency table of frequencies of responses classified by penetration level and region.

---

**Exercise 7.16**   Verify the 'Bought product' percentages in Table 7.4.

---

Technically speaking, this is the *bivariate frequency distribution* of the two categorical variables, region and penetration level. It is called a contingency table because it gives information on how the answers to the questions concerning penetration are *contingent* on region. The hypothesis of homogeneity of penetration patterns across regions is equivalent to the hypothesis of *statistical independence* that is tested in contingency table analysis. The value of the chi-square statistic is the same in each case. Below is typical computer output from a contingency table analysis, showing both absolute and relative frequency distributions and the resulting chi-square value.

```
Rows are levels of      Region
Columns are levels of   Level
No Selector

              B       H       N     total

A            109      55      36     200
            54.5    27.5      18     100

B             49      56      45     150
            32.7    37.3      30     100

C            168      78      54     300
              56      26      18     100

total        326     189     135     650
            50.2    29.1    20.8     100

table contents:
Count
Percent of Row Total

Chi-square =    24.61   with   4   df
p ≤ 0.0001
```

*Implementing the test*

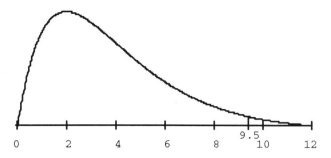

To implement the test, we need the sampling distribution of the test statistic. Assuming the null hypothesis of no difference in regional penetration patterns, it is the 'chi-square distribution with four degrees of freedom'. Its graph is shown here. The calculated value of 24 is not consistent with this reference distribution and, therefore, is not consistent with the null hypothesis. On the basis of these data, therefore, we reject the null hypothesis.

*Degrees of freedom*

The number of degrees of freedom is related to the constraints on the deviations $P - \hat{P}$, already noted.[7] There is a simple rule for determining the number of degrees of freedom appropriate for the chi-square test being applied here; it is

$$(r - 1) \times (c - 1),$$

where $r$ is the number of rows in the frequency table and $c$ the number of columns. Here,

$$(3 - 1) \times (3 - 1) = 2 \times 2 = 4.$$

*Critical value*

As an alternative to referring the calculated value of chi-square to the curve above, when that curve is not readily available, we can read the appropriate critical value from the table of chi-square values in Appendix B and refer the calculated value to it.

---

**Exercise 7.17**  Test the null hypothesis of homogeneous penetration patterns using the appropriate critical value.

---

[7]  As before, the deviations of each column of percentages from the corresponding overall percentage in Table 7.4 are constrained; the three deviations in each column 'lose' one degree of freedom, leaving, essentially, two 'free' deviations in each column, that is, two 'free' rows in the table. However, a similar constraint applies across the rows, so that there are only two 'free' columns in the table, a total of $2 \times 2$ degrees of freedom in all.

### Reporting the results of the analysis

A short management report of the analysis carried out here might go as follows.

> A marketing research survey of 650 respondents in three regions was commissioned to assess market penetration following the recent marketing campaign. Table 7.6 summarises the survey results.
>
> The results for regions A and C were virtually identical. In regions A and C combined, over half the respondents bought the product, just over one quarter had heard of it but did not buy and less than one fifth had never heard of the product. This is reasonably satisfactory.

**Table 7.6**   Responses at each penetration level, per cent in each region

| Region | Bought product | Heard of product, did not buy | Never heard of product | Sample sizes |
|--------|---------|---------|---------|---------|
| A and C | 55 | 27 | 18 | *500* |
| B | 33 | 37 | 30 | *150* |
| Overall | 50 | 29 | 21 | *650* |

> The percentage who bought, at 55% (95% confidence interval 51% to 59.4%), is marginally below the target of 60%; the difference is also marginally statistically significant. The overall penetration rate (those who heard of the product) in regions A and C, at 82% (95% confidence interval 78.6% to 85.4%), is satisfactory, as is the rate of buying among those who heard of the product at almost 80%.
>
> The penetration pattern for region B is less satisfactory; the difference between it and that for regions A and C is considerable and statistically highly significant. The percentage buying is just 33% (95% confidence interval 25% to 40%) and the rate of buying among those who heard of the product is less than 50%. Both the percentage who heard of the product but did not buy and who never heard of the product were considerably higher than the corresponding percentages in regions A and C.
>
> There are serious problems to be addressed in region B; both the percentage who heard of the product and, among them, the percentage who bought are very low. Some consideration might also be given to reducing the one quarter of respondents in regions A and C who heard of but did not buy the product.

---

**Exercise 7.18**   Refer to the relevant preceding exercises for substantiation of the individual conclusions reported above or provide substantiation if not already provided.

---

## 7.4   Multiply classified frequency data

Variation patterns may be influenced by more than one factor. Consider Table 7.7. The numbers of repaid and defaulted bank loans among 715 loans checked in a

**Table 7.7**   Numbers of loans defaulted and repaid classified by type, commercial or non-commercial, and by size, small or large.

| Loan type | Loan size | Default status Defaulted | Default status Repaid | Totals |
|---|---|---|---|---|
| Commercial | <10K | 3 | 176 | 179 |
|  | >10K | 4 | 293 | 297 |
| Non-commercial | <10K | 17 | 197 | 214 |
|  | >10K | 2 | 23 | 25 |
|  | Totals | 26 | 689 | 715 |

bank audit are shown, separately for the four possible combinations of loan type and size.

This display of the basic numerical data is not the most informative that could be made. It is usually easier to detect patterns in frequency data by studying appropriate relative frequencies, or percentages. A more informative display is shown in Table 7.8.

It seems quite clear from Table 7.8 that commercial loans have a much smaller default rate than non-commercial and that the size of the loan is a relatively unimportant factor in determining the default rate. Management reaction to such an analysis might be to study the non-commercial loan business to see what measures can be taken to reduce the high default rate.

There might also be a suggestion that some attention be paid to the smaller commercial loans to attempt to improve the default rate to the level achieved with the larger commercial loans. However, statistical analysis shows that the observed difference in default rates between small commercial and large commercial loans is not statistically significant, so that such a management reaction would amount to reacting to chance variation.

A suitable significance test for this purpose is based on the two-sample $Z$ statistic, introduced in Section 7.2:

$$Z = \frac{\hat{P}_1 - \hat{P}_2}{\sqrt{\dfrac{\hat{P}_1 \times (100 - \hat{P}_1)}{n_1} + \dfrac{\hat{P}_2 \times (100 - \hat{P}_2)}{n_2}}},$$

**Table 7.8**   Numbers of loans and default rates classified by type, commercial or non-commercial, and size, small or large

| Loan type | Loan size | Number of loans | Default rate, % |
|---|---|---|---|
| Commercial | <10K | 179 | 1.7 |
|  | >10K | 297 | 1.3 |
| Non-commercial | <10K | 214 | 7.9 |
|  | >10K | 25 | 8.0 |

confining attention to the 179 small commercial and 297 large commercial loans. The value[8] of the statistic is

$$Z = \frac{1.68 - 1.35}{\sqrt{\dfrac{1.68 \times 98.32}{179} + \dfrac{1.35 \times 98.65}{297}}} = 0.28,$$

not statistically significant by the usual criterion.

---

**Exercise 7.19**   Repeat this test for the non-commercial loans. Also, test the statistical significance of the difference between the observed default rates for commercial and non-commercial loans, separately for small and large loans.

---

It may be suggested that, rather than test separately the differences between default rates, it would be desirable to combine these tests to form one comprehensive test of no difference between default patterns. This would parallel the way in which we combined one-sample tests to form a test of homogeneity of percentages and combined tests of homogeneity of percentages to form a test of homogeneity of percentage patterns. However, when there are more than one explanatory factor, the simple combination suggested may not be valid. The analysis required to deal with these issues is beyond the level of this text. It is noted, however, that the more detailed analysis is more powerful than the separate analyses conducted here.

### A cautionary note; misleading displays

It is clear from the analysis carried out so far that the default rate is critically dependent on loan type, commercial or non-commercial, but virtually not at all on loan size. However, a frequently used approach to displaying data such as these does not permit this conclusion. Frequently, data such as these are displayed as two two-way tables for numbers of loans, one classified by default status and loan type and the second classified by default status and loan size. Consider the latter as shown in Table 7.9. This seems to contradict our previous conclusion that loan size was not a critical factor in determining default rates. A formal test of the statistical significance of the difference between the small loan and large loan default rates yields a $Z$ statistic value of

$$Z = \frac{5.09 - 1.86}{\sqrt{\dfrac{5.09 \times (100 - 5.09)}{393} + \dfrac{1.86 \times (100 - 1.86)}{322}}} = \frac{3.23}{1.34} = 2.41,$$

which is statistically significant according to the usual convention.

---

[8]   Note that the values substituted for the sample percentages are rounded to two decimal places, rather than the one reported in Table 7.8. The latter is appropriate for reporting but leads to inaccuracy when used in further calculations. The calculated value of $Z$ using the percentages as reported in Table 7.8 is 0.34 giving a rounding error of 0.06 or 21%.

**Table 7.9** Numbers of loans defaulted and repaid, and default rates, classified by size, small or large.

| Loan size | Default status | | Totals | Default rate, % |
|---|---|---|---|---|
| | Defaulted | Repaid | | |
| <10K | 20 | 373 | 393 | 5.1% |
| >10K | 6 | 316 | 322 | 1.9% |
| Totals | 26 | 689 | 715 | 3.6% |

---

**Exercise 7.20** Construct a table of loans defaulted and repaid, and default rates, classified by type, commercial or non-commercial. Test the statistical significance of the difference between commercial and non-commercial loan default rates.

---

It seems as if both factors, loan type and loan size, have a significant effect on default rate, contradicting the previous analysis. Which of these analyses is correct?

### Resolving the problem; Simpson's paradox

The 5.1% small loan default rate shown in Table 7.9 may be calculated directly from the combined frequencies shown in that table:

$$5.1 = \frac{20}{393}$$

Alternatively, it may be represented as a weighted average of the two 'Small loan' default rates 1.7% and 7.9% shown in Table 7.8, the weights being in proportion to the totals, 179 and 214, on which each percentage is based:[9]

$$5.1 = \frac{179}{179 + 214} \times 1.7 + \frac{214}{179 + 214} \times 7.9$$

Evaluating the weights, we find

$$5.1 = 0.46 \times 1.7 + 0.54 \times 7.9$$

Similarly, the 1.9% default rate in Table 7.9 may be represented as a weighted average of the two 'Large loan' default rates of 1.3% and 8.0% shown in Table 7.8. Similar calculations lead to the representation

$$1.9 = 0.92 \times 1.3 + 0.08 \times 8.0$$

---

[9] This representation is confirmed by representing the rates 1.7 and 7.9 in terms of the original frequencies in Table 7.7; $1.7 = \frac{3}{179}$ and $7.9 = \frac{17}{214}$, respectively. Substituting these in the weighted average formula leads to $5.1 = \frac{179}{179 + 214} \times \frac{3}{179} + \frac{214}{179 + 214} \times \frac{17}{214} = \frac{3}{179 + 214} + \frac{17}{179 + 214} = \frac{3 + 17}{179 + 214} = \frac{20}{393}$, the original calculation.

Observe that in both representations, the weights sum to 1:

$$0.46 + 0.54 = 1; \qquad 0.92 + 0.08 = 1$$

We can now see why the 'Small loan' and Large loan' default rates are different when calculated from the frequencies for both loan types combined, although they are virtually the same within each loan type. The 5.1% rate is a weighted average of two rates in which the lower rate, 1.7%, is weighted slightly less than the higher rate, 7.9%; 0.46 is slightly less than 0.54. On the other hand, the 1.9% rate is a weighted average of a similar pair of rates, but the lower rate is weighted much more than the higher rate; 0.92 is much larger than 0.08. Thus, the higher rate dominates in the first average and the lower rate dominates in the second.

The weights in each 'Loan size' calculation reflect the 'Commercial–Non-commercial' pattern or frequency distribution within each loan size. When these patterns are different, combining 'Loan type' categories is hazardous.

In the end, we conclude that Table 7.8 gives the more reliable and revealing view of these data.

The phenomenon exemplified above is known as Simpson's paradox. It occurs when an apparent overall relationship between two variables takes on different forms at different levels of a third variable. The possibility of its occurring indicates that special care needs to be taken when studying the results of sample surveys involving many categorical variables which may be interrelated in complex ways. Many reports of such surveys consist of a series of two-way tables, which may be seriously misleading if Simpson's paradox applies. The problem is not confined to frequency data. It will turn up again when we study multiple regression in detail, where it is associated with a problem known as 'multicollinearity'.

The problem is exaggerated when there are more than two factors which may influence a response pattern. Although, in theory, it is possible to set out appropriate rates or proportions in a higher dimensional table, in practice, it requires more and more space, and the study of such tables to find critical patterns and differences in patterns becomes increasingly difficult.

This problem is largely overcome by the use of appropriate models for frequency data, particularly the *logistic regression* model. However, the study of such models is beyond the scope of this text.

## 7.5   Review exercises

7.1 (a) A large banking organisation engaged a market research company to monitor the attitudes of its staff towards proposals for changes in work practices. The market research company sampled 500 staff members at random and found 45% in favour of accepting the changes. Calculate a 95% confidence interval for the proportion of staff in favour.

(b) Following six months of stalemate in negotiations, the bank commissioned another survey. This time, they required that the proportion in favour be estimated to within 2 percentage points, with 95% confidence. What sample size was required? (Note: An approach to sample size determination was given in Section 5.4, page 183–5.)

(c) The bank agreed to a sample size of 1,000 for the second survey. 481 favourable responses were counted. Is this result significantly different from the previous one?

(d) A month later, the staff union conducted a complete ballot of its members and found 44% in favour. Are you surprised?

7.2 Of 294 urban residents selected for interview in a market research sample survey, 29% refused to participåte. Of 1,015 rural residents selected for the same survey, 17% refused. Are urban and rural response rates different? Explain the basis for your answer. Explain the derivation of the formula for the standard error of the difference between two sample percentages, $\hat{P}_1$ and $\hat{P}_2$ and discuss the correspondence between that derivation and the derivation of the standard error of the difference between two sample means, $\bar{X}_1$ and $\bar{X}_2$.

7.3 In an experiment to investigate the effect of the wording of questions on survey responses, two versions of a question concerning gun control in the USA were asked of two subsamples of the survey sample. The versions were:

Version 1: Would you favour or oppose a law that would require a person to obtain a police permit before purchasing a gun?

Version 2: Would you favour or oppose a law that would require a person to obtain a police permit before purchasing a gun, or do you think that such a law would interfere too much with the right of citizens to own guns?

The results were reported as follows:

|                       | Version 1 | Version 2 |
|-----------------------|-----------|-----------|
| Sample size           | 615       | 585       |
| Number who favour     | 463       | 403       |
| Percentage who favour | 75.3%     | 68.9%     |

Test the significance of the difference between the sample percentages and report the result of the test both in statistical terminology and in ordinary English.

7.4 40 males and 40 females were interviewed for 12 positions. Seven males and five females were selected. Is this difference statistically significant?

(a) Test the difference between proportions selected using a two-sample Z test.

(b) Test the homogeneity of the proportions selected using a chi-square test.

(c) Make a 'contingency table' for these data, that is, a table of frequencies categorised by both gender and selection status. Test the statistical significance of the association between the categorising factors using a chi-square test.

(d) Discuss the relationships between all three tests

7.5    In a study of 400 trials relating to 'white collar' crime, the numbers jailed or not were recorded for each of three categories of crime, as follows:

|  | Embezzlement | Fraud | Forgery | Totals |
|---|---|---|---|---|
| **Sent to jail** | 22 | 130 | 20 | 172 |
| **Not sent to jail** | 56 | 146 | 25 | 228 |
| *Totals* | 79 | 276 | 45 | 400 |

Provide a more informative display. Carry out a chi-square analysis to test whether jailing pattern varied between the crime categories. Provide a brief (one or two sentences) verbal report on the data, directed towards a non-technical readership.

7.6    A sample of professional economists was asked whether they agreed or disagreed with each of 27 statements, to see if there was consensus or dissension within the profession. Here are their responses, by country, to the statement 'Inflation is primarily a monetary phenomenon'.

|  | Agree | Mixed | Disagree | total |
|---|---|---|---|---|
| United States | 55 | 61 | 87 | 203 |
| Austria | 12 | 25 | 51 | 88 |
| France | 17 | 30 | 110 | 157 |
| Germany | 67 | 84 | 117 | 268 |
| Switzerland | 62 | 70 | 65 | 197 |
| total | 213 | 270 | 430 | 913 |

table contents: Count

Chi-square = 59.29

Make a new table or tables which facilitates intercountry comparisons; explain your choice of form of table. Briefly summarise the comparisons.

Test the homogeneity of the proportions agreeing with the statement.

Test the significance of the association between views (agree, mixed, disagree) and country.

7.7    A student engaged on a project for a printed circuit board manufacturer examined 500 defective boards to determine defect patterns. The defective boards had come from three different machines, 250 from machine A and 125 from each of machines B and C, with the following breakdown into defect types:

Rows are levels of        Machine
Columns are levels of      Defect Type

|  | Damaged | Missing | Raised | total |
|---|---|---|---|---|
| A | 80 | 50 | 120 | 250 |
| B | 55 | 60 | 10 | 125 |
| C | 45 | 65 | 15 | 125 |
| total | 180 | 175 | 145 | 500 |

table contents: Count

Chi-square = 98.35

Are there significant differences between machines? In the light of your answer, prepare a more effective display of the information in the above table, with a brief commentary.

7.8 A technical report on a survey of the economic outlook (favourable, neutral or unfavourable) of 309 restaurant owners (classified as large company, partners or sole owner) included the following table. The column headings, F, N, U, indicate economic outlook and the row labels, LC, P, SO, indicate type of owner. Provide a more informative presentation of the basic data and a brief non-technical verbal summary which includes a suitable reference to the result (not the details) of a chi-square analysis.

|       | F  | N   | U  | total |
|-------|----|-----|----|-------|
| LC    | 20 | 64  | 35 | 119   |
| P     | 23 | 49  | 12 | 84    |
| SO    | 17 | 53  | 36 | 106   |
| total | 60 | 166 | 83 | 309   |

table contents: Count

Chi-square = 11.61

When surprise was expressed at the variation in response patterns among the three owner types, the raw data were re-examined. It was discovered that the outlook responses for partners had been miscoded, favourable being recorded as unfavourable and vice versa. A new analysis was done, with the following result.

|       | F  | N   | U  | total |
|-------|----|-----|----|-------|
| LC    | 20 | 64  | 35 | 119   |
| P     | 12 | 49  | 23 | 84    |
| SO    | 17 | 53  | 36 | 106   |
| total | 49 | 166 | 94 | 309   |

table contents: Count

Chi-square = 1.54 with 4 df

Revise your data display and report in the light of this.

Explain what a chi-square analysis is intended to achieve and explain the difference between the results of the two analyses in this example.

7.9 Consider the following artificial 'bank loan' data.

*Numbers of loans defaulted and repaid classified by type, commercial or non-commercial, and by size, small or large.*

| Loan type | Loan size | Default status | | Default rate, % |
|-----------|-----------|----------------|--------|-----------------|
|           |           | Defaulted      | Repaid |                 |
| Commercial | <10K | 1 | 9 | 10 |
|            | >10K | 1 | 9 | 10 |
| Non-commercial | <10K | 9 | 10 | 90 |
|                | >10K | 90 | 100 | 90 |

(i)   Construct a table giving the default status of the loans classified by loan size, irrespective of loan type, with the default rates.

(ii)  Calculate the average of the small loan default rates using the corresponding counts as weights. Repeat for the large loans.

(iii) Compare the default rates of part (i) with the averages of part (ii). Comment and explain.

7.10    Magazine publishers carefully monitor rates of renewal of expiring subscriptions. One publisher noted 23,545 renewals out of 45,955 subscriptions due in January and 5,869 renewals out of 9,157 subscriptions due in February of the same year. Calculate the corresponding renewal rates, per cent. Formally test the statistical significance of the difference between these two percentages, using the standard test for comparing sample percentages, assuming that the assumptions appropriate to that test were satisfied. What are the appropriate assumptions referred to? Were they satisfied in this case? Assuming that they were, briefly discuss the statistical significance test in this case.

The following table shows frequency data on subscriptions categorised according to Month, January or February, and Source, which may be one of gift, previous renewal, direct mail, subscription service, catalogue agent.

*Expiring Subscriptions, Renewals, and Renewal Rates,*
*by Month and Subscription Category*

| Month | Gift | Previous Renewal | Direct Mail | Subscription Service | Catalogue Agent | Overall |
|---|---|---|---|---|---|---|
| | | | | Source of Current Subscription | | |
| January | | | | | | |
| Total | 3,594 | 18,364 | 2,986 | 20,862 | 149 | 45,955 |
| Renewals | 2,918 | 14,488 | 1,783 | 4,343 | 13 | 23,545 |
| Rate | .812 | .789 | .597 | .208 | .087 | .512 |
| February | | | | | | |
| Total | 884 | 5,140 | 2,224 | 864 | 45 | 9,157 |
| Renewals | 704 | 3,907 | 1,134 | 122 | 2 | 5,869 |
| Rate | .796 | .760 | .510 | .141 | .044 | .641 |

Note that the January renewal rates exceed those for February in every category but the overall rates are in the reverse order. Explain the discrepancy between the overall comparison and the individual category comparisons.

The publisher gives a substantial commission for new subscriptions (but not for renewals) to the catalogue agent and the proprietors of the subscription service. Comment.

7.11    In a study of gender as a determinant of small business success and survival, the following data were assembled.

| Industry | Businesses headed by men | | Businesses headed by women | |
|---|---|---|---|---|
| | **Number of successes** | **Number of failures** | **Number of successes** | **Number of failures** |
| Food and drink | 91 | 15 | 35 | 7 |
| Computers | 99 | 23 | 13 | 1 |
| Health | 72 | 12 | 36 | 7 |
| Totals | 262 | 50 | 84 | 15 |

Prepare a report with suitable tables and/or graphs showing the key comparisons to be made in these data and outlining the main conclusions. Include a section on reservations about your conclusions, keeping in mind other variables that might have been measured.

Collapse the three-way table to two two-way tables. Do any anomalies arise? If so, explain them.

## 7.6   Laboratory exercise: Frequency data analysis

This exercise is based on the data on perceived extent of uses of mobile phones, discussed at the beginning of this chapter. The data are stored in the Excel file 'Extent of use.xls' on the book's website.

Make a table of responses, per cent, to perceived extent of use, categorised by region. Make a corresponding profile chart. Describe the pattern of extent of use and the variation in pattern between regions.

Carry out a chi-square test of homogeneity of patterns of extent of use. State the null hypothesis tested by the chi-square test. Draw a rough diagram of the corresponding sampling distribution, indicating on it the calculated value of chi-square. Use Excel to find the 5% critical value and to find the p-value corresponding to the value of chi-square calculated from the data; check your answers against the chi-square table appended. Report formally on the result of the chi-square test.

Carry out a chi-square test of the homogeneity of the percentages of 'Enough' responses using the contingency table approach. First, use an 'If' function to create a new variable whose values are 'Enough' and 'Too much or too little'. Illustrate and report on the result.

# 8
# Multiple linear regression

Multiple linear regression is an extension of simple linear regression, as discussed in Chapter 6, to the case where a response variable may be related to several possible explanatory variables, rather than just one. The multiple linear regression model was introduced in Section 1.6, in the context of a sales forecasting problem. There, we made various uses of a prediction formula that had been developed through multiple linear regression. In this chapter, we show how that formula was developed. The method involves two phases, referred to as *model fitting* and *model checking*. Model fitting involves choosing a version of the multiple linear regression model that best fits the data available, using the method of least squares introduced in Chapter 6. Model checking involves using graphical diagnostic checks to determine whether the model chosen by least squares is satisfactory. For simple linear regression, model checking was based on inspection of the scatterplot. With several explanatory variables, simple scatterplots are not enough so a more sophisticated approach is required.

The ideas are introduced in the context of a production prediction problem and then illustrated in the context of the stamp sales case study introduced in Chapter 1. A number of important issues arise in the context of multiple linear regression including some consequences of the degree of control that may be applied to the process under study and of problems arising with very large datasets. These are briefly discussed.

### Learning objectives

After completing this chapter, students should understand the basis for and application of multiple linear regression, and demonstrate this by being able to:

- illustrate the need for a prediction formula relating a response variable to several explanatory variables;

- write down an equation representing the multiple linear regression model, identify the parameters of the model, describe the least squares criterion for choosing estimates for the linear parameters and use Data Desk to calculate parameter estimates;
- explain Data Desk regression output and calculate a prediction formula with error bounds from the output;
- explain the formulas for estimating standard deviation and for measuring explained variation;
- explain what is meant by model criticism and illustrate the need for it by example;
- describe the diagnostic plot and explain its ideal form;
- illustrate by example problems that may be detected in a diagnostic plot and in a Normal plot and time series plot of residuals, and their resolution;
- outline an iterative procedure for fitting and testing regression models;
- discuss issues related to degree of control of the study environment, stability of relationships, extrapolation, prediction of explanatory variables and large datasets.

## 8.1   A prediction problem

A metal fabrication company makes a variety of metal products to order for a range of customers. Customers' production schedules depended on the fabrication company's delivery dates. It was important that the delivery dates quoted by the fabrication company at the time of placing orders were met; if not, customers could suffer severe losses. The company had available data on the time taken to complete 20 successive orders received, along with data on other variables thought to influence the completion time. These were the number of units ordered, the number of operations involved in manufacturing a unit and an indication of whether the job had received a 'rushed' priority status or was a normal job. The data are shown in Table 8.1.

These data were collected as part of a study of a production control system. During that study, it was suggested that a new variable, Total operations, defined as the product of Units and Operations per unit, would be a sensible measure of the size of a job. The company now proposed to use these data to develop a prediction equation for predicting the time to complete a new order, which could be used by their sales executives when negotiating with potential customers.

Multiple linear regression is an appropriate tool to apply to a problem such as this. The task is to find a prediction formula for Job time, the *response* variable, based on Units, Operations per unit, Total operations and 'Normal'/'Rushed', the potential *explanatory* variables.

Before proceeding to the task of finding a prediction formula, we first undertake an important step in any statistical problem solving exercise, that is, initial data analysis.

**Table 8.1**    Times, in hours, to complete jobs with varying numbers of units, numbers of operations per unit and priority status (normal or rushed)

| Order number | Jobtime (hours) | Units | Operations per unit | Normal (0) or Rushed (1)? |
|---|---|---|---|---|
| 1 | 153 | 100 | 6 | 0 |
| 2 | 192 | 35 | 11 | 0 |
| 3 | 162 | 127 | 7 | 1 |
| 4 | 240 | 64 | 12 | 0 |
| 5 | 339 | 600 | 5 | 1 |
| 6 | 185 | 14 | 16 | 1 |
| 7 | 235 | 96 | 11 | 1 |
| 8 | 506 | 257 | 13 | 0 |
| 9 | 260 | 21 | 9 | 1 |
| 10 | 161 | 39 | 8 | 0 |
| 11 | 835 | 426 | 14 | 0 |
| 12 | 586 | 843 | 6 | 0 |
| 13 | 444 | 391 | 8 | 0 |
| 14 | 240 | 84 | 13 | 1 |
| 15 | 303 | 235 | 9 | 1 |
| 16 | 775 | 520 | 12 | 0 |
| 17 | 136 | 76 | 8 | 1 |
| 18 | 271 | 139 | 11 | 1 |
| 19 | 385 | 165 | 14 | 1 |
| 20 | 451 | 304 | 10 | 0 |

## Initial data analysis

The dot plots in Figure 8.1 give a preliminary view of the individual variation in the variables. We note that there is considerable variation in job times from job to job. Job times vary from less than 150 hours to almost 850 hours. Assuming a 40 hour, five day working week, this approximates to 3½ weeks to 21 weeks. However, note the two jobs at around 800, separated from the remainder whose highest value is less than 600. Judging from the concentration of points at the low end and the spread at the higher end, the distribution appears strongly skewed, with a considerably higher frequency of smaller rather than larger jobs.

The number of units per job ranges from close to 0 to over 800. However, we note that the latter is considerably higher than the rest, whose maximum is around 600. If we regard the number of units as a rough measure of job size, we might anticipate that job times would be proportional to the number of units although, with some of the very small jobs, initial productivity problems might affect the entire job, thus leading to relatively higher job times.

Operations per unit vary from 5 to 16. If we regard the number of operations per unit as a measure of complexity of the job, we would expect job times to increase with the number of operations per unit. Again, Total Operations vary from around 200 to over 6000 and we would expect job times to be roughly proportional. Note the two or three exceptionally high values.

We also note that there are 10 normal and 10 rushed jobs.

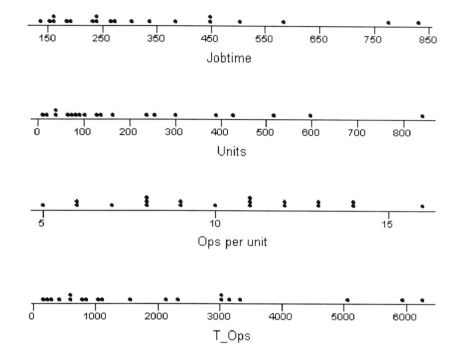

**Figure 8.1**   Dotplots of Job time, Units, Operations per unit and Total operations.

*Time series plots*

With time ordered data, an important view of the data is through time series plots; recall Figures 1.26–1.28 in Chapter 1 where time series plots of the variables involved in the stamp sales case study were informative. Here, the jobs are listed according to the times orders were received. Time series plots are shown in Figure 8.2. It should be noted that, although jobs are evenly spaced along the horizontal axis, the times at which orders were received were almost certainly not evenly spaced.

Apart from noting that bigger jobs appear later in the time order, there is nothing remarkable about these plots.

*Scatterplot matrix*

While these individual summaries provide basic reference information, the key to finding a prediction formula is in the relationships between the variables. When studying relationships between variables, an important graphical display is the *scatterplot matrix,* shown in Figure 8.3 for the Job time data. This is an array of scatterplots of all pairs of variables, arranged by variable in rows and columns, with the scatterplots involving the response variable, Job time, in the top row and scatter-plots involving the remaining variables underneath.

Looking at the first row, there appears to be a strong positive relationship between

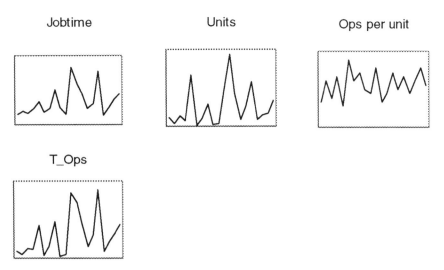

Figure 8.2    Run order plots for Job time, Units, Ops per unit and Total Ops.

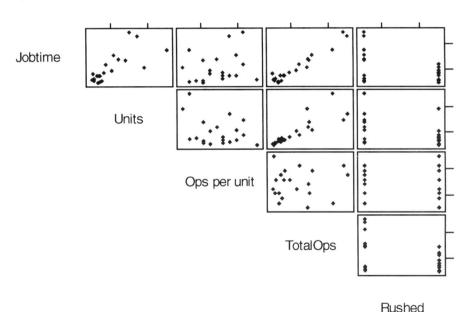

**Figure 8.3**    Scatterplot matrix of Job time, Units, Operations per unit, Total operations and 'Rushed'.

Job time and Units, with two possible exceptional values seen on the right side of the plot. There is no clear relationship between Job time and Operations per Unit. There is a strong relationship between Job time and Total operations. Note the cluster of points in the bottom left corner and the two (or three) separated points in the top right. The scatterplot of Job time against 'Rushed' shows, in effect, dotplots of Job time for the 'Normal' and 'Rushed' jobs. As expected, the Normal jobs (coded 0, on the left) tend to take longer.

Looking at the lower rows, we find a strong correlation between Units and Total operations, but no clear relationship between either and Operations per unit. We also see that Units and Total operations tend to be higher for 'Normal' jobs than for 'Rushed'; this may well explain why 'Normal' jobs take longer.

This view of the relationships between variables gives us preliminary ideas about the importance of the explanatory variables for 'explaining' variation in Job time. It also shows that there are relationships between the explanatory variables themselves. This may cause problems in disentangling their individual explanatory effects.

## 8.2   The multiple linear regression model

The multiple linear regression model suggests that the time to complete a job may be represented as a linear combination of the four explanatory variables, plus chance variation:

$$\text{Job time} = \alpha + \beta_{\text{Units}} \times \text{Units} + \beta_{\text{Ops}} \times \text{Ops} + \beta_{\text{T\_Ops}} \times \text{T\_Ops} + \beta_{\text{Rushed}} \times \text{Rushed} + \varepsilon$$

Here, obvious abbreviations have been used for the names of the explanatory variables. In the equation, $\alpha$ and the $\beta$'s are the *parameters* of the regression model; different values of these parameters give different versions of the model, and different prediction formulas. $\varepsilon$ represents unexplained variation. We assume this to behave like chance variation. As such, it is assumed to follow the Normal model, centred on 0. The corresponding standard deviation, $\sigma$, is a parameter of this Normal model; different values of $\sigma$ correspond to different amounts of spread of unexplained variation.

*A prediction formula for Job time*

Before turning to the details of the model fitting process, we focus first on interpretation of the fitted model. The final choice of values for the regression coefficients will turn out to be

$$\hat{\alpha} = 44, \quad \hat{\beta}_{\text{Units}} = -0.07, \quad \hat{\beta}_{\text{Ops}} = 9.8, \quad \hat{\beta}_{\text{T\_ops}} = 0.10, \quad \hat{\beta}_{\text{Rushed}} = -38$$

with

$$\hat{\sigma} = 7.4.$$

The estimated coefficients are designated as such by a circumflex or 'hat' (^) on top, and are referred to as 'alpha hat', 'beta Units hat', etc.

Substituting these values in the multiple regression model formula leads to the prediction formula

$$\text{Job time} = 44 - 0.07 \times \text{Units} + 9.8 \times \text{Ops} + 0.1 \times \text{T\_Ops} - 38 \times \text{Rushed} \pm 15$$

If we take as a typical job one with 200 units and 10 operations per unit, the prediction interval for Job time is, for a normal job,

$$44 - 0.07 \times 200 + 9.8 \times 10 + 0.1 \times 200 \times 10 - 38 \times 0 \pm 15,$$

that is

$$328 \pm 15,$$

that is

$$313 \text{ to } 343 \text{ hours.}$$

If the job was rushed, the prediction interval would be 38 hours less:

$$44 - 0.07 \times 200 + 9.8 \times 10 + 0.1 \times 200 \times 10 - 38 \times 1 \pm 15$$

which evaluates as

$$290 \pm 15,$$

that is

$$275 \text{ to } 310 \text{ hours.}$$

---

**Exercise 8.1**   Use the prediction formula above to calculate prediction intervals for jobs with the same characteristics as the first three jobs in Table 8.1. How do the actual job times compare?

---

*Indicator variables*

Note how the 'Rushed' variable entered into the prediction formulas. For a normal job, no adjustment was made; for a rushed job, 38 hours were subtracted. This is the result of multiplying the 'Rushed' variable by its estimated regression coefficient:

if Rushed = 0, that is, the job is normal, then $-38 \times$ Rushed = 0,

if Rushed = 1, that is, the job is rushed, then $-38 \times$ Rushed = $-38$.

The variable 'Rushed' is a special kind of variable, called an *indicator variable*.[1] It has only two possible values, 0 and 1. A value of 1 indicates that the corresponding job is rushed; a value of zero indicates normal.

**The least squares method**

We need to develop a basis for choosing and validating prediction formulas such as those exemplified above. The first step is to find a way of arriving at estimates for the regression coefficients. To do this, we seek the prediction formula that best matches the historical data, using the least squares criterion. This is a straightforward extension of the least squares method as applied to simple linear regression in Chapter 6.

---

[1]   Such variables were first encountered in Section 1.7, pages 48–49, where their values indicated the appropriate season of the year.

*Fitted values*

Given values for the estimated regression coefficients $\hat{\alpha}$, $\hat{\beta}_{Units}$, $\hat{\beta}_{Ops}$, $\hat{\beta}_{T\_Ops}$ and $\hat{\beta}_{Rushed}$, we can apply those values to the successive values of the explanatory variables, resulting in a set of *fitted values* which are represented as

$$\hat{J}_1 = \hat{\alpha} + \hat{\beta}_{Units} \times Units_1 + \hat{\beta}_{Ops} \times Ops_1 + \hat{\beta}_{T\_Ops} \times T\_Ops_1 + \hat{\beta}_{Rushed} \times Rushed_1,$$
$$\hat{J}_2 = \hat{\alpha} + \hat{\beta}_{Units} \times Units_2 + \hat{\beta}_{Ops} \times Ops_2 + \hat{\beta}_{T\_Ops} \times T\_Ops_2 + \hat{\beta}_{Rushed} \times Rushed_2,$$
$$\hat{J}_3 = \hat{\alpha} + \hat{\beta}_{Units} \times Units_3 + \hat{\beta}_{Ops} \times Ops_3 + \hat{\beta}_{T\_Ops} \times T\_Ops_3 + \hat{\beta}_{Rushed} \times Rushed_3,$$

$$\hat{J}_{20} = \hat{\alpha} + \hat{\beta}_{Units} \times Units_{20} + \hat{\beta}_{Ops} \times Ops_{20} + \hat{\beta}_{T\_Ops} \times T\_Ops_{20} + \hat{\beta}_{Rushed} \times Rushed_{20}$$

Here, $\hat{J}$ represents *fitted job time*, that is, the value of job time given by the *fitted model*, and $\hat{J}_1$, $\hat{J}_2$, $\hat{J}_3$, ... $\hat{J}_{20}$ represent the successive fitted Job time values for the 20 jobs. $Units_1$, $Units_2$, $Units_3$, ... , $Units_{20}$ represent the successive values of Units for the 20 jobs, and similarly for Ops, T_Ops and Rushed.

---

**Exercise 8.2**   Three sets of trial values for the regression coefficients, corresponding to candidate formulas that will arise later, are as follows

(i)   $\alpha = 77$, $\beta_{Units} = -0.15$, $\beta_{Ops} = 7.2$, $\beta_{T\_Ops} = 0.11$, $\beta_{Rushed} = -25$;
(ii)  $\alpha = 42$, $\beta_{Units} = -0.08$, $\beta_{Ops} = 10$, $\beta_{T\_Ops} = 0.11$, $\beta_{Rushed} = -38$;
(iii) $\alpha = 44$, $\beta_{Units} = -0.07$, $\beta_{Ops} = 9.8$, $\beta_{T\_Ops} = 0.10$, $\beta_{Rushed} = -38$;

set (iii) is the final choice introduced earlier.
    Substitute the data from the first three jobs in Table 8.1 into each of the corresponding prediction formulas and calculate the corresponding fitted values.

---

*Residuals*

The idea behind the least squares method is to seek values for $\alpha$, $\beta_{Units}$, $\beta_{Ops}$, $\beta_{T\_Ops}$ and $\beta_{Rushed}$ which minimise the set of *residuals*

$$e_1 = Job\ time_1 - \hat{J}_1,$$
$$e_2 = Job\ time_2 - \hat{J}_2,$$
$$e_3 = Job\ time_3 - \hat{J}_3,$$

$$e_{20} = Job\ time_{20} - \hat{J}_{20},$$

that is, deviations of successive fitted values from corresponding values of Job time, for the 20 jobs involved in the study.

**Exercise 8.3**   For each of formulas (i), (ii) and (iii) in Exercise 8.2, calculate the residuals for the first three jobs in Table 8.1. Compare the sizes of the residuals calculated using the three formulas. On the basis of these sets of residuals, which formula is best? Which is worst?

In the case of simple linear regression, we were able to illustrate such deviations or residuals, calculated from trial values of the parameters, on a scatterplot; recall Figure 6.4, page 194. That form of visualisation is not possible here; there are too many variables. However, we can illustrate the residuals separately, as shown in Figure 8.4.

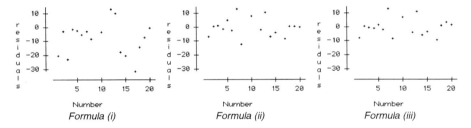

**Figure 8.4**   Residuals from three prediction formulas.

Clearly, formula (i) produces much larger residuals, that is, deviations from actual Job time, than either formula (ii) or formula (iii). There is little to choose between the latter.

The least squares method seeks the values of $\alpha$, $\beta_{\text{Units}}$, $\beta_{\text{Ops}}$, $\beta_{\text{T\_Ops}}$ and $\beta_{\text{Rushed}}$ which minimise the sum of the squares of the residuals, that is,

$$\Sigma e_i^2 = \Sigma[\text{Observed Job times} - \text{Fitted Job times}]^2$$
$$= \Sigma[\text{Job time}_i - (\alpha + \beta_{\text{Units}} \times \text{Units}_i + \beta_{\text{Ops}} \times \text{Ops}_i + \beta_{\text{T\_Ops}} \times \text{T\_Ops}_i + \beta_{\text{Rushed}} \times \text{Rushed}_i)]^2,$$

where the sum extends over the 20 jobs, $i = 1, 2, \ldots, 20$. The solution to this mathematical optimisation problem may be found using differential calculus or appropriate algebraic manipulations. It is possible to write down algebraic formulas for the solution; however, that will not be done here. Instead, we rely on a suitable software package to provide the numerical solutions for us. In fact, if we enter the observed data into the software and select the regression option, we find the following output.

```
Dependent variable is:    Jobtime
No Selector
R squared = 97.3%      R squared (adjusted) = 96.6%
s =  37.46  with  20 - 5 = 15  degrees of freedom
```

| Source | Sum of Squares | df | Mean Square | F-ratio |
|---|---|---|---|---|
| Regression | 756055 | 4 | 189014 | 135 |
| Residual | 21050.1 | 15 | 1403.34 | |

| Variable | Coefficient | s.e. of Coeff | t-ratio | prob |
|---|---|---|---|---|
| Constant | 77.2415 | 44.76 | 1.73 | 0.1049 |
| Units | -0.150744 | 0.1121 | -1.34 | 0.1989 |
| Ops | 7.15154 | 4.305 | 1.66 | 0.1174 |
| T_Ops | 0.114596 | 0.01322 | 8.67 | ≤ 0.0001 |
| Rushed | -24.9441 | 19.11 | -1.31 | 0.2115 |

## *The least squares prediction formula*

From the bottom left corner of the computer output, we find the *estimated* regression coefficients to be

$$\hat{\alpha} \quad = \quad 77,$$
$$\hat{\beta}_{\text{Units}} \quad = \quad -0.15,$$
$$\hat{\beta}_{\text{Ops}} \quad = \quad 7.2,$$
$$\hat{\beta}_{\text{T-Ops}} \quad = \quad 0.11,$$
$$\hat{\beta}_{\text{Rushed}} \quad = \quad -25,$$

with appropriate rounding. The corresponding prediction formula is, symbolically,

$$\hat{J} = \hat{\alpha} + \hat{\beta}_{\text{Units}} \times \text{Units}_1 + \hat{\beta}_{\text{Ops}} \times \text{Ops} + \hat{\beta}_{\text{T\_Ops}} \times \text{T\_Ops} + \hat{\beta}_{\text{Rushed}} \times \text{Rushed},$$

that is,

Predicted Job time $= 77 - 0.15 \times \text{Units} + 7.2 \times \text{Ops} + 0.11 \times \text{T\_Ops} - 25 \times \text{Rushed}$.

This is formula (i) encountered in Exercise 8.2.

---

**Exercise 8.4**   Equipped with such a formula, the company can anticipate the job times for a range of jobs. Use the least squares prediction
formula given above to calculate the predicted job times for small,
medium and large jobs, defined as 100 units and five operations per
unit, 300 units and 10 operations per unit, 500 units and 15 operations
per unit respectively. Calculate predictions for both rushed and normal
jobs.

---

## Assessing uncertainty

As with the simple linear regression model, the next step is to assess the uncertainty
associated with these estimated coefficient values and with predictions made using
this prediction formula. In the multiple linear regression model the uncertainty is represented by the chance component $\varepsilon$. In many problems, it is reasonable to assume
that the values taken on by $\varepsilon$ are generated by a process for which the Normal model

for chance variation is appropriate, with mean 0 and some standard deviation, $\sigma$, to be estimated from the data to hand.

The residuals from the fitted model provide a basis for estimating $\sigma$, the standard deviation of the chance variation component of the model. In fact, the equation defining the residuals can be written

$$\text{Residual} = \text{Job time} - \text{Fitted Job time,}$$

which can be rewritten as

$$\text{Job time} = \text{Fitted Job time} + \text{Residual}$$

or, symbolically,

$$\text{Job time} = \hat{\alpha} + \hat{\beta}_{\text{Units}} \times \text{Units} + \hat{\beta}_{\text{Ops}} \times \text{Ops} + \hat{\beta}_{\text{T\_Ops}} \times \text{T\_Ops} + \hat{\beta}_{\text{Rushed}} \times \text{Rushed} + e,$$

This echoes the original model formula,

$$\text{Job time} = \alpha + \beta_{\text{Units}} \times \text{Units} + \beta_{\text{Ops}} \times \text{Ops} + \beta_{\text{T\_Ops}} \times \text{T\_Ops} + \beta_{\text{rushed}} \times \text{Rushed} + \varepsilon.$$

We may view the calculated residuals, $e_1$ to $e_{20}$, as historical data on $\varepsilon$, the chance component of the model and view their calculated standard deviation as an estimate for $\sigma$. The calculated standard deviation of the residuals is given by $s$ in the fourth row of the computer output on page 257; $s = 37.46$ in this case.[2]

### Prediction error

As in simple linear regression, we need to allow for prediction error when predicting a new value for Job time; it is not enough to calculate a value from the prediction formula. As in simple linear regression, a commonly used simplified error band is $\pm 2s$. Applying this to the prediction of Job time calculated in Exercise 8.4 above for small jobs, that is, jobs of 100 units each requiring five manufacturing operations gives

$$155 \pm 2 \times 37.5 \text{ for normal,} \qquad 130 \pm 2 \times 37.5 \text{ for rushed,}$$

that is

$$80 \text{ to } 230 \text{ for normal,} \qquad 55 \text{ to } 205 \text{ for rushed.}$$

These intervals are disappointingly wide. Assuming a working week of 40 hours, the interval width is almost four weeks. This is not very useful to a customer preparing a work schedule.

---

[2]   The reference to degrees of freedom in the computer output is a technical one. The mathematical derivation of the five regression coefficient estimates involves the solution of five algebraic equations involving the residuals. The fact that the residuals satisfy these five equations places five constraints on the residuals. Mathematically, they are not free to vary; they have lost five 'degrees of freedom',

one for each equation. This is reflected in the formula for $s$: $s = \sqrt{\dfrac{\sum e_i^2}{n-5}}$. Note that $\bar{e}$ does not occur

in the sum of squares part of the formula, as in a normal standard deviation formula. This is because one of the equations specifies that the sum of the residuals is 0. Note also the divisor of $n - 5$; because five degrees of freedom are 'lost', there are, in a mathematical sense, only $n - 5$ squared deviations to be averaged.

### Assessing statistical significance of regression coefficient estimates

The regression output on page 257 which shows the estimates of the regression coefficients also shows their estimated standard errors, $t$-values for testing their statistical significance and corresponding p-values. A similar interpretation applies to these quantities as to the corresponding quantities in Chapter 6. The argument is as follows.

The standard error of an estimate reflects the extent of chance variation affecting that estimate. Using the multiple regression model implies assuming that there are ideal values for the regression coefficients which characterise the relationship between Job time and the explanatory variables. We have sampled the Job time process and observed corresponding data on the explanatory variables. On the basis of the twenty sets of measurements available, we have calculated *estimates* of the ideal regression coefficients. However, as the observed data are subject to chance variation, so are the coefficient estimates based on the data. Thus, $\hat{\beta}_{Units} = -0.15$ is an estimate of $\beta_{Units}$. As such, being based on chance data, it is also subject to chance variation, and this is reflected in its standard error, the standard deviation of its sampling distribution. The value of the standard error reported here is

$$SE(\hat{\beta}_{Units}) = 0.11$$

The reported $t$-value is the ratio of the estimate to its standard error and tests the statistical significance of the deviation of the estimate from 0. If $\beta_{Units}$ is 0, then Units has no role in the regression model. Here, the $t$-value of $-1.32$ indicates that the deviation of $\hat{\beta}_{Units}$ from 0 can be explained in terms of chance variation and suggests that Units can be excluded from the model. This is reflected in the corresponding relatively large p-value of 0.1, or 10%. (Recall that p-values are discussed in Section 5.2.)

Corresponding assessments of the other parameter estimates suggest that $\hat{\beta}_{Ops}$ and $\hat{\beta}_{Rushed}$ are also not statistically significant while $\hat{\beta}_{T-Ops}$ is highly statistically significant.

*A cautionary note*

On the basis of this analysis, it may be suggested that $\beta_{Units}$, $\beta_{Ops}$ and $\beta_{Results}$ should be removed from the equation, leaving us with a simple linear regression which is much easier to handle and to interpret. However, this is unwise for at least two reasons. In the first place, we have already noted the relationships between explanatory variables. When explanatory variables are correlated, their individual effects on the response variable are difficult to disentangle. Such relationships affect the regression coefficient estimates and their standard errors which can, therefore, be misleading.

Secondly, data such as these frequently include cases that do not fit the pattern of the rest, as we have seen several times. Including such exceptional cases in the model fitting process will lead to biased estimates of the model parameters and, therefore, a biased prediction formula. It will also lead to an inflated estimate of $\sigma$, the error process standard deviation and also, therefore, of the coefficient standard errors. Both biases can substantially affect $t$-values, and related interpretations.

Checking for the presence of such exceptional cases and patterns is a little more sophisticated when there are several variables involved than it is in the simpler situations dealt with up to now. The tools appropriate for making such checks are referred to as *regression diagnostics* and are the subject of the next section.

## 8.3  Regression diagnostics

With simple linear regression, a quick look at the scatterplot will indicate whether there are any exceptional cases that do not conform to the simple linear model. With multiple regression, this simple diagnostic tool is not sufficient and may be mislead-ing.[3] Instead, a more sophisticated approach based on the residuals is required. The residuals reflect departures of the data from the fitted regression model. Ideally, the residuals will reflect just chance variation. This implies that they should be centred on 0 and that the pattern of variation around 0 should appear haphazard. Exceptional cases that do not conform to this pattern represent departures of the data from the linear regression model that are not due to chance variation and, therefore, must be

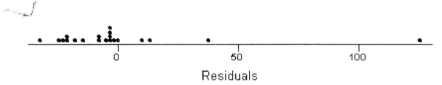

**Figure 8.5**  Dotplot of residuals.

due to some assignable cause, in Shewhart's terminology. Such causes of variation need investigation and possible action.

The simplest approach to identifying the presence of exceptional cases is make a dotplot of the residuals. Figure 8.5 shows the result.

This clearly shows the presence of an exceptional case, represented by the dot on the right. In the case of simple linear regression, a residual dotplot such as this would correspond to a scatterplot such as that shown in Figure 8.6. As discussed in Chapter 6, this exceptional case cannot be accommodated by the simple linear regression model; it must be deleted and dealt with separately. In the present case, a similar conclusion applies: the exceptional point cannot be accommodated by the multiple linear regression model; it must be deleted and dealt with separately.

The scatterplot in Figure 8.6 provides us with some additional information which may be helpful in attempting to discover the 'assignable cause' that creates the exception. We see that the exceptional case, when referred to the $X$ axis or the $Y$ axis individually, is not exceptional. This suggests that either the $X$ value, though small, is not exceptional but, given that value, the $Y$ value is exceptionally large, or, vice versa, the $Y$ value, though large, is not exceptional but, given that value, the $X$ value

---

[3]  In particular, the plots in the scatterplot matrix of Figure 8.3 show cases that appear exceptional there, in the context of a series of simple linear regressions, but, as will be seen, are not exceptional in the context of a multiple linear regression model. It will also be seen that the most exceptional case identified here does not appear to be particularly exceptional in the scatterplot matrix. These points will be dealt with later, in the light of the analysis that is to follow.

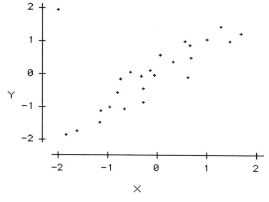

**Figure 8.6** Scatterplot based on artificial data with a highly exceptional case.

is exceptionally small. In a real study, such information gives us a starting point for seeking an explanation for the exception.

A plot that is frequently found to be helpful in this way in the context of multiple regression is the so-called *diagnostic plot*.

## The diagnostic plot

The scatterplot of residuals against fitted values is shown in Figure 8.7 for the model fitted to the job times data in the previous section. The fitted values are included in the plot because it is often the case that unusual patterns in the residuals are related to the response variable and this relationship will be seen in a plot of the residuals against the fitted response values. Knowledge of such a relationship can be helpful in diagnosing the 'assignable cause' of an unusual pattern.

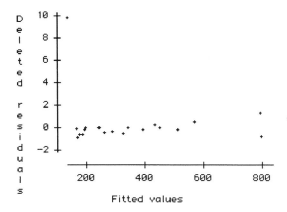

**Figure 8.7** Job time diagnostic plot.

Note that it is *deleted residuals* that are plotted. These are specially standardised versions of the residuals[4] which should follow the *standard* Normal model. Thus, their values should be centred on 0, most of their values (95%) should fall between −2 and +2 and almost all values (99.7%) should fall between −3 and +3.

From this it follows that the expected pattern in the diagnostic plot of Figure 8.7, assuming that the multiple regression model fits the data well, is haphazard variation above and below 0, with most if not all of the 20 residuals lying between −2 and +2.

Clearly, there is an exceptional case in Figure 8.7; the case at the top left of the diagnostic plot is almost 10 standard deviations from 0. Looking at the remaining cases, there are two on the right that show rather more residual variation than the rest.

When considering how to react to these observations, we must keep in mind that a single highly exceptional case such as that in the top left of Figure 8.7 will seriously bias the multiple linear model. We can illustrate this effect in the case of a simple linear regression model.

### Illustrating the effect of an outlier via simple linear regression

Figure 8.8 shows a scatterplot of artificial data, with a strong linear pattern and an obvious exception. It also shows the diagnostic plot for the corresponding simple linear regression, with the exceptional case showing as a large deviation on the residual scale.

The scatterplot shows the regression line based on the data excluding the exceptional case, passing through the middle of the main scatter, and also the regression based on all the data, which is biased upwards on the left side and downwards on the right. This bias occurs because the least squares criterion is heavily influenced by the deviation of the line from the exceptional case; moving the line closer to the exceptional cases reduces this influence.

The bias seen in the scatterplot in Figure 8.8 is reflected in the diagnostic plot, which shows a slight upward trend from left to right in the non-exceptional residuals.

An identical effect is observed in the diagnostic plot shown in Figure 8.7. We may infer a similar bias in the prediction formula fitted to the full dataset. Although we have no explanation available to us for this exceptional behaviour, it does not make sense to include the exceptional case in fitting the multiple linear regression model as it will result in a biased fit. Consequently, we should delete that case and refit.

When seeking an explanation for the exception, we might start by noting that the fitted value was low, suggesting that this was a small job that took an exceptionally long time to complete, for such jobs.

---

[4]    The use of deleted residuals is another application of the deletion principle already encountered in Chapter 4, in calculating $\sigma$ for setting up control charts. Here, each of the residuals is subject to chance variation and this is reflected in its standard error. The standardised residual is the residual divided by its standard error. The formula for this involves $\sigma$. Including an exceptional case will bias the calculation of the standardised residual, with the effect of reducing its exceptional appearance. Consequently, when standardising a residual for inclusion in the diagnostic plot, the corresponding case is deleted from the data before the necessary calculations are done.

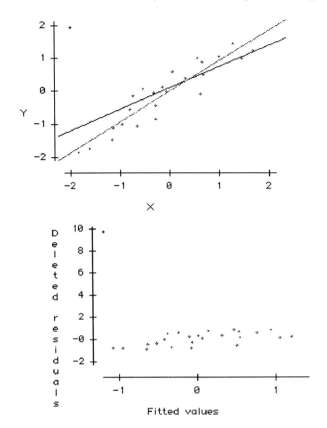

**Figure 8.8** Scatterplot and diagnostic plot for artificial data.

**Exercise 8.5** In subsequent analysis, we will find that the exceptional case in the top left of Figure 8.7 corresponds to case number 9. From Table 8.1 find the corresponding values for each of the variables. Use the least squares prediction formula to calculate the fitted value and, hence, the residual for case 9.

**Additional diagnostic tools**

Before proceeding to refit, we introduce two additional diagnostic tools, designed to check other assumptions of the linear model. The first is a Normal plot, to check Normality of residuals. Significance tests, confidence intervals and, more critically, prediction intervals depend on Normality of the error component, $\varepsilon$, in the multiple linear regression model. The residuals reflect the variation associated with $\varepsilon$ and so a Normal plot of residuals provides a useful check on the Normality assumption.

The second additional plot is a time series plot of residuals, designed to check for any effects related to the order of the cases. This plot is used to detect serial correlation, that is, correlations between successive cases. Such a correlation pattern will mean that successive residuals will tend to have similar values (assuming positive correlation), thus reducing the apparent extent of chance variation. This means that prediction intervals will be narrower than they should be, resulting in over-optimistic predictions. (It also means that the prediction formula is less than optimal, but this is a less serious problem.)

Figure 8.9 shows the Normal plot and time series plot for the deleted residuals.

Both plots reflect the presence of the exceptional case already detected. There is a suggestion in the Normal plot of curvature in the remaining cases when a linear pattern is expected, assuming Normality. There are also suggestions of runs of similarly valued residuals in the time series plot, suggesting an order effect. However, both plots could be considerably distorted by the presence of the exceptional case, so any judgement on these possible effects should be suspended until this case has been deleted.

Note also that the time series plot assists us in identifying the exceptional case; it is case number 9.

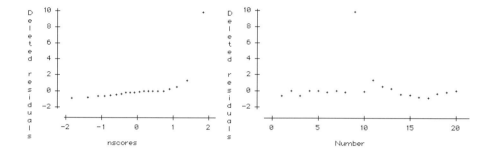

**Figure 8.9**   Normal plot and time series plot for deleted residuals.

### Reviewing the diagnosis

These relatively simple diagnostic devices have revealed a number of potential problems with fitting this model to these data. There is a clear exceptional case. There are two cases, corresponding to larger jobs, with apparently more variation than the remaining cases. There is possible non-linearity in the Normal plot and possible evidence of order effects in the time series plot.

The most severe problem is the exceptional residual of case 9. Experience shows that extreme cases such as this can cause apparent problems in other areas as well. Hence, it makes sense to deal with this problem first. Accordingly, case 9 is deleted from the data and the entire analysis, regression and diagnostics, repeated.

## 8.4   Iterating the analysis

The regression output resulting from fitting the regression model to the 19 cases with case 9 deleted follows.

```
Dependent variable is:                   Jobtime
No Selector
20 total cases of which 1 is missing
R squared = 99.7%      R squared (adjusted) = 99.6%
s =  13.8  with  19 - 5 = 14  degrees of freedom

Source        Sum of Squares    df    Mean Square    F-ratio
Regression    767198            4     191799         1.01e3
Residual      2664.31           14    190.308

Variable    Coefficient    s.e. of Coeff    t-ratio      prob
Constant    41.7152        16.87            2.47         0.0269
Units       -0.0834938     0.04186          -1.99        0.0659
Ops         10.0215        1.612            6.22         ≤ 0.0001
T_Ops       0.110016       0.004891         22.5         ≤ 0.0001
Rushed      -38.2167       7.166            -5.33        0.0001
```

The revised regression coefficient estimates may be read from the bottom left corner of the output. They are shown in Table 8.2 along with the original estimates, based on the full dataset, for ease of comparison.

**Table 8.2**  Coefficient estimates from two fits

| Coefficient | $\alpha$ | $\beta_{Units}$ | $\beta_{Ops}$ | $\beta_{T\_Ops}$ | $\beta_{Rushed}$ |
|---|---|---|---|---|---|
| Original fit | 77 | −0.15 | 7.2 | 0.11 | −25 |
| Revised fit | 42 | −0.08 | 100 | 0.11 | −38 |
| Difference | 35 | 0.07 | 2.8 | 0 | 13 |
| Revised s.e. | 17 | 0.04 | 1.6 | 0.005 | 7 |

Substantial changes are evident, with the intercept ($\hat{\alpha}$) and $\hat{\beta}_{Units}$ reduced in magnitude by almost half, $\hat{\beta}_{Ops}$ and $\hat{\beta}_{Rushed}$ increased by almost half, while $\hat{\beta}_{T\_Ops}$ remains unchanged. On the other hand, comparing the changes to the corresponding standard error, the changes appear only marginally statistically significant, by the usual criterion.[5] However, this will change; in a later fit, a smaller estimated standard deviation will emerge.

We can assess the effects of these changes on prediction by calculating new predicted job times for small, medium and large jobs and comparing them with the corresponding predictions using the original prediction formula as calculated in Exercise 8.4. The results are shown in Table 8.3.

For normal jobs, predictions are reduced for small jobs, unchanged for medium jobs and increased for large jobs. For rushed jobs, all predictions are reduced, with those for smaller jobs being more substantially reduced. These changes reflect the removal of the bias towards the exceptional case seen in the diagnostic plot of Figure 8.5. Note, however, that, in parallel with the changes in the coefficients, the biggest change is not much bigger than prediction error

---

[5]  This informal 'test' is equivalent to using a popular diagnostic test statistic called DFFITS. Details are given in the Supplements and Extensions page of the book's website.

**Table 8.3**  Original and revised predicted job times for small, medium and large jobs

|        |          | Small | Medium | Large |
|--------|----------|-------|--------|-------|
| Normal | Original | 155   | 447    | 969   |
|        | Revised  | 138   | 447    | 975   |
| Rushed | Original | 130   | 422    | 944   |
|        | Revised  | 100   | 409    | 937   |

### Revised prediction error

Returning to the revised regression output, note that the value for $s$, the estimate of $\sigma$, is reduced by a factor of almost 3, to 13.8. This makes for a major improvement in prediction interval width. Thus, predictions may now be claimed to be within 3–4 days of actual, assuming a 40 hour week of five 8 hour days, with 95% confidence.

Before accepting these revised estimates, however, we need to run the diagnostic checks again.

### Revised diagnostics

Figure 8.10 shows revised diagnostics, the diagnostic plot, a Normal plot and a time series plot, for the residuals and fitted values calculated from the revised regression.

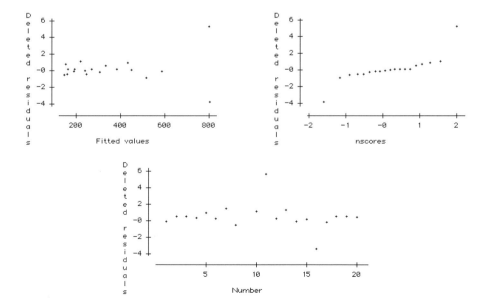

**Figure 8.10**   Job times diagnostics, case 9 deleted.

The diagnostic plot now reveals two exceptional cases, with deleted residuals of around −4 and +5, respectively. We see from the diagnostic plot that these are associated with the two longest jobs, with fitted job times of around 800 hours or 20 weeks; the next longest job is less than 600 hours, or 15 weeks. This suggests the possibility that long jobs are subject to more variation than shorter jobs although, with such little evidence, we are not in a position to come to any conclusion on this. Nevertheless, these two jobs clearly do not fit the pattern of the rest. Accordingly, it makes sense to delete these jobs and refit, keeping in mind, however, that any revised prediction formula may not be appropriate for longer jobs.

### A further iteration

From the run chart in Figure 8.10, we see that the cases for deletion are cases 11 and 16. The results and diagnostics from the third fit are shown in Figure 8.11. There is nothing remarkable about the diagnostics. Consequently, we accept the regression output as satisfying the model assumptions. Table 8.2 is extended in Table 8.4 to

**Table 8.4**  Coefficient estimates from three fits

| Coefficient | $\alpha$ | $\beta_{Units}$ | $\beta_{Ops}$ | $\beta_{T\_Ops}$ | $\beta_{Rushed}$ |
|---|---|---|---|---|---|
| Original fit | 77 | −0.15 | 7.2 | 0.11 | −25 |
| Revised fit | 42 | −0.08 | 10 | 0.11 | −38 |
| Final fit | 44 | −0.07 | 9.8 | 0.11 | −38 |
| Final s.e. | 9 | 0.03 | 0.9 | 0.004 | 4 |

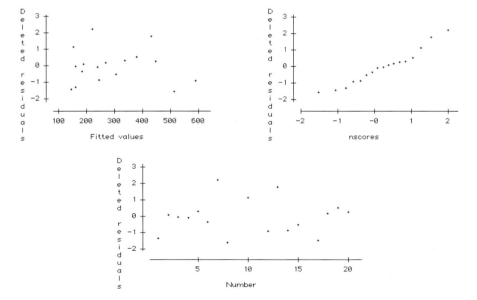

**Figure 8.11**  Job times diagnostics, cases 9, 11 and 16 deleted.

include the coefficient estimates from the final fit, with corresponding standard errors. There is very little difference between the revised and final coefficient estimates. In retrospect, this makes sense. Visualise a simple linear regression with two exceptional cases with similar $X$ values and with $Y$ values on either side of the fitted regression line and equidistant from it; deleting them will make little or no difference to the fit.

```
Dependent variable is:                    Jobtime
No Selector
20 total cases of which 3 are missing
R squared = 99.8%       R squared (adjusted) = 99.7%
s =  7.413  with   17 - 5 = 12   degrees of freedom

Source        Sum of Squares    df    Mean Square    F-ratio
Regression    299165             4       74791.2      1.36e3
Residual      659.381           12       54.9484

Variable      Coefficient    s.e. of Coeff    t-ratio      prob
Constant      44.2165        9.08              4.87       0.0004
Units         -0.0693069     0.02853          -2.43       0.0318
Ops           9.82859        0.8873           11.1      ≤ 0.0001
T_Ops         0.107795       0.004114         26.2      ≤ 0.0001
Rushed        -37.9601       3.857            -9.84     ≤ 0.0001
```

What is different is the estimated standard deviation, $s$, whose value has been almost halved from 13.8 to 7.4. Predictions can now be made with prediction limits of $\pm 2$ working days, with 95% confidence. However, while we can make predictions which are likely to be valid for small, medium and large jobs, the associated prediction limits are valid for small and medium jobs but not for large jobs. Further investigation is needed to check whether the wider spread for large (long) jobs encountered in these data persists and, if so, why, and what can be done to improve it. However, this is beyond the scope of the present study.

---

**Exercise 8.6**   Extend Table 8.3 to include predictions based on the final fit. Compare and contrast.

---

## 8.5   Alternative measures of goodness of fit

The regression output displayed in earlier sections includes, along with $s$ and the regression coefficients, additional features which we have not discussed. Specifically, it includes values of 'R-squared' and 'R-squared (adjusted)', in the line above the line showing the value for s, and, below that line, a table called the 'analysis of variance' table. The latter need not concern us here.

R-squared may be interpreted as the proportion of variation in actual job times which is explained by the variation in the explanatory variables, through the fitted job time values. In the final fit, we see that 99.8% of the variation in job times is explained by the variation in the numbers of units per job, the numbers of operations per unit, the total numbers of operations per job and whether the job was normal or rushed. In most applications, 99.8% would be regarded as highly satisfactory.

However, neither R-squared nor R-squared (adjusted) are entirely satisfactory. The reader is referred to the discussion in Section 6.4, pages 211–2, concerning arbitrariness in setting criteria for satisfactory values of the correlation coefficient, $r$. In simple linear regression, R-squared is simply the square of $r$.

*Reduction in prediction error*

The ultimate problem with R-squared and R-squared (adjusted) is the lack of an operational interpretation. This is overcome by focusing on the value of $s$, the estimated standard deviation of chance variation, which determines the width of the standard prediction interval. As noted earlier, the value of $s$ in the first fit was impractically large; predicting time to complete a job to within two weeks is not very useful to a customer with a tight schedule to meet. On the other hand, the value of $s = 7.4$ from the final fit is much more satisfactory.

There is another interpretation of $s$ that is related to that of R-squared (adjusted). In the absence of any explanatory variables, the best prediction of job times would be the average of the observed job times, while the best estimate of $\sigma$, the standard deviation of chance variation, would be that based on the observed job times, $\hat{\sigma}_{\text{Jobtime}}$, so that the naive prediction interval calculated in the absence of explanatory variables would be

$$\text{Average(Job time)} \pm 2 \times \hat{\sigma}_{\text{Jobtime}}.$$

Expressing $s$ as a proportion of $\hat{\sigma}_{\text{Jobtime}}$ thus shows the reduction in prediction error achieved by using the explanatory variables. Similarly, values of $s$ from successive equations can be compared with each other.

In the first fit, $s$ was 37.5. Calculating $\hat{\sigma}_{\text{Jobtime}}$ from all the data gives $\hat{\sigma}_{\text{Jobtime}} = 202$. Thus, introducing the explanatory variables gives a reduction in prediction error by a factor of more than 5. In the final fit, $s$ was 7.4, $\hat{\sigma}_{\text{Jobtime}}$ based on the data with the three exceptional cases removed was 137, so the prediction error was reduced by a factor of almost 20. Similarly, moving from the first equation to the final fit brought a reduction by a factor of around 5.

While these statistical measures of goodness of prediction are qualitatively helpful, the ultimate criterion is by reference to the requirements of the user of the prediction. In this case, the final fit provided a useful prediction in this regard.

## 8.6 Outlining the model fitting and testing procedure

In this section, we outline the steps taken in a standard regression analysis.

Step 1: Initial data analysis:
- standard single variable summaries, to determine the extent of variation in the variables and possible exceptional values;
- a scatterplot matrix, to view pair-wise relationships between the response and the

explanatory variables and to view pair-wise relationships between the explanatory variables themselves.

Step 2: Least squares fit and interpretation:
• calculate the best fitting regression coefficients, check meaningfulness and statistical significance;
• calculate $s$, check its usefulness for prediction, and its usefulness relative to alternative estimates of the standard deviation of chance variation.

Step 3: Diagnostic analysis of residuals:
• diagnostic plot, check for exceptional residuals or patterns of residuals and possible explanations in terms of the fitted values;
• Normal plot, check for exceptional residuals or non-linear patterns in the residuals;
• where appropriate, time series chart, check for patterns of residual variation related to case order, particularly tracking of successive residuals.

Step 4: Iterate fit and check:
• determine cases for deletion, and repeat steps 2 and 3 until checks are passed.

## 8.7    Another application: the stamp sales case study

In Section 1.6, the problem of forecasting annual postage stamp sales was addressed. Three variables, thought to be related to stamp sales, were chosen as predictors, Gross National Product (GNP), Real Letter Price (RLP) and Real Phone Charge (RPC). The relevant data are reproduced in Table 8.5.

We have already undertaken some initial data analysis in Section 1.6. Here, we consolidate that in the manner applied to the job times study.

### Initial data analysis

Dotplots of the four variables follow in Figure 8.12. Most remarkable is the exceptionally low value of stamp sales. Referring to Table 8.12, this corresponds to the year 1979 when, as already noted in Section 1.6, there was an industrial dispute which badly affected sales in that year. There also appear to be two well separated subsets in each of RLP and RPC.

### *Time series plots*

Time series plots of the four variables are shown in Figure 8.13. There are clear trends in all four plots. Up to 1961, there was an upward trend in stamp sales, ended by a large drop in 1962. Sales remained more or less steady from then until 1968, which marked the beginning of a strong negative trend until 1983, punctuated by the large drop in 1979 due to the industrial dispute in that year. GNP shows three phases, a slow upward trend to 1958, a faster trend to 1966 and a further increase in trend from 1967 onwards. It is tempting to associate the three phases of change in stamp

**Table 8.5**  Annual postage stamp sales, GNP, Real Letter Prices and Real Phone Charges, 1949–83

| Year | Stamp sales | GNP | RLP[a] | RPC[b] |
|------|------|------|------|------|
| 1949 | 245.2 | 552.6 | 1.047 | 0.419 |
| 1950 | 224.4 | 557 | 1.031 | 0.413 |
| 1951 | 241.3 | 564.3 | 0.957 | 0.383 |
| 1952 | 251.3 | 580.1 | 0.88 | 0.352 |
| 1953 | 236.7 | 598.1 | 0.946 | 0.501 |
| 1954 | 231.6 | 603.9 | 0.998 | 0.499 |
| 1955 | 235.8 | 616 | 0.974 | 0.487 |
| 1956 | 253 | 608.3 | 0.934 | 0.622 |
| 1957 | 262.6 | 611.8 | 0.897 | 0.598 |
| 1958 | 265.4 | 600.9 | 0.859 | 0.572 |
| 1959 | 266 | 626.6 | 0.859 | 0.572 |
| 1960 | 278.4 | 658.9 | 0.855 | 0.57 |
| 1961 | 277.7 | 690.9 | 0.832 | 0.554 |
| 1962 | 235.9 | 716 | 0.997 | 0.532 |
| 1963 | 230 | 749.6 | 1.039 | 0.519 |
| 1964 | 234.8 | 780.7 | 1.113 | 0.73 |
| 1965 | 228.8 | 800.7 | 1.158 | 0.695 |
| 1966 | 230.1 | 806.8 | 1.124 | 0.675 |
| 1967 | 234.3 | 848.4 | 1.09 | 0.654 |
| 1968 | 238.6 | 919.4 | 1.04 | 0.624 |
| 1969 | 242.7 | 970.7 | 1.164 | 0.582 |
| 1970 | 226.4 | 1,002.6 | 1.206 | 0.714 |
| 1971 | 199.4 | 1,037.3 | 1.57 | 0.655 |
| 1972 | 205.4 | 1,112.5 | 1.453 | 0.603 |
| 1973 | 201.6 | 1,154.5 | 1.464 | 0.541 |
| 1974 | 191.1 | 1,201.7 | 1.526 | 0.557 |
| 1975 | 181 | 1,223.5 | 1.616 | 0.544 |
| 1976 | 174.9 | 1,229.7 | 1.764 | 0.626 |
| 1977 | 181 | 1,316.2 | 1.677 | 0.551 |
| 1978 | 188.2 | 1,388.4 | 1.598 | 0.639 |
| 1979 | 112.5 | 1,422.8 | 1.526 | 0.564 |
| 1980 | 163.7 | 1,462.2 | 1.607 | 0.577 |
| 1981 | 162.1 | 1,492.6 | 1.835 | 0.58 |
| 1982 | 148.9 | 1,473.2 | 2.114 | 0.601 |
| 1983 | 151.2 | 1,462.6 | 1.993 | 0.651 |

[a] The Real Letter Price is the price of a standard sealed internal letter divided by the Consumer Price Index (CPI).
[b] The Real Phone Charge (RPC) is the price of a local telephone call divided by the CPI.

sales with the almost coinciding phases of change in GNP and suggest a causal link.

RLP and RPC exhibit contrasting behaviour. RLP shows relatively little change up to 1970 with a strong upward trend after that; RPC shows a strong underlying trend up to around 1970 followed by relatively little change after that. Both variables display unusual behaviour at times, consisting of sudden upward jumps followed by steady downward trends. These have been identified as due to occasional nominal

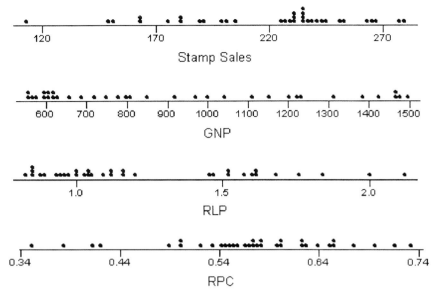

**Figure 8.12**　Dotplots of stamp sales, GNP, RLP and RPC.

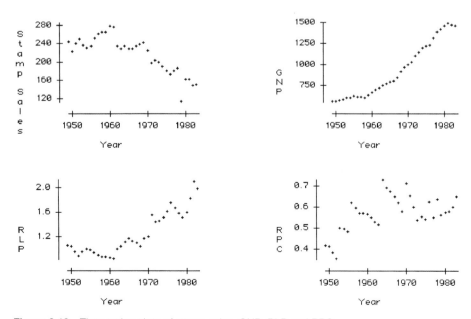

**Figure 8.13**　Time series plots of stamp sales, GNP, RLP and RPC.

price increases followed by periods of constant nominal price, corresponding to slowly falling real prices. Note that RLP shows real increases in most years after 1970, suggesting that nominal prices were being raised annually for most of this period. This contrasts with the behaviour before 1970. RPC shows similar behaviour to a lesser extent. Thus, there appears to have been a change in pricing practice around 1970.

We can also see that the separated subsets noted in the RLP and RPC dotplots correspond to the first four years, 1949–53, in the case of RPC and the years up to 1970 in the case of RLP.

*Scatterplot matrix*

The scatterplot matrix for these variables is shown in Figure 8.14. The first row shows stamp sales strongly related to both GNP and RLP, with little or no relationship with RPC. The cluster of points in the top left of the stamp sales/GNP scatterplot corresponds to the early years when GNP was low and showed little variation. When fitting a linear regression model, we should be aware of the possible influence a non-linear pattern such as this may have on the results. Apart from this, there are other suggestions of non-linear behaviour, but straight line relationships are likely to provide good approximations. The set of four points in the top left corner of the stamp sales/RPC plot are of little consequence in the context of the lack of relationship exhibited by the rest of the data. They correspond to the low values of RPC in the years 1949–53. The exceptional 1979 case shows up on all plots.

Turning to the remaining plots, note the strong relationship between GNP and RLP and the weak relationships elsewhere. The former may create problems in

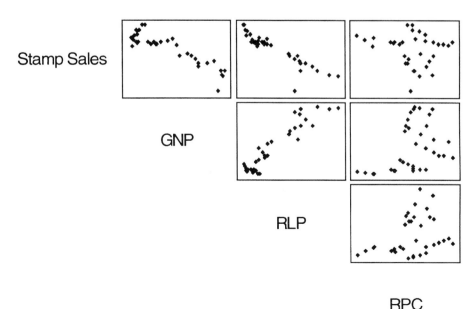

**Figure 8.14**   Scatterplot matrix of stamp sales, GNP, RLP and RPC.

separating any explanatory effects of the two variables involved and make interpretation of the individual regression coefficients difficult.

## Multiple linear regression

Having observed some trends, relationships and exceptional patterns in the data, we
make a more formal analysis using the multiple linear regression model. This model
suggests that variation in stamp sales may be represented as a linear combination of
the three explanatory variables, plus chance variation:

$$\text{Stamp sales} = \alpha + \beta_{GNP} \times GNP + \beta_{RLP} \times RLP + \beta_{RPC} \times RPC + \varepsilon.$$

Here, $\alpha$ and the $\beta$'s are the *parameters* of the regression model; different values of
these parameters give different versions of the model, and different forecasting for-
mulas. In Section 1.6, we used the values $\alpha = 340$, $\beta_{GNP} = -0.03$, $\beta_{RLP} = -70$, $\beta_{RPC} = 0$
in our forecasting formula:

$$\text{Stamp sales} = 340 - 0.03 \times GNP - 70 \times RLP \pm 8$$

The extra element of $\pm 8$ at the end of the formula represents the allowance we must
make for chance variation. This reflects an additional model parameter, the standard
deviation, $\sigma$, of the Normal model which we assume for chance variation. In fact, our
best estimate for $\sigma$ was 4; 8 is twice that estimate.

It is typically assumed that the parameters $\alpha$, $\beta_{GNP}$, $\beta_{RLP}$, $\beta_{RPC}$ and $\sigma$ remain constant over the period of observation of the variables Sales, GNP, RLP and RPC and
also for any period for which predictions of sales are to be made, given new values
of GNP, RLP and RPC. This corresponds to the assumption that the process remains
in statistical control.

To find estimates of the regression parameters, $\alpha$, $\beta_{GNP}$, $\beta_{RLP}$ and $\beta_{RPC}$, we seek the
forecasting formula that best matches the historical data, using the least squares
criterion. Using appropriate statistical software to achieve this yields output such as
the following.

```
Dependent variable is:   Stamp Sales
No Selector
R squared = 86.6%     R squared (adjusted) = 85.3%
s =  15.3  with  35 - 4 = 31  degrees of freedom
```

| Source | Sum of Squares | df | Mean Square | F-ratio |
|--------|---------------|-----|-------------|---------|
| Regression | 46806.6 | 3 | 15602.2 | 66.7 |
| Residual | 7256.45 | 31 | 234.079 | |

| Variable | Coefficient | s.e. of Coeff | t-ratio | prob |
|----------|-------------|---------------|---------|------|
| Constant | 300.257 | 19.34 | 15.5 | ≤ 0.0001 |
| GNP | -0.060328 | 0.02406 | -2.51 | 0.0176 |
| RLP | -54.5674 | 21.15 | -2.58 | 0.0148 |
| RPC | 73.515 | 32.83 | 2.24 | 0.0325 |

Substituting the regression coefficient estimates in the bottom left corner into the
symbolic prediction formula

$$\text{Forecast\_Sales} = \hat{\alpha} + \hat{\beta}_{GNP} \times GNP + \hat{\beta}_{RLP} \times RLP + \hat{\beta}_{RPC} \times RPC \pm 2 \times \hat{\sigma}$$

yields the prediction interval formula

$$\text{Forecast\_Sales} = 300 - 0.06 \times \text{GNP} - 55 \times \text{RLP} + 73.5 \times \text{RPC} \pm 30.6$$

---

**Exercise 8.7** Use the prediction formula given above to make predictions for 1984 and 1985. Note that the forecasts of GNP and inflation given in Chapter 1 were:

|            | 1984    | 1985    |
|------------|---------|---------|
| GNP:       | + 1.5%  | + 1.5%  |
| Inflation: | + 8.6%  | + 5.5%  |

and assume that the nominal letter price and nominal phone charge did not change. Compare the forecasts with each other and with the actual outcomes.

---

**Exercise 8.8** Discuss the value of the prediction interval width in the context of (i) the current level of stamp sales, (ii) annual changes in stamp sales in recent years, excluding the effect of 1979 and (iii) the value of $\hat{\sigma}_{\text{Sales}}$, the estimate of $\sigma$ based on the sales data alone.

---

Note that this prediction interval formula differs from the prediction formula used earlier to calculate predictions for stamp sales in 1984 and 1985. The earlier values were calculated following a careful analysis which involved identifying exceptional cases and other non-standard patterns, in which the calculation of the parameter estimates given here was just the first step. The remaining steps in this process are described next.

*Diagnostic analysis of residuals*

The standard diagnostics are shown in Figure 8.15. The variation in the vertical direction in the diagnostic plot of Figure 8.15 should correspond to chance variation according to the standard Normal model. Clearly, there is an exceptional case; the case at the bottom of the diagnostic plot is almost eight standard deviations from 0. This corresponds to the year 1979 when there was an industrial dispute and sales were down substantially because of this. Clearly, a model intended to reflect the relationship of sales to GNP, RLP and RPC cannot cope with an exceptional case such as this. It should be deleted from the data and a second regression equation fitted.

There appears to be further unusual behaviour of the residuals in this diagnostic plot. Apart from the exceptional case identified above, there appear to be two groups

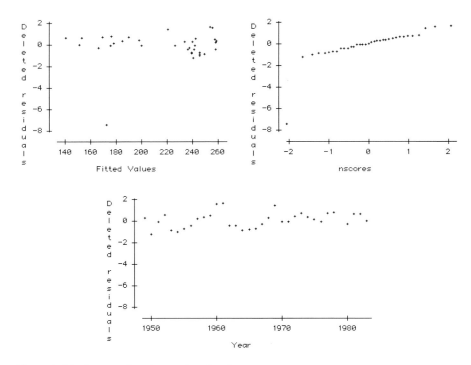

**Figure 8.15**   Stamp sales diagnostics, first fit.

of residuals, one on the left side of the plot corresponding to smaller fitted values and another on the right corresponding to larger fitted values, with a gap in the middle. It appears that there is considerably more variation in the residuals on the right than there is in the residuals on the left. Recalling from Figure 8.13 that stamp sales decreased over the years and anticipating that the fitted values will follow suit, we associate the smaller fitted values with the later years and the larger fitted values with the earlier years. We surmise that there may have been more chance variation in stamp sales in the early years than in the later years. This does not conform to the standard process model which assumes steady variation over time. If it is confirmed, then suitable action will be needed.

Our initial data analysis may suggest a possible explanation. Noting that there are 13 points in the left side subset, it follows that the gap occurred around 1970, 13 years back from 1983. Our initial data analysis suggested changes in behaviour of the price variables around that time.

However, there is always the possibility that the exceptional case uncovered above is distorting the fitted model in a way that leads to this unequal variation effect; we suspend judgement until after the second fit.

Both the Normal plot and the time series plot reflect the presence of the 1979 exceptional case. However, the time series plot suggests cyclical variation of the residuals, consistent with serial correlation. While this will have some biasing effect on the prediction formula, its main effect will be to bias downwards the estimate of prediction error, thus giving prediction intervals that are too optimistic. There is also a suggestion that three points at the top right of the Normal plot may need attention.

The diagnostics have revealed a number of potential problems with fitting this model to these data. The most severe problem is the exceptional residual of 1979. Experience shows that extreme cases such as this can cause apparent problems in other areas as well. Hence, it makes sense to deal with this problem first. Accordingly, the 1979 case is deleted from the data and the entire analysis, regression and diagnostics, repeated.

## Iterating the analysis

Applying the regression analysis with case 1979 deleted gives the following output.

```
Dependent variable is:                    Stamp Sales
No Selector
35 total cases of which 1 is missing
R squared = 94.0%      R squared (adjusted) = 93.4%
s =  9.225  with  34 - 4 = 30  degrees of freedom

Source        Sum of Squares    df    Mean Square    F-ratio
Regression    40040.2            3     13346.7        157
Residual      2552.8            30       85.0933

Variable    Coefficient    s.e. of Coeff    t-ratio    prob
Constant    317.96         11.9             26.7       ≤ 0.0001
GNP         -0.00770814    0.015614         -0.478     0.6364
RLP         -92.177        13.72            -6.72      ≤ 0.0001
RPC         43.2861        20.21            2.14       0.0405
```

Note the substantial fall in the value of s and, therefore, in prediction interval width. Also, there have been substantial changes in the regression coefficient estimates. $\hat{\beta}_{GNP}$ has changed from $-0.06$ to $-0.008$. Furthermore, it is less than half its standard error in magnitude ($t = -0.478$) and so is judged to be statistically insignificant. The other coefficients have also changed substantially. Before using these new values for prediction, however, we need to apply the diagnostic tests. The diagnostic plot and the Normal probability plot and time series plot of residuals follow in Figure 8.16.

The diagnostic plot now suggests a possible exceptional point, whose deleted residual is close to $-3$. The time series plot identifies that point to be 1980. Conceivably, the difficulties caused by the 1979 industrial dispute could have affected sales in 1980; recovering the previous market position may have taken some time. The Normal plot suggests nothing extraordinary beyond 1980 being exceptional. The pattern in the time series plot is now much less consistent than earlier, although there are some aspects, such as the run of seven residuals from 1962 to 1968 with almost identical values, which may arouse suspicion.

The evidence in the diagnostic plot concerning the difference in the extent of chance variation up to and after 1970 now appears stronger than before. Visual inspection suggests that the spread in the early residuals, on the right, exceeds that in the more recent residuals, on the left, by a factor of 2 or 3. One possibility is that there was a change in the way the sales process worked; recall the suggestions made

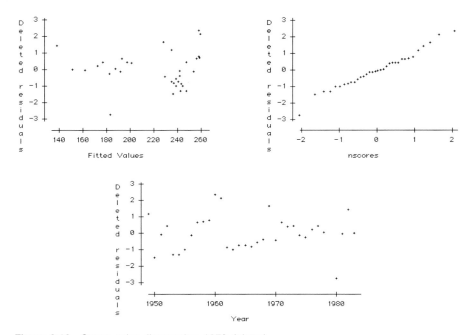

**Figure 8.16**    Stamp sales diagnostics, 1979 deleted.

in the course of the initial data analysis regarding changes in pricing behaviour. The same model cannot be expected to work for different processes. This suggests modelling the corresponding subsets of the data separately. It was decided to fit a new model to the recent data as it was more relevant to current (1984) forecasting needs.

### Modelling recent data

The results of regressing stamp sales on GNP, RLP and RPC using only the data for the years 1971–83, with 1979 omitted, together with corresponding diagnostics, are shown below and in Figure 8.17.

```
Dependent variable is:                    Stamp Sales
cases selected according to               Recent
35 total cases of which 23 are missing
R squared = 93.2%      R squared (adjusted) = 90.6%
s =  5.892  with   12 - 4 = 8   degrees of freedom

Source       Sum of Squares    df    Mean Square    F-ratio
Regression   3800.5             3     1266.83        36.5
Residual     277.768            8       34.721

Variable     Coefficient    s.e. of Coeff    t-ratio      prob
Constant     327.987        29.03            11.3      ≤ 0.0001
GNP          -0.0547952     0.01664          -3.29       0.0110
RLP          -56.6475       13.45            -4.21       0.0029
RPC          29.502         46.78            0.631       0.5459
```

The diagnostics continue to show 1980 to be exceptional, with a deleted residual of around 3.5. Since there is a plausible explanation for this exceptional value, it may be deleted. The regression results follow; the diagnostics (not shown) did not change appreciably, apart from the deletion of the case 1980 from the plots.

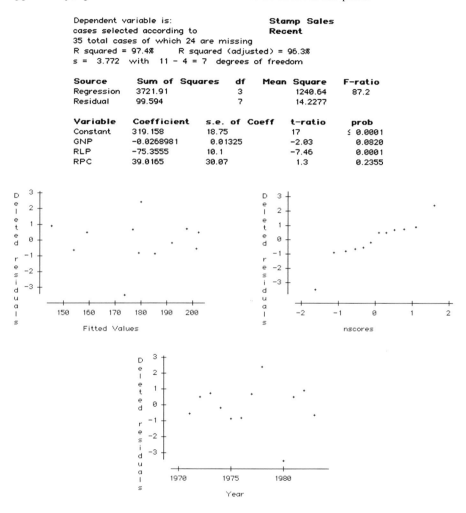

Dependent variable is:               **Stamp Sales**
cases selected according to               **Recent**
35 total cases of which 24 are missing
R squared = 97.4%       R squared (adjusted) = 96.3%
s = 3.772   with   11 - 4 = 7   degrees of freedom

| Source | Sum of Squares | df | Mean Square | F-ratio |
|---|---|---|---|---|
| Regression | 3721.91 | 3 | 1240.64 | 87.2 |
| Residual | 99.594 | 7 | 14.2277 | |

| Variable | Coefficient | s.e. of Coeff | t-ratio | prob |
|---|---|---|---|---|
| Constant | 319.158 | 18.75 | 17 | ≤ 0.0001 |
| GNP | -0.0268981 | 0.01325 | -2.03 | 0.0820 |
| RLP | -75.3555 | 10.1 | -7.46 | 0.0001 |
| RPC | 39.0165 | 30.07 | 1.3 | 0.2355 |

**Figure 8.17**   Stamp sales regression results and diagnostics, 1971–83, 1979 deleted.

*Simplifying the model; removing an insignificant variable*

Note that the *t*-ratio for RPC is considerably smaller than 2, indicating that $\hat{\beta}_{RPC}$ is statistically insignificant, consistent with the null hypothesis that $\beta_{RPC} = 0$. If $\beta_{RPC} = 0$, then RPC plays no part in the regression model or the forecasting formula. In fact, keeping $\hat{\beta}_{RPC}$ in the forecasting formula merely adds chance variation to the formula, which is not desirable. On the other hand, removing RPC simplifies the model and the formula which is, in itself, desirable. It makes sense, therefore, to remove RPC from the model and refit. The results, with diagnostics, follow.

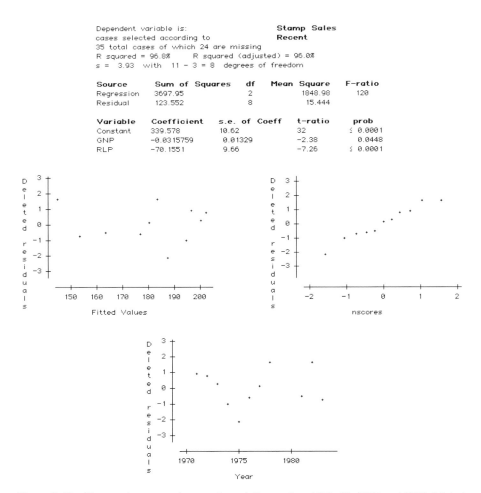

**Figure 8.18**    Stamp sales regression results and diagnostics, 1971–83, 1979 and 1980 deleted and RPC removed.

### Using reference plots to check perceived patterns

The time series plot shows some apparently unusual behaviour with a suggestion of 'tracking' on the left side. However, given the small number of cases, this behaviour could not be described as exceptional. In these circumstances, it can be helpful to see what might be expected with pure chance variation. Simulating random data gives some insight into what might happen. Figure 8.19 shows nine time series plots of

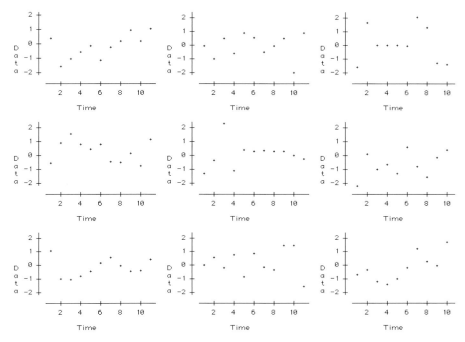

**Figure 8.19**    Reference time series plots of simulated pure chance variation.

randomly generated data corresponding to processes subject to pure chance variation. By reference to these, the time series plot in Figure 8.18 is not exceptional.

*Final fit*

There are no exceptions visible in either the diagnostic plot or the Normal plot.
Hence, we take the equation in the regression results as an acceptable fit, based on the
recent data, and use it to construct a forecasting formula:

$$\text{Sales} = 340 - 0.0316\,\text{GNP} - 70.2\,\text{RLP} \pm 8.$$

This is the final formula chosen as a result of the analysis reported here and is the
formula used in Section 1.6.

## Checking the effect of removing an insignificant variable

We decided to remove RPC from the prediction formula on the basis that the
estimated value of the corresponding regression coefficient, when included, was not
statistically significant. We can now check directly the effect of the removal on
actual predictions and judge in the light of that whether the removal was justified. In
Section 1.6, we have already used the final formula to make predictions for 1979 (in
retrospect), 1984 and 1985; see pages 41–2. The results are reproduced in Table 8.6.

**Table 8.6**   Stamp sales prediction for 1979, 1984 and 1985 using the final prediction formula

|                         | 1979 | 1984 | 1985 |
|-------------------------|------|------|------|
| Lower confidence bound  | 180  | 156  | 162  |
| Point prediction        | 188  | 164  | 170  |
| Upper confidence bound  | 196  | 172  | 178  |

The prediction formula with RPC included is

$$\text{Sales} = 319 - 0.0269\,\text{GNP} - 75.4\,\text{RLP} + 39.0\,\text{RPC} \pm 7.6$$

Substituting the 1979 values for the explanatory variables

$$\text{GNP}(79) = 1422.8, \quad \text{RLP}(79) = 1.526 \quad \text{and} \quad \text{RPC}(79) = 0.564$$

leads to a prediction of

$$319 - 0.0269 \times 1422.8 - 75.4 \times 1.526 + 39.0 \times 0.564 \pm 7.6$$

that is

$$187.7 \pm 7.6$$

that is

$$180.1 \text{ to } 195.3$$

When rounded to whole numbers, these results are identical to the 1979 prediction results in Table 8.6.

---

**Exercise 8.9**   Use the prediction formula with RPC included to predict stamp sales for 1984 and 1985, assuming the predicted values of GNP and inflation given in Chapter 1, page 42, and that there was no change in the nominal prices of stamps or telephone calls. Compare the results with those in Table 8.6.

---

The conclusion from these comparisons is that the removal of RPC on the grounds of statistical insignificance was justified in terms of prediction. The simpler formula is confirmed.

### Comparing models based on early and recent data

We need to check the possibility that there was a change around 1970 in the way the sales process worked. If there was no change, then the data prior to 1970 are still relevant and should be considered for inclusion in a forecasting formula. If not, then the formula just derived is the best we can do. To decide this issue, we model the early data (this is the subject of Review exercise 6 at the end of the chapter) and compare the fitted model with the model just derived. In the course of the analysis of the early data, two exceptional residuals appear. Although there are no rational explanations available for their presence, they are deleted to allow a fair comparison with the model derived from the recent data. When the two cases were deleted, the diagnostics show no strongly suggested patterns. However, the GNP coefficient was not statistically significant and so was removed from the equation. The final estimated regression coefficients were

$$\hat{\alpha} = 371, \hat{\beta}_{RLP} = -176, \hat{\beta}_{RPC} = 84$$

with

$$\hat{\sigma} = 5.5$$

The resulting prediction formula is

$$\text{Sales} = 371 - 176\ \text{RLP} + 84\ \text{RPC} \pm 11$$

*Comparing early and recent residual spread*

Recalling that the decision to separate early and recent data was based on the appearance that there was more variability among the early residuals than among the recent, we see that the values of $s$ in the two regressions, 5.5 and 3.9, respectively, appear to be consistent with this suggestion, although their ratio of 1.4 is considerably smaller than the ratio suggested by the diagnostic plot in Figure 8.16. This raises the question of whether the difference is due to chance variation; there will be a difference in the residual standard deviations even if the underlying process standard deviations are the same. According to standard tests which may be applied here, the result is that the observed difference in residual standard deviations is not statistically significant. However, we will not pursue this here; rather, we will turn to the more interesting differences that may be seen between prediction formulas.

*Comparing early and recent prediction formulas*

The prediction formulas appear quite different from each other. While there are formal tests for comparing the formulas (and they are statistically significantly different according to these tests), we will examine the differences in actual predictions for 1979, 1983 and 1984, as above. Substituting the relevant data into the final early prediction formula

$$\text{Sales} = 371 - 176\ \text{RLP} + 84\ \text{RPC} \pm 11$$

leads to the extension to Table 8.6 in Table 8.7.

Clearly, the predictions are completely different; all pairs of prediction intervals are well separated.

Our conclusion is that the process operated differently before and after 1970, although not in the way suggested by the initial diagnostic plot: while there is no significant difference in residual spread, there are substantial differences between the prediction formulas.

**Table 8.7**   Stamp sales prediction for 1979, 1984 and 1985
using the final prediction formula based on early and recent data

|      |        | Lower confidence bound | Point prediction | Upper confidence bound |
|------|--------|-----------------------|-----------------|------------------------|
| 1979 | Early  | 139                   | 150             | 161                    |
|      | Recent | 180                   | 188             | 195                    |
| 1984 | Early  | 88                    | 99              | 110                    |
|      | Recent | 156                   | 164             | 172                    |
| 1985 | Early  | 102                   | 113             | 124                    |
|      | Recent | 162                   | 170             | 178                    |

### Evaluating the final model

Having decided that the earlier data correspond to a different sales process, we are left with a regression equation involving two explanatory variables, GNP and RLP, based on 11 cases, and apparently satisfying standard tests for acceptability. However, there is a question as to the ultimate value of the resulting prediction formula. In the first place, 11 is a small number of cases. This affects prediction in two main ways. In using $\hat{\sigma}$ as the standard error of prediction, we have ignored the fact that the regression coefficients are themselves subject to chance variation. The contribution to prediction standard error from this source is roughly proportional to $\frac{1}{\sqrt{n}}$. When $n$ is large, this is negligible. However, for smaller values of $n$, this may be considerable.[6]

The second effect of small sample size is to query the validity of using 2 as a multiplier of $\hat{\sigma}$ in calculating the prediction; it assumes that the prediction error process follows the Normal model with process mean 0 and process standard deviation $\hat{\sigma}$. However, $\hat{\sigma}$ is itself just an estimate of the actual process standard deviation, which we denote by $\sigma$, and, as such, is subject to chance variation. When $n$ is large, this source of variation is negligible. However, when $n$ is small, we need to use a wider prediction interval to allow for it.

Another major consideration is the model selection process that has been followed. While it is well known that the validity of the final model is affected by this process, little is known about how it is affected.

Currently recommended practice is to use the final model for prediction but recognise that the confidence we are entitled to have in our predictions is likely to be somewhat less than the 95% suggested by the use of the error bounds $\pm 2\hat{\sigma}$.

---

[6]   This issue is discussed and exemplified in the Supplements and Extensions page of the book's website, in the context of simple linear regression. Identical considerations apply here, though the technical details vary.

## 8.8   General issues

The multiple regression model can be very effective in assisting us in understanding and exploiting relationships between variables. However, care is needed in applying the model. Diagnostic analysis is an essential adjunct to model fitting. Without it, we may be seriously misled. For example, in the job times study, ignoring the diagnostics may lead to ignoring important explanatory variables and ending up with a spuriously simple but badly biased prediction formula. Recall the cautionary note on page 259.

In the stamp sales study, it is unlikely that the 1979 exceptional case would be overlooked, since the industrial dispute of that year was a recent event in 1984. However, the possibility that its effect carried over into 1980, suggested by the exceptional residual corresponding to that year, would be likely to go unnoticed without diagnostic analysis, as would the fact that the same model does not apply across the entire period under study.

In this section, some other issues which statistical analysts need to be aware of in the context of multiple linear regression are addressed briefly.

### Degree of control of the study environment

Most industrial processes are subject to high degrees of control, in the sense that the inputs to the process can be set at desired levels with a view to controlling the outputs. For example, we have seen how adjusting the input pressure for the tennis ball core presses results in changing the diameters of the tennis balls produced. Furthermore, there is a presumption that other variables that may affect diameter may be controlled and not allowed to vary so that, apart from pressure, only chance causes will affect diameter. In such circumstances, we may presume a cause-and-effect relationship between pressure and diameter and use it to our advantage.

By contrast, socio-economic processes are not subject to such degrees of control. While governments and central banks attempt to control various aspects of national economies, their success in doing so is limited. Economic processes are subject to many complex, interacting influences. Economic forecasters build very complex models (of which the multiple linear regression model is a basic building block) in order to assist them in making predictions. However, as we will see in Chapter 9, their record of success is poor.

We may compare and contrast the job time process and the stamp sales process in this regard. We may regard the job time process as subject to a high degree of control in this sense, at least potentially, assuming that an effective production control system is in place. Although it might not be practical, there is the possibility in principle of conducting controlled experiments in which key variables are changed in a controlled way and the effects of the changes may be measured. Experimentation of this kind is discussed in Chapter 11.

By contrast, the variables which we have identified as the key variables affecting stamp sales are not controllable in this way; there is no possibility of conducting controlled experiments with the national economy. Consequently, there is no way of unambiguously drawing inferences from such data concerning cause and effect regarding relationships between economic variables.

Data collected as they occur, without intervention to control the values of key variables, are referred to as 'observational data'. Attempts to draw causal inferences from such data are fraught with danger. A quotation from industrial statistician K.A. Brownlee is appropriate:

> The justification sometimes advanced that a multiple regression analysis on observational data can be relied upon if there is an adequate theoretical background is utterly specious and disregards the unlimited capability of the human intellect for producing plausible explanations by the carload lot.

> (K.A. Brownlee, *Statistical Theory and Methodology in Science and Engineering*, Wiley, 1965, page 454.)

### Stability of relationships

Relationship can be expected to remain stable in a controlled environment and to change in an uncontrolled environment. Indeed, we have seen evidence of this with the stamp sales process as noted in the discussion in Section 8.7. More critically, given the substantial changes that have occurred in communications, particularly with the introduction of facsimile and e-mail (1984 is said to be the year of the 'birth of the internet'), any prediction formula derived from pre-1984 data is likely to become unsatisfactory not long after 1984. By contrast, assuming that the metal fabrication company's production system remains in control, job time predictions can be relied on to a much greater extent than stamp sales forecasts.

### Extrapolation

Extrapolation beyond the range of data for the explanatory variables brings with it the risk that the fitted model may not be valid outside that range. Figure 6.6, page 196 shows some possibilities for this in the case of simple linear regression. This almost invariably applies to forecasting in an economic environment. Extrapolation is inevitable, with no way of checking on the validity of the model. Extrapolation may also apply in an industrial environment, but interpolation is common there and extrapolation may be anticipated by experimental studies in many cases.

### Predicting explanatory variables

A related issue arises when the values of the explanatory variables are not known in advance of using them for prediction. In that case, the values for the explanatory variables must themselves be predicted. This adds to the uncertainty of prediction of the response variable. More often than not, this source of uncertainty is ignored, as we did in the stamp sales study. In the job times study, by contrast, the values for the explanatory variable are known as soon as an order is received.

### Large datasets

The problems addressed in this chapter have involved quite small datasets. This allowed us to consider each case in detail and to consider each variable and relationships between variables in detail. The ability to do this lessens as the volume of data increases. This may happen because of an increase in the number of cases, the number of variables, or both.

*Many cases*

The diagnostics used in this chapter have focussed on individual cases or small numbers of cases. With very many cases, the conventional critical values for standardised residuals are not relevant. Table 8.8 shows the numbers of cases we might anticipate will exceed different critical values for a range of sample sizes. Thus, we might prefer to use a critical value of 4 for samples around 10,000 and 5 for samples of around 1,000,000.

**Table 8.8** Expected numbers of cases exceeding critical values for varying sample sizes

| | Critical value | | | |
| --- | --- | --- | --- | --- |
| | 2 | 3 | 4 | 5 |
| Sample size | | | | |
| 100 | 5 | 0 | 0 | 0 |
| 1,000 | 46 | 3 | 0 | 0 |
| 10,000 | 455 | 27 | 1 | 0 |
| 100,000 | 4,550 | 270 | 6 | 0 |
| 1,000,000 | 45,500 | 2,700 | 63 | 1 |

More than this, however, individual cases, even if obviously exceptional, will not influence the prediction formula very much; their influence will be outweighed by the very many other cases. Consequently, the effort would be better directed at seeking exceptional subsets. However, research in and practical experience of this approach are still at an early stage.

*Many variables*

If there are very many variables, it is likely that they will be highly correlated. This implies that many variables or sets of variables are measuring similar things. If included in a prediction formula, there will be considerable redundancy, with many variables merely contributing to the chance variation in the formula. The task of selecting a reasonable subset of variables is not easy. While there are a number of more or less automatic techniques available, they are notoriously unstable and susceptible to influence by exceptional cases.

In addition, causal interpretations of prediction formulas in terms of the variables remaining after a selection procedure are unreliable. For purely prediction purposes, this is not a serious problem. However, attempts to use such causal interpretations are likely to mislead.

## 8.9   Review exercises

8.1   A study of the relationship between price and quality of vegetables involved collecting the prices of 200 lots of asparagus over a three month period and inspecting the lots to assess their quality. The variables chosen to represent quality were:

- 'Number of stalks', the average number of stalks per bunch in a lot;
- 'Diameter spread', the interquartile range of the diameters of stalks in a lot;
- 'Greenness', the average length, in hundredths of an inch, of the green part of the stalks in a lot.

Greenness is a desirable quality in asparagus. Number of stalks per lot is an indirect measure of weight per stalk, as the asparagus was made up in standard lots weighing about 18 ounces. Diameter spread measures the uniformity of the stalks in the lot; a small value indicates a high degree of uniformity.

The regression of price on the three quality variables resulted as follows:

```
Dependent variable is:   Price
No Selector
R squared = 72.7%     R squared (adjusted) = 72.3%
s =  15.52  with  200 - 4 = 196  degrees of freedom
```

| Source | Sum of Squares | df | Mean Square | F-ratio |
|--------|----------------|-----|-------------|---------|
| Regression | 125648 | 3 | 41882.8 | 174 |
| Residual | 47230.7 | 196 | 240.973 | |

| Variable | Coefficient | s.e. of Coeff | t-ratio | prob |
|----------|-------------|---------------|---------|------|
| Constant | 40.7613 | 5.328 | 7.65 | ≤ 0.0001 |
| Greenness | 0.137598 | 0.007099 | 19.4 | ≤ 0.0001 |
| Number of ... | -1.35726 | 0.1508 | -9 | ≤ 0.0001 |
| Diameter sp... | -0.345283 | 0.1297 | -2.66 | 0.0084 |

A full diagnostic analysis revealed no serious discrepancies.

Give a formal interpretation in context of the 'Greenness' coefficient; note that prices are expressed as percentages of the daily average price per lot for each day on which data were collected.

Explain the calculation and interpretation of the $t$-ratio for 'Greenness'. How does its value relate to the other numbers in the same row? How does the $t$-ratio relate to statistical significance testing? Give a full explanation including references to null hypothesis, sampling distribution, significance level.

Two of the coefficients are negative. Explain the significance of this in terms of the variables concerned, which are intended to measure quality.

A grower thinks he can increase the amount of greenness of asparagus stalks by about 1 inch on average by using extra fertiliser. Assuming that the daily average price per lot of asparagus is £20, how much should he be willing to pay to achieve this increase? Give an error bound on your estimate. State the level of confidence you have in this bound; give a full formal explanation of the basis for your confidence.

8.2   A car leasing company, in order to be able to set lease charges which are both profitable and competitive, needs to be able to forecast at time of purchase the prices its cars will realise when sold. To this end, they have assembled data on over 800 cars that they have handled in recent years. As part of a more comprehensive study of the data, a regression analysis was conducted on the 41 Ford cars in the dataset. The response variable was Selling Value; the explanatory variables were Cost Price, Age in days and Mileage. The first fit of explanatory variables to response led to the following output.

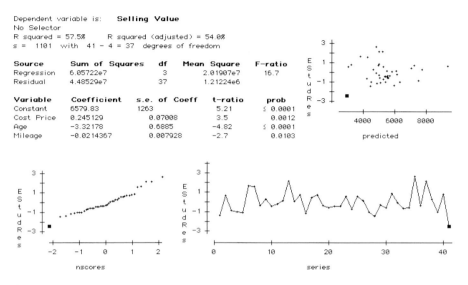

```
Dependent variable is:   Selling Value
No Selector
R squared = 57.5%     R squared (adjusted) = 54.0%
s =  1101  with  41 - 4 = 37  degrees of freedom

Source        Sum of Squares    df    Mean Square    F-ratio
Regression    6.05722e7          3    2.01907e7      16.7
Residual      4.48529e7         37    1.21224e6

Variable      Coefficient    s.e. of Coeff    t-ratio    prob
Constant      6579.83         1263              5.21      ≤ 0.0001
Cost Price    0.245129        0.07008           3.5       0.0012
Age          -3.32178         0.6885           -4.82      ≤ 0.0001
Mileage      -0.0214367       0.007928         -2.7       0.0103
```

$\hat{\sigma}_{\text{SellingValue}} = £1,623$

Write a short report providing an interpretation of the key features of the regression output and a prediction formula with prediction error. Also, provide a report on diagnostic analysis and a recommendation for action.

On investigation of the case corresponding to the highlighted point in the diagnostic plots, it was found that the selling price was recorded as £675 instead of £6750. When this was corrected, the updated diagnostic plots showed no unusual behaviour. The Mileage coefficient appeared statistically insignificant and so was deleted. The final regression output was:

```
Dependent variable is:   Selling Value
No Selector
R squared = 44.4%     R squared (adjusted) = 41.5%
s =  1111  with  41 - 3 = 38  degrees of freedom

Source        Sum of Squares    df    Mean Square    F-ratio
Regression    3.74333e7          2    1.87167e7      15.2
Residual      4.68765e7         38    1.23359e6

Variable      Coefficient    s.e. of Coeff    t-ratio    prob
Constant      6656.03         1216              5.47      ≤ 0.0001
Cost Price    0.188344        0.0697            2.7       0.0102
Age          -3.46996         0.6695           -5.18      ≤ 0.0001
```

Revise your first report above. Noting that the revised $\hat{\sigma}_{\text{SellingValue}}$ was £1,452, comment on the usefulness of the final prediction formula.

8.3

Warning: This and the following two exercises are based on a very small dataset. The main purposes of the exercises are to provide experience in interpreting and acting on diagnostics, in the danger of premature simplification of equations and in dealing with problems relating to exceptional cases whose presence is masked by others.

A savings and loan association needs validation of property prices negotiated by prospective clients before sanctioning loans. A study commissioned from a consultant suggests

- living area;
- tax liability;
- swimming pool, presence or absence;

as useful predictors for price, and data on these variables were sampled from recent transactions.

| Price ($ thousands) | Living area (Sq. ft. hundreds) | Tax liability ($hundreds) | Pool or not? (1 or 0) |
|---|---|---|---|
| 145 | 15 | 1.9 | 1 |
| 228 | 38 | 2.4 | 0 |
| 150 | 23 | 1.4 | 0 |
| 130 | 16 | 1.4 | 0 |
| 160 | 16 | 1.5 | 1 |
| 114 | 13 | 1.8 | 0 |
| 142 | 20 | 2.4 | 0 |
| 265 | 24 | 4.0 | 0 |

The consultant used the following regression output of price on the other three variables as the basis for a prediction formula.

```
Dependent variable is:    Price
No Selector
R squared = 90.4%      R squared (adjusted) = 83.2%
s =  21.31  with  8 - 4 = 4  degrees of freedom
```

| Source | Sum of Squares | df | Mean Square | F-ratio |
|---|---|---|---|---|
| Regression | 17132.6 | 3 | 5710.87 | 12.6 |
| Residual | 1816.88 | 4 | 454.219 | |

| Variable | Coefficient | s.e. of Coeff | t-ratio | prob |
|---|---|---|---|---|
| Constant | 2.32903 | 29.72 | 0.0784 | 0.9413 |
| Area | 3.52648 | 1.151 | 3.06 | 0.0375 |
| Tax | 40.4834 | 10.23 | 3.96 | 0.0167 |
| Pool | 26.6888 | 19.16 | 1.39 | 0.2360 |

What formula did he use? What allowance did he make for prediction error? Are these useful? Using this formula, predict the price for a house of 2,000 sq. ft. with tax liability of $200 and a pool; allow for prediction error.

How much extra would you expect to pay for a house with an additional 100 sq. ft., again allowing for prediction error?

Provide an interpretation of the estimated Pool coefficient. Formally test the null hypothesis that the Pool coefficient is 0. Explain what is meant by this hypothesis.

A re-analysis of the data was carried out. Relevant computer output follows. In the scatterplots, two exceptional points have been marked '+' and '×'.

*Preliminary scatterplots:*

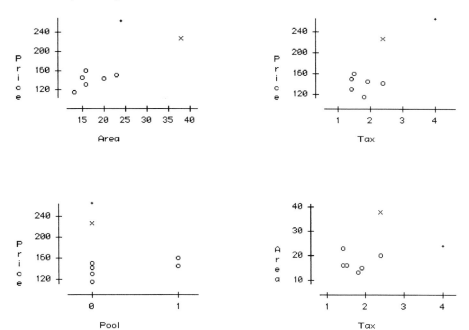

Comment on the relationships shown in the above scatterplots. Make special reference to the exceptional cases and their possible influence on perceived relationships.

*Diagnostic plot:*

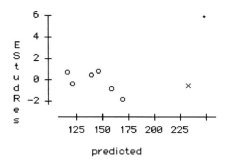

Provide an interpretation of the diagnostic plot from the earlier regression, shown above. How do you respond to the point marked '+'? How do you respond to the point marked '×'?

*Second fit, with diagnostic plot, exceptional point marked '+' deleted.*

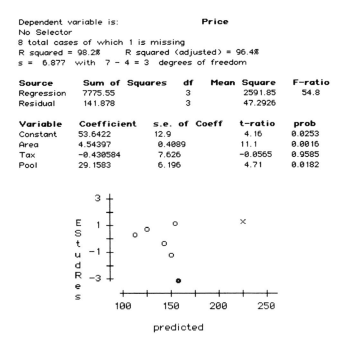

```
Dependent variable is:                    Price
No Selector
8 total cases of which 1 is missing
R squared = 98.2%      R squared (adjusted) = 96.4%
s =  6.877  with  7 - 4 = 3  degrees of freedom

Source        Sum of Squares    df    Mean Square    F-ratio
Regression    7775.55            3                   2591.85      54.8
Residual      141.878            3                   47.2926

Variable      Coefficient    s.e. of Coeff    t-ratio    prob
Constant      53.6422        12.9              4.16       0.0253
Area          4.54397        0.4089           11.1        0.0016
Tax           -0.430584      7.626            -0.0565     0.9585
Pool          29.1583        6.196             4.71       0.0182
```

Explain the rationale for deleting the point marked '+'. Give a commentary on the changes in the regression, in particular, the change in *s* and in the apparent statistical significance of the coefficients. Give an interpretation of the diagnostic plot. How do you respond to the point marked '•'?

*Third fit, point marked '•' deleted, with diagnostic plot*

```
Dependent variable is:                    Price
No Selector
8 total cases of which 2 are missing
R squared = 99.7%      R squared (adjusted) = 99.3%
s =  3.422  with  6 - 4 = 2  degrees of freedom

Source        Sum of Squares    df    Mean Square    F-ratio
Regression    7885.41            3                   2628.47      224
Residual      23.4224            2                   11.7112

Variable      Coefficient    s.e. of Coeff    t-ratio    prob
Constant      68.4572        7.93              8.63       0.0132
Area          4.849          0.2249           21.6        0.0021
Tax           -10.2114       4.885            -2.09       0.1717
Pool          26.2428        3.216             8.16       0.0147
```

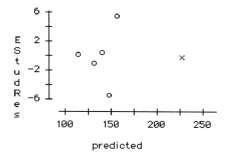

Explain the rationale for deleting the point marked '•'. Give a commentary on the changes in the regression, in particular, the change in *s* and in the apparent statistical significance of the coefficients. Give an interpretation of the diagnostic plot. Note that deletion of exceptional points is not feasible at this stage, as it leaves just four cases to estimate four regression coefficients and *s*.

## 8.4 Continuation of Exercise 8.3

Suppose the point marked '×' had been deleted first, followed by deletion of the point marked '+'. The resulting regression outputs and diagnostic plots follow.

```
Dependent variable is:                    Price
No Selector
8 total cases of which 1 is missing
R squared = 88.9%      R squared (adjusted) = 77.9%
s =   23.25   with   7 - 4 = 3   degrees of freedom
```

| Source | Sum of Squares | df | Mean Square | F-ratio |
|--------|----------------|-----|-------------|---------|
| Regression | 13040.9 | 3 | 4346.97 | 8.04 |
| Residual | 1621.08 | 3 | 540.36 | |

| Variable | Coefficient | s.e. of Coeff | t-ratio | prob |
|----------|-------------|---------------|---------|------|
| Constant | -19.7216 | 48.91 | -0.403 | 0.7138 |
| Area | 5.10552 | 2.908 | 1.76 | 0.1774 |
| Tax | 37.2253 | 12.4 | 3 | 0.0576 |
| Pool | 29.8031 | 21.53 | 1.38 | 0.2602 |

```
Dependent variable is:                    Price
No Selector
8 total cases of which 2 are missing
R squared = 94.1%      R squared (adjusted) = 85.3%
s =  6.202  with  6 - 4 = 2  degrees of freedom
```

| Source | Sum of Squares | df | Mean Square | F-ratio |
|--------|---------------|-----|-------------|---------|
| Regression | 1227.91 | 3 | 409.302 | 10.6 |
| Residual | 76.9273 | 2 | 38.4637 | |

| Variable | Coefficient | s.e. of Coeff | t-ratio | prob |
|----------|-------------|---------------|---------|------|
| Constant | 74.4277 | 19.78 | 3.76 | 0.0639 |
| Area | 3.605 | 0.8112 | 4.44 | 0.0471 |
| Tax | -3.03867 | 7.165 | -0.424 | 0.7127 |
| Pool | 27.3606 | 5.756 | 4.75 | 0.0415 |

Comment on the changes in *s*, in the coefficients and in the residuals. Comment on the effect of the presence or absence of the point marked '×' on the effect of deleting the point marked '+'.

## 8.5    Continuation of Exercise 8.3

In the first fit, Exercise 8.3, the Pool coefficient is apparently not statistically significant. Removing the Pool variable from the equation gives the following regression output and diagnostic plot.

```
Dependent variable is:    Price
No Selector
R squared = 85.8%      R squared (adjusted) = 80.1%
s =  23.23  with  8 - 3 = 5  degrees of freedom
```

| Source | Sum of Squares | df | Mean Square | F-ratio |
|--------|---------------|-----|-------------|---------|
| Regression | 16251.1 | 2 | 8125.55 | 15.1 |
| Residual | 2698.41 | 5 | 539.682 | |

| Variable | Coefficient | s.e. of Coeff | t-ratio | prob |
|----------|-------------|---------------|---------|------|
| Constant | 24.1657 | 27.52 | 0.878 | 0.4201 |
| Area | 3.0141 | 1.189 | 2.54 | 0.0522 |
| Tax | 38.2946 | 11.02 | 3.48 | 0.0178 |

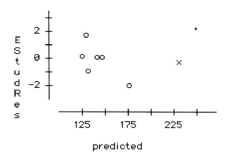

Comment on the changes in *s*, in the coefficients and in the residuals.

In the second fit in Exercise 8.3, the Tax coefficient appears insignificant. Removing the Tax variable from the equation gives the following regression output and diagnostic plot.

```
Dependent variable is:                    Price
No Selector
8 total cases of which 1 is missing
R squared = 98.2%      R squared (adjusted) = 97.3%
s =  5.959  with  7 - 3 = 4  degrees of freedom

Source       Sum of Squares    df    Mean Square    F-ratio
Regression   7775.4            2         3887.7        109
Residual     142.029           4         35.5071

Variable   Coefficient   s.e. of Coeff    t-ratio    prob
Constant   53.088        7.246            7.33       0.0018
Area       4.53236       0.3063           14.8       0.0001
Pool       29.1604       5.368            5.43       0.0056
```

Comment on the changes in *s*, in the coefficients and in the residuals.

In both cases, refer to the patterns apparent in the preliminary analysis for clues about reasons for changes.

8.6 Carry out the analysis of stamp sales data prior to 1970 leading to the prediction formula discussed in the subsection on 'Comparing models based on early and recent data', page 283.

## 8.10    Laboratory Exercise: Prediction of meter sales

Recall Section 1.6, where the stamp sales case study was introduced. Included in Table 1.4 were data on meter sales. They are in Excel file Meter Sales.xls on the book's website, along with the data on GNP, RLP and RPC.

Carry out a full regression analysis of the meter sales data, with a view to developing a prediction formula. Report on each step along the way, with detailed commentary on regression output and diagnostics and justification for each step taken. Provide a concluding report on the value of the data for providing a prediction formula.

# 9
# Time series

Processes vary with time. However, in most of the problems addressed so far, time has not played an explicit role in our analysis. Exceptions have been the seasonal variation in bar sales noted in Section 1.1, the random walk model for share index variation considered in Section 1.2 and the possibility of serial correlation of residuals raised in Section 8.7. In this chapter, we focus on problems where time plays a key role which must be accounted for in any analysis.

We consider two types of problem where time plays a role, one where time may be regarded as an explanatory variable and a second where correlations across time are important. In the first case, the most commonly encountered sources of variation are trend and seasonal variation. We will find that straightforward application of regression methods provides a useful approach in dealing with trend and seasonal variation, assuming that there are no significant correlation patterns across time. We will also explore an alternative approach to trend and seasonal variation which does allow for the presence of serial correlation. This involves the use of *smoothers* which may be chosen to average out the effects of chance variation, leaving trend and seasonal variation. They may also be used to average the seasonal variation, leaving just the trend.

Both of these approaches may be combined and extended, thus allowing the involvement of complex combinations of response and explanatory variables, using regression type methods, and complex correlation patterns, using smoothing methods.

## Learning objectives

After completing this chapter, students should know the definition of the classical model for time series variation, understand the use of smoothing formulas in exploratory analysis of time series data, understand the application of multiple regression in estimating trend and seasonal components of a time series and producing corresponding forecasting formulas, understand the construction of simple and exponentially weighted moving averages and the combination of moving averages into forecasts incorporating trend and seasonality, and appreciate how such approaches to forecasting may be combined and extended to produce more complex forecasting models and formulas, and demonstrate this by being able to:

- describe the additive and multiplicative versions of the classical model for business time series;
- determine linear trends using simple linear regression;
- define indicator variables corresponding to different seasons;
- determine linear trends and constant seasonal effects using multiple linear regression;
- calculate simple moving averages to smooth seasonal effects;
- describe and illustrate the use of the Lowess smoother for exploratory analysis of time series data;
- calculate simple moving averages for forecasting;
- describe the construction and calculation of exponentially weighted moving averages;
- describe the combination of exponentially weighted moving averages of level and slope of a time series with trend to produce Holt's formula;
- outline the extension of Holt's method to the Holt–Winters forecast incorporating trend and seasonal effects;
- outline the extension of regression based forecasts and moving average based forecasts to econometric and ARIMA models and forecasts.

## 9.1   A sales forecasting problem

Southern Oil Products are primary processors of vegetable oils made from a variety of vegetable species which they acquire from a variety of sources, depending on the season of the year. They sell their produce in bulk in 50 litre drums. Sources tend to be limited during the first quarter of each year, so production tends to be lowest then. During the past year, they had a major problem in the second quarter due to political unrest in the country from which they get the bulk of their supplies during that time of the year. As a result, they have carried out a review of their whole operation and have decided that they need quarterly forecasts one year ahead so that they can plan their budgeting and staff allocation and hiring strategies to take account of the seasonal nature of the business. They also want to quantify the impact of the second quarter problem last year; they feel that, by having a better understanding of this crisis, they will be in a better position to handle the next crisis, whenever it comes along. Quantifying the extent of the crisis is one aspect of this.

Table 9.1 gives production figures, in numbers of 50 litre drums, for the past six years. As with any statistical data analysis problem, the first step is to conduct an initial data analysis.

**Table 9.1**　Quarterly production of vegetable oil, in numbers of 50 litre drums, for a six year period

| Year | Quarter | Production | Annual | Year | Quarter | Production | Annual |
|------|---------|-----------|--------|------|---------|-----------|--------|
| 1 | 1 | 1,102 | | 4 | 1 | 1,407 | |
| | 2 | 1,352 | | | 2 | 1,778 | |
| | 3 | 1,333 | | | 3 | 1,750 | |
| | 4 | 1,426 | | | 4 | 1,852 | |
| | | | *5,213* | | | | *6,787* |
| 2 | 1 | 1,204 | | 5 | 1 | 1,602 | |
| | 2 | 1,463 | | | 2 | 1,907 | |
| | 3 | 1,472 | | | 3 | 1,833 | |
| | 4 | 1,528 | | | 4 | 2,009 | |
| | | | *5,667* | | | | *7,351* |
| 3 | 1 | 1,352 | | 6 | 1 | 1,694 | |
| | 2 | 1,648 | | | 2 | 1,657 | |
| | 3 | 1,519 | | | 3 | 2,185 | |
| | 4 | 1,602 | | | 4 | 2,139 | |
| | | | *6,121* | | | | *7,675* |

## Initial data analysis

Figure 9.1 shows a line plot or time series plot of quarterly production for the 24 quarters, numbered 1–24, of the six year period.

The most striking aspect of this plot is the positive trend. More careful inspection shows a seasonal pattern with production in the first quarter being relatively low, fourth quarter highest in all but year 6, second quarter usually next highest, usually

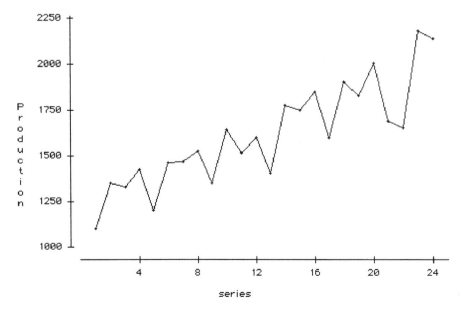

**Figure 9.1**　Quarterly production of vegetable oil, in numbers of 50 litre drums, for a six year period.

followed by third quarter. The uncharacteristic low value in the second quarter of year 6 corresponds to the known problem that occurred in that period. Note also that third quarter production is uncharacteristically high in year 6; this occurred as a result of efforts made to reduce the backlog caused by the second quarter problem.

Given the dominance of the trend in Figure 9.1, the plot may be enhanced by adding a straight line to represent the underlying trend. The result is Figure 9.2.

Quarter 1 production is now seen to be always well below the trend, with production in the other three quarters being usually above the trend, to varying degrees.

The added trend line suggests the possibility of forecasting future production by extrapolating the trend and making adjustments for each quarter (seasonal adjustment). A variety of more or less *ad hoc* ways of doing this has been suggested. Two variations are indicated in Review Exercises 9.1 and 9.2. In the next section, a more formal approach is introduced, based on formal modelling of the trend and seasonal effects, using a multiple regression model as in Chapter 8. This approach was illustrated in Section 1.7.

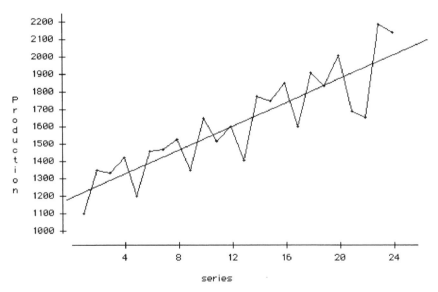

**Figure 9.2**   Quarterly production of vegetable oil, in numbers of 50 litre drums, for a six year period, with trend line added.

## 9.2   Modelling trend and seasonality

A version[1] of the classical model for business time series is expressed as

---

[1]   This version is referred to as *additive* because the individual components are added to give the series. Alternatives include *multiplicative*, where Series = T × S × C × I, using obvious abbreviations. Focusing on trend and seasonality, this model indicates that the seasonal effect is *proportional* to trend; in many applications, variation around a trend will grow with the trend.

Series = Trend + Seasonal effect + Cyclical effect + Irregular fluctuation.

In the production forecasting problem, we have visually identified a trend and seasonal effects. The term 'seasonal' is also used in reference to fixed periods of other than a year For example, daily bar sales in the sports and social club discussed in Section 1.1 tend to be highest at weekends, decreasing towards the middle of the week and increasing again towards the weekend. Figure 9.3 shows daily sales for the first quarter of 1990, corresponding to weeks 1–13 in Figure 1.1.

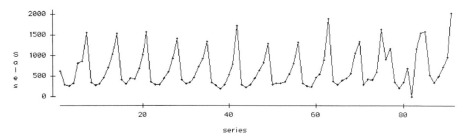

**Figure 9.3**    Daily sales in a sports and social club for the first quarter, 1990.

The weekly pattern is striking. On seeing this, the club management committee decided to organise mid-week special events, to attract more members and improve mid-week business.

Cyclical effects are usually associated with the so-called *business cycle* in which periods of economic prosperity lasting several years are followed by recessions. However, the length of the cycle varies and, specifically, is very difficult to predict.[2] Consequently, its use in forecasting formulas is questionable.

The final component, irregular fluctuation, corresponds to what we have described as chance variation.

## A simple linear model for trend

The trend in the vegetable oil data appears to be linear and may be expressed in the standard simple linear regression form:

$$\alpha + \beta \times \text{Time},$$

where Time is here measured in units of a quarter of a year. In this case, Time varies from 1 to 24. If we ignore seasonality for the moment, we can model the trend by fitting a simple linear regression model to the data. In fact, because of the known exceptional variation in year 6, we fit the model to the data from the first five years.

---

[2]    In the late 1980s and again in the late 1990s, both times which had been preceded by relatively long periods of prosperity, several analysts published claims or suggestions that the business cycle was dead, only to have their claims undermined by the recessions that quickly followed. A highly informative article entitled 'Why the Chancellor is always wrong' published in *New Scientist* magazine in 1992 gives an account of the false predictions of the end of the early 1990s recession by British Treasury forecasters. This article is reproduced, with permission, on the book's website.

Figure 9.4 shows the data for the first five years with the fitted trend line added. The corresponding regression output follows.

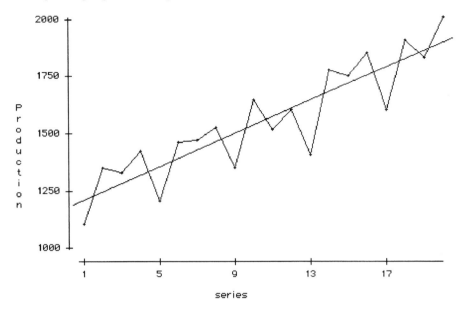

**Figure 9.4**  Quarterly production of vegetable oil, in numbers of 50 litre drums, for a five year period, with trend line added.

```
Dependent variable is:                    Production
No Selector
24 total cases of which 4 are missing
R squared = 78.4%      R squared (adjusted) = 77.3%
s =   115.4  with   20 - 2 = 18  degrees of freedom
```

| Source | Sum of Squares | df | Mean Square | F-ratio |
|--------|----------------|-----|-------------|---------|
| Regression | 872565 | 1 | 872565 | 65.5 |
| Residual | 239728 | 18 | 13318.2 | |

| Variable | Coefficient | s.e. of Coeff | t-ratio | prob |
|----------|-------------|---------------|---------|------|
| Constant | 1176.61 | 53.61 | 21.9 | ≤ 0.0001 |
| Time | 36.2233 | 4.475 | 8.09 | ≤ 0.0001 |

Thus, the fitted trend is

$$\text{Production} = 1\,177 + 36 \times \text{Time}.$$

This is of limited value, since it ignores the obvious quarterly effect. However, it does tell us that production has been growing at an average rate of 36 drums per quarter, or $4 \times 36 = 134$ drums per year.

### An estimate for seasonal effect

The next step is to adjust this trend formula to allow for seasonal variation. The first quarter production data, corresponding to the points labelled 1, 5, 9, 13 and 17 on the horizontal axis in Figure 9.4, all deviate from the trend by similar negative amounts. Further inspection suggests similar patterns in each of the other three quarters, with one or two possible exceptions.

In Section 1.7, special variables Q1, Q2, Q3 and Q4 called *indicator variables* were introduced and added to the simple regression model to produce a multiple regression model incorporating the seasonal effects. Quarterly indicators may be introduced here as well; their values in this case are shown in Table 9.2.

**Table 9.2** Quarterly production of vegetable oil, in numbers of 50 litre drums, with time and quarterly indicators, for a five year period

| Year | Quarter | Production | Time | Q1 | Q2 | Q3 | Q4 |
|------|---------|------------|------|----|----|----|----|
| 1 | 1 | 1,102 | 1 | 1 | 0 | 0 | 0 |
|   | 2 | 1,352 | 2 | 0 | 1 | 0 | 0 |
|   | 3 | 1,333 | 3 | 0 | 0 | 1 | 0 |
|   | 4 | 1,426 | 4 | 0 | 0 | 0 | 1 |
| 2 | 1 | 1,204 | 5 | 1 | 0 | 0 | 0 |
|   | 2 | 1,463 | 6 | 0 | 1 | 0 | 0 |
|   | 3 | 1,472 | 7 | 0 | 0 | 1 | 0 |
|   | 4 | 1,528 | 8 | 0 | 0 | 0 | 1 |
| 3 | 1 | 1,352 | 9 | 1 | 0 | 0 | 0 |
|   | 2 | 1,648 | 10 | 0 | 1 | 0 | 0 |
|   | 3 | 1,519 | 11 | 0 | 0 | 1 | 0 |
|   | 4 | 1,602 | 12 | 0 | 0 | 0 | 1 |
| 4 | 1 | 1,407 | 13 | 1 | 0 | 0 | 0 |
|   | 2 | 1,778 | 14 | 0 | 1 | 0 | 0 |
|   | 3 | 1,750 | 15 | 0 | 0 | 1 | 0 |
|   | 4 | 1,852 | 16 | 0 | 0 | 0 | 1 |
| 5 | 1 | 1,602 | 17 | 1 | 0 | 0 | 0 |
|   | 2 | 1,907 | 18 | 0 | 1 | 0 | 0 |
|   | 3 | 1,833 | 19 | 0 | 0 | 1 | 0 |
|   | 4 | 2,009 | 20 | 0 | 0 | 0 | 1 |

Each quarterly indicator takes the value 1 in the relevant quarter and 0 otherwise. Note that, in each row, only one of the quarterly indicators takes the value 1, while the other three take the value 0. We have encountered this kind of variable in Chapter 8, Section 8.2, where the 'Rushed' variable indicates by its value, 1 or 0, for a particular job whether that job is rushed or not. Its coefficient in the regression formula represented the adjustment to be made to the corresponding job time prediction.

The regression model introduced in Section 1.7 to represent seasonal effects was

$$\text{Production} = \alpha_1 \times Q1 + \alpha_2 \times Q2 + \alpha_3 \times Q3 + \alpha_4 \times Q4 + \beta \times \text{Time} + \varepsilon.$$

Fitting this model to the data leads to

```
Dependent variable is:    Production
No Selector
R squared = ●%      R squared (adjusted) = ●%
s =  40.97  with   20 - 5 = 15  degrees of freedom

Source          Sum of Squares    df    Mean Square   F-ratio
Regression      4.9569e7           5      9.9138e6     5.91e3
Residual        25172.4           15       1678.16

Variable     Coefficient    s.e. of Coeff     t-ratio      prob
Q1           1029.87         23.41             44          ≤ 0.0001
Q2           1292.35         24.45             52.9        ≤ 0.0001
Q3           1210.42         25.55             47.4        ≤ 0.0001
Q4           1278.7          26.71             47.9        ≤ 0.0001
Time         33.725           1.619            20.8        ≤ 0.0001
```

and thus the prediction formula

$$\text{Production} = 1\,030 \times Q1 + 1\,292 \times Q2 + 1\,210 \times Q3$$
$$+ 1\,279 \times Q4 + 34 \times \text{Time} \pm 2 \times 41$$

The first point to note is that a prediction range of 164, corresponding to the prediction limits of $\pm 2 \times 41$, is not unsatisfactory in the context of a data range of 907, being less than 20%.

Next, the prediction formula can be represented more explicitly as four separate prediction formulas, one for each quarter. In quarter 1, Q1 is 1 while Q2, Q3 and Q4 are zero. Substituting these values in the formula leads to

$$\text{Production} = 1\,030 + 34 \times \text{Time} \pm 2 \times 41,$$

as a prediction formula for first quarter production in a future year.

Similar formulas apply to second, third and fourth quarter prediction; simply replace the intercept value with the coefficient of the corresponding quarterly indicator.

---

**Exercise 9.1**   Write down the second, third and fourth quarter prediction formulas. Predict production for the four quarters of year 6.

---

### Diagnostic analysis

Before accepting these formulas, we need to conduct a diagnostic analysis. Figure 9.5 shows a standard set of diagnostics, as discussed in Chapter 8.

---

**Exercise 9.2**   Review the criteria for evaluating residual plots; see Step 3 in the model fitting and testing procedure described in Section 8.6, page 270.

---

There is one residual larger than 2 in magnitude; its value is −2.6. When referred to the time series plot of residuals in Figure 9.5, it forms part of a suggestive set of three in a row, corresponding to quarters 3 and 4 of year 3 and quarter 1 of year 4,

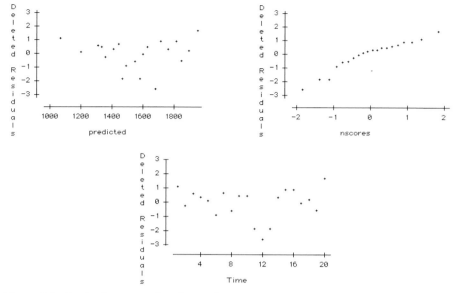

**Figure 9.5**    Production regression diagnostics.

which appear low, by comparison with the rest. This suggests the possibility of a three quarter downturn in the business. However, this is highly speculative. In any case, short term downturns are inevitable in most businesses. Apart from this, the diagnostic plots appear unexceptional.

Deletion of the three points identified makes little difference to the forecast formulas although it does substantially reduce the value of $s$; the corresponding regression results follow.

```
Dependent variable is:                    Production
No Selector
20 total cases of which 3 are missing
R squared = •%       R squared (adjusted) = •%
s =   24.45  with   17 - 5 = 12  degrees of freedom
```

| Source | Sum of Squares | df | Mean Square | F-ratio |
|---|---|---|---|---|
| Regression | 4.27336e7 | 5 | 8.54671e6 | 1.43e4 |
| Residual | 7174.12 | 12 | 597.843 | |

| Variable | Coefficient | s.e. of Coeff | t-ratio | prob |
|---|---|---|---|---|
| Q1 | 1041.25 | 14.53 | 71.7 | ≤ 0.0001 |
| Q2 | 1287.41 | 14.7 | 87.6 | ≤ 0.0001 |
| Q3 | 1220.59 | 16.31 | 74.8 | ≤ 0.0001 |
| Q4 | 1293.12 | 16.98 | 76.2 | ≤ 0.0001 |
| Time | 34.2194 | 0.982 | 34.8 | ≤ 0.0001 |

**Exercise 9.3**    Compare the values of the regression coefficients above with the corresponding values given earlier; informally refer the differences to the corresponding standard errors shown above.

In the circumstances, it is probably safer not to delete the three points and accept the extra prediction error as reasonable.

## Using the forecasting formulas

We can 'forecast' the first quarter of year 6 and compare with actual production. In this case, Time takes the value 21, so the quarter 1 forecast formula gives

$$1\,030 + 34 \times \text{Time} = 1\,030 + 34 \times 21 = 1\,744 \text{ drums.}$$

The actual value, from Table 9.2, was 1,694 drums. Thus, the forecast exceeds actual by 50 drums. This is well within the '$2\sigma$ limits' of $\pm 82$.

---

**Exercise 9.4**    Compare the forecast for year 6, quarter 4 with actual.

---

The second quarter forecast formula should indicate the level of production we would have expected to achieve if the problem had not occurred and production growth continued as evidenced in years 1–5. Substituting Time = 22 in the second quarter formula gives

$$1\,292 + 34 \times 22 = 2\,040.$$

The actual value, from Table 9.2, was 1,657, which is 384 drums less than anticipated, that is, approximately 19% less and well outside the '$2\sigma$ limits'. This gives us a measure of the impact of the second quarter problem.

Having noted that quarter 3, year 6, was well up on what we might anticipate from third quarter production levels for previous years, we can measure how well production recovered in the third quarter.

---

**Exercise 9.5**    Calculate the forecast for year 6, quarter 3, compare with actual, compare the difference with the shortfall in quarter 2 and, hence, quantify the third quarter recovery.

---

## Different time units

Many business series are recorded monthly. In that case, monthly seasonal adjustments are needed. These may be calculated by adding indicator variables for the 12 months to the basic linear trend (excluding intercept) and using the corresponding estimated coefficients as monthly intercepts.

In cases where the 'seasonality' is not annual, the basic time units within each cycle may be represented by indicators in the same way. For example, in the case of the weekly pattern of daily sales illustrated in Figure 9.3, indicators for the days of the week may be defined. The corresponding analysis is the subject of Review Exercise 9.3.

## 9.3 Smoothing for exploratory analysis

The trend line fitted to the production data in Section 9.2 may be regarded as a *smoother*, smoothing the effects of seasonal and chance variation to leave just the trend, which may then be projected forward for forecasting purposes. However, the linear trend smoother, as such, is rather inflexible. In the next section, the use of more flexible families of smoothers for forecasting purposes is described. To introduce smoothers generally, this section describes the use of smoothers for graphical exploratory analysis to emphasise or enhance underlying patterns in data. Recall the use of a smoother in Figure 1.2, page 4, to emphasise the seasonal effect on sales and in Figure 1.30, page 46, to highlight changes in the pattern of housing completions. The section begins with the introduction of *moving averages.*

### Moving averages

A simple way to remove the seasonal effect from a series is to average successive values in the series four at a time. The average of the first four values is

$$1\,303.25 = \frac{1\,102 + 1\,352 + 1\,333 + 1\,426}{4};$$

the average of the second four, that is, quarters 2, 3 and 4 of year 1 and quarter 1 of year 2, is

$$1\,328.75 = \frac{1\,352 + 1\,333 + 1\,426 + 1\,204}{4}.$$

The results of these calculations are shown in Table 9.3 and illustrated in Figure 9.6.

---

**Exercise 9.6**  Calculate the missing entries in column 4 of Table 9.3.

---

The effect of this smoother is to smooth out the quarterly effect and some chance variations and leave an underlying trend. Note that the entries in Table 9.3 are centred between quarters; the average of four successive values is considered to represent a value in the middle of the time range. This makes no essential difference in the context of graphical exploratory analysis, where the emphasis is on understanding the overall pattern of variation. However, if further numerical work is needed as in, for example, decomposing the series into its components, a smoothed value is needed at time points corresponding to actual data. To achieve this, another device is used involving a weighted moving average of *five* values.

Table 9.4 is a reworked version of Table 9.3, showing the new relocated moving averages. The first value in column 4, 1,316.00, is an average of the first five numbers in column 3, with the first and last numbers carrying half weight:

$$1\,316 = \frac{\frac{1}{2} \times 1\,102 + 1\,352 + 1\,333 + 1\,426 + \frac{1}{2} \times 1\,204}{4}.$$

**Table 9.3**   Quarterly production data, with moving averages of order 4

| Year | Quarter | Production | 4MA | Year | Quarter | Production | 4MA |
|------|---------|-----------|------|------|---------|-----------|------|
| 1 | 1 | 1,102 | | 4 | 1 | 1,407 | |
| | | | | | | | 1,576.50 |
| | 2 | 1,352 | | | 2 | 1,778 | |
| | | | 1,303.25 | | | | 1,634.25 |
| | 3 | 1,333 | | | 3 | 1,750 | |
| | | | 1,328.75 | | | | 1,696.75 |
| | 4 | 1,426 | | | 4 | 1,852 | |
| | | | | | | | 1,745.50 |
| 2 | 1 | 1,204 | | 5 | 1 | 1,602 | |
| | | | | | | | 1,777.75 |
| | 2 | 1,463 | | | 2 | 1,907 | |
| | | | 1,416.75 | | | | 1,798.50 |
| | 3 | 1,472 | | | 3 | 1,833 | |
| | | | 1,453.75 | | | | 1,837.75 |
| | 4 | 1,528 | | | 4 | 2,009 | |
| | | | 1,500.00 | | | | |
| 3 | 1 | 1,352 | | | | | |
| | | | 1,511.75 | | | | |
| | 2 | 1,648 | | | | | |
| | | | 1,530.25 | | | | |
| | 3 | 1,519 | | | | | |
| | | | 1,544.00 | | | | |
| | 4 | 1,602 | | | | | |

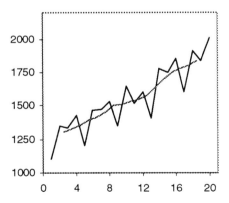

**Figure 9.6**   Quarterly production with moving averages centred between quarters.

The reason for this is that the first and fifth numbers are both first quarter values. If included with full weight, the first quarter effect would be included twice in the average. By giving each half weight, the first quarter effect counts just once. Because this average involves *five* successive quarters, the centre of that time period corresponds to an actual time point and the moving average may be located there, as shown in Table 9.4.

**Table 9.4**   Quarterly production data, with moving average smoothing

| Year | Quarter | Production | 2 × 4*MA* | Year | Quarter | Production | 2 × 4*MA* |
|---|---|---|---|---|---|---|---|
| 1 | 1 | 1,102 | | 4 | 1 | 1,407 | 1,605.38 |
|   | 2 | 1,352 | | | 2 | 1,778 | 1,665.50 |
|   | 3 | 1,333 | 1,316.00 | | 3 | 1,750 | 1,721.13 |
|   | 4 | 1,426 | 1,342.63 | | 4 | 1,852 | 1,761.63 |
| 2 | 1 | 1,204 | | 5 | 1 | 1,602 | 1,788.13 |
|   | 2 | 1,463 | | | 2 | 1,907 | 1,818.13 |
|   | 3 | 1,472 | 1,435.25 | | 3 | 1,833 | |
|   | 4 | 1,528 | 1,476.88 | | 4 | 2,009 | |
| 3 | 1 | 1,352 | 1,505.88 | | | | |
|   | 2 | 1,648 | 1,521.00 | | | | |
|   | 3 | 1,519 | 1,537.13 | | | | |
|   | 4 | 1,602 | 1,560.25 | | | | |

Similarly, the second value is a weighted average of the first five numbers excluding the first, that is,

$$1\,342.63 = \frac{\frac{1}{2} \times 1\,352 + 1\,333 + 1\,426 + 1\,204 + \frac{1}{2} \times 1\,463}{4}$$

This weighted average includes two second quarter values, each half weighted. The middle of the time period involved is quarter 4, where the average is located, as in Table 9.4.

---

**Exercise 9.7**   Calculate the missing entries in column 4 of Table 9.4.

---

Figure 9.7 shows the adjusted moving averages. For graphical exploratory analysis purposes, both smoothers are effectively identical. The heading, 2 × 4MA, in column 4 of Table 9.4 reflects the fact that the weighted average calculated above may also be represented as the average of the first and second moving averages in

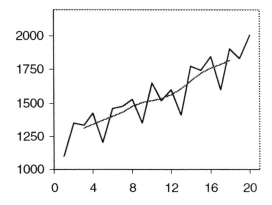

**Figure 9.7**   Quarterly production with centred moving average.

Table 9.3. The first is the average of quarters 1–4, the second is the average of quarters 2–5; their average includes time periods 2–4 twice and time periods 1 and 5 once each.

Many variations on this simple idea of combining simple smoothers into more complicated forms have been proposed, with varying degrees of success. A problem faced by all such smoothers is how to deal with end points, with a variety of solutions mainly involving weighted averages of data near the ends. Choosing among the vast array of smoothers available is not easy. However, an increasingly popular choice is the so called Lowess smoother, which is the smoother used earlier in Chapter 1.

**The Lowess smoother**

Figure 1.30, reproduced below as Figure 9.8, shows the number of houses completed in Ireland in each quarter from 1978 to 2000. The line chart is enhanced with a version of the Lowess smoother and suggests four distinct patterns, an erratic period during the first three years, a strong negative trend from 1981 until 1988, a large jump followed by a period of relative stability from the third quarter of 1989 and, starting in 1993, a very strong upward trend.

The choice of smoother in Figure 9.9 was the culmination of a series of choices of versions of Lowess which assisted, through exploratory analysis, in arriving at an informative description of the changing patterns of variation in the data. Figures 9.7 and 9.8 show earlier trial versions involving greater degrees of smoothness which, however, do not reveal as much detail as the finally chosen version shown in Figure 9.8.

Lowess is an acronym for **LO**cally **WE**ighted regression **S**catterplot **S**moothing. It extends the moving average idea to *moving lines.* At each point in the time series, a straight line is fitted to a span of data points on either side of the chosen point, using a form of regression in which points close to the chosen point are weighted more heavily than more remote points and in which an automatic adjustment is made to

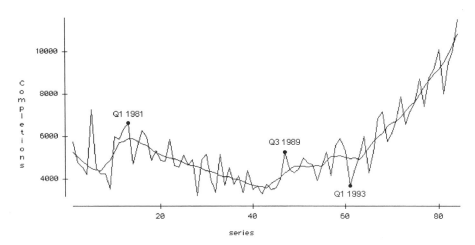

**Figure 9.8**   Housing completions, quarterly, 1978–2000, with Lowess smoother.

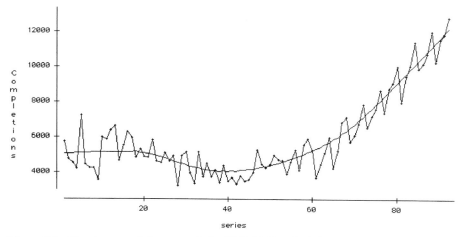

**Figure 9.9** Housing completions, quarterly, 1978–2000, with default span Lowess smoother.

reduce the influence of exceptional values. The lines corresponding to each data point are suitably joined together to give the final smoother.

A key parameter in deciding which version of Lowess to use is the *span,* that is, the distance on either side of the chosen point that determines the points to be included in the calculation; the larger the span, the smoother will be the resulting curve. Typically, the default value in standard software gives a relatively smooth curve. Figure 9.9 shows the default used by Data Desk, Figure 9.10 shows the version with span half the default while the final choice in Figure 9.8 above shows the version with span one quarter of the default. (Minitab gives virtually identical results.)

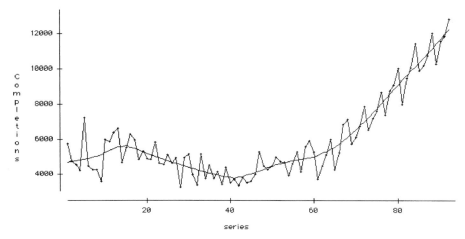

**Figure 9.10** Housing completions, quarterly, 1978–2000, with half default span Lowess smoother.

> **Exercise 9.8** Figure 9.11 shows line plots of the weekly sales data discussed in Section 1.1 enhanced with Lowess smoothers using four different degrees of smoothing. Discuss arguments for and against selecting each one.

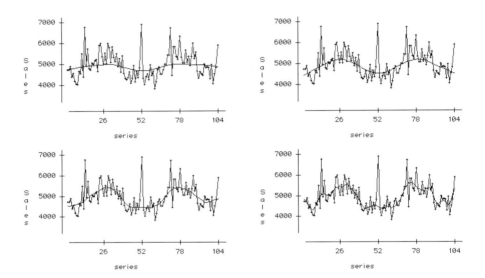

**Figure 9.11** Line plots of weekly sales in a sports and social club for two years, 1990–91, with Lowess smoothers using 1.5 times default span, default span, half default span and quarter default span, respectively.

## 9.4 Forecasting with smoothers; the Holt–Winters method

A widely used class of forecasting methods is based on smoothing the data and building forecasts from the smoothed data. In this section, we introduce smoothers which are designed to be sensitive to trend and seasonality but are also sensitive to changes in patterns of trend and seasonality. These smoothers have the advantage that they can take account of certain patterns of serial correlation in the data, something which ordinary multiple regression methods do not attempt. Recall that, in Section 8.3, on additional diagnostic tools, the use of time series plots of residuals was advocated with a view to detecting serial correlation if present but with the hope of demonstrating its absence and, therefore, the validity of the standard methods.

The development starts with a simple moving average, noting its shortcomings. By using a suitable weighted average, this can be adapted to weigh more on recent data and less on past data. This leads to the *exponentially weighted moving average* or *exponential smoothing*. These smoothers are still not capable of coping with trend and seasonality, however. Holt's method involves adapting the exponential smoothers to take account of linear trend. Finally, the Holt–Winters method introduces a further adaptation to take account of seasonal effects.

## Moving averages

The simplest possible time series forecasting formula, given up-to-date historical data, is to use the current value of the series as a forecast of the next value. Among professional forecasters, this is known as the *naive forecast*. In the case of a series which has no trend and no seasonal variation, the naive forecast is not without its merits. For example, recalling the analysis of the FTSE 100 share index in Section 1.2, the naive forecast is as good as any when the change from one period to the next appears to behave like pure chance variation. However, in the presence of trend, the naive forecast will always be one step behind the trend; with seasonal variation, it will be one year behind the season to season variation. If naive forecasts were made at each time period as the series evolved, the result would be as illustrated in Figure 9.12.

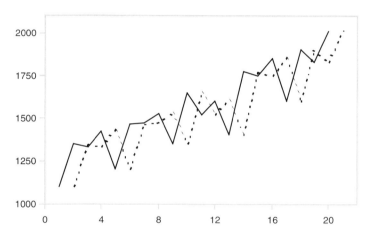

**Figure 9.12**   Quarterly production, years 1–5 (solid) with naive forecasts (dashed).

A simple improvement that makes some allowance for seasonal variation is to use the average of the last four values in the series as the forecast of the next value. This tends to average out quarterly effects, thus allowing the forecast to get closer to the underlying trend, but still one step behind. The result of applying this forecast at each time period as the series evolves is shown in Figure 9.13. Note that each average is placed one quarter ahead of the time period on which it is based, reflecting the fact that the interest here is in *forecasting*, and not exploratory analysis.

Of necessity, no forecasts are available for the first four time points. However, at time 4, the average of the first four points provides a forecast for time 5. When time five comes, the average of the values at times 2 to 5 provide a forecast for time 6. Proceeding in this way, one imagines the current selection of four points moving forward as time evolves, providing a forecast for one step ahead of the current time

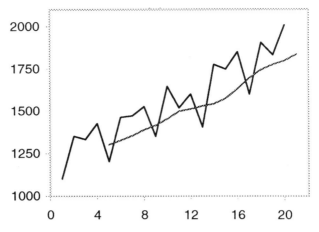

**Figure 9.13**   Quarterly production, years 1–5 with MA(4) forecasts.

point, whence the phrase *moving average*. Table 9.5 shows the production data with moving averages of order 4. Thus, the first entry in column 4 is the average of the first year's data, the second entry is the average of quarters 2, 3 and 4 in year 1 and quarter 1 in year 2, etc. The notation MA(4) is conventional when the moving average is used for forecasting.

> **Exercise 9.9**   Calculate the missing entries in column 4 of Table 9.5.

The moving average forecasts are closer to the underlying trend than the naive forecasts, because the quarterly effects have been *smoothed* out. However, they remain one step behind the trend, which partially explains why the forecasts appear consistently below the trend. Also note that the same moving average used as an exploratory smoother was located three time periods to the left; recall Figure 9.6.

**Table 9.5**   Quarterly production data, with moving average forecasts

| Year | Quarter | Production | MA(4) | Year | Quarter | Production | MA(4) |
|------|---------|-----------|----------|------|---------|-----------|----------|
| 1 | 1 | 1,102 | | 4 | 1 | 1,407 | 1,530.25 |
| | 2 | 1,352 | | | 2 | 1,778 | 1,544.00 |
| | 3 | 1,333 | | | 3 | 1,750 | 1,576.50 |
| | 4 | 1,426 | | | 4 | 1,852 | 1,634.25 |
| 2 | 1 | 1,204 | 1,303.25 | 5 | 1 | 1,602 | 1,696.75 |
| | 2 | 1,463 | 1,328.75 | | 2 | 1,907 | 1,745.50 |
| | 3 | 1,472 | | | 3 | 1,833 | 1,777.75 |
| | 4 | 1,528 | | | 4 | 2,009 | 1,798.50 |
| 3 | 1 | 1,352 | 1,416.75 | 6 | 1 | | 1,837.75 |
| | 2 | 1,648 | 1,453.75 | | | | |
| | 3 | 1,519 | 1,500.00 | | | | |
| | 4 | 1,602 | 1,511.75 | | | | |

Averaging reduces the effect of irregular or chance variation on the forecasts. As we have seen in earlier chapters, we can further reduce the effects of chance variation on an average by increasing the number of values included in the average. A simple way to do this is to use a moving average of order 8, 12, or higher.

A drawback with this approach is that we have to wait some time before we can make any forecasts, two years in the case of MA(8), three years in the case of MA(12), etc. A second drawback is that values of the time series from the past have the same influence on the forecast as current values; with a changing series, it may be argued that older data are less relevant to forecasting than current data.

## Exponentially weighted moving average

A solution to the first of these drawbacks is to 'anchor' the moving average at the start of the series, allowing it to move at the front end only. Thus, the forecast at time 2 is the first value, the forecast at time 3 is an average of the first two values, the forecast at time 4 is an average of the first three values, etc. Thus, succeeding values of the moving average are based on increasing numbers of values of the time series. A solution to the second is to use a weighted average, weighting recent data more heavily than earlier data. A form of moving average that achieves both of these is the *exponentially weighted moving average* or EWMA. This is defined by the following formula, which appears more formidable than it is:

$$\hat{Y}_{t+1} = \frac{Y_t + cY_{t-1} + c^2 Y_{t-2} + c^3 Y_{t-3} + \cdots + c^{t-1} Y_1}{1 + c + c^2 + c^3 + \cdots c^{t-1}}.$$

Here, $Y$ is the variable of interest, values $Y_1, Y_2, Y_3, \ldots, Y_t$, $t$ in number, have been observed and $\hat{Y}_{t+1}$ represents the forecast of the next value, $Y_{t+1}$.

The formula shows, in the numerator, a weighted combination of the observed values and, in the denominator, the sum of the weights, thus giving a weighted average. The form of the weights is special. The constant, $c$, which must be specified in any application, is always between 0 and 1. The most recent value, $Y_t$, gets the highest weight. $Y_{t-1}$ gets weight $c$, smaller than 1. Because $c$ is smaller than 1, it follows that $c^2$ is smaller than $c$, $c^3$ is smaller than $c^2$, etc. (For example, $(\frac{1}{2})^2 = \frac{1}{4}$, smaller than $\frac{1}{2}$, $(\frac{1}{2})^3 = \frac{1}{8}$, smaller than $\frac{1}{4}$, etc.) Thus, the values further back in the series are weighted less and less. The early values have very small weights. In the case of the Production series, there are 20 values available in the first five years. The earliest weight is $(\frac{1}{2})^{19} = 0.000002$.

In mathematical terminology, the numbers of times $c$ is multiplied by itself in the successive weights are called the *exponents* of $c$; hence the phrase *exponentially weighted*.

## Updating formula for calculating EWMA

The formula given above is rather complicated for computation purposes. Fortunately, there is an equivalent formula which is easy to compute. It may be shown that, to a high degree of approximation,

$$\hat{Y}_{t+1} = \alpha Y_t + (1 - \alpha)\hat{Y}_t,$$

where $\alpha = 1 - c$. This means that the next forecast is a simple weighted average of the current value and the current forecast. This version of the EWMA is referred to as the *updating formula*.

To implement the formula, a value for $\alpha$ must be chosen. The values of $\alpha$ are always between 0 and 1. Values of $\alpha$ less than 0.5 weigh the current value less than the current forecast and vice versa for values exceeding 0.5. In practice, the current forecast is invariably favoured more, incorporating, as it does, all the preceding data, as opposed to the single current value. The current forecast is an average of several data values and thus smooths out chance variation; the current value is just a single value, containing an unsmoothed chance variation component. One approach to choosing a suitable value for $\alpha$ is to apply the method of least squares, as used for choosing values for regression equation parameters. As with regression, this is best left to suitable software.[3] Alternatively, in the absence of other indications, a default value of $\alpha = 0.2$ is recommended by some.

An initial 'forecast' is also required. $\hat{Y}_2$ equals $\alpha Y_1 + (1 - \alpha)\hat{Y}_1$. However, there is no $\hat{Y}_1$. A simple and usually effective solution is to use $Y_1$ for $\hat{Y}_1$. Alternatively, the average of the first few values may be used. Other options are available.

---

**Exercise 9.10**    Use the updating formula (repeatedly) to calculate the EWMA forecast for quarter 1, year 2. Use $\alpha = 0.2$ and $Y_1$ as the 'initial' forecast. Compare the result with the corresponding MA(4) forecast.

---

Given values for $\alpha$ and an initial 'forecast', the updating formula is easily programmed in Excel.

---

**Exercise 9.11**    The quarterly production data are available in an Excel spreadsheet named Production.xls on the book's website. Implement the EWMA forecasting formula in Excel using $\alpha = 0.2$ and $Y_1$ as the 'initial' forecast. Compare the results with the MA(4) forecasts shown in Table 9.5.

---

Figure 9.14 shows the result of applying the EWMA forecast at each time period as the series evolves, along with the MA(4) forecasts shown earlier. Note that the EWMA forecasts underestimate the trend effect, increasingly as the series evolves. It appears that the EWMA forecast is seriously affected by the big difference between quarter 4 and the following quarter 1. This is because of the unequal weighting built into the EWMA formula.

---

[3]    Minitab has extensive time series modelling and forecasting facilities, including exponentially weighted moving averages with optimal selection of $\alpha$. Excel and Data Desk do not have such facilities, although Excel 'Add-in' functions are available. Other general purpose statistical software packages with time series facilities are SAS and SPSS.

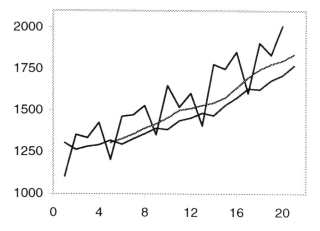

**Figure 9.14** Quarterly production, years 1–5 with MA(4) forecasts (upper) and EWMA forecasts (lower).

### Holt's method for incorporating trend

Neither the simple moving average forecast nor the EWMA forecast adequately deal with trend. Holt's method of incorporating trend is an extension of the EWMA method. It is most simply described in terms of an extension of the updating formula

$$\hat{Y}_{t+1} = \alpha Y_t + (1 - \alpha)\hat{Y}_t,$$

given above. The series may be expressed as a combination of *level, L,* and *trend,* taken to be linear with slope, say, *b*. Both level and slope may be estimated using exponentially weighted moving averages. The level and slope estimates may then be recombined to forecast the series. Thus, given current estimates of level and slope, we can forecast one or more steps ahead using the forecast formula

$$\hat{Y}_{t+s} = L_t + b_t \times s,$$

where $L_t$ is the current level, $b_t$ is the current slope and $s$ is the number of steps ahead. The formulas for the EWMA estimates of current level and slope are

$$L_t = \alpha Y_t + (1 - \alpha)(L_{t-1} + b_{t-1})$$

and

$$b_t = \beta(L_t - L_{t-1}) + (1 - \beta)b_{t-1}$$

respectively. The rationale for these formulas is similar to that for the single EWMA updating formula. The current level estimate is a weighted average of the current series value and the previous level updated by the slope. The current slope estimate is a weighted average of the difference in current and previous levels (itself a naive estimate of slope), and the previous slope. Again, both updating formulas and the combined forecasting formula are easily implemented in Excel. A suggested default value for both $\alpha$ and $\beta$ is 0.2. Suggested initial values for $L_1$ and $b_1$ are $Y_1$ and $Y_2 - Y_1$, respectively. An alternative suggestion is to calculate the simple linear regression of Series ($Y$) against Time ($T$) and use the intercept and slope from that regression as initial values for $L_1$ and $b_1$, respectively.

---

**Exercise 9.12**   Implement Holt's forecasting formula in Excel setting $\alpha = 0.2$, $\beta = 0.2$, $L_1$ to the intercept of the simple linear regression of production against time and $b_1$ to the corresponding slope. (These have already been calculated in Section 9.2; see page 301.) Compare the results with the MA(4) and EWMA forecasts calculated earlier.

---

Figure 9.15 shows the effect of adding in the trend component to the forecast. It appears to over-compensate and the impact of seasonality is still present.

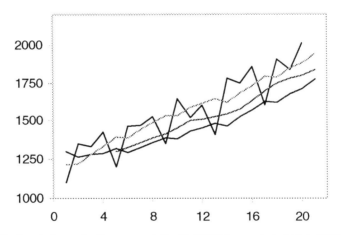

**Figure 9.15**  Quarterly production, years 1–5 with MA(4) forecasts (middle), EWMA forecasts (lower) and Holt forecasts (upper).

### The Holt–Winters forecast incorporating trend and seasonality

If there is a seasonal component in the time series, then neither simple EWMA nor Holt's double EWMA forecast will be adequate. A further extension to Holt's method is needed. This is the Holt–Winters method. An extra updating equation is needed for the seasonal effect. Denoting the current seasonal effect by $S_t$ and letting $n$ denote the number of seasons, the three updating equations are:

$$L_t = \alpha(Y_t - S_{t-n}) + (1 - \alpha)(L_{t-1} + b_{t-1}),$$
$$b_t = \beta(L_t - L_{t-1}) + (1-\beta)b_{t-1}$$

and

$$S_t = \gamma(Y_t - L_t) + (1 - \gamma)S_{t-n},$$

and the combined $s$ step ahead forecasting formula is

$$\hat{Y}_{t+s} = L_t + b_t \times s + S_{t-n+s}.$$

Once again, the three updating formulas and the combined forecasting formula are easily implemented in Excel, although the initialisation process is rather more tedious in this case. Figure 9.16 shows the result of applying the Holt–Winters method as the series evolves. The initialisation was the same for $L$ and $b$. A simple initialisation for $S$ is $S_1 = Y_1 - L_n$, $S_2 = Y_2 - L_n$, ... , $S_n = Y_n - L_n$; recall that $n$ is the number of seasons. Because quarterly effects are included, the final forecasts are made for 1, 2, 3 and 4 steps ahead, that is, for year 6.

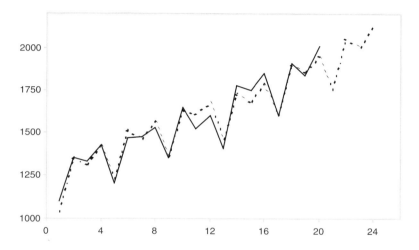

**Figure 9.16**   Quarterly production, years 1–5 (solid) with Holt–Winters forecasts (dashed).

Clearly, the Holt–Winters method performs much better than the other smoother-based methods.

### Additive versus multiplicative models

As noted at the beginning of Section 9.2, the Production series was assumed to be additive. This seems entirely reasonable in this case. In many economic time series, or any series which involves growth, some or all of the components may combine multiplicatively. In that case, this must be taken into account when calculating suitable versions of the various forecasting formulas discussed here. Details are not pursued here.

### Comparison with regression based method

A simple comparison of the Holt–Winters method with the regression based method is shown in Table 9.6. Forecasts of the four quarters of year 6 using both methods,

**Table 9.6**    Holt–Winters and regression based forecasts

| Time | Holt–Winters | Regression | Difference |
|------|------|------|------|
| 21 | 1,755 | 1,738 | 17 |
| 22 | 2,058 | 2,034 | 24 |
| 23 | 2,008 | 1,986 | 22 |
| 24 | 2,116 | 2,088 | 28 |

with the difference between forecasts, are shown. In all four seasons, the Holt–Winters forecasts are slightly higher, but by no more than 1.3%.

Qualitatively, the regression based method is more transparent, in that it readily provides estimates of the various effects. In this respect, it is more useful than Holt–Winters as an exploratory tool, where the aim includes gaining an understanding of the factors influencing the time series, rather than focusing purely on forecasting. This is likely to be the case in one-off studies such as the one undertaken here or the Grafton Group case study of Section 1.7.

For ease of use in ongoing forecasting, the Holt–Winters updating formula is considerably easier to implement. Thus, if there is a need for ongoing forecasting of many series, the Holt–Winters method may readily be automated while the multiple regression based method is impractical. The classic situation where this arises is when a company needs frequent forecasts of inventory requirements for very many raw material items; exponential smoothing methods were developed initially in a production planning and inventory control environment.

More extensive comparisons of the two methods are beyond the scope of this text.

## 9.5    Advanced time series analysis

The methods of analysis used in Sections 9.2 and 9.4, respectively, may be regarded as prototypes for a vast array of more and more complicated methods for analysing time series data which have mushroomed in the last half century.

### Decomposition methods

Both approaches in Sections 9.2 and 9.4 recognised the presence of trend, seasonal effect and irregular fluctuations. In longer series such as the housing completions series, we may anticipate long term cyclical effects as well. These are represented in the classical additive model for business and economic time series,

Series = Trend + Seasonal effect + Cyclical effect + Irregular fluctuation.

or its multiplicative counterpart,

$$Series = T \times S \times C \times I,$$

using obvious abbreviations. There have been many approaches to decomposing series of this form into their basic components. The best known of these is the X-11 method developed by the US Bureau of the Census. The basic decomposition method involves a series of steps involving the use of a variety of moving averages to isolate components and diagnostic checks to identify exceptional cases. The method is applied iteratively to gradually refine the estimates of the components.

Various enhancements to the basic decomposition method of X-11 are continually being developed and new versions of the software emerge. The latest version is called X12-ARIMA. The ARIMA add-on is discussed below.

## Extending multiple regression; econometric methods

An obvious extension to the multiple regression approach to the decomposition of Section 9.2 is to add further explanatory variables which we may anticipate will affect the response. We have already seen this with the annual stamp sales data, analysed in Section 8.7, where no attempt was made to isolate trend-cycle effects. Econometricians have taken this approach to great lengths, adding not just additional variables but also additional equations linking the variables. As a simplistic illustration, consider the following model involving the variables

C = Consumption,
I = Investment,
D = Disposable National Income,
P = Profits,
G = Government Expenditure,
GNP = Gross National Product,
T = Taxes,

where

$$GNP = C + I + G,$$

and

$$D = GNP - T,$$

with the variables being related through the series of equations

$$C_t = a_1 + b_1 D_t + Z_{1t}$$
$$I_t = a_2 + b_2 P_t + Z_{2t}$$
$$T_t = b_3 GNP_t + Z_{3t}$$
$$P_t = a_4 + b_4 D_t + c_4 I_{t-1} + Z_{4t}$$

Here, the Z variables represent irregular or chance variation, or disturbances in the language of econometrics.

Econometricians have gone considerably further than this. A recent article (see footnote 2, page 301) described one very elaborate model of the UK economy, built by a team of 75 econometricians in the British Treasury, which at one stage involved 1,275 variables and 500 equations.

## Extending EWMA-based forecasting; ARIMA and extensions

The forecasting methods of Section 9.3 are related to simple examples of a powerful class of models called ARIMA models. The basic idea behind such models is that current values of time series may be related to past values. This happens in two ways. In the first place, a series $Y$ may satisfy a relationship of the kind

$$Y_t = a + b_1 Y_{t-1} + b_2 Y_{t-2} + b_3 Y_{t-3} + \cdots + b_p Y_{t-p} + \varepsilon_t.$$

Here, the current value of $Y$ is regressed against its own past values. This is referred to as *autoregression* or AR.

It may also happen that the current value of $Y$ depends on past values of the error term, $\varepsilon_t$;

$$Y_t = a + b_1 \varepsilon_{t-1} + b_2 \varepsilon_{t-2} + b_3 \varepsilon_{t-3} + \cdots + b_q \varepsilon_{t-q} + \varepsilon_t.$$

Traditionally, this form of relationship of $Y$ with past error terms has been referred to as a *moving average* or MA model.

When both forms of model apply simultaneously, the result is referred to as an ARMA model. However, ARMA models require that the series have no trend-cycle component. Traditionally, such components are removed by *differencing,* that is by working with the series

$$Y'_t = Y_t - Y_{t-1}$$

the first difference or, if that still has a trend-cycle component, differencing again to get a second or higher difference that has no trend-cycle component. Then, ARMA models are applied to the differenced series.

In mathematical terminology, the original series may be recovered from the differenced series by summing or *integrating* the differenced series. Consequently, applying ARMA models to the differenced series is considered to be applying ARIMA models to the original series, where the I stands for *integrated.*[4]

ARIMA models have considerable flexibility, deriving from the choice of $p$, the number of regression coefficients in the autoregression part of the model, $q$, the order of the moving average part and $d$, the number of differencing operations required. Once the appropriate choices have been made, that is, once the appropriate ARIMA model has been *identified,* optimal values for the model parameters which give a *best fit* of model to data must be found. As with multiple regression models, it is essential to apply diagnostic analysis to the residuals from the best fitting models. All three steps of identification, fitting and diagnostics may need to be iterated until a satisfactory fit is found. The result is a formula which may be used for forecasting, providing both point forecasts and prediction intervals.

A relatively straightforward extension of the ARIMA models allows seasonal effects to be incorporated.

The exponential smoothing forecast formulas of Section 9.4 may be seen as optimal forecasts in the context of specific ARIMA models. In this respect, they have an advantage over the multiple linear regression approach of Section 9.2, as they can accommodate some degree of correlation among the error terms. The valid application of standard multiple regression requires that the error terms are un-correlated.

---

[4]   It would seem simpler to have used S for *summed* but the resulting acronym might not have been acceptable!

**Combinations and extensions**

Regression models have the advantage of being able to accommodate explanatory variables which, in the light of knowledge of the application area, may be considered to have some value in making forecasts of the response variable. However, as noted, ordinary regression cannot accommodate time series correlation patterns. ARIMA models, on the other hand, were specifically designed to accommodate such time series correlation patterns. However, they suffer from the defect that they make no attempt to identify causal or explanatory mechanisms that might lie behind such correlations. In this regard, they are often described as *black box* models. An obvious next step is to combine regression and ARIMA models. Strategies for doing just this have been developed and computer software to allow its implementation in practice is widely available. Econometricians have extended this to incorporate ARIMA modelling into econometric models.

Further developments along these lines and development of a range of radically different approaches to time series modelling and forecasting continue apace, limited only by computing power and the imagination and capability of the statistical and econometric mathematicians involved. Considerable empirical experience has been assembled on the effectiveness of many of these forecasting methods. The general conclusion is disappointing. One frequently occurring characteristic is that forecasters regularly change their models when they find their forecasts are wrong, making adjustments based on *post hoc* analysis of what was deemed to have gone wrong with their forecasts. To some extent, this is analogous to adjusting business or manufacturing processes in the light of deviations that may be ascribed to chance variation and is, therefore, not to be recommended.

Further evidence of the extent of chance variation in forecasting is the wide range of forecasts of the same thing by different forecasters. In the larger developed economies, several hundred forecasters publish forecasts of key economic variables. There is considerable variation in such forecasts, with the pattern of variation closely resembling the Normal model. This leads naturally to the suggestion of using averages of such forecasts, referred to as *consensus forecasting*. This usually leads to more accurate and precise forecasts. However, even consensus forecasts cannot deal with turning points at the start or end of a business cycle.

Related to this is the combination of several methods applied to the same data. Again, the empirical evidence suggests that this leads to improved forecasting performance.

## 9.6 Review exercises

9.1 The first 20 cases of the quarterly data shown in Table 9.1 are available in an Excel file, Production5.xls on the book's website. Create a new variable, Time, which simply numbers the quarters from 1 to 20. Calculate the simple linear regression of Production against Time. This provides an estimate of the underlying trend.

Calculate the average production for each quarter and the deviations of the quarterly averages from the overall average for the five years. These deviations will give quarterly *adjustments* to the underlying trend; for quarters when Production is typically relatively high, the corresponding deviations will be positive and, for quarters when Production is typically relatively low, the corresponding deviations will be negative.

Calculate a separate trend line for each quarter by adding the corresponding quarterly adjustment (including sign, where appropriate) to the intercept of the underlying trend.

9.2    Calculate the ordinary residuals from the simple linear regression of Exercise 9.1; recall the definition of residuals in Section 6.1 in Chapter 6. Calculate the quarterly averages of the residuals. Use these to adjust the underlying trend as in Exercise 9.1.

9.3    Data on daily sales in the sports and social club mentioned earlier are in an Excel spreadsheet, DailySales.xls on the book's website. Use the multiple regression method to quantify the daily effects seen in Figure 9.3. Note that there are some apparently exceptional cases in Figure 9.3. Use diagnostic analysis to confirm these and check for others.

9.4    The article 'Why the Chancellor is always wrong' by Robert Chote, was published in *New Scientist,* October 1992. Read the article and prepare answers to the following questions:

• Why does the Treasury need forecasts?
• What is the most important single forecast? Why?
• What are the four main requirements for econometric forecasting? Explain the errors that can arise in each case, how they can arise and how they affect forecasts.
• Discuss the difficulties arising from scarcity of data in modelling changing economic systems.
• Discuss the effect of human factors on economic systems and forecasts thereof.

## 9.7    Laboratory exercise: Housing completions

The private house completions data are stored in an Excel file named Grafton.xls in the book's website. Your first step is to determine what data are available. How many variables (fields) are in the file? What is/are the key substantive variable(s). How many cases (records)? What time period is covered? How frequently?

Make a line plot of 'Completions'. Add a smoother. Describe the trend. Visually determine when you think changes in trend occurred.

The last few years' data (from 1993) appear to have a consistent pattern. Describe the trend and seasonal patterns that you see in them.

Assuming the model

$$\text{Completions} = \text{Trend} + \text{Seasonal effect} + \text{Irregular component},$$

the components of the model may be estimated by regression methods. First, calculate the simple linear regression of Completions on Time, where Time is measured in quarters. What is the slope of the trend? How do you interpret its value, in terms of quarterly trend and annual trend? What is the intercept? How do you interpret its value? (Hint: What does $t = 0$ correspond to?)

Generate indicator variables to indicate the quarters. Calculate the multiple regression of Completions on the indicators, with no 'constant' term. Read off the seasonal effects from the resulting report. How do you interpret a positive seasonal effect? How do you interpret a negative seasonal effect? How do you interpret the first quarter effect? How do you interpret the second quarter effect?

Conduct a full diagnostic analysis, as in Chapter 8, and adjust the data and model accordingly. Re-interpret the results.

Use the model of trend and seasonal effects you have estimated to forecast Completions for each quarter of 2001. Using the internet, locate the actual housing completions; go to website www.irlgov.ie, navigate to the Department of the Environment website and locate the relevant data.

What are your predicted completions for each quarter of 2001? How do they compare with the actual data? Comment.

# 10

# Simple statistical models in finance

In Section 1.2, two aspects of the statistical variation evident in stock market data were remarked upon. In the first place, it was noted that the day-to-day changes in the leading stock market indices appeared to behave as pure chance variation. This was illustrated in the case of the FTSE 100 index of the 100 leading shares traded on the London Stock Exchange. This chapter begins by applying two simple tests of this suggestion. In the first place a Normal diagnostic plot of the day-to-day changes is studied. Then, a simple test of the *random walk model,* as applied to the index itself, is implemented.

The second key observation concerning financial data was that the principle of *diversification* applied to the selection of shares for inclusion in an investment port-folio led to a remarkable degree of reduction of *risk* while giving a satisfactory level of *return* on the investment. This idea leads to a specific measure of risk in the context of portfolio construction, called *beta,* which arises out of the development of the *capital asset pricing model (CAPM),* a model that has a long history. There has been much debate about the role (if any) of the CAPM. Here, reference is made to some reasonable applications of the model. Also, some simple tests of the model are suggested, although it should be noted that even the area of testing this model has not been without controversy.

## Learning objectives

After completing this chapter, students should understand the relevance of the Normal model for chance variation and the random walk model as they apply to share indices and individual share prices, the definition of risk and return and the role of diversification in reducing risk, and the role and some limitations of the capital asset pricing model, and demonstrate this by being able to:

- evaluate Normal diagnostic plots of daily changes in the FTSE 100 share index;
- explain how the random walk model is a special case of simple linear regression;
- use simple linear regression as a basis for testing the random walk model;
- define absolute and relative returns on investments;
- explain the relation between return and risk;
- describe diversification and demonstrate, by example, how diversification reduces risk;
- explain the risk free rate and define risk premium;
- write the equation representing the capital asset pricing model;
- explain how the $\beta$ term in the model represents relative risk;
- define the security market line and explain its potential use for detecting incorrectly priced securities;
- explain how the CAPM may be used to evaluate the return on capital required by a company considering investing in a new project;
- describe the use of simple linear regression applied to historical data to calculate company betas;
- describe how simple linear regression may be used to test the CAPM and implement the test;
- discuss limitations of the CAPM and limitations on fitting and testing the CAPM.

## 10.1  The random walk model for variation in the Stock Exchange

Figures 1.10 and 1.11 of Section 1.2 suggested that daily changes in the FTSE 100 index followed the Normal model for chance variation. This suggestion led to proposing the *random walk* model for the FTSE 100 itself. A simple test of the Normal model is a Normal diagnostic plot, as developed in Section 3.6. Given the evidence of changing volatility evident in Figures 1.10 and 1.11, it is not reasonable to apply the Normal model test to the full data set; the Normal diagnostic plot works on the assumption that volatility remains constant. However, inspection of the 1996 daily changes shown in Figure 1.10a suggests that volatility was reasonably stable during that period.

Figure 10.1 shows the Normal diagnostic plot for the 1996 daily changes in FTSE 100. Figure 10.2 shows nine corresponding plots based on simulated Normal data, for reference. These provide strong corroboration for the adequacy of the Normal model in this case.

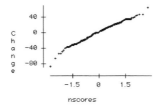

**Figure 10.1**   Normal diagnostic plot of 262 daily changes in FTSE 100, 1996.

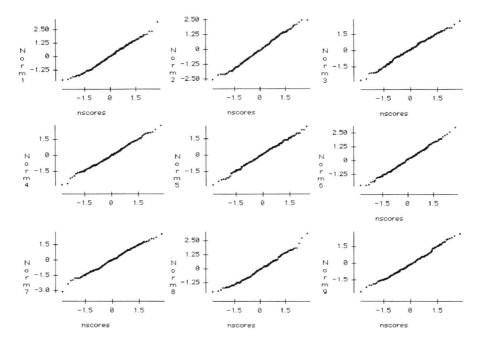

**Figure 10.2**   Nine simulated Normal diagnostic plots based on samples of 262.

**Exercise 10.1**   Data on daily values of FTSE 100 for the year September 1999 to August, 2000 may be found in the Excel file FTSE 99_00.xls in the book's website. Make a line plot of the daily changes. How would you describe the volatility in the daily changes? Make a Normal diagnostic plot of the daily changes and several reference plots based on simulated Normal data. Make an assessment of the appropriateness of the Normal model in this case.

### Testing the random walk model

The random walk model for variation in FTSE 100 may be represented as

$$FTSE_t = FTSE_{t-1} + \varepsilon_t$$

Here, $FTSE_t$ represents the value of the FTSE 100 index on trading day $t$, $FTSE_{t-1}$ represents its value on the previous trading day and $\varepsilon_t$ represents the change from day $t - 1$ to day $t$. An obvious approach to assessing the actual relationship between $FTSE_t$ and $FTSE_{t-1}$ is to make a scatterplot. Figure 10.3 shows the result of doing this for the 262 values of $FTSE_t$ and $FTSE_{t-1}$ of 1996.

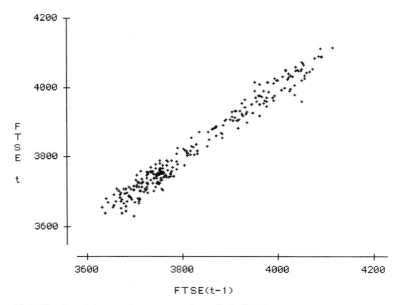

**Figure 10.3**   Scatterplot current versus previous day's FTSE.

This strongly suggests a straight-line relationship corresponding to a simple linear regression model, as in Chapter 6:

$$FTSE_t = \alpha + \beta FTSE_{t-1} + \varepsilon_t$$

The random walk model corresponds to the version of this given by setting $\alpha = 0$ and $\beta = 1$. To test this, the first step is to fit the full simple linear regression model. This results in

```
Dependent variable is:    FTSE t
No Selector
R squared = 97.1%    R squared (adjusted) = 97.0%
s =  22.22  with  262 - 2 = 260  degrees of freedom
```

| Source | Sum of Squares | df | Mean Square | F-ratio |
|---|---|---|---|---|
| Regression | 4.23743e6 | 1 | 4.23743e6 | 8.59e3 |
| Residual | 128319 | 260 | 493.535 | |

| Variable | Coefficient | s.e. of Coeff | t-ratio | prob |
|---|---|---|---|---|
| Constant | 29.8866 | 41.02 | 0.729 | 0.4669 |
| FTSE(t-1) | 0.992619 | 0.01071 | 92.7 | $\leq$ 0.0001 |

Note that the intercept term, 29.8866, is smaller than its standard error, 41.02, and so the data are consistent with the hypothesis that $\alpha = 0$. To test the hypothesis that $\beta = 1$, we construct the test statistic

$$Z = \frac{\hat{\beta} - \beta_0}{SE(\hat{\beta})} = \frac{0.992619 - 1}{0.01071} = 0.6898$$

Once again, the deviation of $\hat{\beta}$ from the null hypothesis value of 1 is less than the standard error of $\hat{\beta}$ and so the data are consistent with the hypothesis that the slope is 1. If we accept the results of these two tests simultaneously,[1] we find that the data are consistent with the random walk hypothesis.

The fact that we found the data consistent with the random walk model is not proof that the random walk model is true. There is a range of values of the two parameters, $\alpha$ and $\beta$, with which the data are consistent. We can easily construct individual 95% confidence intervals for $\alpha$ and $\beta$:

$$\hat{\alpha} \pm 2\, SE(\hat{\alpha}) = 30 \pm 82 = -52 \text{ to } 112; \quad \hat{\beta} \pm 2\, SE(\hat{\beta}) = 0.99 \pm 0.02 = -0.97 \text{ to } 1.01$$

Whether or not deviations of such an extent from the random walk model are of substantive interest is a question that cannot be answered through statistical analysis; it is a matter for financial analysts. However, the result of this test of the random walk model does call into question the value of mass broadcasting of changes in Stock Exchange indices on prime time radio and television, as suggested in Section 1.2.

---

**Exercise 10.2**  Continuation of Exercise 10.1. Repeat the above analysis for the 1999–2000 data. Does the presence of an apparently exceptional case make a difference to the results?

---

### Random walk test for individual shares

Individual shares are likely to fluctuate considerably more than the index, which is a weighted average of the individual shares. Consequently, it may be felt that the random walk model is less likely to apply. To check this, we can look at a selection of shares from among those included in the index. Figure 10.4 shows the scatterplot of current versus previous day values of Abbey National, followed by corresponding simple linear regression output.

---

[1]    There is a danger in accepting the results of two or more tests of individual coefficients simultaneously; recall the cautionary note in Section 8.2. However, further analysis shows that the danger is unfounded in this case.

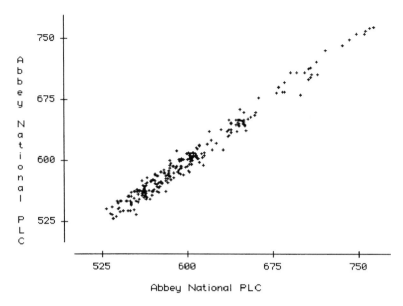

**Figure 10.4** Current versus previous day's Abbey National.

```
Dependent variable is:    Abbey National PLC
No Selector
R squared = 97.7%     R squared (adjusted) = 97.7%
s =  7.542  with  253 - 2 = 251  degrees of freedom
```

| Source | Sum of Squares | df | Mean Square | F-ratio |
|---|---|---|---|---|
| Regression | 6 16982 | 1 | 6 16982 | 1.08e4 |
| Residual | 14278. 1 | 251 | 56.8847 | |

| Variable | Coefficient | s.e. of Coeff | t-ratio | prob |
|---|---|---|---|---|
| Constant | -4.94785 | 5.846 | -0.846 | 0.3981 |
| Abbey Natio... | 1.00906 | 0.009689 | 104 | ≤ 0.0001 |

The intercept is not statistically significantly different from 0 according to the usual criterion. The statistic for testing the hypothesis that the slope is 1 takes the value

$$\frac{1.00906 - 1}{0.009689} = 0.935,$$

not statistically significant. This suggests that the values of Abbey National share prices in 1996 were consistent with the random walk model.

In fact, the random walk model fits many stocks well and most stocks moderately well. However, this is not universal. For example, another stock included in the FTSE 100 index is Diageo. A similar analysis of the Diageo share values leads to test statistic values of 3.06 and −3.07 for testing the hypotheses $\alpha = 0$ and $\beta = 1$, respectively, suggesting that the Diageo share values did not follow the random walk model in 1996.

---

**Exercise 10.3**   Regression of today's Diageo prices against yesterday's for 1996 yielded the results that follow. Confirm the calculation of the test statistic values given above.

```
Dependent variable is:    Diageo PLC
No Selector
R squared = 86.3%       R squared (adjusted) = 86.3%
s =  5.082  with  253 - 2 = 251  degrees of freedom

Source        Sum of Squares     df     Mean Square    F-ratio
Regression    40986               1          40986      1.59e3
Residual      6482.69           251        25.8275

Variable      Coefficient    s.e. of Coeff    t-ratio      prob
Constant      33.3802         10.89              3.06      0.0024
Diageo PLC    0.928429         0.02331          39.8     ≤ 0.0001
```

---

In some cases, exceptional values may influence the calculations. This is illustrated in the following exercise.

---

**Exercise 10.4**   Data on the share values for Sainsbury in 1996 are available in Excel file Sainsbury96.xls in the book's website. Make a scatterplot of current vs. previous day's values. Comment. Calculate the corresponding simple linear regression. Test the random walk hypothesis and note your conclusion. Delete the obvious exceptional values, recalculate and retest. Comment.

---

### Random walks and efficient markets

A good fit is consistent with what is referred to in the theory of Finance as the *efficient market hypothesis,* a simple version of which states

> *All information relevant to a stock is quickly factored into its price.*

This means that information such as an announcement concerning profits is simultaneously available to all traders so that none of them can take unique advantage of that information. For example, if a trader knows before others that a positive profit announcement is due, that trader can buy shares before the announcement and sell afterwards when the share price has gone up, thereby making a profit through possession of special knowledge not shared with others. Stock exchanges have strict rules about 'insider trading' in order to prevent such eventualities.

A not so good fit of the random walk model means there is some inefficiency in the market. In that case, diligent traders may be able to find some obscure information not widely known and use it to advantage. This is referred to as an *arbitrage opportunity.*

## 10.2 Risk and return

The *return* on a stock is the difference between its price at a given time and its price at a later time, usually expressed in relative terms. For example, at the beginning of 1996, the price of a share in Abbey National was 639p while at the beginning of 1997 it was 744.5. Thus, the absolute return over the year was

$$744.5 - 639 = 105.5,$$

and the relative return was

$$\frac{744.5 - 639}{639} = \frac{105.5}{639} = 0.165$$

or 16.5%.

---

**Exercise 10.5** The price of a Diageo share was 477.61 at the beginning of 1996 and 455.39 at the beginning of 1997. Calculate the absolute and relative annual returns.

---

A negative return means that an investor who bought at the start of the period and sold at the end has made a loss.

For a single stock, risk is synonymous with variation, also called volatility. A highly volatile stock may give a high positive return today but could give a high negative return tomorrow; the chance of a large gain today is offset by the chance of a large loss tomorrow. Low volatility means a small chance of either a large profit or a large loss, that is, low risk.

A basic principle of investment is that high risk attracts high return. Thus, high-risk investments tend to have higher returns in the long run than low-risk investments. This may be seen by studying the relationship between average return and standard deviation of returns over a period of time. Figure 10.5 shows the scatterplot of average daily relative return against standard deviation for the constituents of the FTSE 100 for the year September 1999 to August 2000.

Apart from one clear exception and a few possible exceptions, there appears to be a reasonably strong relationship between mean return and standard deviation. It may be argued that the returns being achieved by the highlighted exceptional point are out of line with the returns being achieved by the rest of the shares, given its exceptionally high risk, as represented by the very high standard deviation. The company in question is Freeserve, an Internet information and trading company. Companies in that sector are notoriously volatile.

### Diversification

In choosing between two stocks to invest in, an investor must seek to balance risk and return. However, in choosing a range of stocks, that is a *portfolio,* another principle, that of *diversification,* comes into play. Diversification is a means of

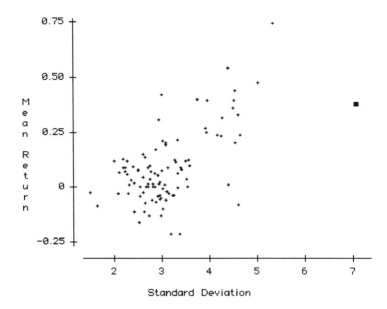

**Figure 10.5**  Average daily relative return against standard deviation for the constituents of the FTSE 100, September 1999 to August 2000.

reducing risk while maintaining a level of return. Recalling the example of a two-stock portfolio consisting of equal shares in an ice cream company and an umbrella company discussed in Section 1.2, when profits from one are high, profits from the other are low and vice versa. In statistical language, returns from the two companies are negatively correlated.

As a further illustration, consider three investors who may invest in two companies, one of which is destined to thrive and the other is destined to fail. Suppose an investment of £100 in the successful company brings a return of £300 while an investment of £100 in the failing company is lost completely. Suppose investor 1 invests £100 in Company A, investor 2 invests £100 in Company B and investor 3 invests £50 in each company. If Company A succeeds (and Company B fails), then investor 1 ends up with £400, investor 2 has nothing while investor 3 has £200. If Company B succeeds, investors 1 and 2 reverse positions while investor 3 still has £200. Thus, an investor who plumps for one company either makes a big profit or loses everything, depending on circumstances, while the diversifier makes a modest profit, regardless.

The preceding illustrations over-simplify what happens in practice. In the real world, returns on investments tend to move together in line with general economic conditions. On the Stock Exchange, this is reflected in the way share prices in general move which, in turn, is reflected in the various Stock Exchange indices such as FTSE 100 (London), S&P 500 (New York), Nikkei (Tokyo), etc. In fact, such indices, being averages of a wide range of share prices, represent close to the ultimate in diversification. The risk involved in investing in a portfolio that parallels such an index is close to as low as can be achieved by diversification. This level of risk is referred to as *undiversifiable* or *systematic* risk.

A corollary to this is that the risks attached to individual shares may be evaluated in terms of their relationships to an overall index. This view of investment risk is encapsulated in the *capital asset pricing model* or CAPM.

## 10.3   The capital asset pricing model

The capital asset pricing model was developed by finance theorists as part of a strategy for selecting optimal portfolios of investments. As such, it has had a controversial history, with heated debates about both its theoretical foundations and its practical applicability. Here, we focus on some simple statistical analyses related to the model. Details on the finance background may be found elsewhere.[2]

The model is concerned with the *risk premium,* that is, the difference between actual rate of return (relative return) on an investment and the rate of return that can be achieved on a risk free investment, called the *risk free rate.* Typically, this is represented by short term (one day) Government bonds that the national central bank (Bank of England in the UK, Federal Reserve Bank in the USA) uses to control the money supply by selling or buying back at a fixed base interest rate. The CAPM says that the risk premium appropriate to a risky investment is proportional to the market risk premium, that is, the risk premium achievable by investing in a portfolio representing the entire market. More formally, the CAPM is given by the equation

$$R - R_F = \beta(R_M - R_F) + \varepsilon,$$

where

$R$ = return on a risky investment
$R_F$ = return on a risk free investment (the *risk free rate* )
$R_M$ = return on a market portfolio
$\beta$ = slope in simple linear regression.

If the model holds, then $\beta$ may be interpreted as a measure of the risk of adding the investment to a portfolio. If the return on the market portfolio changes, up or down, by 1, then the investment risk premium changes by a factor of $\beta$. If $\beta$ is greater than 1, then the investment is more volatile than the market, if $\beta$ is less than 1, then the investment is less volatile than the market.

### Applications

One of the applications originally conceived for the CAPM was to check whether the current price of an asset was as predicted by the model, given the asset's $\beta$. This is done by recasting the equation as:

---

[2]   See, for example, *Finance* by Zvi Bodie and Robert Merton, Prentice Hall, 1998, especially Chapter 13.

$$R = R_F + (R_M - R_F)\beta + \varepsilon,$$

plotting the corresponding line on a graph of $R$ versus $\beta$ and checking whether the current value of $R$ is on the line, as predicted, or above or below the line.

The line is determined by the fact that $R = R_F$ when $\beta = 0$, that is, zero risk, and $R = R_M$ when $\beta = 1$, the market portfolio risk. It is referred to as the *security market line,* or SML. It is illustrated in Figure 10.6 for the case when the (annual) risk free rate is 6% and the annual return on the market is 10%.

Note that the returns being achieved by asset A are lower than those of asset B. Relative to the risks involved, however, asset A is under-priced, given that its returns are more than would be predicted from the state of the market, based on its beta risk level. An investor noting this could borrow money at the risk free rate and buy the asset, wait until the market adjusts its price and then sell at a profit, having paid back the debt. This action of purchasing and reselling knowing that there is a profit to be made is known as *arbitrage.* According to finance theory, the possibility of arbitrage is one of the forces that keep markets efficient.

Asset B, although giving higher returns than asset A, is actually over-priced since the returns it is giving are less than predicted by the market, given its high level of beta risk. An investor holding shares in asset B would be well advised to sell as quickly as possible, before the market takes notice.

This form of application of the CAPM is not widely used these days. Rather, the CAPM may be seen as providing an explanation for why the market works relatively efficiently.

A more widely used application is in evaluating the cost of capital to a company and, therefore, the return that a new project must make in order to justify it. If the company's beta, which measures the risk of investing in the company's shares, is also regarded as measuring the risk of investing in the new project, then the projected rate of return on the investment is, simply,

$$R_F + \beta(R_M - R_F).$$

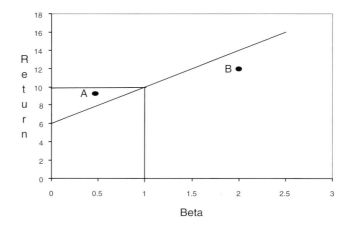

**Figure 10.6**   The Security Market Line.

Alternatively, the company might take the view that the risk in taking on a project that is one of many activities it engages in is more in line with the risk of investing in a smaller company in its sector. As investment in smaller companies tends to have higher risk, research into the betas of small companies in the sector will lead to a higher value of β to include in the model and, therefore, a more realistic assessment of the rate of return required to justify the risk.

## 10.4   Evaluating β

The CAPM takes the form of a simple linear regression equation where the intercept, $\alpha$, is predetermined as 0. This suggests a method for calculating β; given data on successive rates of return on a company's shares and corresponding data on market return and the risk free rate, calculate the regression of $R - R_F$ on $R_M - R_F$, with the intercept set to 0. Here, we apply the method to data on a portfolio of shares formed on a more or less *ad hoc* basis which involved selecting one FTSE 100 company from each of several sectors in the FTSE Global Classification System, which provides a classification of industries in sectors.[3] For convenience, we use the FTSE 100 index as the market index.

The fourteen stocks selected were chosen with a view to having broad representation of the various sectors or, in the language of finance, a diversified portfolio. The companies chosen, and their sectors, are shown in Table 10.1.

The data chosen as a basis for calculating the companies' beta values were the relative daily returns for the year September 1999 to August 2000. This differs from the usual choice of data for calculating betas, which is monthly returns over a five or ten year period. However, the evident volatility over the last half of the 1990s makes

**Table 10.1**

| Company | Sector |
|---|---|
| Abbey National | Banks |
| Blue Circle Industries | Building & Construction Materials |
| British American Tobacco | Tobacco |
| British Sky Broadcasting Group | Cable & Satellite |
| Diageo | Beverages – Distillers & Vintners |
| GKN | Auto Parts |
| Glaxo Wellcome | Pharmaceuticals |
| Marconi | Telecommunications Equipment |
| Marks & Spencer | Retailers – Multi-department |
| Rio Tinto | Mining |
| Rolls-Royce | Aerospace |
| Sainsbury | Food & Drug Retailers |
| Vodafone Group | Wireless Telecomm Services |
| 3i Group | Investment Companies |

---

[3]   Full details can be found on the FTSE website at www.ftse.com

the longer period unsuitable. On the other hand, twelve monthly returns is a rather small number on which to base the calculations, and so daily returns were used. Also required were the daily returns on FTSE 100 and a daily risk free rate computed from the base rate set by the Bank of England.[4] The latter changed several times during the year.

The risk of each company in the portfolio can be assessed through its beta value. Before carrying out the calculation, it is highly desirable to view scatterplots to identify possible outliers which will distort the calculation. The details are not shown here; they are left to be completed as part of a laboratory exercise at the end of the chapter.

The betas calculated for each company are, in order, as shown in Table 10.2.

**Table 10.2**

| Company | Beta | SE(Beta) |
|---|---|---|
| Blue Circle Industries | 0.11 | 0.12 |
| Diageo | 0.11 | 0.12 |
| GKN | 0.28 | 0.11 |
| Sainsbury | 0.33 | 0.17 |
| British American Tobacco | 0.49 | 0.12 |
| Rio Tinto | 0.49 | 0.15 |
| Rolls-Royce | 0.52 | 0.12 |
| Marks & Spencer | 0.56 | 0.15 |
| Glaxo Wellcome | 0.68 | 0.11 |
| Abbey National | 0.93 | 0.15 |
| 3i Group | 0.98 | 0.14 |
| British Sky Broadcasting Group | 1.72 | 0.22 |
| Marconi | 1.74 | 0.19 |
| Vodafone Group | 1.79 | 0.15 |

It appears that the selection was somewhat conservative with most companies having beta values less than 1. On the other hand, three companies appear to have quite high risk. Note, however, that the standard errors are relatively large. This reflects the fact that there is considerable chance variation in the system.

The portfolio made up of equal investments in the 14 companies may also be assessed for risk. In fact, the portfolio beta is 0.94, with a standard error of 0.04. Both numbers reflect an averaging effect, the beta value reflecting the centring effect and the standard error showing a reduction due to averaging.[5] The portfolio's beta value also reflects diversification. In fact, it may be verified that as few as 20 or 30 well-diversified shares are sufficient to closely approximate the behaviour of the market index.

This leads to the suggestion that beta calculations are not very useful for individual companies but may be quite effective for evaluating portfolios. This in turn suggests that they may be used effectively to evaluate the risk levels of investment fund managers. This is widely done in practice.

---

[4]    The data may be found in the file Portfolio 99_00.xls in the book's website.

[5]    In fact, the average of the individual standard errors divided by the square root of 14 is 0.04.

## 10.5 Testing the CAPM

We have calculated betas for 14 companies from daily returns over a year. According to the theory, the relationship between risk premium and beta should satisfy

$$R - R_F = (R_M - R_F)\beta + \varepsilon.$$

This provides a means of testing the model; fit average risk premiums, calculated from the same data, to corresponding betas and test whether the resulting intercept and slope are 0 and average market risk premium, respectively. The scatterplot made from these data is shown in Figure 10.7.

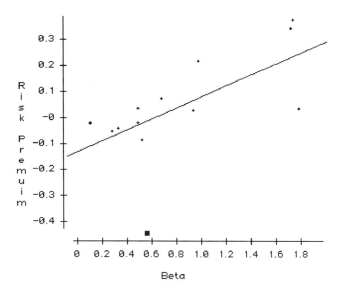

**Figure 10.7** Scatterplot of risk premium against beta for 14 companies.

There is one clear exceptional case. There is also evidence of increasing spread as beta increases. Both of these phenomena undermine the application of simple linear regression to these data. The first is easily solved by deletion, with expert financial investigation of why the company (Marks & Spencers) was so exceptional. The second needs more sophisticated treatment.[6] However, for the purpose of calculating regression coefficients and their standard errors, the ordinary regression is reasonably satisfactory; where it fails is in providing valid prediction limits. The results of the simple linear regression are:

---

[6] One suggestion is to calculate the *logarithms* of the risk premiums and regress these on the betas. In fact, many analysts use an alternative to the relative return used here, that is, the logarithm of ratios of successive prices, for reasons related to the unequal spread problem as well as financial reasons.

```
Dependent variable is:                    Risk Premuim
No Selector
15 total cases of which 2 are missing
R squared = 59.3%       R squared (adjusted) = 55.6%
s =  0.09999  with   13 - 2 = 11  degrees of freedom

Source       Sum of Squares    df    Mean Square    F-ratio
Regression   0.160479           1       0.160479      16.1
Residual     0.109975          11     0.00999774

Variable     Coefficient   s.e. of Coeff    t-ratio    prob
Constant     -0.0787823       0.04621         -1.7     0.1163
Beta          0.18912         0.0472           4.01    0.0021
```

According to the theory, the intercept should be 0 and the slope should be 0.01, the average of the market portfolio (FTSE 100) risk premium. Taking the estimates and their standard errors at face value, it appears that the intercept is not significantly different from 0 according to the usual criteria but the slope of 0.18912 is very far from the market risk premium value of 0.01, when referred to a standard error of 0.0472.

**Commentary**

There are many reasons why the CAPM might fail the test applied here. Among them is the use of the FTSE 100 as a market index, when it represents the less risky part of the market. Small company shares behave somewhat differently and, in particular, are much more volatile. Also, 14 companies chosen deliberately are unlikely to be a representative sample of all companies traded on the London Stock Exchange. A fairer test would include all companies.

There is a more fundamental statistical reason why the CAPM is likely to fail any test, which is that there is clear evidence in some of the scatterplots of company risk premiums against market risk premium that there are exceptional cases that do not conform to the simple linear regression model. This means that the simple linear regression model cannot adequately represent these data. In a problem solving environment, as in Chapter 6, the way of dealing with this difficulty was to delete the exceptional cases from the regression calculation and deal with them separately, as evidence of assignable causes of variation. Here, where the goal is to establish a measure of risk, that approach is not satisfactory. The exceptional points correspond to exceptional risk that should be accounted for. However, it is not clear how to combine the level of risk represented by a validly calculated $\beta$, excluding the exceptional cases, with the level of risk represented by the exceptional cases themselves.

One possible solution is to confine calculation of $\beta$ to companies where this problem does not arise.

## 10.6   Laboratory exercise: Statistical analysis of a portfolio of stocks

In this laboratory, we will study the variation patterns in selected stocks included in the FTSE 100 index. The 14 stocks selected were chosen with a view to having broad representation of the various sectors or, in the language of finance, a diversified port-folio. Data on the stocks and on FTSE 100 for the year September 1999 to August 2000 are in an Excel file named Portfolio 99_00.xls in the book's website. The data are in four worksheets named Daily Prices, Daily Changes, Returns% and Risk Premiums. The Returns% worksheet also contains daily risk free rates computed from the Bank of England base rate.

Summarise and compare price variation for the year September 1999 to August 2000 in the selected stocks. Make a scatterplot of mean versus standard deviation. Comment on the relations between means and standard deviations, including details on the obvious exceptional case.

Make Normal diagnostic plots of the daily changes in FTSE 100, along with simulated Normal reference plots. Comment.

Test the random walk hypothesis for FTSE 100 and (selected) stocks by calculat-ing the regression of stock prices against prices lagged one day. Report on the results of your tests; does the random walk hypothesis hold?

Construct the portfolio made up of £1 invested in each of the selected stocks on September 1, 1999. Test the random walk hypothesis for the portfolio.

Make scatterplots of each of the risk premiums of the portfolio and its constituents against the market risk premium. Comment generally on the scatterplots; make individual comments on any that depart from linearity.

Assuming that simple linear regression is appropriate, calculate the regression in each case. Check whether the intercepts are significantly different from 0. Note the corresponding slopes, for later use.

Calculate the mean annual risk premiums for the year 1999–2000 and regress on the betas. Report on exceptional stocks. With exceptions deleted, test the CAPM; is the intercept 0? Is the slope the market premium? Report on the CAPM test.

# 11

# Data production; surveys, experiments, archives

This chapter contains a review of selected issues in the area of data production. It differs from the earlier chapters, where the focus was on the practice of statistical analysis. It considers a number of important issues that need to be borne in mind both when producing data and when analysing data produced by someone else.

The chapter begins with a short introduction to sample surveys, via selected examples and a brief account of the survey process. A range of issues is covered under the heading 'Errors in surveys', using a series of examples to illustrate the pitfalls involved and to indicate how to avoid them.

The key distinction between observational and experimental studies, having regard to conclusions regarding cause and effect, forms the backdrop for introducing experimentation. Three examples are introduced and used to illustrate key issues in the design of experiments, leading to two basic principles of design: blocking and randomisation, along with replication. The examples involve just one design variable thought to influence the key response variable. Issues arising when there is more than one design variable are discussed. The traditional one-variable-at-a-time approach common in engineering experimentation is criticised, by comparison with the statistical approach, which focuses on all design variables simultaneously. The latter is shown to be more efficient in estimating the effects of changing design variable settings and also explicitly accounts for interactions between design variables.

The chapter concludes with a brief overview of archive data, particularly internet sources.

### Learning objectives

After completing this chapter, students should understand the roles of sample surveys, experimentation and archive search in data production, and demonstrate this by being able to:

- describe illustrative examples of sample surveys, experiments and archive searches;
- outline the steps in implementing a survey;
- illustrate by example the procedures needed to minimise errors in sample surveys;
- compare and contrast observational experimental studies;
- explain the roles of control, blocking, randomisation and replication in experimentation;
- explain the advantages of statistical designs for multi-factor experiments;
- discuss issues related to the implementation of experiments.

## 11.1   Sample surveys

Sample surveys are used extensively to collect useful business information. In Section 1.8, a market research survey referred to as Generation T was described. The key elements were the *target population,* in that case all 15–24 year olds, the *sample,* a representative quota-controlled sample of 309 individuals, the *questionnaire,* a series of questions designed to provide a basis for answering the research questions of the client(s), the *collection mode,* in this case, face-to-face interview in the respondent's home, *data processing and analysis,* resulting in a series of reports for clients. Further examples of sample surveys follow.

### Market share surveys

There are many examples of sample surveys where the key elements differ from those described in Section 1.8. For example, one of the research questions addressed in the Generation T survey was the market share of mobile phones. Other research companies that focus specifically on market share and related issues for different types of consumer products, for example, alcoholic drinks, take as their target 'population' all retail outlets for alcoholic drinks. (The term *population* is used even though the individual retail outlets involved are not people.) Typically, *random sampling* is used, at two levels. First, the country (state, region) is divided into *strata* or survey areas classified as large urban areas (towns/cities), small urban areas, rural areas. Typically, random samples of small urban areas and rural areas are selected while all large urban areas are included. Then within each selected area, retail outlets are selected at random, where the chance of selection of an outlet is proportional to the size (total volume of sales) of the outlet. The questionnaire is relatively straightforward, essentially, a list of brand names and pack sizes with spaces for entering quantities sold. Traditionally, fieldwork was conducted via telephone interview with the retail outlets' product managers and direct entry of data to a database. Increasingly, the world wide web is used for direct data capture. Following data analysis, reports giving overall market share for all brands are circulated to all subscribers, with much more detailed 'own brand' reports being prepared for individual subscribers.

## Audit sampling

Auditors carry out examinations of all aspects of a business to ensure proper conduct of the business and proper reporting of results This may involve examining individual transactions, documentation and reports, stocks and inventory. Statistical sampling is routinely used in many audit activities. For example, when auditing a bank's client loan accounts, accounts will be stratified by size into, say, small, medium and large, with all large accounts being audited, perhaps a 10% randomly selected sample of medium accounts and a 1% sample of small accounts. In auditing inventory in a warehouse where components are stored in bins that are stacked on shelves that are arranged in bays, auditors may select a sample of bays and, within each sampled bay, select a sample of shelves and, within each sampled shelf, select a sample of bins.

In recent years, detailed guidelines have been developed for audit sampling, with considerable input from survey statisticians. The requirements of an audit sample are frequently stated as being *representative* in the statistical sense discussed in Section 1.8, *protective* in the sense of minimising audit reporting error, and *preventive* of possible fraud.

Random sampling plays a key role in achieving these. The role of random sampling in achieving the first of these has been discussed briefly in Section 1.8. Random sampling provides a basis for statistical inference and, hence, for selection of a sample design that will control the chances of audit reporting error. Random sampling also makes it impossible for potential fraudsters to anticipate the auditor.

The 'questionnaire' in audit sampling consists of audit tests applied to the sampled items. Two types of audit testing may be considered, *compliance testing* and *substantive testing*. Compliance testing amounts to establishing whether the sampled items comply with standard requirements. Results may be summarised in the form of proportions of non-compliances. Standard statistical methods for proportions or percentages apply with little modification. Substantive testing involves checking whether recorded amounts (of money, inventory, etc.) are correct and, if not, by how much they are in error. There are potential problems in applying standard statistical methods to the results of substantive testing, however; audit 'populations' (of accounts, bins, etc.,) tend to have frequent zero errors and substantially non-Normal frequency distributions of non-zero errors.

## Sampling in accountancy

A classic example of sampling used in the accountancy area is the Chesapeake and Ohio Freight study.[1] The Chesapeake and Ohio railway company was one of many companies operating in the United States. Before the formation of Amtrak, different

---

[1]    See the article by J. Neter, 'How accountants save money by sampling' in *Statistics: A Guide To The Unknown* (pages 249–58), edited by J. M. Tanur, San Francisco: Holden Day, 1978.

companies owned and operated different segments of rail track. When one company accepted freight for transfer to a distant destination, a waybill was prepared which detailed the route by which the freight was transported to its destination. The route frequently involved using the rail track of several different companies, each of which was entitled to a share in the fee charged to the customer. Determining this share out was an expensive business, adding around 8% to the costs involved in delivering the freight. In order to reduce this accountancy cost, sampling was suggested, whereby the cost share out would be determined from a small sample of waybills rather than through examination of all. Although there are valid theoretical arguments to support this suggestion, the Chesapeake and Ohio company decided to conduct a special study of waybills it originated. A sample of 2,072 waybills was selected from 22,984 waybills for which the amount due to Chesapeake and Ohio had been determined, a sample of approximately 1 in 11 waybills. The amount due on the sample waybills was determined and grossed up (multiplied by 11) to give an estimate of the total amount due. The results of the two approaches and the corresponding costs were as follows.

|  | Estimated Amount due | Cost of estimate |
|---|---|---|
| Complete examination: | $64,651 | ≈ $5,000 |
| Examination of sample: | $64,568 | ≈ $1,000 |
| Difference: | $83 | ≈ $4,000 |
| % difference: | .13% | 80% |

Clearly, in this case, sampling proved extremely accurate and also cost effective, with the accountancy cost being reduced to less than 2% of delivery costs.

## Customer satisfaction surveys

Customer satisfaction is a key element for business success. The expressed level of satisfaction of a company's customers with the company's products and services provides an essential measure of past company performance. More specifically, customer satisfaction is a key determinant of customers' current purchase decisions and long-term loyalty. Many companies are spending increasing amounts on conducting customer satisfaction surveys. A range of survey techniques may be used, including in-depth interviews with a small number of customers, on-the-spot collection of customer feedback at each stage of customer contact (initial contact, sales/ordering, delivery, service), regular surveys of customers' needs, attitudes and intentions regarding the company. Considerable amounts of data are generated by such surveys. For such data to be useful, careful analysis is required to extract the maximum information. An important consideration in designing the data collection is that the information produced is actionable. This means that questions are focused on discovering what needs to be done to improve customer satisfaction, rather than merely monitoring whether the company is doing what it thinks will please the customer.

## 11.2   The survey process

The steps involved in a typical sample survey were listed in Section 1.8:

- specifying objectives and identifying data requirements;
- measurement instrument design;
- sample design;
- field work; and
- data processing, analysis and reporting.

The term *measurement instrument* is a general one. For *social* surveys (of people), the measuring instrument is a questionnaire. In auditing and accounting surveys, the measurement will involve an accounting task, for example, evaluating the shareout of the freight charge in the Chesapeake and Ohio Railroad study discussed in Section 11.1.

The steps listed above have much in common with the steps involved in statistical problem solving, as listed in Section 1.6. The first step parallels the problem formulation phase in statistical problem solving. For social surveys, step 2 involves deciding on the structure of the questionnaire, the detailed wording of individual questions and the communication method to be used, all of which can have significant influences on the survey process. Sample design is, perhaps, the most straightforward part of the process. It is also the most heavily researched and documented. Preparation for fieldwork involves selection and training of interviewers when this is part of the process and a pilot survey to fully test all aspects of design and implementation before committing to full implementation. Traditionally, the main modes of deployment of social survey questionnaires are face-to-face interview, telephone interview and mail. More recently, interactive response to taped telephone messages, electronic mail and the world wide web have found increasing use. Data processing may include more or less complex database manipulations and also error checking prior to statistical data analysis.

It is not the intention to give a full account of the survey process here; there are many specialist texts devoted to the subject. Here, the focus is on selected issues related to errors in surveys and the intention is to provide criteria by which individual surveys may be evaluated.

## 11.3   Errors in surveys

In reviewing the sample survey process, it is convenient to consider the errors that can occur grouped under four broad headings:

- coverage error
- measurement error
- sampling error
- non-response error

Coverage error arises when the sampled population differs from the intended or target population. If the salient characteristics of those not covered are different from those covered, then the results of the survey will be biased. Measurement error is concerned with issues that arise in getting the desired information from survey respondents, including interviewer effect, respondent effect, questionnaire effect, communication mode effect. Sampling error refers to the error that arises because the sample is not the population. If *random* sampling is employed, then the differences between sample characteristics and corresponding population characteristics may be regarded as due to chance variation and all the techniques of statistical inference become available to quantify the extent of sampling error. Non-response error arises because some members of the selected sample may not respond. As with coverage error, if the salient characteristics of those not responding are different from those responding, then the results of the survey will be biased.

## Coverage error

Perhaps the most quoted survey ever undertaken is the pre-election opinion poll commissioned by the *Literary Digest* prior to the 1936 US presidential election. In spite of the fact that the sample size was over 1,000,000, the survey predicted the wrong result. The Republican candidate, Alf Landon, was predicted to have a 'landslide' victory over the Democrat incumbent President Roosevelt. In the event, Roosevelt won by a substantial majority. Part of the problem was that the sample was selected from telephone listings and automobile registration lists. At the time, only a minority of US households had either telephones or automobiles and these were predominantly relatively wealthy households who would be more likely to vote Republican. This differential coverage of the population of electors virtually guaranteed an incorrect prediction.

In 1936, only 35% of US households had telephones. Nowadays, telephone coverage in developed countries is much closer to 100% of households. For example, in the UK in 1998, 96% of households had telephones. However, the 4% without a telephone are likely to be socially or economically deprived, thus creating some bias in telephone surveys. This may not be important in market research, since the purchasing power of such groups is low, by definition. However, another problem with telephone surveys is the number of unlisted telephone numbers, over one third in the UK in 1998 and over half in London. A potential solution to this problem is to use random digit dialling (RDD), that is, dial randomly selected numbers within the range of possible telephone numbers. In this way, unlisted numbers are covered as well as listed ones. Unfortunately, many ineligible numbers are also covered, such as numbers not in use and business numbers. This adds considerably to the fieldwork burden. Various mechanisms have been developed to deal with these difficulties. However, even with such mechanisms, many ineligible numbers are still selected, typically more than 50%.

The examples of coverage error discussed above arose because of the communication mode employed. While telephone coverage is now much improved, internet surveys, the use of which is rapidly increasing, suffer considerably from coverage problems. For example, it is estimated that the number of US households with e-mail access is not much more than the 35% of US households that had telephones in 1936, when the *Literary Digest* survey failed so dramatically. On the other hand, some populations have virtual complete coverage by internet. For example, in most universities in developed countries, all staff and students have internet access. As another example, an internet service provider has access to all its customers and so can easily carry out customer satisfaction surveys. In fact, such surveys are likely to be complete so that sampling error will not arise.

## Measurement error

In surveys of people, or *social* surveys, the questionnaire is the basic measurement instrument. Drafting questions for a questionnaire appears initially to be very simple and straightforward. Apparently obvious guidelines for questionnaire design include

- questions should be related to objectives;
- questions should be easily and unambiguously understood;
- respondents should know or have ready access to the information required to answer the question;
- respondents should be capable of selecting the appropriate answer.

Research aimed at understanding how respondents answer questions breaks the task of answering a question into four components:

- comprehending the question;
- retrieving relevant information;
- making a judgement based on the information; and
- making a response.

However, there are very many pitfalls awaiting questionnaire designers. Here, a few illustrations of the difficulties are provided.

### Ambiguity effects

Many would consider the question

> Do you exercise regularly?

to be easily understood, as in the first guideline above, because it is so short and (apparently) simple. However, consideration of the alternative question

> Aside from any work you do at home or at a job, do you do anything regularly – that is, on a daily basis – that helps you keep physically fit?

shows up the ambiguity of the first; 'exercise' and 'regularly' are not defined so that respondents must provide their own definitions. Consequently, the answers that are given are answers to a range of different questions; any analysis of such answers is meaningless.

### Memory recall

Common sense suggests and there is abundant research evidence to show that the quality of answers that depend on recall of memory of past events deteriorates the longer the period. The following example shows that the memory recall problem is more complex than that. In a survey, respondents were asked

During the last year, how many times did you see or talk to a medical doctor?

followed by a secondary question to ascertain the recall strategy used by respondents, whether count based, rate based or a guess. A count based strategy involves recalling individual visits and counting them. Rate based means thinking in terms of periods less than a year, say monthly, making a judgement on the typical number of visits per month and grossing up to a year. The results are shown in Table 11.1. The contrasts are self-evident.

**Table 11.1** Average reported visits for different recall strategies

| Recall strategy | Per cent using strategy | Average reported visits |
|---|---|---|
| Count based | 51 | 3 |
| Rate based | 43 | 10 |
| Guess | 6 | 7 |

Memory recall error is an example of respondent error. While it may not be possible to eliminate such errors, reducing them should be borne in mind when designing questionnaires.

*Question order*

There have been many demonstrations of the effect of question ordering. In one experiment, a random sample of students at an American university were asked whether they agreed or disagreed with the statements

Cheating is a widespread problem at this university

Cheating at universities throughout the United States is a widespread problem

presented in that order. Respondents in a second random sample were asked the same questions in the reverse order. The results are summarised in Table 11.2.

**Table 11.2** Levels of agreement with questions on cheating

| Order | Agree | Disagree | No opinion |
|---|---|---|---|
| 'USA' first | 65 | 20 | 15 |
| 'This' second | 60 | 24 | 16 |
| | | | |
| 'This' first | 44 | 27 | 29 |
| 'USA' second | 49 | 13 | 38 |

It appears that, when asked about U.S. universities first, students have relatively strong opinions, (the 'No opinion' rate was 15–16%), and many believe that cheating is a problem, though slightly less believe it of their own university than of U.S. universities in general. However, when asked about their own university first, not as many have strong opinions and correspondingly less believe that cheating is a problem, the differential between 'This' and 'USA' being the same as before. Thus, a simple reversal of question order appears to have a relatively complex effect. In both orders, the first question appears to 'anchor' the second.

*Sensitive issues and interviewer effect*

Survey respondents are sensitive to some issues and may not wish to answer questions on such issues honestly. This is borne out by the following example, where the responses varied depending on whether the questionnaire was administered by an interviewer or self-administered. Respondents were asked to report the number of sexual partners they had over three time periods. In approximately half the sample, the questionnaire was administered by an interviewer while, for the rest, the questionnaire was self-administered. The average numbers, classified by method of administration, were as shown in Table 11.3. Clearly, issue sensitivity is a factor and respondents are more sensitive in the presence of an interviewer.

**Table 11.3**   Average numbers of sexual partners reported, by mode and time period

|  | Self-administered | Administered by interviewer |
|---|---|---|
| Past year | 1.7 | 1.4 |
| Past five years | 3.9 | 2.8 |
| Lifetime | 6.5 | 5.4 |

Conceivably, this may also be a case where interviewer effect played a role. For example, an interviewer who disapproves of having more than one sexual partner may, even unwittingly, convey such feelings by a change in tone of voice or body language. A respondent who picks up such signals may report lower then actual numbers of sexual partners.

*Scale effects*

Many questions require answers to be provided using rating scales. For example, the Generation T survey introduced in Section 1.8 included questions seeking expressions of interest in using various services that might be possible using mobile (cellular) phones. In an early draft of the questionnaire, the possible answers were listed as follows:

| Very interested | Somewhat interested | Not very interested | Not at all interested | Don't know |
|---|---|---|---|---|
| 1 | 2 | 3 | 4 | 5 |

However, it was recognised that there were potential problems with this format. The interpretation of the phrases used may not be uniform; they may mean different things to different people. Specifically, they may indicate different propensities to buy for different people. Also, the meaning of 'Don't Know' may be ambiguous. For some, it may indicate a position in the middle of the interest scale, for others, it may represent an inability to choose between the four levels of interest. There is also a potential problem with the analysis of data recorded using such a scale. Unsophisticated analysts may be tempted to interpret the numbers 1–4 as representing magnitudes of interest (or disinterest in this case), which may lead to spurious applications of inappropriate statistical analysis methods.

## Communication mode effects

The way in which data are collected can influence survey results in a number of ways, including affecting responses and affecting response rates. The main communication modes may be listed as:

- face-to-face interview
  - in house, or
  - on street,
- telephone interview
  - live, or
  - interactive voice response,
- mail surveys,
- internet surveys,
  - email, or
  - web.

Here, we illustrate just two problems, relating to questionnaire design and responses to sensitive issues. Effects on response rates are dealt with in a later section.

### *Impact on questionnaire design*

Data collection mode can influence questionnaire structure. The need for structuring questionnaires may arise for a number of reasons. For example, it is usually desirable to direct different subgroups of respondents to different questions. This requires a questionnaire that directs respondents to appropriate questions depending on responses to earlier questions. This is feasible with interviews and mail surveys, can be most effectively done with web-based questionnaires but is severely constrained with email questionnaires.

With complex questions or questions with complex responses, traditionally, face-to-face interviewers have used printed cards to show respondents the questions and possible answers. Much more sophisticated display methods are available with web-based questionnaires, including drop down boxes that can hold very many possible answers and direct respondents seamlessly to the next appropriate question. However, such aids are not available to telephone interviewers nor with either mail nor email questionnaires.

### *Sensitive issues*

Responses to sensitive issues can be influenced substantially by the data collection mode. In particular, the presence of an interviewer can substantially affect responses.

Recall, for example, the results reported in Table 11.3, where there was a clear distinction between results obtained with self-administered questionnaires and results obtained with interviewer-administered questionnaires. With a relatively innocuous issue such as rating respondents' health, the rate of positive responses (that is, health is 'good' or better) tends to be highest for face-to-face interview, less with telephone interview and less again with mail interview.

## Sampling error

Sampling error is probably the easiest form of survey error to deal with. For this reason, it is frequently the only form considered. Here, we review some different forms of sampling and related issues. The first issue relating to sampling concerns its advantages and disadvantages relative to a complete survey (or census) of all the individuals in the target population. The most obvious disadvantage is sampling error; a sample cannot provide exactly correct answers regarding the sampled population. More precisely, the chances of such an event are very low indeed. On the other hand, statistical theory and considerable empirical evidence indicate that, with a correctly designed sampling plan, values calculated from the sample will be close to corresponding population values.

### Cost saving

The most obvious advantage of sampling is the cost saving involved, particularly for very large populations. As an illustration, note that opinion pollsters conducting national pre-election surveys of voters can get satisfactory results using a sample of around 1,000 voters whether the national population is around 4 million (4m), as in the Republic of Ireland, over 30m, as in Canada, around 60m, as in the UK, or heading for 300m, as in the USA. This is because the formula for standard error, the standard yardstick of sampling error, depends significantly on the sample size but not at all on population size, provided the latter is relatively large.

### Timeliness

Timeliness is another key advantage of sample surveys. For example, the simplest summaries of national censuses take weeks if not months to produce, even in the best organised national statistical offices, and this takes no account of the extensive preparation prior to census day. In-depth analyses take one or several years to produce. If market research were to take this long, the market would have changed so much in the meantime that results would be out of data by the time they were produced.

### Improved quality

A third advantage, arising from the first, is that data quality can be improved by spending some of the cost saving on, for example, improved interviewing, improved field supervision, improved checking and validation of data, improved follow-up of non-responders.

## Random sampling

Theoretically, selection of a sample from a designated population should be done in such a way that every member of the population has a specified chance of being included in the sample. If this is done, then statistical theory indicates that sample based estimates of population characteristics will be both *accurate* and *precise*. Here, accuracy and precision have to do with the spread of values in a sample:

- if the spread is centred in the right place, the sampling is accurate;
- if the extent of the spread is small, the sampling is precise.

The degree of precision is determined by the *size* of the sample; the bigger the number included in the sample, the more precise will be the sample estimates. Recall the formulas for standard error of a sample mean:

$$\frac{\sigma}{\sqrt{n}},$$

and for a sample percentage:

$$\sqrt{\frac{P \times (100 - P)}{n}},$$

where, in each case, the sample size, $n$, occurs in the denominator.

Random sampling also makes possible formal *statistical inference*, for example, reporting sample based estimates of population characteristics in the form of *confidence intervals*. All the properties of sample statistics that flow from the *assumptions* concerning chance variation in processes, as detailed in Chapters 4 and 5, here flow from the *fact* of random sampling from the population. Purists argue that random sampling is the only valid method of sampling. However, in some circumstances, particularly face-to-face interviewing of people sampled from national (or regional) populations, random sampling can be prohibitively expensive and compromises must be made. In making such compromises, the use of judgement sampling, discussed next, should be kept to a minimum and strictly controlled.

## *Judgement sampling*

The problems with judgement sampling may be illustrated with two simple examples. In the case of on-street interviewing with quota controls on age groups, interviewers may be tempted to select individuals who appear to be in the middle of an age group, to minimise the possibility of approaching a potential respondent and finding that he or she was outside the desired age group. For example, if a number of respondents are required in the 15–24 age group, there may be a tendency to select people who appear to be around 20 years of age. If this happens, people whose ages are near age group boundaries are likely to be under-represented in the sample. This problem may be detected by careful analysis of respondents' actual ages, if given, and avoided by careful training and supervision of interviewers.

Again, if interviewers avoid selecting poorly dressed individuals for interview, the sample average of a variable such as income is likely to err on the high side. In this case, the *accuracy* of the sample average is in question; the sample average is seen to have an upwards *bias*. If the selection focuses on what are regarded as *typical* individuals, then extremes at both ends are likely to be avoided, in which case the sample spread is likely to be downwards biased so that the *precision* of the sample is exaggerated.

## Structured sampling

While random sampling is recommended to ensure representative samples, there are many situations where structure in the population being sampled should be reflected in the sample design. Two examples of structured sampling are *stratified* sampling and *cluster* sampling.

### Stratified sampling

Populations may be stratified by region. In that case, it may be administratively convenient to conduct separate sampling exercises within each region. In addition, precision of estimation can be assured within each region by fixing the sample size for each region in advance, rather than allow the regional sample sizes to be determined randomly in case stratified sampling is not used.

Financial populations may be stratified by size for the purposes of a financial audit. Typically, all large items will be audited, a percentage of medium size items will be sampled and a much smaller percentage (although, perhaps, a much larger number) of small items will be sampled. The primary aim of such stratification in audit sampling is to be *protective* in the sense of minimising audit reporting error; the biggest errors are likely to be associated with the biggest accounts.

### Monetary unit sampling

An alternative form of sampling frequently used with financial populations is *monetary unit sampling,* or, as it is called in the USA, dollar unit sampling. To illustrate, consider an artificial example where an accounting population consists of ten *line items,* with book values listed as

$2     $5     $6     $4     $1     $8     $5     $6     $3     $4,

and a sample of four items is required. The monetary unit sampling may be viewed as listing the individual dollar units with each line item:

| $2 | $5 | $6 | $4 | $1 |
|---|---|---|---|---|
| (1 1) | (1 1 1 1 1) | (1 1 1 1 1 1) | (1 1 1 1) | (1) |

| $8 | $5 | $6 | $3 | $4 |
|---|---|---|---|---|
| (1 1 1 1 1 1 1 1) | (1 1 1 1 1) | (1 1 1 1 1 1) | (1 1 1) | (1 1 1 1), |

and then applying *systematic sampling*. In this case, the total number of monetary units is 44, the sum of the book values, and a systematic sample of size 4 is obtained by selecting every eleventh unit. If we start with the first unit, this yields the first, third, sixth and eighth line items with book values $2, $6, $8 and $6, respectively. As this guarantees inclusion of the first line item, it may be thought wise to use a *random start,* that is, select one unit at random from the first 11 and proceed systematically from there.

With monetary unit sampling, the chance of inclusion in the sample for each population item is proportional to its size. (In general applications, this form of sampling is referred to as sampling with *probability proportional to size.*) Hence, monetary unit sampling is protective in the sense that the chances of incurring very large errors are minimised, although it does not rule out the possibility, as stratified sampling with 100% inclusion of the largest items does.

### Cluster sampling

It may be administratively convenient to select items in close proximity to each other, either in place or in time. For example, in auditing a traditional paper based book-keeping system, a random sample of pages may be selected from a ledger and all line items in the selected pages audited. In sampling inventory in a warehouse, auditors may select a sample of bays and, within each sampled bay, select a sample of shelves and then audit all the bins on the selected shelves.

A danger with cluster sampling is that the extent of variation as calculated from the data using standard formulas may under-represent the variation in the population. This is because variation within clusters may be constrained. As an illustration, consider a survey of school pupils to determine their opinions on safety of a range of different sports, with schools or classes within schools taken as clusters. Within a school, opinion is likely to be relatively homogeneous, tending to favour the sports played in the school; there will be much greater variation between schools, particularly between those where different sports are played. It should be noted, however, that suitable formulas that allow for clustering exist; they are built into reputable statistical software.

## Response error

In parallel with inadequate coverage, inadequate response rates can also cause serious problems for surveyors. As with low coverage rates, the main problem with low response is differential non-response rates. In the *Literary Digest* presidential election poll referred to earlier, page 347, ten million questionnaires were sent out but less than two and a half million were returned, a response rate of less than 25%. *Post hoc* analysis suggests that Landon supporters were much more likely to return the questionnaires; a higher response rate among Landon supporters gave the impression of a higher support rate for Landon.

### Response rates in practice

Rates of response to many kinds of surveys are very low. In some cases, response rates have been decreasing over time. A recent study found that typical response rates in the surveys included in the study fell from over 80% in the middle of the last century to just over 60% close to its end for face-to-face surveys, with telephone surveys having a slightly lower rate over that period. Other studies have found even more alarming declines. This is causing serious concern among survey researchers as, if it continues, it will undermine the credibility of survey research.

By contrast, response rates for mail surveys have been generally lower over this period but appear to be increasing, albeit very slowly from around 58% around 1950 to around 64% in 1992, according to the study quoted earlier. If these trends continue, mail surveys will give better response rates in the future than the other two. There is as yet not enough evidence to assess response rates from internet surveys.

Apart from variation in response rates between survey modes, other factors that affect survey response rates include saliency, that is, degree of interest or importance for the respondent; the research organisation, e.g., government, market research, academic; the surveyed population, e.g. national surveys vs. surveys of businesses. In some cases, response rates of 40% or lower are being achieved. There is a case to be made that the value of such surveys is questionable at best. In particular, the use of standard statistical inference in the analysis of data arising from such surveys is dubious; the requirement of representative sampling seems unlikely to be fulfilled.

*Improving response rates*

Several procedures are used in attempting to improve response rates. It is generally acknowledged that the most successful method is multiple contacts. If a response is not received at the first contact, a second contact is made and this is repeated until either a response is achieved or it is judged that further attempts will be worthless. Varying the form of contact at each attempt can be effective. For example, with self-administered surveys, the first contact might be an advance notice indicating the importance of the survey, the second includes the questionnaire with a covering letter explaining the purpose and importance of the survey, the third a brief reminder, the fourth a copy of the questionnaire, with an appropriate covering letter, and, finally, use of a different contact mode, for example, for a mail survey, a telephoned reminder if the telephone number is available or a special delivery letter.

Other techniques include small financial incentives; careful drafting of the introduction to the survey, whether verbal in the case of interview modes or written in the case of self administered surveys; using a simple but interesting question to begin the questionnaire.

## 11.4   Observational studies and experimentation

The vast majority of sample surveys implemented nowadays may be classified under the broad heading of *observational studies*. Measurements are made on a range of variables across a range of individuals (the sample). Given the values of the variables that happen to have been *observed*, relationships between variables will frequently emerge. In fact, in a sensibly planned survey, such relationships will be expected and the purpose of the survey is to quantify them. For example, in researching attitudes to and interest in using a range of new mobile services, interest may focus on *whether* individuals are likely to purchase one or other proposed new mobile services and, if so, *how much* individuals are likely to be prepared to pay for such services. Answers to such questions may influence decision making about introducing new products. Given a positive decision, when it comes to deciding on marketing strategies for such a new product, then the *relationships* of such variables with other variables, for example, income, age, leisure activities, that might be thought to influence them, will become important. However, there is an assumption being made here that the so-called *response* and *explanatory* variables are in a *cause–effect* relationship. This means that changes in the values of the explanatory variables, income, age, leisure activities etc., actually cause changes in the response variables, rather than being merely statistically or numerically related to the observed changes in the responses.

Such assumptions, while essential if progress is to be made in business decision-making, are fallible in the absence of properly designed and controlled experiments. Recall the discussion of Simpson's paradox in Section 7.4, pages 241–2, where a simplistic analysis suggested that there was a relationship between loan size and default rate but where the relationship disappeared when the influence of a third variable, loan type, was taken into account. While the paradox was resolved in that situation, because the so-called 'lurking variable' had in fact been observed, there is no guarantee in an observational study that a lurking variable has not been over-looked and, therefore, no guarantee that an observed statistical relationship corresponds to cause and effect. It cannot be stressed enough that statistical relationships, *of themselves,* do *not* imply cause and effect. It must also be said that the temptation to infer cause and effect relationships using business judgement is fraught with danger; recall Brownlee's remark quoted in Section 8.8, page 286.

To ensure as far as possible that an observed relationship does correspond to cause and effect requires a properly designed experiment in a properly controlled environment. The simplest form of experiment involves studying the effect of a single change. In the experiment described in Section 1.9, pages 54–58, the change was from one version of a process to another. A classic experiment in retail marketing is comparing sales of goods in large retail stores, using either mid-aisle or end-aisle displays. Drugs manufacturers conduct extensive trials to evaluate new drug treatments. The simplest of these involves comparison of a new treatment with a 'placebo', that is, a version of the treatment that omits the active drug ingredient.

In all these examples, two key ingredients are the *factor* (or *design variable*) changes in which may bring about a desired effect and the *experimental unit* to which the factor is applied. In the examples described, the factors (and their *levels*) were

- process (old or new);
- display location (mid-aisle or end-aisle);
- drug (present or absent),

respectively.

The experimental unit in the case of the process change experiment described in Section 1.9 was a working day, chosen primarily for convenience. It could be argued that shorter time periods could have been chosen as experimental units, with a view to minimising variation within units, thus allowing possible variation between units associated with the process change to be more evident. However, economic and logistical considerations conspire against this.

In the retail marketing example, the experimental unit could be a time period such as a week, with the factor levels, mid-aisle and end-aisle display, alternating in successive pairs of weeks in a design similar to that used in the process change experiment. Ideally, the alternating pattern is chosen at random, with a view to reducing the effect of any other systematic pattern of variation that might be present without our knowledge. To achieve maximum homogeneity of experimental units, the experiment should be run entirely within a single store, necessarily over several weeks.

Alternatively, in a chain of retail stores, a store could constitute an experimental unit with the entire experiment being run in one week using several stores. However, there are likely to be considerable differences between stores, other than a possible factor effect difference, thus making it difficult to detect a factor effect if present. It may be possible to reduce such differences by pairing stores with known similarities, then randomly allocating factor levels to stores within pairs to minimise the possibility of unknown systematic differences between stores affecting the result of the experiment.[2]

In the drug testing example, the obvious experimental unit is the individual patient. The reason for administering an inactive form of the drug to those not receiving the active form is to allow for the well established *placebo* effect whereby, in many cases, patients show some improvement when they think they have received a treatment, even when the treatment is inactive. Thus the placebo is administered so that all patients think that they are receiving the treatment.

However, there is another factor involved, the doctor who prescribes the treatment for the patient, and there is a major ethical problem in that the doctor is required to prescribe a placebo for some patients that might well benefit from the real treatment. Another problem is that, in evaluating the result, the doctor making the diagnosis may be influenced by knowledge of which patient got which treatment. To overcome these difficulties, treatments are allocated randomly to patients and identified with the patients' names in such a way that the doctor involved does not know which patient gets which treatment. Such experiments, in which neither patient nor doctor knows who got which treatment, are referred to as *double blind* experiments. They have the effect of sharing the ethical problem with the whole research team and avoiding possible doctor bias, either in prescription or subsequent evaluation.

### Randomised blocks

These three apparently simple examples illustrate the care that is needed in designing satisfactory experiments so as to achieve the level of control necessary to be able to infer a cause and effect relationship; there are many more complex issues that arise in different circumstances. Two basic principles that emerge are those of *blocking* and *randomisation*. When there are known differences between experimental units, it makes sense to group the units into *blocks*[3] that are as similar to each other

---

[2]   There is a third possibility in which the effects of differences over time and differences between stores both can be minimised. This involves the use of what is called a *Latin square* design. This is not pursued here. Details may be found in the Supplements and Extensions page of the book's website.

[3]   The term originated in agricultural experimentation where neighbouring experimental plots of land were grouped into relatively homogeneous blocks.

(*homogeneous*) as possible. In the examples discussed above, blocks consist of pairs. If, in the process change experiment, there were six versions of the process to be compared, it would be sensible to form blocks of the six days in a week and apply each version of the process on one of the days. In order to minimise the effect of any other systematic pattern of variation that might exist unknown to the experimenter, versions of the process are allocated to days of the week *at random*.

*Replication*

This whole scheme may then be *replicated,* that is, repeated over a number of weeks. In theory, the number of replications is chosen so as to give desirable *power,* in the sense discussed in Section 5.3; the more replications, the better the chances of detecting real effects of the experimental changes. Replication also makes it more likely that random allocation of factor levels to experimental units will deliver the protection it promises. In practice, more often than not, the number of replications is determined by available resources.

The *randomised block* experimental design is a basic form of design that may be elaborated on in many ways. The design allows valid comparisons between levels of the experimental factor within each block, which may be combined across blocks. In this way, systematic differences between blocks do not interfere in the assessment of factor effects, while randomisation gives some protection against unknown sources of systematic variation.

## 11.5   Multi-factor experiments

In Section 11.4, attention was confined to just one experimental factor. In many cases, there are many factors that may potentially affect a process. In this section, we address some of the issues that arise in multi-factor experiments. The first issue concerns whether factor effects should be studied one factor at a time or whether several factors should be studied simultaneously. The 'one-factor-at-a-time' approach has been used traditionally in much scientific investigation. Here, we show that it is inferior to the multi-factor approach, recommended by statisticians, in at least two ways.

### Traditional versus statistical design

Consider a process that may be affected by two factors, say a chemical manufacturing process where the yield of the process may be affected by operating pressure and operating temperature. A choice is to be made between two possible temperature levels, say 'low' and 'high', as well as between low and high levels of pressure. Suppose available resources allow that the process may be run in experimental mode 12 times. It is easily demonstrated that the two-factor approach makes more efficient use of the data in determining the best level for each factor.

*Efficiency*

The traditional approach involves two steps:

- keep one factor fixed at its standard level, say temperature at 'low', run the process at each level of pressure and choose the best level;
- with pressure set at its best level, run the process at the 'high' level of temperature and choose the best level of temperature.

With 12 experimental runs, it is natural to run the process four times at each factor level combination, that is

- low temperature, low pressure;
- low temperature, high pressure;
- high temperature, best pressure.

In the first step, the effect of changing pressure is assessed by comparing the average of the four measurements of yield at low pressure with the average of the four measurements at high pressure, with temperature at its low level in each case.

In the second step, the effect of changing temperature is assessed by comparing the better of those two averages of four measurements with the average of the four measurements at high temperature.

Now, consider the statistically recommended design, which looks at all combinations of level of both factors in a single study. This may be illustrated as in Figure 11.1 where the subscripted $Y$'s represent the 12 yield measurements made.

In this design, there are six measurements made at each level of each factor:

$Y_1$, $Y_2$, $Y_3$, $Y_4$, $Y_5$ and $Y_6$ at low pressure, compared to
$Y_7$, $Y_8$, $Y_9$, $Y_{10}$, $Y_{11}$ and $Y_{12}$ at high pressure;

$Y_1$, $Y_2$, $Y_3$, $Y_7$, $Y_8$ and $Y_9$ at low temperature, compared to
$Y_4$, $Y_5$, $Y_6$, $Y_{10}$, $Y_{11}$ and $Y_{12}$ at high temperature.

Thus, the effect of changing the levels of each factor is assessed by comparing an average of six measurements with an average of six. This represents a considerable improvement on the comparison of four with four employed in the traditional approach. To achieve the same quality of comparison with the traditional approach, 18 measurements, divided into three subsets of six, would be required. Looking at it in another way, with the two-factor design, all 12 measurements are used twice in assessing the factor effects whereas, with the one-at-a-time approach, four

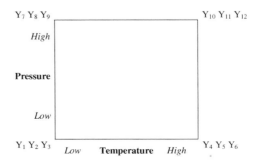

**Figure 11.1**   Illustration of a full factorial design.

measurements are used twice while eight are used only once. Thus, the two-factor approach makes much more efficient use of the 12 measurements available.

*Interaction*

There is a more subtle difference between the two approaches, which is demonstrated here with the aid of some hypothetical data. Suppose that, in a study following the traditional approach, the average response at low and high pressure, with temperature low in both cases, were 65 and 60, respectively. On this basis, low pressure gives the higher process yield and so the next step is to keep pressure low and run the process at high temperature. Suppose that the average yield under these conditions is 70. Assuming that the standard operating conditions are low temperature and low pressure, the conclusion from this experiment is that an improvement can be achieved by running the process at high temperature while retaining pressure at its low level (Figure 11.2).

There is a potential flaw in this approach, however, arising from the fact that process performance has not been evaluated with both factors at their high levels. Conceivably, the yield in this case could be higher than at any other factor level combination, for example, as illustrated in Figure 11.3.

If, using the one-at-a-time approach, temperature rather than pressure had been studied first, then the best combination of levels would have been found; at the first

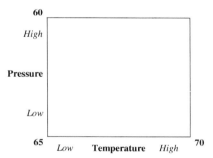

**Figure 11.2** Hypothetical results using the traditional approach.

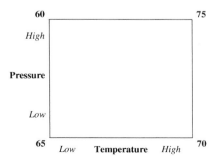

**Figure 11.3** Hypothetical results using the recommended approach.

step, high temperature would have been chosen as best and the second step, comparing low and high pressure at high temperature, would have led to the best combination. However, it cannot be regarded as satisfactory that locating the optimum conditions depends on having the good fortune to pick the right factor to study first. Here, the choice is between two factors. With several factors, there are very many sequences of factors that might be chosen to study one at a time and, typically, very few sequences will lead to the optimum conditions. An experimental strategy that has just a small chance of locating the optimal conditions can hardly be recommended.

An explanation for the possible failure of the one-factor-at-a-time approach in this case may be found in the pattern of changes illustrated in Figure 11.3. Note that process yield increases by 5, from 65 to 70, when temperature changes from low to high at the low level of pressure. However, at the high level of pressure, the effect of changing from low to high temperature is 15, that is, from 60 to 75. Correspondingly, at the low level of temperature, yield decreases by 5, from 65 to 60, when pressure is changed from low to high, whereas, at the high level of temperature, yield increases by 5, from 70 to 75.

In short, the effect of changing the level of one factor depends on the level of the other factor. In statistical terminology, this is referred to as an *interaction* between the factors.

### Several levels

When each factor has just two levels, there are just four possible combinations. If there are more than two levels per factor, the number of combinations increases. For this reason, it is advisable to keep the number of levels to a minimum. For many purposes, two levels are adequate. If the relationship between the response variable and the factors is non-linear, however, three levels may be advisable. Consider the following example.

Suppose an experimental change of temperature from 50 (low) to 60 (high) resulted in a yield improvement from 65 to 69. This may be depicted as in Figure 11.4, as commonly seen in statistical software.

Implicit in choosing the high level of temperature in this case is an assumption that the yield curve relating yield to temperature is linear, as depicted. Suppose, however, that the process had been run at a third temperature level, say 55, intermediate between low and high, with results as depicted in Figure 11.5.

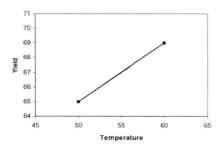

**Figure 11.4**   Effects plot for one-factor experiment.

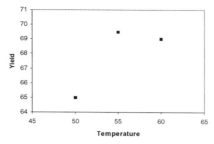

**Figure 11.5**  Effects plot for one-factor experiment with three factor levels.

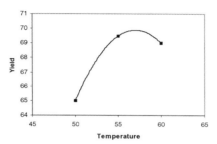

**Figure 11.6**  Effects plot for a one-factor experiment and a possible response curve.

This clearly shows that the intermediate level is better. Conceivably, there may be other better levels, possibly as depicted in Figure 11.6.

With two factors, the response relationship may be depicted as a *response surface*. With more than two factors, graphical representation becomes virtually impossible. However, multi-factor designs with three or more levels may be used to assist in identifying optimal conditions.

## Several factors

Two-factor experiments are relatively simple. To allow for interaction, all that is needed is to ensure that all possible factor level combinations are included in the experiment. The principles of blocking and randomisation apply just as readily; all that is required is to ensure that each possible combination of factor levels occurs once within each homogeneous block with random assignment of combinations to experimental units within a block.

As the number of factors increases, the number of level combinations rapidly increases. With three factors, each with two levels, the number of level combination is $2 \times 2 \times 2 = 8$. If blocking and replication are required, the number of experimental runs required builds up very quickly. In such circumstances, not only do resources become a problem but also the task of controlling the experimental environment over the length of time necessary to complete the experiment becomes increasingly diffi-cult. In addition, there are now three possible two-factor interactions and a possible three-factor interaction, whose presence will complicate any analysis carried out.

With four two-level factors, the number of possible level combinations is 16; with 5, it is 32; with 6, 64, etc. Effectively, so-called *full factorial experiments,* where the process is run with all possible level combinations quickly become impossible. Nevertheless, when a process is subject to possible influence of several factors, it is important to be able to distinguish the few (it is hoped) factors that have substantial effects. Fortunately, suitable designs have been devised for this purpose, sometimes referred to as *screening designs.* Carefully selected fractions, half, quarter, eighth, or less, of the full set of possible combinations may be chosen which give the necessary information when implemented experimentally. These designs are also referred to as *fractional factorial designs.* Their success depends on an assumption that there are no high order interactions or, in other words, that the response relationship is not too complicated.

## 11.6   Implementing experiments

A number of considerations need to be borne in mind when implementing experiments. A few are considered briefly here.

Most experimentation is sequential in the sense that the results of one experiment inform the design of a new experiment; one experiment may give indications of the *direction* of process improvement, further experimentation is likely to be required to explore the effects of specific changes in the desired direction. In those circumstances, it may be desirable to make relatively large changes in the factors under study, to ensure that *some* effect is seen. This is particularly the case when resources are constrained so that more than minimal replication is not feasible.

A consequence of choosing large factor changes is that such experiments must be conducted offline, either in the laboratory or in special runs of the process where the resulting product may not be usable. A consideration here is that, because the experimental conditions are special, care must be taken to ensure that results are transferable to the online process. An alternative approach is to conduct experiments during normal operation, ensuring that any changes that are made are sufficiently small that they will not threaten product quality but continuing the experiment for long enough so that real effects will be detected. This approach is called EVolutionary OPeration, or EVOP for short. The experiment described in Section 1.9, pages 54–58, and further discussed above was of this kind. As it transpired, the change made no significant difference so that no disruption of the process took place. On the other hand, this was valuable information, as the 'new' process was cheaper than the 'old', so that a saving could be made by making the change permanent without reducing the level of quality.

The logistics of experimentation need careful consideration and planning. In particular, the allocation of factor levels to experimental units must be strictly adhered to. This requires adequate supervision as, particularly when randomisation is involved, it may appear more efficient to those setting up the process to change the experimental run order to make implementation more convenient. Unfortunately, such unplanned changes could undermine the whole experiment.

Another aspect of logistics is concerned with the difficulty or expense of some factor level changes. For example, in an experiment to assess the effect on rupture strength of automobile tyres of changes to key factors, one factor of substantive interest was tyre size. However, to change this required disassembly and reassembly of the tyre moulds used in a critical stage of the process. As this was a major operation, it was not feasible to make the change as frequently as levels of the other factors could be changed. Consequently, the full set of planned changes in the other factors was implemented for each tyre size. A consequence of this is that the effective number of replications applicable to tyre size was a fraction of the effective replications applicable to the other factors, resulting in less power for detecting a tyre size effect. Designs of this kind are called *split-plot designs,* a term originating in agricultural experimentation.

Finally, the analysis of data arising from experiments needs careful attention. In relatively simple factorial experiments where each factor has just two levels, the analysis can be conducted as a series of comparisons of two sample means, as discussed in Section 5.1; refer to the discussion of efficiency in Section 11.4. Frequently, however, the sample sizes arising in experiments are considerably smaller than those arising in the context of process capability assessment, as in Section 5.1. A consequence of this is that the use of the standard Normal distribution as the reference distribution for significance testing purposes may not be appropriate. Instead, another distribution, called *Student's t-distribution,*[4] may be needed. The key issue here is whether the value of the process standard deviation as it occurs in test statistic formulas is considered known, for example from historical data, or determined from current experimental data, typically involving small sample sizes. In the former case, it is safe to use the Normal reference distribution. In the latter, however, the extra degree of uncertainty involved in estimating $\sigma$ undermines the use of the Normal reference distribution. In particular, test statistic critical values need to be bigger (and, correspondingly, confidence intervals are wider). In fact, when the effective sample size on which the estimate of $\sigma$ is based is large, the Normal reference distribution provides an adequate approximation to Student's *t*-distribution. For small[5] sample sizes, however, it may be necessary to refer to special tables to find the appropriate critical value. It is also conventional to use the letter *t* rather than *Z* to designate the relevant test statistic.

When there are more than two levels per factor, simple comparison of means is cumbersome. An alternative approach is to use the technique of *analysis of variance,* (ANOVA for short) which seeks to apportion the total extent of variation in the experimental data to the designed changes in the experimental factors as well as to chance variation. Assessing whether or not changes in a given factor affect the results is done using a test statistic that compares the extent of variation apportioned to that factor with the extent of chance variation. In simple experiments, this is

---

[4]   This form of sampling distribution was discovered by W.S. Gossett, Head Brewer at the Guinness brewery in Dublin, who conducted extensive experimentation with raw materials, particularly barley, and who realised the significance of using estimates of $\sigma$ based on the small samples typically used in agricultural experiments. His employers barred him from publishing the results of his researches under his own name, for reasons of confidentiality, and so he used the pseudonym 'Student'.

[5]   A conventional cut off point is 30, which may be justified on the basis that the 5% critical value for *t* based on an effective sample size of 30 is 2.04 which is as close to the conventional critical value of 2 as the exact 5% critical value for *Z*, 1.96.

reasonably straightforward. However, with complex designs, great care must be exercised in order to ensure the correct apportionment of variation to the experimental factors and, especially, to chance.

## 11.7   Archive data

Before undertaking any data collection exercise such as a survey or an experiment, a careful search of a variety of data archives should be conducted. Conceivably, the answers to the research questions of interest will already be known. This is more likely to be true at a macro-economic level. At a micro-economic level, individual businesses and organisations are likely to be sufficiently different that an answer appropriate to one will not meet the needs of another. However, a preliminary data search is almost certain to produce information that will inform the definition and design of a survey or experiment.

The most obvious starting point in an archive search is in house. All businesses keep some records, even if only those, such as financial accounts, that they are required to keep by law. Many businesses keep extensive business records on a variety of variables, ideally organised in one or more databases. Modern manufacturing businesses keep extensive process performance data. Where quality improvement is part of the organisational culture, there will be records of previous quality improvement studies. The increasing use and sophistication of customer satisfaction surveys provides increasingly valuable data.

A key source of macro level data is the national government. Invariably, national governments maintain a national statistics office which maintains extensive archives of all kinds including national censuses of population, labour force surveys, several business surveys, key economic data including GNP / GDP, various price indices, consumers' disposable income, and many more. More than that, however, individual government departments, state agencies, local government agencies, etc. maintain archives relevant to their own activities, many of which may be relevant to business and industry. For example, the data on housing completions in the Republic of Ireland, which is the subject of Section 1.7, was obtained from the Irish Government Department of the Environment.

Two recent relevant books are:

Steve Hurd and Jean Mangan, editors, *Essential Data Skills for Business and Management*, Statistics for Education Ltd, 2001, ISBN 1 872849 83 0;

N. Frumkin, *Guide to Economic Indicators*, 3rd ed., M.E. Sharpe, 2000, ISBN 0 7656 0437 X.

The first is a 'guide to using official data sources' which provides not only extensive coverage of UK sources but also provides extensive discussion on their make-up and guidance on their interpretation and use. The second is a compendium of over 70 different economic indicators of domestic and international perspectives of the US economy, with details on sources, definitions and uses.

In recent years, particularly with the advent of large memory computers and the internet, there has been a substantial growth in data service providers in many areas of business, but especially in finance and marketing. Current data on changes in prices in the major stock exchanges of the world are provided free, with a fifteen-minute time lag, by many finance houses; a fee is charged for up-to-the-minute data. Detailed corporate data on the companies whose stocks are traded are also available for a fee, including, for example, companies' β values, as in the capital asset pricing model discussed in Chapter 10.

There is also a huge range of market related information available, usually for a substantial fee. A recent development in this area is the advent of market data brokers who act as middlemen, maintaining extensive lists of suppliers of market related data, and who make the data available to clients at a fee. One of their main advantages is the extensive range of data suppliers that they source and maintain. In the USA, two main players are MindBranch.com and MarketResearch.com, while ResearchandMarkets.com have launched a corresponding European service.

In the area of forecasting, the idea of consensus forecasting mentioned in Section 9.5 has been implemented as a form of archive by a firm called Consensus Forecasts They assemble monthly the forecasts made by over 200 prominent financial and economic forecasters for their estimates of a range of variables including future growth, inflation, interest rates and exchange rates, covering more than 30 countries. Their web address is www.consensuseconomics.com.

Most publicly available data archives are available via the internet. Apart from those referred to above, there are many more awaiting discovery by those with commensurate internet search skills.

# 12
# Statistical analysis in context

In this chapter, general remarks are made concerning the place of statistical thinking and analysis in the management of companies, the relationship of statistical thinking and analysis with mathematics and computing and a brief guide to further development beyond the boundaries of this book. Reference is made to the Business Excellence Model as a framework in which to accommodate statistical thinking. There is also a brief discussion of Six Sigma Quality, as promoted by Motorola, which is distinguished as an approach to quality management by the key role it gives to statistics.

Both mathematics and computing are essential for the theory and practice of statistics. However, students need to be aware of important reservations concerning their roles, which are sometimes overplayed.

To assist students wishing to pursue further development of the material in this book, the chapter ends with a short annotated list of textbooks recommended for further study in areas of interest to the student

**Learning objectives**

After completing this chapter, students should understand the place of statistics in a management context, the roles and limitations of mathematics and computing and sources of material for further study and demonstrate this by being able to:

- describe the Business Excellence Model and its components;
- indicate how statistics fits into the model;
- give a brief outline of Six Sigma Quality;
- describe the roles and limitations of mathematics and computing in the development and use of statistical methods;
- identify appropriate sources for further development in areas of interest.

## 12.1 The management context

Statistical analysis for business and industry is concerned with problem solving and assisting decision making. To be effective, statistical analysis needs a conducive management environment. In recent decades, there has been a series of management movements, all focused on quality and quality improvement, with titles such as Total Quality Management, World Class Manufacturing, Business Process Re-engineering, 'gurus' such as J.M. Juran (Managerial Breakthrough), W.E. Deming (14 Points for Management), the international quality system standard ISO 9000, and the 'Six Sigma Quality' movement pioneered by Motorola. Statistical thinking, involving a focus on processes, understanding variation and using data to guide action, features to varying extents in these movements. For example, statistics receives merely token mention in ISO 9000 (at least, prior to 2000), Deming was an ardent advocate of statistical thinking while the Six Sigma movement places statistical thinking very firmly in centre stage.

### The Business Excellence Model

All these movements were based, either explicitly or implicitly, on business models, which took a very comprehensive view of what was needed to ensure that a company was successful. A convenient explicit representation that encapsulates the essence of these models is the *Business Excellence Model,* promoted by the European Foundation for Quality Management (EFQM). This was originally based on a model that formed a basis for the Baldridge Award scheme, a scheme to assess companies in terms of quality and quality improvement developed by the US Government and used to recognise excellence. An outline of the model is shown in Figure 12.1. The percentages shown in the figure correspond to a marking scheme used in the EFQM assessment scheme.

According to the EFQM,

The EFQM Model for Business Excellence . . . is based on the following premise:

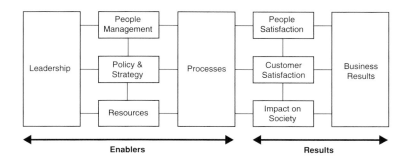

**Figure 12.1**   The Business Excellence Model.

Customer Satisfaction, People Satisfaction and Impact on Society are achieved through Leadership driving Policy and Strategy, People Management, Resources and Processes, leading ultimately to excellence in Business Results.

The criteria in the model have been classified as *Enablers*, concerned with *how* the organisation approaches each of the criterion parts, and *Results,* concerned with *what* the organisation has achieved and is achieving. The criteria may be described as follows.[1]

## *Leadership*

Leadership is concerned with the behaviour and actions of the executive team and all other leaders in an organisation to inspire, support and promote a culture of total quality management and improvement.

## *Policies and strategies*

An organisation must formulate policy and strategy and turn these into action plans based on internal goals and information about the competition and economic climate. It is important that everyone knows what the overall goals and strategies are and how they can contribute.

## *People management*

Managing and developing people has become a priority in many organisations as they realise that this will ultimately determine their success and competitive advantage. Openness and participation will create innovations through matching or developing competencies.

## *Resource management*

This is concerned with effective deployment of equipment, materials, finances, energy and time.

## *Processes*

Processes are 'how things are done'. Quality standards have always included the discipline of measuring key processes. This is a key part of any business improvement exercise.

## *Customer satisfaction*

An organisation must strive to satisfy its customers according to criteria that are important to them and measure its achievement in this regard through a reliable method of collecting customer information. This information must be used as a key part of the strategic planning process.

---

[1]   This description is based on a pamphlet produced by the UK Department of Trade and Industry, © 1999.

*Impact on society*

Satisfying the needs and expectations of the community at large is becoming an important criterion in measuring a company's sense of success and self-esteem. In addition to environmental issues, it includes the relationship the company has with its industry and its community.

*People satisfaction*

A company's strength lies in the contribution its people are making to its strategies and performance. This relates directly to how satisfied they are with their job, their working environment, their future and their sense of self-worth. Policies and systems are needed to ensure that people are effectively developed and managed.

*Business results*

Business results are what the organisation is achieving in relation to its planned objectives. Analysis of past and current performance can show directions for the future and thus business results become an important planning tool, not just a reporting mechanism. In order for the analysis to become integrated throughout the organisation, there must be measures in place that can monitor achievements and highlight weak areas as they develop.

Effective use of the model entails extensive measurement of the organisation under all nine criteria. Thus, statistical thinking fits very neatly into the model. Increasing emphasis is being put on the appreciation of statistical thinking at all levels of an organisation and the extensive use of statistical analysis within and between the various elements of the model. It is important that statistical analysis is effective and, in particular, that it is action oriented. A useful device in this regard is the Shewhart PDCA cycle, developed by Walter Shewhart, the father of modern quality improvement.

## Shewhart's PDCA cycle

The cycle is illustrated in Figure 12.2.

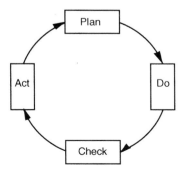

**Figure 12.2**   The Shewhart PDCA Cycle.

The stages in the cycle are:

**Plan:**  Plan a change to the process, predict its effect, plan to measure the effect.
**Do:**    Implement the change as an experiment and measure the effect.
**Check:** Study the results to learn what effect the change had, if any.
**Act:**   Make the change permanent if successful, proceed to plan the next improvement;
           or
           proceed to plan an alternative change

A related cycle that may help convey the message is:

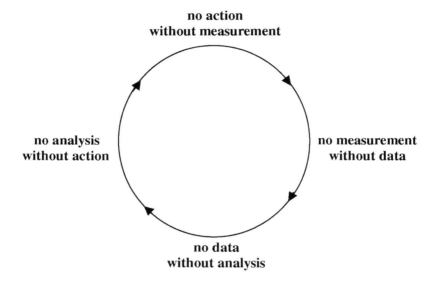

**no action
without measurement**

**no analysis
without action**

**no measurement
without data**

**no data
without analysis**

### Six Sigma quality

The Six Sigma quality movement pioneered by Motorola has attracted considerable attention and comment. In its full form, it embodies all the key characteristics of the other quality management approaches, as reflected in the Business Excellence Model, with the key distinction that it gives a highly visible role to statistical thinking and analysis.

The name itself refers to the fact that processes for which the specification limits are at least $6\sigma$ from their mid-point (possibly with $\mu$ at a distance of $1.5\sigma$ from the mid-point) have very low non-conformance rates of the order of parts per million. Thus, Six Sigma quality is synonymous with exceptionally high quality.

The approach lays heavy emphasis on the use of statistical analysis at all levels of an organisation. To this end, a strong corps of personnel trained in the use of such methods and in training others is built up. They are also trained in a range of problem solving tools including tools for teamwork. (There is also a heavy emphasis on teamwork for problem solving.) To emphasise the status of these personnel, they are given titles like Green Belt, indicating a moderate level of expertise, or Black Belt, indicating a more advanced level.

To many, it appears that this is all there is to Six Sigma. One manifestation of this is the appearance of textbooks by self-styled authorities which amount to no more than procedures manuals in teamwork, problem solving and statistical tools. These authors ignore the fact that the full Six Sigma recognises the need for a comprehensive approach such as that embodied in the Business Excellence Model. Recent accounts of companies where the Six Sigma approach failed point to the same kinds of causes that have been associated with failure of other quality management approaches, chief among them being a lack of commitment and leadership at the top.

## 12.2   The role of mathematics

Mathematics is essential for the research and development of statistical methods. However, it is claimed that mathematics, beyond the most basic levels, is not needed for the effective use of elementary statistical analysis; it is hoped that this text is a testament to that. In particular, the use of formal probability theory, up to recently an apparently essential component of elementary statistics texts, is seen to be unnecessary. Students are entitled to feel relieved at this because recent research in the field of mathematics education has found that probability theory is one of the most difficult areas of mathematics to teach at an elementary level.

Nevertheless, for those who intend to develop their statistical analysis expertise beyond the elementary, probability theory becomes an increasingly important tool. For example, in the study of reliability, which may be regarded as the time related dimension of quality, the interplay between time to failure and number of failures at a given time is very important but, without the use of probability theory, becomes very difficult to exploit. It is also true to say that there is more to chance variation then the Normal model. For example, the Normal model is typically not appropriate in reliability. The basic models appropriate there are the so-called Poisson and Exponential models and other more complicated models are needed once we go past the simplest problems.

On the other hand, students need to be aware that there are crucial differences between mathematical thinking and statistical thinking. An illustration of this is the difference between the two in their approach to dealing with exceptional cases that do not fit the basic model, as in regression, for example. Mathematical thinking seeks to accommodate an exceptional case within the standard model framework by either extending the model in a special way or by down-weighting the influence of the exceptional case in estimating the model parameters, leading to what is referred to as *robust estimation*. By contrast, statistical thinking tends to regard the exceptional case as being due to an assignable cause of variation, which needs separate investigation and explanation; the exceptional case should *not* be accommodated in the modelling process.

There is an increasing consensus among those engaging in research in statistical education that the unnecessary emphasis on mathematics robs time from the study of statistics. A stronger viewpoint is that, for those who understand it, mathematics simplifies; for those who don't, it mystifies.

## 12.3   The role of computing

Computing is essential for the application of statistical methods and, increasingly, also for their research and development. In this text, we have seen how user-friendly menu driven statistical software can, with little difficulty, execute all the necessary computation, including the generation of effective graphs. We also insisted on using extensive diagnostic analysis, to help ensure that the results of our computations were valid. Statistical software that does not incorporate diagnostic tools is dangerous as its use will lead, almost invariably, to wrong results. This author has never encountered a real statistical problem that did not have cases needing special treatment. Such experience seems to be common among practising statisticians, though not, it seems, among many textbook authors. For example, the distinguished industrial statistician, Cuthbert Daniel, gave an account in his influential book *Fitting Equations to Data*, (co-authored with F.S. Wood)[2] of his quest to find examples of 'clean' data to illustrate the methods he was expounding. He reported that every textbook example he examined had some quirk in it, not noticed by the textbooks' authors, which made it unsuitable for use as 'clean' data.

Computer simulation, as expounded in several of the Laboratory exercises in this text, has long been used in researching statistical methods when the mathematical approach is too difficult. It has also been used when the necessary mathematical analysis required to develop ad hoc methodology in a problem solving environment is too time consuming when a speedy answer is needed, although this use appears to be not widespread.[3]

The classic use of computer simulation is for generating the sampling distribution of a statistic of interest. This is done by repeatedly simulating sample data from a theoretical process or population distribution, calculating the value of the statistic of interest and assembling its frequency distribution over the long run of simulations. A clever variation on this theme is now beginning to provide us with an alternative approach to implementing statistical inference. The idea is that the actual sample in hand is the closest thing we have to the actual process or population distribution so that, by repeatedly drawing subsamples from the actual sample and calculating the statistic of interest each time, we can build up a sampling distribution, using a simple adjustment to allow for the subsample size. This idea, known as the *bootstrap*, is beginning to appear in elementary textbooks. However, until software to implement this that is sufficiently friendly and comprehensive becomes widely available, its use in elementary texts is probably premature.

---

[2]   C. Daniel, and F.S. Wood, *Fitting Equations to Data*, New York: Wiley-Interscience (1971, 2nd ed. 1980).

[3]   This issue is explored in 'Simulation as an aid in practical statistical problem solving', by E. Mullins and M. Stuart, *The Statistician,* No. 41, pp. 17–26, 1992.

The power of computers has also made possible the practice of *Bayesian statistical inference,* an alternative to the classical approach to statistical inference presented in this text. Subject to one proviso, Bayesian inference is a more satisfactory approach than the classical, based on sampling distributions. The Bayesian approach attempts to incorporate into the inference information available prior to acquiring data. Such information is invariably present and the approach has many attractions for business decision makers. The one proviso referred to is that the methods for eliciting such prior information are underdeveloped. However, once that hurdle is crossed, and comprehensive user-friendly software is widely available, we may anticipate Bayesian inference becoming the approach of choice.

## 12.4 Extensions and developments

In this section, we give some references to texts that take the developments in this book a stage further, and make some concluding remarks. The references are personal, but may be seen as compatible in spirit with this book

### Quality

A modern text covering statistical aspects of quality is

*Introduction to Statistical Quality Control,* by Douglas C. Mongomery, 4th ed., Wiley, 2001, ISBN 0 471 31648 2.

A rather different text which is a slightly fictionalised account of a quality consultant at work and which gives useful insights into the way statistical analysis may be applied in industry is

*Achieving Quality Improvement, a Practical Guide,* by Roland Caulcutt, Chapman and Hall, 1995, ISBN 0 412 55930 7.

### Frequency data

Most of the specialist texts in this area focus on scientific, mainly medical, applications. An authoritative introductory general text is

*An Introduction to Categorical Data Analysis,* by Alan Agresti, Wiley, 1996, ISBN 0 471 11338 7.

### Regression

Typically, a second course in statistics involves further development of regression. There are many fine texts available. Of those available, the one closest to the style of this book is

*Regression with Graphics, a Second Course in Applied Statistics,* Lawrence C. Hamilton, Duxbury Press, 1992, ISBN 0 534 15900 1.

## Time series

A good review with a strong orientation to business and economic problems is

*Forecasting: Methods and Applications,* by S. Makradakis, S.C. Wheelwright and R.J. Hyndman, 3rd ed., Wiley, 1998, ISBN 0 471 53233 9.

## Finance

There has been a plethora of textbooks in the mathematical finance area recently. However, most of them are (i) beyond the reach of most readers of this text and (ii) of dubious practical value. The finance industry has been very active in trying out the methods developed by financial mathematicians, but with mixed success, including some spectacular failures such as that of LTCM discussed in Section 1.2. A recent textbook that appears reasonably authoritative in areas such as the theory and application of the CAPM is

*Finance,* by Zvi Bodie and Robert C. Merton, Prentice Hall, 1998, ISBN 0 137 81345 7.

A more or less layman's account of finance, consisting of a series of special articles published in the *Financial Times*, is

*Mastering Finance,* edited by George Bickerstaff, Pitman Publishing, 1998, ISBN 0 273 63091 1.

## Sample surveys

A practical modern reference for mail, email and Internet surveys is

*Mail and Internet Surveys,* by Don A. Dillman, 2nd ed., Wiley, 2000, ISBN 0 471 32354 3.

There are useful references therein to classic and modern texts in the sample survey area.

## Experiments

The reference closest in spirit to this book is

*Statistics for Experimenters,* by G.E.P Box, W.G. Hunter and J.S. Hunter, Wiley, 1978, ISBN 0 471 09315 7.

A comprehensive and authoritative alternative is

*Design and Analysis of Experiments,* by Douglas C. Mongomery, 5th ed., Wiley, 2001, ISBN 0 471 31649 0.

## Statistical thinking

While statistical thinking has been laid down as a *sine qua non* for success in business and industrial problem solving, statistical thinking *per se* has not been extensively developed. However, a highly informative book on the subject is

*Statistical Thinking: Improving Business Performance,* by Roger W. Hoerl and Ronald D. Snee, Duxbury, 2002, ISBN 1 800 423 0563.

A text in the closely related area of statistical problem solving is

*Problems, a Statistician's Guide,* by Chris Chatfield, 2nd ed., Chapman and Hall, 1995, ISBN 0 412 60630 5.

The writing style is somewhat uneven, with some topics being more extensively covered than others. However, it is still highly readable and there is much practical wisdom to be found within its pages.

## 12.5 Conclusion

This text will be a success if students of it can appreciate the following quotation from two masters of the art of statistics, Frederick Mosteller and John W. Tukey, in their book *Data Analysis and Regression* (Addison Wesley, 1977):

> One hallmark of the statistically conscious investigator is his firm belief that however the survey, experiment, or observational program actually turned out, it could have turned out somewhat differently. Holding such a belief and taking appropriate actions make effective use of data possible.

# Appendix A Areas under the standard Normal curve

The table gives the area to the left of $z$. For example, if $z = 1.23$, the area, shaded in the illustration below, is 0.8907.

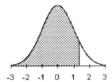

| z | 0.00 | 0.01 | 0.02 | 0.03 | 0.04 | 0.05 | 0.06 | 0.07 | 0.08 | 0.09 |
|---|------|------|------|------|------|------|------|------|------|------|
| 0.0 | 0.5000 | 0.5040 | 0.5080 | 0.5120 | 0.5160 | 0.5199 | 0.5239 | 0.5279 | 0.5319 | 0.5359 |
| 0.1 | 0.5398 | 0.5438 | 0.5478 | 0.5517 | 0.5557 | 0.5596 | 0.5636 | 0.5675 | 0.5714 | 0.5753 |
| 0.2 | 0.5793 | 0.5832 | 0.5871 | 0.5910 | 0.5948 | 0.5987 | 0.6026 | 0.6064 | 0.6103 | 0.6141 |
| 0.3 | 0.6179 | 0.6217 | 0.6255 | 0.6293 | 0.6331 | 0.6368 | 0.6406 | 0.6443 | 0.6480 | 0.6517 |
| 0.4 | 0.6554 | 0.6591 | 0.6628 | 0.6664 | 0.6700 | 0.6736 | 0.6772 | 0.6808 | 0.6844 | 0.6879 |
| 0.5 | 0.6915 | 0.6950 | 0.6985 | 0.7019 | 0.7054 | 0.7088 | 0.7123 | 0.7157 | 0.7190 | 0.7224 |
| 0.6 | 0.7257 | 0.7291 | 0.7324 | 0.7357 | 0.7389 | 0.7422 | 0.7454 | 0.7486 | 0.7517 | 0.7549 |
| 0.7 | 0.7580 | 0.7611 | 0.7642 | 0.7673 | 0.7704 | 0.7734 | 0.7764 | 0.7794 | 0.7823 | 0.7852 |
| 0.8 | 0.7881 | 0.7910 | 0.7939 | 0.7967 | 0.7995 | 0.8023 | 0.8051 | 0.8078 | 0.8106 | 0.8133 |
| 0.9 | 0.8159 | 0.8186 | 0.8212 | 0.8238 | 0.8264 | 0.8289 | 0.8315 | 0.8340 | 0.8365 | 0.8389 |
| 1.0 | 0.8413 | 0.8438 | 0.8461 | 0.8485 | 0.8508 | 0.8531 | 0.8554 | 0.8577 | 0.8599 | 0.8621 |
| 1.1 | 0.8643 | 0.8665 | 0.8686 | 0.8708 | 0.8729 | 0.8749 | 0.8770 | 0.8790 | 0.8810 | 0.8830 |
| 1.2 | 0.8849 | 0.8869 | 0.8888 | 0.8907 | 0.8925 | 0.8944 | 0.8962 | 0.8980 | 0.8997 | 0.9015 |
| 1.3 | 0.9032 | 0.9049 | 0.9066 | 0.9082 | 0.9099 | 0.9115 | 0.9131 | 0.9147 | 0.9162 | 0.9177 |
| 1.4 | 0.9192 | 0.9207 | 0.9222 | 0.9236 | 0.9251 | 0.9265 | 0.9279 | 0.9292 | 0.9306 | 0.9319 |
| 1.5 | 0.9332 | 0.9345 | 0.9357 | 0.9370 | 0.9382 | 0.9394 | 0.9406 | 0.9418 | 0.9429 | 0.9441 |
| 1.6 | 0.9452 | 0.9463 | 0.9474 | 0.9484 | 0.9495 | 0.9505 | 0.9515 | 0.9525 | 0.9535 | 0.9545 |
| 1.7 | 0.9554 | 0.9564 | 0.9573 | 0.9582 | 0.9591 | 0.9599 | 0.9608 | 0.9616 | 0.9625 | 0.9633 |
| 1.8 | 0.9641 | 0.9649 | 0.9656 | 0.9664 | 0.9671 | 0.9678 | 0.9686 | 0.9693 | 0.9699 | 0.9706 |
| 1.9 | 0.9713 | 0.9719 | 0.9726 | 0.9732 | 0.9738 | 0.9744 | 0.9750 | 0.9756 | 0.9761 | 0.9767 |
| 2.0 | 0.9772 | 0.9778 | 0.9783 | 0.9788 | 0.9793 | 0.9798 | 0.9803 | 0.9808 | 0.9812 | 0.9817 |
| 2.1 | 0.9821 | 0.9826 | 0.9830 | 0.9834 | 0.9838 | 0.9842 | 0.9846 | 0.9850 | 0.9854 | 0.9857 |
| 2.2 | 0.9861 | 0.9864 | 0.9868 | 0.9871 | 0.9875 | 0.9878 | 0.9881 | 0.9884 | 0.9887 | 0.9890 |
| 2.3 | 0.9893 | 0.9896 | 0.9898 | 0.9901 | 0.9904 | 0.9906 | 0.9909 | 0.9911 | 0.9913 | 0.9916 |
| 2.4 | 0.9918 | 0.9920 | 0.9922 | 0.9925 | 0.9927 | 0.9929 | 0.9931 | 0.9932 | 0.9934 | 0.9936 |
| 2.5 | 0.9938 | 0.9940 | 0.9941 | 0.9943 | 0.9945 | 0.9946 | 0.9948 | 0.9949 | 0.9951 | 0.9952 |
| 2.6 | 0.9953 | 0.9955 | 0.9956 | 0.9957 | 0.9959 | 0.9960 | 0.9961 | 0.9962 | 0.9963 | 0.9964 |
| 2.7 | 0.9965 | 0.9966 | 0.9967 | 0.9968 | 0.9969 | 0.9970 | 0.9971 | 0.9972 | 0.9973 | 0.9974 |
| 2.8 | 0.9974 | 0.9975 | 0.9976 | 0.9977 | 0.9977 | 0.9978 | 0.9979 | 0.9979 | 0.9980 | 0.9981 |
| 2.9 | 0.9981 | 0.9982 | 0.9982 | 0.9983 | 0.9984 | 0.9984 | 0.9985 | 0.9985 | 0.9986 | 0.9986 |
| 3.0 | 0.9987 | 0.9987 | 0.9987 | 0.9988 | 0.9988 | 0.9989 | 0.9989 | 0.9989 | 0.9990 | 0.9990 |
| 3.1 | 0.9990 | 0.9991 | 0.9991 | 0.9991 | 0.9992 | 0.9992 | 0.9992 | 0.9992 | 0.9993 | 0.9993 |
| 3.2 | 0.9993 | 0.9993 | 0.9994 | 0.9994 | 0.9994 | 0.9994 | 0.9994 | 0.9995 | 0.9995 | 0.9995 |
| 3.3 | 0.9995 | 0.9995 | 0.9995 | 0.9996 | 0.9996 | 0.9996 | 0.9996 | 0.9996 | 0.9996 | 0.9997 |
| 3.4 | 0.9997 | 0.9997 | 0.9997 | 0.9997 | 0.9997 | 0.9997 | 0.9997 | 0.9997 | 0.9997 | 0.9998 |

# Appendix B   Selected critical values of the chi-square distribution

| $\alpha$ | 0.2 | 0.1 | 0.05 | 0.025 | 0.01 | 0.005 |
|---|---|---|---|---|---|---|
| $v = 1$ | 1.6 | 2.7 | 3.8 | 5.0 | 6.6 | 7.9 |
| 2 | 3.2 | 4.6 | 6.0 | 7.4 | 9.2 | 11 |
| 3 | 4.6 | 6.3 | 7.8 | 9.4 | 11 | 13 |
| 4 | 6.0 | 7.8 | 9.5 | 11 | 13 | 15 |
| 5 | 7.3 | 9.2 | 11 | 13 | 15 | 17 |
| 6 | 8.6 | 11 | 13 | 14 | 17 | 19 |
| 7 | 9.8 | 12 | 14 | 16 | 18 | 20 |
| 8 | 11 | 13 | 16 | 18 | 20 | 22 |
| 9 | 12 | 15 | 17 | 19 | 22 | 24 |
| 10 | 13 | 16 | 18 | 20 | 23 | 25 |
| 12 | 16 | 19 | 21 | 23 | 26 | 28 |
| 15 | 19 | 22 | 25 | 27 | 31 | 33 |
| 20 | 25 | 28 | 31 | 34 | 38 | 40 |
| 24 | 30 | 33 | 36 | 39 | 43 | 46 |
| 30 | 36 | 40 | 44 | 47 | 51 | 54 |
| 60 | 69 | 74 | 79 | 83 | 88 | 92 |
| 20 | 133 | 140 | 147 | 152 | 159 | 164 |

# Index

alternative hypothesis 160, 171
analysis of variance 205, 268, 365–6
aspect ratio 70, 71, 92
assignable causes of variation 19
  and control charts 120–1
  illustrated 3–5, 6–7, 17–19
Automotive Industry Action Group (AIAG)
  127

Bayesian inference 375
beta (financial risk criterion) 335–7
  evaluating beta 337–8
boxplot 63–64
Business Excellence Model 369–71

capital asset pricing model (CAPM) 14,
  335–7,
  testing the CAPM 339–340
cause and effect 41, 207, 285–6, 357,
  358
centre line (CL), *see* control limits
chance variation 19
  explained by example 20
  illustrated 4, 6–7, 11–13, 17
  Normal model for 95
chi-square tests 231–7
coefficient
  correlation 208
  multiple linear regression 41, 43–4
  simple linear regression 49, 192
confidence bounds 177
confidence interval
  and sample size 178, 181, 183–185
  for a process mean 176–177
  for a process proportion 182

for a process/population percentage 183,
  229
for a simple linear regression coefficient
  205
confidence level 177
  choice of 180–181
contingency table 236
control chart 9, 65, 120–158
  action rules 129–130
control limits
  for individual measurements 119, 121,
    126
  for np charts 151
  for range charts 131, 143–4
  for regression control charts 199
  for X-bar charts 129, 140, 145–6
correlation 207–212
  and reduction of prediction error
    208–210
  and simple linear regression 208
  conventional interpretations 211
  pitfalls 212–213
critical value 161
  for chi-square 234–5, 237

Daniel, C. 374
degrees of freedom 199, 233–5, 237, 258
Deming, W.E. 369
detection rate 170–175
diversification 14, 333–5
dotplot 61–62, 64, 251, 260

effective digits 78, 226
  and rounding error 79, 81
efficient market 14, 332

estimation　41, 45, 108, 122–5, 141, 142–148, 175, 194, 197–199, 203
evolutionary operation (EVOP)　364
experimentation　55–58, 357–366
　and observational studies　356–7
　blocking　358–9, 363
　experimental factors　357–8
　experimental units　357–8
　factor levels　357–8, 362–3
　implementation issues　364–5
　interaction　361–2
　one-factor-at-a-time versus multi-factor　359–62
　randomisation　58, 358–9, 363
explanatory variable　24, 41, 249, 357

false alarm rate　122, 167, 202
Fisher, R.A.　9, 167–8
fitted values　194, 198, 255
five number summary　72
flowchart　16
frequency data analysis　221–247
　multiply classified data　238–242
frequency distribution　22–23,　69
FTSE 100　10–14, 327–30
　daily changes　11
　　Normal plot　328
　　random walk model　14, 328–330

Gosset, W.S. ('student')　365
graphical perception　67, 71, 72,
guidelines for graph making　85
　graphical codes　70, 85, 89–92
guidelines for table making　78

histogram　7, 61, 64–69
　histogram view　7–8

indicator variables　48, 254, 303
initial data analysis　24–29, 32–36, 45–47, 250–3, 270–4, 299–300
interquartile range　73
ISO 9000　369

Juran, J.M.　369

least squares method　193–5, 256
line chart　70–72
lower control limit (LCL), *see* control limits

mean　73, 74, 100, 102, 105, 107–108
median　63, 72–73
multiple linear regression　32–44, 248–296
　comparing models　283–4

correlated explanatory variables (multicollinearity)　253, 259, 273–4
　diagnostics　261–264, 266–8, 275–9
　general issues　285–7
　iterative procedure　269–270
　model　41, 48, 253
　model parameters　41, 253, 274
　prediction error　41, 253, 258, 266, 268, 275, 277
　　caveats　284
　　operational interpretation　258, 269
　prediction formula　41–43, 253–4, 257, 274–5
　regression coefficients　41, 253
　　interpretation of　43–44

Normal diagnostic plot　109
Normal frequency curve　7–8, 20, 21, 23, 98–100
Normal frequency distribution　23, 69, 74
　standard Normal frequency distribution　100, 101
Normal model　20, 95–116
NORMDIST spreadsheet function　100, 102–103, 106, 107, 115
np chart　148–152
N-scores　109
null hypothesis　160, 171

observational studies　285–6, 356–7
observed significance level　169

parameters
　multiple regression model　41, 253, 274
　Normal model　108, 253
　process　108
　simple linear regression model　30, 192
PDCA　371–2
power of a significance test　170–175
prediction formula　31, 41–43, 49, 50, 196, 257
problem formulation, illustration　32–40
problem solving, statistical approach　ix, 44–45
process capability　142
process parameters　108
　estimating　108, 142, 148
process variation, sources of, illustrated　17
process view　3–4, 8
　advantages　5–6
profile charts　91
p-value　169

quartile　63, 72
questionnaire design　53

random walk model   14, 328–332
range   72
range chart   127, 130–131, 142–144
reference plots
    for Normal diagnostic plots   111–13,
        328
    for time series residual plots   280–1
regression, see simple linear regression,
    multiple regression
regression control chart   199–203
    advantages   201
    and variance control chart   201–2
    applications   202–3
    choice of false alarm rate   202
    control limits   199
    residuals   198, 255–6
        deleted   262
response relationship   24, 223, 226, 357
response variable   24, 41, 249, 357
return, financial   333
risk, financial   333
R-squared   268–9
    and reduction in prediction error   269

sample size, choice of   175, 178, 181,
        183–85, 353
sample surveys   50–54, 343–56
    errors in   346–56
        coverage error   347–8
        measurement error   53, 348–52
        response error   355–6
        sampling error   352–5
    in auditing and accounting   344–5
    in market research   50–52, 343
    of customer satisfaction   345
    questionnaire design   53, 348, 351
    sample design   53–4, 353–5
    steps in   52, 346
sampling
    demonstration of effectiveness   345–6
    preventive   344
    protective   344
    random   53–4, 343–4, 347, 353–5
        as a basis for inference   54, 353
    representative   53, 344, 354, 356
sampling distribution   132
    of chi-square   233
    of the sample error count   150
    of the sample mean   141, 161–2
    simulation of   132–139
scatterplot   26–27, 30, 39–40, 109–10,
        192, 208–11, 212, 260–1
    aspect ratio   71
scatterplot matrix   251–3, 273–4
seasonal effects   3–5, 25, 47–50, 297–325

serial correlation   263–4
Shewhart, W.S.   7, 9, 19, 27, 41, 122, 129,
        130, 167–168, 372
significance level   168
    and sample size   175
    conventional choices   168
simple linear regression   30–32, 190–220
    and the capital assets pricing model
        337, 339–40
    and the random walk model   329–30
    interpreting results   204–5
    model   30, 47, 191–2
    model parameters   30, 192
    pitfalls   212–3
    prediction formula   31, 196
    regression coefficients   49, 192
        interpretation 195
    *see also* regression control chart
Simpson's paradox   241–2
simulation   132–139, 179–180, 374
Six Sigma   369, 372–3
smoothing
    for exploratory analysis   4, 46, 56–57,
        307–12
        linear trend smoother   300
        lowess   310–12
        moving averages   307–10
    for forecasting   312–20
        exponentially weighted moving
            average (EWMA)   315–6
        moving averages   313–5
specification limits   98
standard deviation   69, 73, 74, 100, 102,
        105, 107–108, 198–9, 258
standard error   132
    of a difference between sample means
        165, 231
    of a difference between sample
        percentages   231
    of a multiple regression coefficient   259
    of a sample mean   141, 163
    of a sample percentage   183
    of a sample proportion   182
    of a simple linear regression coefficient
        205
    of an error count   151
standardisation   102
statistic   108, 161
statistical control   120
statistical significance   122, 160
    and substantive significance   207
    test of
        consequences of errors in
        for a difference between two sample
            means   165–6

statistical significance – *contd*
  test of – *contd*
    for a difference between two sample
      percentages   230
    for a percentage   227–228
    for a regression coefficient   206, 259,
      279–80, 330, 331, 340
    for a sample mean   163
    for differences between several sample
      percentages   232–3
    for differences between several sets of
      percentages   235–7
    for proportions   166
statistical thinking   ix, xi, xii, 369, 371,
  372, 376–7
  and mathematical thinking   373
stratification   17
survey sample design   53–54

tally sheet   66
t-distribution   365
test statistic   161
time series analysis
  ARIMA   321–2
    comparison with regression   323
  classical model   301, 319
  consensus forecasting   323
  decomposition   320–321

econometric methods   321
Holt's method for forecasting trend
  317–8
Holt-Winters method for trend and
  seasonality   318–9
  comparison with regression   319–20
linear model for trend   47–8, 301–2
  prediction formula   48, 302
multiple regression model for trend and
  seasonal effect   48, 303–4
  diagnostic analysis   304–6
  prediction formula   49–50, 304,
    306
post hoc analysis   323
Total Quality Management   369
trend   11, 32, 35, 46–9, 297–325

upper control limit (UCL,)   *see* control
  limits

variance control chart   201–2

website address   xiii
'what-if' analysis   100, 105–107, 175
World Class Manufacturing   369

X-bar chart   127, 129–130, 131, 140,
  145–147